Lecture Notes in Computer Science 9407

Commenced Publication in 1973
Founding and Former Series Editors:
Gerhard Goos, Juris Hartmanis, and Jan van Leeuwen

More information about this series at http://www.springer.com/series/7408

Michael Butler · Sylvain Conchon
Fatiha Zaïdi (Eds.)

Formal Methods and Software Engineering

17th International Conference
on Formal Engineering Methods, ICFEM 2015
Paris, France, November 3–5, 2015
Proceedings

 Springer

Editors
Michael Butler
Electronics and Computer Science
University of Southampton
Southampton
UK

Fatiha Zaïdi
Université Paris-Sud
Orsay
France

Sylvain Conchon
Université Paris-Sud
Orsay
France

ISSN 0302-9743 ISSN 1611-3349 (electronic)
Lecture Notes in Computer Science
ISBN 978-3-319-25422-7 ISBN 978-3-319-25423-4 (eBook)
DOI 10.1007/978-3-319-25423-4

Library of Congress Control Number: 2015950921

LNCS Sublibrary: SL2 – Programming and Software Engineering

Springer International Publishing AG Switzerland is part of Springer Science+Business Media
(www.springer.com)

Preface

The International Conference on Formal Engineering Methods (ICFEM) is a premier conference for research in all areas related to formal engineering methods, such as verification and validation, software engineering, formal specification and modeling, software security, and software reliability. Since 1997, ICFEM has been serving as an international forum for researchers and practitioners who have been seriously applying formal methods to practical applications. Researchers and practitioners, from industry, academia, and government, are encouraged to attend, present their research, and help advance the state of the art. We are interested in work that has been incorporated into real production systems, and in theoretical work that promises to bring practical and tangible benefit.

In recent years, ICFEM has taken place in Luxembourg (2014), Queenstown, New Zealand (2013), Kyoto, Japan (2012), Durham, UK (2011), Shanghai, China (2010), and Rio de Janeiro, Brazil (2009). The 17th edition of ICFEM took place in Paris during November 3–5, 2015. The Program Committee (PC) received 78 full research papers and four tool papers. Each paper received at least three reports from PC members or external reviewers. On the basis of these reports, each submission was extensively discussed in the virtual meeting of the PC, and the PC decided to accept 27 papers, among them two tool papers. The proceedings also include short presentation from the three keynote speakers, Ana Cavalcanti (York University), Sava Krstic (INTEL), and Rupak Majumdar (MPI).

ICFEM 2015 was organized and supported by the LRI and the CNAM Paris. The conference would not have been possible without the contributions and the support of the following organizations: The Digiteo-Digicosme foundation, the CNRS Scientific Research Group GDR GPL, the French National Agency of Research (ANR), the Systematic Paris Region Systems and ICT Cluster, the W4 software company, and OCamlPRO. We thank also the Local Organizing Committee for their hard work in making ICFEM 2015 a successful and exciting event.

The main event was followed by the 4th International Workshop on Formal Techniques for Safety-Critical Systems (FTSCS 2015) and the 5th International Workshop SOFL+MSVL.

We would like to thank the numerous people who contributed to the success of ICFEM 2015: the Steering Committee members, the PC members and the additional reviewers for their support in selecting papers and composing the conference program, and the authors and the invited speakers for their contributions without which, of course, these proceedings would not exist. We would like also to thank Springer for their help during the production of this proceedings volume and the EasyChair team for their great conference system.

July 2015

Michael Butler
Sylvain Conchon
Fatiha Zaïdi

Organization

Program Committee

Étienne André	University of Paris 13, France
Keijiro Araki	University of Kyushu, Japan
Nikolaj Bjorner	Microsoft Research, USA
Ahmed Bouajjani	University of Paris Diderot, France
Michael Butler	University of Southampton, UK
Sylvain Conchon	University of Paris-Sud, France
Tristan Crolard	Cnam, France
Frank De Boer	CWI, The Netherlands
Rémi Delmas	ONERA, France
Zhenhua Duan	Xidian University, China
Stefania Gnesi	ISTI-CNR, Italy
Radu Grosu	Vienna University of Technology, Austria
Ian J. Hayes	University of Queensland, Australia
Rob Hierons	Brunel University, UK
Michaela Huhn	Technische Universität Clausthal, Germany
Alexei Iliasov	University of Newcastle, UK
Fabrice Kordon	University of Paris 6, France
Yassine Lakhnech	University of Joseph Fourier, Grenoble, France
Peter Gorm Larsen	Aarhus University, Denmark
Pascale Le Gall	Ecole Centrale Paris, France
Xuandong Li	Nanjing University, China
Shang-Wei Lin	National University of Singapore, Singapore
Shaoying Liu	University of Hosei, Japan
Yang Liu	Nanyang Technological University, Singapore
Stephan Merz	INRIA Nancy, France
Mohammadreza Mousavi	Halmstad University, Sweden
Shin Nakajima	National Institute of Informatics, Japan
Manuel Nuñez	University Complutense, Madrid
Jun Pang	University of Luxembourg, Luxembourg
Jan Peleska	University of Bremen, Germany
Ion Petre	Åbo Akademi University, Finland
Shengchao Qin	University of Teesside, UK
Zongyan Qiu	Peking University, China
Silvio Ranise	FBK, Italy

Jing Sun	University of Auckland, New Zealand
Jun Sun	Singapore University of Technology and Design, Singapore
Kenji Taguchi	AIST, Japan
Viktor Vafeiadis	MPI-SWS, Germany
Jaco Van De Pol	University of Twente, The Netherlands
Wang Yi	Uppsala University, Sweden
Fatiha Zaïdi	University of Paris-Sud, France
Gianluigi Zavattaro	University of Bologna, Italy
Huibiao Zhu	East China Normal University, China

Additional Reviewers

Aiguier, Marc
Ballarini, Paolo
Bannour, Boutheina
Bezirgiannis, Nikolaos
Blanchette, Jasmin Christian
Borde, Etienne
Bu, Lei
Chen, Xin
Ciancia, Vincenzo
De Masellis, Riccardo
Delahaye, David
Dokter, Kasper
Dragoi, Cezara
Dreossi, Tommaso
Fang, Huixing
Fantechi, Alessandro
Feng, Ruitao
Ferreira, Joao F.
Frehse, Goran
Frömel, Bernhard
Giallorenzo, Saverio
Gratie, Cristian
Gratie, Diana-Elena
Hallerstede, Stefan
Han, Tingting
Hillah, Lom Messan
Hu, Tingting
Huang, Yanhong
Islam, Md. Ariful
Jaksic, Stefan
Kamali, Maryam

Katoen, Joost-Pieter
Keshishzadeh, Sarmen
Khakpour, Narges
Kitamura, Takashi
Kong, Weiqiang
Kromodimoeljo, Sentot
Kuperberg, Denis
Kuruma, Hironobu
Le, Ton Chanh
Levy, Nicole
Li, Qin
Lienhardt, Michael
Liu, Haiyang
Maximilien, Colange
Meijer, Jeroen
Mizera, Andrzej
Mohammad Hasani, Ramin
Mostowski, Wojciech
Murthy, Abhishek
Okano, Kozo
Pan, Minxue
Petre, Luigia
Qu, Hongyang
Sciarretta, Giada
Semini, Laura
Serbanescu, Vlad Nicolae
Singh, Neeraj
Solin, Kim
Su, Wen
Susini, Jean-Ferdy
Taktak, Sami

Tan, Tian Huat
Tapia Tarifa, Silvia Lizeth
Ter Beek, Maurice H.
Vandin, Andrea
Wang, Linzhang
Wijs, Anton
Winter, Kirsten
Xu, Zhiwu

Zhang, Min
Zhang, Tian
Zhao, Jianhua
Zhao, Yongwang
Zhu, Longfei
Ziane, Mikal
Zwolakowski, Jakub

Invited Talks

Can Java Ever Be Safe?
The hiJaC Project Abstract

Ana Cavalcanti

University of York, UK

For its popularity, both in academia and industry, Java [11] is a language that dispenses introductions. It has a wide base of programmers, an impressive collection of libraries, and continues to evolve with the support of a very large number of companies. The real-time community has, however, at first, completely rejected it. Issues included poor support for absolute time, timeouts, management of threads waiting on a lock, and priorities.

Ten years later, the tremendous success of Java lead to a reversal of this situation: the Real-Time Specification for Java (RTSJ) [28] was developed to address the main concerns of the community. It adapts and extends the programming model of Java to support real-time programming abstractions. It also has adequate memory management based on the use of scoped memory areas, which are not subject to garbage collection. With these developments, it is possible to write Java programs with predictable time properties.

This is essential to allow the use of Java in the context of safety-critical applications, since the requirements for many of them involve timed as well as functional properties. RTSJ is not enough in this application domain, though. Some sort of certification is typically needed, and that prescribes a controlled engineering process to obtain programs that are reliable, robust, maintainable, and traceable. For that, the safety-critical industry usually resorts to controlled language subsets [1, 22]. In this context, RTSJ is far too rich, encompassing the whole of Java as well as the novel constructs to support real-time programming.

To address this issue, an international effort has been more recently producing an Open Group standard for a high-integrity real-time version of Java: Safety-Critical Java (SCJ) [17]. It is a subset of the RTSJ; its execution model is based on missions and event handlers, and it restricts the memory model to prohibit use of the heap and define a policy for the use of memory areas. The SCJ design is organised in Levels (0, 1, and 2), with a decreasing amount of restrictions.

The standardisation work includes the production of a reference implementation, but no particular design or verification technique. We have addressed this using the *Circus* [4] family of languages for refinement [7] as part of the hiJaC (High-Integrity Java Applications using *Circus*) project. The *Circus* languages are based on a flexible combination of elements from Z [31] for data modelling, CSP [24] for behavioural specification, and standard imperative commands from Morgan's calculus [21]. Variants and extensions of *Circus* include *Circus Time* [25], which provides facilities for time modelling from Timed CSP [23], and *OhCircus* [5], which is based on the Java model of object-orientation. The most recent variant is *SCJ-Circus* [20], which caters

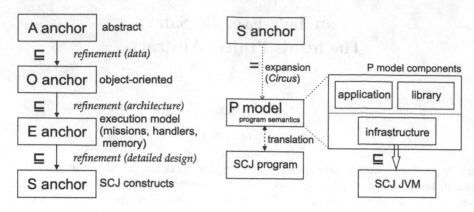

Fig. 1. Our approach to development and verification

for modelling using the abstractions of the SCJ paradigm: missions, handlers, memory areas, and so on.

Circus has been used for modelling and verification of control systems specified in Simulink [3, 19], including virtualisation software by the US Naval Research Laboratory [10]. The semantics of the *Circus* family of languages is based on the Unifying Theories of Programming (UTP) [15]. This is a framework that supports refinement-based reasoning in the context of a variety of programming paradigms. It supports the independent treatment of programming theories, with associated techniques for their combination. This makes it possible for us to consider a rich language for refinement that supports the use of object-oriented and SCJ constructs as well as the modelling and verification of time properties.

A *Circus*-based formalisation of the SCJ execution model [32] and a UTP theory for the SCJ memory model [6] are available. In [7], we have presented a refinement strategy for deriving SCJ programs from *Circus* specifications that builds on these results and UTP theories for references [5, 13, 30].

Our refinement strategy supports the stepwise development of SCJ Level 1 programs based on specification models that do not consider the details of either the SCJ mission or memory models. SCJ Level 1 corresponds roughly to the Ravenscar profile for Ada [2]. It is not as restrictive as Level 0, which is based on a cyclic executive programming model, but is controlled enough to impose a reasonable challenge in the development of a programming theory.

As shown in Figure 1, four *Circus* specifications characterise the major development steps of our strategy. We call them anchors, as they identify the (intermediate) targets for refinement and the design aspects treated in each step. Each anchor is written using a different combination of the *Circus* family of notations. The first anchor is the abstract specification model. The last is so close to an SCJ program as to enable automatic code generation. It is written in *SCJ-Circus*, a new version of *Circus* extended with constructs that correspond to the components of the SCJ programming paradigm. They are syntactic abbreviations for definitions introduced in [32] to characterise the SCJ infrastructure and applications; they use a combination of the variants of *Circus* to cater for time, object-orientation, and the SCJ memory model.

Our development strategy establishes, by construction, that the *SCJ-Circus* model is a refinement of the specification used as the first anchor. This means that safety, liveness, and timing properties are preserved. Safety requires that the sequences of interactions (traces) of the program are possible for the specification. Liveness requires that deadlock or divergence in the program can occur only if allowed in the specification. Finally, preservation of the timing properties requires that the deadlines and budgets defined in the specification are enforced by the deadlines and budgets defined for the components of the program. Our long-term goal is to provide for Safety-Critical Java at least the same level of support that the SPARK tools, for instance, provide for Ada.

Regarding time, our strategy makes use of decomposition via refinement. It is inspired by the work in [14], which introduces time into Morgan's refinement calculus so that derivation of code from specifications is similar to that for untimed specifications. In our approach, the requirements in the first anchor are localised in the SCJ components of the final target anchor. It is, in this way, annotated with the machine-independent timing requirements that every correct implementation (for a specific platform) needs to satisfy. Verifying that they do may require, for instance, schedulability analysis.

By extending *Circus* with SCJ constructs, we can model SCJ programs in the unified framework of a refinement language. We are tackling translation from *SCJ-Circus* model to Java code as separate work in line with what we have previously achieved for low-level *Circus* models and corresponding Java implementations [9]. Another interesting line of work uses the part of the model of an *SCJ-Circus* program that gives an abstract specification of the SCJ paradigm to support verification of an SCJ virtual machine (SCJVM).

Ongoing work includes formalisation of the requirements for an SCJVM and the verification of the only SCJVM that is publicly available and up to date with the SCJ standard [26]. We are also pursuing the extension of our approach to SCJ Level 2 [29]. Our starting point is the extension of the model in [32] for the SCJ infrastructure and applications.

Complementary efforts in the SCJ community provide support for static analysis of SCJ programs. There are annotation-based [8, 27] and annotation-free [18] techniques for checking memory safety. The use of JML to support worst case execution time analysis considers an important non-functional property [12]. Testing has also been investigated [16].

So, can Java ever be safe? Can we ever consider the use of Java for programming safety-critical applications? The answer is "a version of Java, namely, SCJ, is already being used in this domain". As explained, it is necessary to perform some essential changes and restrictions to Java. With these, however, it is possible to achieve certification and it is possible to develop a programming theory to support formal development and verification.

Acknowledgements. This work is funded by EPSRC grant EP/H017461/1. Much of what is described here has been developed jointly with James Baxter, Leo Freitas,

Matthew Luckcuck, Chris Marriott, Alvaro Miyazawa, Pedro Ribeiro, Andy Wellings, Jim Woodcock, and Frank Zeyda.

References

1. Barnes, J.: High Integrity Software: The SPARK Approach to Safety and Security. Addison-Wesley (2003)
2. Burns, A.: The Ravenscar profile. Ada Letters **XIX**, 49–52 (1999)
3. Cavalcanti, A.L.C., Clayton, P., O'Halloran, C.: From control law diagrams to Ada via *Circus*. Formal Aspects Comput. **23**(4), 465–512 (2011)
4. Cavalcanti, A.L.C., Sampaio, A.C.A., Woodcock, J.C.P.: A refinement strategy for *Circus*. Formal Aspects Comput. **15**(2–3), 146–181 (2003)
5. Cavalcanti, A.L.C., Sampaio, A.C.A., Woodcock, J.C.P.: Unifying classes and processes. Software and System Modelling **4**(3), 277–296 (2005)
6. Cavalcanti, A.L.C., Wellings, A., Woodcock, J.C.P.: The safety-critical Java memory model formalised. Formal Aspects Comput. **25**(1), 37–57 (2013)
7. Cavalcanti, A.L.C., Zeyda, F., Wellings, A., Woodcock, J.C.P., Wei, K.: Safety-critical Java programs from *Circus* models. Real-Time Systems **49**(5), 614–667 (2013)
8. Dalsgaard, A.E., Hansen, R.R., Schoeberl, M.: Private memory allocation analysis for safety-critical java. In: 10th International Workshop on Java Technologies for Real-time and Embedded Systems, pp. 9–17. ACM (2012)
9. Freitas, A., Cavalcanti, A.: Automatic translation from *Circus* to Java. In: Misra, J., Nipkow, T., Sekerinski, E. (eds.) FM 2006. LNCS, vol. 4085, pp. 115–130. Springer, Heidelberg (2006)
10. Freitas, L., McDermott, J.P.: Formal methods for security in the xenon hypervisor. Int. J. Softw. Tools Technol. Transfer **13**(5), 463–489 (2011)
11. Gosling, J., Joy, B., Steele, G.: The Java Language Specification. Addison-Wesley (1996)
12. Haddad, G., Hussain, F., Leavens, G.T.: The design of SafeJML, a specification language for SCJ with support for WCET specification. In: 8th International Workshop on Java Technologies for Real-time and Embedded Systems. ACM (2010)
13. Harwood, W.T., Cavalcanti, A., Woodcock, J.: A theory of pointers for the UTP. In: Fitzgerald, J.S., Haxthausen, A.E., Yenigun, H. (eds.) ICTAC 2008. LNCS, vol. 5160, pp. 141–155. Springer, Heidelberg (2008)
14. Hayes, I.J., Utting, M.: A sequential real-time refinement calculus. Acta Informatica **37**(6), 385–448 (2001)
15. Hoare, C.A.R., J., He: Unifying Theories of Programming. Prentice-Hall (1998)
16. Kalibera, T., Parizek, P., Malohlava, M., Schoeberl, M.: Exhaustive testing of safety critical Java. In: 8th International Workshop on Java Technologies for Real-time and Embedded Systems, pp. 164–174. ACM (2010)
17. Locke, D., Andersen, B.S., Brosgol, B., Fulton, M., Henties, T., Hunt, J.J., Nielsen, J.O., Nilsen, K., Schoeberl, M., Tokar, J., Vitek, J., Wellings, A.: Safety Critical Java Specification, First Release 0.76. The Open Group, UK (2010). jcp.org/aboutJava/communityprocess/edr/jsr302/index.html
18. Marriott, C., Cavalcanti, A.: SCJ: memory-safety checking without annotations. In: Jones, C., Pihlajasaari, P., Sun, J. (eds.) FM 2014. LNCS, vol. 8442, pp. 465–480. Springer, Heidelberg (2014)

19. Miyazawa, A., Cavalcanti, A.L.C.: Refinement-oriented models of Stateflow charts. Sci. Comput. Program. **77**(10–11), 1151–1177 (2012)
20. Miyazawa, A., Cavalcanti, A.L.C.: *SCJ-Circus*: a refinement-oriented formal notation for Safety-Critical Java. In: REFINE Workshop (2015)
21. Morgan, C.C.: Programming from Specifications. 2nd edn. Prentice-Hall (1994)
22. Motor Industry Software Reliability Association Guidelines. Guidelines for Use of the C Language in Critical Systems (2012)
23. Reed, G.M., Roscoe, A.W.: A timed model for communicating sequential processes. Theoret. Comput. Sci. **58**, 249–261 (1988)
24. Roscoe, A.W.: The Theory and Practice of Concurrency. Prentice-Hall Series in Computer Science. Prentice-Hall (1998)
25. Sherif, A., Cavalcanti, A.L.C., He, J., Sampaio, A.C.A.: A process algebraic framework for specification and validation of real-time systems. Formal Aspects Comput. **22**(2), 153–191 (2010)
26. Søndergaard, H., Korsholm, S.E., Ravn, A.P.: Safety-critical Java for low-end embedded platforms. In: Schoeberl, M., Wellings, A., (eds.) 10th International Workshop on Java Technologies for Real-time and Embedded Systems, pp. 44–53. ACM (2012)
27. Tang, D., Plsek, A., Vitek, J.: Static checking of safety critical Java annotations. In: 8th International Workshop on Java Technologies for Real-time and Embedded Systems. ACM (2010)
28. Wellings, A.: Concurrent and Real-Time Programming in Java. Wiley (2004)
29. Wellings, A.J., Luckcuck, M., Cavalcanti, A.L.C.: Safety-critical Java level 2: motivations, example applications and issues. In: Siebert, F., Nilsen, K., (eds.) The 11th International Workshop on Java Technologies for Real-time and Embedded Systems, pp. 48–57. ACM (2013)
30. Woodcock, J.: The miracle of reactive programming. In: Butterfield, A. (ed.) UTP 2008. LNCS, vol. 5713, pp. 202–217. Springer, Heidelberg (2010)
31. Woodcock, J.C.P., Davies, J.: Using Z—Specification, Refinement, and Proof. Prentice-Hall (1996)
32. Zeyda, F., Cavalcanti, A., Wellings, A.: The safety-critical Java mission model: a formal account. In: Qin, S., Qiu, Z. (eds.) ICFEM 2011. LNCS, vol. 6991, pp. 49–65. Springer, Heidelberg (2011)

Specification and Analysis of SoC Flows
(Abstract)

Sava Krstić

Intel Corporation

Systems-on-chip are mindbogglingly complex mass-produced machines with a set of characteristics that make them worthy of dedicated, domain-specific study. We build these machines with a lot of effort, per specs that are largely informal, and they work more-or-less as desired. The hope is that with better understanding of what we're creating, it can be created more efficiently and it will work better.

As a state machine, a system-on-chip (SoC) is composed of multiple IP blocks (state machines themselves) that communicate by messaging. Thus, at the top level of the SoC specification, we have a graph whose nodes are IP blocks and whose edges represent interfaces over which messages get passed from block to block. The role of messages is central: at any point in the SoC execution, every IP block contains a set of messages, and these (structured) sets are a crucial part of the SoC state. Message creation, destruction, and transfer from block to block are basic state changes that happen in an SoC. The only other kind of a basic state change is an update of the value of an IP block's repository (register or memory range).

When can an agent (IP block) send a specific message, and what should an agent do when it receives a specific message? Answers to these questions define the most important aspects of global SoC behavior. Consider for a moment just one aspect: powering down of an agent. It gets accomplished by a sequence of messages and actions of several participants, including the agent itself, the power management engine, and perhaps the memory module where the current state of the agent is saved in order to be restored later when the agent is powered up again. It's a protocol, and at Intel the architects would typically specify it as a "flow diagram"—an informal message sequence chart with perhaps some additional information, that in one picture shows the messages involved, their ordering etc. Specification of other protocols, like cache coherence, may require a large number of flow diagrams.

The number of protocols executed in a given SoC is huge and no single person understands them all. Multiple protocols and multiple instances of the same protocol may execute concurrently in an SoC. Things can easily go wrong here, and when they go wrong it is not always clear even who is responsible. For example, if two concurrently executing protocols can lead to a deadlocked state (where none of the two can make progress towards completion), the deadlock bug may be possible to fix by making a change in either of the protocols, which may mean making a change in either of two agents. Lack of programming and logic rigor in SoC protocol specification makes parts of SoC system-level validation and debugging nightmarish and costly.

At Intel, we are trying to raise the level of precision and analyzability of SoC protocol specs by promulgating the use of the in-house experimental graphical

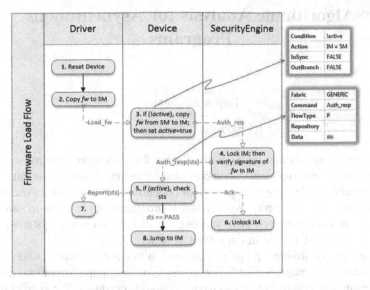

Fig. 1. IFLOW for a version of the firmware load protocol for a microcontroller (Device) in an SoC. Attributes of one flow task and one message are shown in boxes on the right.

language IFLOW. The basic compilation unit of the language is the *flow* (protocol fragment), with an example shown in Figure 1. A flow has a graphical part consisting of various geometric shapes (agent "lanes", control-flow arcs, message arcs, "task" rectangles, etc.) and the textual part which the user supplies in shape *annotations*, and which becomes visible by mouse clicking on the shape. (English text written on the shapes is just comments.)

IFLOW has a well-developed semantics and a compiler that creates an executable system given any set of flows as input. The more information the user puts in the annotations, the more detailed model gets generated.

In our presentation, we will cover the elements of the IFLOW language and its semantics, and show its use on two examples: (1) model checking with *Spin* back-end that finds a subtle security vulnerability of the protocol in Figure 1, which manifests itself only when three instances of the flow are executing concurrently; (2) a static analysis method for deadlock detection in systems of flows, which extracts dependencies between flow events and was capable of finding vicious cycles responsible for some of the most pernicious SoC deadlocks at Intel.

Acknowledgment. Thanks to Flemming Andersen, Jesse Bingham, Sylvain Conchon, John Erickson, John O'Leary, David Palmer, Eran Talmor, and Jin Yang for their flows-related work and thoughts.

Algorithmic Analysis for Asynchronous Programs

Rupak Majumdar

MPI-SWS, Germany

Asynchronous programming is a generic term for concurrent programming with co-operative task management. Asynchronous programs allow efficient resource management and low-latency management of concurrent requests and are used in many diverse settings. For example, asynchronous programming is used in smartphone applications, in clientside web programming, in high-performance systems software such as servers, in GUIs, and in embedded systems.

There are several different programming models that are all clubbed together by the term "asynchronous programming." For example, in one implementation, the underlying programming system exposes an *asynchronous* procedure call construct (either in the language or using a library), which allows the programmer to post a procedure for future execution in case a certain event occurs. An event scheduler manages asynchronously posted procedures. When the corresponding event occurs, the scheduler picks the associated procedure and runs it to completion. These procedures are sequential code, possibly with recursion, and can post further asynchronous procedures. This model is used, e.g., in systems software such as memcached or nginx. In a different implementation, asynchronous tasks provide a way for pipelined processing of requests, and asynchronously posted tasks are processed first-in-first-out but without any external event management. This model is used, e.g., in low level embedded systems. In yet another implementation, several concurrent worker threads may run in parallel, each with its own queue of events, and the threads can send tasks to each other. This model is used, e.g., in Android and iOS.

In all these scenarios, while programs can be very efficient, the manual management of resources and asynchronous procedures can make programming quite difficult. The natural control flow of a task is obscured and the programmer must ensure correct behavior for all possible orderings of external events. Specifically, the global state of the program can change between the time an asynchronous procedure is posted and the time the scheduler picks and runs it.

In this talk, I will describe algorithmic analysis techniques for asynchronous programs. On the one hand, I will talk about formal models for different styles of asynchronous programs and their decidability properties. On the other, I will talk about our attempts to build model checking and program analysis tools for programs written in this style.

For formal models, I will describe a surprising decidability result for a rich model of asynchronous programming by showing a connection between the model and Petri data nets, a well-studied infinite-state concurrency model.

For tool development, I will describe three recent attempts: one using coverability analysis of Petri nets, one using rely-guarantee reasoning, and one using systematic exploration with partial order refinement.

Acknowledgements. My work on asynchronous programs has been informed by collaborations with many wonderful colleagues. I would like to thank Michael Emmi, Javier Esparza, Pierre Ganty, Ivan Gavran, Ranjit Jhala, Aditya Kanade, Johannes Kloos, Pallavi Maiya, Filip Niksic, Fernando Rosa-Velardo, Viktor Vafeiadis, and Zilong Wang.

Contents

Domain-Specific Languages with Scala

Cyrille Artho[1]([✉]), Klaus Havelund[2], Rahul Kumar[2], and Yoriyuki Yamagata[1]

[1] AIST, Amagasaki, Japan
c.artho@aist.go.jp
[2] Jet Propulsion Laboratory, California Institute of Technology, Pasadena, CA, USA

Abstract. Domain-Specific Languages (DSLs) are often classified into external and internal DSLs. An external DSL is a stand-alone language with its own parser. An internal DSL is an extension of an existing programming language, the host language, offering the user of the DSL domain-specific constructs as well as the constructs of the host language, thus providing a richer language than the DSL itself. In this paper we report on experiences implementing external as well as internal formal modeling DSLs with the Scala programming language, known in particular for its support for defining DSLs. The modeling languages include monitoring logics, a testing language, and a general purpose SysML inspired modeling language. We present a systematic overview of advantages and disadvantages of each option.

Keywords: External and internal domain-specific language · DSL · Scala · Modeling · Programming · Language design · Evaluation

1 Introduction

A domain-specific language (DSL) is a language specialized to a particular domain [10]. DSLs are for example popular in the formal methods and testing communities. A DSL is designed to make the modeling or programming task easier and sometimes eliminates the need for a full-fledged programming language altogether. DSLs are classified into external and internal DSLs. An *external DSL* is a stand-alone language with a customized parser. Examples are XML [7] for representing data and DOT [12] for drawing graphs, for example state machines. In contrast to this, an *internal DSL* extends an existing programming language, the *host language*. A user may employ the host language in addition to the DSL. On the implementation side, the compiler and run-time environment of the host language are reused. Internal DSLs are furthermore divided into shallow and deep embeddings. In a *shallow embedding,* the host language's features are used directly to model the DSL. The constructs have their usual meaning. Conversely,

---

Part of the work was supported by the Japanese Society for the Promotion of Science (*kaken-hi* grants 23240003 and 26280019), and by NSF Grant CCF-0926190. Part of the work was carried out at Jet Propulsion Laboratory, California Institute of Technology, under a contract with the National Aeronautics and Space Administration.

M. Butler et al. (Eds.): ICFEM 2015, LNCS 9407, pp. 1–16, 2015.
DOI: 10.1007/978-3-319-25423-4_1

in a *deep embedding*, a separate internal representation is made of the DSL (an abstract syntax), which is then interpreted or compiled as in the case of an external DSL. The reuse of an existing programming language reduces development time but can also manifest itself as a constraint for an internal DSL.

Both external and internal DSLs therefore have their own trade-offs. In this paper, we systematically examine these advantages and disadvantages, based on our own practical experience in building numerous external as well as internal modeling and testing DSLs with the Scala programming language. Scala is a modern strongly typed programming language combining object-oriented and functional programming [22]. Scala has several libraries and features that make it suited for DSL development. For external DSLs these include parser combinators, and for internal DSLs these include implicit function definitions, which allow values of one type to be lifted to values of a different type, the ability to call methods on objects without dots and parentheses, case classes, partial functions, call-by-name, user-defined operators composed of symbols, operator overloading, as well as other features such as higher-order functions and lambda expressions.

Our contributions are: (a) a report on our experiences on using Scala to implement external and internal DSLs for formal modeling, three of which have been incorporated into real production systems, (b) a summary of the pros and cons of each type of DSL, and (c) a survey of the various tools and techniques used for creating DSLs with Scala. A higher-level contribution is the message that Scala, as a high-level programming language, can be used for modeling in general, possibly augmented with internal modeling DSLs.

Much work has been carried out studying the development of DSLs [10,21]. The literature is too vast to be surveyed here. Other programming languages have been popular as a platform for DSLs, such as Ruby, Python, and Haskell. One of our through-going themes is DSLs for event monitoring. Such internal DSLs have also been developed in Haskell [29] and Java [6]. Focusing specifically on Scala, an internal DSL for rule-based programming, which we will also present, is presented in [11]. Numerous internal DSLs have been developed in Scala for testing, including for example ScalaTest [30]. Technologies that we have not yet explored, and therefore will not evaluate, include Scala macros [28], Scala virtualized [25], and SugarScala [19], a framework for extending Scala's syntax.

The paper is organized as follows: Sect. 2 covers the design and implementation of external DSLs, while Sect. 3 covers internal DSLs. Section 4 compares the key points of different approaches, and Sect. 5 concludes.

2   External DSLs

An external DSL is a stand-alone language. With Scala, one can develop an external DSL using either a *parser library* or a *parser tool.*

2.1   The Parser Library Approach

Existing parser libraries for Scala include *parser combinators* [13,24] and *parsing expression grammars* [23]. A parser combinator is a higher-order function that accepts zero or more parsers and returns a new parser. A parser is a function that accepts a string and returns a user-defined data object, typically a parse tree. Parser combinators are based on recursive descent and facilitate modular construction.[1] Generalized LL (GLL) combinators [13] are an alternative to Scala's original parser combinators. The GLL algorithm allows left-recursion and ambiguity, and also provides more elegant handling of semantic actions. Note that the parser combinator libraries in Scala themselves are internal DSLs for writing grammars. A yet different library is Parboiled2, a high-performance Parsing Expression Grammar library [23]. It uses macros to generate a parser at compile time from a grammar written in an internal Scala DSL.

Example: Data Automata. *Data Automata* (Daut) [15] monitor program executions at run time; execution traces are checked against specifications in Daut's logic. A trace is a sequence of events, each of which is a named tuple of values. The logic is defined using Scala's original parser combinators [24]. Assume as an example that a multi-threaded program has been instrumented to emit events reflecting the acquisition and release of locks: $acquire(t, l)$ and $release(t, l)$ represent events where thread t acquires or releases lock l, respectively. A simple way of detecting deadlock potentials between two threads is to monitor whether threads take locks in a circular manner: one thread acquiring some lock l_1 and then some lock l_2 without having released l_1, and another thread acquiring these two locks in the opposite order. Even if a deadlock does not occur, the circular pattern represents a potential for it to occur. The monitor shown in Fig. 1, formulated in the DSL named Daut, detects such potentials.

```
monitor LockOrder {
  acquire(t1,a) -> {
    release(t1,a) -> ok
    acquire(t1,b) :: !(b = a) -> {
      acquire(t2,b) -> {
        release(t2,b) -> ok
        acquire(t2,a) -> error } } } }
```

Fig. 1. External Daut DSL: lock order monitor.

Constructing a parser for a language usually begins with designing an abstract syntax: data structures that represent the result of parsing. In Scala we usually define such as case classes, as shown in Fig. 2 (top) for the first few top-level case classes for this DSL.[2] In this example, a specification is a list of automata; an automaton has a name and contains a lists of states. A state is defined by a collection of state modifiers (specifying the kind of state, for example whether

---

[1] The standard Scala library [26] originally included a parser combinator package. However, because it is rarely used, it was moved to an external library [24].

[2] A case class in Scala is like a class with the additional properties that it supports pattern matching over objects of the class, that the **new** keyword is not needed to create objects of the class, and equality is pre-defined based on the arguments.

it is an initial state or final state); a name; possible formal parameters (states can be parameterized with data); and transitions. A transition in turn consists of a pattern that must successfully match an incoming event, and an optional condition which must evaluate to true, for the transition to be taken, resulting in the right-hand side (a state expression) to be executed.

AST.scala:
```
case class Specification(automata: List[Automaton])

case class Automaton(name: Id, states: List[StateDef])

case class StateDef(modifiers: List[Modifier], name: Id,
   formals: List[Id], transitions: List[Transition])

case class Transition(pattern: Pattern, condition: Option[Condition],
   rhs: List[StateExp])
```

Grammar.scala:
```
def specification: Parser[Specification] =
   rep(automaton) ^^ {case automata => transform(Specification(automata))}

def automaton: Parser[Automaton] =
   "monitor" ~> ident ~
   ("{ " ~> rep(transition) ~ rep(statedef) <~ "}") ^^
   {case name ~ (transitions ~ statedefs) =>
       if (transitions.isEmpty) Automaton(name, statedefs) else { ... } }

def transition: Parser[Transition] =
   pattern ~ opt("::" ~> condition) ~ ("->" ~> rep1sep(stateexp, ",")) ^^
   {case pat ~ cond ~ rhs => Transition(pat,cond,rhs)}
```

Fig. 2. External Daut DSL: part of the Scala AST and parser combinator grammar.

Figure 2 (bottom) shows part of the parser expressed using Scala's parser combinator library. The parser generates an abstract syntax tree (AST) in the above-mentioned data structure. A specification is a Parser, which when applied to an input (as in specification(*input*)) produces an object of the (case) class Specification. A specification consists of zero or more (rep) automaton. The code after the ^^ symbol is a function, which takes as argument the parsed sub-data structures and returns the Specification object, in this case obtained by a transformation. An automaton is introduced by the keyword monitor, followed by an identifier, and a block delimited by { and }, which contains a sequence of transitions and a sequence of state definitions. Finally, a transition consists of a pattern, an optional guard condition, and one or more target states following the arrow. Transitions at the top level of a monitor represent an initial state. The symbols ~>, <~, , and ~ are methods in the parser combinator DSL that are used to represent spaces. This illustrates one of the drawbacks of using an internal DSL such as parser combinators: the notation can get slightly inconvenient, lowering readability.

2.2 The Parser Tool Approach

In the parser tool approach, a tool generates the parser program from a grammar. Parser tool frameworks that can be used with Scala include ScalaBison [27] and ANTLR [1]. ScalaBison [27] is a Scala parser generator, and hence allows Scala code to be written directly as the actions generating Scala objects. ANTLR [1] is Java-based and generates a parse tree as a Java object. This then has to be traversed (visited) by a Scala program and translated into a Scala tree. The advantage of ANTLR is its robust parsing algorithm. We use ANTLR for implementing the K language—a SysML-inspired language for specifying both high-level system descriptions as well as low-level implementations of a system. Note that ANTLR itself provides an external DSL for writing grammars.

Example.k:
```
class Instrument {
  var id : Int
  var name : String
  var powerLevel : Real }

class Spacecraft {
  var id : Int
  var instruments : [Instrument]
  req InstrumentsCount :
    instruments.count > 0 &&
    forall i,j:instruments . i != j => i.id != j.id }

assoc SpacecraftInstrument {
  part Spacecraft : Spacecraft
  part instruments: Instrument 1 .. 10 }
```

Grammar.g4:
```
grammar K;

classDeclaration:
  'class' Identifier extends? '{' memberDeclarationList? '}';

assocDeclaration:
  'assoc' Identifier  '{' assocMemberDeclarationList? '}';

expression:
  '(' expression ')' #ParenExp
  | Identifier #IdentExp
  | expression '.' Identifier #DotExp
...
```

Fig. 3. External K DSL: example of a model and ANTLR grammar.

Example: The K Language. Figure 3 shows an example model in K. Class Instrument specifies the instrument id, name, and power level. Class Spacecraft models the spacecraft, which contains several instruments with a unique id, as specified by constraint InstrumentsCount. Definition SpacecraftInstrument specifies that each Spacecraft can be *associated* with a maximum of 10 instruments, i.e., each Instrument contains a reference to the Spacecraft and the Spacecraft contains references to all instruments that are a *part* of it.

Using ANTLR, we create a tool chain to parse and process K artifacts. ANTLR accepts grammars specified in *Extended Backus-Naur-Form* (see Fig. 3). Patterns are specified using rules and sub-rules that can be marked optional (?) and repetitive (*, +). Each rule can also be named using the # notation at the end of a rule. Keywords are specified in single quotes. In the example, rule classDeclaration specifies how classes are defined by an identifier, an optional *extends* declaration, and an optional class member declaration list enclosed within curly brackets. Similarly, we define the grammar for associations. The expression rule specifies how expressions can be constructed in K. Rule precedence is determined by the order of the occurrence of the rules.

Given a grammar, ANTLR produces a lexer and parser (in Java). ANTLR further enables one to create a *visitor* to visit the nodes in the generated parse tree. We implement a visitor in Scala by importing the required Java libraries and *stitching* the code together to access the ANTLR parse tree in Scala. Figure 4 shows a snippet of the visitor for the K language. The visitor makes use of classes defined in the K AST, also shown in Fig. 4. Both snippets correspond to visiting expression nodes in the parse tree and creating expression declarations in the AST. For example, the visitor function visitDotExp takes as input a context ctx of type DotExpContext. This is used to extract the expression e and the identifier ident from the ANTLR parse tree. Together, these are used to create an instance of DotExp, which is defined in the K Scala AST. The K Scala visitor produces the complete AST, which can be used for code generation and analysis. We currently use the AST to transform K code to JSON and back. The robustness of ANTLR is a benefit, but there is also significant effort involved in creating the visitor that produces the Scala AST from the Java AST. A small change in the grammar can produce a cascading series of changes to the visitor.

Visitor.scala:

```scala
override def visitDotExp(ctx: ModelParser.DotExpContext): AnyRef = {
  var e: Exp = visit(ctx.expression()).asInstanceOf[Exp]
  var ident: String = ctx.Identifier().getText()
  DotExp(e, ident) }

override def visitParenExp(ctx: ModelParser.ParenExpContext): AnyRef = {
  ParenExp(visit(ctx.expression()).asInstanceOf[Exp]) }
```

AST.scala:

```scala
trait Exp
case class ParenExp(exp: Exp) extends Exp
case class DotExp(exp: Exp, ident: String) extends Exp
case class IdentExp(ident: String) extends Exp
```

Fig. 4. External DSL: part of the ANTLR visitor and AST for K.

3   Internal DSLs

An internal DSL extends the host language with custom constructs. We cover three variants: Annotations, shallow embedding, and deep embedding.

With *annotations,* a host program is annotated with information on existing language constructs. The host language needs to permit annotations, as is the case for Java and Scala. When using embedding, the extension is implemented as a library in the host language without any additional techniques. Here we distinguish between shallow and deep embedding. *Shallow embedding* uses the host language's features directly to model the DSL. The constructs have their usual meaning. In contrast, in a *deep embedding* one creates a separate representation of the DSL: an abstract syntax (AST), which is then interpreted or translated, as in the case of an external DSL.

3.1   Annotations

Annotations in Java or Scala associate extra information with classes, fields, and methods. Java annotations accept a possibly empty list of key-value pairs of parameters, where parameters can be of primitive types, strings, classes, enumerations, and arrays of the preceding types. To be used at run-time with Scala, annotations have to be defined as Java annotations with run-time retention since Scala's annotations currently do not persist past the compilation stage.

Example: Modbat's Configuration Engine. Many command line programs allow options to be set via environment variables or command line arguments. Existing libraries parse command line arguments, but still leave it to the user to check semantic correctness, such as whether a value is within a permitted range. This problem also occurs for Modbat, a model-based test tool [2].

```
@Doc("overrides environment variable CLASSPATH if set")
var classpath: String = "."

@Choice(Array("one", "two", "many"))
var simpleNumber = "one"

@Range(dmin = 0.0, dmax = 1.0) @Shorthand('p')
var defaultProbability = 0.5
```

Fig. 5. Example of annotations for configuration variables.

In Modbat, configuration options are expressed as annotated Scala variables. An internal library analyzes the annotations and parses command line arguments, checking whether a parameter matches the name of an annotated variable. If so, the default value of the right variable is overridden by the new value. For example, the value for `defaultProbability` can be overridden by command line option `--default-probability=0.6`. Figure 5 shows an example. `@Doc` provides a documentation string for a usage/help output; `@Choice` limits options to a predetermined set; `@Range` defines the allowed range of a value; and `@Shorthand` defines a one-letter shorthand for a command line option.

It is also possible to use inheritance, naming conventions, or library calls, to represent or set certain attributes. However, these solutions are more limiting than annotations or require more code. Indeed, when Java annotations became available, many tools (such as JUnit [20]) adapted them.

3.2   Shallow Embedding

In a shallow embedding the host language's features are used directly, with their usual meaning, to model the DSL, which is typically presented as an application programming interface (API).

Example: Data Automata. Recall the lock order monitor expressed in an external DSL in Fig. 1. Figure 6 shows a version of this monitor expressed in an internal shallow DSL, also described in [15], and variants of which are described in [4,14]. Event types are defined as case classes sub-classing a trait Event.[3] The monitor itself is defined as a class sub-classing the trait Monitor, which is parameterized with the event type. The trait Monitor offers various constants and methods for defining monitors, including in this case the methods **whenever** and **state**, and the constants **ok** and **error**, which are not Scala keywords. The LockOrder monitor looks surprisingly similar to the one in Fig. 1.

```
trait Event
case class acquire(thread:String,lock:String) extends Event
case class release(thread:String,lock:String) extends Event

class LockOrder extends Monitor[Event] {
  whenever {
    case acquire(t1, a) => state {
      case release('t1', 'a') => ok
      case acquire('t1', b) if b != a => state {
        case acquire(t2, 'b') => state {
          case release('t2', 'b') => ok
          case acquire('t2', 'a') => error } } } } }
```

Fig. 6. Internal shallow Scala DSL: lock order event definitions and monitor.

The complete implementation of the internal DSL is less than 200 lines of code, including printing routines for error messages. Conversely, the similar external DSL is approximately 1500 lines (nearly an order of magnitude more code) and less expressive. The parts of the implementation of the internal shallow DSL directly relevant for the example in Fig. 6 are shown in Fig. 7.

A monitor contains a set of currently active states, the *frontier*. All the states have to lead to success (conjunction semantics). A transition function is a *partial function* (a Scala concept), which maps events to a set of target states. A state object (of the case class **state**) contains a transition function, which is initialized with the **when** function. A state is made to react to an event using apply.[4] There are several forms (sub-classes) of states, including **error**, **ok**, and **always** states

---

[3] A trait in Scala is a module concept closely related to the notion of an abstract class, as for example found in Java. Traits, however, differ by allowing a more flexible way of composition called mixin composition, an alternative to multiple inheritance.

[4] The apply method in Scala has special interpretation: if an object O defines a such, it can be applied to a list of arguments using function application syntax: O(...), equivalent to calling the apply method: O.apply(...).

```
class Monitor[E <: AnyRef] {
  private var states: Set[state] = Set()
  type Transitions = PartialFunction[E, Set[state]]

  class state {
    private var transitions: Transitions = noTransitions

    def when(transitions: Transitions) {
      this.transitions = transitions }

    def apply(event: E): Option[Set[state]] =
      if (transitions.isDefinedAt(event))
        Some(transitions(event)) else None }

  case object error extends state
  case object ok extends state
  class always extends state

  def state(transitions: Transitions): state = {
    val e = new state; e.when(transitions); e }

  def always(transitions: Transitions): state = {
    val e = new always; e.when(transitions); e }

  def whenever(transitions: Transitions) {
    states += always(transitions) } }
```

Fig. 7. Internal shallow Scala DSL: part of implementation.

that stay active even if the transition function applies to an event. Functions **state** and **always** take a transition function and return a new state object with that transition function. Function **whenever** creates an **always** state from the transition function and adds it to the set of initial states of the monitor.

The type of a transition function suggests that it returns a set of states. In Fig. 6, however, the result of transitions (on the right of =>) are single states, not sets of states. This would not type check was it not for the definition of the implicit function convSingleState, which lifts a single state to a set of states, here shown together with a selection of other implicit conversion functions:

```
implicit def convSingleState(state: state): Set[state] = Set(state)
implicit def convBool(b: Boolean): Set[state] = Set(if (b) ok else error)
implicit def convUnit(u: Unit): Set[state] = Set(ok)
implicit def convStatePredicate(s: state): Boolean = states contains s
```

These other implicit functions support lifting for example a Boolean value to an **ok** or **error** state (such that one can write a Boolean expression on the right-hand side of =>); the **Unit** value to **ok** (such that one can write statements with side-effects on the right-hand side); and finally a state to a Boolean, testing whether the state is in the set of active states, used in conditions.

Example: CSP$_E$. CSP$_E$ (CSP for events) is a run-time verification tool that uses a notation similar to Hoare's Communicating Sequential Processes (CSP) [18]. CSP$_E$ allows specification of "concurrent" processes. The top of Fig. 8 shows the lock order monitor in CSP$_E$. Compared to the lock monitor of Fig. 1, the major difference is that parallel composition of the top level process (p || ...) is required to run the monitor continuously. The similarity to data automata in the previous example is evident. The role of p || ... is similar to **always** and **process** is similar

Example monitor:

```
val lock_order = process (p => ?? {
  case acquire(t1, a) =>
    p || ?? { case release('t1', 'a') => STOP
              case acquire('t1', b) if a != b =>
                ?? { case acquire(t2, 'b') =>
                  ?? { case release('t2', 'b') => STOP
                       case acquire('t2', 'a') => FAIL }}}})
```

CSP$_E$ implementation:

```
abstract class Process { ... }

class Rec (f: Process => Process) extends Process {
  override def acceptPrim(e: AbsEvent): Process = f(this).accept(e) }

object CSPE {
  def process (f: Process => Process) = new Rec (f)
  def ??(f: PartialFunction[AbsEvent, Process]) = new ParamPrefix(f) }

class ParamPrefix(f: PartialFunction[AbsEvent, Process]) extends Process {
  override def acceptPrim(e: AbsEvent): Process =
    if (f.isDefinedAt(e)) f(e) else this }
```

Fig. 8. Example monitor written in CSP$_E$ and partial implementation.

to whenever in data automata. The pattern match clauses are almost the same, except for ??.

In CSP$_E$, recursive definitions are implemented by functions that take a process and return a new process (see Fig. 8, bottom). Function ?? takes a partial function from events to processes (monitors), and creates a new process. That process evaluates the given function if it is defined for a given event, and waits otherwise. The monitor specification supplies the event as the first argument of a process (before =>) and the behavior of the process to be executed after receiving the event, as the second one. Internally acceptPrim takes the first argument and executes f to continue monitoring the right-hand side of the expression.

CSP$_E$ is implemented as an internal DSL. The main reason for this is to interface with external logging tools. The shallow embedding furthermore simplifies the implementation. However, due to this, the grammar of CSP$_E$ slightly deviates from the standard CSP notation. For example, parametric events and the recursive definition of processes are more complicated than in standard CSP.

3.3 Deep Embedding

In a deep embedding, a DSL program is represented as an abstract syntax tree (AST), which is then interpreted or translated as in the case of an external DSL. The AST is generated via an API. We shall show two deep DSLs, one for writing state machine driven tests, and one for rule-based trace monitoring.

Example: Modbat. The model-based test tool Modbat generates test cases from extended finite-state machines [2]. Modbat has been used to verify a Java model library and a SAT solver [2]. A Modbat model contains definitions of

Example.scala:
```scala
import Model._

class Example {
  def action { /* code */ }

  "a" -> "b" := { action } }
```

Transition.scala:
```scala
class Transition(val src: String,
                 val tgt: String) {
  var transfunc: () => Any = null

  def := (action: => Any) {
    transfunc = () => action
    Model.addTrans(this) } }
```

Model.scala:
```scala
object Model {
  /* implicit conversion for
     transition declaration */
  implicit def stringPairToTrans
    (tr: (String, String)) = {
    new Transition(tr._1, tr._2) }

  /* model data */
  val transitions =
    ListBuffer[Transition]()

  def addTrans(tr: Transition) {
    transitions += tr } }
```

Fig. 9. Implementation of a deep DSL: a miniaturized version of Modbat, given as an example (**Example.scala**) and two classes showing a partial implementation.

transitions: source and target states, and transition actions (code to be executed when a transition is taken). Figure 9 shows a simple example model and a minimalist implementation that registers the model data at run time. The key Scala features that are used for deeply embedding the DSL are the definition of a custom operator := in Transition.scala, together with an implicit conversion of a string pair "a" -> "b", to a transition (in Model.scala).

The design of Modbat's DSL mixes deep embedding for transitions, with annotations and shallow embedding for code representing transition actions on the system under test. The main goal is to make the syntax more declarative and concise where possible (e. g., to declare transitions), while avoiding too many new constructs when Scala code is used (hence the use of annotations and API functions where appropriate). Shallow embedding is ideal for transition actions as they have to interact with the Java run-time environment during test execution.

Example: LogFire. LogFire is an internal (mostly) deep Scala DSL [16]. It was created for writing trace properties, as were the earlier described data automata DSLs in Sects. 2.1 and 3.2 respectively. LogFire implements the Rete algorithm [9], modified to process instantaneous events (in addition to facts that have a life span), and to perform faster lookups in a fact memory. A monitor is specified as a set of rules, each of the form:

```
name -- condition1 & ... & conditionN |-> action
```

Figure 10 illustrates the lock order property expressed as rules in LogFire. The rules operate on a database of facts, the *fact memory*. Rule left-hand sides check incoming events, as well as presence or absence of facts in the fact memory. Right-hand sides (actions) can modify the fact memory, issue error messages, and generally execute any Scala code (here the DSL becomes a shallow DSL). Class **Monitor** defines features for writing rules, for example the functions: event, fact, --, &, |->, insert, remove, and fail. Recall that in Scala, method names can be sequences of symbols, and dots and parentheses around method

```
class LockOrder extends Monitor {
  val acquire, release = event
  val Locked, Edge = fact

  "acquire" -- acquire('t, 'l)                        |-> insert(Locked('t, 'l))
  "release" -- Locked('t, 'l) & release('t, 'l)       |-> remove(Locked)
  "edge"    -- Locked('t, 'l1) & acquire('t, 'l2)     |-> insert(Edge('l1, 'l2))
  "cycle"   -- Edge('l1, 'l2) & Edge('l2, 'l1)        |-> fail() }
```

Fig. 10. Internal deep Scala LogFire DSL: lock order monitor.

arguments are optional. Each rule definition in the monitor above is a sequence of method calls, that last of which is the call of the method |->, which produces an internal representation (an abstract syntax tree) of the rule as an object of a class `Rule`, which is then passed as argument to a method `addRule(rule: Rule)` in the Rete module. The abstract syntax class `Rule` is in part defined as:

```
case class Rule(name: String, conditions: List[Condition], action: Action)
case class Action(code: Unit => Unit)
```

A rule consists of a name; a left-hand side, which is a list of conditions, interpreted as a conjunction; and a right-hand side, which is an action. Conditions use deep embedding for optimization purposes. Actions are implemented as Scala code using a shallow embedding (functions from `Unit` to `Unit`).

```
implicit def R(name: String) = new {
  def --(c: Condition) = new RuleDef(name, List(c)) }

class RuleDef(name: String, conditions: List[Condition]) {
  def &(c: Condition) = new RuleDef(name, c :: conditions)

  def |->(stmt: => Unit) {
    addRule(Rule(name, conditions.reverse, Action((x: Unit) => stmt))) } } }
```

Fig. 11. Internal deep Scala LogFire DSL: rule syntax implementation.

The definitions in Fig. 11 support the transformation of a rule entered by the user to an AST object of the class `Rule`. The implicit function R, lifts a string (a rule name) to an anonymous object. That object defines the -- operator, which when applied to a condition returns an object of the class `RuleDef`. This class in turn defines the condition conjunction operator & and the action operator |-> defining the transition from left-hand side to right-hand side of the rule. This operator calls `addRule`, which adds the rule to the Rete network. The implicit function R gets invoked by the compiler automatically when a string is followed by the symbol --, to resolve the type "mismatch" (as no -- operator is defined on strings). The individual conditions in a rule are similarly constructed with the help of the following implicit function, which lifts a symbol (the name of an event or fact) to an object, which defines an `apply` function:

```
implicit def C(kind: Symbol) = new {
  def apply(args: Any*): Condition = ... }
```

The complete interpretation by the Scala compiler of the rule `"release"` in Fig. 10 becomes:

```
R("release").--(C('Locked).apply('t,'l)).&(
  C('release).apply('t,'l)).|->(remove('Locked))"")
```

4 Discussion

We discuss the characteristics of five approaches to DSL implementation from our experience with DSLs for formal modeling (see Table 1 for a summary).

Table 1. Characteristics of different DSL implementation approaches. Signature: $\sqrt{}$ means yes, × means no, ⊗ means no unless an effort is made to make it happen, and ++, +, −, −− rank different approaches from best to worst.

	External		Internal		
	Tool	Lib	Annotations	Deep	Shallow
Parser generation	$\sqrt{}$	×	×	×	×
AST generation	$\sqrt{}$	$\sqrt{}$	$\sqrt{}$	$\sqrt{}$	×
Enables transformation, analysis	$\sqrt{}$	$\sqrt{}$	$\sqrt{}$	$\sqrt{}$	×
Directly executable	×	×	×	×	$\sqrt{}$
Turing complete	⊗	⊗	×	$\sqrt{}$	$\sqrt{}$
Ease of development	−−	−	++	+	++
Flexibility of syntax	++	++	−−	−	−−
Quality of syntax error messages	+	+	++	−−	−
Ease of use	++	++	+	−	−−

Parser Generation. The external tool approach requires an extra *parser generation* and compilation stage, where a parser is first generated from a grammar specification, and then compiled. The other approaches have no code generation stage, which slightly facilitates development.

AST Generation. All approaches except the internal shallow approach generate ASTs. AST generation can complicate matters and at the same time be a facilitator. It influences topics such as transformation analysis, executability, Turing completeness, ease of development, and flexibility of syntax, as discussed below.

Enables Transformation and Analysis. An AST allows us to transform and analyze the DSL. Specifically, it allows us to optimize any code generated from the AST, a capability particularly important for the shown monitoring DSLs. This is not directly possible in the internal shallow approach, which is one of its main drawbacks. One could potentially use reflection, but the Scala reflection API does not support reflection on code. Alternatively one can use a bytecode analysis library such as ASM [8] or the Scala compiler plugin. However, these solutions require a great level of sophistication of the developer.

Directly Executable. The internal shallow approach has the advantage that the DSL is directly executable since the host language models the DSL. There is no AST to be interpreted/translated. This again means that internal shallow DSLs are faster to develop, often requiring orders of magnitudes less code.

Turing Complete. Annotations typically carry simple data, and are usually not Turing complete (although they can be made to be). Internal DSLs are by definition Turing complete since they extend a Turing complete host language (in our case, Scala). For internal shallow DSLs the host language is directly part of the DSL, thus making the DSL itself Turing complete. Our experience with internal DSLs is that the user of the DSL will use the host language constructs in case the DSL is not applicable to a particular problem. As an example, an internal DSL lends itself to writing "glue code" to connect the DSL with another system, such as the system under test in case of a test DSL. It is more challenging to turn external DSLs into Turing complete languages.

Ease of Development. External DSLs developed using a library (such as Scala's parser combinators) seem easier to develop than using a parser generator tool (such as ANTLR) due to the reduced parser generator step. However, using a parser generator such as ANTLR facilitates grammar development itself since ANTLR accepts more grammars than for example Scala's parser combinators. Annotations-based DSLs are easy to develop since the Java compiler and the core libraries support annotations. However, it is not possible to extend the syntax or scope of annotations in any way. It furthermore appears that internal DSLs are easier to develop than external DSLs, and that internal shallow DSLs are the easiest to develop.

Flexibility of Syntax. Our experience with internal DSLs is that it can be a struggle to achieve the optimal syntax. This is mostly due to limitations in operator composition and precedence in Scala. In an external DSL one is completely free to create any grammar as long as it is accepted by the parser.

Quality of Syntax Error Messages. External DSLs have a potential for good error messages, depending on the toolkit used. Internal DSLs often result in error messages that can be intimidating to users, especially if not used to the host language. In the case of deep internal DSLs, conversion functions may show up in compiler errors; or a missing symbol may result in a lack of conversion, in which case no error message is shown or a completely wrong one. Furthermore, for a deep internal DSL a type checker has to be developed from scratch. In contrast, shallow internal DSLs have the advantage that Scala's type system takes care of type checking.

Ease of Use. Annotations and internal DSLs are usually adopted easily if the users are already host language programmers. As an illustration, in spite of being originally a research tool, TraceContract [4], a variant of the internal data automaton DSL illustrated in Sect. 3.2, was used throughout NASA's LADEE

Moon mission for checking all command sequences before being sent to the space-craft [5]. Similarly, the internal DSL LogFire [16], illustrated in Sect. 3.3, also originally a research tool, is currently used daily for checking telemetry from JPL's Mars Curiosity Rover [17]. These adoptions by NASA missions were not likely to have happened had these DSLs been external limited stand-alone languages. On the other hand, if a user is not already a host language programmer (and is not willing to learn the host language), it may be easier to adopt an external DSL. For example, we developed an external monitoring DSL much along the lines of data automata, and had non-programmers use it for testing without much training [3]. More interestingly perhaps, the SysML-inspired external modeling DSL K, illustrated in Sect. 2.2, is planned to be adopted by a JPL's future mission to Jupiter's Moon Europa, for modeling mission scenarios.

5 Conclusions

We have presented five approaches to implementing domain-specific languages (DSLs) in Scala, illustrated by application to formal modeling and testing languages. External DSLs use either (1) a parser generator, or (2) a parser library. Internal DSLs extend the host language by (3) annotations of existing language elements, (4) deep embedding where an abstract representation of the program is computed, or (5) shallow embedding of functions that directly execute. Our experience shows that each approach has its strengths; in particular, external DSLs can offer a fully flexible syntax while internal DSLs are easier to develop and in the case of shallow embedding, are directly executable. Mixed approaches are common, in particular for internal DSLs. Future work includes leveraging macro-based and compiler-based approaches, which promise to combine some of the strengths of the techniques discussed here.

References

1. ANTLR: http://www.antlr.org
2. Artho, C.V., Biere, A., Hagiya, M., Platon, E., Seidl, M., Tanabe, Y., Yamamoto, M.: Modbat: A model-based API tester for event-driven systems. In: Bertacco, V., Legay, A. (eds.) HVC 2013. LNCS, vol. 8244, pp. 112–128. Springer, Heidelberg (2013)
3. Barringer, H., Groce, A., Havelund, K., Smith, M.: Formal analysis of log files. J. Aerosp. Comput. Inf. Commun. 7(11), 365–390 (2010)
4. Barringer, H., Havelund, K.: TraceContract: A scala DSL for trace analysis. In: Butler, M., Schulte, W. (eds.) FM 2011. LNCS, vol. 6664, pp. 57–72. Springer, Heidelberg (2011)
5. Barringer, H., Havelund, K., Kurklu, E., Morris, R.: Checking flight rules with TraceContract: Application of a Scala DSL for trace analysis. In: Scala Days 2011. Stanford University, California (2011)
6. Bodden, E.: MOPBox: A library approach to runtime verification. In: Khurshid, S., Sen, K. (eds.) RV 2011. LNCS, vol. 7186, pp. 365–369. Springer, Heidelberg (2012)

7. Bray, T., Paoli, J., Sperberg-McQueen, M., Maler, E., Yergeau, F.: Extensible markup language (XML). World Wide Web Consortium Recommendation REC-xml-19980210 (1998)
8. Bruneton, E., Lenglet, R., Coupaye, T.: ASM: a code manipulation tool to implement adaptable systems. In: Adaptable and Extensible Component Systems, Grenoble, France (2002)
9. Forgy, C.: Rete: A fast algorithm for the many pattern/many object pattern match problem. Artif. Intell. **19**, 17–37 (1982)
10. Fowler, M., Parsons, R.: Domain-Specific Languages. Addison-Wesley, Boston (2010)
11. Fusco, M.: Hammurabi–a Scala rule engine. In: Scala Days 2011. Stanford University, California (2011)
12. Gansner, E., North, S.: An open graph visualization system and its applications to software engineering. Softw. Pract. Exper. **30**(11), 1203–1233 (2000)
13. GLL combinators: https://github.com/djspiewak/gll-combinators
14. Havelund, K.: Data automata in Scala. In: Leucker, M., Wang, J. (eds.) Proceedings of 8th International Symposium on Theoretical Aspects of Software Engineering (TASE 2014), Changsha, China. IEEE Computer Society Press (2014)
15. Havelund, K.: Monitoring with data automata. In: Margaria, T., Steffen, B. (eds.) ISoLA 2014, Part II. LNCS, vol. 8803, pp. 254–273. Springer, Heidelberg (2014)
16. Havelund, K.: Rule-based runtime verification revisited. Softw. Tools Technol. Transf. (STTT) **17**(2), 143–170 (2015)
17. Havelund, K., Joshi, R.: Experience with rule-based analysis of spacecraft logs. In: Artho, C., Ölveczky, P.C. (eds.) FTSCS 2014. CCIS, vol. 476, pp. 1–16. Springer, Heidelberg (2015)
18. Hoare, C.: Communicating sequential processes. Commun. ACM **26**(1), 100–106 (1983)
19. Jakob, F.: SugarScala: Syntactic extensibility for Scala. Master's thesis, Technische Universität Darmstadt (2014)
20. Link, J., Fröhlich, P.: Unit Testing in Java: How Tests Drive the Code. Morgan Kaufmann Publishers Inc., Sebastopol (2003)
21. Mernik, M., Heering, J., Sloane, A.: When and how to develop domain-specific languages. ACM Comput. Surv. **37**(4), 316–344 (2005)
22. Odersky, M., Spoon, L., Venners, B.: Programming in Scala: A Comprehensive Step-by-step Guide, 2nd edn. Artima Inc., USA (2010)
23. Parboiled: https://github.com/sirthias/parboiled2
24. Parser combinators: https://github.com/scala/scala-parser-combinators
25. Rompf, T., Amin, N., Moors, A., Haller, P., Odersky, M.: Scala-virtualized: linguistic reuse for deep embeddings. High. Order Symbolic Comput. **25**, 1–43 (2013)
26. Scala: http://www.scala-lang.org
27. ScalaBison: https://github.com/djspiewak/scala-bison
28. Scala macros: http://scalamacros.org
29. Stolz, V., Huch, F.: Runtime verification of concurrent Haskell programs. In: Proceedings of the 4th International Workshop on Runtime Verification (RV 2004), ENTCS, vol. 113, pp. 201–216. Elsevier (2005)
30. Venners, B.: ScalaTest (2014). http://www.scalatest.org

Formal Verification of Programs Computing the Floating-Point Average

Sylvie Boldo$^{(\boxtimes)}$

LRI, Bâtiment 650, Inria, Université Paris-Sud, 91405 Orsay Cedex, France
Sylvie.Boldo@inria.fr

Abstract. The most well-known feature of floating-point arithmetic is the limited precision, which creates round-off errors and inaccuracies. Another important issue is the limited range, which creates underflow and overflow, even if this topic is dismissed most of the time. This article shows a very simple example: the average of two floating-point numbers. As we want to take exceptional behaviors into account, we cannot use the naive formula (x+y)/2. Based on hints given by Sterbenz, we first write an accurate program and formally prove its properties. An interesting fact is that Sterbenz did not give this program, but only specified it. We prove this specification and include a new property: a precise certified error bound. We also present and formally prove a new algorithm that computes the correct rounding of the average of two floating-point numbers. It is more accurate than the previous one and is correct whatever the inputs.

1 Introduction

Floating-point computations are everywhere in our lives. They are used in control software, used to compute weather forecasts, and are a basic block of many hybrid systems: embedded systems mixing continuous, such as sensors results, and discrete, such as clock-constrained computations. Which numbers and how operations behave on them is standardized in the IEEE-754 standard [13] of 1985, which was revised in 2008 [14].

Computer arithmetic [11], is mostly known (if known at all) to be inaccurate, as only a finite number of digits is kept for the mantissa. A more ignored fact is that only a finite number of digits is kept for the exponent. This creates the underflow and overflow exceptions, that are often dismissed, even by floating-point experts. We are here mostly interested in handling overflow, even if underflow will also play its part.

The chosen example is very simple: how to compute the average of two floating-point numbers:

$$\frac{x+y}{2}.$$

This work was supported by both the VERASCO (ANR-11-INSE-003) and the FastRelax (ANR-14-CE25-0018-01) projects of the French National Agency for Research (ANR).

M. Butler et al. (Eds.): ICFEM 2015, LNCS 9407, pp. 17–32, 2015.
DOI: 10.1007/978-3-319-25423-4_2

The naive formula (x+y)/2 is quite accurate, but may fail due to overflow, even if the correct result is in the range. For example, consider the maximum floating-point number M, then (M+M)/2 overflows while the correct result is M. This problem has been known for decades and has been thoroughly studied by Sterbenz [17], among some examples called "carefully written programs".

This study is especially interesting as Sterbenz does not fully give a correct program: he specified what it is required to do, such as symmetry and gives hints about how to circumvent overflow. We are interested in writing and proving the behavior of such a program, that produces an accurate result without overflowing. And of course, we look for an improved algorithm which would give a correct result, also without overflowing.

All the theorems stated in this article correspond to Coq theorems. This development, meaning the C codes and full proofs are available from the following web page https://www.lri.fr/~sboldo/research/.

The outline of this article is as follows. Basics about floating-point arithmetic are given in Sect. 2. The methodology of the verification, and what is supposed to be verified are in Sect. 3. The formal proofs about the algorithms are described in Sect. 4. The annotations of the C programs and the corresponding proofs, including overflow, are in Sect. 5. Section 6 concludes and gives a few perspectives.

2 Basics About Floating-Point Arithmetic

The IEEE-754 standard [13] of 1985, which was revised in 2008 [14] describes the floating-point formats, numbers and roundings and all modern processors comply with it. We adopt here the level 3 vision of the standard: we do not consider bit strings, but the representation of floating-point data. The format will then be $(\beta, p, e_{min}, e_{max})$, where e_{min} and e_{max} are the minimal and maximal unbiased exponents, β is the radix (2 or 10), and p is the precision (the number of digits in the significand).

In that format, a floating-point number is then either a triple (s, e, m), or an exceptional value: $\pm\infty$ or a NaN (Not-a-Number). For non-exceptional values, meaning the triples, we have additional conditions: $e_{min} \leq e \leq e_{max}$ and the significand m has less than p digits. The triple can be seen as the real number with value

$$(-1)^s \times m \times \beta^e.$$

We will consider m as an integer and we therefore require that $m < \beta^p$. The other possibility is that m is a fixed-point number smaller than β. In this setting, the common IEEE-754 formats are binary64, which corresponds to (2, 53, −1074, 971) and binary32, which corresponds to (2, 24, −149, 104).

Non-exceptional values give a discrete finite set of values, which can be represented on the real axis as in Fig. 1. Floating-point numbers having the same exponent are in a binade and are at equal distance from one to another. This distance is called the unit in the last place (ulp) as it is the intrinsic value of the last bit/digit of the significand of the floating-point number [15]. When going

from one binade to the next, the distance is multiplied by the radix, which gives
this strange distribution. Around zero, we have the numbers having the smallest
exponent and small mantissas, they are called subnormals and their ulp is that
of the smallest normal number.

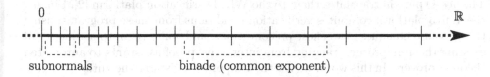

Fig. 1. Distribution of the floating-point numbers over the real axis.

Floating-point arithmetic tries to mimic real arithmetic but, in many cases,
the exact result of an operation on two floating-point numbers is not a floating-
point number. For example, in `binary64`, 1 and 2^{-53} are floating-point numbers,
but $1 + 2^{-53}$ is not, as it would require 54 bits for the significand. The value
therefore needs to be rounded. The IEEE-754 standard defines 5 rounding modes.
We will here only use the default rounding mode: rounding to nearest ties to even,
denoted by $\circ$. Rounded addition will be denoted by $\oplus$, rounded subtraction by
$\ominus$ and rounded division by $\oslash$.

The main rule of the IEEE standard of floating-point computation for basic
operations is the following one, called *correct* rounding: each operation gives the
same result as if it was first performed with infinite precision, and then rounded
to the desired format. This is a very strong mathematical property that has two
essential consequences: portability and accuracy. It also implies that rounding is
non-decreasing. A last property is the fact that division by the radix is an exact
operation, provided the input is not subnormal.

For some ugly details, as for the difference between signaling and quiet NaNs,
the sign of $0 - 0$ or the value of $\left(\sqrt{-0}\right)$, we refer the reader directly to the
standard [14]. Other major references are an article by Goldberg [11] and the
Handbook of Floating-Point Arithmetic [15].

3   Methodology and Desired Specification

3.1   Methodology

To give a high guarantee on our mathematical results and programs, we rely on
formal methods. Floating-point arithmetic that has been formalized since 1989
in order to formally prove hardware components or algorithms [8,12,16]. We use
the Flocq library [7], a formalization in Coq which offers a multi-radix and multi-
precision formalization for various floating- and fixed-point formats (including
floating-point with or without gradual underflow, meaning subnormals) with a
comprehensive library of theorems.

Following the methodology described in [3–5], we use the Frama-
C/Jessie/Why3 chain and the ACSL language to perform formal verification

of C programs at the source-code level. Frama-C is an extensible framework which combines static analyzers for C programs, written as plug-ins, within a single tool. In this work, we use the Jessie plug-in for deductive verification. C programs are annotated with behavioral contracts written using the ANSI C Specification Language [1] which tries to be as near C statements as possible. The Jessie plug-in translates them to the Why3 verification platform [2]. Finally, the Why3 platform computes verification conditions from these programs, using traditional techniques of weakest preconditions, and emits them to a wide set of existing theorem provers, ranging from interactive proof assistants to automated theorem provers. In this work, we use the Coq proof assistant, the automated theorem prover Gappa [10] which uses interval arithmetic to prove properties that occur when verifying numerical applications, and the SMT prover Alt-Ergo [9].

3.2 Desired Specification

The first point we want to specify is the accuracy of the ideal average function. In principle, we would like an error less than half a unit in the last place, which corresponds to correct rounding. But this is very difficult to achieve while preventing overflow as noted by Sterbenz [17]. This requirement will be weakened to a few ulps for the first program, as long as several other properties are kept. More precisely, we require:

- the program never overflows,
- $average(x, y)$ is within a few ulps of $\frac{x+y}{2}$,
- $\min(x, y) \leq average(x, y) \leq \max(x, y)$,
- $average(x, y) = average(y, x)$,
- $average(-x, -y) = -average(x, y)$,
- $average(x, y)$ has the same sign as $\frac{x+y}{2}$.

Sterbenz specified two facts related to underflow. First, $average(x, y) = 0$ if and only if $y = -x$, except in case of underflow. Second, the program should not underflow unless $0 < \left|\frac{x+y}{2}\right| < \eta$, where $\eta = 2^{p-1+E_i}$ is the smallest normalized positive number. Our specifications are stronger than Sterbenz's and will be detailed in Sect. 4.

This paper will formally prove the previous assumptions, and will determine and prove the accuracy of two programs: an accurate one based on Sterbenz's hints and a correct one. We will also weaken the underflow assumptions. For that, we will first need to write a correct program. Sterbenz suggested several ways to compute the average:

- $(x \oplus y) \oslash 2$, which is very accurate (see below for the error bound), but may overflow when x and y share the same sign.
- $(x \oslash 2) \oplus (y \oslash 2)$ is also accurate, and may underflow. Moreover, it requires an additional operation.
- $x \oplus ((y \ominus x) \oslash 2)$ is less accurate than the first one, but it does not overflow if x and y have opposite signs.
- As for underflow, Sterbenz suggests a scaling. We will prove that it is useless.

On the internet, we found a reference to Sterbenz's book and a corresponding program in the user notes on Fortran programming[1]. An excerpt of this program is given:

```
real function average (x, y)
      real   x, y, zero, two, av1, av2, av3, av4
      logical    samesign
      parameter (zero = 0.0e+00, two = 2.0e+00)

      av1(x,y) = (x + y) / two
      av2(x,y) = (x / two) + (y / two)
      av3(x,y) = x + ((y - x) / two)
      av4(x,y) = y + ((x - y) / two)

[...definition of samesign...]

      if (samesign) then
        if (y .ge. x) then
           average = av3(x,y)
        else
           average = av4(x,y)
        endif
      else
        average = av1(x,y)
      endif
      return
      end
```

The problem is that this program is incorrect: it does not fulfill one of Sterbenz's requirement: $average(-x, -y) = -average(x, y)$. For example, consider the IEEE binary64 format and the values $x = -2^{53}$ and $y = -1.25$, then $average(-x, -y) = average(2^{53}, 1.25) = average4(2^{53}, 1.25) = 2^{52} + 1$, but $-average(x, y) = -average(-2^{53}, -1.25) = -average3(-2^{53}, -1.25) = 2^{52}$. The reason is the test $y \geq x$ that should be $|y| \geq |x|$ to preserve the symmetry.

4   Formal Proof of the Algorithms

This formal proof was done in the FLT format of the Flocq library [7]. This corresponds to a generic floating-point format with gradual underflow and no overflow. This may seem strange as we are mostly interested in overflow here, but overflow will be taken into account at the program level in the next Section. The reason is that underflow happens and can be handled, while overflow must be prevented. We will use radix 2 and rounding to nearest, ties to even $\circ$. We will denote by p the precision and E_i the minimal exponent, so that 2^{E_i} is the smallest positive floating-point number and 2^{p-1+E_i} is the smallest normal positive floating-point number.

---
[1] http://www.ibiblio.org/pub/languages/fortran/ch4-9.html.

We will here define the algorithms at the Coq level, and prove that they fulfill all the stated properties. For that, we will study all the algorithms in all the different cases. But we will be smarter as far as formal proofs are concerned: as $average4(x, y)$ is exactly $average3(y, x)$, we will only have to study the $average1$, $average2$ and $average3$ functions.

The interesting points here will be first the rounding error of the functions, and then the handling of underflow. In fact, we will prove that scaling is useless and that gradual underflow behaves perfectly. For sign correctness, the most problematic case is computing the average of 0 and 2^{E_i} which gives 0, even if computed correctly, as rounding is to nearest, ties to even. In the other cases, the sign is correct. We will therefore prove the following properties concerning underflow: if the average is exactly 0, then the algorithm returns 0. If the absolute value of the average is greater or equal to 2^{E_i}, then the returned value is non-zero.

4.1   The $average1$ Function

The $average1$ function is the simplest one, the naive one to compute the average.

```
Definition average1 (x y : R) :=round_flt(round_flt(x+y)/2).
```

That is to say $average1(x, y) = (x \oplus y) \oslash 2$.
In fact, this function is correct: it computes the correctly-rounded exact average.

Theorem 1. *For all floating-point numbers x and y,*

$$(x \oplus y) \oslash 2 = \circ \left(\frac{x + y}{2} \right).$$

This holds in our algorithmic model without overflow.

Proof. Let us denote by r the floating-point number $r = (x \oplus y) \oslash 2$. We have two sub-cases. When $|x + y| \leq 2^{p+E_i}$, then $x \oplus y$ has the minimal exponent, meaning a subnormal number or just above. It is therefore computed without error [7,11]. Then, $r = (x \oplus y) \oslash 2 = (x + y) \oslash 2 = \circ(\frac{x+y}{2})$.

When $|x + y| > 2^{p+E_i}$, then $|x \oplus y| \geq 2^{p+E_i}$. In this case, the division by 2 is exact as $x \oplus y$ is a normal number. Then $r = (x \oplus y) \oslash 2 = \frac{x \oplus y}{2} = \circ(\frac{x+y}{2})$. □

This correct rounding easily implies all the basic requirements on this function: $average1(x, y) = average1(y, x)$, $average1(-x, -y) = -average1(x, y)$, $average1(x, y)$ has the same sign as $\frac{x+y}{2}$. The fact that $average1(x, y)$ is between $\min(x, y)$ and $\max(x, y)$ is slightly more difficult as rounding is involved. The facts that $\frac{x+y}{2} = 0$ implies $average1(x, y) = 0$ and that $2^{E_i} \leq |\frac{x+y}{2}|$ implies $average1(x, y) \neq 0$ are also quite simple from basic floating-point properties of the rounding.

The rounding error here is very small as it is equivalent to only one rounding:

$$\left| average1(x, y) - \frac{x + y}{2} \right| \leq \frac{1}{2} \mathrm{ulp} \left(\frac{x + y}{2} \right).$$

An interesting point is the fact that this algorithm requires x and y to be of different signs in order to not overflow. But the preceding proofs do not require it and are valid (in our model without overflow) whatever the values of x and y.

4.2   The average3 Function

The *average3* function is the more complex one, designed to prevent overflow when x and y share the same sign.

```
Definition average3 (x y : R) :=
        round_flt(x+round_flt(round_flt(y-x)/2)).
```

That is to say $average3(x, y) = x \oplus ((y \ominus x) \oslash 2)$.

Some of the basic requirements on this function are not difficult to prove: $average3(-x, -y) = -average3(x, y)$ is easy, so is the fact that $\frac{x+y}{2} = 0$ implies $average3(x, y) = 0$ and *vice versa*. Proving that $average3(x, y)$ has the same sign as $\frac{x+y}{2}$ is slightly more difficult.

The fact that $\min(x, y) \leq average3(x, y) \leq \max(x, y)$ is more difficult as many roundings are involved, including possible underflows. Without loss of generality, we assume that $x \leq y$. We have left to prove that $x \leq x \oplus ((y \ominus x) \oslash 2) \leq y$. The first inequality is simple: as $y \geq x$, then $y \ominus x \geq 0$, then $(y \ominus x) \oslash 2 \geq 0$. Then $x \leq x + ((y \ominus x) \oslash 2)$, and then $x \leq x \oplus ((y \ominus x) \oslash 2)$ as x is in the floating-point format.

The difficult part is $x \oplus ((y \ominus x) \oslash 2) \leq y$. We split into two different subcases: either the rounding down of $y - x$, that is denoted by $\triangledown(y - x)$ equals 0, or is positive. It is non-negative as $y \geq x$. When $\triangledown(y - x) > 0$, this amounts to prove that $\circ \left(\frac{\circ(y-x)}{2} \right) \leq y - x$. When $y - x$ is in the format, this is trivial. When not, then we prove that $\circ \left(\frac{\circ(y-x)}{2} \right) \leq \triangledown(y - x)$ by real number inequality manipulations, and the study of whether $\circ(y - x)$ is the rounding up or down. Then we have left to prove that $\triangledown(y - x) \leq y - x$, which holds by definition. When $\triangledown(y - x) = 0$, we have two cases: if $x = y$, the result holds. The only remaining case corresponds to $x < y$ and $\triangledown(y - x) = 0$. As x and y are in the floating-point format, this is impossible as $y - x \geq 2^{E_i}$.

Another difficult point is that $2^{E_i} \leq \left| \frac{x+y}{2} \right|$ implies $average3(x, y) \neq 0$. This relies on the intermediate fact that, for all positive floating-point number f, then $\circ(f/2) < f$, even when underflow occur.

The proof of $\circ(f/2) < f$ for a positive floating-point number f is a case split: if the exponent of f is greater than E_i, then $\circ(f/2) = f/2 < f$. When $f = n2^{E_i}$ with $|n| < 2^p$, then we have left to prove that the integer rounding to nearest even of $n/2$ is strictly smaller than n. This is done by studying n: as $f > 0$, then $n \geq 1$. When $n = 1$, the result holds as $0 < 1$. For bigger n, we prove that this integer rounding is smaller than $n/2 + 1/2$ which is smaller than n.

Given this lemma, we assume that x and y share the same sign and that $2^{E_i} \leq \left| \frac{x+y}{2} \right|$. Without loss of generality, we assume $x \leq y$. We prove that $x \oplus ((y \ominus x) \oslash 2) \neq 0$ by contradiction. If a floating-point addition is zero, it is exact, therefore we know that $x + ((y \ominus x) \oslash 2) = 0$. Therefore $x = -((y \ominus x) \oslash 2) \le 0$ as $y - x \ge 0$. We split into two subcases: if $x < 0$, we will prove the contrary of the previous lemma applied to $-x$. We have left to prove that $-x \le -x \oslash 2$. But $-x = ((y \ominus x) \oslash 2)$. As $y \le 0$, we have $y - x \le -x$, then $y \ominus x \le -x$, hence the result. Now, we assume that $x = 0$. Then the hypotheses are rewritten into $2^{E_i} \le |\frac{y}{2}|$ and $y \oslash 2 = 0$, which is impossible as 2^{E_i} cannot round to 0. This property is the first to rely on the fact that x and y share the same sign.

The last property is the bound on the rounding error. The first subcase is when $|\frac{x+y}{2}|$ is exactly $\frac{2^{E_i}}{2}$. It corresponds to $x = 0$ and $y = \pm 2^{E_i}$ or *vice versa*. This very special case is not difficult, but must be studied differently from the general case. The general case corresponds to $average3(x, y)$ being non-zero. Then, following the idea of the previous subsection, we have either $\circ(y - x)$ or $\circ\left(\frac{\circ(y-x)}{2}\right)$ that is computed exactly. The final rounding error is therefore small and bounded as follows:

$$\left| average3(x, y) - \frac{x+y}{2} \right| \le \frac{3}{2}\text{ulp}\left(\frac{x+y}{2}\right)$$

provided x and y share the same sign.

The last missing property is the link between the values of $average3(x, y)$ and $average3(y, x)$. But they may not be equal, contrary to what happens with $average1$. Symmetry is achieved otherwise, by the sign study.

4.3   The average2 Function

The $average2$ function is rather simple, even if it contains 2 multiplications. This is not a problem on recent architectures as the cost of addition and multiplication is nearly the same.

```
Definition average2 (x y : R) :=
    round_flt(round_flt(x/2) + round_flt(y/2)).
```

That is to say $average2(x, y) = (x \oslash 2) \oplus (y \oslash 2)$.

In fact, this function is correct provided x is not too small: it computes the correctly-rounded exact average.

Theorem 2. *For all floating-point numbers x and y such that $2^{E_i + 2p + 1} \le |x|$,*

$$(x \oslash 2) \oplus (y \oslash 2) = \circ\left(\frac{x+y}{2}\right).$$

This holds when x is not too small. Consider for example $x = y = 2^{E_i}$. Then, the average is also 2^{E_i} while the algorithm returns 0.
Note also that the assumption $2^{E_i + 2p + 1} \le |x|$ can be replaced by $2^{E_i + 2p + 1} \le |y|$ by symmetry.

Proof. Let us denote by r the floating-point number $r = (x \oslash 2) \oplus (y \oslash 2)$. As x is big enough, we have $x \oslash 2 = \frac{x}{2}$. Then we have two subcases, depending on the magnitude of y.

If $|y| \geq 2^{p+E_i}$, then we have the same property: $y \oslash 2 = \frac{y}{2}$. Then $r = (x \oslash 2) \oplus (y \oslash 2) = \frac{x}{2} \oplus \frac{y}{2} = \circ\left(\frac{x+y}{2}\right)$.

If $|y| < 2^{p+E_i}$, then it is subnormal and the division may be inexact. But x is big enough so that this error is too small to impact the result. More precisely, we prove that $r = (x \oslash 2) \oplus (y \oslash 2) = \frac{x}{2} \oplus (y \oslash 2) = \frac{x}{2} = \circ\left(\frac{x+y}{2}\right)$.

This is proved by using twice the following result: given a floating-point number f and a real h such that $2^{p+e_i} \leq |f|$ and $|h| \leq \frac{\text{ulp}(f)}{4}$, then $\circ(f + h) = f$. $\square$

As for the *average*1 function, the correct rounding implies all the previous requirements and gives a half ulp error bound. This hold provided either x or y is big enough.

4.4   Putting All Parts Together: The Average Functions

Accurate Sterbenz Algorithm. Following Sterbenz's ideas and the previous definitions, here is the definition of an accurate average function:

```
if x and y do not have the same sign
        return (x ⊕ y) ⊘ 2
else
        if |x| ≤ |y|
                return x ⊕ ((y ⊖ x) ⊘ 2)
        else
                return y ⊕ ((x ⊖ y) ⊘ 2)
```

Then the properties are easily derived from the properties of *average*1 and *average*3. They may be sometimes long as many subcases have to be studied, but the proofs are straightforward. The worst case is the proof that $average(-x, -y) = -average(x, y)$, as all sign possibilities (positive, negative and zero) have to be considered. The formal proof of the whole algorithm is a Coq file about 1,400 lines long.

What is left to prove is that no overflow occurs. Another difficulty is the specification of this program that will be described in Sect. 5.

Correct Algorithm. From the previous properties of *average*1 and *average*2, another algorithm can be defined, that will return the correctly-rounded average:

```
let C := 2^{E_i+2p+1}
if C ≤ |x|
        return (x ⊘ 2) ⊕ (y ⊘ 2)
else
        return (x ⊕ y) ⊘ 2
```

This program returns $\circ\left(\frac{x+y}{2}\right)$. This means that the specification reduces to this property, as it easily implies everything Sterbenz could wish for a correctly written average function. What is left to prove is that no overflow occurs.

Another point is the value of C. The correct rounding will hold whatever C greater or equal to 2^{E_i+2p+1} in our model without overflow. We may therefore increase this value as long as overflows are prevented. The advantage is efficiency: it would more often use 3 operations instead of 4.

5   Specifications and Formal Verification of the Programs

5.1   Absolute Value

Both programs require an absolute value for tests. This may come from a standard library or playing with the first bit. As long as the specification is the same, any function will make the following programs work. We choose to define and prove it using a condition.

```
/*@ ensures \result == \abs(x); */
double abs(double x) {
   if (x >= 0) return x;
   else return (−x);
}
```

The corresponding proof is automatically done by Alt-Ergo.

5.2   Accurate Average

The accurate program to be proved is the following one, written in C. It corresponds to Sterbenz's hints.

```
1    /*@ axiomatic Floor {
2    @   logic integer floor (real x);
3    @   axiom floor_prop: \forall real x; floor(x) <= x < floor(x)+1;
4    @ } */
5
6    /*@ logic real ulp_d (real x) =
7    @   \let e = 1+ floor (\log(\abs(x)) / \log(2));
8    @       \pow(2,\max(e−53,−1074)); */
9
10   /*@ logic real l_average (real x, real y) =
11   @     \let same_sign =
12   @     (x >= 0) ? ((y >=0) ? \true : \false) : ((y >=0) ? \false : \true);
13   @     (same_sign) ? ((\abs(x) <= \abs(y)) ?
14   @        \round_double(\NearestEven, x+\round_double(\NearestEven,
15   @             \round_double(\NearestEven, y−x)/2))   :
16   @ \round_double(\NearestEven, y+\round_double(\NearestEven,
17   @             \round_double(\NearestEven, x−y)/2)))  :
18   @        \round_double(\NearestEven,\round_double(\NearestEven, x+y)/2);
19   @ */
20
21   /*@   lemma average_sym: \forall double x; \forall double y;
22   @            l_average(x,y) == l_average (y,x);
23   @   lemma average_sym_opp: \forall double x; \forall double y;
24   @            l_average(−x,−y) == − l_average (x,y);
25   @
26   @ lemma average_props: \forall double x; \forall double y;
27   @         \abs(l_average(x,y) − (x+y)/2) <= 3./2*ulp_d((x+y)/2)
28   @     &&  (\min(x,y) <= l_average(x,y) <= \max(x,y))
29   @     && (0 <= (x+y)/2 ==> 0 <= l_average(x,y))
30   @     && ((x+y)/2 <= 0 ==> l_average(x,y) <= 0)
31   @     && ((x+y)/2==0 ==> l_average(x,y)==0)
32   @     && (0x1p−1074 <= \abs((x+y)/2) ==> l_average(x,y) != 0);
```

```
33     @ */
34
35
36    /*@     ensures \result == l_average(x,y);
37     @      ensures \abs((\result - (x+y)/2)) <= 3./2*ulp_d((x+y)/2);
38     @      ensures \min(x,y) <= \result <= \max(x,y);
39     @      ensures 0 <= (x+y)/2 ==> 0 <= \result;
40     @      ensures (x+y)/2 <= 0 ==> \result <= 0;
41     @      ensures (x+y)/2 == 0 ==> \result == 0;
42     @      ensures 0x1p-1074 <= \abs((x+y)/2) ==> \result != 0;
43     @ */
44
45    double average(double x, double y) {
46      int same_sign;
47      double r;
48      if (x >= 0) {
49         if (y >=0) same_sign=1;
50         else same_sign=0; }
51      else {
52         if (y >=0) same_sign=0;
53         else same_sign=1; }
54      if (same_sign ==1) {
55         if (abs(x) <= abs(y)) r=x+(y-x)/2;
56         else r=y+(x-y)/2; }
57      else r=(x+y)/2;
58      //@ assert r==l_average(x,y);
59      return r;
60    }
```

The full annotated program is given above. Here are some details about the annotations. We only consider the **double** type meaning the binary64 type of the IEEE-754. First, the floor function, which rounds down a real number to an integer, is specified at lines (1–4). The ulp function, which gives the unit in the last place in double precision ulp_d, is then defined at lines (6–8). An interesting point is that it takes a real number as input, and not only a floating-point number. We want to compare the result to the ulp of the exact result.

The next big block at lines (10–19) defines a logic function that computes the average following the algorithm described in Sect. 4.4 (Accurate Sterbenz Algorithm). In the ACSL syntax, it exactly describes what the program does. Why is it needed? The reason is that we want to prove that $average(x, y) = average(y, x)$ and this means two calls of the function. As a generic C function may have side effects, this cannot be stated as is. Therefore, we had to define a logic function, that has forcefully no side effects and prove properties on this logic function called l_average. We will also of course prove it is equivalent to the real C program. Then comes the various properties of the l_average function: symmetry, sign, rounding error, and so on at lines (21–33).

Next comes the specification of the average C function: its equivalence with the logical function, the rounding error, the fact that the result is between the minimum and the maximum of x and y, the fact that the sign is correct and that the result is non-zero when the exact average is big enough. Last is the C program with an assertion at line (58), that serves as logical cut to ensure the program is equivalent to its logical counterpart.

Now that the program is fully written, specified and annotated, we have to prove it. The toolchain generates a bunch of theorems, we have to prove all of them in order to verify that the program will not fail, and that it will respect its specification. The "not fail" point is crucial here as it will require to prove there is no overflow, without assuming range values for the inputs.

Proof obligations		Alt-Ergo	Coq Nb lines		Gappa
Previous Coq proof (spec + proof)			7.83	1,432	
VC for model lemmas	Lemma average_sym		5.39	3	
	Lemma average_sym_opp		5.45	6	
	Lemma average_props		7.60	125	
VC for average_ensures_default	1. assertion	0.17			
	2. postcondition	0.61			
	3. assertion	0.23			
	4. postcondition	0.42			
	5. assertion	0.06			
	6. postcondition	0.04			
	7. assertion	0.06			
	8. postcondition	0.06			
	9. assertion	0.06			
	10. postcondition	0.06			
	11. assertion	0.08			
	12. postcondition	0.99			
	13. assertion	0.05			
	14. postcondition	0.06			
	15. assertion	0.06			
	16. postcondition	0.06			
	17. assertion	0.09			
	18. postcondition	1.21			
	19. assertion	0.06			
	20. postcondition	0.51			
	21. assertion	0.07			
	22. postcondition	0.54			
	23. assertion	0.06			
	24. postcondition	0.04			
VC for average_safety	1. floating-point overflow				0.00
	2. floating-point overflow				0.00
	3. floating-point overflow		10.43	8	
	4. floating-point overflow				0.00
	5. floating-point overflow				0.00
	6. floating-point overflow		9.41	8	
	7. floating-point overflow				0.00
	8. floating-point overflow				0.00
	9. floating-point overflow				0.00
	10. floating-point overflow				0.00
	11. floating-point overflow				0.00
	12. floating-point overflow				0.00
	13. floating-point overflow				0.00
	14. floating-point overflow				0.00
	15. floating-point overflow				0.00
	16. floating-point overflow				0.01
	17. floating-point overflow				0.00
	18. floating-point overflow				0.00
	19. floating-point overflow				0.00
	20. floating-point overflow				0.00
	21. floating-point overflow				0.00
	22. floating-point overflow				0.01
	23. floating-point overflow				0.00
	24. floating-point overflow				0.00
	25. floating-point overflow				0.00
	26. floating-point overflow				0.00
	27. floating-point overflow		9.72	8	
	28. floating-point overflow				0.00
	29. floating-point overflow				0.00
	30. floating-point overflow		9.75	8	
	31. floating-point overflow				0.00
	32. floating-point overflow				0.00

Let us now detail the VC (verification conditions) we have to prove. The list of theorems is given in the table above. Timings are in seconds, and the number of lines of Coq proofs is also given. The previous proofs described in Sect. 4 are given, just to give an order of magnitude of the respective proofs. Then comes the proofs of what is in the logic annotations: the lemmas. There are three of them and all are easily proved using the previous algorithm proofs. Two difficulties arose: the first one is to prove that the ulp defined in the C annotations is the same as in the Coq formalization. The second difficulty is to prove that the Coq definition is the same as the logical definition in the annotations. Then comes the postconditions of the average C function. Given the previous lemmas, they are straightforward and proved automatically.

Last but not least, are the proofs related to overflow, as this is the only possible way for this program to fail (for example, there is no pointer access or division by zero). Near all of them are proved automatically. Indeed, most operations do not overflow due to the case study of the signs of x and y and this is handled automatically using Gappa. For a few operations, it is not sufficient and we need to rely on the fact that $\min(x, y) \leq average(x, y) \leq \max(x, y)$, and a small Coq proof is then necessary.

5.3   Correct Average

The correct program for computing the average is the following one, with hypotheses on the value of C.

```
1   /*@    requires 0x1p-967 <= C <= 0x1p970;
2   @      ensures \result == \round_double(\NearestEven, (x+y)/2) ;
3   @ */
4
5   double average(double C, double x, double y) {
6     if (C <= abs(x))
7       return x/2+y/2;
8     else
9       return (x+y)/2;
10  }
```

This specification is quite simpler. The result is the correct rounding of the average. Note that the value of C must be between 2^{-967} and 2^{970}. The 2^{-967} exactly corresponds to 2^{E_i+2p+1} in the binary64 format as $E_i = -1074$ and $p = 53$. As for 2^{970}, the reason is overflow (see below).

Proof obligations		Alt-Ergo	Coq Nb lines	Gappa
Previous Coq proof (spec + proof)			3.82	536	
VC for average_ensures_default	1. postcondition		5.96	20	
	2. postcondition		2.71	9	
VC for average_safety	1. floating-point overflow				0.00
	2. floating-point overflow				0.00
	3. floating-point overflow				0.00
	4. floating-point overflow		14.32	64	
	5. floating-point overflow				0.00

Proofs of behavior are quite simple as they are calls to the previously studied *average*1 and *average*2 functions. The difficult part, as expected, is overflow.

It is handled automatically by Gappa, except the proof that $x + y$ does not overflow, provided that $|x| < C \leq 2^{970}$. More precisely, even if y is the biggest floating-point number, if $|x| < 2^{970}$, then $x \oplus y$ will not overflow as it will round to y.

6   Conclusion and Perspectives

The initial goal was to prove a program computing the average without overflow. This has first been achieved using Sterbenz's hints. This program has been successfully written, specified and proved. All the wanted properties have been proved, and a very good error bound on the rounding error is given. Even if the program is tricky, the proofs are not that long, even if some are tricky. Then another program is presented, which is both new, simpler to write and to prove. It is more efficient and more accurate. It handles all overflow and underflow cases, and gives the most accurate possible result: a correct rounding of the exact average.

The usual method to handle exceptional cases is scaling. This means computing the order of magnitude of the inputs (for example their exponent), and multiplying by a chosen power of the radix before and after the computation, in order to prevent any underflow or overflow during the computation. In particular, Sterbenz recommends scaling on this example to prevent underflow. We have proved this scaling to be useless, which causes a much more efficient program as scaling is costly.

An interesting point is that the overhead to prove the program, compared to the algorithm proofs, is rather low. When the program is specified (which was a difficult task), the proof is either automatic, or simple calls to the previous proofs. Surprisingly, the overflow proofs were not difficult: they were either automatic using Gappa or easily deduced from previous properties. The only difficult one was explained in the previous Section. We did not expect the other 36 theorems to be so easily handled. This case study shows that the difficult point about overflow is not proving it does not happen, but finding the algorithms such that it does not happen. This example is among Sterbenz's "carefully written programs", and this is the reason why it behaves as expected. We did not expect this well-behavior to extend to the overflow proofs.

An unexpected difficulty was in the formalizations that describe the average computation of the accurate program. There are three of them:

- the Coq formalization, written directly in Coq and given in Sect. 4. It was written to be short and easily used in the formal proof assistant.
- the l_average logic function, written in the ACSL syntax in the annotations of the C program. It was written to ensure that this function is free from side effects, so that we can state that l_average(x,y) == l_average (y,x). Its translation in Coq is much longer and much more tedious to use.
- the average C function, written in the C program. Its translation in Coq depends upon the path taken in the program and its definition is based on floating-point operation postconditions. On a typical goal, the definition of

the result of the C function average relies on about 20 hypotheses and 40 lines, which makes it difficult to read.

In the proofs, we handle these three different formalizations. They are very near, so the equivalence proofs are straightforward, but rather long and cumbersome.

As for the perspectives, the first one is to consider radix 10. Unfortunately, the same properties do not hold with the same algorithm. More precisely, the accurate program can produce a result smaller than the minimum of the values when using radix 10 [17] and the correct program is not correct anymore. Therefore, other algorithms have to be created, so that they could fulfill all the requirements, without overflowing. Correct rounding may probably be achieved using odd rounding [6], but it will probably be much more costly than in radix 2.

Another perspective is how to handle overflow in everyday programs. A method for the formal verification is to put preconditions that give ranges on the inputs and let Gappa prove the overflow requirements. This method is sometimes not optimal, but it works very well with satisfactory results. But on basic blocks from libraries, such as Two-Sum or Fast-Two-Sum, we want the best possible results. It means we want to have the tightest precondition, in order to cover all cases that do not fail. And this requires additional work.

Unfortunately, programs are often not carefully written with overflow in mind. There are overflowing examples in an overwhelming proportion of them. Our work is therefore either to give precise conditions for them to work correctly, or to rewrite them.

Acknowledgments. The author is indebted to a referee of a previous version of this work, who rightfully pitied the fact that no program existed for a correctly-rounded average and pointed out the previously dismissed average2 function. The author is also thankful to P. Zimmermann and V. Lefèvre for constructive discussions that turned $E_i + 2p + 2$ into $E_i + 2p + 1$ in Theorem 2.

References

1. Baudin, P., Cuoq, P., Filliâtre, J.C., Marché, C., Monate, B., Moy, Y., Prevosto, V.: ACSL: ANSI/ISO C Specification Language, version 1.9 (2013). http://frama-c. cea.fr/acsl.html
2. Bobot, F., Filliâtre, J.C., Marché, C., Paskevich, A.: Why3: Shepherd your herd of provers. In: Boogie 2011: First International Workshop on Intermediate Verification Languages. Wrocław, Poland, August 2011
3. Boldo, S.: Deductive formal verification: how to make your floating-point programs behave. Thèse d'habilitation, Université Paris-Sud, October 2014
4. Boldo, S., Filliâtre, J.C.: Formal verification of floating-point programs. In: Kornerup, P., Muller, J.M. (eds.) Proceedings of the 18th IEEE Symposium on Computer Arithmetic, pp. 187–194. Montpellier, France, June 2007
5. Boldo, S., Marché, C.: Formal verification of numerical programs: from C annotated programs to mechanical proofs. Math. Comput. Sci. **5**, 377–393 (2011)

6. Boldo, S., Melquiond, G.: Emulation of FMA and correctly-rounded sums: proved algorithms using rounding to odd. IEEE Trans. Comput. **57**(4), 462–471 (2008)
7. Boldo, S., Melquiond, G.: Flocq: a unified library for proving floating-point algorithms in Coq. In: Antelo, E., Hough, D., Ienne, P. (eds.) 20th IEEE Symposium on Computer Arithmetic, pp. 243–252. Tübingen, Germany (2011)
8. Carreño, V.A., Miner, P.S.: Specification of the IEEE-854 floating-point standard in HOL and PVS. In: HOL95: 8th International Workshop on Higher-Order Logic Theorem Proving and Its Applications. Aspen Grove, UT, September 1995
9. Conchon, S., Contejean, E., Iguernelala, M.: Canonized rewriting and ground AC completion modulo Shostak theories : design and implementation. Logical Methods Comput. Sci. **8**(3), 1–29 (2012)
10. Daumas, M., Melquiond, G.: Certification of bounds on expressions involving rounded operators. Trans. Math. Softw. **37**(1), 1–20 (2010)
11. Goldberg, D.: What every computer scientist should know about floating-point arithmetic. ACM Comput. Surv. **23**(1), 5–48 (1991)
12. Harrison, J.V.: Formal verification of floating point trigonometric functions. In: Johnson, S.D., Hunt Jr, W.A. (eds.) FMCAD 2000. LNCS, vol. 1954, pp. 217–233. Springer, Heidelberg (2000)
13. IEEE standard for binary floating-point arithmetic. ANSI/IEEE Std 754–1985 (1985)
14. IEEE standard for floating-point arithmetic. IEEE Std 754–2008, August 2008
15. Muller, J.M., Brisebarre, N., de Dinechin, F., Jeannerod, C.P., Lefèvre, V., Melquiond, G., Revol, N., Stehlé, D., Torres, S.: Handbook of Floating-Point Arithmetic. Birkhäuser, Boston (2010)
16. Russinoff, D.M.: A mechanically checked proof of IEEE compliance of the floating point multiplication, division and square root algorithms of the AMD-K7 processor. LMS J. Comput. Math. **1**, 148–200 (1998)
17. Sterbenz, P.H.: Floating Point Computation. Prentice Hall, Englewood Cliffs (1974)

Formalization and Verification of Declarative Cloud Orchestration

Hiroyuki Yoshida[1]([✉]), Kazuhiro Ogata[1,2], and Kokichi Futatsugi[2]

[1] School of Information Science, Tokyo, Japan
yuki.yoshida@jaist.ac.jp
[2] Research Center for Software Verification (RCSV),
Japan Advanced Institute of Science and Technology (JAIST),
1-1 Asahidai, Nomi, Ishikawa 923-1292, Japan

Abstract. Automation of cloud system operations, for example, which set up, monitor, and back up such systems, is called Cloud Orchestration. A standard specification language, TOSCA (Topology and Orchestration Specification for Cloud Applications), has been proposed to define topologies of cloud applications. A topology is a static structure of resources, such as VMs and software components, and a TOSCA conforming tool is expected to automate system operations based on the topologies. The current TOSCA standard, however, does not yet explicitly provide any way to formally define behavior of a topology (how to automate a topology). This paper proposes how to specify behavior of TOSCA topologies as state transition systems and to verify that orchestrated operations always successfully complete by proving the transition systems enjoys leads-to (a class of liveness) properties. We report on a case study in which we have specified and verified a setup operation to demonstrate the feasibility and usefulness of the proposed solution.

1 Introduction

Cloud computing has recently emerged as an important infrastructure supporting many aspects of human activities. In former days, it took several months to make system infrastructure resources (computer, network, storage, etc.) available, while in these days, it takes only several minutes to do so. This situation accelerates the whole life cycle of system usage where much flexible automation is required for system operations. Correctness of automated operations of cloud systems is much more crucial than that of the former systems because cloud systems serve to much more people in much longer time than the former systems used mainly inside of companies.

A system on cloud consists of many "parts," such as virtual machines (VMs), storages, and network services as well as software packages, configuration files, and user accounts in VMs. These parts are called *resources* and the management of cloud resources is called *resource orchestration*, or *cloud orchestration*.

This work was supported in part by Grant-in-Aid for Scientific Research (S) 23220002 from Japan Society for the Promotion of Science (JSPS).

© Springer International Publishing Switzerland 2015
M. Butler et al. (Eds.): ICFEM 2015, LNCS 9407, pp. 33–49, 2015.
DOI: 10.1007/978-3-319-25423-4_3

The most popular cloud orchestration tool is *CloudFormation* [1] provided as a service by Amazon Web Services (AWS) and a compatible open source tool is being developed as *OpenStack Heat* [10]. CloudFormation can manage resources provided by the IaaS platform of AWS, such as VMs, block storages (EBS), and load balancers (ELB). CloudFormation automatically sets up these resources according to declaratively defined dependencies of resources. However, CloudFormation does not directly manage resources inside VMs and instead it allows to specify any types of scripts for initially setting up VMs, such as installing Apache Httpd package, creating configuration files, copying HTML contents, and activating an Httpd component. Shell command scripts were commonly used for this layer of management and recently several open source tools become popular such as *Puppet* [11], *Chef* [4], and *Ansible* [2].

Currently people have to learn and use these several kinds of tools in actual situations, which results in much elaboration to guarantee its correctness. In an actual commercial experience of the first author, more than 50 % of troubles are caused by defects in those dependency definitions and scripts.

While orchestration tools are specialized into two management layers on IaaS and inside VMs, there is a unified standard specification language, *OASIS TOSCA* [7] that can be used to describe the structure of any type of resources. The resource structure is called a *topology* and a TOSCA tool is expected to automate system operations based on resource dependencies declaratively defined in topologies. Currently, however, there is no practical implementation of declarative specifications of TOSCA because it has not yet explicitly provided any way to specify behavior of a topology, i.e. how to automate a topology.

The contributions of this paper are as follows; (1) modeling and specifying automation of TOSCA topologies as state transition systems in CafeOBJ [3], an algebraic specification and verification system, and (2) verifying that the specification enjoys a desired property of surely reaching a goal state.

The rest of the paper is organized as follows. Section 2 briefly introduces OASIS TOSCA. Section 3 describes a model of the TOSCA topology and automation. Section 4 describes how we specify the model in CafeOBJ. Section 5 presents proof scores that verify a liveness property of a setup operation as an example. Section 6 explains related work and future issues.

2   TOSCA: Topology and Orchestration Specification for Cloud Application

TOSCA is a language to define a *service template* for a cloud application. A service template consists of a *topology template* and optionally a set of *plans*. A topology template defines the resource structure of a cloud application. Note that a topology template can be parameterized to give actual environment parameters such as IP addresses. It is the reason why named as "template" and in this paper we simply say a topology for the sake of brevity. A plan is an imperative definition of a system operation of the cloud application, such as a setup plan, written by a standard process modeling language, such as BPMN.

In TOSCA, a resource is called a *node* that has several *capabilities* and *requirements*. A topology consists of a set of nodes and a set of *relationships* of nodes. A capability is a function that the node provides to another node, while a requirement is a function that the node needs to be provided by another node. A relationship relates a requirement of a source node to a capability of a target node. Note that nodes and relationships in a topology template can also be parameterized, thus the exact terms of TOSCA are node templates and relationship templates. Figure 1 shows a typical example of topology that consists of nine nodes and nine relationships. White circles represent capabilities and black ones are requirements.

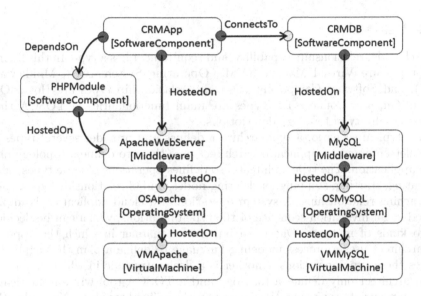

Fig. 1. An example of TOSCA topology

The current version of TOSCA is an XML-based language. The following is a part of the topology template of Fig. 1.

```
<TopologyTemplate>
  <NodeTemplate id="VMApache"name="VM for Apache"
              type="VirtualMachine">
    <Capabilities>
      <Capability id="VMApacheOS"name="OS"
                type="OperatingSystemContainerCapability"/>
    </Capabilities> </NodeTemplate>
  <NodeTemplate id="OSApache"name="OS for Apache"
              type="OperatingSystem">
    <Requirements>
      <Requirement id="OSApacheContainer"name="Container"
```

```
                    type="OperatingSystemContainerRequirement"/>
    </Requirements>
    <Capabilities>
      <Capability id="OsApacheSoftware"name="Software"
                  type="SoftwareContainerCapability"/>
    </Capabilities> </NodeTemplate>
  <RelationshipTemplate id="OSApacheHostedOnVMApache"
                        name="hosted on"type="HostedOn">
    <SourceElement ref="OSApacheContainer"/>
    <TargetElement ref="VMApacheOS"/>
  </RelationshipTemplate>
...
</TopologyTemplate>
```

Each node, relationship, capability, and requirement has a type. In this figure, node types are Virtual Machine (VM), Operating System (OS), Middleware (MW), and Software Component (SC) and relationship types are HostedOn, DependsOn, and ConnectsTo. Types are main functionalities of TOSCA that enable reusability of topology descriptions.

In a typical scenario, a type architect defines and provides several types of those elements and an application architect uses them to define a topology of a cloud application. The type architect also defines operations of node types, such as creating, starting, stopping, or deleting nodes, and of relationship types, such as attaching relationships. A system operation of a cloud application is implemented as an invocation sequence of the type operations, which can be decided in two kinds of manners. One is an imperative manner in which the application architect uses a process modeling language to define a plan that explicitly invokes these type operations. Another is a declarative one in which the application architect only defines a topology and a TOSCA tool will automatically invoke appropriate type operations based on the defined topology. Naturally, the declarative manner is a main target of OASIS TOSCA because it promotes more abstract and reusable descriptions of topologies.

In this paper, *behavior of topologies* means when and which type operations should be invoked in automation. It is important to notice that behavior of a topology depends on types of included nodes and relationships. We also say *behavior of a type* to mean that the conditions and results of invoking its type operations, which is defined by a type architect. Usually, different types of nodes are provided by different vendors and so specified by different type architects. An application architect is responsible for behavior of a topology whereas type architects are responsible for behavior of their defined types.

Currently there are no practical implementations of the declarative manner of TOSCA and one of the reasons is that no standard set of type operations of nodes or relationships are defined and there is no way for type architects to define behavior of their own types.

3   Model of Automation of Topologies

We model a topology of a cloud application as a set of four kinds of objects corresponding to the four main kinds of elements of a topology; nodes, relationships, capabilities, and requirements. Each object has a type, an identifier, a (local) state and may have links to other objects. There is an additional object, a message pool, to represent messaging between resources inside of different VMs because they cannot communicate directly. The message pool is simply a bag of messages, which abstracts implementations of messaging.

A type of nodes defines invocation rules of its operations. Each rule specifies when an operation can be invoked and how it changes the state of the node. A type of relationships also defines invocation rules of its operations. We assume that a state of a relationship is a pair of the states of its capability and requirement in this paper for the sake of simplicity. Thereby, an operation of a relationship type changes the state of its capability or requirement. As described in Sect. 2, type operations and their invocation rules should be defined by type architects. When an application architect defines a topology, a set of all type operations and a set of all invocation rules of referred node/relationship types collectively define behavior of the topology.

Let us use a typical example where four node types and three relationship types in Fig. 1 participate in automation of a setup operation. In this example, we assume that behavior of four node types is the same focusing on when a node is created and started because they are the most essential for setup operations.

On the other hand, behavior of relationship types usually varies according to their nature; they may be in the IaaS layer or in the inside of VM layer, "local" or "remote", "immediate" or "await". Three relationship types of this example typically cover the variation. A HostedOn relationship is one between resources in the IaaS layer. It is "immediate", i.e. it can be established as soon as the target node is created. Each of DependsOn and ConnectsTo relationships is between resources inside of VMs and is "await", i.e. it should wait for the target node to be started. A DependsOn relationship is "local" in the same VM, while a ConnectsTo is "remote" to a different VM and should use some messages to notice the states of its capability to its requirement. We also assume that types of capabilities and requirements are the same as relationships that link them in this example for the sake of simplicity.

Behavior of these types is depicted in Fig. 2. A solid arrow represents a state transition of each object and a dashed arrow represents an invocation of a type operation or a message sending.

Initial States: Every node is initially in a state named as *initial*, every capability of the node is *closed*, and every requirement is *unbound*.
Invocation Rule of Node Type Operations:

- *create* operation can be invoked if all of the HostedOn requirements of the node become *ready* and changes the state from *initial* to *created*.
- *start* operation can be invoked if all of the requirements become *ready* and changes the state from *created* to *started*.

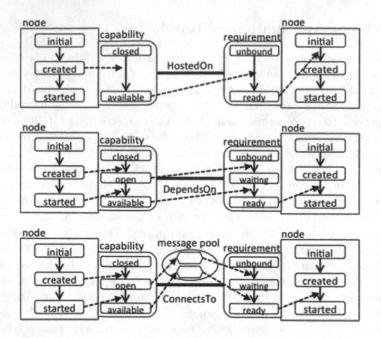

Fig. 2. Typical behavior of relationship types

Invocation Rule of Operations of HostedOn Relationship Type:

– *capavailable* operation can be invoked if the target node is already created, i.e. *created* or *started* and changes the state of its capability from *closed* to *available*.
– *reqready* operation can be invoked if its capability is *available* and changes the state of the requirement from *unbound* to *ready*.

Invocation Rule of Operations DependsOn Relationship Type:

– *capopen* operation can be invoked if the target node is already created and changes the state of its capability from *closed* to *open*.
– *capavailable* operation can be invoked if the target node is *started* and changes the state of its capability from *open* to *available*.
– *reqwaiting* operation can be invoked if its capability is already activated, i.e. *open* or *available*, and the source node is *created*. It changes the state of its requirement from *unbound* to *waiting*.
– *reqready* operation can be invoked if its capability is *available* and changes the state of its requirement from *waiting* to *ready*.

Invocation Rule Operations of ConnectsTo Relationship Type:

– *capopen* operation can be invoked if the target node is already created. It changes the state of its capability from *closed* to *open* and also issues an open message of the capability to the message pool.

- *capavailable* operation can be invoked if the target node is *started*. It changes the state of its capability from *open* to *available* and also issues an available message of the capability to the message pool.
- *reqwaiting* operation can be invoked if it finds an open message of its capability and the source node is *created*. It changes the state of its requirement from *unbound* to *waiting*.
- *reqready* operation can be invoked if it finds an available message of its capability and changes the state of its requirement from *waiting* to *ready*.

4   CafeOBJ Specification of Model

CafeOBJ [3] is a formal specification language that inherits many advanced functionalities from OBJ [8] and OBJ3 [9] algebraic specification language. CafeOBJ specifications are executable by regarding equations and transition rules in them as left-to-right rewrite rules, and this executability can be used for interactive theorem proving.

Let l and r be terms of the same sort including a set of variables X, and let c be a term of sort *Bool*, then $(\forall X)(l=r \text{ if } c)$ is called a (conditional) equation. Let *State* be a sort of states, l and r be terms of sort *State* including a set of variables X, and let c be a term of sort *Bool*, then $(\forall X)(l \rightarrow r \text{ if } c)$ is called a transition rule. Let St be an sorted quotient term algebra of *State* by equality, and let Tr be a set of transitions on the states where $Tr \subseteq St \times St$. A transition sequence is a sequence of states $(S_0, S_1, ...)$ where each adjacent pair $(S_i, S_{i+1}) \in Tr$.

A model of automation of a topology is specified as a transition system in CafeOBJ. A node is represented as a term `node(type,idND,state)` whose sort is `Node` where `idND` is its identifier. Similarly, a capability as `cap(type,idCP,state, idND)`, a requirement as `req(type,idRQ,state,idND)`, and a relationship as `rel(type,idRL,idCP,idRQ)` where `idCP`, `idRQ`, and `idRL` are identifiers of the capability, requirement, and relationship, respectively. In order to specify the whole application, let a global state S be a tuple < `nodes,caps,reqs,rels,mp` > whose sort is `State` where `nodes`, `caps`, `reqs`, and `rels` are sets of nodes, capabilities, requirements, and relationships respectively and `mp` is a message pool.

The model described in the previous section is specified by twelve transition rules two of which are for node operations, two are for operations of HostedOn relationship, and eight are for four operations of two relationship types. The followings show three of them for *create* and *start* operation of nodes (R01, R02) and *reqready* operation of ConnectsTo relationship (R12):

```
-- Create an initial node if all of its hostedOn requirements are ready.
ctrans [R01]:
    < (node(TND,IDND,initial) SetND), SetCP, SetRQ, SetRL, MP >
=> < (node(TND,IDND,created) SetND), SetCP, SetRQ, SetRL, MP >
    if allRQOfNDInStates(filterRQ(SetRQ,hostedOn),IDND,ready).

-- Start a created node if all of its requirements are ready.
ctrans [R02]:
    < (node(TND,IDND,created) SetND), SetCP, SetRQ, SetRL, MP >
```

```
=> < (node(TND,IDND,started) SetND), SetCP, SetRQ, SetRL, MP >
   if allRQOfNDInStates(SetRQ,IDND,ready).

-- Let a waiting ConnectsTo requirement be ready
-- if there is an available message of the corresponding capability.
trans [R12]:
   < SetND, SetCP,
     (req(connectsTo,IDRQ,waiting,IDND) SetRQ),
     (rel(connectsTo,IDRL,IDCP,IDRQ) SetRL),
     (avMsg(IDCP) MP) >
=> < SetND, SetCP,
     (req(connectsTo,IDRQ,ready,  IDND) SetRQ),
     (rel(connectsTo,IDRL,IDCP,IDRQ) SetRL), MP >.
```

Here, all terms staring with capital letters are pattern-matching variables. Since a blank character represents an associative, commutative, and idempotent operator to construct sets with the identity, (ND1 ND2 ND3) represents a set of nodes and (ND SetND) also represents a set of nodes when NDn are nodes and SetND is a set of nodes. Predicate allRQOfNDInStates(SetRQ,IDND,ready) checks whether every requirement in SetRQ is *ready* if the identifier of its node is IDND. filterRQ (SetRQ,hostedOn) is a subset of SetRQ which elements are HostedOn requirements. Note that allRQOfNDInStates(SetRQ,IDND,ready) always holds when node IDND has no requirements in SetRQ. (avMsg(IDCP) MP) means the message pool includes at least one available message of capability IDCP. All CafeOBJ codes of this example can be downloaded at http://goo.gl/s9fJXq.

5   Verification of Setup Operation

A typical property of an automated system setup operation, which we want to verify, is that the operation surely brings a cloud application to the state where all of its component nodes are *started*. We say "surely" to mean total reachability, i.e. any transition sequence from any initial state always reaches some final state. Total reachability is one of the most important properties of practical automation of cloud applications.

The initial and final states are represented as predicates $init(S)$ and $final(S)$ that can be specified by equations in CafeOBJ as follows.

```
eq init(< SetND,SetCP,SetRQ,SetRL,MP >)
   = not (SetND = empND) and wfs(< SetND,SetCP,SetRQ,SetRL,MP >) and
     (MP = empMsg) and allNDInStates(SetND,initial) and
     allCPInStates(SetCP,closed) and allRQInStates(SetRQ,unbound).
eq wfs(< SetND,SetCP,SetRQ,SetRL,MP >)
   = allCPHaveND(SetCP,SetND) and allRQHaveND(SetRQ,SetND) and
     allRLHaveCP(SetRL,SetCP) and allRLHaveRQ(SetRL,SetRQ) and
     allRQHaveRL(SetRQ,SetRL) and allRLNotInSameND(SetRL,SetCP,SetRQ).
eq final(< SetND,SetCP,SetRQ,SetRL,MP >) = allNDInStates(SetND,started).
...
eq allRLNotInSameND(empRL,SetCP,SetRQ) = true.
```

```
eq allRLNotInSameND((RL SetRL),SetCP,SetRQ)
  = (node(getCapability(SetCP,RL))
      = node(getRequirement(SetRQ,RL))) = false
    and allRLNotInSameND(SetRL,SetCP,SetRQ).
```

Here, we omitted definitions of several predicates; `allNDInStates(SetND, initial)` means that every node in `SetND` is *initial*, `allCPHaveND(SetCP,SetND)` means that every capability in `SetCP` has its node in `SetND`, and so on. Note that predicate `wfs` (well-formed state) specifies conditions that should hold in not only initial states but also any reachable states.

When automation is modeled as a transition system, total reachability is formalized as (*init* leads-to *final*) which means that any transition sequence from any initial state reaches some final state no matter what possible transition sequence is taken. Let *cont* be a state predicate representing whether the transition system continues to transit, *inv* be a conjunction of some state predicates, and *m* be a natural number function of a global state. Then the following six conditions are sufficient for proving that (*init* leads-to *final*) holds [6].

(1) $(\forall s \in St)\,(init(s)$ implies $cont(s))$
(2) $(\forall(s, s') \in Tr)$
    $((inv(s)$ and $cont(s)$ and $(\text{not } final(s)))$ implies $(cont(s')$ or $final(s')))$
(3) $(\forall(s, s') \in Tr)$
    $((inv(s)$ and $cont(s)$ and $(\text{not } final(s)))$ implies $(m(s) > m(s')))$
(4) $(\forall s \in St)$
    $((inv(s)$ and $(cont(s)$ or $final(s))$and $(m(s) = 0))$ implies $final(s))$
(5) $(\forall s \in St)\,(init(s)$ implies $inv(s))$
(6) $(\forall(s, s') \in Tr)\,(inv(s)$ implies $inv(s'))$

When condition (5) and (6) hold, each state predicate included in *inv* is called an invariant. And *m* is called a state measuring function.

Condition (1) means an initial state should be a continuing state, i.e. it should start transitions. Conditions (2) means transitions continue until $final(s')$ holds. Condition (3) implies that $m(s)$ keeps to decrease properly while $final(s)$ does not hold, but $m(s)$ is a natural number and should stop to decrease in finite steps, and should get to the state s' with $((cont(s')$ or $final(s'))$ and $(m(s') = 0))$. Condition (4) asserts that it implies $final(s')$.

CafeOBJ provides a built-in search predicate $(s =(*,1)=+ s')$ which returns true for state s if there exists state $s' \in St$ such that $(s, s') \in Tr$. Since $cont(s)$ means that state s has at least one next state, it can be specified as follows.

```
eq cont(S) = (S =(*,1)=>+ S').
```

As to state measuring function $m(s)$, we should find a natural number function that properly decreases in transitions. For this purpose, we intentionally designed the transition system where every transition rule changes local states of at least one objects. Function *m* can be the weighted sum of counting local states of three sorts of objects as follows.

```
eq m(< SetND,SetCP,SetRQ,SetRL,MP >)
  = (( (#NodeInStates(initial,SetND) * 2)
  +      #NodeInStates(created,SetND))
  + ( (#CapabilityInStates(closed,SetCP) * 2)
  +      #CapabilityInStates(open,SetCP)))
  + ( (#RequirementInStates(unbound,SetRQ) * 2)
  +      #RequirementInStates(waiting,SetRQ)).
```

For example, when rule R01 is applied, (#NodeInStates(initial,SetND) * 2) decreases by two while #NodeInStates(created,SetND) increases by one and thus $m(s') = m(s) - 1$ holds. When $m(s)$ becomes 0, all nodes are not *initial* or *created*, i.e. are *started* which means the state is final. Defining $m(s)$ as above makes conditions (3) and (4) naturally hold.

The rest of this section presents proofs for these conditions. Although it is an interactive process, it is based on very systematic way of thinking and achieves structural and deep understanding of models, which is required in order to develop trusted systems.

5.1   Proof Score for Condition (1)

One of interesting features of CafeOBJ is that theorems to be proved and their proofs are written in the same executable specification language. A proof written in CafeOBJ is called a proof score.

The proof score for condition (1) begins with defining a theorem to be proved, i.e. *initcont*(S).

```
eq initcont(S) = init(S) implies cont(S) .
```

The most general case we can consider is when state S is < sND,sCP,sRQ,sRL,mp > where sND is an arbitrary constant representing a set of nodes and similarly so sCP, sRQ, sRL, and mp. But this case is too general for CafeOBJ to determine whether *initcont*(S) does or does not hold.

Thinking through meanings of the model, we know that rule R01 is firstly applicable to an initial state. R01 can be applied when there is at least one *initial* node and all of its HostedOn requirements are *ready*. The proof score is hence split into five cases; there is no node, at least one *created* node, one *started* node, one *initial* node whose HostedOn requirements are *ready*, and one *initial* node one of whose HostedOn requirements is not *ready*. Let tnd be an arbitrary constant representing any type of node and let sND' be any set of nodes, then the proof score for the first four cases is as follows:

```
-- Case 1: There is no node.
  eq sND = empND .
  reduce initcont(< sND, sCP, sRQ, sRL, mp >).
  --> to be true because init(S) does not hold.
...
-- Case 2: There is at least one created node.
  eq sND = (node(tnd,idND,created) sND').
  reduce initcont(< sND, sCP, sRQ, sRL, mp >).
```

```
    --> to be true because init(S) does not hold.
  ...
-- Case 3: There is at least one started node.
    eq sND = (node(tnd,idND,started) sND').
    reduce initcont(< sND, sCP, sRQ, sRL, mp >).
    --> to be true because init(S) does not hold.
  ...
-- Case 4: There is at least one initial node
--          all of whose HostedOn requirements are ready.
    eq allRQOfNDInStates(filterRQ(sRQ,hostedOn),idND,ready) = true.
    eq sND = (node(tnd,idND,initial) sND').
    reduce initcont(< sND, sCP, sRQ, sRL, mp >).
    --> to be true because cont(S) holds.
```

5.2 Cyclic Dependency

The fifth case requires more consideration.

When the *initial* node has one requirement that is not *ready*, there should be another node that has the corresponding capability. According to the state of such node, this case is split into four more cases. However, if at least one of its requirements is not *ready*, the case falls into a cyclic situation and the case splitting becomes endless.

Thinking through meanings of the model, we know that dependency of nodes should not be cyclic. We need to specify that a global state does not include any cyclic dependency, which is represented by state predicate *noCycleInState(S)* specified as follows:

```
eq noCycleInState(S) = noCycle(getAllNodeInState(S),empND,S).
eq noCycle(empND,V,S) = true.
eq noCycle((ND SetND),V,S)
   = (not (state(ND) = initial) or
      if ND \in V then false else noCycle(DDS(ND,S),(ND V),S) fi)
     and noCycle(SetND,V,S).
```

Here, DDS(ND,S), *Directly Depending Set* of node ND in global state S, is a set of nodes whose local states are *initial* and on which ND is hosted. For example, let S be an initial state of the topology of Fig. 1, then DDS(CRMApp,S) = (ApacheWebServer) whereas DDS(VMApache,S) = empND. Predicate noCycle(SetND, V,S) traverses all transitive closures of DDS of all nodes in SetND and checks whether it does not reach some already visited node in V. In order to ensure that the acyclic property holds for any reachable states, *noCycleInState(S)* should be included in *init(S)* and also in *inv(S)* and condition (6) should be proved.

Theorem: For any node N in state S, if *noCycleInState(S)* holds and the local state of N is *initial*, then there exists node N' in S such that the local state of N' is also *initial* and DDS(N',S) is empty.

Proof: If there is no such N' then noCycle will reach some already visited node because it traverses finite number of nodes.   □

Let us return to the proof score of *initcont*(S). When there is an *initial* node in state S and *noCycleInState*(S) holds, the theorem above allows us to assume that DDS of the node is empty. When the node has at least one requirement that is not *ready*, there is another node that has the corresponding capability and there are three more cases as follows:

```
-- When there is at least one initial node whose DDS is empty,
--       and at least one of whose HostedOn requirements is not ready,
-- there should be another node that has the corresponding capability.
  eq sND = (node(tnd,idND,initial) sND').
  eq sRQ = (req(hostedOn,idRQ,srq,idND) sRQ').
  eq (srq \in (unbound waiting)) = true.
  eq sRL = (rel(hostedOn,idRL,idCP,idRQ) sRL').
  eq sCP = (cap(hostedOn,idCP,scp,idND1) sCP').
-- Case 5: The corresponding node is created.
  eq sND' = (node(tnd',idND1,created) sND'').
  reduce initcont(< sND, sCP, sRQ, sRL, mp >).
  --> to be true because init(S) does not hold.
...
-- Case 6: The corresponding node is started.
  eq sND' = (node(tnd',idND1,started) sND'').
  reduce initcont(< sND, sCP, sRQ, sRL, mp >).
  --> to be true because init(S) does not hold.
...
-- Case 7: The corresponding node is initial.
  eq sND' = (node(tnd',idND1,initial) sND'').
  reduce (DDS(node(tnd,idND,initial),< sND,sCP,sRQ,sRL,mp >) = empND).
  --> to be false, which is a contradiction,
  --> i.e. this is not a reachable state.
```

Thereby, *initcont*(S) holds for all cases that are collaboratively exhaustive. Note that we do not explain several irrelevant cases such as inconsistent types, no corresponding capability, and relationship between the same node, because in such cases *wfs*(S) does not hold and thus *initcont*(S) holds.

5.3 Proof Score for Condition (2)

The proof score for condition (2) begins with defining a theorem to be proved, i.e. *contcont*.

```
  eq contcont(S,SS,CC)
    = not (S =(*,1)=>+ SS if CC suchThat
            not ((CC then
                   (inv(S) and cont(S) and not final(S)
                    implies cont(SS) or final(SS))) == true){ ... }).
```

This uses an idiom of a built-in search predicate, =(*,1)=>+ _ if _ suchThat. Given a global state S, contcont(S,SS,CC) searches all possible transitions from S while binding variable SS to each next state and checking condition (2). It holds if and only if condition (2) holds for all such next states.

The most general case, S = < sND,sCP,sRQ,sRL,mp >, is too general because there is no rule to match with it. Thus the proof score should be split into twelve cases in each of which state S is as specific as each transition rule matches with it. This means that condition (2) (also (3) and (6)) can be proved rule by rule. For example, in the case of rule R01, state S should be as specific as its left-hand-side, < (node(tnd,idND,initial) sND),sCP,sRQ,sRL,mp >.

This situation is very instructive for us because we can find that the next state includes a *created* node and can expect that rule R02 will be applicable. The proof score of rule R01 is split into three cases; (1) the condition of R01 does not hold, (2) it holds and the condition of R02 holds, and (3) it does not hold. The proof score of the first two cases is as follows:

```
-- Case 1: The condition of R01 does not hold for S.
  eq allRQOfNDInStates(filterRQ(sRQ,hostedOn),idND,ready) = false.
  reduce contcont(< (node(tnd,idND,initial) sND),sCP,sRQ,sRL,mp >,SS,CC).
  --> to be true because cont(S) does not hold.
...
-- Case 2: The condition of R01 holds for S and
--         the condition of R02 holds for SS.
  eq allRQOfNDInStates(filterRQ(sRQ,hostedOn),idND,ready) = true.
  eq allRQOfNDInStates(sRQ,idND,ready) = true.
  reduce contcont(< (node(tnd,idND,initial) sND),sCP,sRQ,sRL,mp >,SS,CC).
  --> to be true because cont(SS) holds.
```

The last case means that the *initial* node in S becomes *created* in SS but at least one of its requirements is not *ready* (and is not HostedOn). There are thirty-six such cases, (2 relationship types, not HostedOn) × (2 requirement states, not *ready*) × (3 states of the corresponding capability) × (3 states of the corresponding node). Half of them are not reachable states because *reqwaiting* operation is never invoked when the source node is *initial* and thus the requirement should not be *waiting* in S. This property is required to be proved as an invariant. In each of other sixteen cases, one of twelve transition rules can be applicable and so *cont(SS)* holds. For example, if a DependsOn requirement is *unbound* and the corresponding capability is *open*, then *reqwaiting* operation can be invoked in SS because the source node becomes *created*.

Remaining two cases are where a DependsOn or ConnectsTo requirement is *unbound*, the corresponding capability is *closed*, and its node is *initial*. Again we use the cyclic dependency theorem to assume that there is *initial* node X where DDS(X,S) is empty. Then, we repeat similar systematic case splitting as describe above, but this time we can reject another *initial* node.

5.4   Proof Scores for Condition (3), (4), (5) and (6)

As mentioned above, condition (3) can also be proved rule by rule. The following is a piece of the proof score for rule R01, in which a theorem of natural numbers is required:

```
eq mesmes(S,SS,CC)
   = not (S =(*,1)=>+ SS if CC suchThat
          not ((CC then
                (inv(S) and cont(S) and not final(S)
                implies m(S) > m(SS))) == true){ ... }).
```

```
-- A theorem of natural numbers
-- s(N) is a successor of N, i.e. s(N) = N + 1.
   eq (s(N) > N) = true.
...
-- Case for R01:
   reduce mesmes(< (node(tnd,idND,initial) sND),sCP,sRQ,sRL,mp >,SS,CC).
```

For condition (4), we need a lemma such that if the number of *created* or *initial* nodes is zero, then all nodes are *started*. This lemma can be proved using mathematical induction about a set of nodes. The following is a part of the proof score for condition (4), where it also requires another natural number theorem.

```
-- Another theorem of natural numbers
   eq (N1 + N2 = 0) = (N1 = 0) and (N2 = 0).
   eq lemma(SetND)
      = ((#NodeInStates(created,SetND) = 0) and
          #NodeInStates(initial,SetND) = 0)
        implies allNDInStates(SetND,started).
   reduce lemma(sND) and (m(< sND,sCP,sRQ,sRL,mp >) = 0)
          implies final(< sND,sCP,sRQ,sRL,mp >).
```

In order to prove conditions (1) and (2), we need more than ten invariants including *noCycleInState(S)*. Theorems to be proved are defined as follows:

```
eq initinv(S) = init(S) implies inv(S).
eq invinv(S,SS,CC)
   = not (S =(*,1)=>+ SS if CC suchThat
          not ((CC then
                (inv(S) implies inv(SS))) == true){ ... }).
```

Similarly as described above, we can prove them using systematic case splitting and mathematical induction.

6   Related Work and Conclusion

Related Work

OASIS TOSCA TC currently discusses the next version (v1.1) to define a standard set of nodes, relationships, and operations. It is planned to use state machines to describe behavior of the standard operations, which is a similar approach as ours. However, the usage is limited to clarify the descriptions of the standard and the way for type architects to define behavior of their own types is out of the scope of standardization. We provide the formal specification of behavior of types and show that it can be used for verification.

CloudFormation and OpenStack Heat can manage resources on the IaaS layer, however, they support to manage dependencies between resources in VMs. For example, suppose a software component(SC_1) on a VM(VM_1) can be activated only after waiting for activation of another component(SC_2) on another VM(VM_2), CloudFormation requires a pair of special purpose resources, namely, *WaitCondition* and *WaitConditionHandle*. VM_1 should be declared to depend on the WaitCondition resource. The corresponding WaitConditionHandle resource provides a URL that should be passed to the script for initializing VM_2. When SC_2 is successfully activated, the script sends a success signal to the URL, which causes the WaitCondition become active and then creation of dependent VM_1 starts. This style of management includes several problems. Firstly, it forces complicated and troublesome coding of operations. Secondly, although only SC_1 should wait for SC_2, all other components on VM_1 are also forced to wait. This causes unnecessary slowdown of system creation. Thirdly, it tends to make cyclic dependencies. Suppose SC_2 should also wait for another component SC_3 on VM_1. Although the dependency among components, SC_1, SC_2, and SC_3 is acyclic, the dependency between VMs is cyclic. This may be solved by splitting VM_1 to two VMs, one is for SC_1 and another is for SC_3, but it causes increased cost and delayed creation. Our formalization can manage any types of resources and solve this kind of problems in a smarter way because it can manage finer grained dependencies, which is shown as invocation rules described in Sect. 3.

Salaün, G., et al. [5,12,13] designed a system setup protocol and demonstrated to verify a liveness property of the protocol using their model checking method. Although their setup protocol is essentially the same as behavior of our example topology in this paper, there are two main differences. Firstly, their protocol is based on a specific implementation which challenges distributed management of cloud resources while current popular implementations, e.g. CloudFormation, implement centralized management. On the other hand, our model is rather abstract without assuming distributed or centralized implementations. Secondly, they used model checking while we use theorem proving. They checked about 150 different models of system including from four to fifteen components in which from 1.4 thousand to 1.4 million transitions are generated and checked. They found a bug of their specification because checked models fortunately included error cases. The model checking method can verify correctness of checked models and so they should include all boundary cases. In our formalization, the specification itself is verified by interactive theorem proving in which all boundary cases are necessary in consideration in a systematic way. It achieves structural and deep understanding that is required to develop trusted systems.

Future Issues

TOSCA supports type inheritance of any elements such as nodes, relationships, capabilities, and requirements. When a new type is defined and inherits a part of behavior from some existing type, it is desired that the corresponding part of the existing proof can be reused and only extended part of specification needs to be verified. While transition rules shown in this paper directly use type literals such as `hostedOn` or `connectsTo`, it is required to introduce some mechanism to use the rules for inherited types. The next version of TOSCA will define a set of standard types and we will introduce some inheritance mechanism to reuse proof scores of the standard types, which will significantly reduce efforts of proving behavior of topologies using inherited types.

The current version of TOSCA does not manage operation failures and it focuses on declaratively defining expected configurations of cloud applications. In many of failure cases, it is desired to roll back to the initial states, which does not depend on correctness of topologies but on correctness of implementation of automation tools. A possible extension of TOSCA may be to define alternative configurations in failure cases, which we think we can easily extend our formalization to handle.

Conclusion

TOSCA topologies and automation are modeled, formalized, and verified with theorem proving. The specification and verification are demonstrated to prove total reachability of a typical set of relationship types. The proved specification is in a high abstraction level without depending on implementations of distributed or centralized managements, however, it provides a smarter solution than that of the most popular implementation. A related work proved similar problem by their model checking method, in which many of finite-state systems were checked. We use an interactive theorem proving method and verify applications of unlimited number of states in a significantly systematic way. Several general predicates and theorems are presented to be usable for common problems such as Cyclic Dependency.

References

1. Amazon Web Services: AWS CloudFormation: Configuration Management & Cloud Orchestration. http://aws.amazon.com/cloudformation/. Accessed 03 April 2015
2. Ansible: Ansible is Simple IT Automation. http://www.ansible.com/home/. Accessed 03 April 2015
3. CafeOBJ (2014). http://www.ldl.jaist.ac.jp/cafeobj/
4. Chef Software: IT automation for speed and awesomeness. https://www.chef.io/chef/. Accessed 03 April 2015
5. Etchevers, X., Coupaye, T., Boyer, F., Palma, N.D.: Self-configuration of distributed applications in the cloud. In: IEEE CLOUD, pp. 668–675 (2011)
6. Futatsugi, K.: Generate & check method for verifying transition systems in CafeOBJ. In: De Nicola, R., Hennicker, R. (eds.) Software, Services, and Systems. LNCS, vol. 8950, pp. 171–192. Springer, Heidelberg (2015)
7. OASIS: TOSCA - Topology and Orchestration Specification for Cloud Applications Version 1.0. http://docs.oasis-open.org/tosca/TOSCA/v1.0/os/TOSCA-v1.0-os.pdf. Accessed 03 April 2015
8. OBJ (2003). http://cseweb.ucsd.edu/goguen/sys/obj.html

9. OBJ3 (2005). http://www.kindsoftware.com/products/opensource/obj3/
10. OpenStack.org: Heat - OpenStack Orchestration. https://wiki.openstack.org/wiki/Heat/. Accessed 03 April 2015
11. Puppet Labs: IT Automation Software for System Administrators. https://puppetlabs.com/. Accessed 03 April 2015
12. Salaün, G., Boyer, F., Coupaye, T., Palma, N.D., Etchevers, X., Gruber, O.: An experience report on the verification of autonomic protocols in the cloud. ISSE 9(2), 105–117 (2013)
13. Salaün, G., Etchevers, X., De Palma, N., Boyer, F., Coupaye, T.: Verification of a self-configuration protocol for distributed applications in the cloud. In: Cámara, J., de Lemos, R., Ghezzi, C., Lopes, A. (eds.) Assurances for Self-Adaptive Systems. LNCS, vol. 7740, pp. 60–79. Springer, Heidelberg (2013)

Consistency Verification of Specification Rules

Thai Son Hoang, Shinji Itoh[✉], Kyohei Oyama, Kunihiko Miyazaki,
Hironobu Kuruma, and Naoto Sato

Center for Technology Innovation, Hitachi Ltd.,
Yokohama, Kanagawa 244-0817, Japan
{hoang.thaison.ex,shinji.itoh.wn,kyohei.oyama.ec,kunihiko.miyazaki.zt,
hironobu.kuruma.zg,naoto.sato.je}@hitachi.com

Abstract. This paper focuses on the consistency analysis of specification rules expressing relationships between input and expected output of systems. We identified the link between Minimal Inconsistent Sets (MISes) of rules and Minimal Unsatisfiable Subsets (MUSes) of constraints. For practical consistency verification of rules, we developed a novel algorithm using SMT solvers for fast enumeration of MUSes. We evaluated the algorithm using publicly available benchmarks. Finally, we used the approach to verify the consistency of specifications rules extracted from real-world case studies.

Keywords: Specification rules · Consistency verification · Minimal Inconsistent Sets (MISes) · Minimal Unsatisfiable Subsets (MUSes) · SMTs

1 Introduction

In financial and public sectors, regulations and policies are often specified in terms of rules *describing relationships between input and expected output*. As an example, consider a rewarding policy for a vehicle insurance company. Beside the normal contracts, the company offers two special rewards in the form of *discounts* (in percentages) for the insurance and shopping *coupons*. The availability of the rewards to customers depends on the *duration* (number of years) of the contracts, their online *account* status (whether or not they already have an online account), and their *VIP* membership status. The policies on how rewards are offered to a customer are as follows.

(R1) If the customer has an online account then either a discount of 3 % or a 100$ coupon is offered.

(R2) If the customer is a VIP then a discount of at least 5 % and a coupon valued between 50$ and 100$ are offered.

(R3) If the customer is not a VIP and the contract duration is less than 2 years then either a discount of less than 5 % or a coupon valued between 30$ and 50$ is offered.

(R4) If the customer is a VIP and the duration of the contract is at least 2 years then a discount of at least 7 % and a 50$ coupon are offered.

© Springer International Publishing Switzerland 2015
M. Butler et al. (Eds.): ICFEM 2015, LNCS 9407, pp. 50–66, 2015.
DOI: 10.1007/978-3-319-25423-4_4

Each rule comprises a constraint on the input and a constraint on the output, imitating logical implication. In particular, the rules are *non-deterministic*, *i.e.*, given a rule and some input, there could be more than one satisfying output. This type of *specification rules* is particularly useful in the early system design process, where requirements are obscure and the system details cannot be decided. Non-determinism is essentially what makes specification rules different from *production rules* used in *production rules used in Business Rule Management Systems* (BRMSes) [7]. Production rules are designed for execution, and hence they are necessarily deterministic. More discussion on the similarities and differences between specification rules and production rules can be seen in Sect. 6.

Given a set of rules, *i.e.*, a rule base, various properties can be statically analysed. One of the most important properties of a rule base is *consistency*: the rule base should be conflict-free, *i.e.*, there must be some possible output for any valid input. Otherwise, the regulations represented by the rule base are infeasible and cannot be implemented. In the example of the vehicle insurance company, the policy is inconsistent. More specifically, when a customer is a VIP with a 3-year contract and an online account, there are no possible values for the insurance discount and the shopping coupon satisfying the rewarding policy.

This paper focuses on the *consistency analysis* of a special type of specification rules, namely those where the output constraints do not refer to the input (*e.g.*, the vehicle insurance example). This type of specification rules is sufficient to stipulate many policies in financial and public sectors such as taxation regulations or insurance policies. Consistency analysis of this type of rules is a challenging problem. In the worst cases, there can be exponentially many set of inconsistent rules within a rule base. Moreover, even in the case where the rule base is consistent, one (potentially) has to consider every combination of the rules. Our motivation is to develop some program for *efficiently validating the consistency of specification rules*.

Within our knowledge, there are no existing technologies for formally verifying consistency of non-deterministic specification rules. However, given the fact that each rule is made up of an input constraint and an output constraint, the consistency of rules is related to the *satisfiability* of constraints. Recent advancement in the field of SMT solvers enables the possibility of checking satisfiability for a large and complex set of constraints of different types [4]. In particular, SMT solvers have been showed to be applicable to hardware designs, programs verification, etc. Various SMT-based problems have been investigated. Amongst them is "infeasibility analysis", the study about constraint sets for which no satisfying assignments exist. Given an unsatisfiable constraint set, useful information about this set includes to identify where the "problem" occurs. There exist efficient algorithms for extracting a *Minimal Unsatisfiable (sub-)Set* (MUS), i.e., the *unsat-core*, of an unsatisfiable constraint set [6,13,15]. Recently, algorithms for finding all MUSes have been proposed [3,10,11].

In order to validate the consistency of a rule base, we enumerate all *Minimal Inconsistent Sets* (MISes) of the rule base. A MIS is a set of inconsistent rules that is minimal, with respect to the set-inclusion ordering. Similar to the MUSes of constraints, the MISes of rules identify where the problems occur within the rule base. By exploring the relationship between the MISes of the rule base, the MUSes of the output constraints, and satisfiability of individual input constraint, we reduce the problem of enumerating the MISes to that of the MUSes of the output constraints. We use SMT solvers as black-boxes for solving satisfiability problems. Furthermore, our approach is constraint-agnostic, *i.e.*, independent of the type of the input and output constraints.

We identify the relationship between the MISes of the rules, the MUSes of the output constraints, and the satisfiability of the input constraints. Our contribution is a novel algorithm for fast enumeration of MUSes. We compare our algorithm against the state-of-the-art program for MUSes enumeration from [10] using some publicly available benchmarks. The correctness of our approach is ensured by the formalisation of the algorithms using the Event-B modelling method [1] and the mechanical proofs using the supporting Rodin platform [2]. A more detailed version of this paper including the Event-B formalisation can be found elsewhere [9].

The rest of the paper is structured as follows. In Sect. 2, we present some background information including the problem of constraints satisfiability and rules consistency. In Sect. 3, we discuss the relationship between MISes and MUSes, showing that the problem of finding MISes can be reduced to enumerating MUSes. In Sect. 4, we present a novel and efficient algorithm for enumerating MUSes. In Sect. 5, we give our empirical analysis of the new algorithm and its application in finding MISes. Finally, we draw some conclusions in Sect. 6.

2   Background

2.1   Constraints Satisfiability

In this paper, we often discuss satisfiability problems related to different generic sets of constraints. For each set of constraints, the constraint type and variables domain are omitted. In general, we will consider some indexed set of constraints $\mathbb{C} = \{C_1, C_2, \ldots, C_n\}$. Each constraint C_i specifies some restrictions on the problem's variables. Constraint C_i is satisfied by any assignment $\mathbf{A}$ of the variables that meets C_i's restriction. We use the notation $\mathsf{sat}(\mathbf{A}, C)$ to denote the fact that $\mathbf{A}$ satisfies C, and $\mathsf{unsat}(\mathbf{A}, C)$ otherwise.

Given a set of constraints $Cs \subseteq \mathbb{C}$, if there exists some assignment satisfying every constraint in Cs then Cs is said to be satisfiable (SAT). Otherwise, Cs is unsatisfiable (UNSAT). More formally, given a set of constraints Cs, we have

$$\mathsf{SAT}(Cs) \quad \widehat{=} \quad \exists \mathbf{A} \cdot \forall C \in Cs \cdot \mathsf{sat}(\mathbf{A}, C), \text{ and} \tag{1}$$

$$\mathsf{UNSAT}(Cs) \quad \widehat{=} \quad \forall \mathbf{A} \cdot \exists C \in Cs \cdot \mathsf{unsat}(\mathbf{A}, C). \tag{2}$$

In this paper, we will be interested in two special types of sets of constraints, namely: *Maximal Satisfiable (sub-)Set* (MSS) and *Minimal Unsatisfiable (sub-)Set* (MUS). A set of constraints Cs is an MSS if it is a satisfiable subset of $\mathbb{C}$ and cannot be expanded without compromising satisfiability, *i.e.*,[1]

$$\mathsf{MSS}(Cs) \;\hat{=}\; \mathsf{SAT}(Cs) \wedge (\forall S \cdot S \subseteq \mathbb{C} \wedge Cs \subset S \Rightarrow \mathsf{UNSAT}(S)). \tag{3}$$

Conversely, a set of constraints $Cs \subseteq \mathbb{C}$ is a MUS if it is an unsatisfiable subset of $\mathbb{C}$ and is minimal with respect to the set-inclusion ordering, *i.e.*,

$$\mathsf{MUS}(Cs) \;\hat{=}\; \mathsf{UNSAT}(Cs) \wedge (\forall S \cdot S \subseteq \mathbb{C} \wedge S \subset Cs \Rightarrow \mathsf{SAT}(S)). \tag{4}$$

MUSes are valuable since they indicate the core reason for unsatisfiability of a constraint set. In particular, as showed in Sect. 3, MUSes play an important role in verifying rules consistency.

2.2 Rules Consistency

Consider a generic set of rules $\mathbb{R} = \{R_1, R_2, \ldots, R_n\}$, where n is a positive number. Each rule R_i consists of a constraint I_i over the input variables and a constraint O_i over the output variables. The set of input and output variables are disjoint. The types of constraints are not specified.

Definition 1 (Rule Satisfiability). *A rule $R = (I, O)$ is satisfied by an assignment $\mathbf{A}_x$ of the input variables and an assignment $\mathbf{A}_y$ of the output variables —denoted as* $\mathsf{rsat}((\mathbf{A}_x, \mathbf{A}_y), R)$— *if either $\mathbf{A}_x$ does not satisfy I or $\mathbf{A}_y$ satisfies O, i.e.,* $\mathsf{rsat}((\mathbf{A}_x, \mathbf{A}_y), R) \;\hat{=}\; \mathsf{unsat}(\mathbf{A}_x, I) \vee \mathsf{sat}(\mathbf{A}_y, O)$.

A subset of rules $Rs \subseteq \mathbb{R}$ is "consistent" (Consistent) if for every input assignment, there exists some output assignment such that the assignments satisfy all rules in Rs. Otherwise, it is inconsistent (Inconsistent). For convenience, when the generic set of rules $\mathbb{R}$ is known, we identify its subsets by sets of indices, *i.e.*, subsets of the range $1..n$. The consistency definition is lifted accordingly to sets of indices.

Definition 2 (Rule Consistency). *Given a set of indices $S \subseteq 1..n$,*

$$\mathsf{Consistent}(S) \;\;\hat{=}\;\; \forall \mathbf{A}_x \cdot \exists \mathbf{A}_y \cdot \forall i \in S \cdot \mathsf{rsat}((\mathbf{A}_x, \mathbf{A}_y), R_i), \;\; and \tag{5}$$

$$\mathsf{Inconsistent}(S) \;\;\hat{=}\;\; \exists \mathbf{A}_x \cdot \forall \mathbf{A}_y \cdot \exists i \in S \cdot \neg\mathsf{rsat}((\mathbf{A}_x, \mathbf{A}_y), R_i). \tag{6}$$

From now on, we will use *set of rules* and *set of rule indices* interchangeably.

Given an inconsistent rule base $\mathbb{R}$, some indicating facts about $\mathbb{R}$ should be given to "explain" $\mathbb{R}$'s inconsistency. We define the following notion of *Minimal Inconsistent Set* (MIS) of a set of rules, the *inconsistent core* of $\mathbb{R}$.

Definition 3 (MIS). *Given a set of rules $S \subseteq 1..n$, S is a MIS if and only if S is inconsistent and is minimal with respect to the set-inclusion ordering, i.e.,* $\mathsf{MIS}(S) \;\hat{=}\; \mathsf{Inconsistent}(S) \wedge (\forall T \cdot T \subset S \Rightarrow \mathsf{Consistent}(T))$.

---

[1] $S \subset T$ means that S is a proper-subset of T.

Clearly, a rule base $\mathbb{R}$ without any MIS is consistent. In the case where $\mathbb{R}$ is inconsistent, ideally, all MISes of $\mathbb{R}$ should be found. In general, the problem of finding all MISes is intractable: the number of MISes may be exponential in the size of the rule base. Our main objective is to *quickly enumerate MISes*.

Example 1. Consider the rewarding policy mentioned in Sect. 1. The input and output constraints of the rules can be formalised as follows.

Rule	Input constraint	Output constraint
R_1	*account*	$discount = 3 \vee coupon = 100$
R_2	VIP	$discount \geq 5 \wedge coupon \in 50 .. 100$
R_3	$\neg VIP \wedge duration < 2$	$discount < 5 \vee coupon \in 30 .. 50$
R_4	$VIP \wedge duration \geq 2$	$discount \geq 7 \wedge coupon = 50$

In the above example, input assignment "*account, VIP, duration* := F, T, 1" and output assignment "*discount, coupon* := 5, 50" satisfy all rules. The set of rules is inconsistent (as mentioned before) and has one MIS, *i.e.*, $\{R_1, R_4\}$.

3 Relationship Between MISes and MUSes

In this section, we investigate the relationship between MISes and satisfiability problems on the input and output constraints. Since the input and output variables are disjoint, satisfiability problems on input constraints and output constraints are independent. Given a set of rules S, the following lemmas express some relationships between the consistency of S and the satisfiability of S's input and output constraints. The lemmas can be proved directly from the corresponding definitions. Below, we use the notation $C[S]$ for $\{C_i \mid i \in S\}$ (similarly for $I[S]$ and $O[S]$).

Lemma 1. $\mathsf{SAT}(I[S]) \wedge \mathsf{UNSAT}(O[S]) \Rightarrow \mathsf{Inconsistent}(S)$

Lemma 2. $\mathsf{SAT}(O[S]) \Rightarrow \mathsf{Consistent}(S)$

In general, S's consistency cannot be directly determined by the satisfiability/unsatisfiability of its input and output constraints. In particular, when $\mathsf{UNSAT}(I[S])$ and $\mathsf{UNSAT}(O[S])$, S's consistency is determined by the consistency of S's proper-subsets. Consider Example 1, $\{R_1, R_2, R_3\}$ and $\{R_1, R_3, R_4\}$ have unsatisfiable input and output constraints, but only the former one is consistent. To avoid iterating the subsets of rules, we prove the following theorem.

Theorem 1 (MISes and MUSes). $\mathsf{MIS}(S) \Leftrightarrow \mathsf{MUS}(O[S]) \wedge \mathsf{SAT}(I[S])$.

Proof (Sketch).

1. *From left to right*: Assume $\mathsf{MIS}(S)$, we have $\mathsf{Inconsistent}(S)$. We infer that $\mathsf{SAT}(I[S])$ since if $\mathsf{UNSAT}(I[S])$, one of S's proper-subset must be inconsistent, hence S cannot be minimal. We have $\mathsf{UNSAT}(O[S])$ since if $\mathsf{SAT}(O[S])$ then $\mathsf{Consistent}(S)$ (Lemma 2). Subsequently, $\mathsf{MUS}(O[S])$, since otherwise there exists a set $T \subset S$ such that $\mathsf{UNSAT}(O[T])$. From Lemma 1, we have $\mathsf{Inconsistent}(T)$, and hence S is not minimal inconsistent.

2. *From right to left*: Assume $\mathsf{MUS}(O[S])$ and $\mathsf{SAT}(I[S])$. We deduce that Inconsistent(S) from Lemma 1. For every $T \subset S$, we have $\mathsf{SAT}(O[T])$, hence Consistent(T) (Lemma 2). As a result, S is minimal inconsistent.   □

Theorem 1 reduces the problem of enumerating MISes to finding the MUSes of the output constraints, and then checking the satisfiability of the input constraints corresponding to each MUS found. As a result, the quicker output constraints' MUSes are discovered, the faster we can enumerate MISes. In the next section, we present a novel and efficient algorithm for enumerating MUSes.

4 An Efficient Algorithm for Enumerating MUSes

In general, enumerating MUSes is a well-known problem and potentially intractable (since the number of MUSes may be exponential in the number of constraints). A detailed discussion on existing approaches for enumerating MUSes can be found in [10], including both constraint-specific and constraint-agnostic algorithms. In this paper, we present our algorithm for fast enumeration of MUSes, inspired by the state-of-the-art algorithm MARCO [10].

The main feature of MARCO is the use of a powerset manager maintaining a powerset map for selecting subsets to be explored. Given, a constraint set $\mathbb{C}$, the powerset map is a set of propositions Ps over a collection of indexed variables x_i, with $i \in 1..n$ where n is the number of constraints in $\mathbb{C}$. There are three basic operations for the powerset manager (Fig. 1). In getSet, the powerset manager utilises the capability of the constraint solver to return a model for a satisfiable set of constraints, which corresponds to an unexplored subset (a subset required to be validated). Operations addLowerBound and addUpperBound are for pruning the unexplored subsets. Operation addLowerBound (resp. addUpperBound) marks all subsets (resp. supersets) of the input set S as explored (no longer need to be validated).

---

getSet $\hat{=}$
output: **a new unexplored subset** or *null* if all subsets have been explored.

1. if $\mathsf{SAT}(Ps)$	// If there are some unexplored subset, then
2. $m \leftarrow$ getModel(Ps);	// get a model
3. return $\{i \mid m(x_i) = True\}$;	// return the unexplored subset from the model
4. else	// If all subsets have been explored, then
5. return *null*;	// return *null*

---

addLowerBound(S) $\hat{=}$	addUpperBound(S) $\hat{=}$
precondition: $S \subseteq 1..n$	precondition: $S \subseteq 1..n$
effect: **Mark subsets of S explored**	effect: **Mark supersets of S explored**
1. $Ps := Ps \cup \left\{\left(\bigvee_{i \notin S} x_i\right)\right\}$;	1. $Ps := Ps \cup \left\{\left(\neg \bigwedge_{i \in S} x_i\right)\right\}$;

Fig. 1. Operations of the powerset manager

4.1   The MARCO algorithm

Intuitively, for each iteration, MARCO (Fig. 2) gets a new unexplored subset S from the powerset manager. If $\mathbb{C}[S]$ is satisfiable, MARCO uses a grow sub-routine to obtain an MSS, and adds this MSS as a lower bound to restrict future iterations. Otherwise, i.e., if $\mathbb{C}[S]$ is unsatisfiable, MARCO uses a shrink sub-routine to obtain a MUS, yields this MUS, and adds the found MUS as an upper bound. The correctness of the MARCO algorithm relies on the fact that MUS cannot be a subset of an MSS or a (strict-)superset of another MUS. At each iteration, the powerset manager is restricted hence the algorithm terminates.

MARCO $\hat{=}$

effect: **Output MUSes of $\mathbb{C}$ as they are found**

1. $S \leftarrow$ getSet();	// S is an unexplored subset
2. while $S \neq null$	// While there is some unexplored subset S,
3. if SAT($\mathbb{C}[S]$)	// if S is satisfiable,
4. $mss \leftarrow$ grow(S);	// $grow$ S to obtain an MSS
5. addLowerBound(mss);	// add the found mss as a lower bound
6. else	// if S is unsatisfiable,
7. $mus \leftarrow$ shrink(S);	// $shrink$ S to obtain a MUS
8. yields mus;	// yields the found MUS
9. addUpperBound(mus);	// add the found mus as an upper bound
10. $S \leftarrow$ getSet();	// Get a new unexplored subset S

Fig. 2. The MARCO algorithm

The sub-routines grow and shrink can be any off-the-shelf methods for finding an MSS (from a satisfiable seed) and a MUS (from an unsatisfiable seed). For example, the operation growLin in Fig. 3 gradually adds new elements to a satisfiable subset S if this preserves satisfiability. Conversely, shrinkLin removes elements step-by-step from an unsatisfiable subset S if it preserves unsatisfiability. Both growLin and shrinkLin are not the most efficient implementation for grow and shrink sub-routine. For instance, the shrinkBin operation in Fig. 3 and its sub-routine reduce perform binary search and potentially return a MUS faster than shrinkLin. A similar binary search algorithm exists for the grow routine. The MARCO algorithm and various grow and shrink routines are not novel.

Example 2. A possible execution trace for MARCO (using growLin and shrinkBin) applied to the *output constraints* of the rules R_1–R_4 in Example 1 is below. At each step, we show the seed obtained from the powerset manager and its satisfiability status. Depending on the satisfiability status of the seed, a growing or a shrinking sub-routine is called to obtain an MSS or a MUS. We also report the number of SMT calls (the number of times that the SMT solver is called to check the problem constraints) and the number of SAT calls (querying the powerset manager). For example, in Step 2, the powerset manager returns $\{R_3, R_4\}$ (at a cost of 1 SAT call) and checking satisfiability of this seed costs 1 SMT call. Afterwards, it takes 2 SMT calls to grow the seed to obtain the MSS $\{R_2, R_3, R_4\}$.

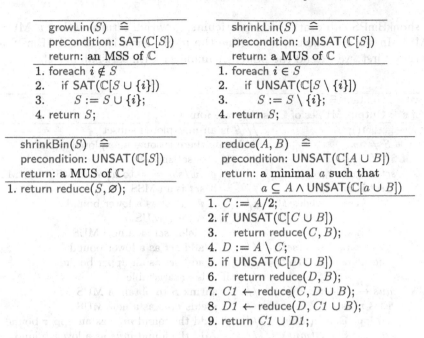

growLin(S) $\triangleq$	shrinkLin(S) $\triangleq$
precondition: SAT($\mathbb{C}[S]$)	precondition: UNSAT($\mathbb{C}[S]$)
return: an MSS of $\mathbb{C}$	return: a MUS of $\mathbb{C}$
1. foreach $i \notin S$	1. foreach $i \in S$
2. if SAT($\mathbb{C}[S \cup \{i\}]$)	2. if UNSAT($\mathbb{C}[S \setminus \{i\}]$)
3. $S := S \cup \{i\}$;	3. $S := S \setminus \{i\}$;
4. return S;	4. return S;

shrinkBin(S) $\triangleq$	reduce(A, B) $\triangleq$
precondition: UNSAT($\mathbb{C}[S]$)	precondition: UNSAT($\mathbb{C}[A \cup B]$)
return: a MUS of $\mathbb{C}$	return: a minimal a such that
1. return reduce($S, \varnothing$);	$a \subseteq A \wedge$ UNSAT($\mathbb{C}[a \cup B]$)
	1. $C := A/2$;
	2. if UNSAT($\mathbb{C}[C \cup B]$)
	3. return reduce(C, B);
	4. $D := A \setminus C$;
	5. if UNSAT($\mathbb{C}[D \cup B]$)
	6. return reduce(D, B);
	7. $C1 \leftarrow$ reduce($C, D \cup B$);
	8. $D1 \leftarrow$ reduce($D, C1 \cup B$);
	9. return $C1 \cup D1$;

Fig. 3. Various grow and shrink routines

Step		Seed (Satisfiability status)	MSS	MUS	SMTs	SATs
1	get seed	$\varnothing$ (SAT)			1	1
	growing		$\{R_1, R_2\}$		4	
2	get seed	$\{R_3, R_4\}$ (SAT)			1	1
	growing		$\{R_2, R_3, R_4\}$		2	
3	get seed	$\{R_1, R_3, R_4\}$ (UNSAT)			1	1
	shrinking			$\{R_1, R_4\}$	4	
4	get seed	$\{R_1, R_2, R_3\}$ (UNSAT)			1	1
	shrinking			$\{R_1, R_2, R_3\}$	4	
5	get seed	$\{R_1, R_3\}$ (SAT)			1	1
	growing		$\{R_1, R_3\}$		2	
6	get seed	null			1	
	Total		3 MSSes	2 MUSes	21	6

4.2 The MUSesHunter Algorithm

Notice that, in the MARCO algorithm, the powerset manager is only used for retrieving unexplored subsets. In particular, during the process of growing and shrinking seeds, many satisfiability checks are spurious: the sets are either supersets of some found MUS or subsets of some found MSS. Satisfiability checking of the problem constraints (possibly involving theories) is more expensive than querying the powerset manager (concerning only Boolean constraints). Furthermore, during the process of growing, often unsatisfiable subsets are found. By calling shrink sub-routine on these unsatisfiable subsets, we can get MUSes faster. The challenge is to ensure that by shrinking immediately, we obtain a *new* MUS.

The MUSesHunter algorithm can be seen in Fig. 4. Compared to MARCO, the main difference is the use of the powerset manager within the growHyb and shrinkBinPS sub-routines. In particular, growHyb returns either a MUS or an MSS. In the subsequent, we outline the implementation of shrinkBinPS and growHyb. First, we extend the powerset manager with satisfiability checking.

MUSesHunter $\mathrel{\widehat{=}}$	
effect: Output MUSes of $\mathbb{C}$ as they are found	
1. $S \leftarrow$ getSet();	// S is an unexplored subset
2. while $S \neq null$	// While there is some unexplored subset S
3. if SAT($\mathbb{C}[S]$)	// if S is satisfiable
4. set $\leftarrow$ growHyb(S);	// grow/shrink S to have an MSS or a MUS
5. if set is an MSS	// if set is an MSS
6. addLowerBound(set)	// Add set as a lower bound
7. else	// if set is a MUS
8. yields set;	// yields set as a new MUS
9. addLowerBound(set);	// add set as a lower bound
10. addUpperBound(set);	// add set as an upper bound
11. else	// if S is unsatisfiable
12. mus $\leftarrow$ shrinkBinPS(S);	// shrink S to obtain a MUS
13. yields mus;	// yields mus as a new MUS
14. addUpperBound(mus);	// Add the found mus as an upper bound.
15. addLowerBound(mus);	// Add the found mus as a lower bound.
16. $S \leftarrow$ getSet();	// Get a new unexplored subset S

Fig. 4. The MUSesHunter algorithm

Satisfiability checking with powerset manager. The following operation is added to the powerset manager in order to check if a set of constraint S need to be explored. This is done by checking the satisfiability of the set of propositions Ps together with the constraint representing S.

isUnexplored(S) $\mathrel{\widehat{=}}$
precondition: $S \subseteq 1 .. n$
output: T if S is an unexplored subset
1. return SAT($Ps \cup \{(\bigwedge_{i \in S} x_i) \wedge (\bigwedge_{i \notin S} \neg x_i)\}$);

Theorem 2 states an important property of MUSesHunter, in particular, for the explored subsets filtered out by the powerset manager.

Theorem 2 (Explored subsets of constraints). *For the* MUSesHunter *algorithm, given a subset of constraints S, we have*

$$\neg \text{isUnexplored}(S) \Leftrightarrow \begin{array}{l} (\exists L \cdot \text{SAT}(\mathbb{C}[L]) \wedge S \subseteq L) \\ \vee \ (\exists M \cdot \text{MUS}(\mathbb{C}[M]) \wedge S \subset M) \\ \vee \ (\exists M \cdot \text{MUS}(\mathbb{C}[M]) \wedge M \subseteq S). \end{array} \tag{7}$$

Proof (Sketch). This fact is trivial invariant of the MUSesHunter algorithm since the set of unexplored subsets can only be pruned in the following two cases:

1. An MSS is added as a lower bound.
2. An MUS is added as a lower bound and an upper bound.

As a result, a set S is explored if and only if either (a) S is a subset of an MSS (some satisfying set L), or (b) S is a subset of some MUS M, or (c) S is a superset of some MUS M.   □

The following Lemmas are consequences of Theorem 2.

Lemma 3 (Satisfiability during shrink**).** *Given sets of constraints S and T, if* isUnexplored(S), $T \subseteq S$, *and* ¬isUnexplored(T), *then* SAT($\mathbb{C}[T]$).

Proof. From ¬isUnexplored(T), apply Theorem 2, we have three cases as follows.

1. There exists L where SAT($\mathbb{C}[L]$) $\wedge T \subseteq L$, we have SAT($\mathbb{C}[T]$) trivially by anti-monotonicity of SAT.
2. There exists M where MUS($\mathbb{C}[M]$) $\wedge T \subset M$, we have SAT($\mathbb{C}[T]$) trivially by definition of MUS (4).
3. There exists M where MUS($\mathbb{C}[M]$) $\wedge M \subseteq T$. From $T \subseteq S$, we obtain $M \subseteq S$. Apply Theorem 2, we have ¬isUnexplored(S) which is a contradiction.

Lemma 4 (Unsatisfiability during grow**).** *Given sets of constraints S and T, if* isUnexplored(S), $S \subseteq T$, *and* ¬isUnexplored(T), *then* UNSAT($\mathbb{C}[T]$).

The proof of Lemma 4 is similar to that of Lemma 3 and is omitted.

Lemmas 3 and 4 allow us to use the powerset manager to replace some of the satisfiability checks during shrinking and growing sub-routines.

The shrinkBinPS *sub-routine.* Comparing the subsequent reducePS with the reduce sub-routine, before checking satisfiability of $C \cup B$ (Line 3) and $D \cup B$ (Line 6), we first check if these subsets are unexplored. Lemma 3 ensures that if they are already explored, they are satisfiable.

shrinkBinPS(S) $\hat{=}$
precondition: UNSAT($\mathbb{C}[S]$) $\wedge$ isUnexplored(S)
output: a MUS of Cs
1. return reducePS($S, \varnothing$);

reducePS(A, B) $\hat{=}$	
precondition: UNSAT($\mathbb{C}[A \cup B]$) $\wedge$ isUnexplored($A \cup B$)	
output: a minimal $a \subseteq A \wedge$ UNSAT($\mathbb{C}[a \cup B]$)	
1. $C := A/2$;	// C is a half of A
2. if isUnexplored($C \cup B$)	// If $C \cup B$ is unexplored,
3. if UNSAT($\mathbb{C}[C \cup B]$)	// if $C \cup B$ is unsatisfiable,
4. return reducePS(C, B);	// recursively reduce C with B
5. $D := A \setminus C$;	// D is the difference between A and C
6. if isUnexplored($D \cup B$)	// If $D \cup B$ is unexplored,
7. if UNSAT($\mathbb{C}[D \cup B]$)	// if $D \cup B$ is unsatisfiable,
8. return reducePS(D, B);	// recursively reduce D with B
9. $C1 \leftarrow$ reducePS($C, D \cup B$);	// $C1$ is the result of reducing C with $D \cup B$
10. $D1 \leftarrow$ reducePS($D, C1 \cup B$);	// $D1$ is the result of reducing D with $C1 \cup B$
11. return $C1 \cup D1$;	// return the union of $C1$ and $D1$

The growHyb *sub-routine.* The following growHyb returns either a new MSS or a new MUS. It is based on the growLin routine showed earlier.

growHyb(S) $\; \widehat{=}$
precondition: SAT($\mathbb{C}[S]$) $\wedge$ isUnexplored(S)
return: an MSS or a MUS of $\mathbb{C}$

1. foreach $c \notin S$	// For each c not in S,
2. if isUnexplored($S \cup \{c\}$)	// if $S \cup \{c\}$ is unexplored
3. if SAT($\mathbb{C}[S \cup \{c\}]$)	// if $S \cup \{c\}$ is satisfiable,
4. $S := S \cup \{c\}$;	// add c to S
5. else	// if $S \cup \{c\}$ is unsatisfiable
6. return shrinkBinPS($S \cup \{c\}$);	// *shrink* to find a MUS
7. return S;	// return S which is an MSS

Similar to the reducePS sub-routine, before checking satisfiability for $S \cup \{c\}$ (Line 3), the growHyb sub-routine checks if it is unexplored. Lemma 4 ensures that if $S \cup \{c\}$ is already explored, it is unsatisfiable. Moreover, the fact that $S \cup \{c\}$ is unexplored guarantees that shrinkBinPS (Line 6) returns a *new MUS*.

Example 3. An example execution trace for the MUSesHunter algorithm (using growHyb and shrinkBinPS) applying to the set of output constraints for the rules R_1–R_4 in Example 1 is below.

Step		Seed (Status)	MSS	MUS	SMTs	SATs
1	get seed	$\varnothing$ (SAT)			1	1
	growing	$\{1, 2, 3\}$ (UNSAT)			3	3
	shrinking			$\{1, 2, 3\}$	2	4
2	get seed	$\{4\}$ (SAT)			1	1
	growing	$\{1, 4\}$ (UNSAT)			1	1
	shrinking			$\{1, 4\}$		2
3	get seed	$\{2, 3, 4\}$ (SAT)			1	1
	growing		$\{2, 3, 4\}$			1
4	get seed	*null*				1
	Total		1 MSSes	2 MUSes	9	15

4.3   Comparing **MARCO** and **MUSesHunter**

The main novelty of MUSesHunter compared to MARCO is the use of the powerset manager for checking satisfiability of the problem constraints. In particular, the powerset manager allows MUSesHunter to produce MUSes even in the case where the original seed is satisfiable, where MARCO must always produce MSSes. For our purpose of enumerating MUSes, finding a MUS is more valuable than MSS. When a MUS is found, MUSesHunter blocks both its super-sets as well as subsets, where MARCO only blocks the super-sets of MUS. As a result, MUSesHunter prunes the search space much faster than MARCO. Comparing the traces for MARCO and MUSesHunter in Examples 2 and 3, MUSesHunter does not need to find all MSSes before termination. In fact MSSes found by MARCO such as $\{R_1, R_2\}$ and $\{R_1, R_3\}$ are spurious, *i.e.*, they are subset of the MUS $\{R_1, R_2, R_3\}$, and does not require to be considered in searching for MUSes. For MARCO, MUS can be also added as a lower bound. Focusing on enumerating MUSes without finding all MSSes was mentioned as future work in [10].

5   Empirical Analysis

We implement our algorithms for finding MUSes and MISes using Java. In particular, for constraint solving (*i.e.*, for the powerset manager and for satisfiability checks of the problem constraints), we use SMTInterpol [8]. We first compare the performance of the MUSesHunter and MARCO algorithms (Sect. 5.1). Afterwards, we evaluate the performance of developed MISes finder program with MUSesHunter using examples extracted from real-world policies (Sect. 5.2).

5.1   MUSesHunter vs. MARCO

Both algorithms were implemented using the same underlying infrastructure, sharing as much code as possible. For growing and shrinking, MARCO uses growLin and shrinkBin sub-routines, whereas MUSesHunter uses growHyb and shrinkBinPS sub-routines. Both algorithms use a powerset manager built on top of SMTInterpol without any modification, *e.g.*, it is not biased towards producing large unexplored sets (which will be beneficial for MARCO). The experiments were performed on a VMWare Virtual Machine with 4×2.7 GHz CPUs running Linux. Each program was executed with 3 GB heap memory limit and an 1800-second timeout. There is no timeout for individual constraints satisfiability check. We selected 473 samples (from 4 to 881 constraints) selected from SMT-LIB for quantifier-free linear integer arithmetic (QF_LIA).[2] Even though our algorithm is constraint-agnostic, we have chosen the QF_LIA fragment of the SMT-LIB benchmarks since the input and output constraints of our rule verification case studies are within this sub-logic. We also restrict our evaluation to the sets of benchmarks where the SMT solver (SMTInterpol in our implementation) can verify their satisfiability in a reasonable time. We plan to evaluate our algorithm against other benchmarks in the future.

Overall. The summary of the results for running the two algorithms is in Table 1. While the numbers of cases where the algorithms terminate and find all MUSes are comparable, MUSesHunter tends to run out of memory (hitting bad seeds) whereas MARCO tends to run out of time (making too many expensive SMT calls) more often. However, in most cases, MUSesHunter usually finds more MUSes than MARCO. In particular, MARCO does not find any MUSes in over 20 % of the samples (105 cases), whereas that percentage for MUSesHunter is 6 % (21 cases). This is the direct effect of growHyb: it can produce MUSes even in the case where the original seed is satisfiable. On average, MUSesHunter found almost twice as many MUSes as MARCO.

Comparing the number of SMT calls for checking satisfiability of the problem constraints and SAT calls for the powerset manager, there is a clear difference between the two programs. MUSesHunter makes heavy use of the powerset manager as a substitute for checking satisfiability of the problem constraints. Even though MUSesHunter's total number of satisfiability calls is twice as many as that

---

[2] Available from http://smtlib.cs.uiowa.edu/benchmarks.shtml.

Table 1. Empirical analysis summary

	MUSesHunter		MARCO	
Find all (no. of samples)	160 (34%)		139 (29%)	
Timeout (no. of samples)	250 (53%)		308 (65%)	
Find none		21 (8%)		104 (34%)
Find 1		33 (13%)		76 (25%)
Find > 1		196 (78%)		128 (42%)
Out-of-memory (no. of samples)	63 (13%)		26 (5%)	
Find none		0 (0%)		1 (4%)
Find 1		9 (14%)		0 (0%)
Find > 1		54 (86%)		25 (96%)
Total (no. of samples)	473		473	
Max MUSes found per sample	29740		18646	
Average MUSes found per sample	1050		533	
Total satisfiability calls	7749472		3127773	
SATs (powerset manager)		6472339 (84%)		82628(3%)
SMTs (constraints satisfiability)		1277133 (16%)		3045145(97%)

of MARCO, solving satisfiability problems in the powerset manager (related to Boolean constraints) are much faster than checking satisfiability of the problem constraints, which are (in our experiments) QF_LIA constraints.

Performance comparison between MUSesHunter and MARCO is as follows.

	MUSesHunter better (%)	MARCO better (%)	Draw (%)
Both terminate	135 (97%)	4 (3%)	
Not both terminate	254 (76%)	52 (16%)	28 (8%)
Total	389 (82%)	56 (12%)	28 (6%)

We separate the benchmarks into two categories according to whether or not both algorithms terminate and find all MUSes. In the first case, an algorithm is better if it terminates faster. In the second case, we compare the number of MUSes that the algorithms found. Overall, MUSesHunter outperforms MARCO by terminating faster or finding more MUSes (82%).

Both programs terminate. The comparison between the (log-scale) speed of MUSesHunter and MARCO in the case where they both terminate can be seen in Fig. 5a. In most cases (97%), MUSesHunter terminates faster than MARCO. Figure 6 compares the percentage of MUSes found against the time, both scaled to the range 0..1 for samples that MUSesHunter and MARCO terminate. For MUSesHunter, it is typical that the MUSes are found early then subsequently, only MSSes are found. For MARCO, in most cases, MUSes are found gradually.

One of the programs does not terminate. We focus on the number of MUSes found by each algorithm. In 76% of cases, MUSesHunter found more MUSes than MARCO. Figure 5b shows the comparison between the numbers of MUSes found by MUSesHunter and MARCO for individual sample.

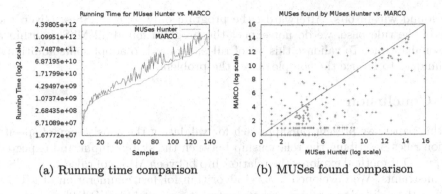

(a) Running time comparison   (b) MUSes found comparison

Fig. 5. Running time and MUSes found comparison

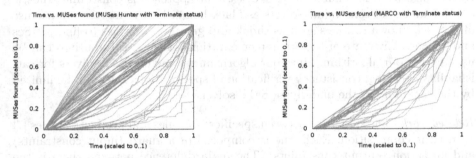

Fig. 6. MUSes found vs. time

5.2 MISes Finder

We evaluate the MISes finder program on the following examples. With the exception of the first one, all of them are extracted from industrial case studies in financial and public sectors. The statistics can be seen as follows.

Example	Size	Time	MUSes	MSSes	MISes	SATs	SMTs
Test sample	8	195 ms	5	12	3	78	57
Vehicle insurance	4	69 ms	2	1	1	9	15
Care insurance	15	403 ms	62	0	10	106	335
Vehicle tax	108	13.4 s	2590	2	0	7223	19345
Registration	725	1800 s	436	1093	0	820455	373767

The performance of the MISes finder program largely depend on the underlying MUSesHunter algorithm on finding MUSes of the output constraints. The last two examples (namely *Vehicle tax* and *Registration*) are consistent. However, MISes finder program does not terminate for the *Registration* example, fails to verify the rule base. In this case, all 436 MUSes (none of them are MISes) are found within 60 s. Afterwards, the program only found MSSes. Given the size of the rule base, we do not expect the program found all MSSes within a reasonable time. To validate this set of rules, we need to adopt some additional techniques to reduce the complexity of the problem.

6   Conclusion

In this paper, we present our approach for validating the consistency of specification rules describing the relationship between the system input and expected output. Our method explores the relationship between MISes of rules and MUSes of constraints. We developed a novel algorithm for fast enumeration of MUSes during the validation process and evaluated it against MARCO [10], a state-of-the-art algorithm for enumerating MUSes. Our approach is constraint-agnostic and makes use of constraints solvers as black-boxes. Furthermore, we make use of the well-known routines such as shrink and grow sub-routines to find MUSes and MSSes. Any state-of-the-art implementation for these sub-routines can be used within our algorithm. Since our algorithm relying on SMT solvers for satisfiability checking, consistency verification of specifications rules will be limited by the capability of the underlying SMT solvers.

Related work. The similarity between specification rules and production rules [7] is in their composition: Each rule is composed of a guard (input constraints) and an action (output constraints). The main difference between them is the fact that specification rules can be non-deterministic while production rules are deterministic. Furthermore, the purpose of specification rules is to stipulate the relationships between input and output of the system, hiding the system state. The production rules often involve systems with explicit state (the working memory). Production rules are also written with some implicit rule execution engine in mind, *e.g.*, firing enabled rules repeatedly. In term of validation, different properties have been considered for production rules [14]. Due to their deterministic nature, minimal inconsistency for production rules can only be pairwise.

In a more general context, *Rule-Based Systems* (RBSes) have been used in the field of Artificial Intelligence and Knowledge Engineering [12] for knowledge representation. Typically, an RBS contains a rule set and an inference control mechanism including some conflict resolution strategy. Each rule imitates logical implication and is used for backward or forward reasoning. Furthermore the conflict resolution strategies ensure that in the case where two or more rules can be activated at a time, only one is selected according to some pre-defined criteria. This is also the main difference between RBSes and the specification rules under our consideration. Verification of RBSes is also extensively discussed in [12]. A taxonomy of verifiable characteristics for RBSes is proposed concerning various anomalies such as consistency, completeness, and (non-)redundancy. In particular, the problem of conflicting and inconsistent rules are considered to be special cases of nondeterminism and is deferred to the conflict resolution mechanism. In fact, in some special representation of RBSes such as tabular systems with no explicit negation, purely logical inconsistency never appears [12].

In order to find all MISes of a set of rules, we need to find all MUSes of its output constraints. Comparison in [10] suggests the CAMUS algorithm [11] can out-perform the MARCO algorithm in finding all MUSes. The disadvantage of CAMUS is its inability to "enumerate" the MUSes, *i.e.*, it can take a long time before outputting any MUS. Hence CAMUS is unsuitable for any application where incremental responses are required. However, its ability of finding all MUSes quickly can be useful to validate a consistent set of rules. We plan to investigate and evaluate CAMUS further.

Future work. Other properties for specification rules include *redundancy* and *completeness*. Similar to consistency, the problem of verifying redundancy and completeness can also be reduced to enumerating MUSes and this is the next logical step of our research. As mentioned before in Sect. 5.2, for the *Registration* example, our MISes finder program does not terminate. The main challenge is in the size of the example (725 rules). A possible solution for validating this set of rule is to syntactically decompose this set of rules into smaller sets. Rule separation will drastically reduce the complexity of the MISes finding problem, hence could be used as a pre-processing step for the current MISes finder program. Moreover, the specification rules can be combined to stipulate system requirements. We are currently investigating how consistency validation can be composed/decomposed for such specification of combined rule bases.

Currently, our implementation uses SMTInterpol [8] as the underlying solver of the powerset manager and for checking satisfiability of the problem constraints. While this is sufficient for our purpose, it would be of our interests to investigate other SMT solvers in place of SMTInterpol. Another possible improvement for our implementation is to take advantage of the incremental checking and backtracking ability of SMT solvers (*i.e.*, using push/pop operations).

Parallelism has been considered for extracting a MUS [5,15]. In a similar fashion, the problem of enumerating MUSes and MISes can take advantage of parallel and/or distributed architectures. In particular, enumeration of MUSes can be parallelised and distributed to a cluster. The essential point to consider is how to correctly and effectively use the powerset manager. Our formal model suggests that having a parallel/distributed version of the program is possible.

Parallel/distributed version of the program is also a solution to another limitation of the current MISes finder program. Currently, our MISes finder program will terminate (without finding all MISes) if the underlying SMT solver cannot solve a satisfiability problem (*i.e.*, return *unknown*). This is often the case when the solver gets a "bad seed" such that its performance is deteriorated. By trying to solve several seeds at once, the MISes program can proceed even if some of the seeds are bad. Moreover, if the bad seeds are not MUSes or MSSes, the program can even terminate finding all MISes.

Often rule bases are developed step-by-step and subject to regular changes. It is necessary for the consistency validation to be carried out in an incremental fashion, where checks are only required to perform on the parts of the rule base that are affected by the changes. This is important for building a practical tool set supporting the development of specification rules.

The correctness of our MISes finder program relies on the separation between input and output constraints, in particular, the output constraints does not refer to any input variable. This is sufficient to model several regulations and policies. In the case where the output constraints refer to the input variables, our program does not guarantee to find all MISes for a rule base. What can be inferred is that any result of the program is an inconsistent set of rules (not necessarily minimal). Further investigation is required to validate this general type of rules, in particular, to consider solving constraints with quantifiers.

References

1. Abrial, J.-R.: Modeling in Event-B: System and Software Engineering. Cambridge University Press, New York (2010)
2. Abrial, J.-R., Butler, M., Hallerstede, S., Hoang, T.S., Mehta, F., Voisin, L.: Rodin: an open toolset for modelling and reasoning in Event-B. STTT **12**(6), 447–466 (2010)
3. Bailey, J., Stuckey, P.J.: Discovery of minimal unsatisfiable subsets of constraints using hitting set dualization. In: Hermenegildo, M.V., Cabeza, D. (eds.) PADL 2004. LNCS, vol. 3350, pp. 174–186. Springer, Heidelberg (2005)
4. Barrett, C.W., Sebastiani, R., Seshia, S.A., Tinelli, C.: Satisfiability modulo theories. In: Handbook of Satisfiability. Frontiers in Artificial Intelligence and Applications, vol. 185, pp. 825–885. IOS Press (2009)
5. Belov, A., Manthey, N., Marques-Silva, J.: Parallel MUS extraction. In: Järvisalo, M., Van Gelder, A. (eds.) SAT 2013. LNCS, vol. 7962, pp. 133–149. Springer, Heidelberg (2013)
6. Belov, A., Marques-Silva, J.: MUSer2: an efficient MUS extractor. JSAT **8**(1/2), 123–128 (2012)
7. Berstel, B., Leconte, M.: Using constraints to verify properties of rule programs. ICST **2010**, 349–354 (2010)
8. Christ, J., Hoenicke, J., Nutz, A.: SMTInterpol: an interpolating SMT solver. In: Donaldson, A., Parker, D. (eds.) SPIN 2012. LNCS, vol. 7385, pp. 248–254. Springer, Heidelberg (2012)
9. Hoang, T.S., Itoh, S., Oyama, K., Miyazaki, K., Kuruma, H., Sato, N.: Validating the consistency of specification rules. http://deploy-eprints.ecs.soton.ac.uk/465/ (2015)
10. Liffiton, M.H., Malik, A.: Enumerating infeasibility: finding multiple MUSes quickly. In: Gomes, C., Sellmann, M. (eds.) CPAIOR 2013. LNCS, vol. 7874, pp. 160–175. Springer, Heidelberg (2013)
11. Liffiton, M.H., Sakallah, K.A.: Algorithms for computing minimal unsatisfiable subsets of constraints. J. Autom. Reasoning **40**(1), 1–33 (2008)
12. Ligeza, A.: Logical Foundations for Rule-Based Systems. Studies in Computational Intelligence, vol. 11, 2nd edn. Springer, Heidelberg (2006)
13. Nadel, A., Ryvchin, V., Strichman, O.: Efficient MUS extraction with resolution. In: FMCAD 2013, pp. 197–200. IEEE (2013)
14. Berstel-Da Silva, B.: Verification of Business Rules Programs. Springer, Heidelberg (2014)
15. Wieringa, S.: Understanding, improving and parallelizing MUS finding using model rotation. In: Milano, M. (ed.) CP 2012. LNCS, vol. 7514, pp. 672–687. Springer, Heidelberg (2012)

Applying Automata Learning to Embedded Control Software

Wouter Smeenk[1], Joshua Moerman[2], Frits Vaandrager[2]([✉]),
and David N. Jansen[2]

[1] Océ Technologies B.V., Venlo, The Netherlands
[2] Faculty of Science, Radboud University Nijmegen, P.O. Box 9010,
6500 GL Nijmegen, The Netherlands
F.Vaandrager@cs.ru.nl

Abstract. Using an adaptation of state-of-the-art algorithms for black-box automata learning, as implemented in the LearnLib tool, we succeeded to learn a model of the Engine Status Manager (ESM), a software component that is used in printers and copiers of Océ. The main challenge that we encountered was that LearnLib, although effective in constructing hypothesis models, was unable to find counterexamples for some hypotheses. In fact, none of the existing FSM-based conformance testing methods that we tried worked for this case study. We therefore implemented an extension of the algorithm of Lee and Yannakakis for computing an adaptive distinguishing sequence. Even when an adaptive distinguishing sequence does not exist, Lee and Yannakakis' algorithm produces an adaptive sequence that 'almost' identifies states. In combination with a standard algorithm for computing separating sequences for pairs of states, we managed to verify states with on average 3 test queries. Altogether, we needed around 60 million queries to learn a model of the ESM with 77 inputs and 3.410 states. We also constructed a model directly from the ESM software and established equivalence with the learned model. To the best of our knowledge, this is the first paper in which active automata learning has been applied to industrial control software.

1 Introduction

Once they have high-level models of the behavior of software components, software engineers can construct better software in less time. A key problem in practice, however, is the construction of models for existing software components, for which no or only limited documentation is available.

The construction of models from observations of component behavior can be performed using regular inference (aka automata learning) techniques [4,19,37]. The most efficient such techniques use the setup of *active learning*, illustrated

---

This work was supported by STW project 11763 Integrating Testing And Learning of Interface Automata (ITALIA) and by the DFG/NWO Bilateral Research Programme ROCKS. An early version of this paper appeared as [35].

M. Butler et al. (Eds.): ICFEM 2015, LNCS 9407, pp. 67–83, 2015.
DOI: 10.1007/978-3-319-25423-4_5

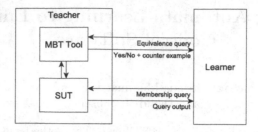

Fig. 1. Active learning of reactive systems

in Fig. 1, in which a "learner" has the task to learn a model of a system by actively asking questions to a "teacher". The core of the teacher is a *System Under Test (SUT)*, a reactive system to which one can apply inputs and whose outputs one may observe. The learner interacts with the SUT to infer a model by sending inputs and observing the resulting outputs ("membership queries"). In order to find out whether an inferred model is correct, the learner may pose an "equivalence query". The teacher uses a model-based testing (MBT) tool to try and answer such queries: Given a hypothesized model, an MBT tool generates a long test sequence using some conformance testing method. If the SUT passes this test, then the teacher informs the learner that the model is deemed correct. If the outputs of the SUT and the model differ, this constitutes a counterexample, which is returned to the learner. Based on such a counterexample, the learner may then construct an improved hypothesis. It is important to note that it may occur that an SUT passes the test for an hypothesis, even though this hypothesis is not valid.

Triggered by various theoretical and practical results, see e.g. [1,7,8,20,26, 28,33], there is a fast-growing interest in automata learning technology. In recent years, automata learning has been applied successfully, e.g., to regression testing of telecommunication systems [22], checking conformance of communication protocols to a reference implementation [3], finding bugs in Windows and Linux implementations of TCP [13], analysis of botnet command and control protocols [9], and integration testing [17,27].

In this paper, we explore whether LearnLib [33], a state-of-the-art automata learning tool, is able to learn a model of the Engine Status Manager (ESM), a piece of control software that is used in many printers and copiers of Océ. Software components like the ESM can be found in many embedded systems in one form or another. Being able to retrieve models of such components automatically is potentially very useful. For instance, if the software is fixed or enriched with new functionality, one may use a learned model for regression testing. Also, if the source code of software is hard to read and poorly documented, one may use a model of the software for model-based testing of a new implementation, or even for generating an implementation on a new platform automatically. Using a model checker one may also study the interaction of the software with other components for which models are available.

The ESM software is actually well documented, and an extensive test suite exists. The ESM, which has been implemented using Rational Rose Real-Time (RRRT), is stable and has been in use for 10 years. Due to these characteristics, the ESM is an excellent benchmark for assessing the performance of automata learning tools in this area. The ESM has also been studied in other research projects: Ploeger [31] modeled the ESM and other related managers and verified properties based on the official specifications of the ESM, and Graaf and Van Deursen [16] have checked the consistency of the behavioral specifications defined in the ESM against the RRRT definitions.

Learning a model of the ESM turned out to be more complicated than expected. The top level UML/RRRT statechart from which the software is generated only has 16 states. However, each of these states contains nested states, and in total there are 70 states that do not have further nested states. Moreover, the C++ code contained in the actions of the transitions also creates some complexity, and this explains why the minimal Mealy machine that models the ESM has 3.410 states. LearnLib has been used to learn models with tens of thousands of states [32], and therefore we expected that it would be easy to learn a model for the ESM. However, finding counterexamples for incorrect hypotheses turned out to be challenging due to the large number of 77 inputs. The test algorithms implemented in LearnLib, such as random testing, the W-method [10,38] and the Wp-method [14], failed to deliver counterexamples within an acceptable time. Automata learning techniques have been successfully applied to case studies in which the total number of input symbols is much larger, but in these cases it was possible to reduce the number of inputs to a small number (<10) using abstraction techniques [2,21]. In the case of ESM, use of abstraction techniques only allowed us to reduce the original 156 concrete actions to 77 abstract actions.

We therefore implemented and extension of the algorithm of Lee and Yannakakis [25] for computing an adaptive distinguishing sequence. Even when an adaptive distinguishing sequence does not exist, Lee and Yannakakis' algorithm produces an adaptive sequence that 'almost' identifies states. In combination with a standard algorithm for computing separating sequences for pairs of states, we managed to verify states with on average 3 test queries and to learn a model of the ESM with 77 inputs and 3.410 states. We also constructed a model directly from the ESM software and established equivalence with the learned model. To the best of our knowledge, this is the first paper in which active automata learning has been applied to industrial control software. Preliminary evidence suggests that our adaptation of Lee and Yannakakis' algorithm outperforms existing FSM-based conformance algorithms.

During recent years most researchers working on active automata learning focused their efforts on efficient algorithms and tools for the construction of hypothesis models. Following [7], our work shows that the context of automata learning provides both new challenges and new opportunities for the application of testing algorithms. All the models for the ESM case study together with the learning/test statistics are available at http://www.mbsd.cs.ru.nl/publications/papers/fvaan/ESM/, as a benchmark for both the automata learning and testing communities.

2   Engine Status Manager

The focus of this article is the *Engine Status Manager (ESM)*, a software component that is used to manage the status of the engine of Océ printers and copiers. In this section, the overall structure and context of the ESM will be explained.

2.1   ESRA

The requirements and behavior of the ESM are defined in a software architecture called Embedded Software Reference Architecture (ESRA). The components defined in this architecture are reused in many of the products developed by Océ and form an important part of these products. This architecture is developed for *cut-sheet* printers or copiers. The term cut-sheet refers to the use of separate sheets of paper as opposed to a *continuous feed* of paper.

An *engine* refers to the printing or scanning part of a printer or copier. Other products can be connected to an engine that pre- or postprocess the paper, for example a cutter, folder, stacker or stapler. Figure 2 gives an overview of the software in a printer or copier. The *controller* communicates the required actions to the engine software. This includes transport of digital images, status control, print or scan actions and error handling. The controller is responsible for queuing, processing the actions received from the network and operators and delegating the appropriate actions to the engine software. The *managers* communicate with the controller using the *external interface adapters*. These adapters translate the external protocols to internal protocols. The managers manage the different functions of the engine. They are divided by the different functionalities such as status control, print or scan actions or error handling they implement. In order to do this a manager may communicate with other managers and functions. A *function* is responsible for a specific set of hardware components. It translates commands from the managers to the function hardware and reports the status and other information of the function hardware to the managers. This hardware can for example be the printing hardware or hardware that is not part of the engine hardware such as a stapler. Other functionalities such as logging and debugging are orthogonal to the functions and managers.

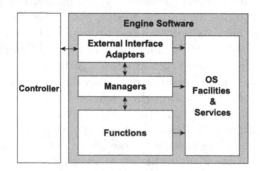

Fig. 2. Global overview of the engine software

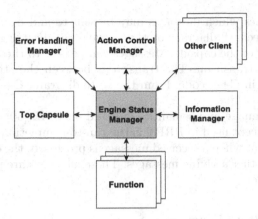

Fig. 3. Overview of the managers and clients connected to the ESM

2.2 ESM and Connected Components

The ESM is responsible for the transition from one status of the printer or copier to another. It coordinates the functions to bring them in the correct status. Moreover, it informs all its connected clients (managers or the controller) of status changes. Finally, it handles status transitions when an error occurs.

Figure 3 shows the different components to which the ESM is connected. The *Error Handling Manager (EHM)*, *Action Control Manager (ACM)* and other clients request engine statuses. The ESM decides whether a request can be honored immediately, has to be postponed or ignored. If the requested action is processed the ESM requests the functions to go to the appropriate status. The EHM has the highest priority and its requests are processed first. The EHM can request the engine to go into the defect status. The ACM has the next highest priority. The ACM requests the engine to switch between running and standby status. The other clients request transitions between the other statuses, such as idle, sleep, standby and low power. All the other clients have the same lowest priority. The Top Capsule instantiates the ESM and communicates with it during the initialization of the ESM. The Information Manager provides some parameters during the initialization.

There are more managers connected to the ESM but they are of less importance and are thus not mentioned here.

2.3 Rational Rose RealTime

The ESM has been implemented using *Rational Rose RealTime (RRRT)*. In this tool so-called *capsules* can be created. Each of these capsules defines a hierarchical *statechart diagram*. Capsules can be connected with each other using *structure diagrams*. Each capsule contains a number of ports that can be connected to ports of other capsules by adding connections in the associated structure diagram. Each of these ports specifies which protocol should be used.

This protocol defines which messages may be sent to and from the port. Transitions in the statechart diagram of the capsule can be triggered by arriving messages on a port of the capsule. Messages can be sent to these ports using the action code of the transition. The transitions between the states, actions and guards are defined in C++ code. From the state diagram, C++ source files are generated.

The RRRT language and semantics is based on UML [30] and ROOM [34]. One important concept used in RRRT is the run-to-completion execution model [12]. This means that when a received message is processed, the execution cannot be interrupted by other arriving messages. These messages are placed in a queue to be processed later.

2.4   The ESM State Diagram

Figure 4 shows the top states of the ESM statechart. The statuses that can be requested by the clients and managers correspond to gray states. The other states are so called *transitory states*. In transitory states the ESM is waiting for the functions to report that they have moved to the corresponding status. Once all functions have reported, the ESM moves to the corresponding status.

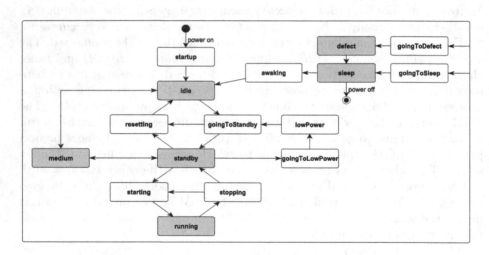

Fig. 4. Top states and transitions of the ESM

The `idle` status indicates that the engine has started up but that it is still *cold* (uncontrolled temperature). The `standby` status indicates that the engine is *warm* and ready for printing or scanning. The `running` status indicates that the engine is printing or scanning. The transitions from the overarching state to the `goingToSleep` and `goingToDefect` states indicate that it is possible to move to the `sleep` or `defect` status from any state. In some cases it is possible to awake from sleep status, in other cases the main power is turned off. The `medium` status is designed for diagnostics. In this status the functions can each be in a different status. For example one function is in standby status while another function is in idle status.

The statechart diagram in Fig. 4 may seem simple, but it hides many details. Each of the states has up to 5 nested states. In total there are 70 states that do not have further nested states. The C++ code contained in the actions of the transitions is in some cases non-trivial. The possibility to transition from any state to the sleep or defect state also complicates the learning.

3 Learning the ESM

In order to learn a model of the ESM, we connected it to LearnLib [29], a state-of-the-art tool for learning Mealy machines developed at the University of Dortmund. A *Mealy machine* is a tuple $M = \langle I, O, Q, q_0, \delta, \lambda \rangle$, where I is a finite set of input symbols, O is a finite set of output symbols, Q is a finite set of states, $q_0 \in Q$ is an initial state, $\delta : Q \times I \rightarrow Q$ is a transition function, and $\lambda : Q \times I \rightarrow O$ is an output function. The behavior of a Mealy machine is *deterministic,* in the sense that the outputs are fully determined by the inputs. Functions δ and λ are extended to accept sequences in the standard way. We say that Mealy machines $M = \langle I, O, Q, q_0, \delta, \lambda \rangle$ and $M' = \langle I', O', Q', q_0', \delta', \lambda' \rangle$ are *equivalent* if they generate an identical sequence of outputs for every sequence of inputs, that is, if $I = I'$ and, for all $w \in I^*$, $\lambda(q_0, w) = \lambda'(q_0', w)$. If the behavior of an SUT is described by a Mealy machine M then the task of LearnLib is to learn a Mealy machine M' that is equivalent to M.

3.1 Experimental Set-Up

A clear interface to the ESM has been defined in RRRT. The ESM defines ports from which it receives a predefined set of inputs and to which it can send a predefined set of outputs. However, this interface can only be used within RRRT. In order to communicate with the LearnLib software a TCP connection was set up. An extra capsule was created in RRRT which connects to the ports defined by the ESM. This capsule opened a TCP connection to LearnLib. Inputs and outputs are translated to and from a string format and sent over the connection. Before each membership query, the learner needs to bring the SUT back to its initial state. This means that LearnLib needs a way to reset the SUT.

Some inputs and outputs sent to and from the ESM carry parameters. These parameters are enumerations of statuses, or integers bounded by the number of functions connected to the ESM. Currently LearnLib cannot handle inputs with parameters; therefore, we introduced a separate input action for every parameter value. Based on domain knowledge and discussions with the Océ engineers, we could group some of these inputs together and reduce the total number of inputs. When learning the ESM using one function, 83 concrete inputs are grouped into four abstract inputs. When using two functions, 126 concrete inputs can be grouped. When an abstract input needs to be sent to the ESM, one concrete input of the represented group is randomly selected, as in the approach of [2]. This is a valid abstraction because all the inputs in the group have exactly the same behavior in any state of the ESM. No other abstractions were found during the research. After the inputs are grouped a total of 77 inputs remain when learning the ESM using 1 function, and 105 inputs remain when using 2 functions.

It was not immediately obvious how to model the ESM by a Mealy machine, since some inputs trigger no output, whereas other inputs trigger several outputs. In order to resolve this, we benefitted from the run-to-completion execution model used in RRRT. Whenever an input is sent all the outputs are collected until quiescence is detected. Next all the outputs are concatenated and are sent to LearnLib as a single aggregated output. In model-based testing, quiescence is usually detected by waiting for a fixed timeout period. However, this causes the system to be mostly idle while waiting for the timeout, which is inefficient. In order to detect quiescence faster, we exploited the run-to-completion execution model used by RRRT: we modified the ESM to respond to a new low-priority test input with a (single) special output. This test input is sent after each normal input. Only after the normal input is processed and all the generated outputs have been sent, the test input is processed and the special output is generated; upon its reception, quiescence can be detected immediately and reliably.

3.2   Test Selection Strategies

In the ESM case study the most challenging problem was finding counterexamples for the hypotheses constructed during learning.

LearnLib implements several algorithms for conformance testing, one of which is a random walk algorithm. The random walk algorithm works by first selecting the length of the test query according to a geometric distribution, cut off at a fixed upper bound. Each of the input symbols in the test query is then randomly selected from the input alphabet I from a uniform distribution. In order to find counterexamples, a specific sequence of input symbols is needed to arrive at the state in the SUT that differentiates it from the hypothesis. The upper bound for the size of this search space is $|I|^n$ where $|I|$ is the size of the input alphabet used, and n the length of the counterexample that needs to be found. If this sequence is long the chance of finding it is small. Because the ESM has many different input symbols to choose from, finding the correct one is hard. When learning the ESM with 1 function there are 77 possible input symbols. If for example the length of the counterexample needs to be at least 6 inputs to identify a certain state, then the upper bound on the number of test queries would be around 2×10^{11}. An average test query takes around 1 ms, so it would take about 7 years to execute these test queries.

Augmented DS-Method. In order to reduce the number of tests, Chow [10] and Vasilevskii [38] pioneered the so called W-method. In their framework a test query consists of a prefix p bringing the SUT to a specific state, a (random) middle part m and a suffix s assuring that the SUT is in the appropriate state. This results in a test suite of the form $PI^{\leq k}W$, where P is a set of (shortest) access sequences, $I^{\leq k}$ the set of all sequences of length at most k, and W is a characterization set. Classically, this characterization set is constructed by taking the set of all (pairwise) separating sequences. For $k = 1$ this test suite is complete in the sense that if the SUT passes all tests, then either the SUT is equivalent to the specification or the SUT has strictly more states than the specification. By increasing k we can check additional states.

We tried using the W-method as implemented by LearnLib to find counterexamples. The generated test suite, however, was still too big in our learning context. Fujiwara et al. [14] observed that it is possible to let the set W depend on the state the SUT is supposed to be. This allows us to only take a subset of W which is relevant for a specific state. This slightly reduces the test suite without losing the power of the full test suite. This method is known as the Wp-method. More importantly, this observation allows for generalizations where we can carefully pick the suffixes.

In the presence of an (adaptive) distinguishing sequence one can take W to be a single suffix, greatly reducing the test suite. Lee and Yannakakis [25] describe an algorithm (which we will refer to as the LY algorithm) to efficiently construct this sequence, if it exists. In our case, unfortunately, most hypotheses did not enjoy existence of an adaptive distinguishing sequence. In these cases the incomplete result from the LY algorithm still contained a lot of information which we augmented by pairwise separating sequences.

As an example we show an incomplete adaptive distinguishing sequence for one of the hypothesis in Fig. 5. When we apply the input sequence I46 I6.0 I10

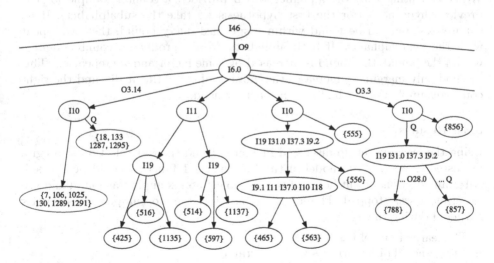

Fig. 5. A small part of an incomplete distinguishing sequence as produced by the LY algorithm. Leaves contain a set of possible initial states, inner nodes have input sequences and edges correspond to different output symbols (of which we only drew some), where Q stands for quiescence.

I19 I31.0 I37.3 I9.2 and observe outputs O9 O3.3 Q ... O28.0, we know for sure that the SUT was in state 788. Unfortunately not all paths lead to a singleton set. When for instance we apply the sequence I46 I6.0 I10 and observe the outputs O9 O3.14 Q, we know for sure that the SUT was in one of the states 18, 133, 1287 or 1295. In these cases we have to perform more experiments and we resort to pairwise separating sequences.

We note that this augmented DS-method is in the worst case not any better than the classical Wp-method. In our case, however, it greatly reduced the test suites.

Once we have our set of suffixes, which we call Z now, our test algorithm works as follows. The algorithm first exhausts the set $PI^{\leq 1}Z$. If this does not provide a counterexample, we will randomly pick test queries from PI^2I^*Z, where the algorithm samples uniformly from P, I^2 and Z (if Z contains more that 1 sequence for the supposed state) and with a geometric distribution on I^*.

Subalphabet Selection. Using the above method the algorithm still failed to learn the ESM. By looking at the RRRT-based model we were able to see why the algorithm failed to learn. In the initialization phase, the controller gives exceptional behavior when providing a certain input eight times consecutively. Of course such a sequence is hard to find in the above testing method. With this knowledge we could construct a single counterexample by hand by which means the algorithm was able to learn the ESM.

In order to automate this process, we defined a subalphabet of actions that are important during the initialization phase of the controller. This subalphabet will be used a bit more often than the full alphabet. We do this as follows. We start testing with the alphabet which provided a counterexample for the previous hypothesis (for the first hypothesis we take the subalphabet). If no counterexample can be found within a specified query bound, then we repeat with the next alphabet. If both alphabets do not produce a counterexample within the bound, the bound is increased by some factor and we repeat all. This method only marginally increases the number of tests. But it did find the right counterexample we first had to construct by hand.

3.3   Results

Using the learning set-up discussed in Sect. 3.1 and the test selection strategies discussed in Sect. 3.2, a model of the ESM using 1 function could be learned. After an additional eight hours of testing no counterexample was found and the experiment was stopped. The following list gives the most important statistics gathered during the learning:

- The learned model has 3.410 states.
- Altogether, 114 hypotheses were generated.
- The time needed for learning the final hypothesis was 8 h, 26 min, and 19 s.
- 29.933.643 membership queries were required, with on average 35,77 inputs per query.
- 30.629.711 test queries were required, with on average 29,06 inputs per query.

4   Verification

To verify the correctness of the model that was learned using LearnLib, we checked its equivalence with a model that was generated directly from the code.

4.1   Approach

As mentioned already, the ESM has been implemented using Rational Rose RealTime (RRRT). Thus a statechart representation of the ESM is available. However, we have not been able to find a tool that translates RRRT models to Mealy machines, allowing us to compare the RRRT-based model of the ESM with the learned model. We considered several formalisms and tools that were proposed in the literature to flatten statecharts to state machines. The first one was a tool for hierarchical timed automata (HTA) [11]. However, we found it hard to translate the output of this tool, a network of Uppaal timed automata, to a Mealy machine that could be compared to the learned model. The second tool that we considered has been developed by Hansen et al. [18]. This tool misses some essential features, for example the ability to assign new values to state variables on transitions. Finally, we considered a formalism called object-oriented action systems (OOAS) [23], but no tools to use this could be found.

In the end we decided to implement the required model transformations ourselves. Figure 6 displays the different formats for representing models that we used and the transformations between those formats. We used the bisimulation checker of CADP [15] to check the equivalence of labeled transition system models in .aut format. The Mealy machine models learned by LearnLib are represented as .dot files. A small script converts these Mealy machines to labeled transition systems in .aut format. We used the Uppaal [6] tool as an editor for defining extended finite state machines (EFSM), represented as .xml files. A script developed in the ITALIA project (http://www.italia.cs.ru.nl/) converts these EFSM models to LOTOS, and then CADP takes care of the conversion from LOTOS to the .aut format.

The Uppaal syntax is not sufficiently expressive to directly encode the RRRT definition of the ESM, since this definition makes heavy use of UML [30] concepts

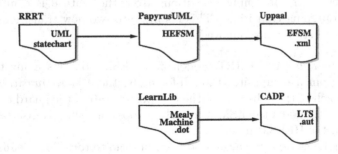

Fig. 6. Formats for representing models and transformations between formats

such as state hierarchy and transitions from composite states, concepts which are not present in Uppaal. Using Uppaal would force us to duplicate many transitions and states.

We decided to manually create an intermediate hierarchical EFSM (HEFSM) model using the UML drawing tool PapyrusUML [24]. The HEFSM model closely resembles the RRRT UML model, but many elements used in UML state machines are left out because they are not needed for modeling the ESM and complicate the transformation process.

4.2   Model Transformations

We explain the transformation from the HEFSM model to the EFSM model using examples. The transformation is divided into five steps, which are executed in order: (1) combine transitions without input or output signal, (2) transform supertransitions, (3) transform internal transitions, (4) add input signals that do not generate an output, and (5) replace invocations of the next function.

1. Empty transitions. In order to make the model more readable and to make it easy to model if and switch statements in the C++ code the HEFSM model allows for transitions without a signal. These transitions are called *empty* transitions. An empty transition can still contain a guard and an assignment. However these kinds of transitions are only allowed on states that only contain empty outgoing transitions. This was done to make the transformation easy and the model easy to read.

In order to transform a state with empty transitions all the incoming and outgoing transitions are collected. For each combination of incoming transition a and outgoing transition b a new transition c is created with the source of a as source and the target of b as target. The guard for transition c evaluates to true if and only if the guard of a and b both evaluate to true. The assignment of c is the concatenation of the assignment of a and b. The signal of c will be the signal of a because b cannot have a signal. Once all the new transitions are created all the states with empty transitions are removed together with all their incoming and outgoing transitions.

Figure 7 shows an example model with empty transitions and its transformed version. Each of the incoming transitions from the state B is combined with each of the outgoing transitions. This results into two new transitions. The old transitions and state B are removed.

2. Supertransitions. The RRRT model of the ESM contains many transitions originating from a composite state. Informally, these *supertransitions* can be taken in in each of the substates of the composite state if the guard evaluates to true. In order to model the ESM as closely as possible, supertransitions are also supported in the HEFSM model.

In RRRT transitions are evaluated from bottom to top. This means that first the transitions from the leaf state are considered, then transitions from its parent state and then from its parent's parent state, etc. Once a transition for which

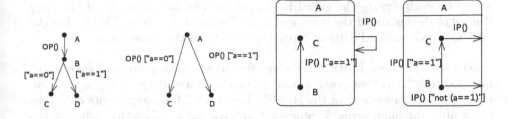

Fig. 7. Example of empty transition transformation. On the left the original version. On the right the transformed version

Fig. 8. Example of supertransition transformation. On the left the original version. On the right the transformed version

the guard evaluates to true and the correct signal has been found it is taken. When flattening the statechart, we modified the guards of supertransitions to ensure the correct priorities.

Figure 8 shows an example model with supertransitions and its transformed version. The supertransition from state A can be taken at each of A's leaf states B and C. The transformation removes the original supertransition and creates a new transition at states B and C using the same target state. For leaf state C this is easy because it does not contain a transition with the input signal IP. In state B the transition to state C would be taken if a signal IP was processed and the state variable a equals 1. The supertransition can only be taken if the other transition cannot be taken. This is why the negation of other the guard is added to the new transition. If the original supertransition is an internal transition the model needs further transformation after this transformation. This is described in the next paragraph. If the original supertransition is not an internal transition the new transitions will have the initial state of A as target.

3. Internal transitions. The ESM model also makes use of *internal transitions* in RRRT. Using such a transition the current state does not change. If such a transition is defined on a composite state it can be taken from all of the substates and return to the same leaf state it originated from. If defined on a composite state it is thus also a supertransition. This is also possible in the HEFSM model. In order to transform an internal transition it is first seen as a supertransition and the above transformation is applied. Then the target of the transition is simply set to the leaf state it originates from. An example can be seen in Fig. 8. If the supertransition from state A is also defined to be an internal transition the transformed version on the right would need another transformation. The new transitions that now have the target state A would be transformed to have the same target state as their current source state.

4. Quiescent transitions. In order to reduce the number of transitions in the HEFSM model quiescent transitions are added automatically. For every state all the transitions for each signal are collected in a set T. A new self transition a is added for each signal. The guard for transition a evaluates to true if and only if none of the guards of the transactions in T evaluates to true. This makes the HEFSM input enabled without having to specify all the transitions.

5. *The next function.* In RRRT it is possible to write the guard and assignment in C++ code. It is thus possible that the value of a variable changes while an input signal is processed. In the HEFSM however all the assignments only take effect after the input signal is processed. In order to simulate this behavior the *next* function is used. This function takes a variable name and evaluates to the value of this variable after the transition.

4.3 Results

Figure 9 shows a visualization of the learned model that was generated using Gephi [5]. The large number of states (3.410) and transitions (262.570) makes it hard to visualize this model. Nevertheless, the visualization does provide insight in the behavior of the ESM. The three protrusions at the bottom of Fig. 9 correspond to deadlocks in the model. These deadlocks are "error" states that are present in the ESM by design. According to the Océ engineers, the sequences of inputs that are needed to drive the ESM into these deadlock states will always be followed by a system power reset. The protrusion at the top right of the figure corresponds to the initialization phase of the ESM. This phase is performed only

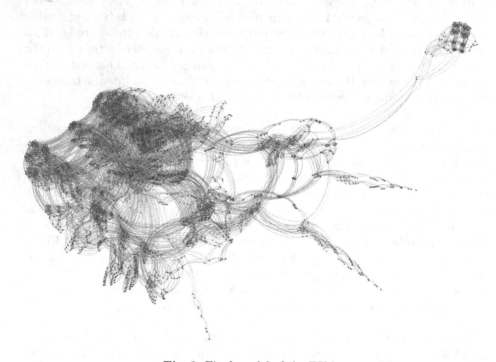

Fig. 9. Final model of the ESM.

once and thus only transitions from the initialization cluster to the main body of states are present.

During the construction of the RRRT-based model, the ESM code was thoroughly inspected. This resulted in the discovery of missing behavior in one transition of the ESM code. An Océ software engineer confirmed that this behavior is a (minor) bug, which will be fixed. We have verified the equivalence of the learned model and the RRRT-based model by using CADP [15].

5   Conclusions and Future Work

Using an extension of the Lee and Yannakakis algorithm for adaptive distinguishing sequences [25], we succeeded to learn a Mealy machine model of a piece of widely used industrial control software. Our extension of Lee and Yannakakis' algorithm is rather obvious, but nevertheless it appears to be new. Preliminary evidence suggests that it outperforms existing conformance testing algorithms. We are currently performing experiments in which we compare the new algorithm with other test algorithms on a number of realistic benchmarks.

There are several possibilities for extending the ESM case study. To begin with, one could try to learn a model of the ESM with more than one function. Another interesting possibility would be to learn models of the EHM, ACM and other managers connected to the ESM. Using these models some of the properties discussed by Ploeger [31] could be verified at a more detailed level. We expect that the combination of LearnLib with the extended Lee and Yannakakis algorithm can be applied to learn models of many other software components.

In the specific case study described in this article, we know that our learning algorithm has succeeded to learn the correct model, since we established equivalence with a reference model that was constructed independently from the RRRT model of the ESM software. In the absence of a reference model, we can never guarantee that the actual system behavior conforms to a learned model. In order to deal with this problem, it is important to define metrics that quantify the difference (or distance) between a hypothesis and a correct model of the SUT, and to develop test generation algorithms that guarantee an upper bound on this difference. Preliminary work in this area is reported in [36].

Acknowledgments. We thank Lou Somers for suggesting the ESM case study and for his support of our research. Fides Aarts and Harco Kuppens helped us with the use of LearnLib and CADP, and Jan Tretmans gave useful feedback.

References

1. Aarts, F.: Tomte: bridging the gap between active learning and real-world systems. Ph.D. thesis, Radboud University Nijmegen, October 2014
2. Aarts, F., Jonsson, B., Uijen, J., Vaandrager, F.: Generating models of infinite-state communication protocols using regular inference with abstraction. Formal Methods Syst. Des. **46**(1), 1–41 (2015)

3. Aarts, F., Kuppens, H., Tretmans, G., Vaandrager, F., Verwer, S.: Improving active mealy machine learning for protocol conformance testing. Mach. Learn. 96(1–2), 189–224 (2014)
4. Angluin, D.: Learning regular sets from queries and counterexamples. Inf. Comput. 75(2), 87–106 (1987)
5. Bastian, M., Heymann, S., Jacomy, M.: Gephi: An open source software for exploring and manipulating networks. In: ICWSM. The AAAI Press (2009)
6. Behrmann, G., David, A., Larsen, K.G., Håkansson, J., Pettersson, P., Yi, W., Hendriks, M.: Uppaal 4.0. In: QEST, pp. 125–126. IEEE Computer Society (2006)
7. Berg, T., Grinchtein, O., Jonsson, B., Leucker, M., Raffelt, H., Steffen, B.: On the correspondence between conformance testing and regular inference. In: Cerioli, M. (ed.) FASE 2005. LNCS, vol. 3442, pp. 175–189. Springer, Heidelberg (2005)
8. Cassel, S., Howar, F., Jonsson, B., Merten, M., Steffen, B.: A succinct canonical register automaton model. J. Log. Algebr. Meth. Program. 84(1), 54–66 (2015)
9. Cho, C.Y., Babic, D., Shin, E.C.R., Song, D.: Inference and analysis of formal models of botnet command and control protocols. In: ACM Conference on Computer and Communications Security, pp. 426–439. ACM (2010)
10. Chow, T.: Testing software design modeled by finite-state machines. IEEE Trans. Softw. Eng. 4(3), 178–187 (1978)
11. David, A., Oliver Möller, M., Yi, W.: Formal verification of UML statecharts with real-time extensions. In: Kutsche, R.-D., Weber, H. (eds.) FASE 2002. LNCS, vol. 2306, pp. 218–232. Springer, Heidelberg (2002)
12. Eshuis, R., Jansen, D.N., Wieringa, R.: Requirements-level semantics and model checking of object-oriented statecharts. Requir. Eng. 7(4), 243–263 (2002)
13. Fiterău-Broştean, P., Janssen, R., Vaandrager, F.: Learning fragments of the TCP network protocol. In: Lang, F., Flammini, F. (eds.) FMICS 2014. LNCS, vol. 8718, pp. 78–93. Springer, Heidelberg (2014)
14. Fujiwara, S., Bochmann, G., Khendek, F., Amalou, M., Ghedamsi, A.: Test selection based on finite state models. IEEE Trans. Softw. Eng. 17(6), 591–603 (1991)
15. Garavel, H., Lang, F., Mateescu, R., Serwe, W.: CADP 2010: a toolbox for the construction and analysis of distributed processes. In: Abdulla, P.A., Leino, K.R.M. (eds.) TACAS 2011. LNCS, vol. 6605, pp. 372–387. Springer, Heidelberg (2011)
16. Graaf, B., van Deursen, A.: Model-driven consistency checking of behavioural specifications. In: MOMPES, pp. 115–126. IEEE Computer Society (2007)
17. Groz, R., Li, K., Petrenko, A., Shahbaz, M.: Modular system verification by inference, testing and reachability analysis. In: Suzuki, K., Higashino, T., Ulrich, A., Hasegawa, T. (eds.) TestCom/FATES 2008. LNCS, vol. 5047, pp. 216–233. Springer, Heidelberg (2008)
18. Hvid Hansen, H., Ketema, J., Luttik, B., Mousavi, M.R., van de Pol, J., dos Santos, O.M.: Automated verification of executable UML models. In: Aichernig, B.K., de Boer, F.S., Bonsangue, M.M. (eds.) FMCO 2010. LNCS, vol. 6957, pp. 225–250. Springer, Heidelberg (2011)
19. de la Higuera, C.: Grammatical Inference: Learning Automata and Grammars. Cambridge University Press, Cambridge, UK (2010)
20. Howar, F., Steffen, B., Jonsson, B., Cassel, S.: Inferring canonical register automata. In: Kuncak, V., Rybalchenko, A. (eds.) VMCAI 2012. LNCS, vol. 7148, pp. 251–266. Springer, Heidelberg (2012)
21. Howar, F., Steffen, B., Merten, M.: Automata learning with automated alphabet abstraction refinement. In: Jhala, R., Schmidt, D. (eds.) VMCAI 2011. LNCS, vol. 6538, pp. 263–277. Springer, Heidelberg (2011)

22. Hungar, H., Niese, O., Steffen, B.: Domain-specific optimization in automata learning. In: Hunt Jr, W.A., Somenzi, F. (eds.) CAV 2003. LNCS, vol. 2725, pp. 315–327. Springer, Heidelberg (2003)

23. Krenn, W., Schlick, R., Aichernig, B.K.: Mapping UML to labeled transition systems for test-case generation. In: de Boer, F.S., Bonsangue, M.M., Hallerstede, S., Leuschel, M. (eds.) FMCO 2009. LNCS, vol. 6286, pp. 186–207. Springer, Heidelberg (2010)

24. Lanusse, A., Tanguy, Y., Espinoza, H., Mraidha, C., Gerard, S., Tessier, P., Schnekenburger, R., Dubois, H., Terrier, F.: Papyrus UML: an open source toolset for MDA. In: Model-Driven Architecture, p. 1 (2009)

25. Lee, D., Yannakakis, M.: Testing finite-state machines: state identification and verification. IEEE Trans. Comput. **43**(3), 306–320 (1994)

26. Leucker, M.: Learning meets verification. In: de Boer, F.S., Bonsangue, M.M., Graf, S., de Roever, W.-P. (eds.) FMCO 2006. LNCS, vol. 4709, pp. 127–151. Springer, Heidelberg (2007)

27. Li, K., Groz, R., Shahbaz, M.: Integration testing of distributed components based on learning parameterized I/O models. In: Najm, E., Pradat-Peyre, J.-F., Donzeau-Gouge, V.V. (eds.) FORTE 2006. LNCS, vol. 4229, pp. 436–450. Springer, Heidelberg (2006)

28. Merten, M., Howar, F., Steffen, B., Cassel, S., Jonsson, B.: Demonstrating learning of register automata. In: Flanagan, C., König, B. (eds.) TACAS 2012. LNCS, vol. 7214, pp. 466–471. Springer, Heidelberg (2012)

29. Merten, M., Steffen, B., Howar, F., Margaria, T.: Next generation LearnLib. In: Abdulla, P.A., Leino, K.R.M. (eds.) TACAS 2011. LNCS, vol. 6605, pp. 220–223. Springer, Heidelberg (2011)

30. Object Management Group (OMG). Unified modeling language specification: Version 2, revised final adopted specification (2004). http://www.uml.org/#UML2.0

31. Ploeger, B.: Analysis of concurrent state machines in embedded copier software. Master's thesis, Eindhoven University of Technology, August 2005

32. Raffelt, H., Merten, M., Steffen, B., Margaria, T.: Dynamic testing via automata learning. STTT **11**(4), 307–324 (2009)

33. Raffelt, H., Steffen, B., Berg, T., Margaria, T.: LearnLib: a framework for extrapolating behavioral models. STTT **11**(5), 393–407 (2009)

34. Selic, B., Gullekson, G., Ward, P.T.: Real-Time Object-oriented Modeling. Wiley, New York (1994)

35. Smeenk, W.: Applying automata learning to complex industrial software. Master thesis, Radboud University Nijmegen, September 2012

36. Smetsers, R., Volpato, M., Vaandrager, F.W., Verwer, S.: Bigger is not always better: on the quality of hypotheses in active automata learning. In: ICGI, JMLR Proceedings, vol. 34, pp. 167–181 (2014)

37. Steffen, B., Howar, F., Merten, M.: Introduction to active automata learning from a practical perspective. In: Bernardo, M., Issarny, V. (eds.) SFM 2011. LNCS, vol. 6659, pp. 256–296. Springer, Heidelberg (2011)

38. Vasilevskii, M.P.: Failure diagnosis of automata. Cybern. Syst. Anal. **9**(4), 653–665 (1973)

A 3-Valued Contraction Model Checking Game: Deciding on the World of Partial Information

Jandson S. Ribeiro[✉] and Aline Andrade

Distributed Systems Laboratory (LaSiD) Computer Science Department –
Mathematics Institute, Federal University of Bahia, Salvador, Bahia, Brazil
jandsonsan@dcc.ufba.br, aline@ufba.br
http://www.lasid.ufba.br

Abstract. In this work we address the problem of model checking a
desired property specified in Computation Tree Logic (CTL) in the presence of partial information. The Kripke Modal Transition System (KMTS)
is used for modelling due its capacity to represent indefinitions explicitly
which enables a KMTS interpretation as a set of Kripke structures. In
this interpretation a specific model checking algorithm is required that
can return one of the three possible values: *true* when all Kripke models
of the set satisfy the property, *false* when no Kripke models of the set
satisfy the property and *indefinite* when some models satisfy and others do not. To the best of our knowledge the literature lacks a KMTS
model checking algorithm that fits this interpretation and in this paper
we present an algorithm based on a game approach called a Contraction
Model Checking algorithm for this purpose.

Keywords: Kripke Modal Transition System (KMTS) · Model checking
game · Partial information

1 Introduction

In this work, we address the problem of verifying whether a model of a system in
the presence of partial information satisfies a required property. It is desirable to
express partial information explicitly, mainly in the preliminary phases of system
development, in order to better give support to the evolution of the model as
new information is acquired.

Model checking tools use algorithms that in general are defined over Kripke
structures that do not express partial information explicitly. However, 3-valued
model checking has been proposed which returns an undetermined value besides
True and False to work with modal transition systems which express indeterminations explicitly. An example of such a structure is the Kripke Modal Transition
System - KMTS [8].

J.S. Ribeiro—This author is supported by the grant # 4576/2014, Bahia Research
Foundation (FAPESB).

A. Andrade—This author is supported by the grant # 447178/2014-8, Brazilian
Research Council (CNPq).

© Springer International Publishing Switzerland 2015
M. Butler et al. (Eds.): ICFEM 2015, LNCS 9407, pp. 84–99, 2015.
DOI: 10.1007/978-3-319-25423-4_6

The Kripke Modal Transition System structures express indetermination in states and in transitions, which induce a set of possible Kripke models by transforming indeterminations into determinations. In this work we propose a KMTS model checking algorithm according to this interpretation. This KMTS model checking algorithm should consider three possible results when verifying a property: *true* (T) when all Kripke models of the set satisfy the property, *false* (F) when no Kripke models of the set satisfy the property and *indefinite* ($\perp$) when some models satisfy and others do not. In [5], Grumberg proposes a 3-valued model checking algorithm based on games to verify CTL properties over KMTS using Kleene three-valued logic [8,10]. The algorithm uses a colouring function over a game board for model checking. We take this algorithm as a reference to develop the model checking algorithm presented in this paper. However, the interpretation of a KTMS considered in [5,11] is different from ours. There a KMTS is interpreted as an abstraction of a concrete Kripke structure and the Kleene three valued logic is suitable for this. In interpreting a KMTS as a set of Kripke models, however, we cannot reason with this logic because the $\perp$ value will not be compositional over conjunctions and disjunctions, i.e., if φ is $\perp$ and ψ is $\perp$, $\varphi \wedge \psi$ is not necessarily $\perp$.

In order to achieve a model checking that fits our interpretation, we consider the truth value of a formula in the model checking process represented as a set of KMTSs. Over truth values (sets of KMTS models) of two formulas φ and ψ we define a contraction operation that can calculate the truth value of formulas composed of φ and ψ. A proper colouring function is defined over a game board using this contraction operation.

The initial motivation of this work is to support the framework for KMTS revision combined with a model checking game proposed in [6], where a KMTS is interpreted as a set of Kripke models. The algorithms for revision in [6] took as reference the Grumberg 3-valued model checking game and can only give partial results because of the difference in semantics reported above. Our Contraction Model Checking algorithm solves this problem enabling a KMTS complete revision. We forecast that this algorithm can also be used in other contexts and can be adjusted to other logics unlike CTL.

With regards to the organization of this paper, in Sect. 2 we present CTL, Kripke structures and KMTS interpreted as a set of CTL models. Section 3 presents the semantics of CTL w.r.t KMTS interpreted as a set of Kripke structures. In Sect. 4 we present KMTS set operations, including the contraction operation. We present in Sect. 5 our Contraction Model Checking and finally in Sect. 6 we present related works and make some final considerations.

2   Computation Tree Logic and Kripke Structures

Computation Tree Logic (CTL) [3,9] is a temporal logic that presupposes a branched representation of the future over sequences of states of a Kripke structure which forms a computation tree. Path quantifiers can be used to make reference to a future or all futures.

Definition 1. *A Kripke structure is a tuple $K = (AP, S, S_0, R, L)$ where AP is a set of atomic propositions; S is a finite set of states, $S_0 \subseteq S$ is the set of initial states, $R \subseteq S \times S$ is the transition relation over S, and $L : S \rightarrow 2^{AP}$ is a labelling function of truth assignment over states.*[1]

We denote a transition $(s, s') \in R$ of a Kripke structure K by $s \rightarrow s'$. Furthermore, to inform that $s \rightarrow s'$ belongs to the set transitions of K we write $s \rightarrow s' \in K$.

Definition 2. *Let l be a literal. A CTL formula ϕ in its negation normal formal is defined as follows:*

$$\phi ::= \top \mid F \mid l \mid (\phi \vee \phi) \mid (\phi \wedge \phi) \mid EX\phi \mid AX\phi \mid$$
$$E[\phi U \phi] \mid A[\phi U \phi] \mid E[\phi R \phi] \mid A[\phi R \phi]$$

In Definition 2, A and E are path operators meaning for all paths and exists a path, respectively. The operators X, U and R mean, respectively, next state, until (in the sense that the left ϕ must hold along the path until the right ϕ holds) and release (the until dual operator). Excluding the conjunction and the disjunction, all the other operators must be bound by path operators. The complete semantics of the CTL formulas can be found in [3,9]. As the CTL semantics are defined over Kripke structures, we will also call these structures CTL models.

2.1   Kripke Modal Transition System

The Kripke Modal Transistion System is capable of representing incomplete system information explicitly. A KMTS has two kinds of transitions, must transitions and may transitions, that express transitions that must occur (certain behaviour) and transitions that may occur (the behaviour is uncertain) in the system. Incomplete information can be also expressed in the states of a KMTS, because in any state of the model an atomic property can be defined or undefined (uncertain state).

Definition 3. *Let AP be a set of atomic propositions and $Lit = AP \cup \{\neg p \mid p \in AP\}$ the set of literal over AP. A Kripke modal transition system (KMTS) is a tuple $M = (AP, S, R^+, R^-, L)$, where S is a set of finite sates, $R^+ \subseteq S \times S$ and $R^- \subseteq S \times S$ are transition relations such that $R^+ \subseteq R^-$, and $L : S \rightarrow 2^{Lit}$ is a label function, such that for all state s and $p \in AP$, at most one between p and $\neg p$ occurs.*

In the definition above the transitions R^+ and R^- correspond to the transitions *must* and *may* respectively.

---

[1] Although the CTL semantics consider Kripke structures with total relation transition, such a requirement can be released and we assume a Kripke structure with a partial transition relation instead.

2.2   KMTS as a Set of Kripke Structures

In [6] the authors interpret a KMTS as a set of Kripke structures. According to this interpretation, a (s_i, s_j) *may* transition can lead to two CTL models, one with a (s_i, s_j) transition and another without this transition, and an indefinite literal l in a state s_i can lead to two CTL models: one which has l labelled in the correspondent state s_i and another one with $\neg l$ labelled in s_i. The authors define a KMTS expansion in CTL models with respect to all their indetermination leading to an exponential set with 2^m Kripke structures, where m is the number of indeterminations.

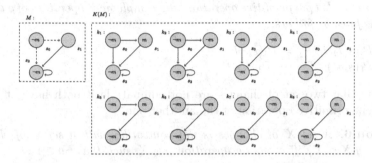

Fig. 1. Expansion K(M) of the KMTS M. The dashed arrows represent *may* transitions and the solid ones represent *must* transitions.

Let M be a KMTS, we denote by $K(M)$ the set of Kripke structures represented by M. Figure 1 illustrates a KMTS M and its expansion set $K(M)$. Since the state s_1 of M is neither labelled with m nor $\neg m$, and the KMTS has two *may* transitions ($s_0 \rightarrow s_1$ and $s_0 \rightarrow s_2$), M leads to eight CTL models.

Definition 4. *Let M_1 and M_2 be two KMTSs. We say M_1 is an instance of M_2 denoting by $M_1 \sqsubseteq M_2$ iff $K(M_1) \subseteq K(M_2)$.*

An instance of a KMTS M represents a subset of Kripke structures from K(M) and in order to represent this subset, an instance of M can be addressed. To do so, we use some change operations that change a KMTS M into an instance of it. We argue that sets of instances represented by change operations have some desired properties which allow the definition of some set operations, defined in Sect. 4, such as the contraction operation which are the key for the contraction model checking.

There are 3 primitive change operations to generate KMTS instances:

P_1 (s, s'): which removes the pair (s, s') from the relation R^-
P_2 (s, s'): which transforms (s, s') of R^- to (s, s') of R^+
P_3 (s, l): which assigns a literal l to the state s if l is undefined in $L(s)$

As for example, the application of the operation $P_2(s_0, s_2)$ over the KMTS M presented in Fig. 1 generates a KMTS that exactly represents the Kripke structures k_1, k_2, k_3 and k_4 presented in the same figure. Likewise, the application of the operations $P_2(s_0, s_2)$ and $P_3(s_1, \neg m)$ generates a KMTS that exactly represents the Kripke structures k_2 and k_3.

The application of a change over a KMTS is sometimes not encouraged. For example, we cannot apply the operations $P_3(s, l)$ and $P_3(s, \neg l)$ over a KMTS nor can we apply $P_1(s, s')$ and $P_2(s, s')$ because we cannot define a KMTS that has a transition $s \rightarrow s'$ that belongs to the set R^+, but it does not belong to the set R^-. We call such operations complement operations.

Definition 5. *Let p a primitive operation, the complement operation of p denoted by $\neg p$ is defined as follows:*

(i) $p = P_3(s, l)$ iff $\neg p = P_3(s, \neg l)$
(ii) $p = P_1(s, s')$ iff $\neg p = P_2(s, s')$

We say that two set of changes are not compatible if both have at least a complement primitive operation of the another one.

Definition 6. *A set X of changes is not compatible with a set Y of changes, denoting by $X \not\simeq Y$, iff exists an operation $p \in X$ such that $\neg p \in Y$.*

3   Semantics of CTL with Respect to KMTS

In this section we consider some notations, definitions and properties used to define the semantics of CTL for KMTS interpreted as a set of Kripke structures which is presented at the end of this section.

Definition 7. *Let M be a KMTS. The set of M states reachable from a state $s \in S$ of M is the set $\overrightarrow{S}(s) = \{s' \in S | s \rightarrow s' \in R^-\}$.*

Definition 8. *Let M be a KMTS, $s \rightarrow s' \in R^-$ a may transition of it. The subset of Kripke structures in $K(M)$ that does not have the transition $s \rightarrow s'$ is the set $[R/]_M(s, s') = \{k \in K(M) \mid s \rightarrow s' \notin k\}$.*

Definition 9. *Let M be a KMTS and φ a CTL formula. The subset of Kripke structures represented by M that satisfies φ starting at a state $s \in S$ is the set $[\varphi]_M^s = \{k \in K(M) \mid k, s \models \varphi\}$.*

Definition 10. *Let M be a KMTS and φ a CTL formula. We define the sets successive union $([\bigcup]_M^s(\varphi))$ and successive intersection $([\bigcap]_M^s(\varphi))$ as follows:*

$$[\bigcup]_M^s(\varphi) = \bigcup_{s' \in \overrightarrow{S}(s)} ([\varphi]_M^{s'} \setminus [R/]_M(s, s'));$$

$$[\bigcap]_M^s(\varphi) = \bigcap_{s' \in \overrightarrow{S}(s)} ([\varphi]_M^{s'} \cup [R/]_M(s, s')).$$

The set successive union captures all the Kripke structures represented by M that satisfy φ starting at a state s' reachable from a state s through the transition $s \rightarrow s'$, excluding those ones that do not have such a transition. On the other hand, the set successive intersection captures all Kripke structures that satisfy φ starting at every state s' reachable from s through the transition $s \rightarrow s'$. Indeed, the sets successive union and successive intersection capture those models that satisfy the CTL formulas $EX\varphi$ and $AX\varphi$, respectively.

Proposition 1. *Let M be a KMTS, s a state of it and φ a CTL formula. A Kripke structure k belongs to $\left[\bigcup\right]_M^s(\varphi)$ iff $k \in K(M)$ and $k, s \models EX\varphi$.*

Proof. $k, s \models EX\varphi$ iff $\exists s \rightarrow s' \in k$ s.t $k, s' \models \varphi$ (I).

"$\Rightarrow$" *From Definition 9, we have* $\forall k \in [\varphi]_M^{s'}$; $k, s \models \varphi$ and $k \in K(M)$. *So,* $\forall k \in \left([\varphi]_M^{s'} \setminus [R/]_M(s, s')\right)$; $k, s' \models \varphi$ and $s \rightarrow s' \in k$ (II). *Thus, from (II) and (I), we have* $\forall k \in \left([\varphi]_M^{s'} \setminus [R/]_M(s, s')\right)$; $k, s \models EX\varphi$. *This way,* $\forall k \in \bigcup_{s' \in \vec{S}(s)} \left([\varphi]_M^{s'} \setminus [R/]_M(s, s')\right)$; $k, s \models EX\varphi$ and $k \in K(M)$. *Therefore,* $\forall k \in \left[\bigcup\right]_M^s(\varphi)$; $k, s \models EX\varphi$ and $k \in K(M)$.

"$\Leftarrow$" *Let us suppose* $k, s \models EX\varphi$ and $k \in K(M)$. *From (I),* $\exists s \rightarrow s' \in k$, $k, s' \models \varphi$. *Thus,* $k \in [\varphi]_M^{s'}$ and $k \notin [R/]_M(s, s')$. *So,* $k \in [\varphi]_M^{s'} \setminus [R/]_M(s, s')$. *Therefore,* $k \in \bigcup_{s' \in \vec{S}(s)} [\varphi]_M^{s'} \setminus [R/]_M(s, s')$ and $k \in \left[\bigcup\right]_M^s(\varphi)$.

Definition 11. *The semantics of a CTL formula φ in its negation normal form w.r.t a KMTS is presented in Table 1.*

Table 1. Semantics of a CTL formula φ w.r.t a KMTS M.

Formula	$\top$	F	$\perp$
$\|l\|_M(s)$	$l \in L(s)$	$\neg l \in L(s)$	Otherwise
$\|\varphi_1 \wedge \varphi_2\|_M(s)$	$[\varphi_1]_M^s \cap [\varphi_2]_M^s = K(M)$	$[\varphi_1]_M^s \cap [\varphi_2]_M^s = \emptyset$	Otherwise
$\|\varphi_1 \vee \varphi_2\|_M(s)$	$[\varphi_1]_M^s \cup [\varphi_2]_M^s = K(M)$	$[\varphi_1]_M^s \cup [\varphi_2]_M^s = \emptyset$	Otherwise
$\|EX\varphi\|_M(s)$	$\left[\bigcup\right]_M^s(\varphi) = K(M)$	$\left[\bigcup\right]_M^s(\varphi) = \emptyset$	Otherwise
$\|AX\varphi\|_M(s)$	$\left[\bigcap\right]_M^s(\varphi) = K(M)$	$\left[\bigcap\right]_M^s(\varphi) = \emptyset$	Otherwise
$\|E[\varphi_1 U\varphi_2]\|_M(s)$	$[\varphi_2]_M^s \cup ([\varphi_1]_M^s \cap \left[\bigcup\right]_M^s(E[\varphi_1 U\varphi_2])) = K(M)$	$[\varphi_2]_M^s \cup ([\varphi_1]_M^s \cap \left[\bigcup\right]_M^s(E[\varphi_1 U\varphi_2])) = \emptyset$	Otherwise
$\|A[\varphi_1 U\varphi_2]\|_M(s)$	$[\varphi_2]_M^s \cup ([\varphi_1]_M^s \cap \left[\bigcup\right]_M^s(A[\varphi_1 U\varphi_2])) = K(M)$	$[\varphi_2]_M^s \cup ([\varphi_1]_M^s \cap \left[\bigcup\right]_M^s(A[\varphi_1 U\varphi_2])) = \emptyset$	Otherwise
$\|E[\varphi_1 R\varphi_2]\|_M(s)$	$[\varphi_2]_M^s \cap ([\varphi_1]_M^s \cup \left[\bigcup\right]_M^s(E[\varphi_1 U\varphi_2])) = K(M)$	$[\varphi_2]_M^s \cap ([\varphi_1]_M^s \cup \left[\bigcup\right]_M^s(E[\varphi_1 U\varphi_2])) = \emptyset$	Otherwise
$\|A[\varphi_1 R\varphi_2]\|_M(s)$	$[\varphi_2]_M^s \cap ([\varphi_1]_M^s \cup \left[\bigcup\right]_M^s(A[\varphi_1 U\varphi_2])) = K(M)$	$[\varphi_2]_M^s \cap ([\varphi_1]_M^s \cup \left[\bigcup\right]_M^s(A[\varphi_1 U\varphi_2])) = \emptyset$	Otherwise

Proposition 2. *Let M be a KMTS and φ a CTL formula, then*

$$\|\varphi\|_M(s) = \begin{cases} \top & \text{iff } \forall k \in K(M); k, s \models \varphi = T; \\ F & \text{iff } \forall k \in K(M); k, s \models \varphi = F; \\ \bot, & \text{otherwise} \end{cases}$$

Proof. It follows straight from the semantics.

4   KMTS Operations

The CTL semantics over KMTS interpreted as a set of Kripke structure deals directly with set operations. Thus, in order to decide if a set of Kripke structures represented by a KMTS M satisfies a CTL property, we should decide if every CTL model in $K(M)$ satisfies such a property. However, it is not necessary because we can deal directly with M, instead of K(M). Therefore, in this section, we define set operations over KMTSs and we prove some properties and some limitations as well.

We write $M(X)$ to denote an instance generated by the application of a set X of changes over a KMTS M.

Definition 12. *Let M, M_1, M_2 be KMTSs, X_1 and X_2 two set of changes, such that $M_1 \sqsubseteq M, M_2 \sqsubseteq M$ and $M_1 = M(X_1), M_2 = M(X_2)$. We define the operations intersection, union and difference, with respect to KMTS as:*

Union: $M_1 \sqcup M_2 = \{M_1, M_2\}$

Intersection: $M_1 \sqcap M_2 = \begin{cases} \emptyset, & \text{iff } X_1 \not\sim X_2 \\ \{M(X_1 \cup X_2)\}, & \text{otherwise} \end{cases}$

Difference: $M_1 \setminus M_2 = \begin{cases} \{M_1\} & \text{iff } X_1 \not\sim X_2 \\ \bigcup\limits_{p_i \in (X_2 \setminus X_1)} \{M(X_1 \cup \{\neg p_i\})\} & \text{otherwise} \end{cases}$

The difference operation $M_1 \setminus M_2$ generates a set of KMTS such that the CTL models represented by them are present in $K(M_1)$ but are not present in $K(M_2)$. As M_1 and M_2 are instances of M, i.e., they can be defined from changes over M then the models resulting from the difference can be defined from the set of changes that generate M_1 and M_2, i.e., X_1 and X_2, respectively. As a result, if X_1 and X_2 are not compatible the intersection between the models is empty and the difference is M_1. If they are compatible, then the models resulting from the difference are obtained from M by the set of changes X_1 (X_1 generates M_1 from M) together with the complementary primitive operations in X_2 which do not belong to X_1 ($X_1 \cup \{\neg p_i\}$) to eliminate the intersection between $K(M_1)$ and $K(M_2)$. For example, for the KMTS M_2 and M_3 illustrated in Fig. 2, $M_2 \setminus M_3$ generates a set containing only the top Kripke structure of the set $K(M_2)$. This model is defined by the set of changes $X' = \{P_1(s_0, s_2), P_2(s_0, s_1)\} \cup \{P_3(s_1, m)\}$ since $M_2 = M(\{P_1(s_0, s_2), P_2(s_0, s_1)\})$ and $M_3 = M(\{P_2(s_0, s_1), P_3(s_1, \neg m)\})$ and $P_3(s_1, \neg m)$ does not belong to X_1.

The intersection operation $M_1 \sqcap M_2$ generates a single set with a KMTS that only represents the CTL models in $K(M_1) \cap K(M_2)$. The union operation is simple and no further explanation is needed.

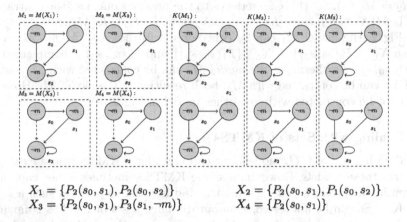

$$X_1 = \{P_2(s_0, s_1), P_2(s_0, s_2)\} \qquad X_2 = \{P_2(s_0, s_1), P_1(s_0, s_2)\}$$
$$X_3 = \{P_2(s_0, s_1), P_3(s_1, \neg m)\} \qquad X_4 = \{P_2(s_0, s_1)\}$$

Fig. 2. Instances M_1, M_2, M_3 and M_4 from the KMTS M illustrated in the Fig. 1 and the expansion sets $K(M_1), K(M_2)$ and $K(M_3)$.

Sometimes the set of Kripke structures represented by two KMTS can be represented by a single KMTS. For example, the expansion set of the KMTS M_4 in Fig. 2 is exactly the union of the expansion set of the KMTSs M_1 and M_2, i.e., $K(M_4) = K(M_1) \cup K(M_2)$, as a result $\{M_1, M_2\}$ can be expressed by a single KMTS, which is in this case M_4. In this sense, we define a contraction operation which is a specific kind of union for these cases. If two KMTSs cannot be contracted into a single one, then the contraction operation will be equivalent to the union operation.

Definition 13. *Let M be a KMTS, M_1 and M_2 instances of M generated, respectively, by the set of changes X_1 and X_2. The contraction operation, denoted by $M_1 \sqcup^+ M_2$, is defined as:*

$$M_1 \sqcup^+ M_2 = \begin{cases} \{M(X_1 \cap X_2)\} & \textit{iff } X_1 \subseteq X_2 \textit{ or } X_2 \subseteq X_1 \textit{ or} \\ & \exists p \in X_1 \textit{ s.t } \neg p \in X_2 \textit{ and} \\ & X_1 \setminus \{p\} = X_2 \setminus \{\neg p\} \\ \{M_1, M_2\} & \textit{otherwise} \end{cases}$$

In order to contract two models into a single one, it is necessary (but not enough) that both models have at most one complementary operation w.r.t each other, otherwise the contraction operation results in a set containing exactly the two input models. We explain the contraction operation through an example. Let us suppose KMTSs $M_1 = M(X_1)$ and $M_2 = M(X_2)$ such that $X_1 \subseteq X_2$. Thus, $X_1 \cap X_2 = X_1$ and $K(M_2) \subseteq K(M_1)$ which implies that the contraction results in M_1, i.e., $M_1 \sqcup^+ M_2 = M(X_1 \cap X_2) = M_1$. Consider now X_1 and X_2 such that X_1 has among all its operations only one operation p which is complementary with an operation $\neg p$ in X_2 and X_1 is equal to X_2 unless this operation. The operation p or $\neg p$ can be applied over M leading to the instances $M_1 = M(X_1)$ and $M_2 = M(X_2)$. So, this case reduces to the previous one, i.e., the contraction result is $M(X_1 \cap X_2)$ since $K(M(X_1 \cap X_2)) = K(M_1) \cup K(M_2)$.

In Fig. 2, the model M_1 can be contracted with M_2, i.e., $M_1 \sqcup^+ M_2 = M_4$ because $X_1 \setminus \{P_2(s_0, s_2)\} = X_2 \setminus \{P_1(s_0, s_2)\}$ and $P_1(s_0, s_2)$ is complementary with $P_2(s_0, s_2)$. Furthermore, the model M_1 can be contracted with M_4 and the model M_2 can be contracted with M_4, both resulting in the model M_4. However, M_3 cannot be contracted with any other model in Fig. 2.

4.1   Dealing with Sets of KMTSs

To deal with a set of CTL models, we can consider a KMTS whose expansion represents these models. However, a single KMTS sometimes is not capable of representing a specific set of CTL models and in order to perform such a task a set of KMTSs can be addressed. Computationally, a set of KMTSs is far more convenient because it is preferable to deal directly with a KMTS instead of its expansion set. In order to achieve our contraction model checking we define in this section a partition set and a full partition set over a set of KMTSs and we define some operations over them.

Let M be a KMTS and Γ a set of instances of M. It is always possible to construct a set Γ_p such that each element in it is an instance of M and the intersection of any two instances of Γ is always empty.

Definition 14. *Let M be a KMTS and Γ a set of instances of it. Γ is a Partition Set (PS) of M iff every model in Γ is an instance of M and $\forall M_1, M_2 \in \Gamma, M_1 \sqcap M_2 = \emptyset$.*

Definition 15. *Let Γ and Γ' be two set of instances of a KMTS M. Γ and Γ' are equivalent, denoting by $\Gamma \equiv \Gamma'$, iff $\bigcup_{M_i \in \Gamma} K(M_i) = \bigcup_{M_i \in \Gamma'} K(M_i)$.*

Definition 16. *Let Γ_1 and Γ_2 be two sets of instances of a KMTS. We define the difference $(\backslash\backslash)$, intersection $(\sqcap)$ and union $(\sqcup)$ operations as:*

$$\Gamma_1 \backslash\backslash \Gamma_2 = \bigcup_{\substack{M_i \in \Gamma_1, \\ M_k \in \Gamma_2}} M_i \setminus M_k \qquad \Gamma_1 \sqcap \Gamma_2 = \bigcup_{\substack{M_i \in \Gamma_1, \\ M_k \in \Gamma_2}} M_i \sqcap M_k$$

$$\Gamma_1 \sqcup \Gamma_2 = \Gamma_1 \cup PS(\Gamma_2 \backslash\backslash (\Gamma_1 \sqcap \Gamma_2))$$

where $PS(\Gamma)$ is a Partition Set equivalent to a set of instances Γ.

Let $K(\Gamma)$ be the set of all Kripke structures represented by every KMTS in Γ. The difference, intersection and union operation in Definition 16 calculates respectively the difference, intersection and union of the set with models sets represented by these KMTSs. In relation to the intersection operation defined over two KMTSs sets Γ_1 and Γ_2 it results in a set Γ' such that $K(\Gamma') = K(\Gamma_1) \cap K(\Gamma_2)$. The union and difference operations are interpreted similarly.

Proposition 3. *If Γ_1 and Γ_2 are two PS of a KMTS M, then $\Gamma_1 \sqcap \Gamma_2$ and $\Gamma_1 \sqcup \Gamma_2$ is a PS.*

Proof. It follows straight from the Definition 16.

Theorem 1. *For any set of instances Γ of a KMTS M there is always a PS Γ' such that $\Gamma \equiv \Gamma'$.*

Proof. Let M be a KMTS, Γ a set of instances of M and M_1 a M instance in Γ. Create the set $\Gamma_1 = \Gamma \backslash \{M_1\}$. Then, $\forall M_i \in \Gamma_1, M_i \sqcap M_1 = \emptyset$ by the difference operation and $\Gamma_1 \cup \{M_1\} \equiv \Gamma$. Choose an element $M_2 \in \Gamma_1$, then the set $\Gamma'_1 = \{M_1, M_2\}$ is a PS. Create now the set $\Gamma_2 = \Gamma_1 \backslash \{M_2\}$, then $\forall M_i \in \Gamma_2$, $M_i \sqcap M_2 = \emptyset$ and $M_i \sqcap M_1 = \emptyset$ and $\Gamma_2 \cup \{M_1, M_2\} \equiv \Gamma$. Choose an element M_3 in Γ_2, then $\{M_1, M_2, M_3\}$ is a PS and $\Gamma_3 \cup \{M_1, M_2, M_3\} \equiv \Gamma$. Following this construction we achieve at the end a PS equivalent to Γ.

If a PS of a KMTS M represents all the CTL models of K(M), then we say such a PS is a Full Partition Set.

Definition 17. *Let M be a KMTS and Γ a set of instances of it. We say Γ is a Full Partition Set (FPS) of M iff Γ is a PS and $K(M) = \bigcup_{M_i \in \Gamma} K(M_i)$.*

Corollary 1. *If Γ is a set of instances of a KMTS M and $K(M) = \bigcup_{M_i \in \Gamma} K(M_i)$, then there is a FPS Γ' such that $\Gamma \equiv \Gamma'$.*

Every KMTS M can be obtained from a finite number of contraction operations over a FPS of M. In order to prove it, we first define a Tree Partition Set and show how to represent a PS over this structure.

4.2 Tree Partition Set

A Tree Partition Set (TPS) is a binary tree that represents a partition set Γ from a KMTS M. Each node v of a TPS is labelled by a primitive change operation $L_T(v)$ applicable over M.

Definition 18. *A Tree Partition Set (TPS) of a KMTS M is a tuple $T_M = (N, v_0, E, L_T, Lf, Rg)$, where N is a finite set of nodes, $v_0 \in N$ is the root node, $E \subseteq N \times N$ is the set of edges, L_T is a partial labelling function that maps each node in N to a primitive operation applicable over M such that v_0 is the only node of a TPS that is not defined in L_T; and Lf, Rg are partial functions that map a node to its left and right child respectively. Furthermore, for every non-end node $v \in N$, there are nodes $v_1, v_2 \in N$ such that $Lf(v) = v_1$ and $Rg(v) = v_2$ iff $L_T(v_1) = p$ and $L_T(v_2) = \neg p$.*

Let $\pi = v_0 \rightarrow v_1 \rightarrow \cdots \rightarrow v_n$ be a path between the nodes v_0 and v_n in a TPS, we denote by $\pi \backslash v_0$ the subpath $v_1 \rightarrow \cdots \rightarrow v_n$ of π, and $v \in \pi$ to denote that a node v belongs to a path π. We highlight that each operation that labelled a vertex along a path v_0 to v_n follows from an indetermination of the KMTS.

Definition 19. *Let M a KMTS, $T_M = (N, v_0, E, L_T, Lf, Rg)$ a TPS. We define the operation $Change(v_n)$ that maps the single path $\pi = v_0 \rightarrow v_1 \rightarrow \cdots \rightarrow v_n$ between v_0 and any node $v_n \in T_M$ to a set of changes applicable over M as:*

$$Change(v_n) = \bigcup_{v_k \in \pi \setminus v_0} \{L_T(v_k)\}$$

A change from a node v as defined above considers all primitive changes that occur along the single path from the root to v excluding the root node.

The $Change(v)$ of any node in a TPS T_M when applied over a KMTS M generates an instance of it and we say a node represents an instance of M. The set of instances represented by every end-node of a TPS is a PS.

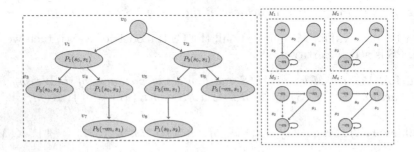

Fig. 3. A Tree Partition Set that represents the PS $\{M_1, M_2, M_3, M_4\}$.

The Fig. 3 illustrates a PS Γ from the KMTS M presented in Fig. 1 and a TPS T_M that represents Γ. M_1, M_2, M_3 and M_4 are generated from changes of TPS end-nodes, i.e., by the application of $Change(v_3), Change(v_7), Change(v_6)$ and $Change(v_8)$ over M, respectively.

Lemma 1. *Let Γ be a PS w.r.t a KMTS M represented by TPS T_M and M' an instance of M. If $\Gamma \cup \{M'\}$ results in a PS, then there is a PS Γ' equivalent to it that can be also represented by a TPS.*

Proof. From the contraction operation we have that for any set of change X and primitive operation p, $M(X \cup \{p\} \sqcup^+ M(X \cup \{\neg p\}) = M(X)$ (I). Create a TPS T'_M equal to T_M. If M' is an instance of M then it is generated from a set X' of changes, i.e., $M' = M(X')$. Select in T'_M the following subpath $\pi = v_0 \rightarrow \cdots \rightarrow v_i$ in such a way $Change(v_i) \subset X'$ and v_i has only one child v_{i+1} such that $L_T(v_{i+1}) \notin X'$ or v_i has two children where $L_T(Lf(v_i)) \notin X'$ and $L_T(Rg(v_i)) \notin X'$.

Case 1. *v_i has only one child v_{i+1} and $L_T(v_{i+1}) \notin X'$. Then there are two cases: $\neg L_T(v_{i+1}) \in X'$ or $\neg L_T(v_{i+1}) \notin X'$.*

(a) $\neg L_T(v_{i+1}) \in X'$. Create a node v_{i+2} to be the other child of v_i and add to T'_M the following path $\pi_1 = v_0 \rightarrow \cdots \rightarrow v_i \rightarrow v_{i+2} \rightarrow \cdots \rightarrow v'$ such that $Change(v')$

$= X'$ and $L_T(v_{i+2}) = \neg L_T(v_{i+1})$. Thus, the resulting T'_M represents the PS $\Gamma' = \Gamma \cup \{M'\}$.

(b) $\neg L_T(v_{i+1}) \notin X'$. Let $X_i = Change(v_i)$, then $X_i \subset X'$ and $X' = X_i \cup (X' \setminus X_i)$. Let $M'_1 = M(X' \cup \{p\})$ and $M'_2 = M(X' \cup \{\neg p\})$, where $p = L_T(v_{i+1})$. From (I) we have $M' = M(X') = M(X' \cup \{p\}) \sqcup^+ M(X' \cup \{\neg p\})$ which means $M' = M'_1 \sqcup^+ M'_2$. Thus, the set $\Gamma' = \Gamma \cup \{M'_1, M'_2\}$ and it is equivalent to $\Gamma \cup \{M'\}$ and by hypothesis it is a PS. So, if we represent M'_1 and M'_2 in T'_M then we achieve a representation of M' in T'_M. To do so, create a node v_{i+2} to be the other child of v_i and add to T'_M the path $\pi_1 = v_0 \rightarrow \ldots v_i \rightarrow v_{i+2} \rightarrow \cdots \rightarrow v'$ such that $L_T(v_{i+2}) = \neg L_T(v_{i+1})$ and $Change(v') = X' \cup \{L_T(v_{i+2})\}$. Thus T'_M represents M'_2. Let $X'_1 = X' \cup \{L_T(v_{i+1})\}$, in order to represent M'_1, we must create a path $\pi_2 = v_0 \rightarrow \cdots \rightarrow v_i \rightarrow v_{i+1} \rightarrow \cdots \rightarrow v'$ such that $Change(v') = X'_1$. To achieve this select in T'_M a subpath $\pi'_2 = v_0 \rightarrow \cdots \rightarrow v_i \rightarrow v_{i+1} \rightarrow \cdots \rightarrow v_k$ in such a way $Change(v_k) \subset X'_1$ and or v_k has only one child v_{k+1} such that $L_T(v_{k+1}) \notin X'_1$ or v_k has two children where $L_T(Lf(v_k)) \notin X'_1$ and $L_T(Rg(v_k)) \notin X'_1$. This reduces to the cases (1) and (2).

Case 2. v_i has two children where $L_T(Lf(v_i)) \notin X'$ and $L_T(Rg(v_i)) \notin X'$. Let $X_i = Change(v_i)$, then $X_i \subset X'$ and $X' = X_i \cup (X' \setminus X_i)$. Let $M'_1 = M(X' \cup \{p\})$ and $M'_2 = M(X' \cup \{\neg p\})$, where $p = L_T(Lf(v_1))$. From (I) we have $M' = M(X') = M(X' \cup \{p\}) \sqcup^+ M(X' \cup \{\neg p\})$ which means $M' = M'_1 \sqcup^+ M'_2$. Thus, the set $\Gamma' = \Gamma \cup \{M'_1, M'_2\}$ is is equivalent to $\Gamma \cup \{M'\}$ and by hypothesis it is a PS. So, we must represent in T'_M the instances M'_1 and M'_2. Let $X'_1 = X' \cup \{L_T(Lf(v_i))\}$ and $X'_2 = X' \cup \{L_T(Rg(v_i))\}$, in order to represent M'_1 we must create a path $\pi_1 = v_0 \rightarrow \cdots \rightarrow v_i \rightarrow Lf(v_i) \rightarrow \cdots \rightarrow v_j$ where $Change(v_j) = X'_1$. Select in T'_M a subpath $\pi'_1 = v_0 \rightarrow \cdots \rightarrow v_i \rightarrow Lf(v_i) \rightarrow \cdots \rightarrow v_k$ in such a way $Change(v_k) \subset X'_1$ and or v_k has only one child v_{k+1} wherein $L_T(v_{k+1}) \notin X'_1$, or v_k has two children where $L_T(Lf(v_k)) \notin X'_1$ and $L_T(Rg(v_k)) \notin X'_1$. This reduces to the cases (1) and (2). To represent M_2 we proceed similary as we have done to M_1. Since a path in a TPS is finite, eventually the cases $1 - (b)$ and 2 will lead to the case $1 - (a)$ and then the TPS T'_M represents the resulting PS Γ'.

From Lemma 1, we prove that for every PS Γ there is always a PS Γ' equivalent to Γ that is represented by a TPS.

Theorem 2. *If Γ is a PS w.r.t a KMTS M, then there is always a PS Γ' equivalent to Γ which can represented by a TPS T_M.*

Proof. Let $\Gamma = \{M_1, \ldots, M_n\}$, each $\{M_i\}$ is also a PS by definition. From Lemma 1, there is a PS $\Gamma_2 \equiv \{M_1\} \cup \{M_2\}$ which can be represented by a TPS. In addition, a PS Γ_3 equivalent to $\Gamma_2 \cup \{M_3\}$ can also be generated and can be represented by a TPS as well. Sucessively, a PS $\Gamma_n \equiv \Gamma_{n-1} \cup \{M_n\}$ that can be represented by a TPS can be generated which is equivalent to $\{M_1, \ldots, M_n\} = \Gamma$.

Theorem 3. *Let M be a KMTS and $T_M = (N, v_0, E, L_T, Lf, Rg)$ a TPS that represents a PS Γ defined from M. If Γ is a FPS then for every non-end node $v_k \in N$ and $X_k = Change(v_k)$ $M_k = M(X_k)$ can be generated from a finite number of contraction operations in Γ.*

Proof. The proof is by induction on the structure of T_M. Let $\pi_k = v_0 \to \cdots \to v_k$ be a path in T_m. If M has m indefinites, then $1 \leq k \leq m$.

Base case: *let* $\pi_k = v_0 \to \cdots \to v_{k-1} \to v_k$ *be a longest path of* T_M. *Then,* v_k *is an end-node. As* π_k *is one of the longest path and* Γ *is a FPS, then the path* $\pi'_k = v_0 \to \cdots \to v_{k-1} \to v'_k$ *belongs to* T_M, *where* $L_T(v_k) = \neg L_T(v'_k)$. *Let* $p = L_T(v_k)$, $X_{k-1} = Change(v_{k-1})$. $Change(v_k) = X_{k-1} \cup \{p\}$ *and* $Change(v'_k) = X_{k-1} \cup \{\neg p\}$. *So we have* $M(X_{k-1}) = M(X_{k-1} \cup \{p\}) \sqcup^+ M(X_{k-1} \cup \{\neg p\})$. *Therefore,* $M(X_{k-1})$ *is obtained by one contraction operation in* Γ.

Induction Step: *let us suppose any* $M(X_k)$ *can be generated by a finite number of contraction operations. We show that* $\forall k - 1$, $M(X_{k-1})$ *can be generated by a finite number of contraction operations as well. The path* $\pi_{k-1} = v_0 \to \cdots \to v_{k-1}$ *has two children* v_k *and* v'_k *where* $L_T(v_K) = \neg L_T(v'_k)$, *due to the fact* Γ *is a FPS. Let* $p = L_T(v_k)$, $X_{k-1} = Change(v_{k-1})$, $X_k = Change(v_k)$ *and* $X'_k = Change(v'_k)$. *Then,* $X_k = X_{k-1} \cup \{p\}$ *and* $X'_k = X_{k-1} \cup \{\neg p\}$. *So,* $M(X_{k-1}) = M(X_k) \sqcup^+ M(X'_k)$. *By the induction hypothesis* $M(X_k)$ *and* $M(X'_k)$ *can be obtained by a finite number of contraction operations and so is* $M(X_{k-1})$.

Theorem 3 implies in the Corollary 2 which guarantees that if we have a FPS of M then it is always possible to produce M from a set of contractions operations over this FPS. The contraction model checking algorithm uses contractions operations over partitions sets and when a full partition set is achieved it means that all Kripke models satisfy the property been verified and consequently M represents the truth values $\top$. The other truth values are represented by PS that is not a FPS and in this case if the PS is not empty then it represents the truth values $\perp$ and if is empty it represents the truth values F.

Corollary 2. *Let M be a KMTS and* Γ *a PS of it. If* Γ *is a FPS then M can be generated from a finite number of contraction operations in* Γ.

Let Γ be a PS and Γ' a PS resulting from a finite number of contraction operations over Γ, we say Γ' is a Maximal Partition Set (MPS) if there is no more contraction applicable over Γ. Therefore, according to Corollary 2 if a PS is in fact a FPS then its MPS is exactly the single set that contains M. We write $\sqcup^+(\Gamma)$ to denote the MPS resulting from Γ.

5   The Contraction Model Checking

Some works such as [5,11] propose model checking game approaches, which consist of a game played over a board by two players: $\exists$ve and $\forall$belard. The former tries to prove that the CTL specification holds, whereas the latter tries to refute the specification. In order to decide the winner of the game (respectively the model checking result), a colouring algorithm that maps each configuration of the game board to one truth value is defined. The colour set for the initial configuration of the board is the model checking result. A model checking game combined with the contraction operation applied in each configuration of the game suffices to determine the model checking result to a KMTS interpreted as a set of CTL models. We call this new approach Contraction Model Checking.

Let M be a KMTS, s_0 a state of it and φ a CTL formula. The model checking game for $M, s_0 \models \varphi$ is played over a board (game-graph) constructed according to the game rules that define the possible moves each player can make in a configuration it owns. A board is a graph of configurations constructed by decomposing φ in its subformulas following the game rules presented in Fig. 4. Every configuration of a game-graph belongs to $S \times sub(\varphi)$, where S is the set of M states and $sub(\varphi)$ is the set of subformulas of φ. We denote a configuration by $s \vdash \psi$, where ψ is a subformula of φ and s is a state of M.

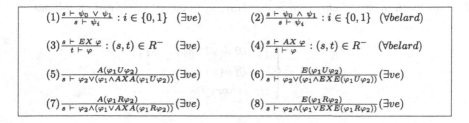

$$(1)\frac{s \vdash \psi_0 \vee \psi_1}{s \vdash \psi_i} : i \in \{0,1\} \quad (\exists ve) \qquad (2)\frac{s \vdash \psi_0 \wedge \psi_1}{s \vdash \psi_i} : i \in \{0,1\} \quad (\forall belard)$$

$$(3)\frac{s \vdash EX \varphi}{t \vdash \varphi} : (s,t) \in R^- \quad (\exists ve) \qquad (4)\frac{s \vdash AX \varphi}{t \vdash \varphi} : (s,t) \in R^- \quad (\forall belard)$$

$$(5)\frac{A(\varphi_1 U \varphi_2)}{s \vdash \varphi_2 \vee (\varphi_1 \wedge AX A(\varphi_1 U \varphi_2))}(\exists ve) \qquad (6)\frac{E(\varphi_1 U \varphi_2)}{s \vdash \varphi_2 \vee (\varphi_1 \wedge EX E(\varphi_1 U \varphi_2))}(\exists ve)$$

$$(7)\frac{A(\varphi_1 R \varphi_2)}{s \vdash \varphi_2 \wedge (\varphi_1 \vee AX A(\varphi_1 R \varphi_2))}(\exists ve) \qquad (8)\frac{E(\varphi_1 R \varphi_2)}{s \vdash \varphi_2 \wedge (\varphi_1 \vee EX E(\varphi_1 R \varphi_2))}(\exists ve)$$

Fig. 4. Game rules for the Model Checking Game

Let G be the game-graph for a KMTS M and CTL formula φ. The contraction model checking is a colouring function $\chi : V \to \{\top, F, \bot\}$, where V is the set of vertices of G, that maps each configuration in G to one truth value. We can observe that the final truth value is calculated from sets of KMTS models that represents truth values in the model checking process. The colouring function is defined over a maximal contraction function δ that maps each configuration of the game-graph to a maximal PS Γ. The expansion of the KMTSs in this PS is exactly the set of Kripke structures that satisfy the formula in the respectively state. As the resulting PS Γ is a MPS, $\Gamma = \{M\}$ iff M satisfies φ in the respectively input configuration, $\Gamma = \emptyset$ if no CTL model in $K(M)$ satisfies φ, and Γ is a PS different from $\{M\}$ and $\emptyset$ otherwise.

Definition 20. *Let M be a KMTS, s and s' states of M, φ a CTL formula and G the board of the game for the model checking $M, s_0 \models \varphi$. The maximal contraction function δ is defined recursively as:*

$$\delta(s \vdash l) = \begin{cases} \{M\} & \text{iff } l \in L(s); \\ \emptyset & \text{iff } \neg l \in L(s); \\ \{M(\{P_3(s,l)\})\} & \text{otherwise} \end{cases}$$

$$\delta(s \vdash EX \varphi) = \sqcup^+ \left(\bigsqcup_{s' \in \vec{S}(s)} \delta(s' \vdash \varphi) \sqcap \{M(\{P_2(s,s')\})\} \right)$$

$$\delta(s \vdash AX\ \varphi) = \sqcup^+ \left(\underset{s' \in \vec{S}(s)}{\boxed{\cdot}}\ \delta(s' \vdash \varphi) \sqcup \{M(\{P_1(s, s')\})\} \right)$$

$$\delta(\varphi_1 \vee \varphi_2) = \sqcup^+ \left(\delta(s \vdash \varphi_1) \sqcup \delta(s \vdash \varphi_2)\right)$$

$$\delta(\varphi_1 \wedge \varphi_2) = \sqcup^+ \left(\delta(s \vdash \varphi_1) \sqcap \delta(s \vdash \varphi_2)\right)$$

The configurations that follow from the rules (5) up to (8) have only one child configuration, thus the value of the function δ in these configurations are equivalent to the value defined in their single child. Hence, if $s \vdash \varphi$ is a configuration defined from one of the rules between (5) and (8) and $s \vdash \psi$ is the single configuration reached from it, then $\delta(s \vdash \varphi) = \delta(s \vdash \psi)$.

Definition 21. *Let M be a KMTS, s and s' states of M, and φ a CTL formula. The contraction model checking is a colouring function χ defined as follows:*

$$\chi(s \vdash \varphi) = \begin{cases} \top & \textit{iff } \delta(s \vdash \varphi) = \{M\} \\ F & \textit{iff } \delta(s \vdash \varphi) = \emptyset \\ \bot & \textit{otherwise} \end{cases}$$

6   Conclusions

In this work we developed a model checking game approach for model checking a KMTS interpreted as a set of CTL models. The works [5,11] interpret a KMTS as an abstraction of a concrete model to deal with the explosion state problem in CTL and μ-calculus model checking and define a 3-valued model checking which we take as reference for our contraction model checking. The works [1,2] also address the abstraction problem through partial Kripke structures which has indeterminations only in their states. The work reported in [12] considers the abstraction approach to deal with partial system specification through partial Kripke structures w.r.t Linear Tree Logic. In [8] the authors extend this structure with transitions that represent possibilities defining the KMTS structures. In [4,7] the authors consider MTS (Modal Transitions Systems) to deal with the abstraction approach. In these works a Kleene 3-valued logic or an equivalent interpretation is applied, while for the KMTS interpretation as a set of CTL models it does not hold. Moreover, none of these approaches interprets a KMTS as a set of CTL models and to the best of our knowledge no other work considers this interpretation.

We argue that in order to verify a set of Kripke structures, model checking a KMTS that represents this set is on average better than model checking each CTL model at a time in the set. Since the determinations of a KMTS M are present in all the CTL models M represents, we can determine the truth value of some property common to all CTL models at once over M and we agree it can lead to a polynomial algorithm on average case. However, in the worst case since a KMTS represents an exponential set of CTL models, model checking a KMTS as a set of Kripke structures is NP-complete as we have already proven. Despite this, the presentation of this proof is beyond the scope of this work. We are investigating polynomial algorithms on average case and we intend to conclude this investigation providing efficient algorithms for model checking a KMTS as a set of CTL models in the future.

References

1. Bruns, G., Godefroid, P.: Model checking partial state spaces with 3-valued temporal logics. In: Halbwachs, N., Peled, D.A. (eds.) CAV 1999. LNCS, vol. 1633, pp. 274–287. Springer, Heidelberg (1999)
2. Bruns, G., Godefroid, P.: Generalized model checking: reasoning about partial state spaces. In: Palamidessi, C. (ed.) CONCUR 2000. LNCS, vol. 1877, pp. 168–182. Springer, Heidelberg (2000)
3. Clarke, E.M., Grumberg, O., Peled, D.A.: Model Checking. MIT press, Cambridge (1999)
4. Godefroid, P., Huth, M., Jagadeesan, R.: Abstraction-based model checking using modal transition systems. In: Larsen, K.G., Nielsen, M. (eds.) CONCUR 2001. LNCS, vol. 2154, pp. 426–440. Springer, Heidelberg (2001)
5. Grumberg, O., Lange, M., Leucker, M., Shoham, S.: When not losing is better than winning: Abstraction and refinement for the full μ-calculus. Inf. Comput. **205**(8), 1130–1148 (2007)
6. Guerra, P.T., Andrade, A., Wassermann, R.: Toward the revision of CTL models through Kripke modal transition systems. In: Iyoda, J., de Moura, L. (eds.) SBMF 2013. LNCS, vol. 8195, pp. 115–130. Springer, Heidelberg (2013)
7. Huth, M.: Model checking modal transition systems using Kripke structures. In: Cortesi, A. (ed.) VMCAI 2002. LNCS, vol. 2294, pp. 302–316. Springer, Heidelberg (2002)
8. Huth, M., Jagadeesan, R., Schmidt, D.A.: Modal transition systems: a foundation for three-valued program analysis. In: Sands, D. (ed.) ESOP 2001. LNCS, vol. 2028, pp. 155–169. Springer, Heidelberg (2001)
9. Huth, M., Ryan, M.: Logic in Computer Science: Modelling and Reasoning About Systems. Cambridge University Press, Cambridge (2004)
10. Kleene, S.C., de Bruijn, N., de Groot, J., Zaanen, A.C.: Introduction to Metamathematics. Van Nostrand, New York (1952)
11. Shoham, S., Grumberg, O.: A game-based framework for CTL counterexamples and 3-valued abstraction-refinement. ACM Trans. Comput. Logic **9**(1), 1 (2007)
12. Wehrheim, H.: Bounded model checking for partial Kripke structures. In: Fitzgerald, J.S., Haxthausen, A.E., Yenigun, H. (eds.) ICTAC 2008. LNCS, vol. 5160, pp. 380–394. Springer, Heidelberg (2008)

Supporting Requirements Analysis Using Pattern-Based Formal Specification Construction

Shaoying Liu[1]([✉]), Xi Wang[2], and Weikai Miao[3]

[1] Department of Computer Science, Hosei University, Tokyo, Japan
sliu@hosei.ac.jp
[2] School of Computer Engineering and Science, Shanghai University, Shanghai, China
[3] SKLTC, East China Normal University, Shanghai, China

Abstract. Requirements analysis for understanding the user's requirements and producing a specification is an important but challenging activity in software development. In this paper, we discuss how the activity can be strengthened by means of pattern-based formal specification construction. We explain the concept of specification pattern and describe how patterns are treated as knowledge stored on computer to guide the user in carrying out the analysis of a functional requirement. Our approach is characterized by the fact that the user only needs to work on natural language level while the computer will automatically select appropriate specification patterns to provide clear instructions on the action to be taken by the user and to eventually form a formal specification or expression as a result. We present a software tool and an experiment to demonstrate the supportability and applicability of our approach, respectively.

1 Introduction

Requirements analysis is an extremely important activity in software engineering, but carrying out a quality requirements analysis in practice is usually not easy [1,2]. Formal methods have been considered as a potential technique for requirements analysis through writing formal specifications [3]. A formal specification is a precise document describing what to be done by the system, but to make it a cost-effective technique for industry, practitioners are required to have sufficient skills for writing formal specifications. Unfortunately, this still remains a challenge in reality [4]. Our experience in collaborations with industry in Japan suggests that one of the major reasons for this situation be the lack of techniques that can effectively support the requirements analysis for accurate understanding through writing formal specifications. Only telling the practitioners a formal notation does not really address the problem; we must tell them how writing a formal specification using the notation can help them understand existing requirements, identify new but necessary requirements, and express the requirements precisely. Providing efficient support for these activities with software tools is also essential for success.

© Springer International Publishing Switzerland 2015
M. Butler et al. (Eds.): ICFEM 2015, LNCS 9407, pp. 100–115, 2015.
DOI: 10.1007/978-3-319-25423-4_7

In this paper, we make a contribution by describing a new technique for requirements analysis through writing formal specifications based on well-defined specification patterns. We call the technique *Pattern-Based Formal Specification for Requirements Analysis* (PBFSRA). The essential idea is that necessary specification patterns are defined and stored on computer beforehand as knowledge, where a specification pattern is an expression that tells how a certain requirement can be translated into a formal expression or specification. Appropriate patterns are then selected by the computer based on the analyst's requests for expressing functional requirements to provide guidance to the analyst for taking further actions in clarifying the requirements. Such interactions continue until every part of the requirement is clarified. As a result, a formal specification or expression of the requirement will be constructed. The very distinct characteristic of this technique is that the analyst only needs to work on the natural language level while the computer understands the analyst's requests to automatically select appropriate specification patterns from the knowledge base to offer clear instructions to the analyst for further actions in analyzing the current level requirement.

The rest of the paper is organized as follows. Section 2 describes the major ideas of the proposed technique. Section 3 presents the definition of specification pattern and pattern system. Section 4 discusses pattern knowledge representation. Section 5 shows an example deriving a formal expression using our approach. Section 6 introduces a tool supporting the proposed technique. Section 7 reports an experiment for evaluation of the performance of the technique. Section 8 gives a brief review of related work. Finally, in Sect. 9, we conclude the paper and point out future research directions.

2   Major Ideas of PBFSRA

In this section, we explain the principle of our approach, and then illustrate the procedure of applying the principle. An assumption for our approach to work in practice is that the analyst understands the formal notation but may not be good at using it to write formal specifications.

2.1   Principle of PBFSRA

Let us use a simple example to explain the underlying principle of PBFSRA. Suppose there is a user's requirement for an Automated Teller Machine (ATM) to describe a relation between two objects as follows:

Input password must be registered in the bank account file.

Such an informal requirement can be written as part of an operation specification in natural language, or can merely be a perception in the client's mind.

To clarify this requirement, the analyst will be guided by the tool we have built (see Sect. 6) to select an appropriate *specification pattern* (see Sect. 3 for definition). By consulting with the client, the analyst confirms that the requirement can be represented by a relation describing that one object is part of another object and tells this information to computer. Since a well-defined "part_whole" pattern is suitable for analyzing such a requirement, the pattern is applied by the computer. This will result in the request for the analyst to clarify what the *input password* and *bank account file* mean. By answering these questions, the analyst will have to analyze the current requirement, possibly by means of consulting with the client. As a result, the analyst may understand that the *input password* is a four-digit natural number and the *bank account file* is a collection of customer bank accounts each of which contains a pre-registered password. After the computer receives these pieces of information in an appropriate manner, another specification pattern will be applied to help clarify the structure of the *bank account file* as an unordered collection of composite objects or as an ordered collection of composite objects. The former can be formalized into a set of objects while the latter can be formalized into a sequence of objects. Continuing this decomposition process by applying appropriate specification patterns, the functional details of the requirement will be clarified and a formal specification or expression will be automatically derived, see Sect. 5 for more details. During the whole process, the analyst only needs to work on the natural language level while the computer works on the specification pattern level to gradually formalize the informal requirements.

2.2   Procedure of Applying PBFSRA

To realize the principle of PBFSRA above, we must deal with several technical issues, such as the informal requirements derivation from the client, clarification of the functional details involved in the requirement, and searching and applying appropriate specification patterns to provide guidance to the analyst and construct the formal expression or specification. Figure 1 depicts the procedure of carrying out requirements analysis and constructing a formal specification using PBFSRA. Basically, the procedure is divided into two stages. The first stage called *Requirements derivation* is for clarifying the informal requirements in the analyst's mind through gradually defining the attributes of the related functions and data types, while the second stage called *Requirements translation* is responsible for automatically translating the clarified requirement into a formal specification. Both stages are performed through interactions between the analyst and computer where computer produces guidance and the analyst responds with necessary inputs for the computer. The response will trigger the computer to produce new guidance for the analyst to take next action in analysis and formalization. Such a process repeats until a formal specification is achieved.

The foundation for the human-machine interaction process is a *specification pattern system* stored on computer. The *specification pattern system* organizes a set of *specification patterns* in a hierarchical structure (see Sect. 3.2 for details) where each pattern carries two kinds of knowledge for formalizing one kind of function: *derivation knowledge* and *transformation knowledge*. The former supports requirements derivation and the latter deals with requirements translation. We adopt *attribute tree* and *hierarchical finite state machine* (HFSM) to represent the above pattern knowledge on computer. The attribute tree is used

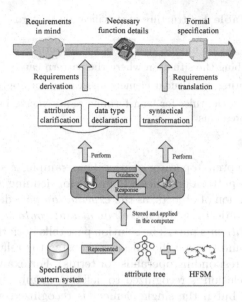

Fig. 1. The procedure of PBFSRA

in *derivation knowledge* to intuitively show the definition of the requirement attributes that need to be clarified, which facilitates the analyst's understanding on the structure of the intended requirements. HFSM is used to describe other parts of the *derivation knowledge* and all *transformation knowledge* since it is easy to be applied by machine and maintained using existing tools. From the next section, we will describe the details of the most important parts of the PBFSRA technique.

3   Specification Pattern and System

Since the essential concept for the technique is specification pattern and the specification pattern system, we introduce them first in this section and then proceed to discuss knowledge representation and application for supporting the two stages mentioned above in the subsequent sections.

3.1   Specification Pattern

Taking the similar idea from the design pattern [5], a specification pattern shows how a required function can be shaped into a formal expression. Informally, a specification pattern is composed of four elements: *name, explanation, constituents*, and *solution*, and their role is explained briefly in Table 1.

Table 2 shows a simplified example of the pattern named "**part_whole**" in which all of the formal expressions are written in SOFL (similar to VDM-SL but most of the operators defined in various data types, such as set, sequence, and

Table 1. Structure of specification pattern

name	Serving as an unique identity of the pattern
explanation	Describing the situation where the pattern can be used
constituents	Presenting constituent elements necessary for applying the pattern
solution	Defining the rules for transforming requirements into formal expressions

map types, adopt the prefix-operator syntax. For example, x *subset* y is written as *subset*(x, y). This pattern provides a template for defining a relation between an object and a collection of objects, as the *explanation* part describes. To define such a relation, two objects, which are *element* and *container*, are needed, as indicated in the *constituents* part. The solution part tells both the general rule for forming the relation and the specific rules for choosing the relational operator ⊛ depending on the corresponding operands (or terms). For example, the operator can be *inset* if the relation is recognized to define a membership of an element in a set of elements, but if the single element is recognized as a subset of the *container*, then the operator can be *subset* to define that one set is a subset of another set.

In general, a specification pattern can be designed to facilitate the construction of the whole structure of a specification, the structure of a single operation, data declarations (including type and variable declarations), or a formal expression, depending on how the four elements of the pattern are defined. For the sake of space, we only concentrate on the issue of formalizing a requirement into a formal expression in this paper. The other issues, which are much simpler than this one, can be addressed similarly.

3.2   Specification Pattern System

In general, a large number of specification patterns need to be designed and stored on computer in order to deal with various functional requirements analysis. How to organize the patterns to facilitate search and application of appropriate patterns therefore becomes an important problem to tackle. In the PBFSRA technique, we divide patterns into distinct categories on the basis of the functions they deal with and organize them in a hierarchical structure in a pattern system. Figure 2 shows the hierarchy where rightmost items represent patterns and others represent categories. The root "Pattern system" owns two sub-items, which indicates that patterns are divided into two categories: one for describing unit functions denoted by UF and the other for depicting compound functions denoted by CF. Their sub-categories are further classified into more specific sub-categories or patterns. Category CF includes the concrete patterns for formalizing compound functions that can be expressed, for example, using the binary choice *if-then-else* or the multiple choice *case* expression. Our studies on many specifications constructed in practice suggest that all the functions used in software systems can be represented by properly combining the three kinds of basic

Table 2. Example of specification pattern

name	**part_whole**
explanation	Relation describing that an object is part of another object
constituents	Three objects are necessary:
	element: the object representing the part
	container: the object representing the whole
	specifier: specific area that the *element* stays in *container*
solution	General rule: *element* ⊛ *container* ∗ *specifier* → *boolean*
	specific rules for choosing operators ⊛ and ∗ depending on
	the type of *element* and *container* and the value of *specifier*:
	(1) $(T, set\ of\ T) \rightarrow$ "*element inset container*"
	(2) $(T, set\ of\ composed\ of\ f_1: T_1, ..., f_n: T_n\ end,$
	$specifier = f) \rightarrow$ "*element = container.f*"
	(3) $(set\ of\ T, set\ of\ T) \rightarrow$ "*subset(element, container)*"
	(4) $(T, set\ of\ T') \rightarrow$ "*exists[v : container]*	
	$part\_whole(element, v)$" where v is a variable in *container*
	and the type of v is T'
	...

functions: *comparison between objects, retrieval of information,* and *update of existing data.* For this reason, we divide category *UF* into three sub-categories: *Relation* patterns, *Retrieval* patterns, and *Recreation* patterns.

Relation patterns can be used to formalize relations between objects, such as greater than (>), less than (<), equality (=), and membership of an object in a set. Retrieval patterns are designed for generating formal expressions that show the meaning of obtaining data items from a compound data structure (e.g., a set, sequence, or map). Recreation patterns offer solutions to formally expressing changes on some data structures (e.g., fields of a composite object, one element of a set or sequence). Currently, there are forty one patterns included in our specification pattern system in which thirty-one patterns belong to category *UF* and ten patterns are classified into category *CF*. It seems difficult to assert the completeness of the pattern system in terms of its capability of expressing all the possible functions in software systems at large, but all of the patterns in the pattern system are designed to cove all of the operators defined on all of the data types available in SOFL. Thus, as long as a function can be expressed in SOFL, there will be sufficient patterns to be used for its formalization.

4   Representation of Pattern Knowledge

The support for PBFSRA requires specification patterns to be stored on computer as knowledge. This raises a question on the notation to be used for knowledge

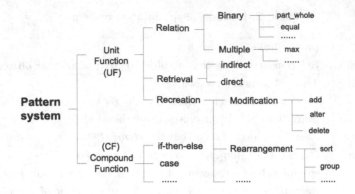

Fig. 2. Pattern system

representation. In our technique, two notations are adopted for representing different aspects of the knowledge. One is called *attribute tree* and the other is known as *Hierarchical Finite State Machine* (*HFSM*). The attribute tree describes the knowledge that needs to be displayed to the analyst during the human-machine interaction, and HFSM represents the knowledge that will be applied by computer to provide guidance to the analyst.

4.1   Attribute Tree

As Fig. 3 shows, an attribute tree provides a visualized view to represent element definitions for a specification pattern. The analyst can relatively easily understand what needs to be provided to the computer based on the tree for analyzing and formalizing elements of the pattern. The root node F of the tree tells that the pattern is used to guide the clarification of the requirement on function F. Its child nodes $e_1, e_2, \ldots$ denote the requirement elements for composing the pattern. Each label $attr_i$ reveals that the element e_i is defined to represent attribute $attr_i$ of F. For each node e_i, its child nodes $d_{i1}, d_{i2}, \ldots$ indicate different ways for clarifying the corresponding element.

An example of the attribute tree for the pattern **part_whole** mentioned previously is given in Fig. 4. The child nodes of the root node indicate that the corresponding three elements (i.e., *element*, *container*, and *specifier*) need to be clarified when applying the pattern. The child nodes of these three elements indicate different ways for clarifying the corresponding elements. For example, nodes d_3 and d_4 indicate two ways for clarifying the element *container*. Specifically, d_3 means to assign the element with a declared variable and d_4 means to assign the element with a formal expression composed of declared variables and operators. The analyst needs to choose one of these child nodes according to the specific requirement. Such a graphical structure facilitates the understanding of the involved functional details to be clarified.

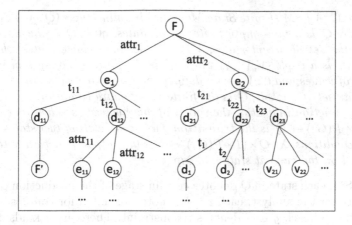

Fig. 3. The structure of attribute tree

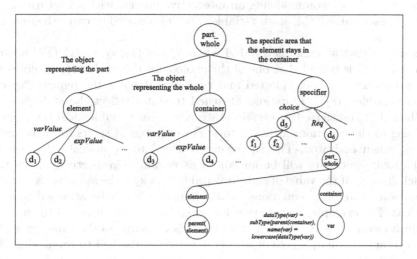

Fig. 4. The attribute tree of the pattern **part_whole**

4.2   HFSM

Apart from the knowledge that is visible to the analyst, a large part of the
pattern knowledge is designed to be applied by computer. Once a pattern is
selected, the application of the pattern will usually take a series of steps to complete. During the steps, necessary guidances need to be produced for the analyst
to take appropriate actions according to the analyst's decision on how the current requirement statement needs to be refined. To realize this mechanism, the
application process of patterns must be represented in the knowledge base. We
adopt an extended finite state machine called HFSM to represent such knowledge, which is formally defined below. Since HFSM is a hierarchical FSM, we
first define the FSM adopted in our approach.

Definition 1. *A FSM (Finite State Machine) is a nine-tuple $(Q, q0, F, VP, I, G,$ $\varphi, \delta, \lambda)$ where Q is a non-empty finite set of states, $q0 \in Q$ is the initial state, $F \subset Q$ is the set of accept states, VP is a set of variable states where each variable state is a triple (V, V', θ) where V is the finite set of system variables, V' is a set of values and $\theta : V \to V'$ defines the associated value for each $v \in V$, I is the finite set of symbols, G is the finite set of guard conditions, $\varphi : Q \to VP$ is the state function indicating the values of the involved variables on each state, $\delta : Q \times (I \times \mathcal{P}(G)) \to Q$ is the transition function relating two states by input and guard conditions, $\lambda : Q \times (I \times \mathcal{P}(G)) \to I$ is the output function determining output based on the current state and input.*

In an FSM, each state in Q denotes certain stage of the production process of the guidance for the analyst, each $i \in I$ denotes a symbol for composing inputs and outputs, and each $g \in G$ denotes a constraint. There are 2 kinds of FSMs: *value FSM* and *process FSM*. The former returns a value when terminated while the latter emphasizes on modeling an interactive process without returning any value. For each value FSM, state variable *return* is created to carry the returned value.

Figure 5 shows an example FSM A where $Q_A = \{s_1, s_2, s_3, s_4\}$ (ΣC denotes that each $c \in C$ is provided as one of the choices for the analyst, $\&c$ denotes the fact that item c has been selected and $req(var_2)$ denotes the request "specify system variable var_2"). Equations attached to states reflect the *state function* φ. When A is transferred to certain state s, system variables will be assigned according to the equations attached to s. For example, A starts from the initial state s_1 when activated. The equations attached to s_1 indicate that system variables var_1 and var_2 will be initialized as v_1 and v_2 respectively. Note that for each state s_i, if the value of certain variable v on s_i is the same as its value on the previous state of s_i, equations for assigning v will not be attached to s_i for simplicity. For example, no equation for assigning var_2 is attached to the state s_2, which means that the value of var_2 on s_2 is the same as the value on s_1. On the acceptance state s_4, "$return = var_1 - var_2$" is attached to reveal that A is a value FSM that will return the value $var_1 - var_2$ when terminated.

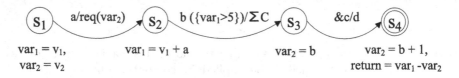

Fig. 5. Example of FSM

Definition 2. *HFSM (Hierarchical FSM) is a pair (F, σ) where F is a set of FSMs and $\sigma : Q \cup I \cup V \to \mathcal{P}(F)$ indicates the hierarchical relations among FSMs in F where lower-level FSMs interpret certain portion of upper-level FSMs iff $\exists_{A_0 \in F} \cdot \forall_{F' \in ran(\sigma)} \cdot A_0 \notin F'$ (A_0 is the root FSM).*

There are two kinds of hierarchical relations in σ: (1) lower-level FSMs demonstrate the inner transitions of states in upper-level FSMs and (2) upper-level FSMs utilize values generated by the FSMs in lower levels. In the second relation, a variable *return* is included in the system variables of each lower-level FSM for carrying the value to be used by the corresponding upper-level FSM. Figure 6 compares the two different relations through two example HFSMs H_1 and H_2. In H_1, FSM A_1 and the only FSM A'_1 in $\sigma_{H_1}(u')$ hold the first relation where the detailed behavior of state u' is described by FSM A'_1. The second relation is held in H_2 where $\sigma_{H_2}(\lambda(s,(i_4,G_4))) = \{A_3\} \wedge \sigma_{H_2}(v) = \{A_3, A_4\}$. Label $i_4(G_4)/A_3$ indicates that if the corresponding transition is activated, the value generated by FSM A_3 will be displayed. We omit the illustration of HFSM here for brievty.

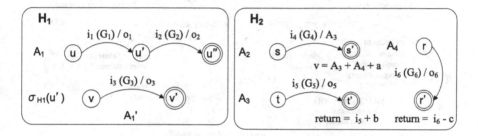

Fig. 6. Example of HFSM

5 Example

We take the formalization of the informal requirement *"Input password must be registered in the bank account file"* mentioned in the beginning of Sect. 2 as an example to briefly illustrate (due to limited space) how the HFSM of the **"part_whole"** pattern as shown in Fig. 7 and the corresponding attribute tree in Fig. 4 help the process of formalizing the informal requirement into the following formal expression:

$exists[account : bank\_account\_file] \mid password = account.password$

The formalization process starts from the initial state s_0 and then transits to state s_1. Then, following the tool's guide, the analyst (the user of the tool) clarifies the *element* as *password* and the *container* as *bank_account_file*. Based on the analyst's clarification, the transition will be made from s_1 to s_2, and then to s_4. According to the analyst's input, the transition moves to state s_8 and then guides the analyst to clarify the field of the composite object according to node d_6 of the attribute tree. Since node d_6 indicates a subtree built by applying the **"part_whole"** pattern, the clarification of the subtree must be carried out using the FSM of the **"part_whole** pattern. Again, we start from the initial state s_0 and then transits to state s_3 (rather than s_2) because the *element* and *container* are already clarified in node d_6 of the attribute tree.

After this, the transition goes on to s_4 and then s_5. The analyst is invited to confirm whether the *password* is the same as the *password* field of *account*. If the answer is positive, the transition will move to s_6 and then to the end state s. Since the low-level FSM is determined, we get back to state s_8 of the high-level FSM and assign the variable *return* with the value returned from the low-level FSM. Finally, the transition goes to the end state s and return the string value that is an internal format of the final formal expression. When it is presented to the analyst in the GUI, it looks exactly the same as the formal expression $exists[account : bank\_account\_file] \mid password = account.password$.

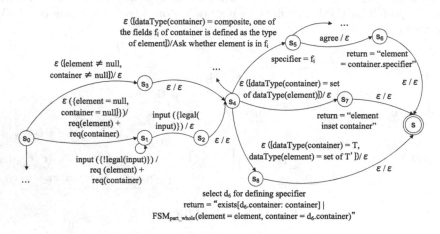

Fig. 7. FSM of the "**part_whole**" pattern

6   A Prototype Tool

We have developed a prototype tool for our PBFSRA technique to demonstrate the tool supportability of the technique. As illustrated in Fig. 8, the tool is mainly composed of four components to provide different functions:

- *Specification pattern knowledge* in an XML file
- *Knowledge extractor* for retrieving knowledge from the XML file
- *Guidance generator* for transforming the retrieved knowledge into explicit guidance to prompt the analyst's response
- *Preprocessor* for collecting input from the analyst and processing it for *knowledge extractor*

When supporting the formalization of an intended requirement, the *knowledge extractor* retrieves appropriate knowledge from the XML file that stores the *specification pattern knowledge*. The retrieved knowledge is then used by the *guidance generator* to produce comprehensible guidance. Following the guidance, the analyst is expected to respond to the tool. After receiving the input response, the *preprocessor* analyzes and processes it within the context of the

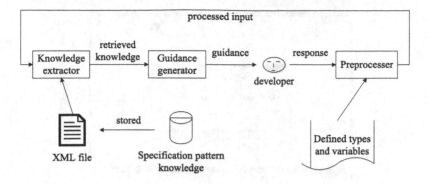

Fig. 8. Illustration of the supporting tool

defined types and variables. The processed input information is used by the *knowledge extractor* to retrieve new knowledge from the XML file for producing new guidance. Such interactions continue until the target formal expression is generated. Figure 9 shows the snapshots of the tool dealing with the analysis and formalization of the example presented in Sect. 5. The upper frame indicates the human-machine interactions while the lower frame shows the finally produced formal expression. The details of the entire case study and the procedure of using the tool are described in [6].

7 Experiment

With the help of graduate students who are experienced in using SOFL, the second author has conducted an experiment aiming to validate the capability and usability of the prototype tool. The result of the experiment is obtained through interviews of the subjects involved. Due to limited resources and many uncertainties, this experiment does not serve as a rigorous assessment of our approach but as a preliminary study. The details can be found in the second author's doctoral dissertation [6].

Six software systems were formally specified using the tool supported technique, which are Hotel reservation system (H), Banking system (B), E-ticket system (E), Suica card system (S), Library information system (L), and Online shopping system (O). Each subject was responsible for one of the six systems. Table 3 shows the result of the experiment. It summaries the collected data for each formal specification and its construction process. The second column indicates the number of the processes included in the specification and the third column records the number of the patterns applied for writing these processes. The column "Simplicity" denotes the rate $((ss/s) + (sg/g))/2$ where ss denotes the number of pattern selection decisions easy to be made, s denotes the total number of the pattern selection activities, sg denotes the number of guidances easy to understand and g denotes the total number of the displayed guidances.

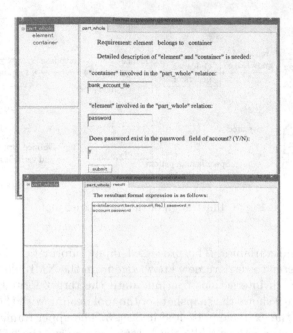

Fig. 9. Snapshots of the supporting tool

After interviewing the subjects of the experiment, we found that the pattern system can cover all the functions in these six systems. The provided categorization of patterns facilitates pattern selection, and the distinct pattern and category names give little chance to wrong selections. The major challenge, however, is how to determine the decomposition of the intended functions into basic functions that are formalized by patterns. The subjects suggest the design of more abstract patterns for domain specific systems to further facilitate pattern selection. Designing such kinds of patterns needs technical support from domain experts and we will extend our framework along this line based on the foundation presented in this paper. We also found that most of the subjects could not fully understand the representation of the provided guidance when formalizing the first several functions, although this difficulty may be mitigated with more experience gained. The last column of the table reveals the number of errors contained in the formal specification. Most of these errors are caused by misunderstanding the displayed guidance when formalizing the first several functions.

8   Related Work

There exist quite a few studies on the formalization of informal requirements and their supporting tools, such as the prototype assistant *NL2ACTL* for translating behavioral requirements in Natural Language to formulae of the action-based temporal logic ACTL developed by Fantechi *et al.* [7] and the Natural Language

Table 3. The result of the first experiment

Software system	Number of processes	Number of applied patterns	Simplicity (%)	Number of errors
H	53	10	89 %	13
B	49	9	85 %	11
E	50	9	89 %	10
S	53	11	87 %	13
L	55	12	90 %	10
O	60	12	85 %	11

processing tool *NLForSpec* that translates software test case descriptions in Natural Language into a formal representation in CSP [8], but there seems no work that has directly addressed the issue of how specification patterns can be used to formalize informal requirements to support requirements analysis and discovery as we have done in this research. For the sake of space, we only introduce the existing work that are strongly related to our study.

Stepney *et al.* describe a pattern language for using notation Z in computer system engineering [9]. The patterns proposed are classified into six types, including presentation patterns, idiom patterns, structure patters, architecture patterns, domain patterns, development patterns. Each pattern provides a solution to a type of problem. Grunske presents a specification pattern system of common probabilistic properties for probabilistic verification [10]. Majority of these patterns cope with formal specification construction at a more abstract level compared with ours. Ding *et al.* propose an approach for specification construction through property-preserving refinement patterns [11]. Konrad *et al.* [12] create real-time specification patterns in terms of three commonly used real-time temporal logics based on an analysis of timing-based requirements of several industrial embedded system applications and offer a structured English grammar to facilitate the understanding of the meaning of a specification. This work is complementary to the notable Dwyer *et al.*'s patterns which are used for presentation, codification and reuse of property specification in a range of common formalisms [13]. In [14], Dong and his colleagues design a set of composable timed automata patterns based on hierarchical constructs in timed enriched process algebras. The patterns facilitate the description of complex systems using Timed Automata and can be used to transform CSP/TCOZ models to Timed Automata to enable the reasoning of TCOZ models. To solve bottom-level problems, these patterns are designed to deal with specific domains. There is a specification pattern similar to ours proposed in [15]. It is also defined with formal semantics for automatic utilization. However, their patterns are designed only for a specific domain: formal specification of OCL constraints. They can only be described in the context of UML and can only be used by UML experts.

By contrast, our patterns are aimed at dealing with commonly used functions and allow new ones to be designed to handle wider range of functions.

9   Conclusions and Future Work

We have described the PBFSRA technique to support the process of analyzing and identifying requirements through constructing formal specifications based on specification patterns. The technique is characterized by supporting the interactive requirements analysis in which the analyst only needs to work on the natural language level while the machine automatically formalizes the requirements into formal specifications. The essential concepts, such as specification patterns, specification pattern system, and pattern knowledge representation, are presented, and the underlying principle of PBFSRA is discussed. In addition, we also describe a prototype tool to demonstrate the tool supportability of our technique and an experiment on the usability of the tool supported approach.

Future work will focus on the extension of the specification pattern system to support broader activities in requirements analysis and formal specification construction. We are also interested in the evaluation of the PBFSRA approach using lager scale experiments and the improvement of our prototype tool.

Acknowledgment. This work was supported by JSPS KAKENHI Grant Number 26240008. It was also partly supported by NSF of China (No. 61402178) and the Shanghai STCSM Project (No. 14YF1404300).

References

1. Knauss, E., Damian, D., Poo-Caamano, G., Cleland-Huang, J.: Detecting and classifying patterns of requirements clarifications. In: 20th IEEE International Conference on Requirements Engineering, pp. 251–260, September 2012
2. Kotonya, G., Sommerville, I.: Requirements Engineering - Processes and Techniques. Wiley, Chichester (1998)
3. Woodcock, J., Larsen, P.G., Bicarregui, J., Fitzgerald, J.: Formal methods: practice and experience. ACM Comput. Surv. **41**(4), 1–39 (2009)
4. Parnas, D.L.: Really rethinking formal methods. Computer **43**(1), 28–34 (2010)
5. Shalloway, A., Trott, J.R.: Design Patterns Explained, 2nd edn. Pearson Education Inc., Boston (2005)
6. Wang, X.: A pattern-based approach to requirements formalization and its supporting tool. Ph.D. thesis, Hosei University, Tokyo, Japan, March 2014
7. Fantechi, A., Gnesi, S., Ristori, G., Carenini, M., Vanocchi, M., Moreschini, P.: Assisting requirement formalization by means of natural language translation. Formal Methods Syst. Des. **4**(3), 243–263 (1994)
8. Leitao, D., Torres, D., Barros, F.: Motorola NLForSpec: translating natural language descriptions into formal test case specifications. available on the Internet, Not officially published but available on the Internet
9. Stepney, S., Polack, F.A.C., Toyn, I.: An outline pattern language for Z: five illustrations and two tables. In: Bert, D., Bowen, J.P., King, S., Waldén, M. (eds.) ZB 2003. LNCS, vol. 2651, pp. 2–19. Springer, Heidelberg (2003)

10. Grunske, L.: Specification patterns for probabilistic quality properties. In: 30th International Conference on Software Engineering, pp. 31–40 (2008)
11. Ding, J., Mo, L., He, X.: An approach for specification construction using property-preserving refinement patterns. In: SAC, pp. 797–803 (2008)
12. Konrad, S., Cheng, B.H.C.: Real-time specification patterns. In: 27th International Conference on Software Engineering, ICSE 2005, pp. 372–381. ACM (2005)
13. Dwyer, M.B., Avrunin, G.S., Corbett, J.C.: Pattern in property specifications for finite-state verification. In: 21th International Conference on Software Engineering, pp. 411–420. ACM, New York (1999)
14. Dong, J.S., Hao, P., Qin, S., Sun, J., Yi, W.: Timed automata patterns. IEEE Trans. Softw. Eng. **34**(6), 844–859 (2008)
15. Ackermann, J., Turowski, K.: A library of OCL specification patterns for behavioral specification of software components. In: Martinez, F.H., Pohl, K. (eds.) CAiSE 2006. LNCS, vol. 4001, pp. 255–269. Springer, Heidelberg (2006)

Dependency Analysis of Functional Specifications with Algebraic Data Structures

Oana F. Andreescu[1,2]([✉]), Thomas Jensen[1,2], and Stéphane Lescuyer[1]

[1] Prove & Run, 75017 Paris, France
{oana.andreescu,thomas.jensen,stephane.lescuyer}@provenrun.com
[2] INRIA Rennes - Bretagne Atlantique, Rennes, France

Abstract. In the context of interactive formal verification of complex systems, much effort is spent on proving the preservation of the systems invariants. However, most operations have a localized effect on the system, which only really impacts few invariants at the same time. Identifying those invariants that are unaffected by an operation can substantially ease the proof burden for the programmer. We present a dependency analysis for a strongly-typed, functional language, which computes a conservative approximation of the input fragments on which the operations depend. It is a flow-sensitive interprocedural analysis that handles arrays, structures and variant data types. For the latter, it simultaneously computes a subset of possible constructors. We have validated the scalability of the analysis to complex transition systems by applying it to a functional specification of the MINIX operating system.

1 Introduction

Algebraic data types (structures and variants) and associative arrays are fundamental building blocks when representing, grouping and handling complex data efficiently. However, operations manipulating them are rarely concerned with the entire compound input data structure. Most frequently, they depend only on a limited subset of their input. A complete specification of such an operation will not only stipulate that the output possesses a certain property but will also include its *framing requirements*, i.e. the part of the input that it operates on. Specifying and proving the preservation of logical properties for the unmodified part is a particular manifestation of the more general *frame problem* [8] – a notoriously cumbersome task in formal software verification, imposing unnecessary manual effort [9].

The verification of a given property can be simplified if we can determine the input fragments on which the property depends. This is the purpose of the dependency analysis presented in this paper. Our analysis targets a functional language that handles immutable algebraic data types and arrays. Furthermore, it is designed to be used on programs as well as on specifications. In contrast to the vast majority of static analyses that are mostly used only on actual code and in an essentially purely automatic setting, our analysis is thought of as a companion tool to be exploited in the middle of *interactive* program verification.

© Springer International Publishing Switzerland 2015
M. Butler et al. (Eds.): ICFEM 2015, LNCS 9407, pp. 116–133, 2015.
DOI: 10.1007/978-3-319-25423-4_8

1.1 A Motivating Example

The work reported in this paper is motivated by the formal verification of operating systems. To illustrate the problem that we are addressing, consider an abstract process manager and the data structures for its fundamental components: `process` and `thread`, shown in Fig. 1a. A *process* is an executing instance of an application that can consist of multiple *threads* that share the same address space. A *thread* is a path of execution within a process and it is modeled as a structure having fields such as the thread's identifier and the memory region for its stack. The current state of a thread is defined as a variant having three alternatives: `READY, BLOCKED, RUNNING`. Similarly, a process is a structure including an identifier for the currently running thread and an array of possibly inactive threads associated with it. Whether a thread in the thread array is active or has terminated is indicated by a variant of type `option_thread = | Some(thread th) | None`.

```
type process = {                       type thread = {
   array<option_thread> threads;          int identifier;
   int pid;                               state current_state;
   int current_thread;                    mem_region stack;
   address_space address_space;        }
}
```

a) Data Structures

```
predicate run_thread(process pr, int new_id)
-> [true: process new_pr | invalid_id]
predicate disjoint_stacks(process pr) -> [true | false]
```

b) Signatures for the Example Functions

Fig. 1. Example - data structures and functions of an abstract process manager

The signature of a Boolean function `disjoint_stacks`, written in a modeling language that we will present in Sect. 2, is shown in Fig. 1b. It verifies a fundamental property of a valid process state, namely that the stack regions of all active threads associated with the input `pr` are disjoint. Its result depends only on the array `threads` of the input `pr` and for each *active thread element* only on the field `stack`. All other input sub-elements are irrelevant to the result.

Another function `run_thread` has two possible execution scenarios: `true` and `invalid_id`. It stops the currently running thread and starts the one having the identifier given as an input. If it is valid, then a new process `new_pr` is returned for which `current_thread` is set to `new_id`. In the array `threads`, the state of the thread identified by `new_id` is set to `RUNNING`. The function's precondition stipulates that the `disjoint_stack` property holds for the input `pr` and that the input thread is `READY`. Proving the property's preservation is intuitively easy once the function's effects and the input subset on which `disjoint_stack` depends are known. Automatically proving the preservation of invariants concerning only fields or elements that have not been altered by a transition in the system would considerably diminish the number of proof obligations.

This is precisely the issue that we are addressing: the delimitation of the input subset on which the output depends, given an operation with a compound input. We define *dependency* as the observed part of a structured domain and strive to obtain type-sensitive results, distinguishing between the sub-elements of arrays and algebraic data types and capturing the dependency specific to each. The targeted results mirror – in terms of dependency – the layered structure of compound data types.

Generally, our dependency analysis targets complex transition systems. These are characterized by states defined by compound data structures and transitions, i.e. state changes, that map an input state to an output state. In particular, we are applying it to an abstract model of an operating system, stemming from *ProvenCore* [6], an ongoing project revolving around a fully secure micro-kernel.

ProvenCore, inspired by MINIX 3.1, is a general-purpose micro-kernel that ensures *isolation*. Its proof is based on multiple refinements between successive models, from the most abstract, on which the *isolation* property is defined and proved, to the most concrete, i.e. the actual model used for code generation.

The *global states* of the abstract layers are complex structures with multiple compound fields. Commands such as *fork, exec, exit* can be executed. Each of these receives as an input the global state before executing the command and returns the state of the system after execution. Most supported commands affect only a handful of invariants, leading to a much more complex, but fundamentally similar version of the situation depicted by our introductory example.

Outline. The rest of this paper is structured as follows: in Sect. 2 we underline the specificities of our modeling language. The defined abstract domain of dependencies is described in Sect. 3. It is followed in Sect. 4 by an in-depth presentation of our analysis at an intraprocedural level and in Sect. 5 by a summary of it at an interprocedural level. In Sect. 6 we discuss the results obtained on two abstract layers of ProvenCore. Finally, in Sect. 7 we review related work.

2   The Modeling Language

In this section we present the unified programming and specification language that we will be analyzing. It is an idealized version of a language developed at *Prove & Run*[1] and designed to facilitate proofs and to allow users to write both the implementation and the specification of programs. It is purely functional, side-effect free and strongly-typed. The basic building blocks of programs written in our language are *predicates*, the equivalent of functions in common programming languages. In addition to the common built-in primitive types traditionally available, structures and variants are also provided. The language is designed to write code that will subsequently be proven, so it allows the definition

---

[1] http://www.provenrun.com/.

of various types of logical specifications, ranging from pre- and postconditions, local assertions and loop invariants to inductive predicates.

2.1 Types and Statements

For defining the language we are working on, we let $\mathbb{T}$ be the universe of type identifiers and $\mathbb{T}_0 \subset \mathbb{T}$ the set of base types identifiers. Furthermore, let $\mathscr{F}$ be the set of structure field identifiers and $\mathscr{C}$ the set of variant constructors.

$$
\begin{aligned}
t := \ & | \ \tau \in T_0 && \text{base types} \\
& | \ \boldsymbol{structure}\{f_1 : t, \ldots, f_n : t\} && f_i \in \mathscr{F}, 1 \le i \le n \ \text{structures} \\
& | \ \boldsymbol{variant}[C_1(t \ e_1) \ | \ \ldots \ | \ C_m(t \ e_m)] && C_i \in \mathscr{C}, 1 \le i \le m \ \text{variants} \\
& | \ \boldsymbol{array}^t \langle t \rangle && \text{arrays}
\end{aligned}
$$

A *structure* is a data type grouping elements of different types called *fields* and represents the *Cartesian product* of its fields' types. A *variant* is the *disjoint union* of different types. It represents data that may take on multiple forms, where each form is marked with a specific tag called the *constructor*. *Arrays* group a collection of data of the same type (given in angle brackets) into a single entity; each element is selected by an index whose type is included (as denoted by the superscript) in the array's definition.

A program in our language is a collection of predicates. A predicate has input and output parameters and a body of statements of the form shown in Table 1.

Table 1. Supported statements

$$
\begin{aligned}
\text{statement} := \ & | \ p(e_1, \ldots, e_n) \ [\lambda_1 : \bar{o}_1 \ | \ldots | \ \lambda_m : \bar{o}_m] && \text{(1)} \quad \text{predicate call} \\
& | \ e_1 = e_2 && \text{(2)} \quad \text{equality test} \\
& | \ o := e && \text{(3)} \quad \text{assignment} \\
& | \ s := \{e_1, \ldots, e_n\} && \text{(4)} \quad \text{create structure } s \\
& | \ \{o_1, \ldots, o_n\} := s && \text{(5)} \quad \text{structure destructuring} \\
& | \ o := s.f_i && \text{(6)} \quad \text{access field } f_i \\
& | \ s' := \{s \ \boldsymbol{with} \ f_i = e_i\} && \text{(7)} \quad \text{update field } f_i \\
& | \ s' = \langle f_1, \ldots, f_k \rangle s'' && \text{(8)} \quad \text{test equality on fields } f_1, \ldots, f_k \\
& | \ v := C_p[e_p] && \text{(9)} \quad \text{create } v \text{ with constructor } C_p \\
& | \ \boldsymbol{switch}(v) \ \boldsymbol{as} \ [o_1| \ldots |o_n] && \text{(10)} \quad \text{variant destructuring} \\
& | \ v \in \{C_1, \ldots, C_k\} && \text{(11)} \quad \text{variant possible} \\
& | \ o := a[i] && \text{(12)} \quad \text{array access at index } i \\
& | \ a' := [a \ \boldsymbol{with} \ i = e] && \text{(13)} \quad \text{array update at index } i
\end{aligned}
$$

The first statement represents a generic predicate call and is described later in Sect. 2.2. All other statements could be seen as special cases of it, representing calls to built-in predicates. Statement (2) is a call to the "=" predicate, that checks whether its two inputs are equal. Similarly, (3) is a call to the assignment predicate ":=". Both are generic and can be applied on any supported type of the language.

The statements (4)–(8) are structure-related. (4) creates a new structure s with $e_1; \ldots; e_n$ as field values. (5) returns the values of all the fields of s in the output parameters $o_1; \ldots; o_n$. Statement (6) returns the value of the f_i field. As previously mentioned, we are focusing on a purely functional language and consider immutable algebraic data structures and arrays. Therefore, setting the value of a structure's field, shown in (7), returns a *new* structure where all fields have the same value as in s, except f_i which is set to e_i. Statement (8) verifies if the values of the given subset of fields of two structures s' and s'' are equal.

Statements (9) − (11) are variant-related. (9) creates a new variant v using the constructor C_p with e_p as an argument. Statement (10) is used for matching on the different constructors of an input variant v. Statement (11) verifies if the input variant v was created with one of the constructors in $\{C_1, \ldots, C_k\}$. This could be obtained with a *variant switch*, but for practical considerations it has been provided as a built-in predicate.

The last two statements are array-related. (12) returns the value of the i-th cell of the input array a. Similarly to (7), updating the i-th cell of an array – shown in (13) – has a functional nature. It returns a *new* array where all cells have the same value as in a, except the i-th cell which is set to e.

2.2 Exit Labels

Besides input and output parameters, the declaration of a predicate also includes a non-empty set of *exit labels*. When called, a predicate exits with one of the specified exit labels, thus summarizing and returning to its callers further information regarding its execution.

Table 2. Statements and their exit labels

Statement	Exit Labels		Statement	Exit Labels	
$p(e_1, \ldots, e_n)$ $[\lambda_1 : \bar{o}_1 \mid \ldots \mid \lambda_m : \bar{o}_m]$	$\begin{bmatrix} \lambda_1 \mapsto \bar{o}_1 \\ \vdots \quad \ddots \quad \vdots \\ \lambda_m \mapsto \bar{o}_m \end{bmatrix}$	(1)	$v := C_p[e_p]$	$\begin{bmatrix} \text{true} \mapsto v \end{bmatrix}$	(9)
$e_1 = e_2$	$\begin{bmatrix} \text{true} \mapsto \emptyset, \text{false} \mapsto \emptyset \end{bmatrix}$	(2)	$switch(v)$ as $[o_1 \mid \ldots \mid o_n]$	$\begin{bmatrix} \lambda_{C_1} \mapsto o_1 \\ \vdots \quad \ddots \quad \vdots \\ \lambda_{C_n} \mapsto o_n \end{bmatrix}$	(10)
$o := e$	$\begin{bmatrix} \text{true} \mapsto o \end{bmatrix}$	(3)		where $C_1, \ldots, C_n$ are the constructors of	
$s := \{e_1, \ldots, e_n\}$	$\begin{bmatrix} \text{true} \mapsto s \end{bmatrix}$	(4)		the type of variant v	
$\{o_1, \ldots, o_n\} := s$	$\begin{bmatrix} \text{true} \mapsto o_1 \ldots o_n \end{bmatrix}$	(5)	$v \in \{C_1, \ldots, C_k\}$	$\begin{bmatrix} \text{true} \mapsto \emptyset, \text{false} \mapsto \emptyset \end{bmatrix}$	(11)
$o := s.f_i$	$\begin{bmatrix} \text{true} \mapsto o \end{bmatrix}$	(6)	$o := a[i]$	$\begin{bmatrix} \text{true} \mapsto o, \text{false} \mapsto \emptyset \end{bmatrix}$	(12)
$s' := \{s \ with \ f_i = e_i\}$	$\begin{bmatrix} \text{true} \mapsto s' \end{bmatrix}$	(7)	$a' := [a \ with \ i = e]$	$\begin{bmatrix} \text{true} \mapsto a', \text{false} \mapsto \emptyset \end{bmatrix}$	(13)
$s' = \langle f_1, \ldots, f_k \rangle s''$	$\begin{bmatrix} \text{true} \mapsto \emptyset, \text{false} \mapsto \emptyset \end{bmatrix}$	(8)			

Exit labels constitute the main specificity of the language. They can denote different exceptional execution scenarios and act as exit codes, similarly to exceptions and exit status return values in other programming languages. For example, the predicate run_thread(process pr, int new_id) introduced in Sect. 1 has two exit labels: true, corresponding to a successful execution and invalid_id, indicating that the given identifier is invalid. Labels also offer a convenient way to model a Boolean result. Frequently, a Boolean output value can be replaced by declaring two possible exit labels: true for a successful execution of the predicate and false for its opposite. This is illustrated by the previously defined property disjoint_stacks(process pr) (in Fig. 1b).

Exit labels play an important role with respect to control flow management. Complex control flow is expressed and directed by catching and transforming labels. Furthermore, they condition the existence of output parameters, as these are associated to the exit labels of a predicate. Whenever a predicate exits with an exit label λ, all the outputs associated to it are effectively produced, whereas all other outputs are discarded. If no output is associated to an exit label, it means that no output is generated when the predicate exits with this particular label. We can now explain the generic predicate call statement (1) from Table 1: the predicate p is called with inputs $e_1, \ldots, e_n$ and yields one of the declared exit labels $\lambda_1, \ldots, \lambda_n$, each having its own set of associated output variables $\bar{o}$.

As shown in Table 2, statement (10) will have an exit label corresponding to each constructor of the given input variant. Statements (2), (8) and (11) are bi-labeled, using true and false as logical values. Statements (12) and (13) are bi-labeled as well. However, unlike the previously mentioned statements, they use the label false as an "out of bounds" exception and generate an output only for the label true.

2.3   The Control Flow Graph

In the following we will work with a control flow graph representation of the predicates' bodies. The nodes represent program states, and the edges are defined by statements with a particular exit label λ.

The control flow graph $G_p = (N, E)$ of a predicate p has a node $n_i \in N$ for each program point. For each statement s at program point n_i that can execute and reach program point n_j with exit label λ_k, an edge (n_i, n_j) is added to G_p and labeled with s and λ_k. G_p has a single *entry node* $n_{in} \in N$ corresponding to the program point associated to the first statement of p. The set of *exit nodes* $n_{out} \subset N$ consists of the nodes associated to each possible exit label λ_k of the predicate.

In practice, all the outgoing edges of a node $n_i \in N$ bear the different cases of the same statement s found at program point n_i. Thus, the edges are labeled with the same statement s and there is an edge labeled s, λ_k for each possible exit label λ_k of s. However, the analysis does not depend on this special case.

The subfigures in Fig. 2 show the control flow graph of the following predicate: predicate thread(process p, int i) -> [true: thread ti | None | oob] which receives a process p and an index i as inputs and returns the i-th active thread of the input process (the process and thread types are defined in Fig. 1a). If the i-th thread is inactive, it exits with the exit label None. In the case of an "out of bounds" exception, the exit label oob is returned. For better readability, Fig. 2b gives the control flow of the same predicate where we

have labeled the nodes with statements of the predicate and the edges with their
exit labels.

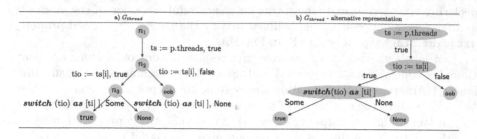

Fig. 2. Example – control flow graph of predicate `thread`

3   Abstract Domain of Dependencies

The goal of our analysis is to detect the input subset on which the outputs of a
predicate *may* depend. More precisely, the analysis makes a conservative approximation and must guarantee that what is marked as not needed is definitely not
needed.

The first step towards such results is the definition of an abstract domain of
dependencies $\mathbb{D}$, shown below. The domain $\delta \in \mathbb{D}$ is defined inductively from the
three atomic cases $\top$, $\oslash$ and $\bot$, mimicking the structure of the concrete types:

$$
\begin{aligned}
\delta := \ & |\ \top\ |\ \oslash\ |\ \bot & \text{atomic cases} & \\
& |\ \{f_1 \mapsto \delta_1; \dots; f_n \mapsto \delta_n\} & f_1, \dots, f_n \text{ fields} & \text{(i)} \\
& |\ [C_1 \mapsto \delta_1; \dots; C_m \mapsto \delta_m] & C_1, \dots, C_m \text{ constructors} & \text{(ii)} \\
& |\ \langle \delta \rangle & & \text{(iii)} \\
& |\ \langle \delta_{default} \rhd i\ :\ \delta_{exc} \rangle & i \text{ array index} & \text{(iv)}
\end{aligned}
$$

For atomic types the dependency is expressed in terms of the domain's atomic
cases: $\top$ (least precise), denoting that *everything* is needed and $\oslash$, denoting that
nothing is needed. The third atomic case $\bot$, denoting *impossible*, is explained
below. The dependency of a structure (i) describes the dependency on each of its
fields. For arrays we distinguish between two cases, namely arrays with a general
dependency applying to all of the cells (iii) and arrays with a general dependency
applying to all but one exceptional cell, for which a specific dependency is known
(iv). For variants (ii), the dependency is expressed in terms of the dependencies
of its constructors, expressed in terms of their arguments' dependencies. Thus,
a constructor having a dependency mapped to $\oslash$ is one for which nothing but
the tag has been read, i.e. its arguments, if any, are irrelevant for the execution.
For variants, we also include the information that certain constructors cannot
occur. The third atomic case – $\bot$ – is introduced for this purpose. We perform
a "possible-constructors" analysis simultaneously, which computes for each execution scenario, the subset of possible constructors for a given value, at a given
program point. All constructors that cannot occur are marked as being $\bot$. This

Table 3. $\sqsubseteq$ – comparison of two domains

$$\frac{}{\delta \sqsubseteq \top} \text{ TOP} \qquad \frac{\delta_1 \sqsubseteq \delta_1' \quad \cdots \quad \delta_n \sqsubseteq \delta_n'}{\{f_1 \mapsto \delta_1; \ldots; f_n \mapsto \delta_n\} \sqsubseteq \{f_1 \mapsto \delta_1'; \ldots; f_n \mapsto \delta_n'\}} \text{ STR}$$

$$\frac{}{\bot \sqsubseteq \delta} \text{ BOT} \qquad \frac{\delta_1 \sqsubseteq \delta_1' \quad \cdots \quad \delta_n \sqsubseteq \delta_n'}{[C_1 \mapsto \delta_1; \ldots; C_n \mapsto \delta_n] \sqsubseteq [C_1 \mapsto \delta_1'; \ldots; C_n \mapsto \delta_n']} \text{ VAR}$$

$$\frac{\oslash \sqsubseteq \delta_1 \quad \cdots \quad \oslash \sqsubseteq \delta_n}{\oslash \sqsubseteq \{f_1 \mapsto \delta_1; \ldots; f_n \mapsto \delta_n\}} \oslash\text{STR} \qquad \frac{\oslash \sqsubseteq \delta_1 \quad \cdots \quad \oslash \sqsubseteq \delta_n}{\oslash \sqsubseteq [C_1 \mapsto \delta_1; \ldots; C_n \mapsto \delta_n]} \oslash\text{VAR}$$

$$\frac{\delta_{def} \sqsubseteq \delta_{def}'}{\langle \delta_{def} \rangle \sqsubseteq \langle \delta_{def}' \rangle} \text{ ADEF} \qquad \frac{\delta_{def} \sqsubseteq \delta_{def}' \quad \delta_{exc} \sqsubseteq \delta_{def}'}{\langle \delta_{def} \triangleright i \,:\, \delta_{exc} \rangle \sqsubseteq \langle \delta_{def}' \rangle} \text{ AIA} \qquad \frac{\delta_{def} \sqsubseteq \delta_{def}' \quad \delta_{def} \sqsubseteq \delta_{exc}'}{\langle \delta_{def} \rangle \sqsubseteq \langle \delta_{def}' \triangleright i \,:\, \delta_{exc}' \rangle} \text{ AAI}$$

$$\frac{\delta_{def} \sqsubseteq \delta_{def}' \quad \delta_{exc} \sqsubseteq \delta_{exc}' \quad \delta_{def} \sqsubseteq \delta_{exc}' \quad \delta_{exc} \sqsubseteq \delta_{def}' \quad i \neq j}{\langle \delta_{def} \triangleright i \,:\, \delta_{exc} \rangle \sqsubseteq \langle \delta_{def}' \triangleright j \,:\, \delta_{exc}' \rangle} \text{ AIJ}$$

$$\frac{\oslash \sqsubseteq \delta_{def}}{\oslash \sqsubseteq \langle \delta_{def} \rangle} \oslash\text{A} \qquad \frac{\delta_{def} \sqsubseteq \delta_{def}' \quad \delta_{exc} \sqsubseteq \delta_{exc}'}{\langle \delta_{def} \triangleright i \,:\, \delta_{exc} \rangle \sqsubseteq \langle \delta_{def}' \triangleright i \,:\, \delta_{exc}' \rangle} \text{ AI} \qquad \frac{\oslash \sqsubseteq \delta_{def} \quad \oslash \sqsubseteq \delta_{exc}}{\oslash \sqsubseteq \langle \delta_{def} \triangleright i \,:\, \delta_{exc} \rangle} \oslash\text{AI}$$

atomic value is the lower bound of our domain and hence, the most precise value. The final abstract domain is a closure of all these combined recursively.

The partial order relation $\sqsubseteq \subseteq \mathbb{D} \times \mathbb{D}$ used to compare dependency domains is detailed in Table 3. The greatest element is $\top$ (TOP) and $\bot$ is the least (BOT). Instances of identical structure and variant types are compared pointwise (STR, VAR). For arrays without known exceptional dependencies we compare the default dependencies applying to all array cells (ADEF). If exceptional dependencies are known for the same cell, these are additionally compared (AI). For arrays with known exceptional dependencies for different cells, we compare each dependency on the left-hand side with each one on the right-hand side (AIJ). The comparison of $\oslash$ with structures ($\oslash$STR), variants ($\oslash$VAR) and arrays ($\oslash$A, $\oslash$AI) is a pointwise comparison between $\oslash$ and the dependency of each sub-element.

Table 4. Join operation

δ' δ''	$\delta' \vee \delta''$
$\top \vee \delta$	$= \top$
$\bot \vee \delta$	$= \delta$
$\{f_1 \mapsto \delta_1; \ldots; f_n \mapsto \delta_n\} \vee \{f_1 \mapsto \delta_1'; \ldots; f_n \mapsto \delta_n'\}$	$= \{f_1 \mapsto \delta_1 \vee \delta_1'; \ldots; f_n \mapsto \delta_n \vee \delta_n'\}$
$[C_1 \mapsto \delta_1; \ldots; C_n \mapsto \delta_n] \vee [C_1 \mapsto \delta_1'; \ldots; C_n \mapsto \delta_n']$	$= [C_1 \mapsto \delta_1 \vee \delta_1'; \ldots; C_n \mapsto \delta_n \vee \delta_n']$
$\langle \delta_{def} \rangle \vee \langle \delta_{def}' \rangle$	$= \langle \delta_{def} \vee \delta_{def}' \rangle$
$\langle \delta_{def} \rangle \vee \langle \delta_{def}' \triangleright i \,:\, \delta_{exc}' \rangle$	$= \langle \delta_{def} \vee \delta_{def}' \triangleright i \,:\, \delta_{def} \vee \delta_{exc}' \rangle$
$\langle \delta_{def} \triangleright i \,:\, \delta_{exc} \rangle \vee \langle \delta_{def}' \triangleright j \,:\, \delta_{exc}' \rangle \begin{cases} i = j \\ i \neq j \end{cases} =$	$\langle \delta_{def} \vee \delta_{def}' \triangleright i \,:\, \delta_{exc} \vee \delta_{exc}' \rangle$ $\langle \delta_{def} \vee \delta_{exc} \vee \delta_{def}' \vee \delta_{exc}' \rangle$
$\oslash \vee \oslash$	$= \oslash$

The defined *join* operation $\vee : \mathbb{D} \times \mathbb{D} \to \mathbb{D}$ is detailed in Table 4. It is a *commutative* operation for which the undisplayed cases are defined with respect to their symmetrical counterparts. The operation is total: joining incompatible domains such as a structure and a variant or two structures having different field identifiers, results in $\top$. Join is applied *pointwise* on each sub-element; $\bot$ is its *identity* element and $\top$ is its *absorbing* element. Joining $\oslash$ and the dependency of a structure, variant or array is applied pointwise. The value obtained by joining δ and δ' is an upper bound of the two:

$$\delta \sqsubseteq \delta \vee \delta' \ \wedge \ \delta' \sqsubseteq \delta \vee \delta', \ \forall \, \delta, \delta' \in \mathbb{D}.$$

It is not a *least upper bound* as a consequence of the *non-monotonic* approximations made for arrays (rule AIJ).

Besides *join*, a reduction operator $\oplus : \mathbb{D} \times \mathbb{D} \to \mathbb{D}$ has been defined as well. This is a recursive, commutative, pointwise operation. The need for such an operator is a consequence of the possible-constructors analysis that we perform simultaneously. Following the same execution path, the same constructors must be possible. Thus, the reduction operator is used in order to combine dependencies on the same execution path and consists in performing the intersection of constructors in the case of variants and the union of dependencies for all other types. Its *identity* element is $\oslash$ and its *absorbing* element is $\bot$. The reduce operator between $\top$, and the dependency of a structure, variant or array is applied pointwise. Two instances of identical variant types are pointwise reduced.

Finally, the projections summarized in Table 5, have been defined on a dependency domain δ and are used to express the data-flow equations of Sect. 4:

.f	$: \mathbb{D} \to \mathbb{D}$	projection of a field's dependency
@C	$: \mathbb{D} \to \mathbb{D}$	projection of a constructor's dependency
$\langle i \rangle$	$: \mathbb{D} \to \mathbb{D}$	projection of a cell's dependency
$\langle * \setminus i \rangle$	$: \mathbb{D} \to \mathbb{D}$	projection of an array's dependency outside cell i
$\langle * \rangle$	$: \mathbb{D} \to \mathbb{D}$	projection of an array's general dependency

Table 5. Dependency projections

$\delta.f, f \in \mathscr{F}$		$\delta @ C, C \in \mathscr{C}$	
$\{f_1 \mapsto \delta_1; \ldots; f_n \mapsto \delta_n\}.f = \delta_i$ if $f = f_i$		$[C_1 \mapsto \delta_1; \ldots; C_m \mapsto \delta_m] @ C = \delta_j$ if $C = C_j$	

$\delta \langle * \setminus i \rangle$	$\delta \langle i \rangle$	$\delta \langle * \rangle$
$\langle \delta_{def} \rangle \langle * \setminus i \rangle = \delta_{def}$ $\langle \delta_{def} \triangleright k : \delta_{exc} \rangle \langle * \setminus i \rangle =$ $\begin{cases} \delta_{def} & \text{when } i = k \\ \delta_{def} \vee \delta_{exc} & \text{otherwise} \end{cases}$	$\langle \delta_{def} \rangle \langle i \rangle = \delta_{def}$ $\langle \delta_{def} \triangleright k : \delta_{exc} \rangle \langle i \rangle =$ $\begin{cases} \delta_{exc} & \text{when } i = k \\ \delta_{def} \vee \delta_{exc} & \text{otherwise} \end{cases}$	$\langle \delta_{def} \rangle \langle * \rangle = \delta_{def}$ $\langle \delta_{def} \triangleright k : \delta_{exc} \rangle \langle * \rangle =$ $\delta_{def} \vee \delta_{exc}$

They are partial functions, and can only be applied on domains of the corresponding kind. For instance, the field projection $.f$ only makes sense for atomic domains or structured domains with a field named f, which should be the case if the domain represents a variable of a structured type with some field f. For any of the atomic domains δ_a, applying any of the defined projections yields δ_a.

4 Intraprocedural Analysis and Data-Flow Equations

Intraprocedural Domains. Dependency information has to be kept at each point of the control flow graph, for each variable of the environment Γ, that maps input, output and local variables to their types. An *intraprocedural* domain Δ : $\mathcal{V} \rightarrow \delta$ is thus a mapping from variables to dependencies, and is associated to every node of the control flow graph, representing the dependencies at the node's entry point. A special case is the mapping which maps all variables to $\bot$, which we call *Unreachable*. In particular it is associated to nodes that cannot be reached during the analysis. Also, if any of the variables of Δ is marked as $\bot$, the entire node collapses, becoming *Unreachable*.

For any node of the control flow graph associated to an intraprocedural domain Δ, $\Delta(x)$ retrieves the dependency associated to the variable x. If a mapping for x does not currently exist, $\Delta(x)$ retrieves $\oslash$. Forgetting a variable x from a reachable intraprocedural domain, $\Delta \setminus x$, removes its mapping. The $\vee$, $\sqsubseteq$ and $\oplus$ operations are extended pointwise to an intraprocedural domain, for each variable and its associated dependency domain δ_v. In particular, *Unreachable* is the bottom of this intraprocedural lattice.

Table 6. Statements – representations and data-flow equations

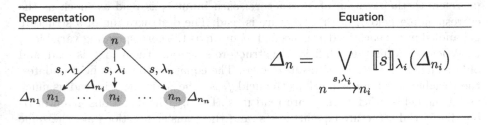

$$\Delta_n = \bigvee_{n \xrightarrow{s,\lambda_i} n_i} [\![s]\!]_{\lambda_i}(\Delta_{n_i})$$

Data-Flow Equations. Our dependency analysis is a *backward* data-flow analysis. For each exit label, it traverses the control flow graph starting with its corresponding exit node and marking all other exit points as *Unreachable*. The intraprocedural domain for the currently analyzed label is initialized with its associated output variables mapped to $\top$. The analysis traverses the control flow graph and gradually refines the dependencies until a fixed point is reached. Table 6 summarizes the representation and general equation of the statements. For each statement, the presented data-flow equation operates on the intraprocedural domains of the statement's *successor* nodes. The intraprocedural domain at the *entry point* of the node is obtained by *joining* the contributions of each *outgoing* edge. The contribution of an edge (n_i, n_j) labeled with s and λ is given by $[\![s]\!]_\lambda(\Delta_{n_j})$ where $[\![s]\!]_\lambda(.)$ is the *transfer function* of the edge labeled s, λ.

Tables 7, 8, 9, 10 define the transfer functions for each built-in statement of our language, whereas the general case of a predicate call and its corresponding equation will be detailed in the following section.

Table 7 presents the transfer functions for statements which are not type-specific. For equality tests (1) both of the inputs e_1, e_2 are completely read, whether the test returns true or false. The transfer functions therefore, reduce the domain of the corresponding successor node with a domain consisting of e_1 and e_2 both mapped to $\top$. In the case of assignment (2), the dependency of the written output variable o is forgotten from the successor's intraprocedural domain, thus being mapped to $\oslash$ and forwarded to the input variable e.

Table 7. Generic statements – data-flow equations

Statement	$[\![s]\!]_{\lambda_i}(\Delta)$
Equality test (1)	$[\![e_1 = e_2]\!]_{\text{true}}(\Delta) = \Delta \oplus dep \quad$ where $[\![e_1 = e_2]\!]_{\text{false}}(\Delta) = \Delta \oplus dep \quad dep = \left\{ \begin{matrix} e_1 \mapsto \top \\ e_2 \mapsto \top \end{matrix} \right\}$
Assignment (2)	$[\![o := e]\!]_{\text{true}}(\Delta) = (\Delta \setminus o) \oplus \{e \mapsto \Delta(o)\}$

The data-flow equations given in Table 8 correspond to structure-related statements. For the Eqs. (3), (4), (5) and (6) we assume that the variable s is of type **structure**$\{f_1 : t, \ldots, f_n : t\}$ for some fields f_i, $1 \leq i \leq n$. The equation (3) refers to the creation of a structure: each input e_i is read as much as the corresponding field f_i of the structure is read. The destructuring of a structure is handled in (4): each field f_i is needed as much as the corresponding variable o_i is. When accessing the i-th field of a structure s (5), only the field f_i is read, and only as much as the access' result o itself. The equation (6) treats field updates: the variable e_i is read as much as the field f_i is. The structure s is read as much as all the fields other than f_i are read in s'. Finally, the equations given in (7) handle partial structure equality tests, and the transfer functions are the same for the labels true or false: for both compared structures s' and s'', all the fields in the given set $f_1, \ldots, f_k$ are completely read, and only those.

The data-flow equations given in Table 9 correspond to variant-related statements. They follow the same principles as those used for structure-related statements above. Note that the transfer functions for the switch (9) and possible constructor test (10) introduce $\bot$ dependencies for constructors which are known to be impossible on the considered edge. In particular, since $\bot$ is an absorbing element for $\oplus$, these transfer functions erase, for every constructor which is known to be locally impossible, all the dependency information possibly attached to said constructor in the successor nodes. This is the actual *raison d'être* for the reduction operator, since using $\vee$ to combine a successor domain and a local contribution would lose this information.

Table 8. Structure-related statements – data-flow equations

Statement	$[\![s]\!]_{\lambda_i}(\Delta)$
Create (3)	$[\![s := \{e_1, \ldots, e_n\}]\!]_{\text{true}}(\Delta) = (\Delta \setminus s) \oplus \bigoplus_{1 \leq i \leq n} \{e_i \mapsto \Delta(s).f_i\}$
Destruct (4)	$[\![\{o_1, \ldots, o_n\} := s]\!]_{\text{true}}(\Delta) = (\Delta \setminus \{o_i \mid o_i \in \bar{o}\}) \oplus \{s \mapsto \{f_i \mapsto \Delta(o_i) \mid 1 \leq i \leq n\}\}$
Access field (5)	$[\![o := s.f_i]\!]_{\text{true}}(\Delta) = (\Delta \setminus o) \oplus \{s \mapsto \{f_1 \mapsto \varnothing; \ldots; f_i \mapsto \Delta(o); \ldots; f_n \mapsto \varnothing\}\}$
Update field (6)	$[\![s' := \{s \text{ with } f_i = e_i\}]\!]_{\text{true}}(\Delta) = (\Delta \setminus s') \oplus \left\{ \begin{array}{l} e_i \mapsto \Delta(s').f_i \\ s \mapsto \{f_j \mapsto \delta_j \mid 1 \leq j \leq n\} \end{array} \right\}$
	where $\delta_j = \left\{ \begin{array}{ll} \Delta(s').f_j & \text{if } j \neq i \\ \varnothing & \text{otherwise} \end{array} \right.$
Equality (7)	$[\![s' = \langle f_1, \ldots, f_k \rangle s'']\!]_{\text{true}}(\Delta) = \Delta \oplus d \quad \text{where } d = \left\{ \begin{array}{l} s' \mapsto \{f_i \mapsto \delta_i \mid 1 \leq i \leq n\} \\ s'' \mapsto \{f_i \mapsto \delta_i \mid 1 \leq i \leq n\} \end{array} \right\}$
	$[\![s' = \langle f_1, \ldots, f_k \rangle s'']\!]_{\text{false}}(\Delta) = \Delta \oplus d \quad \delta_i = \left\{ \begin{array}{ll} \top & \text{if } f_i \in \{f_1, \ldots, f_k\} \\ \varnothing & \text{otherwise} \end{array} \right.$

Table 9. Variant-related statements – data-flow equations

Statement	$[\![s]\!]_{\lambda_i}(\Delta)$
Create variant (8)	$[\![v := C_p[e_p]]\!]_{\text{true}}(\Delta) = (\Delta \setminus v) \oplus \{e_p \mapsto \Delta(v)@C_p\}$
Variant Switch (9)	$[\![\text{switch}(v) \text{ as } [o_1 \mid \ldots \mid o_n]]\!]_{\lambda_i}(\Delta) = (\Delta \setminus o_i) \oplus \{v \mapsto dep_i\}$
	where $dep_i = [C_1 \mapsto \bot; \ldots; C_i \mapsto \Delta(o_i); \ldots; C_n \mapsto \bot]$
	$[\![v \in \{C_1, \ldots, C_k\}]\!]_{\text{true}}(\Delta) = \Delta \oplus \{v \mapsto [C_i \mapsto \delta_i \mid 1 \leq i \leq n]\}$
	where $\delta_i = \left\{ \begin{array}{ll} \Delta(v)@C_i & \text{if } C_i \in \{C_1, \ldots, C_k\} \\ \bot & \text{otherwise} \end{array} \right.$
Possible variant (10)	$[\![v \in \{C_1, \ldots, C_k\}]\!]_{\text{false}}(\Delta) = \Delta \oplus \{v \mapsto [\bar{C}_i \mapsto \bar{\delta}_i \mid 1 \leq i \leq n]\}$
	where $\bar{\delta}_i = \left\{ \begin{array}{ll} \Delta(v)@\bar{C}_i & \text{if } \bar{C}_i \notin \{C_1, \ldots, C_k\} \\ \bot & \text{otherwise} \end{array} \right.$

Finally, the equations for array-related statements are given in Table 10. We assume for both that the context is fixed and that $\mathcal{I}$ is the distinguished set of input variables for the analyzed predicate. This set is used to make sure that exceptions in array dependencies are only registered to variables in $\mathcal{I}$ and not local or output variables. The reason for such a constraint is a pragmatic one: input variables are not assignable in our language, and therefore they always represent the same value intraprocedurally. Otherwise, each time a variable is written by a statement, we would need to traverse all the dependencies in the domain to erase or reinterpret the occurrences where this variable appears as an exception. Only recording exceptions for input variables makes this kind of costly traversal useless, and since only exceptions about input variables make sense at the interprocedural level (see Sect. 5), we do not lose much precision by doing so. The transfer functions for (11) and (12) thus take care of making adequate approximations when exceptions cannot be introduced. As for the cases when the array access exits with the false label, note that the contribution to the array a is $\langle \varnothing \rangle$, which is strictly less precise than $\varnothing$. The operation makes implicit bounds checking and this can thus be seen as accounting for the fact that no cell in a has been read, but the "length" or "support" of a has been read, hence it would not be true to claim that the result of the statement did not depend on a at all. Similarly, a variant dependency $[C_1 \mapsto \oslash, \ldots, C_n \mapsto \oslash]$ mapping all constructors to nothing has not read any value in any of the constructors, but may still depend on the variant's constructor itself.

Table 10. Array-related statements – data-flow equations

Statement	$[\![s]\!]_{\lambda_i}(\Delta)$
Array access (11)	$[\![o := a[i]]\!]_{\mathsf{true}}(\Delta) = \begin{cases} (\Delta \setminus o) \oplus \begin{Bmatrix} i \mapsto \top \\ a \mapsto \langle \oslash \triangleright i : \Delta(o) \rangle \end{Bmatrix} & \text{when } i \in \mathcal{I} \\ (\Delta \setminus o) \oplus \begin{Bmatrix} i \mapsto \top \\ a \mapsto \langle \Delta(o) \vee \oslash \rangle \end{Bmatrix} & \text{when } i \notin \mathcal{I} \end{cases}$
	$[\![o := a[i]]\!]_{\mathsf{false}}(\Delta) = \Delta \oplus \begin{Bmatrix} i \mapsto \top \\ a \mapsto \langle \oslash \rangle \end{Bmatrix}$
Array update (12)	$[\![a' := [a \; \textbf{with} \; i = e]]\!]_{\mathsf{true}}(\Delta) = \begin{cases} (\Delta \setminus a') \oplus \begin{Bmatrix} i \mapsto \top \\ e \mapsto \Delta(a')\langle i \rangle \\ a \mapsto \langle \Delta(a')\langle * \setminus i \rangle \triangleright i : \oslash \rangle \end{Bmatrix} \\ \quad \text{when } i \in \mathcal{I} \\ (\Delta \setminus a') \oplus \begin{Bmatrix} i \mapsto \top \\ e \mapsto \Delta(a')\langle * \rangle \\ a \mapsto \langle \Delta(a')\langle * \rangle \vee \oslash \rangle \end{Bmatrix} \\ \quad \text{when } i \notin \mathcal{I} \end{cases}$
	$[\![a' := [a \; \textbf{with} \; i = e]]\!]_{\mathsf{false}}(\Delta) = \Delta \oplus \begin{Bmatrix} i \mapsto \top \\ a \mapsto \langle \oslash \rangle \end{Bmatrix}$

5   Interprocedural Dependencies

Exit labels, presented in Sect. 2.2, constitute an increased source of expressivity, as they indicate the scenario that was observed while executing a predicate. We incorporate this expressivity in our dependency results, by computing specific dependencies for each possible execution scenario. Therefore, our analysis is performed label by label and interprocedural dependency domains associate an intraprocedural domain to each exit label of the analyzed predicate. The variable key-set of each associated intraprocedural domain comprises the inputs of the analyzed predicate. A label that cannot be returned is mapped to an *Unreachable* intraprocedural domain. This is a form of *path-sensitivity* [10]. However, we favor the term *label-sensitivity* for this characteristic, as it seems to be a more natural choice applied to our case and the language we are working on.

An interprocedural domain of a predicate p is thus defined as follows:

$$\mathscr{D}_p : \Lambda_p \to \Delta, \quad \text{where } \Lambda_p \text{ the set of output labels of predicate } p$$

For each analyzed label of a predicate, the analysis starts by initializing the intraprocedural domain mapped to it, with the output variables associated to the exit label. To avoid making any false supposition, these are initially mapped to the most general dependency, namely $\top$. Subsequently, as described in Sect. 4, the dependency information is gradually refined until a fixed point is reached. The execution scenarios denoted by the exit labels of a predicate are mutually exclusive. Therefore, during the analysis of a particular exit label, all other exit labels of the predicate are mapped to *Unreachable*. After reaching a fixed point, the intraprocedural domain is *filtered* so that only input variables appear in the variable set. As explained in Sect. 4, the intraprocedural domains are built such that only input variables may appear as exception indices in dependencies computed for arrays. This invariant is preserved throughout the analysis.

A substitution must be performed on interprocedural domains. This consists in substituting all occurrences of formal input parameters of a predicate by the corresponding effective input parameters. The substitution operation is denoted by $\blacktriangleleft (\sigma)$ where σ is a substitution from formal to effective parameters.

We proceed by detailing the equation corresponding to a call to a predicate:

$$p(e_1, \ldots, e_n)[\lambda_1 : \bar{o}_1 \mid \ldots \mid \lambda_m : \bar{o}_m]$$

having the following signature:

$$p(\epsilon_1, \ldots, \epsilon_n)[\lambda_1 : \bar{\omega}_1 \mid \ldots \mid \lambda_m : \bar{\omega}_m]$$

The general equation form applies:

$$\Delta_n = \bigvee_{n \xrightarrow{s,\lambda_i} n_i} [\![p(e_1, \ldots, e_n)\, [\lambda_1 : \bar{o}_1 \mid \ldots \mid \lambda_m : \bar{o}_m]]\!]_{\lambda_i}(\Delta_{n_i})$$

The transfer functions for the predicate call statement are deduced from the predicate's interprocedural domain in the following fashion:

$$[\![p(e_1, \ldots, e_n)\, [\lambda_1 : \bar{o}_1 \mid \ldots \mid \lambda_m : \bar{o}_m]]\!]_{\lambda_i}(\Delta) = (\Delta \setminus \bar{o}_i) \bigoplus_{j \in \{1, \ldots, n\}} e_j \mapsto dep_j^i$$

where $\quad dep_j^i = \mathscr{D}_p(\lambda_i)(\epsilon_j) \blacktriangleleft (\bar{\epsilon} \mapsto \bar{e})$

Namely, the mappings for the outputs $\bar{o}$ associated to a label λ_i are removed, and the contribution of a call to each input e_j stems from the contribution of the interprocedural domain for label λ_i and formal input ϵ_j. In these, all the formal input parameters $\bar{\epsilon}$ in array dependency domains are substituted by the corresponding effective input parameters from $\bar{e}$.

Semantics. We conclude this section by briefly presenting the two possible interpretations of the results of our analysis. Considering an intraprocedural result Δ_p^λ for a predicate p and label λ, a first interpretation of our dependency analysis is an equivalence relation on tuples of values $\approx_{\Delta_p^\lambda}$ which relates values that only differ in places on which p, λ does not depend. It can be used for applying *congruence modulo* reasoning to predicate calls. Namely, if we write $p(\bar{v}) \xrightarrow{\lambda:\bar{w}}$ to denote that applying p to the values $\bar{v}$ yields the exit label λ with outputs $\bar{w}$, then if p is applied in turn to two input data structures $\bar{u}$ and $\bar{v}$ that are congruent w.r.t. $\approx_{\Delta_p^\lambda}$, the predicate will exercise the same execution scenario:

$$\bar{u} \approx_{\Delta_p^\lambda} \bar{v} \implies p(\bar{u}) \xrightarrow{\lambda:\bar{w}} \implies p(\bar{v}) \cancel{\xrightarrow{\mu:\bar{z}}}$$

Furthermore, identical outputs will be obtained:

$$\bar{u} \approx_{\Delta_p^\lambda} \bar{v} \implies p(\bar{u}) \xrightarrow{\lambda:\bar{w}} \implies p(\bar{v}) \xrightarrow{\lambda:\bar{z}} \implies \bar{w} = \bar{z}$$

whereas this first interpretation focuses on the dependency part of the analysis, it is also possible to focus on the possible constructors part of the analysis. This additional interpretation is a characteristic function $\mathbb{1}_{\Delta_p^\lambda}$ on input values which constrains the space of inputs that can make p exit with label λ. It denotes the necessary conditions on inputs according to the observed execution scenario and can be used as an *inversion lemma* when reasoning on calls to a predicate:

$$p(\bar{u}) \xrightarrow{\lambda:\bar{w}} \implies \mathbb{1}_{\Delta_p^\lambda}(\bar{u})$$

A detailed presentation of these semantics is out of the scope of this paper but in order to give a good intuition of the adequation between the interpretation and the lattice operations described in Sect. 3, we can give some fundamental properties relating the domain operations and these interpretations:

$$\bar{v} \approx_\top \bar{w} \iff \bar{v} = \bar{w} \qquad \bar{v} \approx_\varnothing \bar{w} \wedge \bar{v} \approx_\bot \bar{w} \;\; \forall \bar{v}, \bar{w} \qquad \mathbb{1}_\top = \mathbb{1}_\varnothing = \_ \mapsto 1$$

$$\mathbb{1}_\bot = \_ \mapsto 0 \qquad \Delta \sqsubseteq \Delta' \implies \approx_\Delta \;\supseteq\; \approx_{\Delta'} \qquad \Delta \sqsubseteq \Delta' \implies \mathbb{1}_\Delta \sqsubseteq \mathbb{1}_{\Delta'}$$

$$\approx_{\Delta \oplus \Delta'} \;\subseteq\; \approx_\Delta \cap \approx_\Delta' \qquad \mathbb{1}_\Delta \wedge \mathbb{1}'_\Delta \implies \mathbb{1}_{\Delta \oplus \Delta'}$$

The soundness of the second interpretation as well as the *well-formedness* of our dependency domains have been proven in Coq[2].

6   Preliminary Results and Experiments

Our analysis has currently been applied on two abstract layers of *ProvenCore*, described in Sect. 1. These are the *Refined Security Model* (RSM), an abstract layer situated just underneath the top-most layer of the refinement chain and the *Functional Specifications* (FSP) layer, a model closely resembling the most concrete layer (*Target of Evaluation Design* – TDS) but using data structures and algorithms that facilitate reasoning. Each layer is characterized by a global state with numerous fields and different transitions, i.e. supported commands. Various invariants and properties characterize their states. For example, the FSP's state contains 14 fields; it is characterized by approximately 50 invariants. In the TDS, these figures are doubled. Each invariant is concerned with a different subset of the global state's fields. Some of the invariants concern all the processes held in the process store. However, most transitions affect only a few of these fields. We have applied our analysis at a medium-scale on the RSM and FSP layers. The results for over 660 predicates having approximately 11000 lines of code have been computed in 1.5 s.

One of the analyzed predicates from the FSP layer is:
predicate proc_mem_auth_ok(proc proc) -> [true | false] verifying a fundamental property that has to hold for all processes in the process store of **proc**. It

---

[2] The corresponding files are provided: http://ajl2015.ddns.net/ajl2015/proveCoq.

refers to the *relevance of memory permissions* and states that every process has permissions covering a valid range of memory addresses inside its virtual space. The `process` type is a structure with 26 fields, of which 11 are compound data types themselves. Among these, 2 fields are arrays, 3 fields are variants and 6 others are structures with a number of fields ranging from 3 to 17 fields.

The dependency results computed by our analysis for this predicate are shown below. The analysis detects that for each of the possible execution scenarios, the outcome depends only on 2 out of the 26 fields, namely the stackframe and the memory permissions. The dependency on the `stackframe` is confined to only one of the 3 fields: the data and stack segment. The memory permissions are given by a variant with 3 constructors, denoting reading and writing permissions or the absence of any permission. Furthermore, besides pinning down the outcome's dependency on 2 out of the 26 fields of the `process` structure, the analysis also detects that the absence of any memory permission, indicated by the constructor `NONE` of the `mem_auth` variant, is $\bot$ for the `false` execution scenario. In other words, unused permissions cannot threaten the property `proc_mem_auth_ok`.

$$
\begin{aligned}
\textbf{false} \rightarrow \{proc \rightarrow \{\ mem\_auth \rightarrow [\ & READ\ \rightarrow \{\ base \rightarrow \top;\ len \rightarrow \top\} \\
& WRITE \rightarrow \{\ base \rightarrow \top;\ len \rightarrow \top\} \\
& NONE \rightarrow\ \ \ \bot] \\
stackframe \rightarrow \{\ ds\ \ & \rightarrow\ \ \ \top\}\}\} \\
\textbf{true}\ \rightarrow \{proc \rightarrow \{\ mem\_auth \rightarrow [\ & READ\ \rightarrow \{\ base \rightarrow \top;\ len \rightarrow \top\} \\
& WRITE \rightarrow \{\ base \rightarrow \top;\ len \rightarrow \top\} \\
& NONE \rightarrow\ \ \ \oslash] \\
stackframe \rightarrow \{\ ds\ \ & \rightarrow\ \ \ \top\}\}\}
\end{aligned}
$$

The *relevant memory permissions* property is thus only threatened by transitions that add memory permissions or change a process' virtual space layout. Only 3 transitions out of the 25 belong to this category: `exec` which resets the process' segments, `do_auth_read` and `do_auth_write` which add permissions. In particular, transitions deleting memory permissions do not impact the property since the absence of permissions, as shown by the dependency of the constructor `NONE` for the `false` label, is an impossible case when the property does not hold. This is one of the practical advantages of tracking constructor possibilities simultaneously.

Space constraints prevent us from discussing other examples here. However, various other examples are provided on the webpage[3] dedicated to our analysis.

7 Related Work

The *frame problem* and its manifestations in the software verification process – detecting program properties that remain unchanged under a certain operation – are notorious. First described in 1969 [8], the frame problem is still a target for full automation in the software verification realm. A *complete specification* of a program will necessarily include *frame properties*. However, though necessary, frame properties are tedious and repetitive. Two prominent solutions to the

---

[3] http://ajl2015.ddns.net/ajl2015/.

frame problem come from *separation logic* [4] and *ownership types* [1]. However, it is argued that the problem itself should not impose such annotation-heavy solutions. Simpler, automatic solutions for their specification and verification would allow programmers to concentrate on the truly challenging part [9].

The dependency results computed by our analysis are similar to *primitive read* and *write effects* used in ownership type systems [1]. Write effects in our case are implicit and include strictly the output variables associated to an exit label. Read effects can only refer to input variables of a predicate. Also, read effects comprise the whole execution of a method even if they are irrelevant for the method's results. We however, ignore read effects on which the output does not depend, reflecting only those which contribute to the observed result. A technique for declaring and verifying read effects in an ownership type system is presented in [1]. We use static analysis to automatically detect them.

Our dependencies are similar to the *influence sets* presented by Leino and Müller [5]. Influence sets are represented as sets of heap locations and they are used to specify the parts of the program state that are allowed to impact the return values. Reasoning about heap locations is beyond the scope of our analysis. We treat mappings between variables and values, analyze their evolution in a side-effect free environment and express dependencies as input-output relations.

Static dependence or liveness analyses are typically used for code optimization, dead code elimination [7] and compile time garbage collection, but only seldom for program verification. One case we are aware of comes from Frama-C [2], where it is used in a purely *automatic* setting and unlike our analysis it does not handle unions and arrays. A plug-in based on the available value analysis [3] computes lists of input and output locations for each function, distinguishing between *operational*, *functional* and *imperative inputs*.

8   Conclusion

We have presented a *flow-sensitive*, *path-sensitive*, interprocedural dependency analysis that handles arrays, structures and variants. For the latter it simultaneously computes a subset of possible constructors. We have defined our own abstract dependency domain and obtain dependency information that mirrors the layered structure of compound data types.

The main original traits of our contribution stem from its design as an analysis meant to be used as a companion tool during interactive program verification, in an unified manner on programs as well as on specifications.

An obvious first challenge is to address the issue of *context-sensitivity*. We plan to introduce lazy components in our interprocedural dependency summaries and to inject in them the current intraprocedural context on an as-needed basis. Early experiments show much promise in terms of improved precision, with only a marginal decrease in performance.

Our long-term goal is to combine the dependency analysis with a correlation analysis, meant to detect relations between inputs and outputs. By uncovering relations (preorders and equivalences) between inputs and outputs, after having detected that a property only depends on unmodified parts and unifying the results, the preservation of invariants for the unmodified parts could be inferred.

Acknowledgments. We would like to thank the anonymous referees for helpful comments and suggestions. For his excellent comments and sharp observations, we are particularly grateful to Olivier Delande. Our article also benefited from the remarks of P. Bolignano, G. Dupéron, L. Hubert and B. Montagu.

References

1. Clarke, D., Drossopoulou, S.: Ownership, encapsulation and the disjointness of type and effect. In: Proceedings of the 17th ACM SIGPLAN Conference on Object-oriented Programming, Systems, Languages, and Applications, OOPSLA 2002, pp. 292–310. ACM, New York, NY, USA (2002)
2. Cuoq, P., Kirchner, F., Kosmatov, N., Prevosto, V., Signoles, J., Yakobowski, B.: Frama-C. In: Eleftherakis, G., Hinchey, M., Holcombe, M. (eds.) SEFM 2012. LNCS, vol. 7504, pp. 233–247. Springer, Heidelberg (2012)
3. Cuoq, P., Prevosto, V., Yakobowski, B.: Frama-c value analysis manual. http://frama-c.com/download/value-analysis-Neon-20140301.pdf
4. Distefano, D., O'Hearn, P.W., Yang, H.: A local shape analysis based on separation logic. In: Hermanns, H., Palsberg, J. (eds.) TACAS 2006. LNCS, vol. 3920, pp. 287–302. Springer, Heidelberg (2006)
5. Leino, K.R.M., Müller, P.: Verification of equivalent-results methods. In: Drossopoulou, S. (ed.) ESOP 2008. LNCS, vol. 4960, pp. 307–321. Springer, Heidelberg (2008)
6. Lescuyer, S.: ProvenCore: Towards a verified isolation micro-kernel (2015)
7. Liu, Y., Stoller, S.: Eliminating dead code on recursive data. Sci. Comput. Program. **47**(2–3), 221–242 (2003). (special Issue on Static Analysis (SAS 1999))
8. Mccarthy, J., Hayes, P.J.: Some philosophical problems from the standpoint of artificial intelligence. In: Machine Intelligence, pp. 463–502. Edinburgh University Press (1969)
9. Meyer, B.: Framing the frame problem. In: Pretschner, A., Broy, M., Irlbeck, M. (eds.) Dependable Software Systems, Proc. of August 2014 Marktoberdorf Summer School. pp. 174–185. D: Information and Communication Security, Springer (2015)
10. Robert, V., Leroy, X.: A formally-verified alias analysis. In: Hawblitzel, C., Miller, D. (eds.) CPP 2012. LNCS, vol. 7679, pp. 11–26. Springer, Heidelberg (2012)

A SysML Formal Framework to Combine Discrete and Continuous Simulation for Testing

Jean-Marie Gauthier[✉], Fabrice Bouquet, Ahmed Hammad, and Fabien Peureux

Institut FEMTO-ST – UMR CNRS 6174, Université Bourgogne Franche-Comté, 16, Route de Gray, 25030 Besançon, France
{jmgauthi,fbouquet,ahammad,fpeureux}@femto-st.fr

Abstract. The increasing interactions between huge amount of software and hardware subsystem (hydraulics, mechanics, electronics, etc.) lead to a new kind of complexity that is difficult to manage during the validation of safety-critical and complex embedded systems. This paper introduces a formal SysML-based framework to combine both discrete and continuous simulation to validate physical systems at the early stage of development. This original modelling framework takes as input a SysML model annotated with Modelica code and OCL constraints. Such a model provides a precise and unambiguous description of the designed system and its environment, involving both discrete and continuous features. This formal framework enables to automatically generate Modelica code to perform real-time simulation. On the basis of a constraint system derived from the discrete SysML/OCL modelling artefacts, it also makes it possible to automatically generate black-box test cases that can be used to validate the simulated system as well as the corresponding physical device. This framework has been validated by conclusive experiments conducted to prototype a new energy manager system for aeronautics.

Keywords: SysML · Model-driven engineering · Real-time system · Discrete & continuous simulation · Modelica · Constraint solving · Model-based testing

1 Introduction

Due to increasing behavioural complexity and growing technology heterogeneity combined with still higher expectations, checking that a software embedded system meets its specifications becomes more and more complex, expansive and time-consuming. Moreover, in the traditional development of such systems, the Verification and Validation (V&V) activities begin only after implementation and integration are completed. Under these conditions, discovered problems are particularly more difficult and more expensive to fix, what is a major concern especially when the systems are critical, such as lots of system for aeronautical, railway, automotive, nuclear or telecommunication domains. In these contexts,

© Springer International Publishing Switzerland 2015
M. Butler et al. (Eds.): ICFEM 2015, LNCS 9407, pp. 134–152, 2015.
DOI: 10.1007/978-3-319-25423-4_9

such systems indeed require to be as trusty as possible because the most little failure could lead to financial as well as human losses, and even so to an irreversible damage of the whole system including its environment.

To mitigate these issues, Model-Based Software Engineering (MBSE) approaches have emerged for several years as a way to improve and automate design, analysis, development, verification and validation of the software embedded in high technology products. Basically, MBSE aims to achieve these software life cycle activities using models that describe the system under development. This kind of approach is mostly supported using (semi-)formal modelling artefacts, which are enough precise to achieve formal verification, but also simulation and testing that provide early practical feedback to validate requirements [1]. Simulation code generation from formal model is increasing as it reduces the gap between high level of abstraction modelling and rapid prototyping, as demonstrated in [2]. Finally, using formal model also enables to apply Model-Based Testing (MBT) approaches [3] that aim to cross-check a model against an implementation, and hence make it possible to provide early validation of functional as well as non-functional properties, such as performance and resource use.

In addition, applying iterative and incremental approaches has also helped the development of critical embedded systems, especially within real-time domain. Such typical approaches are known as *In-the-Loop* processes, and can be performed at different levels: Model-in-the-loop (MIL), hardware-in-the-loop (HIL), processor-in-the-loop (PIL), and software-in-the-loop (SIL) [4]. Simulation and testing are at the core of all these system design processes. For example, within MIL process, at the early stages of the design process, the system (or subpart of the system) and its environment are modelled and simulated using languages such as Modelica[1] or Matlab-Simulink[2] to ensure that the designed (sub)system conforms to its requirements [5]. Another level of simulation and testing concerns the HIL process and consists to test the real hardware platform in combination with its simulated environment (called the *plant* model) [6].

This paper describes an original SysML-based formal framework for simulation and testing of multi-physical and critical systems, that bridges the gap between high-level design model, starting point of MBSE approaches, and real-time execution platform, keystone of the In-the-Loop approaches. In this way, this framework allows system engineers to stay as close as possible of the initial design specifications when achieving all the steps of the development life-cycle. Moreover, it takes advantage of both approaches by ensuring a model centric process enabling validation, simulation and testing from the earliest stage of design. To achieve that, the architecture and the discrete behaviour of the system are described by a Systems Modeling Language (SysML) [7] model, which is annotated with OCL and Modelica code to specify its discrete and continuous features. This model is used to automatically generate real-time Modelica program for simulation, and black-box test cases for validation. The generated test cases can be simulated using the generated Modelica program to validate the

---

[1] https://www.modelica.org/documents/ModelicaSpec33.pdf.
[2] http://www.mathworks.fr/products/matlab/.

design model as well as the the physical system itself. Therefore, the proposed framework can contribute both to MIL process (model against simulated environment), and to HIL process (physical system against simulated environment).

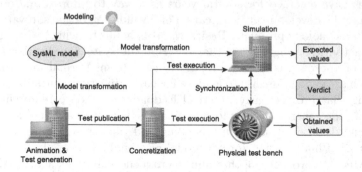

Fig. 1. Overview of the Validation Process from SysML Models

The validation process supporting this formal framework is depicted in Fig. 1. The process starts on the top left with the SysML model that specifies both the system and the plant. This model is expressed using a dedicated subset of the SysML language, which integrates as a whole SysML constructs, Modelica code and OCL annotations. From such a model, a first transformation automatically produces an executable Modelica program to perform real-time simulation. A second transformation allows deriving a set of constraints describing the discrete and abstract behaviours of the system. This set of constraints can be solved to achieve (in a discrete manner) animation of the system as well as test case generation by selecting a subset of trace executions. These abstract test cases are concretized into executable test scripts that can be executed both on Modelica simulation model (within MIL and HIL processes) and physical test bench (within HIL process). During MIL testing, simulation results are manually compared with the initial system requirements and may also be assessed by the domain experts. Once the model is validated, it becomes the test oracle within the HIL testing process: it computes the expected values of the test cases and allows systematic comparison with the real values obtained on the physical test bench (a synchronization step between simulation and test bench environments is required to automate the comparison and the verdict assignment).

The paper is organized as follows. Section 2 introduces the background of the framework to achieve modelling, animation, simulation and test generation from SysML models, and motivates the work presented in the paper. In Sect. 3, we detail the SysML and OCL subset supported by the framework for discrete specifications, and we describe how it is natively combined with Modelica for real-time simulation. Section 4 reports on the conclusive results obtained on a real-life case-study about an helicopter Energy Manager System. Finally, after discussing related work in Sect. 5, we conclude and outline future work in Sect. 6.

2   Background and Motivation

This section clarifies our motivation by introducing preliminaries on the SysML modelling language and the Modelica simulation code, and presents the standard SysML4Modelica that specifies the way to combine them. We also describe the test engine that enables to animate SysML models and apply MBT strategies.

2.1   SysML Modelling Language

The SysML Modelling Language [7], developed within the Object Management Group (OMG) since 2001, enables system engineers to specify all aspects of a complex system using graphical constructs. SysML is a UML profile that adapts the UML semantics to the system engineering field. The semantics of UML, through class and composite structure diagrams, has been moved to the system-level in SysML by the definition of the Block Definition Diagram (BDD) and Internal Block Diagram (IBD). The BDD is based on the UML class diagram. It enables to define component using blocks and their relationships such as associations, generalizations and dependencies. These blocks are instantiated as parts in the IBD, which is a system-level version of the UML composite structure diagram. It specifies the internal organization of a block by describing its parts and the connections between them. Usually, parts are connected through flow ports.

Using SysML allows engineers to achieve MBSE approach to specify, develop and maintain complex systems, notably in the aerospace industry as shown in [8]. In previous work [9], we have proposed to use SysML models to apply MBT strategies to automatically generate functional black-box test cases. To reach this goal, subsets of SysML and OCL, called SysML4MBT and OCL4MBT, have been defined to precisely model the expected behaviour of the System Under Test (SUT) [10]. It contains BDD and IBD to specify the static structure of the SUT and its environment, and state machines with OCL constraints to specify, in a discrete way, behavioural features. Such models are complete and precise enough to automatically derive black-box test cases using the CLPS-BZ test engine.

2.2   Model Animation and Test Generation Using CLPS-BZ

CLPS-BZ [11] is a constraint solver that augments the capabilities of (and co-operates with) the integer finite domain solver of SICStus Prolog[3] by handling constraints over sets, relations and mappings. Initially built to animate and generate test cases from B and Z set-oriented formal specifications [12], it has been extended to manage object-oriented specifications, such as UML/SysML models with OCL constraints [13]. Basically, such models are translated into an internal Prolog-readable syntax, called BZP, which provides special constructs for defining SysML diagrams and OCL expressions as constraints over sets. CLPS-BZ makes it possible to efficiently execute on discrete domains the BZP code, both for model animation and for test computation. Test computation consists to look

---

[3] https://sicstus.sics.se.

into the graph of reachable states of the system described by the constraints to achieve classical test coverage criteria including transition-based, decision-based and data-oriented criteria [9]. Afterwards, a set of execution traces, that define the test cases, is computed by solving the constraints to find the sequences of operation invocations that ensure the given criteria. To achieve that, CLPS-BZ animates the model and computes a reachability graph, whose nodes are the constrained states built during the animation, and whose transitions define an operation invocation. Using constraint solving dramatically reduces the search space during test generation, which allows the method to scale to larger systems.

The constraint system, described using the BZP format, obviously defines a Constraint Satisfaction Problem (CSP) [14], i.e. a set of constraints, which must be satisfied by the solution of the problem it models. Formally, a CSP is a triplet $< V, D, C >$ where V is a set of variables $\{v_1, \ldots, v_n\}$, D is a set of domains $\{d_1, \ldots, d_n\}$, where d_i is the domain associated with the variable v_i, and C is a set of constraints $\{c_1(V_1), \ldots, c_m(V_m)\}$, where a constraint c_j involves a subset V_j of the variables of V. Within CLPS-BZ, which is able to manage sets and integer finite domains, variables of V can be either an *atom*, or a set of atoms (*set(atom)*), or a set of (nested) pairs of atom (*set(pair(atom, atom))*). However, the CLPS-BZ technology is only able to handle constraints on discrete domains and thus can execute neither animation nor test generation based on continuous formula to efficiently address real-time systems. Therefore, CLPS-BZ enables to derive test cases, as sequences of operation invocations, but an other and independent model or program is necessary to execute them in the continuous domain to gather the real and expected results. Moreover, SysML is natively not executable: it does not include an action language, which could allow to simulate SysML model, and even less if equations occur. To overcome this lack, the OMG has proposed an extension to SysML to allow clarifying such mathematical properties into SysML models using Modelica code. Hence, we propose to use this extension to adapt and complete the existing approach to be able to manage in a single model both high-level discrete requirements and low-level continuous behaviours for test generation purpose.

2.3   Modelica and SysML4Modelica

Modelica is an object-oriented and equation-based language adapted to complex physical systems modelling. Indeed, Modelica is built on acausal modelling with mathematical equations and object-oriented constructs, and is designed to support effective library development and model exchange. Since 2012, the OMG promotes a dedicated SysML-Modelica Transformation specification[4] to integrate Modelica semantics into SysML and to provide a bi-directional transformation between the both languages. The specification gives an extension to SysML, called SysML4Modelica, which proposes matching semantics between the SysML constructs and the Modelica code. The integration of Modelica concepts into SysML is based on profiling: the SysML4Modelica constructs enable to stereotype elements, which are parts of the BDD and the IBD of SysML.

---

[4] http://www.omg.org/spec/SyM/.

Hence, to describe complex and heterogeneous systems, the SysML4Modelica profile enables to bring together, in a single model, the non executable graphical high-level SysML modelling and the real-time and continuous Modelica specifications. However, no theoretical framework is given to provide a practical way to combine the architecture and discrete behaviours of SysML models with the continuous aspects described by Modelica formula. This paper bridges this gap by defining such a framework to bring them back together to achieve model-based testing. It integrates constraint solving to address discrete animation and black-box test generation, and Modelica simulation to address continuous needs.

This proposed framework aims (1) to avoid managing several models (at least one for high-level discrete design and one for low-level continuous features) that require to be manually synchronized, (2) to increase the automation level of the model-based testing approach by minimizing the number of testing artefacts and by providing a native link between abstract data (from SysML structures) and executable structures (derived from Modelica code), and (3) to foster the use of MBSE approach by supporting in the same modelling framework all design steps of the real-time system life-cycle activities. The next section precisely introduces the modelling framework we define to efficiently combine discrete and continuous features in a single model for simulation and model-based testing purposes.

3 Combining Continuous and Discrete Modelling

This section gives a formal description of the SysML modelling framework unifying discrete and continuous points of view. As depicted in Fig. 2, the resulting framework is defined by the intersection of the SysML subset for discrete modelling with the one dedicated to continuous modelling. In this section, these both SysML subsets are detailed and we show how the combination of them defines a formal SysML modelling framework for simulation and testing activities. Afterwards, the next section will introduce a proof-of-concept integrated tool chain implementing this theoretical framework. However, this

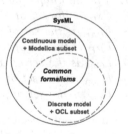

Fig. 2. Overlap of the SysML subsets

framework defines a generic way to combine discrete and continuous SysML modelling, and therefore it can be used and implemented using another similar tooled approaches.

NOTE: in the rest of the paper, to dispel any ambiguity and avoid misunderstanding, *animation* is defined as a discrete evaluation of the model (variables belong to finite domains or sets), i.e. an execution of the model based on constraint solving restricted to the SysML data that belong to finite domains or sets, whereas *simulation* means real-time simulation of the model, i.e. an execution of the Modelica code describing the system in a continuous-time process.

3.1   SysML Subset for Simulation

The SysML subset for simulation purpose focuses on the following diagrams: BDD, IBD and state machine. The structural view of the system is specified in the BDD with blocks, which are connected each other using flow ports that are depicted in the IBD. The behaviour of each system component may be described using state machines. We thus define a SysML model for simulation as a model M_s comprising two kind of blocks (blocks for component definition and blocks that type flow ports) and enumerations. A block that types flow ports only contains properties (no behaviour). SysML enumerations enable declaring abstract types that can be used during a Modelica simulation.

Definition 1 (Model for simulation). *Let M_s, the model for simulation, be given by $M_s = <\eta, \Gamma_{Bs}, \Gamma_{Bf}, \Gamma_{Enum}>$, where η is the name of the model, Γ_{Bs} is the set of SysML blocks that defines components, Γ_{Bf} is the set of SysML blocks that types flow ports and Γ_{Enum} is the set of enumerations.*

A component is defined with attributes and may be composed of other components. Thus, it may have different typed elements (properties, parts and flow ports). Its behaviour may be specified by a state diagram with Modelica code.

Definition 2 (Block for component definition). *We define $\beta \in \Gamma_{Bs}$ to be the tuple $\beta = <\eta, \Gamma_{Att}, \Gamma_{Part}, \Gamma_{FP}, \Gamma_{Cnt}, \Gamma_{Cons}, \Gamma_{SM}>$, where:*

1. *η is the unique name of the block,*
2. *Γ_{Att} is the set of attributes,*
3. *Γ_{Part} is the set of parts,*
4. *Γ_{FP} is the set of flow ports,*
5. *Γ_{Cnt} is the set of connectors,*
6. *Γ_{Cons} is the set of constraints,*
7. *Γ_{SM} is the set of parallel state machines.*

Each attribute, each part and each flow port shall be typed with primitive types (real, integer and Boolean, respectively noted $\mathbb{R}$, $\mathbb{Z}$ and $\mathbb{B}$) or with user-defined type (block for part, block for flow port and enumeration, respectively noted Γ_{Bs}, Γ_{Bf} and Γ_{Enum}). The set of types Γ_T by $\Gamma_T = \{\Gamma_{Bs}, \Gamma_{Bf}, \Gamma_{Enum}, \mathbb{R}, \mathbb{B}, \mathbb{Z}\}$ are defined as follows. Concerning attributes of Γ_{Att}, we have to distinguish several cases: an attribute may be a constant, an equation's unknown or a parameter that defines the initial condition of the simulation. Within Modelica, an equation's unknown, which needs to be solved by integration, can be either continuous or discrete.

Definition 3 (Attribute). *Let $\alpha \in \Gamma_{Att}$ be defined by $\alpha = <\eta, \omega, \upsilon, t>$ where:*

1. *η is the name of the attribute,*
2. *ω is variability such as $\omega \in \{constant, parameter, discrete, continuous\}$,*
3. *υ is the value of the attribute,*
4. *t is the type of the attribute ($\Gamma_{Enum}, \mathbb{R}, \mathbb{B},$ or $\mathbb{Z}$).*

If an attribute is discrete or continuous, then it is necessarily a state variable.

A block that types ports can only have properties, i.e., attributes that describe what flows between ports. Then, the following is the definition of such blocks:

Definition 4 (Block for flow ports typing). *We define $\beta_f \in \Gamma_{Bf}$ to be the tuple: $\beta_f =< \eta, \Gamma_{Att} >$, where η is the unique name of the block and Γ_{Att} is the non-empty set of attributes.*

We need also to formalize the connection between parts of a SysML model. Connections are always between two flow ports, and a flow port has to be connected at least to one other flow port. Then, we define the surjective connecting function as follows:

Definition 5 (Connecting function). *Let f_c, the surjective connecting function, be defined by $f_c : \Gamma_{FP} \times \Gamma_{FP} \twoheadrightarrow \Gamma_{Cnt}$.*

The continuous behaviour of the system is specified by equations over continuous state variables. The SysML constraints (Γ_{Cons}) are written using a subset of the Modelica language that expresses equations. Numerical solvers (embedded in all Modelica frameworks) are able to rewrite such constraints into a set of first-order differential equations in order to compute integration over time.

Finally, state machine diagrams enable to describe the life-cycle of a component. For instance, one may specify several component states depending on time, state variables or user behaviours. The formal definition is given below (it excludes join, fork and history pseudo-states that are not supported).

Definition 6 (State machine). *State machine for simulation is described with its classical definition $SM =< s_0, \Sigma, \Gamma_E, \mathscr{L}_s, \delta >$, where:*

1. *s_0 is the initial state,*
2. *Σ is a finite non-empty set of states composed of three disjoint sets: simple states Σ_{ss}, compound states Σ_{cs} and eventually final states Σ_{fs},*
3. *Γ_E is the set of trigger events,*
4. *$\mathscr{L}_s$ is the alphabet for specifying guard and effect of a transition,*
5. *$\delta : \Sigma \times \Gamma_E \times \mathscr{L}_s \rightarrow \Sigma$ is the transition function.*

The language $\mathscr{L}_s$, used for specifying guards and effects, is a subset of the Modelica language. A guard is a Modelica Boolean expression and an effect is a Modelica statement such as *assignment, if-statement, while-statement* or *for-statement*. Moreover, each state may have *onEntry* and *onExit* actions, which are respectively executed at the entry and the exit of the state. These are defined using Modelica statements. Concerning trigger events Γ_E, we only consider call events, i.e. representing an operation call. The called operations have to be defined in the block that the state machine specifies. However, we do not consider the operations of the blocks for components definition because operations are not translated into Modelica code, only trigger events are.

The above presented subset (summarized in Table 1 in Sect. 3.3) is sufficient to perform Modelica code generation and simulation. This subset enables to validate a system at the earliest stage of a design process by automating the derivation of Modelica code. To provide a modelling framework that enables to perform both simulation and testing from a single SysML model, discrete aspects of the system have also to be integrated in order to use the CLPS-BZ solver for animation and test case generation purposes.

3.2 SysML Subset for Animation and Test Generation

The SysML subset for animation (SysML4MBT with OCL4MBT [9]) enables to formally specify the system to perform a constraint evaluation. Such a SysML model describes the system from an abstract and discrete point of view. The model is abstract in the way that the domain of a variable in $\mathbb{R}$ is discretized using enumeration classes since CLPS-BZ only manages integers, Booleans and finite sets. The behaviour of the model is also discrete as, during animation, we do not know what happen between two stable states of the state machines. Of course, simulation gives us some information about it, but during model animation, each state transition is executed as an atomic and non-breaking computation.

Definition 7 (Model for animation). *The model for animation M_a is defined by $M_a =< \eta, \Gamma_{Ba}, \Gamma_{Enum}, \Gamma_{Asso} >$, where η is the name of the model, Γ_{Ba} is the set of SysML blocks that defines components, Γ_{Enum} is the set of enumerations and Γ_{Asso} is the set of associations between blocks.*

Associations of Γ_{Asso} are translated into relations between instances of classes. The multiplicities of the association determine whether the relationship is a function, and if so, the type of this function (partial or total, and possibly injective, surjective or bijective). Hence, the associations are translated into structures of type $\Gamma_{Part} \times \Gamma_{Part}$.

A block for component definition comprises attributes, parts and operations, which are used to describe actions from the environment.

Definition 8 (Block for component definition). *We define $\beta \in \Gamma_{Ba}$ to be the tuple $\beta =< \eta, \Gamma_{Att}, \Gamma_{Part}, \Gamma_{Op}, \Gamma_{SM} >$, where:*

1. *η is the unique name of the block ,*
2. *Γ_{Att} is the set of attributes,*
3. *Γ_{Part} is the set of parts,*
4. *Γ_{Op} is the set of operations,*
5. *Γ_{SM} is the set of parallel state machines.*

Blocks define variables of the CSP and their domains are defined by the set of instances (Γ_{Part}) of these blocks. With CLPS-BZ, each block is associated with information concerning its instances: the set of instances that can potentially be created (*all_instances* as a *set(atom)*), the set of currently created instances (*instances* as a *set(atom)*), and the current instance, which is the last created instance or treated by an operation (*currentInstance* as an *atom*). Among all the possible instances *all_instances*, a fictitious *none* instance is created. It is used in the case to formalize the absence of current instance. Concerning enumerations, they are translated into *set(atom)*, where the atoms are the literals defined in the enumeration. Thus, enumerations define domains in the CSP.

For animation, the set of types Γ_{Ta} is defined by $\Gamma_{Ta} = \{\Gamma_{Ba}, \Gamma_{Enum}, \mathbb{B}, \mathbb{Z}\}$.

Definition 9 (Attribute). *Let $\alpha \in \Gamma_{Att}$ be defined by $\alpha = < \eta, \omega, \upsilon, t >$ where:*

1. *η is the name of the attribute,*
2. *$\omega \in \{constant, variable\}$, and if $\omega = variable$ then ω is a state variable,*
3. *υ is the value of the attribute during the animation,*
4. *t is the type of the attribute ($\mathbb{Z}$, $\mathbb{B}$ or Γ_{Enum}).*

Each attribute $\alpha \in \Gamma_{Att}$, belonging to a block β, is translated into a total function between all instances of the block β and the domain of α. Considering for example that α is an integer, α is translated into a structure of type $\Gamma_{Part} \times \mathbb{Z}$.

The operations have a name and optional parameters ($in, out, inout, return$). For animation purpose, we only take into account in and $return$ parameters. In addition, operations can also have OCL4MBT precondition and postcondition.

Definition 10 (Operation). *Let $o \in \Gamma_{Op}$ defined as $o = < \eta, \Gamma_{Par}, pre, post >$ where: η is the name of the attribute, Γ_{Par} is the set of parameters, pre is the precondition of the operation and post is the postcondition of the operation.*

State machines are used to specify discrete component behaviours and external, physical or human, actions. For animation purpose, state machines are defined as expressed in the definition 6. However, we define $\mathcal{L}_a$, based on the OCL4MBT subset, as the alphabet for specifying guard and effect of a transition.

Each state (single, composite, initial or final state) of a state machine is translated into a specific context of the CSP. For each state, a variable *status* stores the current state(s) of a block instance: it is a function associating each instance of the block to a Boolean (the function is partial due to the presence of the fictitious *none* instance in its domain). At the beginning of the animation, each instance is in the initial state. In addition, two operations are declared to each state to formalize the possible *onEntry* and *onExit* effects.

Each state machine is associated with the block it specifies the behaviour. Operations of this block can be used as triggers for some transitions of the state machine. To avoid unmanageable infinite loop during animation, three types of transitions are allowed: external (reflexive or not) with trigger, internal with trigger and guarded external or automatic (not reflexive). A variable *opCalled* $\in$ Γ_E, declared to store the last executed operation, enables to fire, from the current state, transition triggered by this operation. We finally add a precondition for all guarded and automatic transitions, expressing that no operation has been called (*opCalled* $=$ *none*). This ensures that the UML "run-to-completion" semantic is satisfied. To sum up, each state gives rise to a variable *status* and constraints related to the *onEntry* and *onExit* actions. Each transition is translated into constraints in the CSP that are defined by its guard and effect. Finally, trigger events of Γ_E define a set of operation triggers *set(atom)* that defines the domain of the variable *opCalled*.

The above formalized subset (summarized in Table 1 in Sect. 3.3) enables to animate a discrete and abstract SysML model by translating it into a CSP. This CSP is defined by a Prolog-readable BZP file such that it is now possible to specify the continuous and discrete behaviour of a complex and critical system for simulation, animation and testing purpose. In the next subsection, we combine these subsets to adress both continuous and discrete features.

3.3 Combined Formalism for Simulation and Animation

Table 1 summarizes the SysML subsets for simulation and animation. Each combined SysML element are derived both to Modelica element and to CSP element (variable V, domain D or constraint C). To propose a unified modelling framework, blocks and enumerations for simulation have to be used for animation. Then, the model for validation M_v is defined as $M_v = M_s \cap M_a = \{\Gamma_{Bv}, \Gamma_{Enum}\}$ where $\Gamma_{Bv} = \Gamma_{Bs} \cap \Gamma_{Ba}$. Blocks for flow port typing (Γ_{Bf}) are not used for animation. Considering now $\beta_1 \in \Gamma_{Bs}$ and $\beta_2 \in \Gamma_{Ba}$, then $\beta_1 \cap \beta_2 = < \eta, \Gamma_{Att}, \Gamma_{Part}, \Gamma_{SM} >$ where each attribute of Γ_{Att} is defined as proposed in definition 9. Indeed, Modelica is able to process discrete and continuous variables whereas the CLPS-BZ solver is not able to manage continuous state variables. Concerning SysML parts, they enable to instantiate Modelica components and to declare block instances in the constraint system.

Finally, state machines for simulation and animation are not totally combined. The language for specifying guard and effect of transitions, as well as *onEntry* and *onExit* actions of states, is indeed not fully equivalent. In one case, the language $\mathscr{L}_s$ is a subset of Modelica and in the other case, the language $\mathscr{L}_a$ is a subset of OCL. However, states, transitions and events are used for both simulation and animation. Thus, every state machines are translated both into Modelica code (using formula of $\mathscr{L}_s$) and CSP (using OCL code of $\mathscr{L}_a$). It should be noted that state machines without OCL code and event trigger are not translated into CSP because it would not impact the CSP solving and could even give a under-constrained CSP (and make it non deterministic).

4   Implementation and Case-Study Evaluation

This section discusses the proposed modelling framework regarding an industrial case-study about a large and complex Energy Manager System (EMS) that delivers energy to a new type of helicopter. Figure 3 shows the architecture of our simulation, animation, and testing environment from SysML models. This Eclipse-based tool chain, that instantiates the intended process given in Fig. 1, strongly relies on Model-Driven Architecture (MDA) approach since model transformation and code generation procedures enable to automatically derive the simulation and testing artefacts from the SysML models [15]. Therefore, the SysML model is translated into Modelica simulation code and into a pivot meta-model, named UML4TST, and next into BZP file. Finally, Papyrus[5]

---

[5] https://www.eclipse.org/papyrus/.

Table 1. SysML for Modelica Simulation and CSP Animation

SysML elements	Modelica elements	CSP <V,D,C>
Model M_v	Root Modelica model	CSP model
Blocks Γ_{Bv}	Model	$\Gamma_{Bv} \in V$
Blocks Γ_{Bf}	Connector	-
Enumerations Γ_{Enum}	Enumeration type	$\Gamma_{Enum} \in D$
Attributes Γ_{Att}	Value property	$\Gamma_{Att} \in V$
Constraints Γ_{Cons}	Equation	-
Parts Γ_{Part}	Component	$\Gamma_{Part} \in D$
FlowPorts Γ_{FP}	Port	-
Connectors	Connect equation	-
Op. Precondition $pre \in \Gamma_{Op}$	-	$pre \in C\ (\mathscr{L}_a)$
Op. Postcondition $post \in \Gamma_{Op}$	-	$post \in C\ (\mathscr{L}_a)$
Op. parameters Γ_{Param}	-	$\Gamma_{Param} \in D$
State-Machines SM	Algorithm section	-
States Σ	Boolean variable	$status$ variable $\in V$
State $Entry$	Statement $(\mathscr{L}_s)$	$Entry \in C\ (\mathscr{L}_a)$
State $Exit$	Statement $(\mathscr{L}_s)$	$Exit \in C\ (\mathscr{L}_a)$
Event triggers Γ_E	Boolean variable	$\Gamma_E \in D$
Transition δ	When statement	-
Transition $guard$	Boolean expr $(\mathscr{L}_s)$	$guard \in C\ (\mathscr{L}_a)$
Transition $effect$	Statement $(\mathscr{L}_s)$	$effect \in C\ (\mathscr{L}_a)$

is used to support the SysML modelling, OpenModelica[6] computes the simulations, and CLPS-BZ (included as a plugin in our Eclipse environment) generates the test cases that are exported as UTP sequence diagrams in the SysML model.

This tool chain has been tested out during the prototyping phase of the EMS system within HIL process. Hence, we distinguish the system under design (the EMS) and its environment called the plant system (a simulation model of some helicopter's instruments). The objective of our experiment was to assess the suitability and the reliability of the combined formalism to perform simulation and test generation. The experiment started from requirement specifications given in natural language. They describe the EMS and the physical limit of its components, and the instruments of the helicopter with their energy request over time during the activation period. We now describe the main results obtained from this experimentation, which was divided into five stages: (1) EMS and plant modelling (using SysML subset for simulation), (2) simulating the system components using a scenario example, (3) adding abstraction and discrete

---

[6] https://www.openmodelica.org.

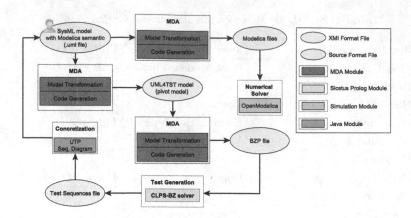

Fig. 3. Overall Architecture of the Simulation and Testing Tool Chain

behaviours (using SysML subset for animation), (4) animating the model and generating test cases, and (5) executing test cases on the simulation model.

SysML Modelling for Simulation. The EMS, depicted in Fig. 4, is composed of an energy source that emulates a permanent power source, an accumulators battery, a battery of super-capacitors, and a bus that connects the energy sources. Each source is described by a specific IBD, which specifies the source and its controller for managing strategies. The helicopter energy requests go through the flow port *Icharge* modelled at the top of the IBD.

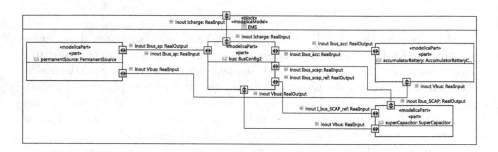

Fig. 4. IBD of the Energy Manager System

The plant model comprises 14 helicopter's instruments that all require energy during a mission. For confidentiality reason, we cannot cite these components and provide more details about the EMS and the plant. However, the IBD of Fig. 5 shows 4 instruments that require energy over time. Each of them is connected to a bus that sums the energy demand. The *outPlant* flow port enables to connect the plant to the *Icharge* flow port of the EMS. The functional and continuous modes of the instruments are specified with state machines and equations.

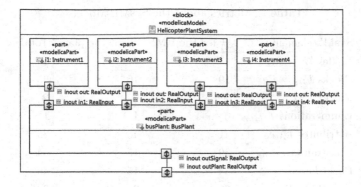

Fig. 5. IBD of the Plant Model

Overall information about the SysML model is provided in Table 2. Note that the bold numbers are the same for the EMS and the plant. This means that the EMS and the plant are specified in the same SysML model ($M_s = 1$) and that blocks for flow port typing ($\Gamma_{Bf} = \{RealInput, RealOutput\}$) are used both in the EMS and in the plant. From this SysML model, 626 lines of Modelica code have been automatically generated for the plant, and 412 lines for the EMS.

Model Animation and Test Generation. The EMS and the plant were translated into a CSP using the BZP format. In this model, no operation pre-conditions and postconditions were used. The discrete behaviour of the helicopter has been specified only using state machines with OCL4MBT and event triggers.

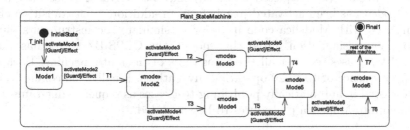

Fig. 6. Excerpt of Plant System State Machine

Basically, a mission of the helicopter is composed of a sequence of several modes. Each mode is an activation of one or more instruments over time that are done by the pilot during the flight. All the possible mode activations have been specified with a state machine, as shown in Fig. 6. The complete state machine contains 17 modes and 55 transitions. Among these 55 transitions, everyone has an event trigger, 17 have OCL4MBT guard and 18 have OCL4MBT effect. OCL4MBT enables to guide the CLPS-BZ solver during test case generation to

Table 2. Metrics about the SysML Model

SysML elements	# for the EMS	# for the plant	Total
Model $M_s = M_a$	1	1	1
Blocks $\Gamma_{Bs} = \Gamma_{Ba}$	19	16	35
Blocks Γ_{Bf}	2	2	2
Enumerations Γ_{Enum}	0	1	1
Attributes Γ_{Att}	41	48	89
Constraints Γ_{Cons}	39	15	54
Parts Γ_{Part}	34	15	49
FlowPorts Γ_{FP}	66	30	96
Connectors	76	15	91
State-Machines SM	3	2	5
States Σ	10	21	31
State $Entry$	0	0	0
State $Exit$	0	1	1
Event triggers Γ_E	0	15	15
Transition δ	11	47	58
Transition $guard$	8	16	24
Transition $effect$	0	47	47

produce sequences verifying the system requirements. For instance, OCL4MBT code has been added on several transitions to satisfy the following requirement: the mode $Mode9$ (not depicted in Fig. 6) may be activated twice only if the mode $Mode6$ has been activated just before. In addition, each transition effect is completed with Modelica code in order to simulate the instruments during the continuous simulation. From this model, the CLPS-BZ solver has generated 154 test cases to cover all the transitions of the state machine. Each test case is a sequence of 10 to 20 operation invocations. Finally, the concretization step consisted in automatically publishing test cases as sequence diagrams, next translated into Modelica procedures to be simulated.

Feedback and Lessons Learned. First of all, it should be noted that these experiments have been conducted by an engineer with a huge expertise in SysML modelling and model-based testing approach, but without any initial knowledge about real-time simulation and EMS specifications. In this way, it might bias us to have an objective view of the scalability of the process, but it does not affect the suitability of the formal framework we aim to evaluate. Moreover, case-study results have been evaluated with scientists specialized in smart energy systems, who are therefore familiar with development and continuous simulation of such complex systems. This enables us to get a solid feedback regarding the relevance of the framework and the related tool-supported overall approach.

Thanks to these experiments, we can conclude that the proposed modelling framework, combining both discrete and continuous features of the designed system, is relevant to achieve efficient model-based testing. On the one hand, the selected SysML formalism is expressive and precise enough to describe the system, generate relevant abstract test cases, and enable early simulation of the system. On the other hand, the framework offers a concrete benefit regarding the model writing and maintenance since the discrete and continuous features are natively mapped and kept consistent within the SysML model, and they can be automatically checked using test case generation and simulation.

As a consequence, the supporting implementation offers a relevant execution platform for a rapid prototyping and an early validation of the real-time designed system. These experiments have also highlighted the high level of automation regarding test case concretization, which is known to be tricky and time-consuming, especially when real-time constraints occur, as observed in previous work [9] where discrete model and continuous program were distinctly and separately managed and synchronized. This benefit stems again from the native link between discrete model elements (basis of the test generation) and the Modelica code (basis of the simulation). Regarding the process, deeper investigations are required to provide a complete report about scalability and efficiency of the overall approach, in particular w.r.t. industrial practices on large-scale systems.

5 Related Work

To the best of our knowledge, there is no reported approach in the literature that supports continuous and discrete SysML modelling for simulation and testing purposes. However, combining discrete and continuous modelling is not a recent topic. The integration of continuous and discrete aspects for modelling and simulation introduced by Zeigler et al. in [16], which defines a coupled Discrete Event and Differential Equation Specified System formalism (DEV&DESS), is close to our proposal. Basically, a such a coupled model is a model, which contains connected components. Components are defined as atomic DEV&DESS. We first tried to map our SysML modelling framework with this coupled DEV&DESS formalism. But this formalism does not support both discrete and continuous states into a coupled model, so a SysML block with parts cannot support a state machine. Some other results have been provided recent years to achieve similar continuous and discrete modeling for simulation. The approach in [17] proposes to combine superdense time, modal models, generalized functions and constructive semantics to get a rigorous approach for modelling discrete physical phenomena that occur on cyber-physical systems. Nevertheless, this approach does not consider test generation for model and physical system validation.

We have to point out that similar black-box testing approaches exist for real-time systems. For instance, Iqbal et al. [18] propose a modelling methodology based on UML and MARTE, in which the UML model is automatically translated into environment simulators implemented in Java. However, this modelling approach does not deal with continuous aspects, and differential and algebraic equations (DAEs) are hidden to the engineers.

About generation of simulation code from UML and SysML models, in [19], the authors propose to derive VHDL specifications from UML classes and state diagrams. Vanderperren et al. [20] propose to translate SysML models into Matlab-Simulink. Other work [21] focuses on generating SystemC from UML models. Each of these approaches enables to simulate a system specified with UML or SysML, but discrete and abstract aspects of such models are not considered for model-based testing. Moreover, our work is original as we propose to combine continuous and discrete modelling in a single model.

6 Conclusion and Future Work

This paper presented a SysML framework that combines continuous features for simulation and discrete aspects for model-based testing. We formally described the SysML subsets for Modelica simulation and CSP solving, and the way to combine them in a single SysML model. This combined approach aims to be used within model-in-the-loop and hardware-in-the-loop processes. In these contexts, the simulation respectively plays two key roles: simulating a component based system and providing test cases and oracles for the model and its concrete product. While preserving the V cycle to address complex and critical system development, we promote a more iterative and incremental approach driven by the early validation and verification activities. Experiments give a conclusive feedback about the suitability and the reliability of this framework, and highlighted its higher automation ability for early design validation of real-time systems.

As future work, we plan to conduct extensive experiments and to extend CLPS-BZ to handle continuous domain in order to investigate new test generation criteria based not only on discrete features, but also on continuous ones. It would be possible to use the CLPQR library. This library considers real valued variables and enables to perform linear equations solving. Furthermore, we have some insights concerning the combined use of CLPS-BZ with a numerical solver. More precisely, the use of interactive simulation, driven by a numerical solver, would enable to explore the continuous state space between two specified discrete states. This combination requires each solver to manipulate the same object, and requires establishing a communication protocol to propagate deductions made by a solver in the other. Such protocol would not only raise issues about concurrency or synchronization: it would obviously require further investigation about more complex algorithms regarding state reachability issues, including meta-heuristics, patterns recognition, fuzzing, etc. These issues open new research topics combining parallel and distributed fields with formal V&V.

References

1. Qamar, A., During, C., Wikander, J.: Designing mechatronic systems, a model-based perspective, an attempt to achieve SysML-Matlab/Simulink model integration. In: International Conference on Advanced Intelligent Mechatronics (AIM 2009). IEEE CS, Singapore, Republic of Singapore, pp. 1306–1311, July 2009

2. Sindico, A., Di Natale, M., Panci, G.: Integrating SysML with Simulink using open-source model transformations. In: 1st International Conference on Simulation and Modeling Methodologies, Technologies and Applications (SIMULTECH 2011). SciTePress, Noordwijkerhout, The Netherlands, pp. 45–56, July 2011
3. Utting, M., Legeard, B.: Practical Model-Based Testing: A Tools Approach. Morgan Kaufmann Publishers Inc., Massachusetts (2007). ISBN 978-0-08-046648-4
4. Broekman, B.M.: Testing Enbredded Software. Addison-Wesley Longman Publishing Co., Inc, Boston, MA (2002). ISBN 0321159861
5. Matinnejad, R., Nejati, S., Briand, L., Bruckmann, T.: MiL testing of highly configurable continuous controllers: scalable search using surrogate models. In: 29th ACM/IEEE International Conference on Automated Software Engineering (ASE 2014). ACM, Vasteras, Sweden, pp. 163–174, September 2014
6. Benigni, A., Monti, A.: Development of a platform for hardware in the loop testing of network controller. In: Grand Challenges on Modeling and Simulation Conference (GCMS 2011). Society for Modeling and Simulation International, Hague, Netherlands, pp. 124–128, June 2011
7. Friedenthal, S., Moore, A., Steiner, R.: A Practical Guide to SysML: The Systems Modeling Language. Morgan Kaufmann, Massachusetts (2009). ISBN 978-0-12-374379-4
8. Graves, H., Bijan, Y.: Using formal methods with SysML in aerospace design. Ann. Math. Artif. Intell. **63**(1), 53–102 (2011)
9. Ambert, F., Bouquet, F., Lasalle, J., Legeard, B., Peureux, F.: Applying a def-use approach on signal exchange to implement SysML model-based testing. In: Van Gorp, P., Ritter, T., Rose, L.M. (eds.) ECMFA 2013. LNCS, vol. 7949, pp. 134–151. Springer, Heidelberg (2013)
10. Bouquet, F., Grandpierre, C., Legeard, B., Peureux, F., Vacelet, N., Utting, M.: A Subset of Precise UML for Model-based Testing. In: 3rd International Workshop on Advances in Model-based Testing, (A-MOST 2007). ACM, pp. 95–104, July 2007
11. Bouquet, F., Legeard, B., Peureux, F.: CLPS-B: a constraint solver to animate a B specification. Int. J. Soft. Tools Technol. Transf. STTT **6**(2), 143–157 (2004)
12. Ambert, F., Bouquet, F., Chemin, S., Guenaud, S., Legeard, B., Peureux, F., Vacelet, N., Utting, M.: BZ-TT: a tool-set for test generation from Z and B using Constraint Logic Programming. In: Hierons, R., Jéron, T. (eds.) Formal Approaches to Testing of Software (FATES 2002), pp. 105–120, August 2002
13. Spataru, C., Gillott, M.: The use of intelligent systems for monitoring energy use and occupancy in existing homes. In: Howlett, R.J., Jain, L.C., Lee, S.H. (eds.) SEB 2010 SIST 7. SIST, vol. 7, pp. 247–256. Springer, Heidelberg (2011)
14. Macworth, A.K.: Consistency in networks of relations. J. Artif. Intell. **8**(1), 99–118 (1977)
15. Gauthier, J., Bouquet, F., Hammad, A., Peureux, F.: Tooled process for earlyvalidation of SysML models using Modelica simulation. In: 6th International Conference on Fundamentals of Software Engineering (FSEN 2015), Tehran, Iran, April 2015
16. Zeigler, B.P., Praehofer, H., Kim, T.: Theory of Modeling and Simulation: Integrating Discrete Event and Continuous Complex Dynamic Systems, 2nd edn. Elsevier Science, San Diego, CA (2000). ISBN: 0-12-778455-1
17. Lee, E.: Constructive models of discrete and continuous physical phenomena. Access, IEEE **2**, 797–821 (2014)

18. Iqbal, M., Arcuri, A., Briand, L.: Environment modeling and simulation for automated testing of soft real-time embedded software. Soft. Syst. Model. **14**(1), 483–524 (2015)
19. McUmber, W.E., Cheng, B.H.C.: UML-based analysis of embedded systems using a mapping to VHDL. In: 4th International Symposium on High-Assurance Systems Engineering (HASE 1999). IEEE CS, Washington, DC, pp. 56–63, November 1999
20. Vanderperren, Y., Dehaene, W.: From UML/SysML to Matlab/Simulink: current state and future perspectives. In: 9th International Conference on Design, Automation and Test in Europe (DATE 2006). EDAA, Munich, Germany, pp. 93–93, March 2006
21. Boutekkouk, F.: Automatic SystemC code generation from UML models at early stages of systems on chip design. Int. J. Comput. Appl. **8**(6), 10–17 (2010)

Mastering the Visualization of Larger State Spaces with Projection Diagrams

Lukas Ladenberger[✉] and Michael Leuschel

Institut Für Informatik, Universität Düsseldorf, Düsseldorf, Germany
{ladenberger,leuschel}@cs.uni-duesseldorf.de

Abstract. State space visualization is a popular technique for supporting the analysis of formal models. It often allows users to get a global view of the system and to identify structural similarities, symmetries, and unanticipated properties. However, state spaces typically become very large, so human inspection of the visualization becomes difficult. To overcome this challenge, we present an approach which can considerably reduce the size of the state space by creating *projection diagrams*. Moreover, we present an approach to link a projection diagram with a domain specific visualization. The projection diagram construction can be initiated directly from user-selected graphical elements without the user having to write formulas or having to know the variables or internal structure of the model. This makes the projection diagram inspection and construction accessible to non-formal method experts. These techniques have been implemented within the PROB toolset, and we demonstrate their benefits and usefulness on several examples.

Keywords: Formal methods · B-Method · State space · Visualization · Human inspection · Domain specific visualization · Tool support

1 Introduction and Motivation

In state-based formal methods, such as the Classical-B method [2] and its successor Event-B [1], the system behaviour is modelled by *states* and *transitions*. A state is a particular configuration of variables, whereas transitions link two states and represent the evolution of the system. Transitions are triggered by the *execution* of an operation (or event in Event-B). Some states are marked as *initial* and the set of states and transitions reachable from the initial state is the *state space* of the model.

The state space can be constructed and validated automatically via model checking [5]. In this process, the validity of temporal properties will be checked, but the state space itself is "invisible" to the user. However, often it is important for the developer or a domain expert to inspect the state space (or parts of it) manually. This can be achieved interactively with animation [7] or by visualizing the state space [23]. The latter can be especially useful to identify structural similarities, symmetries, and unanticipated properties from the system [23]. However, most state space visualization tools and techniques do not

© Springer International Publishing Switzerland 2015
M. Butler et al. (Eds.): ICFEM 2015, LNCS 9407, pp. 153–169, 2015.
DOI: 10.1007/978-3-319-25423-4_10

scale well. Indeed, the number of states and transitions typically becomes very large, especially at more concrete refinement levels, and human inspection of the visualization thus becomes a very difficult task. As an example, consider the state space visualization shown in Fig. 1 (the reader is not expected to be able to read the diagram, just to get a general impression of the problem statement). The visualization was generated with PROB [17], a validation toolset with support for Event-B [1] and Classical-B [2], as well as other formalisms (e.g. [9,18] and [21]). The visualization shows the full state space (145 states and 673 transitions) of the first refinement level of the landing gear system taken from [8] modelled in Event-B. Although the visualization shown in Fig. 1 is produced at an abstract level (the whole model covers 6 refinement steps), it is already hard for humans grasp.

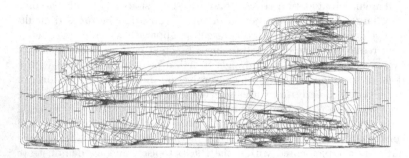

Fig. 1. Full state space visualization of the first refinement of the landing gear system

To overcome this challenge, we present an approach to considerably reduce the complexity of a state space visualization by creating *projection diagrams*. The main objective of the approach is to support human analysis of the system by highlighting relevant aspects of the model (e.g. certain variables or a particular behaviour), while hiding information that is not relevant from the diagram. The approach has been implemented into the PROB toolset with support for Event-B, Classical-B, TLA$^+$ and Z models. However it is generic so that it can also be integrated into another tool that is capable of producing a state space of a formal model.

In the second part of this paper, we present an approach to link a projection diagram to a domain specific visualization developed with BMotion Studio [14]. The resulted projection diagram consists of the basic projection diagram enhanced with graphical elements that come from the linked domain specific visualization. An important insight is the fact that the diagram can be generated from the domain specific visualization directly without the user having to know the variables of the model nor having to type expressions in a formal modelling language. We explain the approach and provide an implementation that comes as an extension of the PROB toolset. In order to demonstrate the approach, we provide a live visualization, that can be tested online at [13]. Finally, we draw conclusions, discuss future improvements for the approach, and compare our work with related work.

2   Basic Projection Diagram Algorithm

In this paper, we explain our approach based on the Event-B method [1] and the PROB tool [17]. The starting point of our approach is to explore the state space of a formal model. This can be achieved via model-checking [5] or interactively with animation [7]. Note that for our approach it is not mandatory to exhaustively explore the full state space of the formal model. The algorithm can also be applied on partial explored state spaces and provides feedback about which states have not yet been fully explored (see Sect. 2.1). As described in [19], the state space can be viewed as a non-deterministic labelled transition system (LTS):

Definition 1 (LTS). *An LTS is a 4-tuple (Q, Σ, q_0, δ) where Q is the set of states, Σ the alphabet for labelling the transitions, q_0 the initial state and $\delta \subseteq Q \times \Sigma \times Q$ is the transition relation. By $q \xrightarrow{a} q'$ we denote that $(q, a, q') \in \delta$.*

Figure 2 shows a simple example of an LTS for an Event-B model with two variables x and y. Each node in the graph represents a state of the model, where each state is defined by a particular configuration of the two variables x and y. In the following, we use the notation $[v_1 = r_1, ..., v_n = r_n]$ to name the configuration of a state, where $v_1 = r_1, ..., v_n = r_n$ are the variables (v_x) and their values (r_x) in the respective state. For instance, the initial state q_0 (the node with the incoming serrated arrow) has the configuration $[x = 0, y = 0]$.

The edges in the graph represent the possible transitions of the LTS (δ). In Event-B, a transition is the execution of an *event*, which is specified as a generalised substitution allowing deterministic and non-deterministic assignments to be specified. Each transition is labelled with the corresponding event name, where $\Sigma = \{set\_x, set\_y, reset\}$ defines the names of the possible events. For instance, the event set_x can modify the value of the variable x from 0 to 1, which is denoted by the transition $[x = 0, y = 0] \xrightarrow{set\_x} [x = 1, y = 0]$ shown in Fig. 2.

The next step in the construction of a projection diagram of an LTS consists of defining a *projection function*. All states with the same value for the projection function are merged into an *equivalence class*. A transition leads from one equivalence class C to another C' if there is a transition from one state $s \in C$ to a state $s' \in C'$. Formally, one can define the projection of an LTS as follows:

Definition 2 (Projection). *Let $L = (Q, \Sigma, q_0, \delta)$ be an LTS and p a projection function with domain Q. The projection of the LTS using p, denoted by L^p, is defined to be the LTS $(Q^p, \Sigma, p(q_0), \delta^p)$, with $Q^p = \{p(s) \mid s \in Q\}$ and $\delta^p = \{p(s) \xrightarrow{ev} p(s') \mid s \xrightarrow{ev} s' \in \delta)\}$.*

Each element in Q^p represents an equivalence class, where each equivalence class merges the states of Q (the states of the original LTS) that have the same

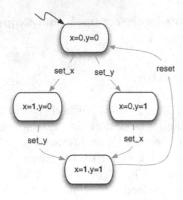

Fig. 2. Simple LTS

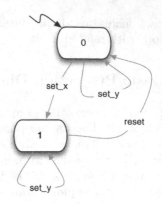

Fig. 3. Projection of the LTS onto the variable x

value for the projection function p. To illustrate the idea of a projection, consider Fig. 3. The diagram shows the projection of the simple LTS of Fig. 2 onto the variable x using the projection function $p([x = vx, y = vy]) = vx$. Obviously, the projection of an LTS may not be equivalent to the original LTS, as the sequences of the events are not necessarily possible in the original LTS. However, all sequences of the original LTS are possible in any projection of it.[1] In order to reduce clutter in the projection diagram, one can also remove self loops, i.e., removing the event set_y. This is useful if a user wants to focus on the transitions that can *change* the value of the projection function.

2.1 Categorizing Edges and Equivalence Classes

To provide a more refined visualization, we categorize the equivalence classes and edges. We distinguish between *definite* and *non-definite*, as well as between *deterministic* and *non-deterministic* edges. In addition, we distinguish between two types of equivalence classes: the equivalence classes that contain only a single state and the equivalence classes that have not yet been fully explored (e.g., if the state space has not been explored exhaustively).

In the following subsections we explain the different types of edges and equivalence classes and illustrate them with an example. To do this, let $L = (Q, \Sigma, q_0, \delta)$ be an LTS and $L^p = (Q^p, \Sigma, p(q_0), \delta^p, E)$ its projection. Given an edge $x \xrightarrow{ev} y \in \delta^p$, we denote x as the *source* and y as the *target* equivalence class. Moreover, we call an edge $x \xrightarrow{ev} y \in \delta^p$ *enabled* for a particular state s, with $s \in x$ if $\exists s' \cdot (s' \in y \wedge s \xrightarrow{ev} s' \in \delta)$.

---

[1] i.e., the original LTS is a trace refinement of the projection LTS.

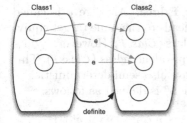

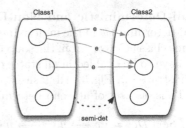

Fig. 4. Definite edge   **Fig. 5.** Semi-deterministic edge

Definite Edges. An edge is definite, iff it is enabled in *all* states of the source equivalence class. Thus, the set of all definite edges of L^P can be defined as follows:

$$Definite = \{x \xrightarrow{ev} y \mid x \xrightarrow{ev} y \in \delta^P \wedge \forall s \cdot (s \in x \Rightarrow \exists s' \cdot (s' \in y \wedge s \xrightarrow{ev} s' \in \delta))\}.$$

Figure 4 illustrates the idea of a definite edge: there is a definite edge between the equivalence classes *Class1* and *Class2* whenever *e* is enabled in all states of the source equivalence class (*Class1*). An edge is non-definite iff it is not definite. In order to distinguish the different edge types in the projection diagram, definite edges are drawn as solid lines, while non-definite edges are drawn as dashed lines.[2] An example can be seen in Fig. 6 adapted from Fig. 3. The set_x edge is possible in all states with $x = 0$, and is the only definite edge in the diagram. All other edges are semi-deterministic as described in the next Section.

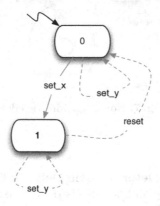

Fig. 6. Projection of the LTS from Fig. 2 onto the variable x, distinguishing definite and semi-deterministic edges

---

[2] In PROB the user can customize the style of the edge types.

Semi-Deterministic and Non-Deterministic Edges. An edge e is called semi-deterministic iff the underlying event always leads to the same target equivalence class ($Class2$) from the source equivalence class ($Class1$). However, it does not have to be enabled in all states of the source equivalence class ($Class1$). This is illustrated in Fig. 5. All dashed edges in Fig. 6 are also semi-deterministic.

Thus, the set of all semi-deterministic edges of L^p is defined as follows:

$$SemiDet = \{x \xrightarrow{ev} y \mid x \xrightarrow{ev} y \in \delta^p \wedge \neg(\exists z \cdot (z \neq y \wedge x \xrightarrow{ev} z \in \delta^p))\}.$$

Furthermore, we denote an edge as non-deterministic if it is *not* semi-deterministic. Thus, the set of all non-deterministic edges of L^p is composed of all edges (δ^p) expect of the semi-deterministic edges ($SemiDet$):

$$NonDet = \delta^p \setminus SemiDet.$$

Figure 7 shows an example of a non-deterministic edge. Given the three equivalence classes $Class1$, $Class2$ and $Class3$, the edge e is non-deterministic if e is enabled and it leads to at least two distinct target equivalence classes (e.g. $Class2$ and $Class3$).

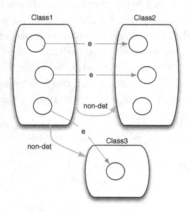

Fig. 7. Non-deterministic edge

Deterministic and Non-Deterministic Definite Edges. The set of all edges of L^p that are deterministic and definite is defined as:

$$DetDef = SemiDet \cap Definite.$$

As an example, the edge e shown in Fig. 4 is definite and deterministic. This is because e is enabled in all states of the source equivalence class ($Class1$) and it leads to the same target equivalence class ($Class2$).

Moreover, edges that are non-deterministic and definite are defined as follows:

$$NonDetDef = NonDet \cap Definite.$$

For instance, the edge shown in Fig. 7 is definite and non-deterministic as it is enabled in all states of the source equivalence class (*Class1*) and it leads to two distinct target equivalence classes (*Class2* and *Class3*).

Non-deterministic, semi-deterministic, deterministic and definite edges are distinguished by their colour (which can be set by the user).

Single State and Partial Equivalence Classes. An equivalence class is *single*, iff one state is merged into the equivalence class. Thus, the set of all single equivalence classes can be defined as follows:

$$Single = \{x \mid x \in Q^p \wedge card(\{s|s \in Q \wedge p(s) = x\}) = 1\}.$$

For instance, the equivalence class *Class3* in Fig. 7 is *single*, as it contains only one state.

Furthermore, we highlight any equivalence classes that have not yet been fully explored, which can happen when not all states of the class have been treated by the model checker yet. This means that additional outgoing edges and new equivalence classes could appear after further exploration of the state space. As in the categorization of edges, the different types of equivalence classes are distinguished by their (user defined) colour. E.g., equivalence classes that have not been fully explored are marked in orange. In this paper, however, we always suppose that the full state space has been explored (and as such no orange equivalence classes appear in the diagrams).

2.2 Application of the Projection Diagram

In this Section we present some example applications of the projection diagram and demonstrate how we have applied it in the process of validating the Event-B model of the ABZ landing gear case study from [8].

Note that from now on we will use projection functions of the form $p(s) = eval(E, s)$, where $s \in Q$, E an expression over the variables and constants of the model, and *eval* is the function that evaluates the expression E in state s. The projection function is thus defined by a "custom" expression E. With this scheme, we can project the state space of a model on a single variable v ($E = v$) but also on a set of variables $v_1, \ldots, v_k$ ($E = (v_1 \mapsto \ldots \mapsto v_k)$). We can also project on particular properties of a variable v, e.g., its cardinality ($E = card(v)$) or its range ($E = ran(v)$).

ABZ Landing Gear Case Study. The landing gear system[3] (LGS) is composed of three parts: a digital part including the control software, a pilot interface, and a mechanical part which contains the doors and gears. The system is

---

[3] The website http://stups.hhu.de/ProB/index.php5/ABZ14 contains the full specification, the Event-B model and a live visualization of the ABZ landing gear system.

in charge of controlling the retraction and extension sequence of the gears with respect to the doors and the pilot handle. The pilot handle and gears of the landing gear system are closely related, since the extension and retraction of the gears can always be interrupted by a counter order of the pilot handle.

A projection on both aspects of the model (the gears and the pilot handle) helped us to inspect their behaviour in the process of modelling the LGS. As an example, consider the visualization of the projection diagram shown in Fig. 8. The visualization was produced with PROB and demonstrates the projection of the fourth refinement level of an earlier version of the Event-B model of the LGS (the full state space covers 6,283 states and 31,299 transitions) using the projection function $p(s) = eval(E, s)$, with $E = ran(gear) \mapsto handle$. Note that $ran(gear)$ is the set of states of the three gears, abstracting away which particular gear is in which state. E.g., $ran(gear)$ has the same value $\{retracted, gear\_moving\}$ for $gear = \{left \mapsto retracted, right \mapsto retracted, front \mapsto gear\_moving\}$ and $gear = \{left \mapsto gear\_moving, right \mapsto gear\_moving, front \mapsto retracted\}$. Each rectangle represents an equivalence class (all states with the same value for the expression E) and is labelled with the associated expression value as well as with the number of states that are merged into the equivalence class. A directed edge between two equivalence classes represents a transition which is labelled with the associated event name. The diagram confirms that in every state the handle can be toggled (the corresponding transitions are definite) and that the only event which can modify the handle is env_toggle_handle. We can also see that the gears do not jump directly from $retracted$ to $extended$ or vice versa. The transitions for changing the gear state are not definite; this is to be expected, as the doors have to put into the correct position first. This again confirms what we intuitively know about the modelled system.

Scheduler Example. Figure 9 illustrates how one can combine various variables into a single expression. The Figure projects the state space of the "standard" scheduler benchmark example from [15] (also used in [19]), which schedules processes and keeps disjoint sets of waiting, ready and active processes. In the Figure we abstract away from the process identities, by computing the cardinality of these sets. Furthermore, we add these sets together, to project on the total number of processes $(E = card(ready) + card(waiting) + card(active))$. One can clearly see that only two events change the total number of processes: new and del. Moreover, new is always enabled when less than 3 processes exist, while del is only possible when more than one process exists and is not always possible. This confirms our intuition, as active processes cannot be deleted straightaway. Figure 9 shows how one can focus on very specific aspects of a model using the projection diagrams. We believe that one should probably generate a variety of projection diagrams for any particular model — a different one for very specific aspects — and that they can or should be incorporated into the documentation accompanying the model.

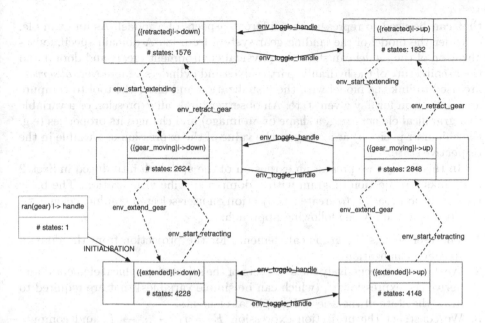

Fig. 8. State space projection of an earlier version of the fourth refinement level on variable handle and range of gears of the landing gear system

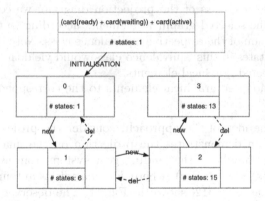

Fig. 9. Projection on expression $card(ready)+card(waiting)+card(active)$ of a process scheduler

In the next Section we show how we can increase the value of these diagrams, by incorporating graphical elements and making them accessible to domain experts not versed in formal modelling.

3   Linking with Domain Specific Visualization

BMotion Studio [14] is a tool for creating domain specific visualizations of formal models. The tool provides various graphical elements (shapes, images, buttons,...)

that can be used to represent the different aspects of a model. As an example, consider the model of the landing gear system from [8]. A domain specific visualization of the model can show the physical environment (gears and doors) and the architecture of the hydraulic part (valves and cylinders). Moreover, *observers* are used to link the model with the visualization and allow the tool to compute a visualization for any given state. An observer binds an expression or a variable to a graphical element (e.g. a shape or an image) and changes its properties (e.g. the colour or position) according to the value of the expression or variable in the respective state.

In this Section we present an extension of the approach introduced in Sect. 2 that links a projection diagram with a domain specific visualization. The basic idea of the approach is to create a projection on user-selected graphical elements. To do this, we apply the following approach:

1. The user selects the graphical elements for the projection from the domain specific visualization.
2. We determine recursively the observers of the selected graphical elements[4] and derive the expressions f_i (which can be simple variables) that are required to draw the state of the selected graphical elements.
3. We construct the projection expression $E = f_1 \mapsto \ldots \mapsto f_n$ and compute the projection diagram using the projection function $p(s) = eval(E, s)$ as described in Sect. 2.
4. For each equivalence class of the projection diagram, we compute the representation of the selected graphical elements according to the value of the projection function of the respective equivalence class. Note that if computed separately, all states in this equivalence class would yield the *same* visualization for the selected graphical elements.
5. We assign the adapted graphical elements to the corresponding equivalence classes.

To illustrate the idea of the approach, consider the projection diagram in Fig. 10. The diagram demonstrates the projection on the image element that represents the pilot handle of the landing gear system from [8] using the projection function $p(s) = eval(E, s)$, where $E = handle$ is automatically derived from the *formula observer* [12] shown in Fig. 11. The observer is registered on the graphical element that matches the selector "#handle"[5] (line 2). Line 3 states that the observer should observe the variable *handle*, i.e. the variable that defines the state of the pilot handle of the landing gear system. In lines 4 to 7 we define the action which is applied on the image element whenever a state change occurred. In this case, the observer sets the path (*src*) of the image element (*origin*) to a new path that is constructed based on the value of the variable handle in the current state (*val[0]*)[6]. To compute the representation of the image

---

[4] In BMotion Studio graphical elements are arranged hierarchically. Thus, we also need to determine recursively the observers of the child graphical elements.

[5] The prefix "#" is used for matching a graphical element by its ID.

[6] The domain specific visualization provides different images to represent the states of the handle (down and up).

element for an equivalence class, we apply the observer using the value of the projection function of the respective class. The adapted image element is then assigned to the equivalence class. For instance, the diagram in Fig. 10 shows the two possible states of the handle (up and down) and its graphical representation.

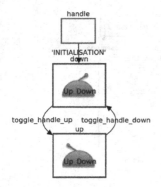

```
1 bms.observe("formula", {
2   selector: "#handle",
3   formulas: ["handle"],
4   trigger: function (origin, val) {
5     origin.attr("src",
6    "handle_" + val[0] + ".png");
7   }
8 });
```

Fig. 10. Projection on handle

Fig. 11. Formula observer for image element that represents the handle

Although developing a domain specific visualization requires extra effort, the benefits of linking it with a projection diagram can be considerable. For instance, it can be used to get a common understanding about the underlying model within a team or to discuss the model with non-formal methods experts. As an example, consider Fig. 12 that shows the projection on the cabin of a simple lift model taken from [13]. One can see at a glance (without knowledge about the underlying model or the used formalism), that the cabin is able to stop and to open the door at all three floors. The diagram also confirms that the cabin door must always be closed (indicated by a gray fill) before the lift can move. This is indicated by the solid edges labelled with the event close_door.

Another example is shown in Fig. 13, illustrating the projection on the graphical elements representing the handle and the front gear cylinder of the fifth refinement level of the landing gear system using the derived projection function $p(s) = eval(E, s)$, with $E = handle \mapsto gears(front)$. The visual feedback may help the user to localize specific equivalence classes for further inspection even if the diagram becomes slightly larger or the layout of the diagram is unflattering. For instance, one can identify at a glance the equivalence classes where the cylinder is extended or where the handle is set to down.

The projection on graphical elements can even support the development of a domain specific visualization. In particular, we have used it while developing the domain specific visualization of the landing gear system, e.g. to check if a particular graphical element represents all relevant states of the model properly and to eliminate undesirable behaviour in the domain specific visualization. For instance, consider the diagram shown in Fig. 10: one can see at a glance that

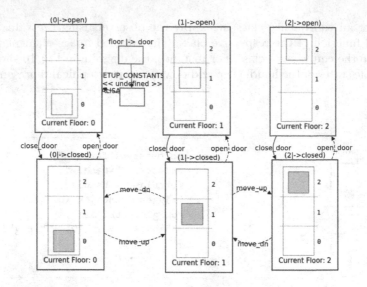

Fig. 12. Projection on cabin of simple lift model

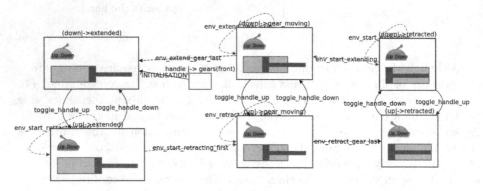

Fig. 13. Projection on handle and front gear of the landing gear system

the handle behaves as expected in the domain specific visualization (and in the formal model). Similar (small) projection diagrams can also be created for other graphical elements (e.g. Figs. 12 and 13).

4   Related Work

Several other approaches exist for state space visualization. In this work we are concerned with reducing the size and complexity of states space visualizations which have a large number of nodes and transitions. However, we are also concerned with supporting the analysis of formal models by producing state space visualizations that are even accessible for non-formal method experts. Thus, we compare our work with other approaches that tend to improve the visualization of larger state spaces, as well as with other approaches that have the goal of making formal models accessible to non-formal method experts. Because our work has a strong focus on the B-method, we first compare our work with state space visualization approaches with support for the B-method. Afterwards, we compare our approach with other related work.

State Space Visualization for the B-Method. Our approach has been implemented into the PROB toolset [17]. PROB also provides further state space visualization features with the motivation to reduce the complexity of the produced graphs. Two of them are presented in [19]: the *signature merge approach* and the *DFA-abstraction algorithm*. The signature merge approach is very similar to our approach: while our approach merges all states based on a projection function, the signature merge approach merges all states with the same enabled events to a common *signature*. While the approach can be tuned by deselecting events from the signature, our approach can be tuned by adapting the projection function. For instance, our approach enables the user to focus on certain variables (or even just properties of those) of a formal model and to see only those events which can modify those variables. On the other hand, the basic idea of the DFA-abstraction algorithm is to abstract the labelling of the edges, i.e., to abstract away from event arguments and to apply the classical minimization algorithm for Deterministic Finite Automaton (DFA). The DFA-abstraction algorithm produces a visualization in which the transitions are equivalent to these in the original state space. However, this produces a larger graph which may still be difficult for humans to grasp [19].

In [11] the authors present two complementary approaches to increase the understanding of formal models by producing *behavioural views* from B models, rather than focusing on reducing the size and complexity of larger state spaces. In particular, the *under-approximation* approach also uses the PROB model-checker [17] to exhaustively explore the state space of a formal model as a first step. While our approach groups nodes based on a projection function, the under-approximation approach produces a graph by grouping concrete states satisfying a same abstract state predicate.

A few other tools provide domain specific visualizations for Event-B models, but without providing any state space visualization: [20, 26] using Flash technology and [27] using web technology.

More State Space Visualization Approaches. The work done in [24, 25] addresses the problem of visualizing large state spaces and presents a tool called *DiaGraphica* with different features for the interactive visual analysis of state spaces. The tool supports the *fsm* input file format[7] for representing state spaces as plain text. It would be interesting to see if the work presented in this paper could be combined with the DiaGraphica tool, i.e. to export the state spaces produced by PROB (the full state space and the state space produced by the

---

[7] http://www.comp.leeds.ac.uk/scsajp/applications/data/fsm.html.

Table 1. Runtime of algorithm for various models and projection functions

Model	States/transitions*	Projection expression	Runtime BP	Runtime EP
Scheduler	36/121	$card(ready)$ $+card(waiting)$ $+card(active)$	0.01 s	-
Landing gear (old), 4th Ref	6,283/31,299	$ran(gear) \mapsto handle$	0.02 s	-
Landing gear, 5th Ref	25,217/149,041	$ran(gears) \mapsto handle$	0.98 s	-
		$gears \mapsto handle$	1.06 s	-
		$handle$	0.77 s	1.59 s
		$handle \mapsto gears(front)$	0.88 s	3.20 s
Simple lift	186/838	$door$	0.03 s	0.70 s
		$floor \mapsto door$	0.03 s	1.10 s

*The states and transitions of the full state space of the corresponding model

basic projection diagram algorithm) into the fsm format and to load it with the DiaGraphica tool.

The muCRL2 system also provides a 3-D state space visualization technique [6,22], which tries to show a large number of nodes as opposed to our approach of projecting the state space onto a smaller refinement of it.

5   Conclusion

In this paper we have presented an approach for state space visualization with *projection diagrams*. The main objective of the approach is to considerably reduce the size of a state space and to support human visual analysis of the system by highlighting relevant aspects of the model. In the second part of this paper, we have presented an extension of the approach to link a projection diagram to a domain specific visualization developed with BMotion Studio. The approach has been implemented into the PROB toolset with support for Event-B, Classical-B, TLA$^+$ and Z models.

We have demonstrated the benefits and usefulness of the approach by applying it on several formal models. For this purpose, various example projection diagrams are presented in this paper. Moreover, we created two live visualizations which can be tested online [13].

Although the produced projection diagram may not be equivalent to the original state space (as far as the sequences of the events are concerned), the projection may achieve a good result in reducing the size of the state space, while still preserving beneficial information. In particular, the categorization of the edges and equivalence classes proved to be very useful in supporting the inspection of the diagram and to infer useful properties of the respective formal model.

Our approach is also flexible, as the user may adjust the underlying projection function. The possibility of defining an individual projection function enables the user to *query* the full state space and to obtain only the information in which the user is interested in (comparable with defining queries on a database).

Moreover, we believe that inspecting multiple small projection diagrams (with a manageable number of nodes and transitions) representing different aspects of the model can be more helpfully than inspecting only one big state space visualization. This was also confirmed by applying our approach on validating the landing gear model. One reason for this is that the user can concentrate on a specific aspect of the model (e.g. on certain variables) or on checking a particular behaviour, while hiding non-relevant information from the diagram.

We also believe that a projection diagram may help to verify properties of the model which are hard to express as invariants. For instance, in the landing gear model we used the diagram to verify that the extension and retraction sequence works as desired and that the controller responds correctly to toggling the pilot handle during both sequences.

Finally, we believe that combining the projection diagram with a domain specific visualization affords further advantages. For example, the graphical representation of a specific aspect or behaviour of the model can be helpful for discussing the specification with non-formal method experts and for the further development of the specification. A non-formal method expert can even use this feature without any knowledge about the notation used in formal methods, since the projection is produced based on graphical elements and the underlying projection function is derived automatically from the attached observers.

Evaluation and Future Work. Table 1 shows some runtime statistics obtained after applying the basic projection approach introduced in Sect. 2 (*runtime BP*) and the extended projection approach described in Sect. 3 (*runtime EP*) on the models presented in this paper. The statistics were obtained after the corresponding state space had been fully explored with PROB. We use the projection function $p(s) = eval(E, s)$, where $s \in Q$ and E is the *projection expression* (third column of Table 1). The measured time includes the actual runtime for both algorithms (implemented in PROB) without the time needed to exhaustively explore the full state space (i.e. the model checking time) and without the time needed for generating and layouting the actual diagram. The model checking and layouting time is not included because it depends on the model checker and layouting tool respectively. Moreover, the state space needs to be explored only once in order to generate multiple projection diagrams.

In general, the runtime of the EP takes longer than the BP. This is because the EP uses the BP to generate the actual data (see Sect. 3) and needs some additional time to generate the graphical representation of the equivalence classes.

Table 1 also confirms that the runtime of both algorithms (EP and BP) increases with the number of nodes and transitions of the state space.

In the future, we plan to apply the algorithms on more case studies to obtain additional statistics. Moreover, a good layout of the nodes and the edges of a projection diagram is crucial for its readability and accessibility [10]. A next step would be also to adapt the underlying layout algorithm of the projection diagrams so that the nodes (the equivalence classes) are ordered based on the defined projection function. As an example, this was already done manually in the diagram shown in Fig. 8. We ordered the nodes so that the left side of the diagram contains the equivalence classes where the handle is set to down, whereas the right side contains the equivalence classes where the handle is set to up.

We also plan to enhance the projection diagram with interactive features. For instance, it would be desirable to "jump" into an equivalence class and to inspect the individual states which have been merged into it. This could be in particular useful to take a closer look at equivalence classes that have unexpected outgoing edges, e.g. if the user expected a definite edge, but the equivalence class has a non-definite edge instead. One could jump into the affected class and inspect the states in which an event is not enabled.

Finally, we plan to symbolically construct a projection diagram statically using the built-in constraint solver of PROB [16] rather than first having to (exhaustively) explore the full state space using the model-checking feature of PROB. This is related to proof-based approaches such as [4] and [3].

References

1. Abrial, J.: Modeling in Event-B: System and Software Engineering. Cambridge University Press, Cambridge (2010)
2. Abrial, J.-R.: The B-Book: Assigning Programs to Meanings. Cambridge University Press, New York (1996)
3. Bendisposto, J., Leuschel, M.: Automatic flow analysis for Event-B. In: Giannakopoulou, D., Orejas, F. (eds.) FASE 2011. LNCS, vol. 6603, pp. 50–64. Springer, Heidelberg (2011)
4. Bert, D., Potet, M.-L., Stouls, N.: GeneSyst: a tool to reason about behavioral aspects of B event specifications. application to security properties. In: Treharne, H., King, S., C. Henson, M., Schneider, S. (eds.) ZB 2005. LNCS, vol. 3455, pp. 299–318. Springer, Heidelberg (2005)
5. Clarke, E.M., Grumberg, O., Peled, D.: Model Checking. MIT press, Cambridge (1999)
6. Groote, J.F., van Ham, F.: Interactive visualization of large state spaces. Int. J. Softw. Tools Technol. Transfer 8(1), 77–91 (2006)
7. Hallerstede, S., Leuschel, M., Plagge, D.: Validation of formal models by refinement animation. Sci. Comput. Program. 78(3), 272–292 (2013)
8. Hansen, D., Ladenberger, L., Wiegard, H., Bendisposto, J., Leuschel, M.: Validation of the ABZ landing gear system using ProB. In: Boniol, F., Wiels, V., Ait Ameur, Y., Schewe, K.-D. (eds.) ABZ 2014. CCIS, vol. 433, pp. 66–79. Springer, Heidelberg (2014)
9. Hansen, D., Leuschel, M.: Translating TLA$^+$ to B for validation with ProB. In: Derrick, J., Gnesi, S., Latella, D., Treharne, H. (eds.) IFM 2012. LNCS, vol. 7321, pp. 24–38. Springer, Heidelberg (2012)
10. Herman, I., Melancon, G., Marshall, M.: Graph visualization and navigation in information visualization: a survey. IEEE Trans. Visual Comput. Graphics 6(1), 24–43 (2000)
11. Idani, A., Stouls, N.: When a formal model rhymes with a graphical notation. In: Canal, C., Idani, A. (eds.) SEFM 2014 Workshops. LNCS, vol. 8938, pp. 54–68. Springer, Heidelberg (2015)

12. Ladenberger, L.: BMotion Studio for ProB Project Website, May 2015. http://stups.hhu.de/ProB/w/BMotion_Studio
13. Ladenberger, L.: Projection Diagram Website, May 2015. http://stups.hhu.de/ProB/w/ProjectionDiagram
14. Ladenberger, L., Bendisposto, J., Leuschel, M.: Visualising Event-B models with B-Motion studio. In: Alpuente, M., Cook, B., Joubert, C. (eds.) FMICS 2009. LNCS, vol. 5825, pp. 202–204. Springer, Heidelberg (2009)
15. Legeard, B., Peureux, F., Utting, M.: Automated boundary testing from Z and B. In: Eriksson, L.-H., Lindsay, P.A. (eds.) FME 2002. LNCS, vol. 2391, pp. 21–40. Springer, Heidelberg (2002)
16. Iordache, O.: Methods. In: Iordache, O. (ed.) Polystochastic Models for Complexity. UCS, vol. 4, pp. 17–61. Springer, Heidelberg (2010)
17. Leuschel, M., Butler, M.: ProB: an automated analysis toolset for the B method. STTT **10**(2), 185–203 (2008)
18. Leuschel, M., Fontaine, M.: Probing the depths of CSP-M: a new fdr-compliant validation tool. In: Liu, S., Araki, K. (eds.) ICFEM 2008. LNCS, vol. 5256, pp. 278–297. Springer, Heidelberg (2008)
19. Leuschel, M., Turner, E.: Visualising larger state spaces in ProB. In: Treharne, H., King, S., C. Henson, M., Schneider, S. (eds.) ZB 2005. LNCS, vol. 3455, pp. 6–23. Springer, Heidelberg (2005)
20. Métayer, C.: AnimB 0.1.1, (2010). http://wiki.event-b.org/index.php/AnimB
21. Plagge, D., Leuschel, M.: Validating Z specifications using the ProB animator and model checker. In: Davies, J., Gibbons, J. (eds.) IFM 2007. LNCS, vol. 4591, pp. 480–500. Springer, Heidelberg (2007)
22. Ploeger, B., Tankink, C.: Improving an interactive visualization of transition systems. In: Proceedings of the 4th ACM Symposium on Software Visualization, SoftVis 2008, pp. 115–124, New York, NY, USA. ACM (2008)
23. Pretorius, A.: Visualization of State Transition Graphs (2008)
24. Pretorius, A., van Wijk, J.: Multidimensional visualization of transition systems. In: Ninth International Conference on Information Visualisation, Proceedings. pp. 323–328, July 2005
25. Pretorius, A., van Wijk, J.: Visual analysis of multivariate state transition graphs. IEEE Trans. Visual Comput. Graphics **12**(5), 685–692 (2006)
26. Servat, T.: BRAMA: a new graphic animation tool for B models. In: Julliand, J., Kouchnarenko, O. (eds.) B 2007. LNCS, vol. 4355, pp. 274–276. Springer, Heidelberg (2006)
27. Yang, F., Jacquot, J., Souquières, J.: JeB: safe simulation of Event-B models in javascript. In: Muenchaisri, P., Rothermel, G.(eds.) 20th Asia-Pacific Software Engineering Conference, APSEC 2013, vol. 1, pp. 571–576, Ratchathewi, Bangkok, Thailand, December 2–5. IEEE Computer Society (2013)

Refinement-Based Verification of the FreeRTOS Scheduler in VCC

Sumesh Divakaran[1,2], Deepak D'Souza[1], Anirudh Kushwah[1],
Prahladavaradan Sampath[3], Nigamanth Sridhar[4],
and Jim Woodcock[5]([✉])

[1] Indian Institute of Science, Bangalore, India
{sumeshd,deepakd,anirudhkushwah}@csa.iisc.ernet.in
[2] Government Engineering College, Idukki, India
[3] MathWorks India, Bangalore, India
prahlad.sampath@gmail.com
[4] Cleveland State University, Cleveland, USA
n.sridhar1@csuohio.edu
[5] University of York, York, UK
jim.woodcock@york.ac.uk

Abstract. We describe our experience with verifying the scheduler-related functionality of FreeRTOS, a popular open-source embedded real-time operating system. We propose a methodology for carrying out refinement-based proofs of functional correctness of abstract data types in the popular code-level verifier VCC. We then apply this methodology to carry out a full machine-checked proof of the functional correctness of the FreeRTOS scheduler. We describe the bugs found during this exercise, the fixes made, and the effort involved.

1 Introduction

The verification of the FreeRTOS real-time kernel was proposed in 2008 as one of the pilot projects of the Verified Software Initiative led by Hoare [19]. FreeRTOS [14] is a priority-based real-time scheduler and is an open-source representative of some of the commonly used kernels in the auto and aviation sectors, like the OSEC and ARINC 653 real-time operating systems. The correctness of applications (many of them safety-critical) that run on such kernels, as well as the analysis of such applications [25,30], crucially depend on the correctness of the kernel and its specification model. With this motivation in mind, we took up the goal of verifying the correctness of the scheduling-related functionality of FreeRTOS. This paper describes the choices made, the methodology developed, and the results achieved in this project.

The first choice to be made was about the kind of proof technique to adopt: one based on the direct use of code-level contracts or one based on the notion of

Supported by grants from the UK-India Education and Research Initiative (UKIERI) and the Robert Bosch Center for Cyber Physical Systems, IISc, Bangalore.

M. Butler et al. (Eds.): ICFEM 2015, LNCS 9407, pp. 170–186, 2015.
DOI: 10.1007/978-3-319-25423-4_11

refinement. While recent verification efforts for functional correctness in the community [3,7,24,28] – with the prominent exception of the seL4 project [23] – have favoured the use of code-level contracts (in the form of **requires** and **ensures** annotations for methods in the program) over refinement-based approaches, we felt that the latter have the potential to ease the verification effort and provide stronger guarantees for verification.

In a refinement-based approach one views the system as an Abstract Data Type (ADT), and begins with an abstract specification of the system's functionality in a concise and mathematically precise modelling language. This specification is then successively refined by adding implementation details to finally obtain an implementation of the system which is guaranteed to "conform" to the high-level specification. The exact meaning of what it means to conform to the specification would vary according to the notion of refinement used, but it could mean for instance that every execution of the concrete implementation can be "matched" or "simulated" by an execution of the abstract model.

There were several reasons to favour a refinement-based approach. To begin with, a refinement-based approach provides a standalone abstract specification (say $\mathcal{A}$) of the implementation (say $\mathcal{C}$), with the guarantee that certain properties proved about a client program P that uses $\mathcal{A}$ as a library (which we refer to as "P with $\mathcal{A}$" and denote by "$P[\mathcal{A}]$") also carry over for P with $\mathcal{C}$ (i.e. $P[\mathcal{C}]$). Thus, to verify that $P[\mathcal{C}]$ satisfies a certain property, it may be sufficient to check that $P[\mathcal{A}]$ satisfies the property. The latter check involves reasoning about a simpler component (namely $\mathcal{A}$) and can reduce the work of a prover by an order of magnitude [22]. Finally, a refinement-based proof is more modular and transparent, since it breaks down the task of reasoning about a complex implementation into smaller tasks, each of which is more manageable for both a human and a prover.

We chose to use a notion of refinement similar to that of VDM [8,20] and Z [2,32], but adapted to a setting in which the client program interacts in a "functional" manner with the ADT (see also [18]). The details of this theory are spelt out in [11]. We propose a methodology for phrasing the refinement conditions from this theory across different models ranging from abstract Z models to concrete C implementations.

We then used this methodology to verify the FreeRTOS scheduler. We view the scheduler-related functionality of the kernel as an ADT, specify its intended behaviour in Z, and then verify that the implementation refines the high-level ADT. We used four levels of models (two in Z and one in VCC [10] ghost code, apart from the C implementation itself), and proved successive refinements between them. Barring a few manual steps, all our refinement conditions were phrased and proved in VCC, using its very useful ghost constructs.

We found a few subtle bugs which were acknowledged by the developers of FreeRTOS [5]. These bugs were fixed with minimal changes to the source code, and the verification of the fixed code was duly completed.

A natural question a VCC expert may ask is why we chose to build a "meta-theory" of refinement on top of VCC, instead of using its internal style of data abstractions as illustrated in [9]. In the latter idiom, to prove an assertion about a client program P with a concrete data type implementation $\mathcal{C}$, one constructs a joint data type $\mathcal{AC}$ which contains a ghost version of the data type called $\mathcal{A}$, and includes a coupling constraint between the states of $\mathcal{A}$ and $\mathcal{C}$. One then proves the assertion in $P[\mathcal{AC}]$. By the restrictions imposed by VCC on ghost code, it follows that the assertion must continue to hold on the original program $P[\mathcal{C}]$ as well. While this style of verification has many of the advantages of a refinement-based approach, it loses out in a couple of aspects. Firstly, VCC must reason about P with the *joint* structure $\mathcal{AC}$ (instead of simply $P[\mathcal{A}]$ in a refinement-based approach). While it is possible to control the portion of the joint state exposed to the prover, this requires expert knowledge of VCC. Secondly, if we want to prove a property of $P[\mathcal{C}]$, like a temporal logic specification, which is not possible with VCC, this idiom is not of much use. On the other hand, using a meta-theory of refinement, we could use VCC to prove that $\mathcal{C}$ refines $\mathcal{A}$, prove the required property about $P[\mathcal{A}]$ using non-VCC means, and then infer the property for $P[\mathcal{C}]$.

In the next few sections we describe our refinement conditions and proposed methodology, before going on to the details of the FreeRTOS verification.

2   ADT's and Refinement

The notion of refinement we use in this paper is essentially that of Z [16,32]. We briefly recall this notion before describing the variant we use.

2.1   Refinement in Z

An ADT *type* is a finite set of operation names N along with a set of "global" states G. An *abstract data type* (ADT) of type (N, G) is a structure $\mathcal{A} = (Q, \mathit{init}, \mathit{fin}, \{op_n\}_{n \in N})$, where Q is the set of states of the ADT, $\mathit{init} \subseteq G \times Q$ is an initialization operation, $\mathit{fin} \subseteq Q \times G$ is a finalization operation, and each $op_n \subseteq Q \times Q$ is a realization of operation n. All operations are allowed to be non-deterministic. A program that makes use of an ADT of type (N, G), called an (N, G)-client program, is a sequence of operations P of the form $\mathit{init}; n_1; \cdots; n_k; \mathit{fin}$, with each $n_i \in N$. Given an ADT $\mathcal{A}$ of type (N, G), the program P with $\mathcal{A}$, written $P[\mathcal{A}]$, induces a relation from G to G in a natural way, obtained by composing the operations of $\mathcal{A}$ according to the sequence given by P. Now given two ADT's $\mathcal{A}$ and $\mathcal{C}$ of type (N, G), we say that $\mathcal{C}$ *refines* $\mathcal{A}$ if, for each (N, G)-client program P, we have $P[\dot{\mathcal{C}}] \subseteq P[\dot{\mathcal{A}}]$, where the "˙" denotes the "totalized" version of the relation in which, essentially, elements outside the domain of the relation are related to all possible elements in the target set. Thus, if $\mathcal{C}$ refines $\mathcal{A}$, then when P uses $\mathcal{C}$ all the behaviours it could observe – in terms of initial global states being transformed to final global states – are also possible behaviours of P with $\mathcal{A}$.

Let $\mathcal{A} = (Q, \mathit{init}, \mathit{fin}, \{op_n\}_{n \in N})$ and $\mathcal{C} = (Q', \mathit{init}', \mathit{fin}', \{op'_n\}_{n \in N})$ be two ADT's of type (N, G). Then a sufficient (and also necessary [16]) condition for

$\mathcal{C}$ to refine $\mathcal{A}$, called "upwards simulation" in [16], which we denote by (RC_Z), is that there should exist an "abstraction" relation $\rho \subseteq Q' \times Q$, satisfying

1. For each $g \in G$, $p' \in init'(g)$, and $p \in Q$ such that $(p',p) \in \rho$: we have $p \in init(g)$.
2. For each $p' \in Q'$ and $p \in Q$, with $(p',p) \in \rho$: we have $fin'(p') \subseteq fin(p)$.
3. For each $n \in N$, $p',q' \in Q'$, and $p \in Q$, with $p \in \text{dom}(op_n)$, $(p',p) \in \rho$, and $(p',q') \in op'_n$: we have there exists $q \in Q$ such that $q \in op_n(p)$ and $(q',q) \in \rho$.

2.2   Our Notion of Refinement

We would like to work in a setting where a client program interacts with an ADT in a *functional* manner, by periodically calling operations of the ADT, each time supplying an argument and using the value returned by the operation to update its local state. Thus, we no longer need a global set of states G in an ADT type, but instead require each operation name n to have an associated *input type* I_n and an *output type* O_n. A realization op_n of operation n in an ADT with state set Q is now a subset of $(Q \times I_n) \times (Q \times O_n)$. An N-client program is a transition system in which some transitions are labelled by local actions, and some by *calls* to the ADT operations, of the form (n,a,b), representing the fact that a call of operation n with argument a returned the value b. We use a notion of refinement based on the sequences of operation calls supported by an ADT, which essentially says that an ADT $\mathcal{C}$ refines an ADT $\mathcal{A}$, written $\mathcal{C} \preceq \mathcal{A}$, if the sequences of operation calls allowed by $\mathcal{C}$ are contained in those allowed by $\mathcal{A}$. Once again, if $\mathcal{C}$ refines $\mathcal{A}$, the "behaviours" seen by a client program using $\mathcal{C}$ are guaranteed to be present when using $\mathcal{A}$. The reader is referred to [11] for the details of the theory.

In the rest of this paper, we restrict our attention to *deterministic* ADT's. One reason for this is that our case study makes use of only deterministic models and implementations. Secondly, the presentation of our methodology is simpler with this assumption, while retaining the essence of what is needed to handle the general case. We model the deterministic operations as functions, by introducing a special *exceptional value*, denoted by e, in each output type O_n, and mapping a state-input pair which was undefined by the operation, to an exceptional state E and return value e. We formally define this below.

A (deterministic) *ADT* of type N is a structure of the form

$$\mathcal{A} = (Q, E, init, \{op_n\}_{n \in N})$$

where Q is the set of states of the ADT, $E \in Q$ is an *exceptional* state, $init :$ $I_{init} \rightarrow (Q \times O_{init})$, and each op_n is a *realisation* of the operation n given by $op_n : Q \times I_n \rightarrow Q \times O_n$ such that $op_n(E,-) = (E,e)$ and $op_n(p,a) = (q,e) \implies q = E$. Thus if an operation returns the exceptional value the ADT moves to the exceptional state E, and all operations must keep it in E thereafter.

Let $\mathcal{A} = (Q, E, init, \{op_n\}_{n \in N})$ and $\mathcal{C} = (Q', E', init', \{op'_n\}_{n \in N})$ be ADT's of type N. We say $\mathcal{A}$ and $\mathcal{C}$ satisfy condition (RC) if there exists a relation $\rho \subseteq Q' \times Q$ such that:

(init) Let $a \in I_{init}$ and let (q_a, b) and (q'_a, b') be the resultant states and outputs after an $init(a)$ and $init'(a)$ operation in $\mathcal{A}$ and $\mathcal{C}$ respectively, with $b \neq e$. Then we require that $b = b'$ and $(q'_a, q_a) \in \rho$.

(sim) For each $n \in N$, $a \in I_n$, $b \in O_n$, and $p' \in Q'$, with $(p', p) \in \rho$, whenever $p \xrightarrow{(n,a,b)} q$ with $b \neq e$, then there exists $q' \in Q'$ such that $p' \xrightarrow{(n,a,b)} q'$ with $(q', q) \in \rho$. This is illustrated in the Fig. 1 below.

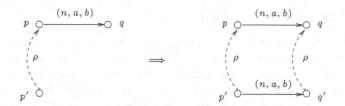

Fig. 1. Illustrating the condition (RC-sim) for refinement.

Notice that this condition is essentially a specialization of the condition (RC_Z) above for deterministic ADT's.

Finally, we will make use of a couple of properties of this notion of refinement from [11]. Firstly, refinement is *transitive*: if $\mathcal{C} \preceq \mathcal{B}$ and $\mathcal{B} \preceq \mathcal{A}$ then $\mathcal{C} \preceq \mathcal{A}$. Secondly, refinement is *substitutive*: if we have a client program $\mathcal{U}$ that implements an ADT, and itself uses a sub-ADT of type M, and if $\mathcal{B}$ and $\mathcal{C}$ are ADT's of type M such that $\mathcal{C} \preceq \mathcal{B}$. Then $\mathcal{U}[\mathcal{C}]$ refines $\mathcal{U}[\mathcal{B}]$.

3   Viewing Z and C Models as ADT's

In this section we show how to view models specified in different modelling languages as ADT's in our setting. We also phrase the refinement condition (RC) in a typical tool/environment for reasoning about these different models.

Z models. A specification $\mathcal{M}$ in the Z modelling language [32] essentially comprises the following: A finite set of variables $Var^{\mathcal{M}}$, with each $v \in Var^{\mathcal{M}}$ having a declared type (set of values) T_v. A state is a valuation s to these variables with $s(v) \in T_v$ for each $v \in Var^{\mathcal{M}}$, which satisfies a constraint $C^{\mathcal{M}}$ given as a first-order logic formula with free variables in $Var^{\mathcal{M}}$. The model has a finite set $Op^{\mathcal{M}}$ of operations. Each operation $n \in Op^{\mathcal{M}}$ has (for simplicity) a single formal input parameter x_n of type $X_n^{\mathcal{M}}$, and a single output variable y_n of type $Y_n^{\mathcal{M}}$; and a before-after-predicate $BAP_n^{\mathcal{M}}$ with free-variables in $Var^{\mathcal{M}} \cup \{x_n, y_n\} \cup Var^{\mathcal{M}'}$, where for a set of variables Var we use the convention that Var' denotes the set of variables $\{v' \mid v \in Var\}$. The set of operations $Op^{\mathcal{M}}$ includes an initialization operation called $init^{\mathcal{M}}$, whose BAP predicate is only on the input variable and primed variables (i.e. it only constrains the post-state). We say the Z model is *deterministic* if for each operation $n \in Op^{\mathcal{M}}$, state p and input value $a \in X_n^{\mathcal{M}}$, we have at most one state q and output value $b \in Y_n^{\mathcal{M}}$ satisfying $BAP_n^{\mathcal{M}}(p, a, q, b)$.

A deterministic Z model like $\mathcal{M}$ above defines an ADT

$$\mathcal{A}_{\mathcal{M}} = (Q', E, init, \{op_n\}_{n \in N}),$$

of type N, where:

- N is the ADT type $Op^{\mathcal{M}}$ with $I_n = X_n^{\mathcal{M}}$ and $O_n = Y_n^{\mathcal{M}} \cup \{e\}$,
- $Q' = Q \cup \{E\}$ where Q is the set of states of $\mathcal{M}$, and E is a new exceptional state;
- the *init* operation is given by $init(a) = (q, b)$ iff $BAP_{init}^{\mathcal{M}}(a, q, b)$; and
- for each $n \in N$, we have $op_n : (Q' \times I_n) \to (Q' \times O_n)$ given by

$$op_n(p, a) = \begin{cases} (q, b) & \text{if} \qquad \exists (q, b) : BAP_n^{\mathcal{M}}(p, a, q, b) \\ (E, e) & \text{otherwise.} \end{cases}$$

Thus we view an operation as returning an exceptional value whenever it is called outside its pre-condition (namely pre_n which is the set of states and input pairs (p, a) such that there exists a state q and output b satisfying $BAP_n^{\mathcal{M}}(p, a, q, b)$).

Given two deterministic Z models $\mathcal{M}_1$ and $\mathcal{M}_2$, we say $\mathcal{M}_2$ *refines* $\mathcal{M}_1$ iff the induced ADT's $\mathcal{A}_{\mathcal{M}_2}$ and $\mathcal{A}_{\mathcal{M}_1}$ are such that $\mathcal{A}_{\mathcal{M}_2}$ refines $\mathcal{A}_{\mathcal{M}_1}$.

C implementations. We assume that an ADT implementation in C is a program P that comprises a set of global variables *Var* with each $v \in Var$ having a declared type T_v. It has a finite set of function names F, with an associated function definition $\mathtt{func}_n$ for each $n \in F$, which could contain local variables. We can view P as an ADT in a natural way, as follows. A program state of P is a valuation for its global variables and local variables that are in scope, together with a location representing the statement number to be executed next. We use a special location "0" to represent the fact that an operation has completed, and the program is not in the middle of executing an operation. We call these program states with location "0" the *complete* program states of P. The states of the ADT induced by P is now the set of *complete* program states of P. As expected, we view each implementation of an operation as starting in a complete program state, taking an argument, transforming the program state – via a number of intermediate steps – from one complete state to another, and returning a value. If the function does not terminate (due to a buggy loop for example), or causes an exception (due to a null dereference for example), we view the operation as returning the exceptional value e.

Finally, we would also like to consider C implementations that have a *precondition* for each operation. We assume that the precondition for operation n is a predicate pre_n on the complete state and input of the operation. We view such a C program as inducing an ADT as defined above, except that for complete states and inputs that don't satisfy pre_n the ADT transitions to a "dead" local state.

With this view of Z and C ADT models we can phrase the refinement conditions (RC) as theorems in tools like Z/Eves or Rodin, or as $\mathtt{requires}$ and $\mathtt{ensures}$ clauses in a tool like VCC (see for instance [12]).

4 Directed Refinement Methodology

We now propose a methodology based on our theory of refinement for proving the functional correctness of an imperative language implementation $\mathcal{P}$ of an ADT-like system.

1. To begin with we view $\mathcal{P}$ as implementing an ADT of a certain type N.
2. Based on a high-level understanding of the code, and documentation like user manual and comments in code, construct an ADT $\mathcal{M}_1$ in a high-level specification language like Z, that captures the intended behaviour of $\mathcal{P}$.
3. In general $\mathcal{P}$ may use several sub-ADT's, say $\mathcal{B}_1, \ldots, \mathcal{B}_n$ of type $M_1, \ldots, M_n$ respectively, and can be viewed as $\mathcal{U}[\mathcal{B}_1, \ldots, \mathcal{B}_n]$, where $\mathcal{U}$ is an $(M_1, \ldots, M_n)$-client program, itself providing an ADT of type N. We now replace each sub-ADT implementation $\mathcal{B}_i$ by a version $\mathcal{A}_i$ of it expressed using the high-level constructs like maps of the ghost language available in tools like VCC. We refer to this abstraction $\mathcal{U}[\mathcal{A}_1, \ldots, \mathcal{A}_n]$ of the implementation as $\mathcal{P}_1$.
4. Refine $\mathcal{M}_1$ towards the implementation $\mathcal{P}_1$, via a sequence of successively refined Z models, that add increasing details of the implementation. Let $\mathcal{M}_2$ be the resulting Z model that is sufficiently "close" to $\mathcal{P}_1$. The refinement conditions for the successive Z models could be checked in Z-Eves [29] or other tools [1,26,27], or by a suitable encoding in VCC.
5. Check that $\mathcal{P}_1$ refines $\mathcal{M}_2$. We can do this by either using a ghost version $\mathcal{M}_2$ if one is available, or by directly importing the before-after predicates from $\mathcal{M}_2$ (see [12] for example), and then checking the resulting annotations in a tool like VCC. At the end of this step, we would have contracts in the form of **requires** and **ensures** annotations, for each ghost implementation $\mathcal{A}_i$ of the sub-ADT's that were used to prove that $\mathcal{P}_1$ refines $\mathcal{M}_2$.
6. Check that each sub-ADT $\mathcal{A}_i$ along with its associated precondition (from the **requires** clause of its contract), is refined by $\mathcal{B}_i$.

If these checks are successful, we can conclude using the transitivity and substitutivity property of refinement, that $\mathcal{P} = \mathcal{U}[\mathcal{B}_1, \ldots, \mathcal{B}_n] \preceq \mathcal{U}[\mathcal{A}_1, \ldots, \mathcal{A}_n] = \mathcal{P}_1 \preceq \mathcal{M}_2 \preceq \mathcal{M}_1$.

5 About FreeRTOS

In the next few sections we describe the case-study (FreeRTOS V6.1.1) on which we apply our verification methodology. FreeRTOS [14] is a real-time kernel meant for use in embedded applications that run on microcontrollers with small to mid-sized memory. It allows an application to organise itself into multiple independent tasks (or threads) that will be executed according to a priority-based preemptive scheduling policy. It is implemented as a set of API functions written in about 3,000 lines of C code, that an application programmer can include with their code and invoke as function calls. These API's provide the programmer ways to create and schedule tasks, communicate between tasks (via message queues, semaphores, etc.), and carry out time-constrained blocking of tasks.

It has been ported to 34 architectures and receives more than 100,000 downloads a year.

Figure 2 shows a simple application that uses FreeRTOS. The application creates two tasks "A1" and "B2" with priorities 1 and 2 respectively (a higher number indicates a higher priority), and starts the FreeRTOS scheduler. We use a naming convention that indicates the task's priority in its name. The scheduler then runs task B2, which immediately asks to be delayed for 2 time units. B2 is now blocked and the lower priority task A1 gets to execute. After 2 time units, B2 is ready to execute and preempts A1. This behaviour continues forever.

```
int main(void) {
  xTaskCreate(foo, "A1", 1,...);
  xTaskCreate(bar, "B2", 2,...);
  vTaskStartScheduler();
}
void foo(void* params) {
  for(;;) { }
}
void bar(void* params) {
  for(;;) {
    vTaskDelay(2);
  }
}
```

Fig. 2. An example FreeRTOS application and its timing diagram.

```
void vTaskDelay(portTickType xTicksToDelay){...    void vListInsert(xList *pxList,
  if(xTicksToDelay > (portTickType) 0){                        xListItem *pxNewItem) {
    xTimeToWake = xTickCount + xTicksToDelay;        ...
    vListRemove(&(pxCurrentTCB->xGenListItem));      xValOfInsertion = pxNewItem->xItemValue;
    listSET_LIST_ITEM_VALUE(                         for(pxIterator = &(pxList->xListEnd);
      &(pxCurrentTCB->xGenListItem),xTimeToWake);      pxIterator->pxNext->xItemValue
    vListInsert(pxDelayedTaskList,                                 <= xValOfInsertion;
      &(pxCurrentTCB->xGenListItem));                  pxIterator = pxIterator->pxNext) {
    ...                                              }
  }                                                  pxNewItem->pxNext = pxIterator->pxNext;
}                                                    pxNewItem->pxNext->pxPrevious = pxNewItem;
                                                     ...
                                                   }
```

Fig. 3. Excerpts from the vTaskDelay API and the xList operation vListInsert.

Figure 3 shows an excerpt from the code of the vTaskDelay API function. It computes the time-to-awake, removes the current task from the ready queue, updates its key value to the time-to-awake, and inserts it in the delayed queue. The last 3 steps are done using calls to a list data-structure called xList which is the core data-structure used in FreeRTOS. It is a circular doubly-linked list of xListItem nodes each of which contains a key field called xItemValue. Based on the invariants it satisfies an xList can be used as a priority queue, a FIFO queue, or a generic list. It provides 13 different operations, including enqueue in a priority queue (vListInsert), head of a FIFO/priority queue, and rotate left.

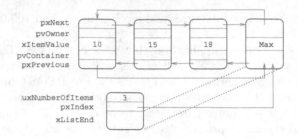

Fig. 4. An example `xList` representing a priority queue with values 10,15, and 18.

Figure 4 shows an instance of `xList`, that represents a (non-decreasing order) priority queue with item values 10,15, and 18. The head of the queue is the node pointed to by the `pxNext` field of the `xListEnd` node of the list header. The second part of Fig. 3 shows part of the `vListInsert` operation of `xList`.

FreeRTOS is architected in a modular fashion. It has a portable part which contains compiler/processor independent code, most of it in 3 C files `tasks.c`, `queue.c`, and `list.c`. The port-specific part is present in a separate directory associated with each compiler/processor pair, and is written in C and assembly.

6   Overview of FreeRTOS Verification

We view the system corresponding to a FreeRTOS application as conceptually having two components: one is an *interpreter* for the application program, which keeps track of the local states of each task, the currently running task, etc.; the other is a component which we call the *scheduler*, whose job it is to maintain the scheduling-related state of the FreeRTOS kernel (the set of tasks created and their priorities, the contents of the ready and delayed queues, the current tick count, etc.). The interpreter component makes calls to the operations (API's) provided by the scheduler (for example `vTaskDelay(d)`), and gets back a return value which typically indicates the task to be run next. Thus, in the terminology of Sect. 2 the interpreter is a scheduler-type-client program, that uses the scheduler component as an ADT.

While in an actual execution of an application API calls could be interleaved in a non-atomic fashion (for example while the `vTaskDelay` function is running, a tick interrupt might arrive causing the `vTaskIncrementTick` to execute before the call to `vTaskDelay` finishes), we assume a limited form of preemption in which interleaving happens only at API boundaries.

In this work our interest lies in this conceptual scheduler component. We restrict ourselves to the task-related API's in the file `task.c` of the FreeRTOS code, and consider the relevant parts of this code to be the implementation $\mathcal{P}$ of the scheduler component. Our aim is to specify and verify this ADT implementation using the methodology outlined in Sects. 2 and 4.

Following the methodology, we first build a high-level deterministic model $\mathcal{M}_1$ of the scheduler in the Z specification language. This model maintains the tick count as a number bounded by $maxNumVal$ and has a single delayed list. Next we observe that the scheduler implementation $\mathcal{P}$ uses a sub-ADT, namely xList, and thus is of the form $\mathcal{U}_S[\text{xList}]$ where $\mathcal{U}_S$ is a xList-type-client program that itself implements an ADT. We replace the sub-ADT xList by a ghost implementation in VCC which we call xListMap. Thus $\mathcal{P}_1$ is a version of the implementation of the form $\mathcal{U}_S[\text{xListMap}]$. Next, we bring $\mathcal{M}_1$ closer to $\mathcal{P}_1$ by adding a separate "overflow-delayed" list to store tasks whose time-to-awake is beyond $maxNumVal$. We call this model $\mathcal{M}_2$. The models $\mathcal{M}_2$ and $\mathcal{P}_1$ are very similar and hence we can import the before-after-predicates from $\mathcal{M}_2$ to $\mathcal{P}_1$, to phrase the refinement conditions. To check these conditions in VCC we come up with pre-conditions in xListMap. Finally we show that xList refines xListMap with its given preconditions. The components in the methodology used to verify FreeRTOS are shown in the figure alongside.

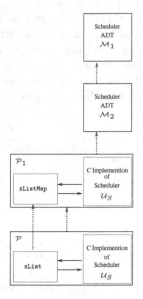

Provided we can check the associated verification conditions (which we address in the next section), we can conclude that $\mathcal{P}$ refines $\mathcal{M}_1$, since $\mathcal{P} = \mathcal{U}_S[\text{xList}] \preceq \mathcal{U}_S[\text{xListMap}] \preceq \mathcal{M}_2 \preceq \mathcal{M}_1$.

7   Details of Steps in the Verification of FreeRTOS

We now describe in some detail the main steps and results of our case-study. The artifacts of this project are available at www.csa.iisc.ernet.in/~deepakd/FreeRTOS/.

7.1   Z Models

We begin by describing our high-level models of the scheduler in Z. To begin with, we tried to understand the "intended" behaviour of the FreeRTOS scheduler. The main input for this understanding was the FreeRTOS user guide [4]. For some API's we had to look at the code and the comments therein to infer the meaning. We also had to re-group some of the functionality in the implementation: for instance, FreeRTOS does not have an explicit API for initialization, but initialization is done partly in the first call to vTaskCreate (calling a private function) and partly in vTaskStartScheduler; so we collected this functionality into a separate initialization API function.

Next we specified this behaviour in a Z model which we call $\mathcal{M}_1$. To represent the state of the scheduler we adopted the basic design of the FreeRTOS implementation, in particular we chose to represent the ready queue as a sequence of sequences resembling the array of FIFO queues (indexed by priorities) used in

FreeRTOS. Figure 5 shows the main elements of the data state of the scheduler and invariants on the state. The variable $maxPrio$ represents the maximum priority, and $maxNumVal$ represents a common bound on values like tick count and time-to-delay, as well as the maximum length of queues like the $ready$ queues. These variables represent corresponding configurable constants in FreeRTOS, and are initialized in the model as shown in Fig. 5.

Scheduler

$maxPrio, maxNumVal, tickCount, topReadyPriority : \mathbb{N}$
$tasks : \mathbb{P}\ TASK$
$priority : TASK \nrightarrow \mathbb{N}$
$running\_task, idle : TASK$
$ready : \text{seq (iseq } TASK)$
$delayed : \text{seq } TASK \times \mathbb{N}$
$blocked : \text{seq } TASK$
$\ldots$

$idle \in tasks \wedge idle \in \text{ran} \frown/(\text{ran } ready)$
$running\_task \in tasks \wedge topReadyPriority \in \text{dom } ready$
$\forall i, j : \text{dom } delayed \mid (i < j) \bullet delayed(i).2 \leq delayed(j).2$
$\forall tcn : \text{ran } delayed \mid tcn.2 > tickCount$
$running\_task = \text{head } ready(topReadyPriority)$
$\text{dom } priority = tasks \wedge tickCount \leq maxNumVal$
$\forall i, j : \text{dom } blocked \mid (i < j) \implies priority(blocked(i)) \geq priority(blocked(j))$
$\ldots$

Init

$maxP? : \mathbb{N}$
$maxN? : \mathbb{N}$

$maxN? > 0$
$maxN? \geq maxP? > 0$
$maxPrio' = maxP?$
$maxNumVal' = maxN?$
$tasks' = \{idle\}$
$running\_task' = idle$
$tickCount' = 0$
$ready'(1) = \langle idle \rangle$
$\ldots$

Fig. 5. Data and invariants of the Scheduler and Init schema.

Figure 6 shows the schema for the `vTaskDelay` API, for the case when there is another ready task of the top ready priority, apart from the running task. The argument `delay` to the operation is required to be at most $maxNumVal$. Since the value of tick count is bounded by $maxNumVal$ the time-to-awake for the running task will be in the range $[0, 2 \cdot maxNumVal]$. The operation for increment-tick increments the value of the tick count modulo $(maxNumVal + 1)$. When it resets the tick count to 0, it reduces the time-to-awake values of the delayed tasks by $maxNumVal + 1$.

The model $\mathcal{M}_2$ refines $\mathcal{M}_1$ by adding two details from the FreeRTOS implementation. FreeRTOS maintains a separate list called "overflow-delayed" for tasks whose time-to-awake values are beyond $maxNumVal$. These tasks are stored in this list with time-to-awake values reduced by $maxNumVal + 1$. This is modelled in $\mathcal{M}_2$ by adding a corresponding list called $oDelayed$. Secondly, the set of tasks blocked on an event (like message arrival in a queue) is modeled in $\mathcal{M}_1$ as a list $blocked$ in which tasks are stored in decreasing order of their priority. In FreeRTOS however they are enqueued with a key value that is the $complement$ of their priority in $maxPrio$. This is done so that a single insert operation of `xList` can be used for both the delayed and blocked lists. $\mathcal{M}_2$ models this by changing the invariant on the $blocked$ list.

We checked that $\mathcal{M}_2$ is a refinement of $\mathcal{M}_1$ using the refinement condition of Sect. 2. The abstraction relation is as follows: the $delayed$ list in $\mathcal{M}_1$ is obtained by increasing the time-to-awake values in $oDelayed$ by $maxNumVal + 1$ and

```
  TaskDelay
  ΔScheduler
  delay? : ℕ
  delayedPrefix, delayedSuffix : seq TASK × ℕ
  running! : TASK

  delay > 0 ∧ delay ≤ maxNumVal ∧ running_task ≠ idle
  #delayed < maxNumVal
  tail ready(topReadyPriority) ≠ ⟨⟩ ∧ delayed = delayedPrefix ⌢ delayedSuffix
  ∀ tcn : ran delayedPrefix | tcn.2 ≤ (tickCount + delay?)
  delayedSuffix ≠ ⟨⟩ ⟹ (head delayedSuffix).2 > (tickCount + delay?)
  running_task' = head tail ready(topReadyPriority)
  ready' = ready ⊕ { ( topReadyPriority ↦ tail ready(topReadyPriority) ) }
  delayed' = delayedPrefix ⌢ ⟨(running_task, (tickCount + delay?))⟩ ⌢ delayedSuffix
  ...
```

Fig. 6. Operation schema for API *vTaskDelay* when another ready task of same priority is available.

appending it to $delayed_{\mathcal{M}_2}$. The corresponding verification conditions for the affected operations were checked using VCC by modelling the relevant parts of $\mathcal{M}_1$ and $\mathcal{M}_2$ in VCC.

7.2   Verifying that $\mathcal{P}_1$ Refines $\mathcal{M}_2$

We now address the task of showing that $\mathcal{P}_1$ (namely the FreeRTOS scheduler C code, with the xList library replaced by the VCC ghost library xListMap) refines $\mathcal{M}_2$, the Z model of the scheduler. As mentioned in Sect. 6, we define a simple list ADT using the ghost programming constructs of VCC, called xListMap, that provides the same intended functionality of xList. Figure 7 shows a part of its definition. Like xList it maintains a list of pointers to xListItem nodes, but as a mathematical "map" from integers to xListItem pointers. The component length records the number of items in the list. The element type keeps track of whether the list is meant to be a FIFO or priority queue. The figure also shows the definition of the operation vListInsert using a lambda construct provided by VCC's ghost language.

```
typedef struct xListMap {                void vListInsert(xListMap *mlist, xListItem *xli)
  _(ghost xListItem *list[unsigned])       _(requires \wrapped(mlist))
  _(ghost unsigned length)                 _(requires mlist->length < maxNumVal) {
  _(ghost enum xListType type)               unsigned index;
  _(invariant length <= maxNumVal)          _(ghost mlist->list = \lambda unsigned i;
  _(invariant (type==PQ)==> (\forall           (i<mlist->length)?
    unsigned i,j; (j<length && i<j)            ((i<index)? mlist->list[i] : ((i == index)?
    ==> (list[i]->xItemValue                     xli: mlist->list[i-1]))) : (xListItem*) NULL)
             <= list[j]->xItemValue)))       _(ghost mlist->length++)
  ...                                         ...
} xListMap;                               }
```

Fig. 7. Excerpts from xListMap and vListInsert. The ghost variable index is constrained to be the required position of xli.

As described in Sect. 3, to check that $\mathcal{P}_1$ refines $\mathcal{M}_2$ we directly import the before-after-conditions from $\mathcal{M}_2$ as `requires` and `ensures` conditions on the API functions in $\mathcal{P}_1$. We manually simplified these conditions to remove the existential quantifiers making use of the fact that $\mathcal{M}_2$ and $\mathcal{P}_1$ were closely related. VCC was able to check most of the annotations in the API's in $\mathcal{P}_1$, except for the `xTaskCreate` API, and a couple of other API's we mention in Sect. 7.4. The problem with `xTaskCreate` was as follows. FreeRTOS follows a convention of keeping the running task at the *end* of the ready queue corresponding to its priority. However this convention leads to inconsistencies like the following. Consider the scenario where tasks A1, B1 (both of priority 1) are ready, with A1 currently executing. By the FreeRTOS convention, the ready queue is the list $\langle B1, A1 \rangle$. Now suppose A1 creates a task C1. The `xTaskCreate` function uses the `xList` operation `vListInsertEnd` to add C1 to the *end* of the queue, to get $\langle B1, A1, C1 \rangle$. Thus the running task A1 is no longer at the end of the queue. If a couple of tick interrupts now arrive, causing A1 and then B1 to be preempted, it will be A1 that runs again (instead of C1!).

We chose to fix this problem in the design of FreeRTOS by following the convention of the Z models to keep the running task at the head of its ready queue. However to do this we needed to add two new functions to the `xList` (and `xListMap`) library: `list-rotate-left` and `list_GET_FIRST_ENTRY` that respectively rotate a FIFO queue by one position to the left, and return the node at the head of the list. The function `list-rotate-left` is used in the case of preemption (time slicing within tasks of the top priority), while `list_GET_FIRST_ENTRY` is used to find the next running task.

With these changes and other fixes mentioned in Sect. 7.4 VCC verifies all the API functions of $\mathcal{P}_1$. This part of the proof required considerable effort, as shown in the table of Fig. 8. As described in Sect. 3 we also need to check that the operations in $\mathcal{P}_1$ all terminate in state-input pairs that satisfy their preconditions. In $\mathcal{P}_1$ all calls to the sub-ADT namely `xListMap` terminate since they are defined declaratively. Further, the only loops present in the $\mathcal{P}_1$ code are in the call to the function `vTaskSwitchContext` whose job is to find the new top ready priority, and consequently the new running task. To verify termination of this function we used a simple ranking function (the value of the `topReadyPriority` variable), and proved that its value decreases in each iteration of the loop, using VCC.

7.3   Verifying that `xList` Refines `xListMap`

We now focus on showing that `xList` is a refinement of `xListMap`. Recall that the preconditions of the `xListMap` operations are derived from the contract (see Fig. 7) used to prove the correctness of $\mathcal{P}_1$ in the previous section. It is sufficient to consider a single pair of instances of `xList` and `xListMap`, and phrase the refinement conditions (RC) on it. We first create a joint structure containing the state components of both `xList` and `xListMap`, and their invariants. In addition we add "gluing" invariants that represent the abstraction map between the two components. These invariants crucially use the `type` field of the `xListMap` component to say how the elements in the two lists correspond. For example, for a non-empty list of type `FIFO`, `pxIndex` points to the *end* of the list, and hence the first element of the list is the one pointed to by `pxIndex->pxNext`. For a priority queue however, the first item is the one after `xListEnd`. In addition, a node in the i-th position of `list` has its `pxNext` field pointing to the one at position $i+1$ in `list`:

```
_(invariant ((type == FIFO) && (length > 0) && (pxIndex->pxNext != (&xListEnd)) ==>
                                    (list[0] == pxIndex->pxNext)))
_(invariant ((type == PQ) && (length > 0)) ==> (list[0] == ((&xListEnd)->pxNext)))
_(invariant (\forall unsigned i; (i < (length-1) ==> (list[i+1] == list[i]->pxNext)))
```

Next, for each list operation we create a joint version of the operation, containing the updates for both `xListMap` and `xList`. The precondition for this operation is inherited from the `xListMap` version, and additionally requires the joint list argument to be "**wrapped**" (that the invariants on the structure hold). The `ensures` clause simply asks for the joint structure to be **wrapped** at the end and return values to be equal. All the assertions were successfully proved by VCC.

The table alongside summarises the number of lines of code (LOC) and annotation effort (LOA) in our case study. The numbers reported exclude comments and blank lines. Of the 2514 LOC in the portable code of FreeRTOS, we have verified 482 LOC mainly from the

Z Model $\mathcal{M}_1$		Z Model $\mathcal{M}_2$		API funcs in $\mathcal{P}$		
Schemas	LOC	Schemas	LOC	Funcs	LOC	LOA
50	766	60	1239	17	361	2347

xListMap			xList		
Funcs	LOC	LOA	Funcs	LOC	LOA (xListJoint)
15	306	1033	15	121	1450

Fig. 8. Size of artifacts in FreeRTOS verification

files `list.c` and `task.c`. This includes 17 core API's from `task.c` (many of the remaining 20 task API's are to do with tracing and other non-core functionality).

7.4 Bugs Found

Apart from the previously mentioned problem with `xTaskCreate`, another related problem is that if the main program creates tasks A1 followed by B1, and then starts the scheduler, the task that runs is B1 (instead of A1). This is due to a problem with the way the `pxCurrentTCB` (the running task) is updated.

A more serious bug was in the `vTaskPrioritySet` function which changes the priority of a given task. When the given task is in the blocked queue (say waiting to receive a message from a message queue), then its priority is updated but its position in the event queue (which is a priority queue) is *not* adjusted. A similar bug exists in the `vTaskPriorityInherit` API function which is used to increase the priority of a task holding a mutex, when a higher priority task wants the mutex. The idea is that the lower priority task temporarily *inherits* the priority of the higher priority task that is waiting for a resource it is holding, so that it can complete sooner and release the resource for the higher priority task.

These functions in turn call list_SET_ITEM_VALUE, which however does not have the desired effect when the lower priority task is in the blocked queue. A simple fix is to implement these API's by first removing the concerned node from the blocked queue, update its priority using list_SET_ITEM_VALUE, and then insert it back in the queue using vListInsert.

We communicated these issues to the developers of FreeRTOS who acknowledged that our understanding of the intended behaviour was correct and that the said behaviours were indeed deviations [5]. They would like to make the proposed fixes provided they do not conflict with other design choices in FreeRTOS: for example a time-consuming priority-based insert operation is ok to do in a lightweight critical section where the scheduler is suspended, but *not* when interrupts are disabled. Finally, the fixes made to obtain the fully verified version of the API's involved only a small part of the code: 19 lines in the API code were modified and 7 lines added to xList.

8   Related Work

We discuss some of the OS verification projects in the literature that are most closely related to ours. In the design-for-verification projects, the most prominent work is the seL4 project [23], where a formally verified microkernel was developed. The scope of their work is larger than ours, addressing among other things memory allocation and interrupts. They also use a refinement-based approach to prove functional correctness of the C implementation with respect to a high-level specification, in Isabelle/HOL. The translation of the C semantics to Isabelle/HOL is validated by checking that the compiled kernel refines the translation to Isabelle/HOL [31]. In contrast, our verification – though far more modest in scope – is "post-facto," and is built on an existing code verification tool like VCC, which has a large user base and hence provides a different dimension of confidence in the verification.

Among the works in post-facto verification, the most related is the Verisoft XT project [7,33] at Microsoft, where the goal was proving the functional correctness of the Hyper-V hypervisor and PikeOS operating systems. While details of the Hyper-V effort are not publicly available (see [21,24]) PikeOS [6] is an embedded OS, similar in nature to FreeRTOS though with a few more features like virtualization. The verification uses VCC and specifications are annotations and correctness is in terms of conformance to ghost code. In contrast, we use a refinement-based approach, and as a result have a standalone abstract specification that can be used to verify clients in other environments.

In a recent and closely related piece of work, Ferreira et al. [13] prove functional correctness and memory safety of some of the FreeRTOS list and task API's, in the HIP/SLEEK verification tool. Their specifications are pre/post annotations on the API code. In contrast we verify all the list API's and the core task API's. We use an abstract specification and correctness is in terms of conformance to the abstract specification. As part of this conformance proof we prove all the functional and safety properties mentioned in [13].

Gotsman and Yang [15] propose a modular way of reasoning about preemptive kernel code by separately arguing correctness of the context-switching and the uninterrupted kernel code. We currently do not model context-switching since this is part of the "interpreter" component that we don't model, but this would be a useful approach in extending this work to a concurrent setting.

In work related to phrasing refinement conditions in code-level verifiers, the work in [17] translates refinement conditions to annotations in C code for the purpose of proving a separation property for an embedded device. Finally, in recent work [12] we propose an efficient 2-step approach to phrasing refinement checks in VCC, and evaluate it against the two approaches proposed here, on a simplified version of FreeRTOS.

References

1. Abrial, J.R., Butler, M., Hallerstede, S., Hoang, T.S., Mehta, F., Voisin, L.: Rodin: an open toolset for modelling and reasoning in Event-B. Softw. Tools Technol. Transf. **12**(6), 447–466 (2010)
2. Abrial, J.R., Schuman, S.A., Meyer, B.: Specification language. In: McKeag, R.M., Macnaughlen, A.M. (eds.) On the Construction of Programs, pp. 343–410. Cambridge University Press, Cambridge (1980)
3. Alkassar, E., Hillebrand, M.A., Paul, W., Petrova, E.: Automated verification of a small hypervisor. In: Leavens, G.T., O'Hearn, P., Rajamani, S.K. (eds.) VSTTE 2010. LNCS, vol. 6217, pp. 40–54. Springer, Heidelberg (2010)
4. Barry, R.: Using the FreeRTOS Real Time Kernel - A Practical Guide (2010)
5. Barry, R.: Personal communication by email (2013)
6. Baumann, C., Beckert, B., Blasum, H., Bormer, T.: Lessons learned from microkernel verification - specification is the new bottleneck. In: SSV, pp. 18–32 (2012)
7. Beckert, B., Moskal, M.: Deductive verification of system software in the verisoft XT project. KI **24**(1), 57–61 (2010)
8. Bjørner, D., Jones, C.B. (eds.): The Vienna Development Method: The Meta-Language. LNCS, vol. 61. Springer, Berlin (1978)
9. Cohen, E.: Data abstraction in VCC. In: Broy, M., Peled, D., Kalus, G. (eds.) Engineering Dependable Software Systems, NATO Science for Peace and Security Series - D: Information and Communication Security, vol. 34, pp. 79–114. IOS Press, Amsterdam (2013)
10. Cohen, E., Dahlweid, M., Hillebrand, M., Leinenbach, D., Moskal, M., Santen, T., Schulte, W., Tobies, S.: VCC: a practical system for verifying concurrent C. In: Berghofer, S., Nipkow, T., Urban, C., Wenzel, M. (eds.) TPHOLs 2009. LNCS, vol. 5674, pp. 23–42. Springer, Heidelberg (2009)
11. Divakaran, S., D'Souza, D., Sampath, P., Sridhar, N., Woodcock, J.: A theory of refinement for ADTs with functional interfaces. Technical report TR-2015-4, Department of Computer Science and Automation, IISc, Bangalore (2015)
12. Divakaran, S., D'Souza, D., Sridhar, N.: Efficient refinement checking in VCC. In: Giannakopoulou, D., Kroening, D. (eds.) VSTTE 2014. LNCS, vol. 8471, pp. 21–36. Springer, Heidelberg (2014)
13. Ferreira, J.F., Gherghina, C., He, G., Qin, S., Chin, W.: Automated verification of the FreeRTOS scheduler in Hip/Sleek. STTT **16**(4), 381–397 (2014)
14. The FreeRTOS Project. www.freertos.org (Accessed on 10 April 2012)

15. Gotsman, A., Yang, H.: Modular verification of preemptive OS kernels. In: Proceeding of the 16th ACM SIGPLAN International Conference on Functional Programming, ICFP 2011, pp. 404–417 (2011)
16. He, J., Hoare, C.A.R., Sanders, J.W.: Data refinement refined. In: Robinet, B., Wilhelm, R. (eds.) ESOP 1986. LNCS, vol. 213, pp. 187–196. Springer, Heidelberg (1986)
17. Heitmeyer, C.L., Archer, M., Leonard, E.I., McLean, J.D.: Formal specification and verification of data separation in a separation kernel for an embedded system. In: 13th ACM Computer and Communications Security (CCS), pp. 346–355 (2006)
18. Hoare, C.A.R., Hayes, I.J., He, J., Morgan, C.C., Sanders, J.W., Sorensen, I.H., Spivey, J.M., Sufrin, B.A.: Data Refinement Refined (DRAFT). Technical report, Oxford University Computing Laboratory, Oxford, UK, May 1985
19. Hoare, C., Misra, J., Leavens, G.T., Shankar, N.: The verified software initiative: a manifesto. ACM Comput. Surv. **41**(4), 22:1–22:8 (2009)
20. Jones, C.B.: Systematic Software Development Using VDM. Prentice Hall International Series in Computer Science. Prentice Hall, Upper Saddle River (1986)
21. Klein, G.: Operating system verification – an overview. Sādhanā **34**(1), 27–69 (2009)
22. Klein, G., Andronick, J., Elphinstone, K., Murray, T.C., Sewell, T., Kolanski, R., Heiser, G.: Comprehensive formal verification of an OS microkernel. ACM Trans. Comput. Syst. **32**(1), 2 (2014)
23. Klein, G., Elphinstone, K., Heiser, G., et al.: sel4: formal verification of an OS kernel. In: Matthews, J.N., Anderson, T.E. (eds.) SOSP, pp. 207–220. ACM (2009)
24. Leinenbach, D., Santen, T.: Verifying the microsoft hyper-V hypervisor with VCC. In: Cavalcanti, A., Dams, D.R. (eds.) FM 2009. LNCS, vol. 5850, pp. 806–809. Springer, Heidelberg (2009)
25. Miné, A.: Static analysis of run-time errors in embedded critical parallel C programs. In: Barthe, G. (ed.) ESOP 2011. LNCS, vol. 6602, pp. 398–418. Springer, Heidelberg (2011)
26. Nipkow, T., Paulson, L.C., Wenzel, M.: Isabelle/HOL - A Proof Assistant for Higher-Order Logic. LNCS, vol. 2283. Springer, Heidelberg (2002)
27. Owre, S., Rushby, J.M., Shankar, N.: PVS: a prototype verification system. In: Kapur, D. (ed.) CADE 1992. LNCS(LNAI), vol. 607, pp. 748–752. Springer, Heidelberg (1992)
28. Penninckx, W., Mühlberg, J.T., Smans, J., Jacobs, B., Piessens, F.: Sound formal verification of Linux's USB BP keyboard driver. In: Goodloe, A.E., Person, S. (eds.) NFM 2012. LNCS, vol. 7226, pp. 210–215. Springer, Heidelberg (2012)
29. Saaltink, M.: The Z/EVES system. In: Till, D., Bowen, J.P., Hinchey, M.G. (eds.) ZUM 1997. LNCS, vol. 1212, pp. 72–85. Springer, Heidelberg (1997)
30. Schwarz, M.D., Seidl, H., Vojdani, V., Lammich, P., Müller-Olm, M.: Static analysis of interrupt-driven programs synchronized via the priority ceiling protocol. In: POPL 2011, pp. 93–104. ACM (2011)
31. Sewell, T.A.L., Myreen, M.O., Klein, G.: Translation validation for a verified OS kernel. In: Boehm, H., Flanagan, C. (eds.) ACM SIGPLAN Conference on Programming Language Design and Implementation, PLDI 2013, 16–19 June 2013, Seattle, WA, USA, pp. 471–482. ACM (2013)
32. Woodcock, J., Davies, J.: Using Z: Specification, Refinement, and Proof. Prentice-Hall, Upper Saddle River (1996)
33. Verisoft XT Project (2010). http://www.verisoftxt.de/

Model Checking μC/OS-III Multi-task System with TMSVL

Jin Cui[1], Zhenhua Duan[1(✉)], Cong Tian[1(✉)], Nan Zhang[1], and Conghao Zhou[2]

[1] ICTT and ISN Laboratory, Xidian University,
Xi'an 710071, People's Republic of China
{ctian,zhhduan}@mail.xidian.edu.cn
[2] College of Information Science and Engineering,
Northeastern University, Shenyang 110819, People's Republic of China

Abstract. μC/OS-III is the third generation of real-time operating systems based on multi-task scheduling for embedded systems. The multi-task system which refers to tasks with the same priority, tasks synchronization and communication, is scheduled by the operating system kernel. It is critical to ensure the timeliness and correctness of related applications using μC/OS-III. This paper proposes a model checking approach to verify a multi-task embedded system running under μC/OS-III. To do so, the multi-task system and its properties are modelled in TMSVL. A model checker built in the toolkit MSV is used to verify the schedulabilty of the μC/OS-III multi-task system. Experiments show that our approach is effective and efficient in verifying embedded systems.

Keywords: Model checking · TMSVL · Multi-task systems · Schedulability · μC/OS-III

1 Introduction

μC/OS-III [10] is a preemptive real-time kernel that manages unlimited number of tasks. It is important to ensure that applications running under μC/OS-III work correctly and timely. μC/OS-III based applications consist of a number of tasks, which are scheduled by the operating system (OS) kernel. How to ensure schedulability of tasks in these applications is critical.

There are two kinds of methods that are often used to determine schedulability of real-time tasks. One is based on mathematical analysis [3–5,11] and the other one is based on formal methods [2,17,18]. Effective solutions for a class of problems can be obtained by mathematical analysis. While for flexible realistic systems, adopting mathematical manual analysis will be quite complex and error prone. As a complement, formal methods are used. The main work is

This research is supported by the NSFC Grant Nos. 61133001, 61272117, 61322202, 61420106004, and 91418201.

to formalize the problem in some formal languages, and determine the schedulability by verifying whether the model possesses the corresponding properties by a supporting tool. The validity of the verification result relies on whether the formalization is consistent with the original problem.

In [9], an abstract formal model to represent AUTOSAR OS programs for determining schedulability properties is proposed where the tasks are periodical and the deadlines and periods of tasks coincide. In [12], schedulability of preemptive event-driven asynchronous real-time systems is analyzed by a conservative approximation method on composable timed automata models. In [1], timed automata is used to find optimal schedules for the classical job-shop problem. In [13], the Uppaal model-checker is applied for schedulability analysis of a system with single CPU, fixed priorities preemptive scheduler, mixture of periodic tasks and tasks with dependencies.

Modeling, Simulation and Verification Language (MSVL) is an executable subset of Projection Temporal Logic (PTL) [7]. TMSVL [8] is a Timed version of MSVL, which is designed to model, simulate and verify real-time systems. A toolkit MSV has been developed to support the above three missions. In particular, a unified model checker can be used to verify whether or not a real-time system satisfies a specified property. An advantage of TMSVL model checking over other model checking approaches is that the model of the system and the property to be verified are both defined in TMSVL. Further, the verification process can be automatically performed with MSV.

In this paper, we verify schedulability of μC/OS-III based applications. The multi-task system consists of independent tasks, synchronous tasks, and tasks with the same priority, which are scheduled by the OS kernel. First, we model the OS scheduler and different kinds of tasks with TMSVL. Then the schedulability of the systems is formalized and the schedulability of tasks is verified with MSV.

The paper is organized as follows. The next section introduces the preliminaries of TMSVL. In particular, how timeout, delay, and timeout after time delay constraints are formalized in TMSVL is introduced. Section 3 gives an overview of μC/OS-III and Sect. 4 discusses the model checking process of a μC/OS-III multi-task application. Finally, conclusion and future work are drawn in Sect. 5.

2   TMSVL

MSVL is a temporal logic programming language consists of conjunction, selection, sequence, parallel, branching, loop as well as projection statements. TMSVL is a real-time extension of MSVL where quantitative temporal constraints are employed to limit the time duration bounded on statements or programs. Real variables T and Ts are used to describe time and time increment, respectively.

2.1   Statements in TMSVL

TMSVL consists of arithmetic expressions, boolean expressions, and basic statements. The arithmetic expression e and boolean expression b are defined by the following grammar:

$$e ::= n \mid x \mid \bigcirc x \mid \ominus x \mid e_0 \, op \, e_1 \, (op::= + \mid - \mid * \mid / \mid mod)$$
$$b ::= true \mid false \mid e_0 = e_1 \mid e_0 < e_1 \mid \neg b \mid b_0 \wedge b_1$$

where n is a constant, x is a variable; $\bigcirc x$ and $\ominus x$ denote the value of x at the next and previous state over an interval, respectively.

1.	MSVL statement	p
2.	Time constraint statment	$(t_1, t_2)tp$
3.	Conjunction statement	$tp_1 \wedge tp_2$
4.	Selection statement	$tp_1 \vee tp_2$
5.	Sequential statement	$tp_1 \, ; \, tp_2$
6.	Parallel statement	$tp \parallel tq$
7.	Conditional statement	if b then $\{tp\}$ else $\{tq\}$
8.	While statement	while (b) $\{ \, tp \, \}$
9.	Projection statement	$(tp_1, \ldots, tp_m)$ prj (tp)

Fig. 1. Basic TMSVL statements

Elementary statements of TMSVL are defined in Fig. 1. First, MSVL statements are included. Suppose t_1 and t_2 are arithmetic expressions and tp a TMSVL statement, the time constraint statement $(t_1, t_2)tp$ means that tp is executed over the time duration from t_1 to t_2. Two possible interpretations of formula $(t_1, t_2)tp$ are shown in Fig. 2. The black dots are states and are represented by $s_0, s_1, \ldots, s_k, \ldots, s_{l_2}$, respectively. We specify s_k as the current state here, thus $s_0, \ldots, s_{k-1}$ are the previous states and $s_{k+1}, \ldots, s_{l_2}$ the future ones. s_{l_2} is the terminal state. An interval is a sequence of states, for example $s_0, s_1, \ldots, s_{l_2}$ constitute an interval. Figure 2(a) shows the case $t_1 > T$ and Fig. 2(b) the case $t_1 = T$. The formula tp in $(t_1, t_2)tp$ must terminate just when $T = t_2$, otherwise $(t_1, t_2)tp$ is $false$. $tp_1 \wedge tp_2$ means that tp_1 and tp_2 are executed concurrently, and terminate at the same time. Selection statement $tp_1 \vee tp_2$ means tp_1 or tp_2 is executed. $tp_1; tp_2$ means that tp_2 is executed after tp_1 finishes. Parallel statement $tp \parallel tq$ means that tp and tq are executed in parallel, while they are not required to terminate at the same time. Conditional and while constructs are consistent with that in general programming languages such as C and $Java$. Projection statement $(tp_1, \ldots, tp_m)$ prj tp means that tp is executed in parallel with $tp_1; tp_2; \ldots; tp_m$ over an interval obtained by taking the endpoints of the intervals over which $tp_1, \ldots, tp_m$ are executed. An endpoint denotes the first or the last state of an interval. Taken (tp_1, tp_2, tp_3) prj tp as an example. We assume tp_3 terminates before tp. The semantics of (tp_1, tp_2, tp_3) prj tp is intuitively depicted in Fig. 3.

2.2   Normal Form and Normal Form Graph for TMSVL

Execution of TMSVL programs depends on the transformation of TMSVL programs into normal forms. A TMSVL program p is in its normal form if p is

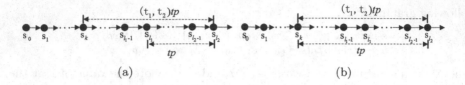

Fig. 2. Semantics of time constraint statement

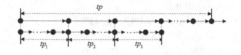

Fig. 3. An example of projection structure

written as:

$$p \equiv \bigvee_{i=1}^{l_1} p_{ei} \wedge \varepsilon \vee \bigvee_{j=1}^{l_2} p_{cj} \wedge \bigcirc p_{fj}$$

where l_1, l_2, i, and $j \in N_0$, $l_1 + l_2 \geq 1$, and p_{fj} is a TMSVL program; p_{ei} and p_{cj} are formulas of the form: $x_1 = e_1 \wedge \ldots \wedge x_m = e_m$. ε means the termination of a program. That is there does not exist a next state. $\bigcirc p_{fj}$ means that p_{fj} will be executed at the next state. It has been proved that any TMSVL program can be transformed into normal form.

Given a TMSVL program p, we can construct a graph named Normal Form Graph (NFG) [6,14,16] that explicitly illustrates the state space of the program. An NFG is a directed graph, denoted as $G =< V, A >$, with a node in the set V of nodes representing a program in TMSVL and an arc in the set A of arcs representing a state. In fact, NFG determines the models that satisfy the corresponding TMSVL program.

Suppose that the sets V and A are empty initially, NFG $G =< V, A >$ of a TMSVL program p can be constructed by determining the set of nodes V and the set of arcs A inductively as follows:

1. $V = V \cup \{p\}$;

2. for any node $q \in V \backslash \{\varepsilon, false\}$, if $q \equiv \bigvee_{i=1}^{l_1} q_{ei} \wedge \varepsilon \vee \bigvee_{j=1}^{l_2} q_{cj} \wedge \bigcirc q_{fj}$, then $V = V \cup \{\varepsilon, q_{fj}\}$ and $A = A \cup \{(q, q_{ei}, \varepsilon), (q, q_{cj}, q_{fj})\}$ for each i and j with $1 \leq i \leq l_1$ and $1 \leq j \leq l_2$.

An element in the set of arcs A is a triple. For instance, (q, q_{ei}, ε) denotes a directed arc from nodes q to ε with the arc labeled with q_{ei}.

2.3   Timeout in TMSVL

It is necessary to confine the time for waiting for a particular condition to become true such that the waiting is terminated when the time expires. Timeout on waiting is a practical method usually adopted in real-time systems and protocols. A maximum waiting time is given in advance, so the waiting process stops finally in one of the following cases: (1) the events waited occur; (2) the event does not occur but the waiting time expires. The two cases are formalized separatively in *time delay* and *timeout* constraints first. Then the constraint named *timeout after time delay* which combines *time delay* and *timeout* constraints is introduced to express the scenario of timeout on waiting or on other process.

Time delay constraint $\{d_1, d_m\}p$ (d_1 and d_m are non-negative reals and $d_1 \leq d_m$) represents that the statement p starts at the current time and terminates after at least d_1 time units and at most d_m time units. d_1 and d_m provides the upper and lower limits of the time that is taken for p to execute. The statement p is the TMSVL formalism of the waiting process or other real-time process. The constraint for *time delay* is expressed as follows:

$$\{d_1, d_m\}p \stackrel{\text{def}}{=} (T, T + d_1)p \vee \ldots \vee (T, T + d_i)p \vee \ldots \vee (T, T + d_m)p$$

where $d_i = d_{i-1} + Ts$ and $1 < i \leq m$. It is a disjunction of time constraint statements starting at T and ending at any time within $T + d_1$ and $T + d_m$.

Timeout constraint $(t_1@t_m)p$ means that p starting at $T = t_1$ terminates when $T = t_m$ naturally or forcibly. If p is not finished when $T = t_m$, it is terminated forcibly. Otherwise, p finishes just when $T = t_1$ naturally. Its definition is given as follows:

$$(t_1@t_m)p \stackrel{\text{def}}{=} (t_1, t_m)\ p_c^1 \wedge (t_2, t_m)p_c^2 \wedge \ldots \wedge (t_m, t_m)(p_e^m \vee p_c^m)$$

where $t_1, \ldots, t_m$ are the time values of m consecutive states respectively. p_c^i represents a state formula obtained by the state reduction on p when $T = t_i$ ($1 \leq i \leq m$). p_e^m represents a terminal state formula indicating that p finishes naturally when $T = t_m$.

Combining the two constraints above, we derive the *timeout after time delay* constraint, denoted as $\{d_1@d_m\}p$. The definition is given as follows:

$$\{d_1@d_m\}p \stackrel{\text{def}}{=} (T, T + d_1)p \vee \ldots \vee (T, T + d_i)p \vee \ldots \vee (T, T + d_{m-1})p \vee (T@T + d_m)p$$

where $d_i = d_{i-1} + Ts$ and $1 < i \leq m$. In the *timeout after time delay* constraint, when the time delay reaches the upper bound d_m but p still does not finish, p will be terminated forcibly.

3 μC/OS-III Overview

μC/OS-III is different from μC/OS-II mainly in two aspects: (1) task management; (2) OS kernel service.

3.1 Task Management

μC/OS-III supports multitasking and allows the applications to have any number of tasks. The maximum number of tasks available only limited by and depends on the configurations of hardware systems. Tasks of embedded systems typically take the form of an infinite loop.

In order to implement a specific functionality, tasks are usually not completely independent in realistic applications. They need to synchronize and communicate. μC/OS-III uses semaphores, task semaphores, event flags, messages and message queues to synchronize and communicate between tasks. Compared with μCOS-II, task semaphore is a newly introduced synchronous mechanism. It can be directly signaled by a task to another one without creation.

3.2 OS Kernel Services

The kernel is an important part of OS and its primary duty is tasks scheduling. μC/OS-III kernel is preemptive and it uses priority-based scheduling. Tasks priority is specified by users when tasks are created. Different μC/OS-III tasks may have the same priority. For this reason, round robin scheduling [15] is adopted in the kernel scheduler. Each task is assigned a duration of time (namely time quantum) to perform. The task is blocked when the time quantum runs out and the following task which is ready gets the turn to execute. A task finishes or being blocked before the quantum running out also yields the processor to other ready tasks. A list is needed for recording the ready tasks and arranges them in order of the earliest ready time. When a task runs out of quantum, it is moved to the end of the list. μC/OS-III scheduler differs from that of μC/OS-II for it utilizes round robin to priority-based scheduling to deal with tasks with the same priority. Task scheduling is triggered in the following situations: (1) a task is added or deleted, or the priority of a task is changed; (2) a task delays itself, or the delay ends; (3) the event a task requests becomes available.

4   Modeling and Verification of a μC/OS-III Multi-task Application

In this section, an abstract μC/OS-III multi-task application is given. In order to verify schedulability, the μC/OS-III kernel is formalized. Then, the TMSVL formalism of different kinds of tasks including dependent (periodic and non-periodic) tasks and tasks with synchronizations is given. Meanwhile, the property to be verified is expressed in TMSVL. Finally, The toolkit MSV is used to verify the schedulability of the tasks in the application.

4.1 A Multi-task Application

The application consists of five user tasks: $task_0$, $task_1$, $task_2$, $task_3$, and $task_4$ with the priorities being 5,6,7,7,8. Larger number represents lower priority.

Thus, $task_0$ has the highest priority, followed by $task_1$, then $task_2$ and $task_3$ which have the same priority, and finally $task_4$. The five tasks are responsible for different functionalities. The relationship of tasks is given in Fig. 4. $task_0$ and $task_2$ are synchronized through task semaphore se_0. $task_0$ sends out se_0 to activate $task_2$. If $task_2$ cannot receive se_0, it waits infinitely. Similarly, $task_1$ and $task_3$ are synchronized through se_1. But $task_3$ waits no more than to time units for se_1. $task_4$ is an independent task.

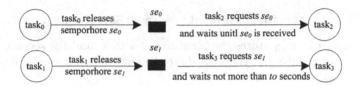

Fig. 4. The relationship between $task_0$ and $task_2$, $task_1$ and $task_3$

In Fig. 5, $task_0$ executes $\texttt{Computation}_1$ first. Then it releases the semaphore se_0 after $\texttt{Computation}_0$. Finally, $task_0$ delays for t_0 time units. The structure of $task_1$ is the same as $task_0$. $task_2$ and $task_3$ share the same priority. They also have similar structures, so we just give the pseudo-code of $task_2$. It requests se_0 first. $\texttt{pend(se}_0\texttt{, }to\texttt{)}$ means that the waiting time for se_0 is at most to time unites, specially, $to < 0$ means there is no time limit on waiting se_0. The first argument se_0 is an integer variable representing the semaphore being requested and the second argument is the time limit for waiting for the signal. For $task_2$, since $to < 0$, it executes $\texttt{Computation}_2$ only after receiving the signal se_0. When the execution of $\texttt{Computation}_2$ is finished, it goes on the requesting for se_0 for the next execution. $task_4$ performs computation and delays for t_4 time units when the computation finishes.

```
task_0()                 task_2()                 task_4()
1. { while(1)            1. { while(1)            1. { while(1)
2.  { Computation_0;     2.  { pend(se_0, to);    2.  { Computation_4;
3.    post(se_0);        3.    Computation_2;     3.    delay(t_4);
4.    delay(t_0);        4.  }                    4.  }
5.  }                    5. }                     5. }
6. }
```

Fig. 5. Tasks pseudo-code

4.2 TMSVL Model of OS Kernel

The OS kernel model consists of the variables which represent the OS objects (e.g. the ready tasks, the highest priority ready task) and the TMSVL model of the OS scheduler.

Kernel Variables. We use an array rd to represent whether each task in it is ready. The index of rd is the task number and smaller index corresponds to higher priority. For index i, if task i is ready, $rd[i] = 1$; otherwise, $rd[i] = 0$. rd is initialized to zero. The variable $runTaskID$ stores the task number of the currently running task. The float variable $Quan$ stores the time quantum for scheduling the same priority tasks in round-robin manner.

A *List* variable l is used to store the ready tasks for each priority when round robin scheduling is enabled. The definition of *List* is as follows:

```
struct{ int taskID; List *nextEL; } List l;
```

The first member in *List* stores the identifier of a task, and the second member is a *List* pointer pointing to the next *List* element. When a task is ready, it is added to the end of l.

Kernel Services. In the TMSVL model of the kernel service, we use Q and M_Robin to represent the OS scheduler and the round robin scheduling modules. Q is given in Fig. 6 and it finds the ready task with the highest priority by conjunctions of the if statements and stores the task's number in $runTaskID$. The number of if statements is the number of priorities used by tasks. For a priority which corresponds to more than one task, an if statement is enough and round robin scheduling M_Robin is invoked in that case. In Fig. 6, $task_2$ and $task_3$ have the same priority.

M_Robin is given in Fig. 7. We use several functions to express the operation on the *List* l. In Line 1, `size(1)` returns the number of elements in l.

$Q \overset{\text{def}}{=}$
```
1.  while(true)
2.  {  if(rd[0]=1) then{runTaskID=0}
3.      and
4.      if(rd[0]=0 and rd[1]=1)
5.      then{runTaskID=1}
6.      and
7.      if(rd[0]=0 and rd[1]=0 and (rd[2]=1 or rd[3]=1))
8.      then{M_Robin }
9.      and
10.     if( rd[0]=0 and rd[1]=0 and rd[2]=0 and rd[3]=0 and rd[4]=1)
11.     then{runTaskID=4 }
12.     and
13.     ...
14.     if( rd[0]=0 and rd[1]=0 and ...)
15.     then{runTaskID=IDEL }
16.     and skip
17. }
```

Fig. 6. TMSVL model of the scheduler

M_Robin $\stackrel{\text{def}}{=}$

    1. if(size(l)>0)
    2. then{ runTaskID=head(l) and
    3.   if(ac[head(l)]+Ts<C[head(l)] and (ac[head(l)]+Ts)%Quan!=0)
    4.   then{runTaskID:=head(l)} }
    5.   and
    6.   if(ac[head(l)]+Ts=C[head(l)])
    7.   then{next popHead(l) and
    8.   if(size(l)>1) then{runTaskID:=head(l)} }
    9.   and
  10.   if(ac[head(l)]+Ts<C[head(l)] and (ac[head(l)]+Ts)%Quan=0)
  11.   then{ next MoveHead2Tail(l) and
  12.   runTaskID:=head(l) }
  13. }

Fig. 7. TMSVL model of the round robin scheduling

If size(l)> 0, l is not empty, the statements in Lines 2–13 are executed. The head of l is running first (Line 2). The function head() is used to obtain the $taskID$ of the first element in l. It takes only one $List$ type argument and returns an integer representing the first element's $taskID$ of the $List$ l. Lines 3–4 show the case where neither does the first element of l run out of the quantum nor does it finish at the next state and the head element goes on running at the next state. Lines 6–8 show the second case where the task corresponding to head(l) finishes. In this case, the task is removed from l. Here we use the function popHead(l) to represent this operation. Next, we need to test whether l is empty after popHead(l) and if l is not empty, the task corresponding to the head of l gets the processor by setting $runTaskID$ to the value of head(l) at the next state. Lines 10–12 show the case where the task is not finished but runs out of the time quantum at the next state. In this case, the task is moved from the head to the tail of l and the task corresponding to the new head gets the chance to run at the next state. The function MoveHeadToTail() moves the head of l to the tail and makes the head of l change (Line 10).

4.3 TMSVL Model of a Multi-task System

The multi-task system consists of five parallel tasks. Let M_task$_i$ represent the user task$_i$ (i=0,1,2,3,4). We denote the model of the multi-task system as M. Thus $M \equiv ||_{i=0}^4 M\_task_i$.

We use float array elements $C[i]$, $ac[i]$ and $acD[i]$ to represent the required computation time, the accumulated running time and the accumulated delay time of $task_i$ in the current period, respectively. Boolean array elements $wait[i]$ and $ex[i]$ are used to indicate whether task$_i$ is at the waiting and the executing state, respectively.

Figure 8 shows the TMSVL model of task$_0$, task$_1$ and task$_4$. A new computation circle starts in Line 2. Then the task waits its turn to run (Line 3).

M_task$_i$ $\overset{\text{def}}{=}$ //i=0,1,4
1. while(true)
2. { ac[i]=0 and
3.   await(runTaskID=i);
4.   while(ac[i]<C[i])
5.   { if(runTaskID=i)
6.   then{ac[i]:=ac[i]+Ts and ex[i]=1 and wait[i]=0 and
7.   if(ac[i]+Ts=C[i] and $i! = 4$) then{se_i:=se_i+1} }
8.   else {ex[i]=0 and skip} };
9.   (T,T+dly[i])keep(next acD[i]=acD[i]+Ts and
10.   rd[i]=0 and ex[i]=0 and wait[i]=1);
11.   acD[i]=0 and rd[i]=1 and empty
12. }

Fig. 8. TMSVL model of tasks 0, 1, 4

M_task$_i$ $\overset{\text{def}}{=}$ //i=2,3
1. while(true)
2. { if($se_{i-2} \leq 0$)
3.   then{rd[i]=0 and ex[i]=0 and wait[i]=1 and
4.   {0@to}await($se_{i-2} > 0$);
5.   rd[i]=1 and wait[i]=0 and empty };
6.   ac[i]=0 and
7.   await(runTaskID=i);
8.   while(ac[i]<C[i])
9.   { if(runTaskID=i)
10.   then{ac[i]:=ac[i]+Ts and ex[i]=1 and wait[i]=0 and
11.   if(ac[i]+Ts=C[i] and $se_{i-2} > 0$)
12.   then{se_{i-2}:=se_{i-2}-1 and
13.   if($se_{i-2} - 1 > 0$)
14.   then {rd[i]:=1 } } }
15.   else {ex[i]=0 and skip} }
16. }

Fig. 9. TMSVL model of tasks signaled by other tasks

Lines 4–8 shows the task starts running in a new circle, during this period, it can be preempted by tasks with higher priorities. Lines 5–7 corresponds to the case where the task is running and Line 8 stands for the situation where the task is preempted. task$_0$ and task$_1$ signal to other tasks and delay themselves upon finishing the computations. task$_4$ just delays after finishing its computation. In Line 7, se_i is increased by 1 at the next state when task$_i$ finishes at the next state, the value of i is 0 or 1. When task$_i$ finishes a computation, namely, ac[i]=C[i], it delays for dly[i] time units. This is represented by the time constraint statement in Lines 9–10. During this period, rd[i] is 0. When the delay ends, task$_i$ becomes ready by setting rd[i] to 1.

The models for $task_2$ and $task_3$ are given in Fig. 9. Before a new computation starts, first, the task needs to test whether the requested task semaphore has been sent out (Line 2). $se_{i-2} \leq 0$ (i=2,3) means that the task semaphore has not been sent out and the task has to wait and be at the waiting state (Lines 3–4). $\{0@to\}$await$(se_{i-2} > 0)$ means the waiting on $se_{i-2} > 0$ is no more than to time units. When the semaphore is received or not received in to time units, the task stops waiting and turns to the ready state by setting $rd[i]$ to 1 and wait[i] to 0 (Line 5). Then the task waits its turn to run (Line 6–7). Lines 8–15 shows the task starts running in a new circle, during this period, it can be preempted by tasks with higher priorities. Lines 10–14 corresponds to the case where the task is running and Line 15 stands for the situation where the task is preempted. When $ac[i] = C[i]$, namely, $task_i$ finishes the computation of the current period, se_{i-2} is decreased. When the computation of the current circle completes, the program goes to Line 2 to repeat the process above.

4.4   Verification of Schedulability

In the previous section, we model the OS scheduler and different kinds of μC/OS-III tasks (independent tasks, synchronous tasks) with TMSVL. Based on the TMSVL model, the property to be verified is formalized.

Schedulability is an important property for real-time multi-task systems. It means that all the tasks scheduled can finish within the given deadline. In other words, each task can finish in a given time duration from the moment it is ready. Schedulability of N tasks is expressed in TMSVL denoted as $PSch$ below.

$$PSch \stackrel{\text{def}}{=} \wedge_{i=0}^{N}(rd[i] = 1 \wedge ac[i] = 0 \rightarrow (\{Ts, D[i]\}true; ac[i] = C[i]))^{+}$$

Here, $D[i]$ is the deadline for $task_i$. $C[i]$ and $ac[i]$ are the computation time and accumulated running time which are given in the previous section. In $PSch$, '+' is derived from the sequential operator ' ; '. Suppose p is a TMSVL statement, p^{+} means that the number of p in $p; p; \ldots ; p$ can be any positive integer.

With the TMSVL model of a μC/OS-III multi-task application and the property described in TMSVL. Whether the property is valid on the application can be automatically checked by the toolkit MSV. In this section, we verify schedulability for the multi-task application given in the previous subsection.

The deadlines for the 5 tasks are stored in the array D where $D[5] = \{0.03, 0.04, 0.13, 0.23, 0.25\}$. The computation time for each task is stored in the array C where $C[5] = \{0.03, 0.04, 0.06, 0.09, 0.12\}$. The delay time of the five tasks are stored in the array dly where $dly[5] = \{0.3, 0.2, 0, 0, 0.3\}$. The waiting time to on request for se_1 is set to 0.03. we assume the tasks are started at the same time $T = 0$.

The verification result for the application is shown in Fig. 10. There are 770 nodes and 770 arcs on the counterexample. Each node represents a program while each arc represents a state which shows the executing of the application at different time. The root node is a double circle, it represents the TMSVL model of the application. Other node represents the future part produced by

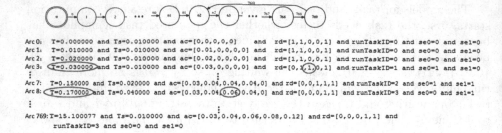

```
Arc 0:  T=0.000000 and Ts=0.010000 and ac=[0,0,0,0,0]      and  rd=[1,1,0,0,1] and runTaskID=0 and se0=0 and se1=0
Arc 1:  T=0.010000 and Ts=0.010000 and ac=[0.01,0,0,0,0] and  rd=[1,1,0,0,1] and runTaskID=0 and se0=0 and se1=0
Arc 2:  T=0.020000 and Ts=0.010000 and ac=[0.02,0,0,0,0] and  rd=[1,1,0,0,1] and runTaskID=0 and se0=0 and se1=0
Arc 3:  T=0.030000 and Ts=0.010000 and ac=[0.03,0,0,0,0] and  rd=[0,1,1,0,1] and runTaskID=1 and se0=1 and se1=0
        :
        :
Arc 7:  T=0.150000 and Ts=0.020000 and ac=[0.03,0.04,0.04,0.04,0] and rd=[0,0,1,1,1] and runTaskID=2 and se0=1 and se1=1
Arc 8:  T=0.170000 and Ts=0.040000 and ac=[0.03,0.04,0.06,0.04,0] and rd=[0,0,0,1,1] and runTaskID=3 and se0=0 and se1=1
        :
        :
Arc 769: T=15.100077 and Ts=0.010000 and ac=[0.03,0.04,0.06,0.08,0.12] and rd=[0,0,0,1,1] and
         runTaskID=3 and se0=0 and se1=0
```

Fig. 10. Verification result

executing the program that the precursor node represents, and the current part is represented by an arc. For example, arc 0 and node 1 are the executing results of node 0. The arcs are state formulas while the nodes are TMSVL programs which are required to be further executed.

In Fig. 10, we can see that arc 0 represents the state that $T = 0$, $task_0$, $task_1$ and $task_4$ are ready since the first, second and fifth elements in rd is 1, and $task_0$ starts executing since $runTaskID = 0$. After 0.03 s, $task_0$ finishes and activates $task_2$, that is, $task_2$ is ready at $T = 0.03$ for the first time. When $T = 0.17$, $task_2$ finishes, for the accumulated time $ac[2]$ is equal to $C[2]$. We can see that $task_2$ finishes after 0.14 s from the time it is activated which is greater than the give deadline. So the schedulability for $task_2$ is violated which leads to the violation of $PSch$.

Fig. 11. Verification result

The property $PSch$ is too strict for it requires all the tasks should finish in the given deadlines. We can relax the schedulability requirements by ignoring the deadline for $task_2$ and $task_3$. Thus the property can be represented as follows:

$$PSch_{0,1,4} \stackrel{\text{def}}{=} \wedge_{i=0,1,4}(rd[i] = 1 \wedge ac[i] = 0 \rightarrow (\{Ts, D[i]\}true; ac[i] = C[i]))^+$$

$PSch_{0,1,4}$ just requires that $task_0$, $task_1$ and $task_4$ always finish in the given deadline. The verification result is shown in Fig. 11, there is no counterexample, so we can conclude that $task_0$, $task_1$ and $task_4$ are always finished in their deadline. When the schedulability of a set of tasks is violated, we need to determine which tasks violated the property. In this case, verifying schedulability of a single task at one time instead of the whole is efficient.

5   Conclusion

We present a unified model checking approach to verify schedulability of multi-task application running under μC/OS-III. The OS scheduler which combines priority based scheduling and round-robin scheduling is modeled in TMSVL. Tasks synchronization with timeout and delay mechanism are also formalized in TMSVL. With the toolkit MSV, a multi-task system running under μC/OS-III is formalized and verified. The mechanism that time intervals are adjustable for modeling improves the efficiency of verification. In the near future, we will put TMSVL into practise and verify more realistic industrial applications.

References

1. Abdeddaım, Y., Asarin, E., Maler, O.: Scheduling with timed automata. Theoret. Comput. Sci. **354**(4), 272–300 (2006)
2. Mokadem, H.B., Berard, B., Gourcuff, V., De Smet, O., Roussel, J.-M.: Verification of a timed multitask system with uppaal. IEEE Trans. Autom. Sci. Eng. **7**(4), 921–932 (2010)
3. Bini, E., Buttazzo, G.C.: Schedulability analysis of periodic fixed priority systems. IEEE Trans. Comput. **53**(11), 1462–1473 (2004)
4. Bini, E., Buttazzo, G.C., Buttazzo, G.M.: Rate monotonic analysis: the hyperbolic bound. IEEE Trans. Comput. **52**(7), 933–942 (2003)
5. Bucci, G., Fedeli, A., Sassoli, L., Vicario, E.: Timed state space analysis of real-time preemptive systems. IEEE Trans. Softw. Eng. **30**(2), 97–111 (2004)
6. Duan, Z., Tian, C.: A unified model checking approach with projection temporal logic. In: Liu, S., Araki, K. (eds.) ICFEM 2008. LNCS, vol. 5256, pp. 167–186. Springer, Heidelberg (2008)
7. Duan, Z., Yang, X., Koutny, M.: Framed temporal logic programming. Sci. Comput. Program. **70**(1), 31–61 (2008)
8. Han, M., Duan, Z., Wang, X.: Time constraints with temporal logic programming. In: Aoki, T., Taguchi, K. (eds.) ICFEM 2012. LNCS, vol. 7635, pp. 266–282. Springer, Heidelberg (2012)
9. Huang, Y., Ferreira, J.F., He, G., Qin, S., He, J.: Deadline analysis of AUTOSAR OS periodic tasks in the presence of interrupts. In: Groves, L., Sun, J. (eds.) ICFEM 2013. LNCS, vol. 8144, pp. 165–181. Springer, Heidelberg (2013)
10. Labrosse, J.J.: uC/OS-III: The Real-Time Kernel. Micrium Press, Weston (2009)
11. Liu, C.L., Layland, J.W.: Scheduling algorithms for multiprogramming in a hard-real-time environment. J. ACM (JACM) **20**(1), 46–61 (1973)
12. Madl, G., Dutt, N., Abdelwahed, S.: A conservative approximation method for the verification of preemptive scheduling using timed automata. In: 2009 15th IEEE Real-Time and Embedded Technology and Applications Symposium, RTAS 2009, pp. 255–264 (2009)
13. Miku00ionis, M., Larsen, K.G., Rasmussen, J.I., Nielsen, B., Skou, A., Palm, S.U., Pedersen, J.S., Hougaard, P.: Schedulability analysis using uppaal: Herschel-planck case study. In: Proceedings of the 4th International Conference on Leveraging Applications of Formal Methods, Verification, and Validation - Volume Part II (2010)

14. Pang, T., Duan, Z., Tian, C.: Symbolic model checking for propositional projection temporal logic. In: 2012 Sixth International Symposium on Theoretical Aspects of Software Engineering (TASE), pp. 9–16. IEEE (2012)
15. Rasmus, R.V., Trick, M.A.: Round robin scheduling-a survey. Eur. J. Oper. Res. **188**(3), 617–636 (2008)
16. Tian, C., Duan, Z.: Propositional Projection Temporal Logic, Büchi Automata and ω-Regular Expressions. In: Agrawal, M., Du, D.-Z., Duan, Z., Li, A. (eds.) TAMC 2008. LNCS, vol. 4978, pp. 47–58. Springer, Heidelberg (2008)
17. Wasziwoski, L., Hanzalek, Z.: Model checking of multitasking real-time applications based on the timed automata model using one clock. Behavioral Modeling for Embedded Systems and Technologies: Applications for Design and Implementation: Applications for Design and Implementation, p. 194 (2009)
18. Waszniowski, L., Krákora, J., Hanzálek, Z.: Case study on distributed and fault tolerant system modeling based on timed automata. J. Syst. Softw. **82**(10), 1678–1694 (2009)

A Predictability Algorithm for Distributed Discrete Event Systems

Lina Ye[1,2(✉)], Philippe Dague[1], and Farid Nouioua[3]

[1] LRI, Université Paris-Sud, 91405 Orsay, France
{lina.ye,philippe.dague}@lri.fr
[2] CentraleSupélec, 91192 Gif-sur-Yvette, France
[3] LSIS, Université Aix-Marseille, Marseille, France
farid.nouioua@lsis.org

Abstract. Predictability is considered as a crucial system property that determines with certainty the future occurrence of a fault based on a sequence of observations on system model. There are very few works done on the predictability problem for discrete event systems, which is however extremely important for developing critical complex systems. In this paper, we propose a formal sufficient and necessary condition for this property before presenting a new algorithm based on it, which is extendible from a centralized framework to a distributed one. Both are formally presented, as well as experimental results that show the efficiency of our approach.

1 Introduction

Fault diagnosis is a crucial and challenging task in the automatic control of complex systems [1,4,5,8,9,14,15,19], whose very possibility depends on a system property called diagnosability. The diagnosability problem has received considerable attention in the literature. Diagnosability describes the system ability to determine whether a fault has effectively occurred based on the observations. In a given system, the existence of two infinite behaviors, with the same observations but exactly one containing the considered fault, violates diagnosability. The existing works search for such ambiguous behaviors both in centralized [3,7,12,16,17] and distributed [13,18,20] ways. The most classical method is to construct a structure called twin plant that captures all pairs of observationally equivalent behaviors to directly check the existence of such ambiguous pairs. However, sometimes it is very expensive to recover the system after fault, which motivates the work on predictability problem, i.e., the system ability to predict with certainty future faults when this system is still in a normal state.

Predictability is an important system property that determines at design stage whether the considered fault can be correctly predicted before its occurrence based on available observations. If a fault is predicted, the system operator can be warned and may decide to halt the system or otherwise take preventive measures. However, up to now, very few works have been done on this subject for discrete event systems (DESs). The authors of [6] proposed a deterministic

© Springer International Publishing Switzerland 2015
M. Butler et al. (Eds.): ICFEM 2015, LNCS 9407, pp. 201–216, 2015.
DOI: 10.1007/978-3-319-25423-4_13

diagnoser approach with exponential complexity as well as a polynomial method that checks predictability directly on a twin plant. Both of them were established in a centralized way and are difficult to be extended for distributed systems due to combinatorial explosion. The first distributed method handling this problem was proposed in [21], which however has the same search space as the centralized one in the worst case.

In this paper, we propose a new efficient algorithm of predictability for DESs. First, we propose and then prove a sufficient and necessary condition for predictability, i.e., characterizing pairs of behaviors violating predictability as two trajectories, exactly one containing the fault, with the same observations before the fault and the normal one being infinite. Totally different from the polynomial method proposed in [6] that reused twin plant, we construct another structure that captures all pairs of trajectories with the same observations only before the fault while preserving the normal trajectories, where the existence of violating pairs can be directly checked. More importantly, we show how to extend this method in a distributed framework with smaller state space even in the worst case. Our distributed algorithm is different from that proposed for checking diagnosability described in [13]. For diagnosability, it suffices to synchronize local twin plants based on communication events in a unique way since the same observations are imposed both before and after the fault. While for predictability, we have to check the same observations only before the fault as well as the infinity of the corresponding normal trajectory, both in an incremental way.

The organization of the rest of the paper is as follows. The next section recalls the definitions and gives a sufficient and necessary condition for predictability. Section 3 proposes a new predictability algorithm before extending it to a distributed framework in Sect. 4. Section 5 gives some experimental results. Then we conclude in Sect. 7 after a discussion in Sect. 6.

2   Preliminaries

In this section, we show how to model a DES, recall the definition of its predictability, and propose a sufficient and necessary condition with a formal proof.

2.1   Models of DESs

We model a DES as a Finite State Machine (FSM), denoted by $G = (Q, \Sigma, \delta, q^0)$, where Q is the finite set of states, Σ is the finite set of events, $\delta \subseteq Q \times \Sigma \times Q$ is the set of transitions (the same notation will be kept for its natural extension to words of Σ^*), and q^0 is the initial state. The set of events Σ is divided into three disjoint parts: $\Sigma = \Sigma_o \uplus \Sigma_u \uplus \Sigma_f$, where Σ_o is the set of observable events, Σ_u the set of unobservable normal events and Σ_f the set of unobservable fault events.

Example 1. The left part of Fig. 1 shows an example of a system model G, where $\Sigma_o = \{O1, O2, O3\}$, $\Sigma_u = \{U1, C1, C2\}$, and $\Sigma_f = \{F\}$.

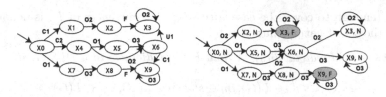

Fig. 1. A system example (left) and its diagnoser (right).

Given a system model G, its prefix-closed language $L(G)$, which describes both normal and faulty behaviors of the system, is the set of words produced by G, $L(G) = \{s \in \Sigma^* | \exists q \in Q, (q^0, s, q) \in \delta\}$. In the following, we call a word from $L(G)$ a trajectory in the system G and a sequence $q_0\sigma_0q_1\sigma_1...$ a path in G, where $\sigma_0\sigma_1...$ is a trajectory in G and we have $\forall i, (q_i, \sigma_i, q_{i+1}) \in \delta$. Given $s \in L(G)$, we denote its set of strict prefixes as $\overline{s}$, i.e., $s \notin \overline{s}$, and the post-language of $L(G)$ after s by $L(G)/s$, formally defined as: $L(G)/s = \{t \in \Sigma^* | s.t \in L(G)\}$. The projection of the trajectory s to observable events of G (resp. G_i in distributed system) is denoted by $P(s)$ (resp. $P_i(s)$). Traditionally, we assume that the system language is always live (any trajectory has a continuation, i.e. is a strict prefix of another trajectory) without unobservable cycle. Precisely, we have at least one transition from any state and every cycle in the system contains at least one observable event. This makes it feasible to check the infiniteness of a trajectory. Given two FSMs G_1 and G_2, their synchronization with respect to the set of synchronized events $\Sigma_s \subseteq \Sigma_1 \cap \Sigma_2$[1] consists in synchronizing only the events in Σ_s, denoted by $G_1 \|_{\Sigma_s} G_2$. All events not in Σ_s can occur independently whenever possible. It is easy to generalize the synchronization for a set of FSMs using its associativity properties [2]. We will need also some infinite objects. So, we denote by Σ^ω the set of infinite words on Σ and by $\Sigma^\infty = \Sigma^* \cup \Sigma^\omega$ the set of words on Σ, finite or infinite. We define in an obvious way $L^\omega(G)$ and $L^\infty(G)$ and thus infinite trajectories and infinite paths.

2.2   Predictability of DESs

Predictability is considered as a crucial property of a DES in the sense that a predictable fault can possibly be avoided. Similar to diagnosability, the predictability algorithm that we will propose has exponential complexity with the number of fault types. For the sake of reducing complexity and simplicity, only one fault type at a time is considered but multiple occurrences of faults are allowed, and the other types of faults are processed as unobservable normal events. However, this framework can be extended in a straightforward way such that a number of different faults can be considered simultaneously. Now we rephrase the predictability definition [6], where a trajectory ending with a first occurrence of the

---

[1] To avoid heavy notations, we will use sometimes $\Sigma_s \nsubseteq \Sigma_1 \cap \Sigma_2$. Synchronization set has then to be understood as $\Sigma_s \cap \Sigma_1 \cap \Sigma_2$.

fault F (enough to cover the case with several occurrences of F) is denoted by s^F and the set of natural numbers by $\mathbb{N}$.

Definition 1 *(Predictability). A fault F is predictable in a DES G, iff*

$$\exists k \in \mathbb{N}, \forall s^F \in L(G), \exists \eta \in \overline{s^F}, \forall p \in L(G), \forall p' \in L(G)/p,$$
$$[(P(p) = P(\eta)) \wedge (F \notin p) \wedge (|p'| \geq k) \Rightarrow (F \in p')].$$

A fault F is predictable iff for any trajectory s^F ending with a first occurrence of F, there exists at least one strict prefix of s^F, denoted by η (thus η does not contain F) such that for each normal trajectory p with the same observations as η, all the long enough (depending only on F) continuations of p should contain F. Only in this way, F can be certainly predicted before its occurrence.

2.3   Sufficient and Necessary Condition

Suppose now that we have two trajectories in a given system such that exactly one, denoted by s^F, ends with the fault F, the other without F has at least one prefix with the same observations as the maximum strict prefix of s^F and is infinite. With such two trajectories, whatever we observe before the occurrence of F, we cannot tell whether F will occur or not since both are possible while only one will contain F in the future. Now we formally define such a pair of trajectories.

Definition 2 *(Pre-Violating Pair (PVP)). Given a system G and a fault F to be predicted, a pair of trajectories $s^F, p.p' \in L^\infty(G)$ is called a Pre-Violating Pair (PVP) with respect to F if the three conditions are satisfied: (1) $P(s^F) = P(p)$; (2) $F \notin p.p'$; (3) p' is infinite.*

Here is the sufficient and necessary condition of predictability.

Theorem 1. *A fault F is predictable in a system G iff there is no PVP in G with respect to F.*

Proof. $\Rightarrow$ Suppose that we have a PVP in G, i.e., s^F and $p.p'$ as in Definition 2. Hence, we have $P(s^F) = P(p)$, i.e., the maximum normal prefix of s^F has the same observations as p since F is not observable. It follows that $\forall \eta \in \overline{s^F}, \exists \eta' \in \overline{p} \cup \{p\}$ such that $P(\eta) = P(\eta')$. Furthermore, η' has at least one normal infinite continuation since $F \notin p.p'$ and p' is infinite. This violates Definition 1, i.e., F is not predictable.

$\Leftarrow$ Now suppose that F is not predictable. It follows that Definition 1 is violated, which can be expressed by the following: $\forall k \in \mathbb{N}, \exists s^F \in L(G), \forall \eta \in \overline{s^F}, \exists p \in L(G), F \notin p, P(p) = P(\eta), \exists p' \in L(G)/p, |p'| \geq k, F \notin p'$. Let η as the maximum normal prefix of s^F. The above formula implies (by taking k greater than $|Q|$) that there must exist a normal infinite trajectory $p.p'$, i.e., $F \notin p.p'$, such that $P(p) = P(\eta)$. This means $P(p) = P(s^F)$ since η is the maximum normal prefix of s^F. Hence, $p.p'$ and s^F constitute exactly a PVP. $\blacksquare$

3   Centralized Framework

Since the predictability verification of a given fault F is to check the existence of PVP, from Definition 2, we take three steps: (1) obtain the set of maximum strict prefixes for all s^F, and actually we can restrict to those s^F which are minimal for the order induced by the prefix relation (with F excluded), which is enough from Theorem 1 as a PVP for $w.w'.F$ is a PVP for w.F; (2) obtain the set of infinite normal trajectories; (3) compare the above two sets in terms of observations to check the existence of PVP. We will construct one FSM for each step. Before this, given a system model, we first construct its non-deterministic diagnoser to explicitly show fault information, which is different from the deterministic diagnoser proposed in [17].

Definition 3 *(Diagnoser). Given a system G, its diagnoser with respect to a considered fault F is a nondeterministic FSM $D = (Q_D, \Sigma_D, \delta_D, q_D^0)$, where (1) $Q_D \subseteq Q \times \{N, F\}$ is the set of states; (2) $\Sigma_D = \Sigma_o$ is the set of events; (3) $\delta_D \subseteq Q_D \times \Sigma_D \times Q_D$ is the set of transitions; (4) $q_D^0 = (q^0, N)$ is the initial state. The transitions of δ_D are those $((q, \ell), e, (q', \ell'))$, with (q, ℓ) reachable from the initial state q_D^0, such that there is a transition path $p = (q \xrightarrow{u_1} q_1 ... \xrightarrow{u_m} q_m \xrightarrow{e} q')$ in G, with $u_k \notin \Sigma_o, \forall k \in \{1, ..., m\}$, $e \in \Sigma_o$ and $\ell' = F$, if $\ell = F \vee F \in \{u_1, ..., u_k\}$, and otherwise, $\ell' = N$.*

The diagnoser preserves all observable information. Then we append the fault label F to those states, up to which the fault has already occurred, and normal label N to those without the fault occurrence. The right part of Fig. 1 depicts the diagnoser of the system in Example 1, where gray nodes represent the states where F has effectively occurred. Based on such a diagnoser, we then construct two different FSMs to capture the set of maximum normal prefixes of all minimal faulty trajectories and the set of normal ones, respectively.

Definition 4 *(Fault-Prefix Diagnoser). Given a diagnoser D, the fault-prefix diagnoser D_{FP} is constructed as follows:*

- *Keep only the minimal paths containing the fault label;*
- *$\forall((q, l), e, (q', l')) \in \delta_D, l = N, l' = F$, it is transformed into $((q, l), \Sigma_o, (q, l)) \in \delta_D$, i.e., (q, l) goes back to itself with any observable event. Such a state (q, l) is called an absorbing state in the following.*

Recall that predictability analysis consists in first checking whether the maximum normal prefix of a faulty trajectory has the same observations with a normal one, and then examining whether the normal one is infinite, which is represented by a cycle in a FSM. This is why in a fault-prefix diagnoser, we keep the exact observable events before the fault and then add to an absorbing state a self-cycle with all observable events. The idea is to make it able to synchronize with a normal trajectory to check whether the latter has a cycle in the future.

Definition 5 *(Normal Diagnoser). Given a diagnoser D, the normal diagnoser D_N is obtained by retaining only normal states with their associated transitions.*

To check the existence of PVP, we synchronize the fault-prefix diagnoser and the normal diagnoser based on the set of observable events. This synchronization is actually the intersection of the maximum normal prefixes of minimal faulty trajectories and the normal trajectories in terms of observations.

Definition 6 *(Pre-Verifier). Given a system, its pre-verifier PV is constructed by synchronizing its fault-prefix diagnoser D_{FP} and its normal diagnoser D_N based on observable events, i.e., $PV = D_{FP} \|_{\Sigma_o} D_N$.*

A state of a pre-verifier s^v is composed of a state of the fault-prefix diagnoser and a state of the normal diagnoser, denoted by $s^v = (q^f, q^n)$. All states in D_{FP}, D_N and thus PV having by construction a normal label N, it will be skipped in the following. If q^f is an absorbing state, then s^v is also called an absorbing state. In a pre-verifier, a path containing a cycle made up of absorbing states is called a violating path. Note that pre-verifier proposed here greatly reduces the state space compared to twin plant used both in [6,13]. The latter is constructed directly by synchronizing the whole diagnoser defined in Definition 3 with itself. Clearly, both fault-prefix diagnoser D_{FP} and normal one D_N are smaller than the diagnoser D. Thus, the pre-verifier $D_{FP} \|_{\Sigma_o} D_N$ is much smaller than $D \|_{\Sigma_o} D$, even in the worst case.

Lemma 1. *A path in PV is a violating one iff it corresponds to a PVP with minimal s^F in the corresponding system.*

Proof. $\Rightarrow$ Let ρ a violating path in PV. Thus $\rho = s_0^v \sigma_0 \ldots s_i^v \sigma_i \ldots s_j^v \sigma_j \ldots s_k^v \sigma_k \ldots$ where $0 \leq i \leq j$, $j < k$, $s_j^v = s_k^v$ and $\forall l < i$ s_l^v is not an absorbing state, $\forall l \geq i$ s_l^v is an absorbing state. By construction of D_{FP}, $\sigma_0 \ldots \sigma_{i-1}$ comes from minimal s^F where $P(s^F) = \sigma_0 \ldots \sigma_{i-1}$. By construction of D_N, $\sigma_0 \ldots \sigma_k$ comes from $p.p' \in L^\omega(G)$ where $P(p) = \sigma_0 \ldots \sigma_{i-1}$, $F \notin p.p'$ and p' is infinite (with $P(p') = \sigma_i \ldots (\sigma_j \ldots \sigma_{k-1})^\omega)$. Thus $s^F, p.p'$ is a PVP in G.
$\Leftarrow$ Let $s^F, p.p'$ a PVP in G with s^F minimal. s^F gives birth in D_{FP} to $q_0^f \sigma_0 \ldots \sigma_{i-1} q_i^f$, $0 \leq i$, where q_i^f is an absorbing state. $p.p'$ gives birth in D_N to $q_0^n \sigma_0 \ldots \sigma_{i-1} q_i^n \ldots q_k^n \sigma_k \ldots$ where $i < k$ and $\exists j, j < k, q_j^n = q_k^n$. Then $\rho = (q_0^f, q_0^n) \sigma_0 \ldots \sigma_{i-1} (q_i^f, q_i^n) \ldots (q_i^f, q_k^n) \sigma_k \ldots$ is a violating path in PV. ∎

Figure 2 shows the two diagnosers and a part of PV for G in Example 1. In PV, a state is composed of a fault-prefix diagnoser state (top) and a normal diagnoser state (bottom). The absorbing states in the fault-prefix diagnoser (X2 and X8) and in PV (all states whose top part is X2 or X8) are bold circles. A violating path in PV, i.e., with an absorbing state cycle, corresponds to a PVP. For example, the path whose trajectory is $O2.O2.O2^\omega$ is a violating path. Its corresponding trajectories in G are $C1.O2.F$ and $C2.O2.U1.O2^\omega$, which are exactly a PVP with $s^F = C1.O2.F$, $p = C2.O2$ and $p' = U1.O2^\omega$. So F is not predictable in G.

The following theorem is from Theorem 1 and Lemma 1.

Theorem 2. *A fault F is predictable in a system G iff there is no violating path in the corresponding PV.*

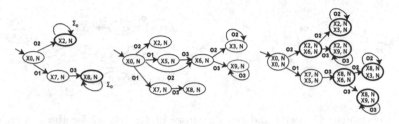

Fig. 2. Fault-prefix diagnoser (left), normal diagnoser (middle) and part of PV (right) of G in Example 1.

4   Distributed Framework

In the previous section, we have presented a centralized approach of predictability analysis. However, it is not realistic to construct a global model for a complex system due to combinatorial explosion. In this section, we will show how to extend our centralized method to a distributed framework.

4.1   Distributed Model

We consider a distributed DES G composed of a set of components $G_1, ..., G_n$ that communicate with each other by communication events. Similar to the system model in the centralized approach, each component is modeled by a FSM, denoted by $G_i = (Q_i, \Sigma_i, \delta_i, q_i^0)$. Differently, the set of events Σ_i is divided into four disjoint parts instead of three: $\Sigma_i = \Sigma_{i_o} \uplus \Sigma_{i_u} \uplus \Sigma_{i_f} \uplus \Sigma_{i_c}$, where Σ_{i_c} is the set of unobservable correct communication events. For any pair of distinct local components G_i and G_j, we have $\Sigma_{i_o} \cap \Sigma_{j_o} = \emptyset, \Sigma_{i_u} \cap \Sigma_{j_u} = \emptyset$, and $\Sigma_{i_f} \cap \Sigma_{j_f} = \emptyset$. In other words, the only shared events between different components are communication ones. Thus, given a considered fault F, it can only occur in one component, denoted by G_F (called the faulty component, the others being the normal ones). Similarly, we assume that the language for each component is always live without unobservable cycle.

Example 2. A distributed system G' is composed of two components G_1 and G_2, where the system in Example 1 is now considered as G_1 with the difference $\Sigma_{1_u} = \{U1\}$ and $\Sigma_{1_c} = \{C1, C2\}$, and G_2 is shown in the left part of Fig. 3 with $\Sigma_{2_o} = \{O4, O5, O6\}$ and $\Sigma_{2_c} = \{C1, C2\}$.

Given a distributed DES, to apply the centralized predictability algorithm, we have first to synchronize all components based on communication events to obtain the global model. The global pre-verifier is calculated by synchronizing the fault-prefix diagnoser with the normal diagnoser, both built from the global model, based on observable events before the fault. The PVP is then checked directly on this global pre-verifier. To save search space but with the same result, the idea of our distributed algorithm is to first construct local structures (e.g., local pre-verifier) by synchronization on local observable events before the fault

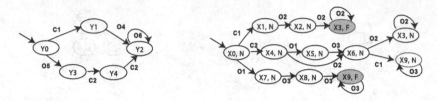

Fig. 3. Component G_2 (left) and the diagnoser of G_1 (right) for the system G' in Example 2.

to search for local version of PVP. The correspondence between this local version and global PVP is then checked by the synchronization based on communication events, which is done partially and incrementally. We will provide a formal proof for the equivalence between centralized and distributed approach.

4.2   Local Analysis

In a distributed DES, since the fault to be predicted can only occur in G_F, we should obtain the original local predictability information from G_F before determining the global decision. For this, we first define the local version of PVP, the projection of s on the local observations in G_F denoted by $P_F(s)$. Different from PVP, local PVP does not require an infinite trajectory, which will be checked from global point of view.

Definition 7 *(Local PVP). In the component G_F, a pair of local trajectories $s^F, p.p' \in L^\infty(G_F)$ is called a local PVP if $F \notin p.p'$ and $P_F(s^F) = P_F(p)$.*

Lemma 2. *Given a distributed DES G, the projection of a PVP on G_F is a local PVP. But conversely, it is not true that all local PVPs can be extended into (global) PVPs.*

Proof. ⇒ Suppose that two global trajectories, denoted by s^F and $p.p'$ are a PVP. We show that the projections of s^F and $p.p'$ on G_F, denoted by $\mathbb{P}_F(s^F)$ and $\mathbb{P}_F(p.p')$, are a local PVP. Since F can only occur in G_F, We must have $\mathbb{P}_F(s^F) = s'^F$, i.e., the projection of s^F on G_F should also be a local trajectory ending with F. From $F \notin p.p'$, we have $F \notin \mathbb{P}_F(p.p')$. Furthermore, $\Sigma_{i_o} \cap \Sigma_{j_o} = \emptyset$ for $i \neq j$ implies that $P(s^F) = P(p) \Rightarrow P_F(\mathbb{P}_F(s^F)) = P_F(\mathbb{P}_F(p))$. From Definition 7, $\mathbb{P}_F(s^F)$ and $\mathbb{P}_F(p.p')$ constitute a local PVP.
⇍ Now consider the two local trajectories $p1 = C1.O2.F$ and $p2 = C2.O2.U1$ in G_1 that constitute a local PVP and show that they are not extendible into a PVP. The reason is that when synchronizing G_1 and G_2, for $p2$, $O5$ occurs necessarily before $O2$ to synchronize on $C2$ while, for $p1$, we have $O2$ without $O5$ before F. Thus, $O5$ distinguishes the normal trajectory from its corresponding faulty one before F. Hence, $p1$ and $p2$ cannot be extended into a global PVP. ∎

From Lemma 2, we know that a local PVP may or may not correspond to a PVP. To verify predictability, it is necessary to check whether a local PVP can be effectively extended into a global PVP. To obtain the set of local PVPs, we construct the local diagnoser exactly as in Definition 3 except that here the set of events retained are not only observable events but also communication events, the latter used to check the extendibility of a local PVP into a PVP in the following step. The right part of Fig. 3 shows the diagnoser of G_1 in Example 2. Then the local fault-prefix diagnoser D_{FP_F} and local normal diagnoser D_{N_F} are constructed in the same way as Definition 4 and Definition 5 with the only difference that their construction is based on the local diagnoser. To obtain the local pre-verifier for G_F, denoted by PV_F, we distinguish the unobservable communication events in D_{FP_F}, prefixed by F, and those in D_{N_F}, prefixed by N, such that PV_F is built by synchronizing D_{FP_F} and D_{N_F} based on the set of observable events. From now on, we call a path of a local PV containing at least one absorbing state a local violating path. The left part of Fig. 4 depicts a part of the local PV for G_1, where absorbing states are represented by bold circles. All paths of length at least 3 shown here are local violating paths.

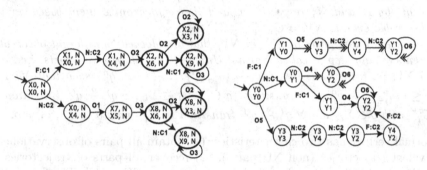

Fig. 4. Part of local PV of G_1 (left) and part of normal verifier of G_2 (right) for the system G' in Example 2.

The proof of Lemma 3 is similar to that of Lemma 1.

Lemma 3. *A path in PV_F is a local violating one iff it corresponds to a local PVP with minimal s^F in G_F.*

4.3   Global Checking

Since a local violating path corresponds to a local PVP, the predictability checking for a distributed system is to check whether a local violating path in PV_F corresponds to a PVP.

Definition 8 *(Global Extendibility of Local Violating Paths). Given a system G, let p_1 and p_2 be the corresponding local trajectories in G_F for a local violating path ρ in the PV_F. ρ is globally extendible if the following two conditions are satisfied: (1) $\exists p_1', p_2' \in L^\infty(G)$, such that $\mathbb{P}_F(p_1') = p_1$ and $\mathbb{P}_F(p_2') = p_2$; (2) p_1' and p_2' constitute a PVP.*

Now the following theorem can be proved from Theorem 1, Lemmas 2, 3 and Definition 8.

Theorem 3. *A fault F is predictable in a system G iff there is no local violating path in PV_F that is globally extendible.*

Checking the extendibility of a local violating path means to check firstly whether the observations in other components can distinguish the corresponding two trajectories before fault occurrence and secondly whether the normal trajectory can be extended into an infinite one. For this, given a normal component, we construct the following structure.

Definition 9 *(Normal Verifier). Given a normal component G_i, its normal verifier NV_i is constructed as follows:*

1. *Construct a coarser model G'_i based on G_i by keeping only the set of communication and observable events;*
2. *Construct two instances G'^F_i and G'^N_i of G'_i by prefixing the communication events by F and N, respectively, and then synchronize them based on the observable events: $NV_i = G'^F_i \parallel_{\Sigma_{i_o}} G'^N_i$;*
3. *Retrieve the lost parts of G'^N_i in NV_i that are blocked by different observable events during step 3, called Normal Unique parts, shortly NU parts. i.e., add to NV_i all transitions $(q^f, q^n_0) \xrightarrow{e_1} (q^f, q^n_1) \ldots \xrightarrow{e_k} (q^f, q^n_k)$ such that: $\forall j, 1 \leq j \leq k, q^n_{j-1} \xrightarrow{e_j} q^n_j$ is a transition in G'^N_i, $e_1 \in \Sigma_{i_o}$, $\exists q^f \xrightarrow{o} q'^f$ transition in G'^F_i with $o \in \Sigma_{i_o}$ and $\forall q^f \xrightarrow{o} q'^f$ transition in G'^F_i with $o \in \Sigma_{i_o}$, $e_1 \neq o$.*

A normal verifier has two characteristics: (1) obtain all pairs of observationally equivalent trajectories (non NU parts); (2) recover all parts of trajectories in G'^N_i that are blocked by different observable events (NU parts). The first one is to check the same observations before the fault while the second is to examine whether the normal trajectory is infinite. The right part of Fig. 4 shows a part of the normal verifier for G_2, where the transitions with double arrows are the NU parts.

Given the local pre-verifier PV_F and a normal verifier NV_i, to check the extendibility of local violating paths in the subsystem composed of G_F and G_i, we take two steps: (1) synchronizing PV_F and the non NU parts of NV_i based on communication events (with the same prefix F or N) until arriving in an absorbing state; (2) from an absorbing state, synchronizing based on communication events only with the prefix N. Intuitively, the first step checks whether the corresponding two trajectories in this subsystem have the same observations before the fault. In NV_i, only the non NU parts have the same observations for both trajectories. Hence, before achieving absorbing states, only the non NU parts should synchronize with PV_F to guarantee the same observations before the fault. The second step extends only the normal trajectory to check its infinity since synchronized events now become the common communication events with the prefix N. If we synchronize PV_F with all NV_i with the two steps without any reduction, then what we get is isomorphic (same set of paths from origin, and thus same language) to the global pre-verifier obtained by the centralized approach.

Theorem 4. *Given a distributed system $G = (G_1, ..., G_n)$, the final synchronized product of PV_F with NV_i for all normal components is isomorphic to the global pre-verifier.*

Proof. (sketch) *Base Case:* We first show this equivalence for n=2, i.e., two components with $G_F = G_1$. Given $G = (G_1, G_2)$, the global pre-verifier is obtained by $PV_2^c = [G_1 \parallel_{\Sigma_c} G_2]^{FP+P_F} \parallel_{\Sigma_o} [G_1 \parallel_{\Sigma_c} G_2]^{N+P_N}$, where $FP + P_F$ (resp. $N + P_N$) means constructing fault-prefix diagnoser (resp. normal diagnoser) and adding prefix of F (resp. N) for communication events. This can be transformed into $PV_2^c = [D_{1_{FP}}^F \parallel_{\Sigma_{F:c}} G_2'^F]^\star \parallel_{\Sigma_o} [D_{1_N}^N \parallel_{\Sigma_{N:c}} G_2'^N]$, where $\star$ represents absorbing state calculation. With our distributed algorithm, the final FSM obtained is $PV_2^d = [D_{1_{FP}}^F \parallel_{\Sigma_{1_o}} D_{1_N}^N] \parallel_{\Sigma_{F:c^\star,N:c}} [G_2'^F \parallel_{\Sigma_{2_o}} G_2'^N]^{\star\star}$, where $\Sigma_{F:c^\star,N:c}$ signifies the synchronized events are F communications events before absorbing states and all N communication events (in particular those in NU parts after absorbing states) and $\star\star$ means the recuperation of NU parts, i.e., 3rd step in Definition 9. From $[D_{1_{FP}}^F \parallel_{\Sigma_{F:c}} G_2'^F]^\star$, in PV_2^c, we only keep F communication events before absorbing states while retaining the rest of normal trajectory. This is transformed in PV_2^d through the set of synchronized events $\Sigma_{F:c^\star,N:c}$ with $\star\star$ operation. Hence, we have $PV_2^c \simeq PV_2^d$.

Inductive Case: Suppose $PV_m^c \simeq PV_m^d$, we now show $PV_{m+1}^c \simeq PV_{m+1}^d$. From above, we have the following demonstration, where the synchronized events are omitted that are similar to the base case: $PV_{m+1}^c = [D_{1_{FP}}^F \parallel \cdots \parallel G_{m+1}'^F]^\star \parallel [D_{1_N}^N \parallel \cdots \parallel G_{m+1}'^N] = [[D_{1_{FP}}^F \parallel \cdots \parallel G_m'^F]^\star \parallel G_{m+1}'^F]^\star \parallel [[D_{1_N}^N \parallel \cdots \parallel G_m'^N] \parallel G_{m+1}'^N] \simeq PV_m^c \parallel [G_{m+1}'^F \parallel G_{m+1}'^N]^{\star\star} \simeq PV_m^d \parallel [G_{m+1}'^F \parallel G_{m+1}'^N]^{\star\star} = PV_{m+1}^d$. ∎

We have proved the equivalence between the centralized result and the distributed one. However, to save search space, in distributed framework, we can partially and incrementally synchronize all local violating paths in PV_F with NV_i for connected components and we have the following theorem.

Theorem 5. *Given a system G, let Θ be the set of connected components containing G_F. After incrementally checking the extendibility of local violating paths in PV_F with NV_i of all normal components in Θ, a local violating path is globally extendible iff there exists a path p in the final FSM satisfying one of the following conditions: (1) p has an absorbing state cycle; (2) p has an absorbing state and $\Theta \neq G$.*

The global checking of predictability is much more complex than that of diagnosability [13]. For the latter, it is enough to construct local twin plants for all components before synchronizing them in a unique way since the violating pair has the same observations in the whole way. While for the former, as shown in this paper, we have to construct different structures for normal and faulty components with different ways of synchronization before and after fault.

Consider the part of PV_F and of NV_2 shown in Fig. 4. The local violating paths whose trajectories are $t1 = F{:}C1.N{:}C2.O2.O2.O2^*$ (resp. $t2 = $

$F{:}C1.N{:}C2.O2.N{:}C1.O3^*$) are not globally extendible because $N{:}C2$ is blocked during extendibility checking with NV_2. The reason is explained in the proof of Lemma 2: observations before F are not the same after synchronization. For the local violating path whose trajectory is $t3 = N{:}C2.O1.O3.N{:}C1.O3^*$, after checking $t3$ with NV_2, the normal trajectory is blocked by $N{:}C1$ after arriving in absorbing states. This means that the trajectories of the corresponding pair have the same observations before F but the normal one cannot be infinite. Thus, $t3$ is not globally extendible. Consider finally the trajectory $t4 = N{:}C2.O1.O3.O2.O2^*$. Its extendibility checking with NV_2 achieves absorbing states and makes the normal trajectory infinite with a cycle, i.e., an absorbing state cycle. Precisely, $O5.C2.O1.O3.U1.O2^\omega$ is an infinite normal trajectory in G' of Example 2, which has the same observable prefix $O5.O1.O3$ with the faulty trajectory $O5.O1.O3.F$. It follows that $t4$ is globally extendible, i.e., F is not predictable in G'.

4.4   Algorithm

Now we formally describe our distributed predictability algorithm based on Theorem 5, which is shown by Algorithm 1. Given the input (line 1) as the set of component models and the fault F in G_F, which is used as initialization of the current subsystem G_S (line 2), we first construct PV_F (see Sect. 4.2 for more details) and reduce it to only retain local violating paths, i.e., with at least one absorbing state (lines 3–4). If the reduced PV_F is not empty and there exists at least one connected component to G_S, i.e., with at least one common communication event (line 5), meaning that the retained PV_F should be further checked in an extended subsystem, then we repeatedly perform the following steps: (1) Select one component G_i not in G_S but connected to it before constructing its normal verifier NV_i as described in Definition 9 (lines 6–7); (2) Check the extendibility of PV_F with NV_i as described in the previous section (line 8); (3) Reduce the newly obtained PV_F to keep only paths containing at least one absorbing state before updating the subsystem G_S by adding G_i (lines 9–10). In the final resulting FSM, if there exists at least one globally extendible violating path (line 11), F is not predictable and PV_F is provided (line 12). Otherwise, F is predictable and predictable information is returned (lines 13–14).

5   Experimental Results

We have proved the correctness of our algorithms from theoretical point of view. To show their efficiency from practical point of view, we have implemented and compared our centralized algorithm with twin plant method in [6] as well as our distributed one with that described in [21] (for this comparison we also implemented algorithms described in [6,21] as codes were not available from the authors). All our experimental results are obtained by running our java program on a Mac OS laptop running on a 1.7 GHz Intel Core i7 processor with 8 Go 1600 MHz DDR3 of memory.

Algorithm 1. Predictability Algorithm for Distributed DES

1: INPUT: component models $G_1, ..., G_n$ in G; F in G_F
2: Initializations: $G_S \leftarrow G_F$(current subsystem)
3: $PV_F \leftarrow ConstructPV_F(G_F)$
4: $PV_F \leftarrow Reduce(PV_F)$
5: **while** $PV_F \neq \emptyset$ and $ConnectComp(G_S, G) \neq \emptyset$ **do**
6: $\quad G_i \leftarrow Select(ConnectComp(G_S, G))$
7: $\quad NV_i \leftarrow ConstructNV_i(G_i)$
8: $\quad PV_F \leftarrow CheckExtendibility(PV_F, NV_i)$
9: $\quad PV_F \leftarrow Reduce(PV_F)$
10: $\quad G_S \leftarrow ADD(G_S, G_i)$
11: **if** $\exists \rho(\rho \in PV_F \wedge GlobExtViolating(\rho))$ **then**
12: $\quad$ return PV_F
13: **else**
14: $\quad$ return "the fault is predictable in G"

Table 1. Experimental comparison results for centralized and distributed algorithms

	Centralized		Distributed			
	S/T (TP) vs. S/T(PV)	T (ms)	T(LPV) [21] vs. O	T(NV) [21] vs. O	T(FP) [21] vs. O	T(ms)
Ex G	36/62　vs. 16/21	26 vs. 21	—			
G_1[6]	9/10　vs. 4/3	16 vs. 9	—			
G_2[6]	10/12　vs. 3/4	17 vs. 10	—			
Ex1 [21]	23/27　vs. 7/7	15 vs. 12	—			
h-c c1	300/566 vs. 21/16	51 vs. 23	—			
Ex G'	—		69　vs. 21	43　vs. 25	86　vs. 28	186 vs. 43
Ex2 [21]	—		68　vs. 21	29　vs. 16	106　vs. 33	81　vs. 33
h-c d1	—		51　vs. 22	204 vs. 20	836　vs. 51	8s　vs. 30
h-c d2	—		226 vs. 16	204 vs. 20	536　vs. 15	6mn vs. 33
h-c d3	—		116 vs. 21	254 vs. 24	1344 vs. 42	1mn vs. 36

Table 1 shows part of our experimental results, where final verdict results, i.e., whether the system is predictable or not, of all examples are omitted, which are exactly the same for all algorithms. For centralized comparison, we give the number of states/transitions of twin plant (S/T(TP)) for algorithm in [6] and that of our pre-verifier (S/T(PV)), for the examples G in this paper, G_1, G_2 in [6], Ex1 in [21] and one hand-craft (h-c c1) example. And for distributed comparison, we have the number of transitions in local pre-verifier(T(LPV)), normal verifier (T(NV)) as well as in the final synchronized product (T(FP)), both for algorithm proposed in [21] and our distributed one (O). The examples that we chose to show here include G' in this paper and the distributed one Ex2 in [21] with some h-c examples to show the scalability. For the sake of simplicity, we use the name of structures defined in this paper to compare the different local structures with the same goal in both algorithms to show the state space that can be saved by our algorithm. To compare running time for all these algorithms, we use millisecond (ms) as time unit by default and s for second and mn for minute.

Our experimental results show that our algorithms can save at least 50 % space for most of our examples. Note that in this figure, we only give the results for systems with two components due to space limit. Actually our experimental results with more components show that more components we have, more space can be saved by our algorithm. Another important observation is that the state space saved by our algorithm also depends on two other factors. One is the percentage of observable events, less this percentage is, more space is saved. For example, h-c c1 has the same structure in terms of observable events as Ex G in this paper but with more unobservable events. We can save state space much more for h-c c1 compared to Ex G. Another one is the position of the fault, earlier the fault occurs, more space is saved. For example, in h-c d1, the fault occurs almost at the latest step while in h-c d2, the fault occurs at the very beginning. The faulty components have the same structure. The results show that our algorithm can save more space in the case of early occurrence of the fault, which is reasonable considering that we introduce absorbing states to not only guarantee the same observations before the fault but also avoid keeping all the events after the fault. The time saved is even more dramatical in the extreme case h-c d2 in terms of the fault position, 6 min vs. 33 ms. Note that the state space saved for big examples (e.g., hand-craft ones) is more clear than for smaller ones (e.g., ones found in the literature).

6   Discussion

In [6], the authors analyzed predictability directly on a global twin plant. They captured the ambiguous behaviors violating predictability in different paths of the twin plant, which is not suitable for a distributed framework. While we propose a different structure where a PVP violating predictability is caught by only one path, which facilitates the distributed extension by enabling the extensibility checking of local violating paths. To verify diagnosability in a distributed way, it is sufficient to construct a local twin plant for each component and then synchronize them to make sure that the two corresponding trajectories of each path in the final product have the same global occurrence of the observations; this is the distributed algorithm proposed in [13]. While to verify predictability, we have to construct a structure where each path captures a pair of trajectories with the same observations only before the fault but where the normal trajectory cannot be blocked after the fault, which is quite different from diagnosability and much more difficult, especially in the distributed case. Another close work is the distributed algorithm in [21], where the condition violating predictability is not formally proved. Moreover, the authors chose to exploit all states after the fault, which is not necessary since predictability concerns the same observations only before the fault. It follows that, in the worst case, the state space could be the same as the centralized approach. While we construct two different diagnosers with absorbing states, which greatly reduce the search space even in the worst case but always with the correct result. As in the previous approaches proposed in the above papers, our predictability checking is also polynomial in the number of system states. But it can practically be much more applicable for large complex systems considering the reduced space. This is confirmed by our experimental results shown in the previous section.

7   Conclusion

In this paper, we propose a new approach for predictability analysis both in a centralized and a distributed framework. First, we formally characterize pairs of trajectories violating predictability. Then, we show how to check the existence of such pairs in a centralized way before adapting it for a distributed framework. Finally, we provide some experimental results to support the efficiency of our algorithms. One perspective of this work is to adapt our approach to deal with fault patterns [11], which is more general in the diagnosis domain. In the literature, only a centralized framework is proposed in [10], which is not extendable to a distributed one since predictability violation is also checked directly on twin plant. Another one is to extend our approach to distributed systems with asynchronous communication events, which is not yet handled in the literature.

References

1. Bertrand, N., Fabre, É., Haar, S., Haddad, S., Hélouët, L.: Active diagnosis for probabilistic systems. In: Muscholl, A. (ed.) FOSSACS 2014 (ETAPS). LNCS, vol. 8412, pp. 29–42. Springer, Heidelberg (2014)
2. Cassandras, C.G., Lafortune, S.: Introduction to Discrete Event Systems, 2nd edn. Springer, New York (2008)
3. Cimatti, A., Pecheur, C., Cavada, R.: Formal verification of diagnosability via symbolic model checking. In: Proceedings of the 18th International Joint Conference on Artificial Intelligence (IJCAI 2003), pp. 363–369. International Joint Conferences on Artificial Intelligence Inc., Menlo Park (2003)
4. Console, L., Picardi, C., Theseider Dupré, D.: A framework for decentralized qualitative model-based diagnosis. In: Proceedings of the 20th International Joint Conference on Artificial Intelligence (IJCAI 2007), pp. 286–291. International Joint Conferences on Artificial Intelligence Inc., Menlo Park (2007)
5. Debouk, R., Malik, R., Brandin, B.: A modular architecture for diagnosis of discrete event systems. In: Proceedings of the 41st IEEE Conference on Decision and Control (CDC 2002), vol. 1, pp. 417–422. IEEE (2002)
6. Genc, S., Lafortune, S.: Predictability of event occurrences in partially-observed discrete-event systems. Automatica 45(2), 301–311 (2009)
7. Germanos, V., Haar, S., Khomenko, V., Schwoon, S.: Diagnosability under weak fairness. In: Proceedings of the 14th International Conference on Application of Concurrency to System Design (ACSD 2014). IEEE Computer Society Press, Tunis, , June 2014
8. Grastien, A., Anbulagan, J.R., Kelareva, E.: Diagnosis of discrete-event systems using satisfiability algorithms. In: Proceedings of the 22th American National Conference on Artificial Intelligence (AAAI 2007), pp. 305–310. AAAI Press, Menlo Park (2007)

9. Haar, S., Haddad, S., Melliti, T., Schwoon, S.: Optimal constructions for active diagnosis. In: Seth, A., Vishnoi, N. (eds.) Proceedings of the 33rd Conference on Foundations of Software Technology and Theoretical Computer Science (FSTTCS 2013). Leibniz International Proceedings in Informatics, vol. 24, pp. 527–539. Leibniz-Zentrum für Informatik, Guwahati, December 2013

10. Jéron, T., Marchand, H., Genc, S., Lafortune, S.: Predictability of sequence patterns in discrete event systems. In: Proceedings of the 17th World Congress, IFAC, pp. 537–453 (2008)

11. Jéron, T., Marchand, H., Pinchinat, S., Cordier, M.O.: Supervision patterns in discrete event systems diagnosis. In: Proceedings of the 8th International Workshop on Discrete Event Systems, pp. 262–268 (2006)

12. Jiang, S., Huang, Z., Chandra, V., Kumar, R.: A polynomial time algorithm for testing diagnosability of discrete event systems. Trans. Autom. Control **46**(8), 1318–1321 (2001)

13. Pencolé, Y.: Diagnosability analysis of distributed discrete event systems. In: Proceedings of the 16th European Conference on Articifial Intelligent (ECAI 2004), pp. 43–47. IOS Press, Nieuwe Hemweg (2004)

14. Pencolé, Y., Cordier, M.O.: A formal framework for the decentralised diagnosis of large scale discrete event systems and its application to telecommunication networks. Artif. Intell. **164**, 121–170 (2005)

15. Reiter, R.: A theory of diagnosis from first principles. Artif. Intell. **32**(1), 57–95 (1987)

16. Rintanen, J.: Diagnosers and diagnosability of succinct transition systems. In: Proceedings of the 20th International Joint Conference on Artificial Intelligence (IJCAI 2007), pp. 538–544. International Joint Conferences on Artificial Intelligence Inc., Menlo Park (2007)

17. Sampath, M., Sengupta, R., Lafortune, S., Sinnamohideen, K., Teneketzis, D.: Diagnosability of discrete event system. Trans. Autom. Control **40**(9), 1555–1575 (1995)

18. Schumann, A., Huang, J.: A scalable jointree algorithm for diagnosability. In: Proceedings of the 23rd American National Conference on Artificial Intelligence (AAAI 2008), pp. 535–540. AAAI Press, Menlo Park (2008)

19. Struss, P.: Fundamentals of model-based diagnosis of dynamic systems. In: Proceedings of the 15th International Joint Conference on Artificial Intelligence (IJCAI 1997), pp. 480–485. International Joint Conferences on Artificial Intelligence Inc., Menlo Park (1997)

20. Ye, L., Dague, P.: Diagnosability analysis of discrete event systems with autonomous components. In: Proceedings of the 19th European Conference on Artificial Intelligence (ECAI 2010), pp. 105–110. IOS Press, Nieuwe Hemweg (2010)

21. Ye, L., Dague, P., Nouioua, F.: Predictability analysis of distributed discrete event systems. In: Proceedings of the 52nd IEEE Conference on Decision and Control (CDC 2013), pp. 5009–5015. IEEE (2013)

History-Based Specification and Verification of Scalable Concurrent and Distributed Systems

Crystal Chang Din[1]([✉]), S. Lizeth Tapia Tarifa[2], Reiner Hähnle[1],
and Einar Broch Johnsen[2]

[1] Department of Computer Science, Technische Universität Darmstadt,
Darmstadt, Germany
{haehnle,crystald}@cs.tu-darmstadt.de
[2] Department of Informatics, University of Oslo, Oslo, Norway
{sltarifa,einarj}@ifi.uio.no

Abstract. The ABS modelling language targets concurrent and distributed object-oriented systems. The language has been designed to enable scalable formal verification of detailed executable models. This paper provides evidence for that claim: it gives formal specifications of safety properties in terms of histories of observable communication for ABS models as well as formal proofs of those properties. We illustrate our approach with a case study of a Network-on-Chip packet switching platform. We provide an executable formal model in ABS of a generic $m \times n$ mesh chip with an unbounded number of packets and verify several crucial properties. Our concern is formal verification of unbounded concurrent systems. In this paper we show how scalable verification can be achieved by compositional and local reasoning about history-based specifications of observable behavior.

1 Introduction

In this paper we address the formal verification of unbounded concurrent systems and show how *scalable* verification of functional behavior can be achieved by means of compositional and local reasoning about history-based specifications of observable behavior. To focus on high-level design, we consider models of the targeted systems. These models should be sufficiently abstract to facilitate reasoning, yet sufficiently concrete to faithfully reflect the data and control flow of the targeted system. ABS is a formal, executable modeling language for concurrent and distributed systems [26], specifically targeting this level of abstraction: (i) it combines functional, imperative, and object-oriented programming styles, allowing intuitive, modular, high-level modeling of concepts, domain and data; (ii) ABS models are fully executable and model system behavior

---

Supported by the EU projects FP7-610582 *Envisage: Engineering Virtualized Services* (http://www.envisage-project.eu) and FP7-612985 *UpScale: From Inherent Concurrency to Massive Parallelism through Type-based Optimizations* (http://www.upscale-project.eu).

M. Butler et al. (Eds.): ICFEM 2015, LNCS 9407, pp. 217–233, 2015.
DOI: 10.1007/978-3-319-25423-4_14

precisely [3]; (iii) ABS can model synchronous as well as asynchronous communication; (iv) ABS has been developed to provide the foundations for scalable formal verification: there is a program logic as well as a compositional proof system [17] that makes possible to prove global system properties by reasoning about object-local invariants; (v) ABS comes with an IDE and a range of analysis as well as productivity tools [41], specifically, there is a formal verification tool called KeY-ABS [18].

For scalable verification, we focus on behavioral properties specified in terms of communication histories. Communication histories have been used to give fully abstract semantics to concurrent object-oriented systems (e.g., [25]), describing observable behavior while abstracting from implementation detail. A fully abstract semantics captures the minimal information needed to characterize equivalence in all program contexts [32]. Hence, communication histories are the natural choice of specification formalism for compositional verification. We specify monitor-like invariants relating local states to local observable behavior, and compose specifications purely in terms of communication histories.

We provide empirical evidence of our scalability claim by way of a case study on a *Network-on-Chip* (NoC) [30] packet switching platform called ASPIN (Asynchronous Scalable Packet Switching Integrated Network) [37]. Our goal is to prove the correctness of an ABS model of an ASPIN NoC of *arbitrary, unbounded size* with respect to safety properties expressed in terms of communication histories. Concretely, we prove that "no packets are lost" and that "a packet is never sent in a circle". The main contributions of this paper are (i) a *formal model* of a generic $m \times n$ mesh ASPIN chip in ABS with unbounded number of packets, as well as a packet routing algorithm; (ii) the *formal specification using communication histories* of safety properties which together ensure that no packets are lost; and (iii) *compositional* and highly automated formal proofs, done with KeY-ABS, that the ABS model of ASPIN fulfills these safety properties.[1]

ABS was developed with the explicit aim to enable scalable verification of detailed, precisely modeled, executable, concurrent systems. Our paper shows that this claim is justified. Our work is the first *compositional* verification (in the sense made precise in Sect. 6) of a generic NoC model unbounded in the number of nodes and packets. It has been achieved with manageable effort and thus shows that our approach based on deductive verification is a viable alternative for the verification of concurrent systems.

Paper overview: Sect. 2 briefly introduces the modeling language ABS and Sect. 3 details formal specification based on communication histories, Sect. 4 provides background on deductive verification with expressive program logics, and Sect. 5 presents the ASPIN NoC case study. Section 6 explains how we achieved the formal specification and verification of the case study and gives details about the exact properties proved as well as the necessary effort. Section 7 sketches some directions for future work, Sect. 8 discusses related work and Sect. 9 concludes.

---

[1] The complete model with all formal specifications and proofs is available at https://www.se.tu-darmstadt.de/se/group-members/crystal-chang-din/noc.

2   The ABS Modeling Language

ABS [26] is a behavioral specification language for developing abstract executable models of concurrent, distributed, and object-oriented systems. ABS offers a clean integration of concurrency and object orientation based on concurrent object groups (COGs). ABS permits synchronous as well as asynchronous communication [27], akin to Actors [1] and Erlang processes [7]. ABS offers a range of complementary modeling alternatives in a concurrent and object-oriented framework that integrates algebraic datatypes and functional and imperative programming styles with a Java-like syntax and a formal semantics [26]. Compared to object-oriented programming languages, ABS abstracts from low-level implementation choices such as imperative data structures. Compared to design-oriented languages like UML diagrams, it models data-sensitive control flow and it is executable. We now briefly introduce the functional and imperative layers of ABS.

The functional layer of ABS is used to model computations on the internal data of concurrent objects. It allows modelers to abstract from implementation details of imperative data structures at an early stage in the software design and thus allows data manipulation without committing to a particular low-level implementation choice. This layer combines a simple language for parametric algebraic data types (ADTs) and a pure first-order functional language which includes *expressions* such as variables, values, constructors, functions, and case expressions. ABS has a library with four predefined basic types (Bool, Int, String and Unit), and parametric datatypes (e.g., lists, sets, and maps). The predefined datatypes come with arithmetic and comparison operators, and the parametric datatypes have built-in standard functions. The type Unit is used as a return type for methods without explicit return value. All other types and functions are user-defined.

The imperative layer of ABS addresses concurrency, communication, and synchronization in the system design, and defines interfaces, classes, and methods in an object-oriented style. In ABS, each concurrent object group (COG) has its own thread of execution where one process is active and the others are suspended on a process queue. Classes can be *active* in the sense that their run method, if defined, automatically triggers a process upon creation. *Statements* are standard for sequential composition $s_1; s_2$, and for **skip, if, while,** and **return** constructs. In addition, ABS includes statements **await** and **suspend** for the explicit suspension of active processes, so scheduling in ABS is *cooperative*. The statement **suspend** unconditionally suspends the execution of the active process and moves this process to the queue. The statement **await** g conditionally suspends execution: the guard g controls thread release and consists of Boolean conditions and return tests (explained in the next paragraph). Just like expressions, the evaluation of guards is side-effect free. However, if g evaluates to false, the process is *suspended* and the execution thread becomes idle. When the execution thread is idle, an enabled task may be selected from the process queue by means of a default scheduling policy. The language also includes COG creation

new $C(\bar{e})$, method calls $o!m(\bar{e})$, and future dereferencing $fr.\mathbf{get}$ (here $\bar{e}$ denotes a lists of expressions).

Communication and *synchronization* are decoupled in ABS. Communication is based on asynchronous method calls, denoted by assignments of the form $fr=o!m(\bar{e})$ to future variables fr. Here, o is an object expression, m a method name, and $\bar{e}$ are expressions providing actual parameter values for the method invocation. (Local calls are written **this**!$m(\bar{e})$.) A future denotes a "mailbox" where the return value to the method call can be retrieved. After calling $fr=o!m(\bar{e})$, the variable fr refers to the corresponding future and the caller may proceed *without blocking*. Two operations on future variables control synchronization in ABS [13]. First, the guard **await** $fr?$ *suspends the active process* unless a return to the call associated with fr has arrived, allowing other processes in the COG to execute. Second, the return value is retrieved by the expression $fr.\mathbf{get}$, which *blocks all execution* in the COG until the return value is available. For example, the statement sequence $fr=o!m(\bar{e});x=fr.\mathbf{get}$ contains no suspension statement and, therefore, encodes commonly used *blocking calls*, abbreviated $x=o.m(e)$ (often referred to as synchronous calls). Futures are first-class citizens of ABS and can be passed around as method parameters. If the return value of a call is of no interest, the call may occur directly as a statement $o!m(e)$ with no associated future variable. This corresponds to asynchronous message passing. The details of the sequential execution of several threads inside a COG are not used in the verification techniques showcased in this paper and therefore we focus on single-object COGs (i.e., concurrent objects) in the sequel.

3   Observable Behavior

A distributed system can be specified by the externally observable behavior of its constituents. The behavior of each component is reflected in the possible *communication histories* over observable events [22]. Theoretically this is justified, because communication histories can be used for fully abstract semantics of object-oriented languages [25]. Here, we strive for *compositional* communication histories of asynchronously communicating systems. Therefore, it is appropriate to record separate events for object creation, method invocation, reaction upon a method call, resolving a future, and for fetching the value of a future. Each of these events is witnessed by merely one object, namely the generating object.

Figure 1 illustrates the relation among the observable events associated with an asynchronous method call. Assume that an object o calls a method m on an object o' with parameter values $\bar{e}$, and assume that u denotes the identity of the associated future. An invocation message is sent from o to o' when the method is invoked. This is reflected by the *invocation event* $invEv(o, o', u, m, \bar{e})$, generated by o. An *invocation reaction event* $invREv(o, o', u, m, \bar{e})$ is generated by o' once m starts to execute. When m has terminated, object o' generates the *future event* $futEv(o', u, m, e)$, reflecting that u receives the return value e. The *fetching event* $fetREv(o, u, e)$ is generated by o once the value of the resolved future is accessed. References u to futures bind all four event types together and allow to filter out those events from an event history that relate to the same method invocation. Since future identities may be passed to other objects o'', these objects may also fetch the future value; this is reflected by the event $fetREv(o'', u, e)$, generated by o'' in Fig. 1. Based on these events, we formalize the notion of a communication history.

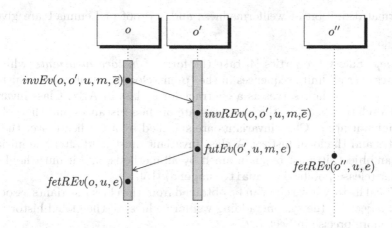

Fig. 1. Communication events and when they occur in the history

Definition 1 (Communication History). *The* communication history H *of a system of objects O is a sequence of events, as defined above, such that each event in H is generated by an object in O.*

For a history H, we let H/o abbreviate the projection of H to the events generated by o. Since each event is generated by a single object, it follows that the projections of a history to two different objects are disjoint.

Definition 2 (Local History). *For a (global) history H and an object o, the projection H/o is the* local history *of o.*

For a method call with future u, the possible ordering of the associated events is described by the regular expression

$$invEv(o, o', u, m, \bar{e}) \cdot invREv(o, o', u, m, \bar{e}) \cdot futEv(o', u, m, e)[\cdot fetREv(\_, u, e)]^*$$

for some fixed o, o', m, $\bar{e}$, e, and where "·" denotes concatenation of events, "_" denotes arbitrary values. Thus, the return value from a method call may be read several times (or not at all), each time with the same value, namely the value given in the preceding future event.

A communication history H is *wellformed* if the order of communication events follows the pattern defined above, the identities of generated futures are fresh, and the communicating objects are non-null.

Lemma 1. *The global history H of a system modeled with ABS and derived from its operational semantics, is wellformed.*

The formal definition of wellformedness and a proof of Lemma 1 are given in [16].

Invariants. Safety properties [4] take the form of *history invariants*, which are predicates over all finite sequences in the (prefix-closed) set of possible histories.

The class invariant serves as a contract for a class in ABS: Class invariants express a relation between the internal state of class instances and their observable communication. Class invariants are specified by a predicate over the class attributes and the local history. A class invariant must hold after the initialization of an object, it must be maintained by all methods, and it must hold at all processor release points (i.e., await, suspend) [15].

A global history invariant can be obtained from the class invariants associated with all objects in the system, adding wellformedness of the global history. This is made more precise in Sect. 6.2.

4   Deductive Verification

KeY-ABS [18] is a deductive verification system for constructing formal proofs about ABS programs, based on the KeY theorem prover [8]. A formal proof is a sequence of reasoning steps to show the truth of a formula (a theorem). The formal proof must lead without gaps from axioms to the theorem by applying proof rules.

The program logic of KeY-ABS is first-order dynamic logic for ABS (ABSDL) [17,18]. For a sequence of executable ABS statements S and ABSDL formulae P and Q, the formula $P \rightarrow [S]Q$ expresses: If the execution of S starts in a state where the assertion P holds and the program terminates normally, then the assertion Q holds in the final state. Thus, given an ABS method m with body mb and a class invariant I, the ABSDL formula $I \rightarrow [mb]I$ expresses that the method m preserves the class invariant. KeY-ABS uses a Gentzen-style sequent calculus to prove ABSDL formulae. In sequent notation $P \rightarrow [S]Q$ is written

$$\Gamma, P \vdash [S]Q, \Delta$$

where Γ and Δ stand for (possibly empty) sets of side formulae. A sequent calculus as realized in ABSDL essentially constitutes a symbolic interpreter for ABS. For example, the assignment rule for local program variables is

$$\frac{\Gamma \vdash \{v := e\}[\text{rest}]\phi, \Delta}{\Gamma \vdash [v = e; \text{rest}]\phi, \Delta}$$

where v is a local program variable and e is a pure (side effect-free) expression. This rule rewrites the formula by moving the assignment from the program into a so-called *update* [8], as {v := e} shown above, which captures state changes. The symbolic execution continues with the remaining program rest. Updates can be viewed as explicit substitutions that accumulate in front of the modality during symbolic program execution. Updates can only be applied to formulae or terms. Once the program to be verified has been completely executed and the modality is empty, the accumulated updates are applied to the formula after the modality, resulting in a pure first-order formula. Below we show a more complex proof rule, which captures asynchronous method invocation:

$$
\text{asyncCall} \quad \frac{\begin{array}{l} \Gamma \vdash (o \neq \texttt{null} \wedge \texttt{wf}(h)), \Delta \\ \Gamma \vdash (\texttt{futureIsFresh}(u, h) \rightarrow \\ \quad \{\texttt{fr} := u \,\|\, h := h \cdot \mathit{invEv}(\mathit{this}, o, u, m, \overline{e})\}[\texttt{rest}]\phi), \Delta \end{array}}{\Gamma \vdash [\texttt{fr} = o!\texttt{m}(\overline{e}); \texttt{rest}]\phi, \Delta}
$$

The rule has two premisses and splits the proof in two cases. The first premiss (on top) ensures that the callee is non-null and the current history h is wellformed. The second case introduces a constant u which represents the future generated for the result of this method invocation. The left side of the implication ensures that u is fresh in h and the right side updates the history by appending the *invocation event* generated by this call. We refer to [17] for the other ABSDL rules as well as soundness and completeness proofs of the ABSDL calculus.

```
type Pos = Pair<Int, Int>; // (x,y) coordinates
type Packet = Pair<Int, Pos>; // (id, destination)
type Buffer = Int;
data Direction = N | W | S | E | NONE;
        // north, west, south, east, the direction for not moving
data Port = P(Bool inState , Bool outState, Router rId, Buffer buff);
        // (input port state, output port state, neighbor router id, buffer size)
type Ports = Map<Direction, Port>;
```

Fig. 2. ADTs for the ASPIN model in ABS

5 The Network-on-Chip Case Study

Network-on-Chip (NoC) [30] is a packet switching platform for single chip systems which scales well to an arbitrary number of resources (e.g., CPU, memory). The NoC architecture is an $m \times n$ mesh of switches and resources which are placed on the slots formed by the switches. The NoC architecture is essentially the on-chip communication infrastructure.

Asynchronous Scalable Packet Switching Integrated Network (ASPIN) [37] is an example of a NoC with routers and processors. ASPIN has physically distributed routers in each core. Each router is connected to four neighboring routers

```
interface Router{
    Unit setPorts(Router e, Router w, Router n, Router s);
    Unit getPk(Packet pk, Direction srcPort);}

class RouterImp(Pos address, Int buffSize) implements Router {
    Ports ports = EmptyMap;
    Set<Packet> receivedPks = EmptySet; // received packages

    Unit setPorts(Router e, Router w, Router n, Router s){
        ports = map[Pair(N, P(True, True, n, 0)), Pair(S, P(True, True, s, 0)),
                    Pair(E, P(True, True, e, 0)), Pair(W, P(True, True, w, 0))];}

    Unit getPk(Packet pk, Direction srcPort){
        if (addressPk(pk) != address) {
            await buff(lookup(ports,srcPort)) < buffSize;
            ports = put(ports,srcPort,increaseBuff(lookup(ports,srcPort)));
            this!redirectPk(pk,srcPort);}
        else { // record that packet was successfully received
            receivedPks = insertElement(receivedPks, pk); } }

    Unit redirectPk(Packet pk, Direction srcPort){
        Direction direc = xFirstRouting(addressPk(pk), address);
        await (inState(lookup(ports,srcPort)) == True)
              && (outState(lookup(ports,direc)) == True);
        ports = put(ports, srcPort, inSet(lookup(ports, srcPort), False));
        ports = put(ports, direc, outSet(lookup(ports, direc), False));
        Router r = rId(lookup(ports, direc));
        Fut<Unit> f = r!getPk(pk, opposite(direc)); await f?;
        ports = put(ports, srcPort, decreaseBuff(lookup(ports, srcPort)));
        ports = put(ports, srcPort, inSet(lookup(ports, srcPort), True));
        ports = put(ports, direc, outSet(lookup(ports, direc), True)); } }
```

Fig. 3. A model of an ASPIN router using ABS

and each core is locally connected to one router. ASPIN routers are split into five separate modules (north, south, east, west, and local) with ports that have input and output channels and buffers. ASPIN uses input buffering for storage: each input channel has an independent FIFO buffer. Packets arriving from different neighboring routers (and from the local core) are stored in the respective FIFO buffer. Communication between routers uses a four-phase handshake protocol with request and acknowledgment messages between neighboring routers to transfer a packet. In ASPIN, the distributed X-first algorithm routes packets from input channels to output channels: packets first move along the X (horizontal) axis of the grid, and afterwards along the Y (vertical) axis to reach their destination. We model the functionality and routing algorithm of ASPIN in ABS starting from a model by Sharifi et al. [35,36], written in Rebeca [38]. In Sect. 6 we will formally verify our model using ABSDL.

We model each router as a concurrent object that communicates with other routers through asynchronous method calls. The algebraic data types used in our model are given in Fig. 2. We abstract from the local communication to cores, so each router has four ports and each port has an input and output channel, the identifier rId of the neighbor router, and a buffer. Packets are modeled as pairs that contain the packet identifier and the final destination coordinate.

```
def Direction xFirstRouting(Pos destination, Pos current) =
case x(current) < x(destination) {
   True => E;
   False => case x(current) > x(destination) {
            True => W;
            False => case y(current) < y(destination) {
                     True => S;
                     False => case y(current) > y(destination) {
                              True => N;
                              False => NONE; }; }; }; };
```

Fig. 4. X-first routing algorithm in ABS

The ABS model of a router is shown in Fig. 3. Method setPorts initializes the ports in a router and connects it to the neighbor routers. Packets are transferred using a protocol expressed by two methods redirectPk and getPk. The internal method redirectPk is called by the router to redirect a packet to a neighbor router. The X-first routing algorithm in Fig. 4 selects the port direc (and consequently the neighbor router). The parameter srcPort determines the local input buffer in which the packet is temporarily stored. As part of the communication protocol, the input channel of srcPort and the output channel of direc are blocked until the neighbor router confirms receipt of the packet, using f = r!getPk(...); **await** f? statements to simulate request and acknowledgment messages (here r is the Id of the neighbor router). The method getPk checks if the final destination of the packet is the current router, if so, it stores the packet, otherwise it temporarily stores the packet in the srcPort buffer and redirects it. The model uses standard library functions for maps and sets (e.g., put and lookup) and observers as well as other functions over the ADTs (e.g., addressPk, inState, decreaseBuff).

6   Formal Specification and Verification of the Case Study

We now formalize and verify safety properties for the ABS NoC model in ABSDL using the KeY-ABS verification tool. The application is based on the theory presented in Sects. 3 and 4, ensuring the correctness of the results. Our approach uses local reasoning about *RouterImp* objects and establishes a system invariant over the global history from invariants over the local histories of each object.

6.1   Local Reasoning

Observe that the four-event semantics for asynchronous communication outlined in Sect. 3 keeps the local histories of different objects disjoint. This makes it possible to reason locally about each object in terms of the local histories. Lemmas 2 and 3 present the history-based class invariants for RouterImp. We then discuss the proof obligations verified by KeY-ABS that stem from reasoning about our model in terms of these class invariants. Figure 5 illustrates the explanations.

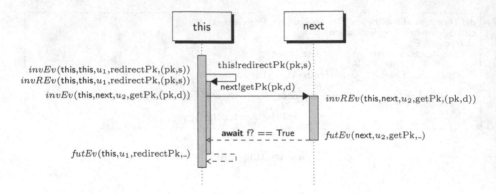

Fig. 5. Communication history between a router and its neighboring router **next**, to which the package is sent

Lemma 2. *Every time a router R terminates an execution of the getPk method, R must either have sent an internal invocation to redirect the packet or have stored the packet in its receivedPks set.*

We formalize this lemma as an ABSDL formula (slightly beautified):

$$\forall i_1, u \, . \, 0 \leq i_1 < len(h) \wedge futEv(this, u, \mathsf{getPk}, \_) = at(h, i_1)$$
$$\Rightarrow$$
$$\exists i_2, pk \, . \, 0 \leq i_2 < i_1 \wedge invREv(\_, this, u, \mathsf{getPk}, (pk, \_)) = at(h, i_2) \, \wedge$$
$$((dest(pk) \neq address(this) \Rightarrow$$
$$\exists i_3 \, . \, i_2 < i_3 < i_1 \wedge invEv(this, this, \_, \mathsf{redirectPk}, (pk, \_)) = at(h, i_3)) \, \vee$$
$$(dest(pk) = address(this) \Rightarrow pk \in \mathsf{receivedPks}))$$

Here, "_" denotes a value without interest. The function $len(s)$ returns the length of sequence s, $at(s, i)$ the element located at index i of sequence s, $dest(pk)$ the destination address of packet pk, and $address(r)$ the address of router r.

This formula expresses that for every future event ev_1 of getPk with future identifier u in history h (capturing a termination of getPk), there is a corresponding invocation reaction event ev_2 that contains the sent packet pk. This is achieved by pattern matching with u in the preceding history. If *this* router is the destination of pk, then pk must be in its receivedPks set, otherwise an *invocation event* of redirectPk containing pk must occur in the history between ev_1 and ev_2. This invariant captures the properties of the state and is prefix-closed.[2]

---

[2] In the heap model of KeY-ABS, a heap value can potentially be modified when a process is released. Therefore, to prove the above property we need a slightly stronger invariant expressing that the address of a router in the heap is *rigid* (cannot be modified by any other process). Due to a current technical limitation of the tool, we proved the invariant for a slightly simplified model where the router address is a parameter of getPk. This modification does not affect the overall behavior of the model and will be lifted in future work.

Lemma 3. *Every time a router R terminates an execution of the redirectPk method, the input and output channels used to redirect the fetched packet are released, and the packet has been redirected to a neighbor router through an invocation of the getPk method.*

Again, we formalize this lemma as an ABSDL formula:

$$\forall u \,.\, futEv(this, u, \mathsf{redirectPk}, \_) = at(h, len(h) - 1)$$
$$\Rightarrow$$
$$\exists i_1, i_2, pk, \mathsf{srcP}, \mathsf{dirP} \,.\, 0 < i_1 < i_2 < len(h) - 1 \,\wedge$$
$$(invREv(this, this, u, \mathsf{redirectPk}, (pk, \mathsf{srcP})) = at(h, i_1) \,\wedge$$
$$invEv(this, \_, \_, \mathsf{getPk}, (pk, opposite(\mathsf{dirP}))) = at(h, i_2)) \,\wedge$$
$$(inState(lookup(ports, \mathsf{srcP})) \,\wedge\, outState(lookup(ports, \mathsf{dirP})))$$

This formula expresses that whenever the last event in the history h is a *future event* of redirectPk method (capturing termination of redirectPk), there are corresponding invocation reaction and invocation events which we find by pattern matching with the same future and packet in the previous history. The source port srcP and the direction port dirP used in the latest execution of redirectPk can be found in these two events. The input channel of srcP and the output channel of dirP must be released in the current state. This invariant captures the properties of the current state and is prefix-closed.

All three methods of RouterImp satisfy both invariants. The statistics for verifying the lemmas by KeY-ABS is given below (in terms of the proof size):

	setPorts		getPk		redirectPk	
	nodes	branches	nodes	branches	nodes	branches
Lemma 2	1638	12	11540	108	27077	200
Lemma 3	214	1	1845	11	4634	34

KeY-ABS provides heuristics and proof strategies that automate large parts of the proof construction. The remaining user input typically consists of universal and existential quantifier instantiations.

6.2   System Specification

A system property of an ABS program can be formulated as a global history invariant, which holds for all finite sequences in the prefix-closed set of possible global histories. The global history of an ABS program consists of the local histories of each object in the system, and is wellformed according to Lemma 1. We now want to derive a global system specification from the history-based class invariants of the system's objects.

The basis for local reasoning in the proof system for ABS is that class invariants must be satisfied at process release points and after method termination (see Sect. 3), but class invariants need not be prefix-closed. Consequently, a local history invariant is in general weaker than the class invariant. For compositional reasoning, we may therefore need to weaken the class invariants in order to transform class invariants into prefix-closed history invariants. The system invariant can then be obtained directly from the history invariants of the composed objects since the local histories are disjoint. The proof rule for compositional reasoning about ABS programs is given and proved sound in [17], by which we obtain a system invariant below for the NoC model.

Let $I_{this}(h)$ denote the conjunction of the class invariants $I_{getPk}(this, h)$ and $I_{redirectPk}(this, h)$, defined in Lemmas 2 and 3, where h is the local history of *this* object. The class invariants are already prefix-closed and need not be weakened. Define a system invariant $I(H)$ as the conjunction of the instantiated class invariants of all RouterImp objects r in the system:

$$I(H) \triangleq \text{wf}(H) \wedge \bigwedge_{(r:\text{RouterImp}) \in new_{ob}(H)} I_r(H/r)$$

Here, H denotes the global history of the system and $I_r(H/r)$ denotes the history invariant of r applied to the local history H/r of a router r as obtained by projection from H (Definition 2). The function $new_{ob}(H)$ returns the set of RouterImp objects generated within the system execution, as captured by H. History wellformedness, denoted $\text{wf}(H)$, ensures a proper ordering of the events that belong to the same method invocation. Each wellformed interleaving of the local histories represents a possible global history. As a consequence, we obtain:

Theorem 1. *Every time a router R terminates an execution of the* redirectPk *method, the pair of input and output channels used to redirect the fetched packet are released, and a neighbor router of R must either have sent an internal invocation to redirect the packet further or have stored the packet in its* receivedPks *set. Hence, the network does not drop any packets.*

More Properties. Besides Theorem 1 we proved in a similar fashion that a packet always moves towards its destination. This follows from two lemmas that hold locally and are proven with KeY-ABS: (i) whenever a router redirects a packet then it moves one step closer to its destination, and (ii) when a packet arrives at its destination then its distance to it becomes zero. The proof of (i) for redirectPk has 5178 nodes and 80 branches, the one of (ii) for getPk has 13401 nodes and 110 branches. As corollary we obtain that a packet is never sent in a circle.

Effort. The modeling of the NoC case study in ABS took ca. two person weeks. Formal specification and verification was mainly done by the first author of this paper who at the time was not experienced with the verification tool KeY-ABS. The effort for formal specification was ca. two person weeks and for formal verification of Lemmas 2, 3 ca. one person month, but this included training to use the tool effectively. Subsequent specification and verification of the property that a packet always moves towards its destination merely took one working day.

7   Future Work

Deadlock Analysis. In addition to history-based invariants, it is conceivable to prove other properties, such as deadlock-freedom. Deadlocks may occur in a system, for example, when a shared buffer between processes is full and one process can decrease the buffer size only if the other process increases the buffer size. This situation is prevented in the ABS model by disallowing self-calls before decreasing the size of the buffer (the method invocation of *getPk* within *redirectPk* in our model is an external call). It is possible to argue informally that our ABS model of NoC is indeed deadlock-free, but a formal proof with KeY-ABS is future work. The main obstacle is that deadlocks are a global property and one would need to find a way to encode sufficient conditions for deadlock-freedom into the local histories. There are deadlock analyzers for ABS [20], but these, like other approaches to deadlock analysis of concurrent systems, work only for a fixed number of objects.

Extensions of the Model. The ASPIN chip model presented in this paper can be extended with time (e.g., delays and deadline annotations) and scheduling (e.g., FIFO, EDF, user-defined, etc.) using Real-Time ABS [9]. A timed model would allow to run simulations and obtain results about the performance of the model. Adding scheduling to the model would make it possible to reason about the ordering of sent packets (using FIFO scheduling) or to express priority of packets. It is also possible to change the routing algorithm (Fig. 4) without the need to alter the RouterImp class (Fig. 3). Then one may compare the performance of different routing algorithms by means of simulations.

8   Related Work

Early work on verifying concurrent systems was non-compositional: interference freedom tests were used for shared variable concurrency [34] and cooperation tests for synchronous message passing [6]. Compositional approaches were introduced for shared variables in the form of rely-guarantee [28] and for synchronous message passing in the form of assumption-commitment [33]. Extending these principles for compositional verification, object invariants can be used to achieve modularity (e.g., [24]). Communication histories first appeared in the object-oriented setting [12] and then for CSP [22]. Soundararajan developed an axiomatic proof system for CSP using histories and projections [39], and Zwiers developed the first sound and complete proof system using histories [43]. Reasoning about asynchronous method calls and cooperative scheduling using histories was first done for Creol [19] and later adapted to Dynamic Logic [2]. Din introduced a proof system based on four communication events, significantly simplifying the proof rules [15] and extended the approach to futures [16,17]. This four-event proof system is the basis for KeY-ABS [18].

The pure history-based proof system of ABS requires strong hiding of local state: the state of other objects can only be accessed through method calls, so shared state is internal and controlled by cooperative scheduling. Consequently, specifications can be purely local. More expressive specifications require significantly more complex proof systems; e.g., modifies-clauses in Boogie [24] or fractional permissions [21] in Chalice [31]. To specify fully abstract interface behavior these systems need to simulate histories in an ad hoc manner (e.g., [24, Fig. 1]). A combination of permission-based separation logic [5] and histories has recently been proposed for modular reasoning about multithread concurrency [42].

Formal analysis of NoC systems is usually done in specialized formalisms. Notably, xMAS is a language with a small set of primitives for specifying abstract microarchitectural models of communication fabrics [14]. It supports, for example, deadlock detection [40], model checking in Verilog by inferring inductive invariants for xMAS models [11], and compositional model-checking of bounded latency properties [23]. Among the approaches based on general specification formalisms, ACL2 has been used for non-compositional analysis of, e.g., message loss and deadlock-free routing (e.g., [10]). Event-B has been used to model and gradually refine 3D NoC systems in [29], and invariants for the models are verified using the Rodin tool. Similar to our work their modeling approach does not assume a specific number of routers. In contrast to our work their approach is based on a global specification of behavior which includes the assumption that a message can only be transferred a finite number of times before it reaches its destination (technically, their *switch* event is "anticipated").

Sharifi *et al.* [35, 36] used the actor-based language Rebeca to study deadlock-freedom and successful package sending for the ASPIN chip and the X-first routing algorithm by means of non-compositional model-checking techniques. They work with configurations of fixed size, which triggered our interest in the verification of ASPIN models in a compositional and scalable manner. Compared to the Rebeca model, the ASPIN model in ABS is decoupled from the routing algorithm and uses object-oriented modeling concepts and high-level concurrency control, which makes it more compact and easier to comprehend. In contrast to most previous work, our approach works for an *unbounded* number of objects and it is valid for *generic* NoC models for any $m \times n$ mesh in the ASPIN chip as well as any number of sent packets.

9 Conclusion

We presented an approach to scalable verification of unbounded concurrent and distributed systems which allows *global safety properties* to be established using *local* verification rules and symbolic execution. The approach is realized in the proof system KeY-ABS, developed for the ABS modeling language. We demonstrated the viability of our verification approach by proving the correctness of safety properties for an ABS model of an ASPIN NoC of arbitrary, unbounded size. This is possible in our proof system, because each class invariant is independent of its class instances and properties are specified in terms of local communication histories. The paper develops a formal model of the case study, explains how local specifications are formalized using communication histories, and uses

KeY-ABS to obtain formal proofs of global properties such as "no packets are lost" and "a packet is never sent in a circle". This is, to the best of our knowledge, the first time that scalable, history-based reasoning techniques have been applied to NoC systems. Our work also shows that a general purpose modeling language and verification framework for concurrent and distributed systems is adequate for NoC systems. After an initial modeling and training effort, system properties can be specified and verified within hours or few days.

Acknowledgements. The authors gratefully acknowledge valuable discussions with Richard Bubel.

References

1. Agha, G.A.: ACTORS: A Model of Concurrent Computations in Distributed Systems. The MIT Press, Cambridge (1986)
2. Ahrendt, W., Dylla, M.: A system for compositional verification of asynchronous objects. Sci. Comput. Program. **77**(12), 1289–1309 (2012)
3. Albert, E., de Boer, F.S., Hähnle, R., Johnsen, E.B., Schlatte, R., Tapia Tarifa, S.L., Wong, P.Y.H.: Formal modeling of resource management for cloud architectures: an industrial case study using real-time ABS. J. SOCA **8**(4), 323–339 (2014)
4. Alpern, B., Schneider, F.B.: Defining liveness. Inf. Process. Lett. **21**(4), 181–185 (1985)
5. Amighi, A., Haack, C., Huisman, M., Hurlin, C.: Permission-based separation logic for multithreaded Java programs. LMCS **11**, 1–66 (2015)
6. Apt, K.R., Francez, N., de Roever, W.P.: A proof system for communicating sequential processes. ACM TOPLAS **2**(3), 359–385 (1980)
7. Armstrong, J.: Programming Erlang. Pragmatic Bookshelf (2007)
8. Beckert, B., Hähnle, R., Schmitt, P.H. (eds.): Verification of Object-Oriented Software. LNCS (LNAI), vol. 4334. Springer, Heidelberg (2007)
9. Bjørk, J., de Boer, F.S., Johnsen, E.B., Schlatte, R., Tapia, S.L.: User-defined schedulers for real-time concurrent objects. Innovations Syst. Softw. Eng. **9**(1), 29–43 (2013)
10. Borrione, D., Helmy, A., Pierre, L., Schmaltz, J.: A formal approach to the verification of networks on chip. EURASIP J. Embed. Syst. **2009**, 2:1–2:14 (2009)
11. Chatterjee, S., Kishinevsky, M.: Automatic generation of inductive invariants from high-level microarchitectural models of communication fabrics. Formal Methods Syst. Des. **40**(2), 147–169 (2012)
12. Dahl, O.-J.: Can program proving be made practical? In: Les Fondements de la Programmation, pp. 57–114. IRIA, December 1977
13. de Boer, F.S., Clarke, D., Johnsen, E.B.: A complete guide to the future. In: De Nicola, R. (ed.) ESOP 2007. LNCS, vol. 4421, pp. 316–330. Springer, Heidelberg (2007)
14. Chatterjee, S., Kishinevsky, M., Ogras, Ü.Y.: xMAS: quick formal modeling of communication fabrics to enable verification. IEEE Des. Test Comput. **29**(3), 80–88 (2012)
15. Din, C.C., Dovland, J., Johnsen, E.B., Owe, O.: Observable behavior of distributed systems: component reasoning for concurrent objects. J. Logic Algebraic Program. **81**(3), 227–256 (2012)

16. Din, C.C., Owe, O.: A sound and complete reasoning system for asynchronous communication with shared futures. J. Logical Algebraic Methods Program. **83**(5–6), 360–383 (2014)

17. Din, C.C., Owe, O.: Compositional reasoning about active objects with shared futures. Formal Aspects Comput. **27**(3), 551–572 (2015)

18. Din, C.C., Bubel, R., Hähnle, R.: KeY-ABS: a deductive verification tool for the concurrent modelling language ABS. In: Felty, A., Middeldorp, A. (eds.) Automated Deduction - CADE-25. LNCS, vol. 9195, pp. 517–526. Springer, Switzerland (2015)

19. Dovland, J., Johnsen, E.B., Owe, O.: Verification of concurrent objects with asynchronous method calls. In: Proceedings of International Conference on Software Science, Technology & Engineering (SwSTE 2005), pp. 141–150. IEEE Press, February 2005

20. Giachino, E., Laneve, C., Lienhardt, M.: A framework for deadlock detection in core ABS. Softw. Syst. Model. 1–36 (2015). Springer. doi:10.1007/s10270-014-0444-y

21. Heule, S., Leino, K.R.M., Müller, P., Summers, A.J.: Abstract read permissions: fractional permissions without the fractions. In: Giacobazzi, R., Berdine, J., Mastroeni, I. (eds.) VMCAI 2013. LNCS, vol. 7737, pp. 315–334. Springer, Heidelberg (2013)

22. Hoare, C.A.R.: Communicating Sequential Processes. Prentice Hall, Upper Saddle River (1985)

23. Holcomb, D.E., Seshia, S.A.: Compositional performance verification of network-on-chip designs. IEEE Trans. CAD Integr. Circ. Syst. **33**(9), 1370–1383 (2014)

24. Jacobs, B., Piessens, F., Leino, K.R.M., Schulte, W.: Safe concurrency for aggregate objects with invariants. In: Proceedings of SEFM, pp. 137–147. IEEE (2005)

25. Jeffrey, A., Rathke, J.: Java JR: fully abstract trace semantics for a core Java language. In: Sagiv, M. (ed.) ESOP 2005. LNCS, vol. 3444, pp. 423–438. Springer, Heidelberg (2005)

26. Johnsen, E.B., Hähnle, R., Schäfer, J., Schlatte, R., Steffen, M.: ABS: a core language for abstract behavioral specification. In: Aichernig, B.K., de Boer, F.S., Bonsangue, M.M. (eds.) Formal Methods for Components and Objects. LNCS, vol. 6957, pp. 142–164. Springer, Heidelberg (2011)

27. Johnsen, E.B., Owe, O.: An asynchronous communication model for distributed concurrent objects. Softw. Syst. Model. **6**(1), 35–58 (2007)

28. Jones, C.B.: Development methods for computer programmes including a notion of interference. Ph.D. thesis, Oxford University, UK, June 1981

29. Kamali, M., Petre, L., Sere, K., Daneshtalab, M.: Refinement-based modeling of 3D NoCs. In: Arbab, F., Sirjani, M. (eds.) FSEN 2011. LNCS, vol. 7141, pp. 236–252. Springer, Heidelberg (2012)

30. Kumar, S., Jantsch, A., Millberg, M., Öberg, J., Soininen, J., Forsell, M., Tiensyrjä, K., Hemani, A.: A network on chip architecture and design methodology. In: Proceedings of VLSI, pp. 117–124 (2002)

31. Leino, K.R.M., Müller, P., Smans, J.: Verification of concurrent programs with Chalice. In: Aldini, A., Barthe, G., Gorrieri, R. (eds.) Foundations of Security Analysis and Design V. LNCS, vol. 5705, p. 195. Springer, Heidelberg (2009)

32. Milner, R.: Fully abstract models of typed λ-calculi. Theoret. Comput. Sci. **4**, 1–22 (1977)

33. Misra, J., Chandy, K.M.: Proofs of networks of processes. IEEE Trans. Softw. Eng. **7**(4), 417–426 (1981)

34. Owicki, S.S., Gries, D.: An axiomatic proof technique for parallel programs I. Acta Informatica **6**, 319–340 (1976)

35. Sharifi, Z., Mohammadi, S., Sirjani, M.: Comparison of NoC routing algorithms using formal methods. In: Proceedings of Parallel and Distributed Processing Techniques and Applications (PDPTA 2013), vol. 2, pp. 474–482. CSREA Press (2013)

36. Sharifi, Z., Mosaffa, M., Mohammadi, S., Sirjani, M.: Functional and performance analysis of network-on-chips using actor-based modeling and formal verification. ECEASST **66**, 16 (2013)

37. Sheibanyrad, A., Greiner, A., Panades, I.M.: Multisynchronous and fully asynchronous NoCs for GALS architectures. IEEE Des. Test Comput. **25**(6), 572–580 (2008)

38. Sirjani, M., Jaghoori, M.M.: Ten years of analyzing actors: Rebeca experience. In: Agha, G., Danvy, O., Meseguer, J. (eds.) Formal Modeling: Actors, Open Systems, Biological Systems. LNCS, vol. 7000, pp. 20–56. Springer, Heidelberg (2011)

39. Soundararajan, N.: Axiomatic semantics of communicating sequential processes. ACM TOPLAS **6**(4), 647–662 (1984)

40. Verbeek, F., Schmaltz, J.: Hunting deadlocks efficiently in microarchitectural models of communication fabrics. In: International Conference on Formal Methods in Computer-Aided Design (FMCAD 2011), pp. 223–231. FMCAD Inc. (2011)

41. Wong, P.Y.H., Albert, E., Muschevici, R., Proença, J., Schäfer, J., Schlatte, R.: The ABS tool suite: modelling, executing and analysing distributed adaptable object-oriented systems. STTT **14**(5), 567–588 (2012)

42. Zaharieva-Stojanovski, M., Huisman, M., Blom, S.: Verifying functional behaviour of concurrent programs. In: Proceedings of 16th Workshop on Formal Techniques for Java-Like Programs (FTfJP 2014), pp. 4:1–4:6. ACM (2014)

43. Zwiers, J.: Compositionality, Concurrency and Partial Correctness: Proof Theories for Networks of Processes, and Their Relationship. LNCS, vol. 321. Springer, Heidelberg (1989)

Regression Verification for Programmable Logic Controller Software

Bernhard Beckert[1], Mattias Ulbrich[1](✉), Birgit Vogel-Heuser[2],
and Alexander Weigl[1]

[1] Karlsruhe Institute of Technology, Karlsruhe, Germany
{beckert,ulbrich,weigl}@kit.edu
[2] Technische Universität München, Munich, Germany
vogel-heuser@ais.mw.tum.de

Abstract. Automated production systems are usually driven by Programmable Logic Controllers (PLCs). These systems are long-living – yet have to adapt to changing requirements over time. This paper presents a novel method for regression verification of PLC code, which allows one to prove that a new revision of the plant's software does not break existing intended behavior.

Our main contribution is the design, implementation, and evaluation of a regression verification method for PLC code. We also clarify and define the notion of program equivalence for reactive PLC code. Core elements of our method are a translation of PLC code into the SMV input language for model checkers, the adaptation of the coupling invariants concept to reactive systems, and the implementation of a toolchain using a model checker supporting invariant generation.

We have successfully evaluated our approach using the Pick-and-Place Unit benchmark case study.

Keywords: Regression verification · Symbolic model checking · Automated production systems · Programmable logic controllers (PLC)

1 Introduction

Motivation and Topic. Automated production systems [34], such as industrial plants and assembly lines, are usually driven by *Programmable Logic Controllers* (PLCs). These computing devices are specially tailored to controlling automated production systems in safety-critical realtime environments. A malfunction may cause severe damage to the system itself or to the payload, or even harm persons within the reach of the system.

The topic of this paper is how to formally verify correctness of the software part of such systems, i.e., the PLC. To be precise, we focus on regression verification of PLC code – as opposed to proving that the PLC code satisfies a functional specification or to proving that the whole production system works correctly. That is, we verify that a version of PLC code after an evolution step shows the same reactive input/output behavior as the old one – allowing only

© Springer International Publishing Switzerland 2015
M. Butler et al. (Eds.): ICFEM 2015, LNCS 9407, pp. 234–251, 2015.
DOI: 10.1007/978-3-319-25423-4_15

desired deviations that are formally specified. The aim of regression verification is to formally prove that existing (good) behavior is retained during system evolution. The old version serves as specification for the new one.

Our Approach and Contribution. This work contributes to the field of formal PLC verification by defining a notion of reactive conditional and reactive relational equivalence together with a proof methodology, also in the presence of environment models. Our main contribution is the design, implementation, and evaluation of a regression verification method for PLC code.

A core element of our verification method is a translation of PLC code into the SMV input language for model checkers. Using this translation on both the old and the new software revision, we can construct a formula expressing that intended behavior is retained. We target PLC code written in the two languages Structured Text (ST) and Sequential Function Chart (SFC), which are part of IEC 61131, the industry standard for PLC software [19]; an adaptation to other languages is easily possible.

A further core element is the use of a model checker supporting invariant generation. It is an important insight that this allows the automatic generation of *coupling invariants*, which are a useful tool for efficient regression verification. Accordingly, we have adapted the concept of coupling invariants to the world of reactive systems. And we have implemented our approach in a toolchain using the model checker nuXmv [9]. It supports techniques for predicate abstraction and invariant generation by interpolant inspection [7,24].

As *full* equivalence of PLC code revisions is *not* the goal in many cases, we have defined and implemented extensions where the behavior of the new code revision may deviate under certain specified conditions and in specified ways.

We have successfully evaluated our approach using the Pick-and-Place Unit, a benchmark case study for the evolution of automated production systems with several evolution scenarios [35]. We were able to demonstrate our method's feasibility for practical evolution scenarios and its ability to uncover regression bugs.

PLCs execute their software in cycles with fixed cycle time. Consequently, PLC code can only cause timing problems if its execution time exceeds the cycle time. Otherwise, the code's exact execution time is irrelevant. Thus, we assume that the cycle time constraint is ensured by other techniques, and we do not consider exact execution time in our method.

Advantages of Regression Verification for PLC Code. The main advantage of regression verification is that no functional or behavioral specification is needed (besides the old code version). In addition, regression verification is particularly well suited for the application area of software in automated production systems for the following reasons.

Automated production systems are designed for long deployment phases, often spanning several decades. But the requirements on production systems change over time. New types of products are to be manufactured. Systems are upgraded to increase throughput or to keep up with technological development. Moreover, flaws in the controlling software or the hardware design may have to be fixed. Production systems therefore frequently *evolve* during their lifetime. Thus, methods and means to safely update their hardware and software – including their PLCs – are of great importance. One has to ensure that a revision does not break existing intended behavior.

As opposed to (regression) testing, regression verification provides an equivalence proof for all possible inputs and not just for individual test cases. Also, while regression testing of PLC software requires either a hardware testbed or an executable hardware model, this is not needed for regression verification. It suffices to provide a formal description of how the hardware has changed during the evolution step (if the hardware has changed at all).

PLC systems can grow rather large, making a (non-regression) correctness verification challenging for fully automatic verification and bisimulation checkers. However, typical changes made during an evolution step are small in comparison to overall system size, so that regression verification is a much easier task.

Structure of this Paper. In Sect. 2, we present a small scenario from our case study as an introductory example. Then, in Sect. 3, we define the formal framework and introduce notions of equivalence between versions of PLC code. In Sect. 4, we discuss the use of environment models to avoid false alarms. The core part of our method, i.e., the translation itself and the toolchain are described in Sect. 5. In Sect. 6, we present the extensive case study that we used to evaluate our approach. We discuss related work in Sect. 7 and draw conclusions in Sect. 8. Some of the ideas presented in the following are adaptations of our regression verification method for imperative programs [11] to the – rather different – world of reactive automated production systems.

2 Introductory Example

As an introductory example, we present a considerably simplified version of a scenario from the case study described in Sect. 6 (see also Fig. 4). A stationary crane moves workpieces from a starting point (A) to one of two target points (B) and (C). In the original version, the plant treats all workpieces in the same way and transports them from the magazine (A) to the conveyor (B).

A new revision of the PLC software is introduced to differentiate the controller's behavior according to the type of workpiece. All metallic workpieces are now first delivered to the stamp (C) where they are treated (signal *stamped*) and are only afterwards delivered to (B). All non-metallic workpieces still go directly to (B). An additional inductive sensor (signal M) is installed at (A) to detect whether a workpiece is metallic or not.

Figure 1 shows sequential function charts (SFCs) for the two versions of the PLC program. The boxes (called *steps*) contain *actions* (blocks of code) and the *transitions* between steps are annotated with guards. In each execution cycle, one step is active and is executed. If at the end of the cycle one of the guards at an outgoing transition is satisfied, the corresponding successor step is made the active step. Otherwise the current step remains active and is repeated in the next cycle. In the example, the actions assign values to output (*Turn, Lift*) and internal variables (*metallic, stamped*). The guard conditions are Boolean input

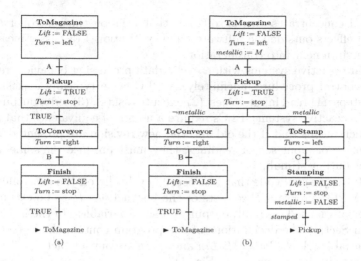

Fig. 1. Sequential Function Charts for the example. (a) Original SFC, (b) SFC after revision.

variables corresponding to sensor input (A, B, C represent input from sensors for crane position) and Boolean internal variables (*metallic*). In the original SFC, the steps correspond to the actions of moving the crane to the magazine, picking up the workpiece, moving the crane to the conveyor, and putting down the workpiece. In the revised SFC, there is a case distinction on *metallic*, and two new steps have been added to move metallic pieces to the stamp and dropping them there. After the workpiece has been stamped, the internal variable *metallic* is set to FALSE and then the step Pickup becomes active, i.e., from there on the SFC continues in the same way as if a non-metallic workpiece has just been picked up at (A).

Note that this is a simple example. In general, actions and guards can be considerably more complex and contain conditional statements and loops.

In case there are metallic workpieces, the behavior of the PLC is obviously different. But in case that only non-metallic workpieces are ever detected by sensor (M), the new software version should do the same as the old version. So this is a scenario for using regression verification to prove conditional equivalence for the unchanged case.

3   Formalizing Equivalence of PLC Programs

We define a formal framework for the behavior of reactive PLC software together with adequate notions of equivalence between them.

There are various possibilities for defining system boundaries when modeling an automated production system. One can model the whole system or only individual components. Even when focusing on the PLC, one could still include models of peripheral hardware components like connecting data buses. However, our method concentrates on the software that runs on the controller and disregards all effects outside the software for now. Section 4 discusses measures to take the environment into consideration.

PLCs are reactive systems with a cyclic data processing behavior, repeating the same control procedure indefinitely. A PLC cycle typically consists of the following steps: (1) read input values, (2) execute task(s), (3) write output values, (4) wait. As reactive systems, PLCs require a notion of equivalence that involves traces, which means that if the old and the new revision are presented with the same *sequence* of input sensor readings, they must produce the same *sequence* of actuator output stimuli.

We call the piece of code that is executed cyclically on the controller a *PLC program*. A PLC program P consists of the instructions Π to be executed and a set of declarations Δ of input, output and state variables. In the introductory example in Sect. 2, the declarations of the program contain the Boolean input (sensor) variables A, B, C and M; *Lift* and *Turn* are output (actuator) variables (the declarations are not shown in Fig. 1).

The internal state of a PLC program consists of an assignment of values to its state variables (in the example, the Boolean variable *metallic*). There is always an implicit state variable *active_step* storing which of the steps in the SFC program is active. The declarations Δ induce an input value space I, an output value space O, and state space S, each as the Cartesian product of the value ranges of the corresponding program variables. In the example, I is *bool* × *bool* × *bool* × *bool*. We assume the initial values of state variables to be determined by their declarations (using default values in case no initial value is given), i.e., the initial state $s_0 \in S$ is fixed by Δ.

Definition 1 (Semantics of PLC programs). *The semantics $\rho(P)$ of a PLC program P is a state transition function $\rho(P) : S \times I \to S \times O$.*

The semantics $\rho(P)$ depends on the instructions in Π. These may read from the state and the input variables (in S and I) and write to the state variables and to the output variables (in S and O).

To be able to consider the effects of a PLC program over time, the above definition needs to be extended to sequences of inputs and outputs. We denote infinite sequences of elements in I (ω-words) with $\bar{i} \in I^\omega$; their components are accessed using subscript indices, i.e., $\bar{i} = \langle i_1, i_2, \ldots \rangle$. The PLC program as a stateful system needs an initial state s_0 from which it is launched. As mentioned above, s_0 is determined by the variable declarations Δ.

Definition 2 (Trace Semantics of PLC Programs). *The behavior $b(P)$ of a PLC program P with initial state $s_0 \in S$ is the function $b(P) : I^\omega \to O^\omega$ defined by $b(P)(\langle i_1, i_2, \ldots \rangle) = \langle o_1, o_2, \ldots \rangle$ where $(s_n, o_n) = \rho(P)((s_{n-1}, i_n))$ for all $n \in \mathbb{N}_{\geq 1}$.*

This definition says that starting from the initial state s_0, the PLC program is executed repeatedly, applying in each cycle $\rho(P)$ to its current state s_{n-1} and the input tuple $i_n \in I$ to produce the output tuple $o_n \in O$ and the new state s_n.

Trace semantics use the internal state in the definition, but when taking an outside look at the semantics, it defines input/output behavior and does not make statements about the internal state space. This is relevant for our initial definition of equivalence where programs are required to produce identical traces.

Definition 3 (Trace Equivalent PLC Programs). *Two PLC programs P, Q whose declarations Δ_P, Δ_Q contain the same input/output variables are called* perfectly equivalent *if they produce the same output sequence when presented with the same input sequence, i.e., $b(P)(\bar{i}) = b(Q)(\bar{i})$ for all $\bar{i} \in I^\omega$.*

They are called conditionally equivalent *modulo the condition $\varphi : I^\omega \to bool$ if they produce the same result for all input sequences that satisfy condition φ, i.e., if $\varphi(\bar{i})$ then $b(P)(\bar{i}) = b(Q)(\bar{i})$ for all $\bar{i} \in I^\omega$.*

It is intuitively evident that replacing a PLC with a new revision whose program is trace equivalent to the original program does not change the observable behavior of the plant, provided everything else remains unchanged and timing effects are left aside.

Conditional equivalence relaxes the strict notion of perfect equivalence by requiring the same output sequence only if a condition φ holds. Intuitively this means that replacing a PLC with a new revision whose program is conditionally equivalent to the original program modulo φ does not change the plant's behavior at least for those traces where all sensor signal readings satisfy φ.

The example given in Sect. 2 is an example of conditional equivalence: The modified controller software (Fig. 1) is conditionally equivalent to the original version *if* every encountered workpiece is non-metallic. This condition can be expressed in Linear Temporal Logic (LTL [26]) as $\varphi_{\text{non-metallic}}(\bar{i}) = \mathbf{G} \neg M$ recalling that M is the signal from the inductive metal detection sensor.

Perfect and conditional equivalence use equality to compare input and output traces. There are many cases, however, where full equality is not required or not appropriate. Equality of outputs may not be required for outputs relating to non-critical components of the system. And equality may not be the appropriate relation if the sensors and/or actuators of the plant have been modified, and thus the input/output spaces of the program revisions are different. It is therefore necessary to generalize the equivalence notion. To this end, we introduce binary relations $\sim_{in}$ and $\sim_{out}$.

Definition 4 (Relational Equivalence of Controllers). *Two PLC programs P, Q with declarations Δ_P resp. Δ_Q are called* relationally equivalent *modulo relations $\sim_{in} \subseteq I_P^\omega \times I_Q^\omega$ and $\sim_{out} : O_P^\omega \times O_Q^\omega$ if they produce related output sequences when presented with related input sequences, i.e.,*

$$\text{if } \bar{i} \sim_{in} \bar{i}' \text{ then } b(P)(\bar{i}) \sim_{out} b(Q)(\bar{i}') \text{ for all } \bar{i} \in I_P^\omega, \bar{i}' \in I_Q^\omega.$$

Note that conditional equivalence can be expressed as relational equivalence (if $I_P = I_Q$ and $O_P = O_Q$) by choosing $(\bar{i} = \bar{i}') \wedge \varphi(\bar{i})$ for the input relation $\sim_{in}$ and $\bar{o} = \bar{o}'$ for the output relation $\sim_{out}$.

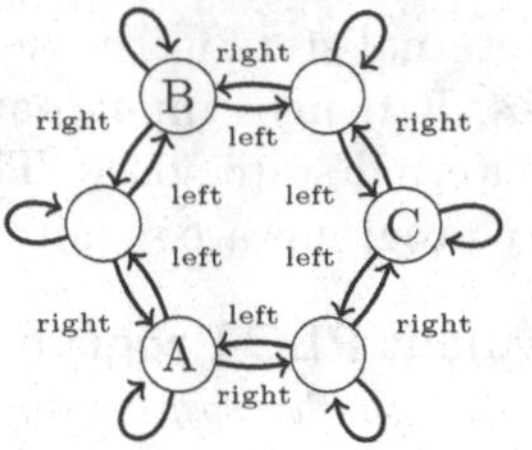

Fig. 2. Finite automaton modeling crane position sensor readings.

If a revision adds or removes existing variables from the declarations, the canonical relations to be considered are the conjoined equalities between all signals shared by both revisions (i.e., the variables in $\Delta_P \cap \Delta_Q$). This is called *projected equivalence*. The introductory example in Sect. 2 is a projected equivalence if the metallic detector is assumed absent in the first version and only introduced in the second. Another example of relational equivalence is shown in the case study in Sect. 6.

4   Environment Models to Increase Precision

False alarms can occur if the two revisions of a PLC program behave differently on input sequences that cannot actually occur in the application. For example, the crane from Sect. 2 can never be in more than one of the positions A, B, C at the same time. Assuming correctly working sensors, not more than one of the Boolean input variables A, B, C can be true at the same time. Thus, it would be irrelevant if the two program revisions were to react differently in case A and B were signaled simultaneously but would still be equivalent for all realistic inputs. It is therefore sensible to add such knowledge on the possible sensor inputs as assumptions to the process and perform a conditional regression verification. In the example, it is possible to encode the assumption in form of the LTL condition $\mathbf{G}(\neg(A \wedge B) \wedge \neg(B \wedge C) \wedge \neg(A \wedge C))$.

But in more involved cases, it is difficult or error-prone to express properties of the physical system correctly in form of temporal logic conditions on the PLC inputs. Then it is more intuitive to use a *model* of the environment taking the output of PLC program as input. This restricts the search space, increases precision of regression verification and avoids false alarms. Figure 2 depicts a model of the crane restricting the input space for the variables corresponding to the crane's position and direction. Besides the three states for positions A, B, C in which the corresponding variable is true, there are three intermediate states between the positions where none of variables is true. The crane behavior model shows that when the crane turns to the right from position A to position B, first variable A is true, then no variable is true, and then B is true. By making environment models non-deterministic (like in the example), one can abstract from details like concrete numbers of waiting cycles.

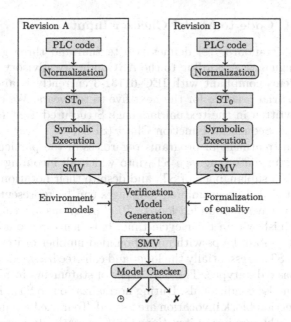

Fig. 3. Overview over the regression verification method.

One evolution scenario of the case study in Sect. 6 describes a case where the PLC program revisions are only equivalent if an environment model is used.

5 Regression Verification Method and Toolchain

This section reports on how we achieve regression verification for PLC software by construction of a verification condition from two PLC program revisions, the equivalence relations $\sim_{in}$, $\sim_{out}$, the condition φ, and environment models.

The workflow of our method – shown in Fig. 3 – covers several transformation steps. The resulting verification condition consisting of a transition system and a property is presented to a model checker that can come back with three possible results: First, it may report that the verification property holds for the transition system in which case the two PLC programs are trace equivalent (modulo the condition, relations, and environment models). Second, it may report a counterexample with a concrete (finite) input trace that leads to the equivalence violation. There are no "false positives": Every reported violation uncovers a case of unequal behavior. However, it may be that the environment is not modeled precisely enough, and that the failure is a false alarm in the sense that it cannot occur in practice with the real hardware. The variables range over finite datatypes and the model checking problem is, in theory, decidable. Depending on the size and complexity of the verification condition, it is still possible that the model checker runs out of resources (time or memory) and does not come back with an answer, which is the third possible result.

5.1   From PLC Code to Model Checker Input

The IEC 61131-3 standard [19] defines two textual and three graphical PLC programming languages. According to the ARC industry advisory group [1], the use of PLC systems compliant with IEC 61131-3 currently is and will remain the state of industrial practice for the next five to ten years. We consider input PLC programs written in the textual language Structured Text (ST) or in the graphical language Sequential Function Chart (SFC).

For a uniform treatment of programs regardless of the particular language, we define an intermediate language ST_0 into which all incoming programs are translated. ST_0 is a sublanguage of ST, and despite their notational differences, programs in all 61131-3 programming languages can be represented in it (provided they do not have unbounded loops). PLC programs are time-critical and are required to finish within their cycle time. It is hence reasonable to assume programs do not contain loops with an unbounded number of iterations.

The language ST_0 is essentially the loop- and call-free fragment of ST reduced to fewer, more basic datatypes. The only types of statements in ST_0 are assignments and if-then-else conditionals. During normalization to ST_0, loops are fully unwound and function block invocation are inlined. To make loop unwinding possible, a bound for the number of iterations must be statically computable for all loops in the code. Inlining is also feasible since recursion is not featured in the IEC 61131-3 framework.

To demonstrate our method, we implemented such translations to ST_0 for ST and SFC. The translation from SFC to ST_0 is problematic since the standard leaves many semantical issues unanswered. We resolved this issue by following the formal semantics for SFCs given in [4] when translating SFC to ST_0.

The normalized code in ST_0 is symbolically executed to derive a state transition system as model checker input. Naïve implementations of symbolic execution (or weakest precondition calculi) may produce program representations whose size is exponential in that of the original program. This is due to an explicit enumeration of all possible paths through the program. Since ST_0 programs resulting from translating SFC code involve many consecutive and nested if-statements to encode the original state machine, the number of paths through the program is huge and explicitly enumerating them is infeasible. For example, the last scenario (Ev14) of our case study (Sect. 6) yields some 13 billion paths, such that the resulting proof obligation would not fit into the available memory.

Instead we produce a smaller program representation by not explicitly enumerating all paths but following the concept of Φ-nodes (known from static single assignment [10]) to merge the effects of the branches of an if-statement. This approach is also similar to the optimized weakest-precondition-calculus from [12].

During symbolic execution, a symbolic variable map $\mathcal{V} : Vars_\Delta \rightarrow Terms_\Delta$ is updated, which assigns to all declared variables their current symbolic value (a term). $Stmt_\Delta$ denotes the set of all ST_0-statements, and $t^\mathcal{V}$ is the symbolic evaluation of an expression t in the symbolic variable assignment $\mathcal{V}$.

Definition 5 (Symbolic Execution). *Symbolic execution of ST_0 code is the operator $se : (Vars_\Delta \rightarrow Terms_\Delta) \times Stmt_\Delta \rightarrow (Vars_\Delta \rightarrow Terms_\Delta)$ with*

$$se(\mathcal{V}, v := t) := \mathcal{V}[v := t^{\mathcal{V}}] \qquad se(\mathcal{V}, S;T) := se(se(\mathcal{V}, S), T)$$
$$se(\mathcal{V}, \text{if } c \text{ then } S \text{ else } T) := \Phi(c^{\mathcal{V}}, se(\mathcal{V}, S), se(\mathcal{V}, T))$$

where the map $\Phi(c, \mathcal{V}_1, \mathcal{V}_2) : Vars_\Delta \rightarrow Terms_\Delta$ is, for all $v \in Vars_\Delta$, defined by:

$$\Phi(c, \mathcal{V}_1, \mathcal{V}_2)(v) := \begin{cases} \mathcal{V}_1(v) & \text{if } \mathcal{V}_1(v) = \mathcal{V}_2(v) \\ \text{if } c \text{ then } \mathcal{V}_1(v) \text{ else } \mathcal{V}_2(v) & \text{otherwise} \end{cases}$$

Essentially, this transformation moves the conditions of if-then-else statements into the variable assignment in form of if-then-else expressions. While this procedure cannot guarantee that the result is not exponentially larger than the input, our experiences show that the results are acceptable in practice.

The state transition system for a program P is computed as follows: The operator *se* is applied to the instructions Π of P with the identity mapping id_Δ as the starting point, resulting in the symbolic variable map $se(\Pi, id_\Delta)$. The symbolic assignments in this map provide the state transition definitions for the state variables and the output terms for the output variables.

5.2   Encoding Regression Verification

The proof obligation handed to the symbolic model checker consists of a state transition system and a property that is to be proved as an invariant for it. The state transition system is a composition of the two systems that result from translating the two PLC program revisions P and Q and the models for the environment as introduced in Sect. 4.

All variables of the input spaces I_P and I_Q make up the input variables of the combined model. If Δ_P and Δ_Q share common input variables, these can also be shared in the combined model, thus reducing the input state space size.

If the sensor readings are constrained by an environment model, the input signals of that model are input signals of the entire state transition system while input signals of the PLC programs corresponding to sensor readings are taken from the outputs of the environment model. In the example environment model for the crane positions (Fig. 2), the PLC program takes the three inputs A, B, C from position sensors, while the composed verification model merely takes as input the indeterministic choice whether to remain in the current model state or whether to move on a step. This has two effects: (1) The input space size is reduced and (2) the modeling is more precise.

The condition φ from Definition 3 and the input and output relations $\sim_{in}, \sim_{out}$ from Definition 4 make up the invariant that is part of the model checking proof obligation. In the current version of our toolchain, we require that the condition φ can be expressed in LTL by a formula of the form $\mathbf{G}\,\psi$, where ψ is a propositional formula over the input variables in I_P without modal operators. That is, it must be possible to express the desired condition on the input sequence as a property of individual inputs. Correspondingly, we require that the relations $\sim_{in}, \sim_{out}$ can be expressed by LTL formulas $\sim_{in} = \mathbf{G}\,\tau_{in}$ resp. $\sim_{out} = \mathbf{G}\,\tau_{out}$, where τ_{in} and τ_{out} are propositional formulas over the variables in $I_P \cup I_Q$ resp. $O_P \cup O_Q$. We then employ a fresh internal state variable $pre : bool$ to model the temporal condition within the invariant as follows:

$$\mathbf{init}(pre) := true \; (1) \quad \mathbf{next}(pre) := pre \wedge \psi \wedge \tau_{in} \; (2) \quad \mathbf{invariant} \; pre \rightarrow \tau_{out} \; (3)$$

The variable pre is initialized to true (1) and is invalidated (2) as soon as input values violate either the condition (ψ) or the input relation (τ_{in}). If the guarded invariant (3) holds for the transition system, then the equivalence of the two programs is guaranteed. What in fact is proved using the auxiliary variable pre is the LTL property $(\neg\psi \vee \neg\tau_{in})\,\mathbf{R}\,\tau_{out}$ stating that the output relation τ_{out} must hold at least as long as neither the condition ψ nor the relation τ_{in} have been violated ($\mathbf{R}$ is the "release" operator of LTL). This entails relational equivalence between P and Q. All relations and conditions occurring in our case study fall into the restricted category of specifications described above. Although this is not implemented at the moment, other classes of LTL constraints can be used in our method by encoding them as invariants along the lines of [27].

5.3   Coupling Invariants

Modern model checkers allow the application of state abstraction methods (like IC3) to find proofs for safety properties more efficiently. Regression verification using symbolic model checkers with such abstractions is particularly promising since the two software revisions are closely related if the newer one results from the adaptation of the older one to a new application scenario. In such cases, it is likely that the old and the new version of the program have a similar – yet not necessary equal – encoding of their state spaces.

The upcoming abstraction theorem allows us to reason about safety properties of two PLC programs P and Q using an invariant $Inv : S_P \times S_Q \rightarrow bool$ over their state spaces S_P and S_Q. Such a predicate, building a bridge between the state spaces, is called a *coupling predicate*.

Theorem 1 (Coupling Invariant Abstraction). *We consider two PLC programs P and Q with common input space I, common output space O, and state spaces S_P and S_Q. Let $s_0 \in S_P$ and $s_0' \in S_Q$ be the initial states.*

Then, P and Q are (perfectly) trace equivalent if and only if there exists a coupling predicate $Inv : S_P \times S_Q \rightarrow bool$ such that, for all states $s \in S_P, s' \in S_Q$ and inputs $i \in I$,

$Inv(s_0, s_0')$ holds, $Inv(s, s')$ implies $Inv(t, t')$, and $Inv(s, s')$ implies $o = o'$,

where $(t, o) = \rho(P)(s, i)$ and $(t', o') = \rho(Q)(s', i)$.

Similar theorems can be formulated for relationally equivalent PLC programs.

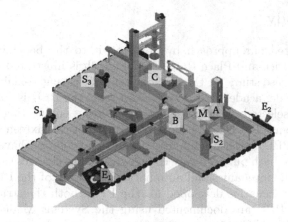

Fig. 4. Schematic of the hardware setup of the PPU case study [35].

The more similar the state space encodings of the old and the new program version are, the closer the coupling predicate is to equality on the state spaces. This becomes evident when a PLC program P is verified against itself. In this case, the equality relation itself can be used as coupling predicate and satisfies the conditions in Theorem 1 regardless of what P computes.

Development of PLC programs is often an incremental process, i.e., the new revision results from a modification of the code in the old version. Often, parts of the state are not affected by the changes (and behave like in the old revision) whereas other parts are affected. An inductive invariant implying equivalence then comprises equality between the unmodified state variables, and a more general coupling invariant must be generated only for the affected variables.

The regression verification method using invariants is complete, but the user of the verification tool would have to find and formalize all coupling invariants which can be large and unintuitive. Instead, we rely upon the capabilities of state-of-the-art symbolic model checkers to automatically infer inductive invariants. In our case, the required system invariant (3) (which usually is not inductive itself) is used as a starting point for an interpolant-based search for a stronger inductive invariant that implies the one given in the problem specification.

We show in our case study that even with large state spaces, this state abstraction mechanism allows us to prove equivalence of non-trivial programs. The model checker nuXmv is capable of coming up with the required coupling predicates using Incremental Construction of Inductive Clauses for Indubitable Correctness (IC3) [7,24]. If this invariant generation mechanism is switched off, the tool relies on more traditional symbolic model checking techniques. Then, even the smaller ones of the problems in the case study could not be solved.

In cases where the search for an inductive invariant takes too long, parts of the coupling invariant can be specified manually (within (3)) – the workload for the invariant generation can thus be shared between user and model checker.

6   Case Study

We have evaluated our approach by applying it to the benchmark evolution scenarios of the Pick-and-Place Unit (PPU), which is illustrated in Fig. 4. The PPU is an open case study for the machine manufacturing domain [35]. Despite being a bench-scale, academic demonstration case, the PPU is complex enough to demonstrate selected challenges that arise during engineering of automated production systems. To explore evolution in this context, sixteen scenarios (i.e., variants of the PPU) covering different aspects of evolution have been defined [22,36]. There are both pure software changes as well as changes that incorporate adaptations to the mechanics and automation hardware of the PPU.

For all of the scenarios developed for the PPU, both the structure and the behavior of the PPU are documented using the Systems Modeling Language (SysML) [35]. Also, IEC 61131-3 automation software code for the PLC is available for each evolution scenario – implemented in CODESYS2, an industrial development tool for automation software executable on PLCs. The PPU has 22 digital input, 13 digital output, and 3 analogue output signals and defines a number of simple discrete event automation tasks [33].

In the following, we discuss three evolution scenarios from the PPU and show how they can be subject to regression verification. More details can be found in [38]; see Table 1 for the time required for verification.

Conditional Equivalence. The evolution scenario Ev3 in [35] has been used as the introductory example in Sect. 2 in a much simplified version. In the full scenario, the new stamping hardware for metallic products brings with it a new emergency stop button E_2 (triggering the same emergency logic as the existing button E_1) and a new start switch S_3 (complementing S_1 and S_2 already present). Only after *all* start switches have been pressed, the plant starts processing workpieces. Trace equivalence between the two revisions of this evolution step can only be shown for traces where these new components do not influence the flow of signals already present in the old software. This is the case if (1) no metallic workpiece is ever detected at M. (2) button E_2 is only pressed if simultaneously E_1 is also pressed, and (3) S_3 is not activated after the other switches S_1 and S_2 have been pressed. The LTL formula over the corresponding input variables for conditional equivalence of the PLC programs is $\mathbf{G}(\neg M \ \wedge \ (E_2 \to E_1) \ \wedge \ (S_1 \wedge S_2 \to S_3))$. Using this condition, equivalence can indeed be proved by our toolchain.

Relational Equivalence. In evolution step Ev14, the three position sensors at A, B and C are replaced by a single angle transmitter that continuously reports the angular position of the crane (in degrees). The input spaces for the PLC programs differ such that relational equivalence is to be shown here.

In correspondence with the hardware setup (see Fig. 4) and the requirements of the production system, we model the relation that binds the old Boolean position inputs A, B, C to the new angular input α as

$$\mathbf{G}((A \leftrightarrow 0 \le \alpha \le 5) \wedge (B \leftrightarrow 90 \le \alpha \le 95) \wedge (C \leftrightarrow 180 \le \alpha \le 185)).$$

In the thus defined input relation $\sim_{in}$ each position switch corresponds to a 5° interval in the angular input space. This also shows that relations in our approach can be more complex than just a biunique mapping between values.

Using an Environment Model. In evolution scenario Ev6, the hardware remains unmodified, but the software is changed to optimize the handling of non-metallic workpieces (see [35] for details). The PLC programs before and after the optimization should be equivalent for traces where only metallic or only non-metallic workpieces are detected, but the programs are *not* equivalent. An inspection of the code reveals that a condition within an SFC has been reformulated. As a first guess one could assume that the two conditions are equivalent and use this as condition for the conditional equivalence proof. Indeed, the equivalence proof succeeds using that assumption (Ev6+A for both cases, Ev6+A_m for metallic and Ev6+A_{nm} for non-metallic pieces only). However, using an ad-hoc assumption about the input state is not satisfactory even if it could be justified by a manual inspection. Instead, a more intuitive and convincing item, an environment model of the crane (essentially the one shown in Fig. 2) can be added, using which the PLC programs are proven equivalent with (Ev6+AEM) and even without the assumption (Ev6+EM).

Results. Using our method and toolchain, automatic regression verification was successful for all scenarios from the PPU case study. Table 1 shows statistics for our experiments. The evolution scenarios were verified using nuXmv version 1.0.1 on an Intel Dual-Core with 2.7 GHz and 4 GB RAM running OpenSUSE 12.2.

Not all evolution scenarios include a modification of the software. The scenarios for which the equivalence verification is trivial have been omitted from the table. The verification times for the same problem on the same machine may vary considerably in multiple runs due to random choices in the symbolic model checker which have a great impact on the verification time.

The regression verification method can not only be used for verifying equivalence of PLC programs up to intended differences, but unintentional differences between programs can also be found using our approach. The evaluation of our approach revealed a few unintentional regressions in the PPU. In four cases, new intermediate code blocks are added into SFCs that cause a regression by delaying the system answer one cycle for each workpiece. Since the cycle time is very short in the PPU (4 ms), the discrepancy between the programs was not found by testing. Moreover, regression verification discovered that a fix for a safety violation was not applied to an earlier version in the PPU evolution sequence. It is possible that the crane tries to grab a workpiece while it is still in motion which might under very unfortunate circumstances cause damages.

7   Related Work

The verification of PLC programs w.r.t. temporal logic specifications (for safety, liveness, and time properties) has been subject of a number of publications

Table 1. Results of the experiments. **scenario** is the name of the evolution scenario in [35], **in** is the size of the sensor input space in bits, **state** the size of the state space in bits, **min/max** show the minimum and maximum time needed for verification using nuXmvin seconds (s), minutes (m) or hours (h). +EM indicates that an environment model has been used.

scenario	in	state	min		max		scenario	in	state	min		max	
Ev1	10	140	4	s	8	s	Ev6+EM	11	299	2	m	21	m
Ev1+EM	12	146	7	s	12	s	Ev8	20	289	13.7 m		20.9 m	
Ev2	11	141	4	s	8	s	Ev9	20	305	50.5 m		1.3 h	
Ev3	19	246	9	s	17	s	Ev10	23	365	13	s	24	s
Ev6+A	19	284	15.1 m		155.4 h		Ev11	28	576	3.5 h		6.3 h	
Ev6+A_m	19	284	8.9 m		9.1 h		Ev12	34	860	22.2 h		56.4 h	
Ev6+A_{nm}	19	284	18.1 m		13 h		Ev13	34	1225	21.9 h		21.9 h	
Ev6+AEM	11	299	25.7 m		104.1 h		Ev14	47	1663	22.1 h		22.1 h	

already. The paper [40] gives an overview of the field, and the survey [21] discusses transformation processes for program languages to verifiable models. Various translations from IEC 6113-3 languages into the input languages of model checkers have been presented: Brinksma et al. [8] present a translation of SFCs into Promela input for the SPIN model checker [17]; De Smet et al. [28] translate all languages within IEC 61131-3 into input for the symbolic model checker Cadence-SMV [25]; and Bauer et al. [3] translate SFCs into timed automata to be used with UPPAAL [5]. This model checker is also used to verify properties of continuous function charts (CFC) in [37]. In [4,6] a unifying semantics for SFC is given where the ambiguities of the standard are addressed in a formal fashion.

Süflow and Drechsler [30] present a framework to verify that the *same* program behaves equivalently on *different* PLC platforms; a scenario closely related to ours. The authors employ a SAT solver to verify the arising proof conditions.

Strichman and Godlin [13–15,29] coined the term *regression verification* and presented a verification methodology based on replacing function calls by uninterpreted function symbols within a bounded software model checking framework for C programs. In [13] they define "reactive equivalence," which is closely related to our notion of perfect trace equivalence. In earlier work [11], we presented an automated approach to regression verification based on invariant generation using Horn clauses. Many other approaches [2,16,31,32,39] exist on regression verification for imperative programming languages.

Equivalence checking is an established issue for the verification of hardware circuits. In *sequential equivalence checking* the perfect trace equivalence between clocked circuits is analysed; see [18] or [20] for an overview. Lu and Cheng [23] present an approach based on inferred invariants, conditional or relational equivalence are not considered.

8 Conclusion and Future Work

We have presented a method and toolchain for the automatic regression verification of PLC software by means of a symbolic model checker. In this process, the old software revision serves as specification for the new one. *Conditions* can be specified under which systems must behave equivalently, *relations* can be specified how the equivalence is to be understood, and *models of environment* can be added to make the process more precise.

Evaluation proved our method to be applicable to non-trivial PPC software. Automatic regression verification was successful for all scenarios from the PPU case study. The evaluation also showed that the use of Φ-nodes in the translation from PPU code to model checking input as well as the automatic generation of coupling invariants is indispensable for non-trivial programs.

Currently, our toolchain supports notions that compare PLC behavior cycle by cycle. Future work will allow for conditions and relations to relate variables of different cycles. Another interesting path of investigation is the use of abstractions to factor out parts of PLCs that have not been touched by evolution and need not be proved equivalent.

Acknowledgement. The authors thank Alberto Griggio for his valuable input on the effective use of nuXmv and Vladimir Klebanov for his feedback on an earlier version of this paper.

This work was supported by the DFG (German Research Foundation) in Priority Programme SPP1593: Design For Future – Managed Software Evolution.

References

1. ARC Advisory Group: PLC & PLC-based PAC worldwide outlook: Five year market analysis and technology forecast through 2016 (2011)
2. Barthe, G., Crespo, J.M., Kunz, C.: Relational verification using product programs. In: Butler, M., Schulte, W. (eds.) FM 2011. LNCS, vol. 6664, pp. 200–214. Springer, Heidelberg (2011)
3. Bauer, N., Engell, S., Huuck, R., Lohmann, S., Lukoschus, B., Remelhe, M., Stursberg, O.: Verification of PLC programs given as sequential function charts. In: Ehrig, H., Damm, W., Desel, J., Große-Rhode, M., Reif, W., Schnieder, E., Westkämper, E. (eds.) INT 2004. LNCS, vol. 3147, pp. 517–540. Springer, Heidelberg (2004)
4. Bauer, N., Huuck, R., Lukoschus, B., Engell, S.: A unifying semantics for sequential function charts. In: Ehrig, H., Damm, W., Desel, J., Große-Rhode, M., Reif, W., Schnieder, E., Westkämper, E. (eds.) INT 2004. LNCS, vol. 3147, pp. 400–418. Springer, Heidelberg (2004)
5. Behrmann, G., Larsen, K., Moller, O., David, A., Pettersson, P., Yi, W.: UPPAAL: present and future. In: CDC. IEEE (2001)
6. Bornot, S., Huuck, R., Lukoschus, B.: Verification of sequential function charts using SMV. In: Arabnia, H.R. (ed.) PDPTA. CSREA Press (2000)
7. Bradley, A.R.: SAT-based model checking without unrolling. In: Jhala, R., Schmidt, D. (eds.) VMCAI 2011. LNCS, vol. 6538, pp. 70–87. Springer, Heidelberg (2011)
8. Brinksma, E., Mader, A., Fehnker, A.: Verification and optimization of a PLC control schedule. STTT 4(1), 21–33 (2002)
9. Cavada, R., et al.: The nuXmv symbolic model checker. In: Biere, A., Bloem, R. (eds.) CAV 2014. LNCS, vol. 8559, pp. 334–342. Springer, Heidelberg (2014)

10. Cytron, R., Ferrante, J., Rosen, B.K., Wegman, M.N., Zadeck, F.K.: An efficient method of computing static single assignment form. In: POPL. ACM (1989)
11. Felsing, D., Grebing, S., Klebanov, V., Rümmer, P., Ulbrich, M.: Automating regression verification. In: ASE. ACM (2014)
12. Flanagan, C., Saxe, J.B.: Avoiding exponential explosion: generating compact verification conditions. In: POPL. ACM (2001)
13. Godlin, B., Strichman, O.: Inference rules for proving the equivalence of recursive procedures. Acta Informatica 45(6), 403–439 (2008)
14. Godlin, B., Strichman, O.: Regression verification. In: DAC. ACM (2009)
15. Godlin, B., Strichman, O.: Regression verification: proving the equivalence of similar programs. JSTVR 23(3), 241–258 (2013)
16. Hawblitzel, C., Kawaguchi, M., Lahiri, S.K., Rebêlo, H.: Towards modularly comparing programs using automated theorem provers. In: Bonacina, M.P. (ed.) CADE 2013. LNCS, vol. 7898, pp. 282–299. Springer, Heidelberg (2013)
17. Holzmann, G.J.: The model checker SPIN. IEEE Trans. Softw. Eng. 23(5), 279–295 (1997)
18. Huang, S.-Y., Cheng, K.-T.: Formal Equivalence Checking and Design DeBugging. Kluwer Academic Publishers, Norwell (1998)
19. International Electrotechnical Commission. IEC 61131-3: Programmable Logic Controllers - Part 3: Programming Languages (2009)
20. Kuehlmann, A., van Eijk, C.: Combinational and sequential equivalence checking. In: Hassoun, S., Sasao, T. (eds.) Logic Synthesis and Verification, pp. 343–372. Springer, New York (2002)
21. Lampérière-Couffin, S., Rossi, O., Roussel, J.-M., Lesage, J.-J.: Formal validation of PLC programs: a survey. In: ECC (1999)
22. Legat, C., Folmer, J., Vogel-Heuser, B.: Evolution in industrial plant automation: a case study. In: Industrial Electronics Society, IECON. IEEE (2013)
23. Lu, F., Cheng, K.-T.: A sequential equivalence checking framework based on k-th invariants. VLSI 17(6), 733–746 (2009)
24. McMillan, K.L.: Interpolation and SAT-based model checking. In: Hunt Jr, W.A., Somenzi, F. (eds.) CAV 2003. LNCS, vol. 2725, pp. 1–13. Springer, Heidelberg (2003)
25. McMillan, K.L.: Symbolic Model Checking. Kluwer, Norwell (1993)
26. Pnueli, A.: The temporal logic of programs. In: FOCS (1977)
27. Schuppan, V., Biere, A.: Efficient reduction of finite state model checking to reachability analysis. STTT 5(2–3), 185–204 (2004)
28. Smet, O.D., Couffin, S., Rossi, O., Canet, G., Lesage, J.-J., Schnoebelen, P., Papini, H.: Safe programming of PLC using formal verification methods. In: Int. PLCopen Conference on Industrial Control Programming (2000)
29. Strichman, O.: Regression verification: proving the equivalence of similar programs. In: Bouajjani, A., Maler, O. (eds.) CAV 2009. LNCS, vol. 5643, p. 63. Springer, Heidelberg (2009)
30. Süflow, A., Drechsler, R.: Verification of PLC programs using formal proof techniques. In: FORMS/FORMAT (2008)
31. Verdoolaege, S., Janssens, G., Bruynooghe, M.: Equivalence checking of static affine programs using widening to handle recurrences. TOPLAS 34(3) (2012). Article No. 11
32. Verdoolaege, S., Palkovic, M., Bruynooghe, M., Janssens, G., Catthoor, F.: Experience with widening based equivalence checking in realistic multimedia systems. J. Electron. Test. 26(2), 279–292 (2010)

33. Vogel-Heuser, B.: Usability experiments to evaluate UML/SysML-based model driven software engineering notations for logic control in manufacturing automation. JSEA **7**(11), 943–973 (2014)
34. Vogel-Heuser, B., Diedrich, C., Fay, A., Jeschke, S., Kowalewski, S., Wollschlaeger, M., Göhner, P.: Challenges for software engineering in automation. JSEA **7**(5), 440–451 (2014)
35. Vogel-Heuser, B., Legat, C., Folmer, J., Feldmann, S.: Researching evolution in industrial plant automation: scenarios and documentation of the pick and place unit. Technical report TUM-AIS-TR-01-14-02, TUM (2014)
36. Vogel-Heuser, B., Legat, C., Folmer, J., Rösch, S.: Challenges of parallel evolution in production automation focusing on requirements specification and fault handling. Automatisierungstechnik **62**(11), 758–770 (2014)
37. Wardana, A., Folmer, J., Vogel-Heuser, B.: Automatic program verification of continuous function chart based on model checking. In: IECON (2009)
38. Weigl, A.: Regression verification of programmable logic controller software. Master's thesis, Karlsruhe Institut of Technology, January 2015
39. Welsch, Y., Poetzsch-Heffter, A.: Verifying backwards compatibility of object-oriented libraries using Boogie. In: FTfJP. ACM (2012)
40. Younis, M.B., Frey, G.: Formalization of existing PLC programs: a survey. In: CESA (2003)

A Logical Approach for Behavioural Composition of Scenario-Based Models

Juliana Küster Filipe Bowles[1]([✉]), Behzad Bordbar[2],
and Mohammed Alwanain[2]

[1] School of Computer Science, University of St Andrews, Jack Cole Building,
North Haugh, St Andrews KY16 9SX, UK
jkfb@st-andrews.ac.uk
[2] School of Computer Science, University of Birmingham, Edgbaston,
Birmingham B15 2TT, UK
{b.bordbar,m.i.alwanain}@cs.bham.ac.uk

Abstract. As modern systems become more complex, design approaches model different aspects of the system separately. When considering (intra and inter) system interactions, it is usual to model individual scenarios using UML's sequence diagrams. Given a set of scenarios we then need to check whether these are consistent and can be combined for a better understanding of the overall behaviour. This paper addresses this by presenting a novel formal technique for composing behavioural models at the metamodel level through *exact metamodel restriction* (EMR). In our approach a sequence diagram can be completely described by a set of logical constraints at the metamodel level. When composing sequence diagrams we take the union of the sets of logical constraints for each diagram and additional behavioural constraints that describe the matching *composition glue*. A formal semantics for composition in accordance with the glue guides our model transformation to Alloy. Alloy's fully automated constraint solver gives us the solution. Our technique has been implemented as an Eclipse plugin SD2Alloy.

Keywords: Sequence diagrams · Behavioural composition · Event structures · Alloy

1 Introduction

As modern systems become more complex, design approaches model different aspects of the system separately. When considering (intra and inter) system interactions, it is usual to model individual scenarios using UML's sequence diagrams. Given a set of scenarios we then need to check whether these are consistent and can be combined for a better understanding of the overall behaviour. The overall behaviour of the system can be obtained step by step by composing individual scenario-based models.

Composing systems manually can only be done for small systems. As a result, in recent years, various methods for automated model composition have

© Springer International Publishing Switzerland 2015
M. Butler et al. (Eds.): ICFEM 2015, LNCS 9407, pp. 252–269, 2015.
DOI: 10.1007/978-3-319-25423-4_16

been introduced [4,6,13,15,18–21,23]. Most of these methods involve introducing algorithms to produce a composite model from smaller models originating from partial specifications [13]. By contrast, in this paper we focus on the composition of models via constraint solvers. This corresponds to producing a number of constraints capturing models and using an automated solver to find a solution that produces the composed model. In this paper, we use Alloy [12] for finding the solution. Using Alloy for model composition is an active area of research [19,23]. Whilst most existing research focuses on static models, the focus of this paper is on dynamic models. The proposed method in this paper consists of two steps. First, create the *logical constraints* that uniquely characterise each model by restricting the metamodels. Second, produce *behavioural constraints* for combining the models. These consist of constraints indicating how elements from both models may be matched and additional constraints such as orderings that may have to be preserved. The augmented model for the composition (if existing) needs to satisfy the *conjunction of all these constraints*. The composed model is semantically equivalent to one obtained by an enriched form of parallel composition with synchronisation and additional constraints on permitted combined behaviour. The automatic generation of such a solution is the main novelty and contribution of this paper.

In general, metamodels represent the model elements and their relationships. Logical statements written in the context of metamodels play a key role in expressing the well-definedness of model elements, defining model equality, and so on. We extend the use of logical constraints and for a given model we produce further constraints to *uniquely* determine the model. We refer to the process of identifying such logical constraints as *Exact Metamodel Restriction* (EMR). As we show in this paper, EMR can be used in the automated instantiation of models via constraint solvers. For example, in [2] starting from any UML sequence diagram, using the Alloy model finder for the sequence diagram metamodel and correct set of constraints, Alloy can be used to automatically recreate the original sequence diagram. Given any two models M_1 and M_2 representing two partial specifications (e.g., two sequence diagrams), through EMR we produce two sets of constrains $\mathcal{L}_1$ and $\mathcal{L}_2$ on their metamodels that uniquely identify them. To compose the two models we may require *all* constraints in the two sets to be true. This would be a very restrictive form of composition. Instead we give the designer a novel way to influence the obtained composition by specifying behaviour that should never occur or sequences of events that must occur in a given order. In other words, it allows the designer to prioritise on specified behaviour. We refer to these additional constraints as *behavioural composition glue* and present a formal semantics for it.

The notion of glue is not new and is also used within software architecture to describe and formalise component connectors [1,8]. Our interpretation of glue here is nonetheless more generic and not only a syntactic matching between component elements. Our behavioural glue gives us a new set of constraints $\mathcal{L}_g$ which specifies how the models should be *glued* together to produce the intended composition. Given the sets of constraints $\mathcal{L}_1$, $\mathcal{L}_2$ and $\mathcal{L}_g$, and provided there are no conflicts between them, the models can be composed automatically using Alloy. If there are conflicts between the constraints, Alloy will point out the conflicting statements so that we can redesign the models or the constraints used for the composition. Although the focus of work is on sequence diagrams, the suggested method can be applied to all models with a trace-based semantics. We have applied the method to sequence diagrams and produced an Eclipse plugin which was described in [2]. This work considerably extends the work in [2] by going beyond composition based on syntactic matching of model elements and focusing on the formalisation of *behavioural glue* for composition.

The paper is organised as follows. Section 2 describes interactions in UML and introduces an example which is used throughout the paper to illustrate our approach. Section 3 introduces labelled event structures (LES), our semantic interpretation of interactions and a guide to the correct composition solution. Section 4 shows the transformation into Alloy. Composition is treated with LES in Sect. 5 and with Alloy in Sect. 6. Related work is described in Sect. 7. Section 8 concludes the paper.

2   Interactions in UML

Sequence diagrams are described in UML's superstructure specification [17] both through a *concrete* and an *abstract syntax*. The concrete syntax consists of the graphical notation for a sequence diagram, whereas the abstract syntax is given by a metamodel which defines all the elements of a sequence diagram model and their possible relationships. An *instance* of the metamodel corresponds to a concrete sequence diagram.

Concrete Syntax: An interaction captured by a sequence diagram involves a group of objects which exchange messages between each other to achieve a particular goal. Each object has a vertical dashed line called *lifeline* showing the existence of the object at a particular time. Points along the lifeline are called *locations* (a terminology borrowed from LSCs [11]) and denote the occurrence of events. The order of locations along a lifeline is significant denoting, in general, the order in which the corresponding events occur. An *interaction* between several objects consists of one or more messages, but may be given further structure through so-called *interaction fragments*. There are several kinds of interaction fragments including **seq** (sequential behaviour), **alt** (alternative behaviour), **par** (parallel behaviour), **neg** (forbidden behaviour), **assert** (mandatory behaviour), **loop** (iterative behaviour), and so on [17].

Consider the following sequence diagrams which show a slightly adapted example from [10]. Figure 1 (left) shows an interaction with two consecutive interaction fragments (a parallel followed by an alternative fragment), and Fig. 1 (right) shows a different interaction involving the same instances and a few additional messages.

In both diagrams, all messages are sent asynchronously between objects a and b (only message *new* is sent by b to a). The locations along the lifeline of object a are shown explicitly in both diagrams. The importance of locations is

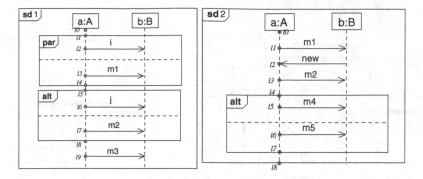

Fig. 1. Two sequence diagrams with fragments involving the same object instances.

described later in the paper. In particular, the distinction between the syntactic notion of a location on a sequence diagram from its semantic counterpart of an event will be clarified. In Fig. 1 messages i and m_1 are sent/received in parallel followed by message j or message m_2 (alternative), and further followed by message m_3 (irrespective of the previous alternative choosen). In Fig. 1, three messages are sent/received before reaching an alternative fragment and choosing between messages m_4 or m_5. These diagrams will be used to show how we can compose diagrams under certain constraints.

Abstract Syntax: A metamodel can be understood as a model of a collection of models. A metamodel is usually a structural model given as a UML class diagram often with additional constraints given in UML's constraint language OCL. Metamodels can be built for both static and dynamic models but focus only on the structural aspects of the model. In this paper we look at sequence diagrams. The metamodel of a sequence diagram, also known as an interaction, shows the structure of such a diagram in terms of the model elements present and their relationships. The dynamic interpretation is not given in the metamodel, and must be defined separately. See ours in Sect. 3.

The UML superstructure specification [17] defines the interaction's metamodel in a package showing different elements and their relationships separately in different diagrams. To make the presentation simpler, we use a subset of the metamodel for interactions and show it as one class diagram in Fig. 2. We capture the main notions that we need for the present paper.

An `Interaction` contains zero or more instances of `Lifeline`, `Message` and `InteractionFragment`. A `Message` usually has a `sendEvent MessageEnd` and a `receiveEvent MessageEnd` associated to it. In the present paper, we assume that `MessageEnd` (an abstract class) is always a special kind of `Occurrence Specification` called `MessageOccurrenceSpecification` (not shown). It is possible for a `Message` to have been *found*, or similarly *lost*, in which case it does not have a `sendEvent` or a `receiveEvent`. A `Message` cannot be simultaneously found and lost. A `Message` has attributes `messageKind` and `messageSort` (not shown in the diagram). These attributes have a type with the same name which are

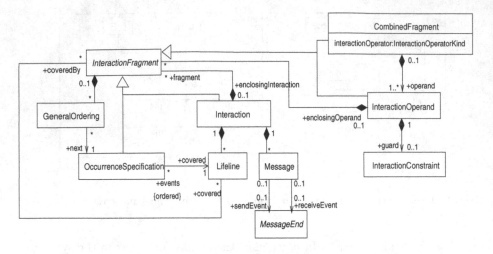

Fig. 2. The interactions metamodel.

enumeration types used to indicate whether a message is lost, found, complete or unknown (`MessageKind`), or a synchronous/asynchronous call, create `Message` and so on (`MessageSort`). A `Lifeline` has attributes for the `name` and `class` associated to the object that is denoted by the lifeline (not shown in the diagram). An `InteractionFragment` is an abstract class which is further specialised into an `OccurrenceSpecification`, an `Interaction`, a `CombinedFragment` or an `InteractionOperand`. The *locations* mentioned in Sect. 2 correspond to instances of `OccurrenceSpecification`. These are the ordered events that cover a `Lifeline`. A `GeneralOrdering` represents a binary relation between two `Occurrence Specifications`. The metamodel contains relations `before` and `after`, but we restrict ourselves to a relation `next` which is all we require for our purposes. A `CombinedFragment` has an attribute `interactionOperator` of enumeration type `InteractionOperatorKind` (par, alt, seq, loop, assert, and so on), and contains one or more `operands` which are `InteractionOperands`. An `InteractionOperand` may have a `guard` which is an `InteractionConstraint`. An `InteractionOperand` encloses either several `OccurrenceSpecifications`, an `Interaction` or another `CombinedFragment` indicating nesting of fragments.

An instance of the metamodel represents a concrete interaction or sequence diagram. The interaction from Fig. 1 can be captured using the abstract syntax as an instance of the metamodel (not shown here).

We have developed a tool **SD2Alloy** that takes a sequence diagram described by its abstract syntax and transforms it into an Alloy model. Alloy [12] is a declarative textual modeling language based on first-order relational logic. Alloy is supported by a fully automated constraint solver **Alloy Analyzer** which enables the analysis of system properties by searching for instances of the model. It is possible to check whether certain properties of the system are present. This is achieved via an automated translation of the model into a Boolean expression, which is then analysed by SAT solvers such as SAT4J [5] embedded within the Alloy Analyzer.

3   Semantics of Interactions

The dynamic interpretation of interactions is done in this paper using labelled event structures [22]. Several possible semantics for sequence diagrams have been defined (see [16] for an overview). Labelled event structures (LESs) are very suitable to describe the traces of execution in sequence diagrams being able to capture directly the notions available such as sequential, parallel and iterative behaviour (or the unfoldings thereof) as well as nondeterminism. For each of the notions we use one of the relations available over events: causality, nondeterministic choice and true concurrency. LESs are the only true-concurrent semantics for sequence diagrams available and first defined in [14]. We recall the main notions used for modelling sequence diagrams with LES. We later extend our semantics to model composition of diagrams with glue constraints.

   Prime event structures [22], or event structures for short, describe distributed computations as event occurrences together with binary relations for expressing causal dependency (called *causality*) and nondeterminism (called *conflict*). The causality relation implies a (partial) order among event occurrences, while the conflict relation expresses how the occurrence of certain events excludes the occurrence of others. From the two relations defined on the set of events, a further relation is derived, namely the *concurrency* relation *co*. Two events are concurrent if and only if they are completely unrelated, i.e., neither related by causality nor by conflict. The formal definition as defined for instance in [22] is as follows.

Definition 1. *An* event structure *is a triple* $E = (Ev, \rightarrow^*, \#)$ *where Ev is a set of events and* $\rightarrow^*, \# \subseteq Ev \times Ev$ *are binary relations called* causality *and* conflict, *respectively. Causality* $\rightarrow^*$ *is a partial order. Conflict $\#$ is symmetric and irreflexive, and propagates over causality, i.e.,* $e\#e' \rightarrow^* e'' \Rightarrow e\#e''$ *for all* $e, e', e'' \in Ev$. *Two events $e, e' \in Ev$ are concurrent, $e \: co \: e'$ iff* $\neg(e \rightarrow^* e' \vee e' \rightarrow^* e \vee e\#e')$.

   We omit further technical details on the model, but note that for the application of event structures as a semantic model for sequence diagrams we use *discrete* event structures. Discreteness imposes a finiteness constraint on the model, i.e., there are always only a finite number of causally related predecessors to an event, known as the *local configuration* of the event (written $\downarrow e$). A further motivation for this constraint is given by the fact that every execution has a starting point or configuration.

   Event structures are enriched with a labelling function $\mu : Ev \rightarrow L$ that maps each event onto an element of the set L. This labelling function is necessary to establish a connection between the semantic model (event structure) and the syntactic model (here a sequence diagram). The labelling function used here is a partial function. Intuitively, each location marked along a lifeline of an object in a sequence diagram corresponds to one (possibly more) event(s) in the labelled event structure. The set of labels used could be the set of locations in a sequence diagram but is usually more concrete information on what the location represents: the initialisation of an object, sending/receiving a message, beginning/ending an interaction fragment, etc.

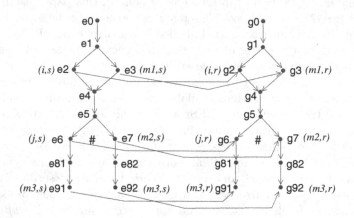

Fig. 3. Model for sequence diagram sd1.

Let I denote the set of objects involved in the interaction described by sequence diagram SD, and Mes the set of asynchronous messages exchanged. Let the set of labels L be given by $L = \{(m, s), (m, r) \mid m \in Mes\}$. An event with label (m, s) corresponds to the sending of message m whereas an event with label (m, r) indicates the receipt of message m.

Definition 2. *A model $M_{SD} = (E, \mu)$ for a sequence diagram SD is obtained by composition of the models $M_a = (E_a, \mu_a)$ of each object instance $a \in I$. In M_{SD}, the set of events is given by $Ev = \bigcup_{a \in I} Ev_a$, and event labels are as before, that is, $\mu(e) = \mu_a(e)$ for $e \in Ev_a$. Let m be a message sent between object a and object b, and let $E_1 \subseteq Ev_a$ with $\mu_a(e_1) = (m, s)$ for all $e_1 \in E_1$, and $E_2 \subseteq Ev_b$ with $\mu_b(e_2) = (m, r)$ for all $e_2 \in E_2$. Then necessarily $|E_1| = |E_2|$ and for each $e_1 \in E_1$ there is a unique $e_2 \in E_2$ for each e_1 such that $e_1 \rightarrow e_2$ and local conflict $\#_a$ propagates over $\rightarrow$ to obtain conflict $\#$ in M.*

More details on the semantics of sequence diagrams using LES can be found in [14].

The overall event structure model for the diagram from Fig. 1 is given in Fig. 3. Conflict propagation is not shown explicitly but is as expected and propagates over the new causality relations gained from communication. For example, $e_6 \#_a e_7$ and consequently $e_6 \# e_7$. In addition, since $e_7 \rightarrow g_7$ by conflict propagation we also have $e_6 \# g_7$.

Definition 3. *Let* $M_{SD} = (E, \mu)$ *be a model for sequence diagram* SD *where* $E = (Ev, \to^*, \#)$ *is an event structure. A subset of events* $C \subseteq Ev$ *is a con-figuration in* E *iff it is both (1) conflict free: for all* $e, e' \in C, \neg(e \# e')$ *and (2) downwards closed: for any* $e \in C$ *and* $e' \in Ev$, *if* $e' \to^* e$ *then* $e' \in C$. *A maximal configuration denotes a trace.*

For example, the following is a trace for Fig. 3: $C = \{e_0, e_1, e_2, e_3, e_4, e_5, e_7, e_{82}, e_{92}, g_0, g_1, g_2, g_3, g_4, g_5, g_7, g_{82}, g_{92}\}$ which denotes the occurrence of m_2 and not j.

4   Exact Metamodel Restriction

We propose a method that considers both the structure and dynamic interpre-tation of a sequence diagram when producing an Alloy model. The model is obtained by *exact metamodel restriction*, that is, by considering the abstract syntax of a diagram and constraints obtained from the dynamic (LES based) interpretation we generate the exact solution in Alloy that corresponds to the intended sequence diagram. This approach is also used to obtain a composed model for two (or more) sequence diagrams later on.

Alloy's syntax and semantics will be apparent in the following rules and code snippets, but we recall some main notions beforehand. Data domains are defined using signatures (keyword `sig`) and represented as sets. Just as in object-oriented languages, a signature may extend another signature, in which case the domain defined by the first is a subset of the domain of the extended signature. A signa-ture that is declared independently of any other is called a *top-level* signature. Extensions of a signature are mutually disjoint, as are top-level signatures. A signature can also be `abstract` in which case its domain only contains elements that belong to its extending signatures. In addition, signatures may contain fields which are captured by relations. Axioms in Alloy are called `facts` which can be given a name. These must hold at any time. Alloy formulae often use the atomic predicate `in` (inclusion), standard connectives from first-order logic, and quanti-fiers `all` (universal) and `some` (existential). In general, expressions in Alloy are built using set theoretical relational operators and constants.

All interaction metamodel elements of Fig. 2 are transformed into top-level signatures in Alloy, and separate transformation rules treat each one. We omit the basic rules for Lifeline, Message and Event (denoting `Occurrence Specification`). It suffices to say that the lifeline transformation rule cre-ates a domain called `Lifeline` as an abstract signature. Furthermore, each lifeline object has fields `name` and `class`. For each concrete instance declared in a sequence diagram we obtain declarations. The `Event` signature has a field `cover` which corresponds to a relationship with a lifeline it belongs to, and a field `next` which corresponds to a relationship with a set of events. This rela-tionship corresponds to the *immediate* causality relation from our labelled event structures. The `Message` signature has two fields `send` and `receive` both cor-responding to one event. We have additional facts to indicate the order of the events associated to a message. Messages also have a name which are introduced when creating a concrete message as shown below.

```
1 one sig sd1_i extends Message {name:one i}
2 one sig sd1_m1 extends Message {name:one m1}
3 lone sig sd1_m2 extends Message {name:one m2}
4 lone sig sd1_j extends Message {name:one j}
5 one sig sd1_m3 extends Message {name:one m3}
```

The lines above show the declaration of the messages from **sd1** (see Fig. 1 on the left). In Alloy, we cannot have two signatures with the same name. Since messages may be repeated accross different sequence diagrams we avoid this problem by adding the information from which diagram it belongs to, in this case **sd1**. Similarly for **sd2**.

```
one sig sd2_m1 extends Message {name:one m1}
one sig sd2_m2 extends Message {name:one m2}
```

Some of the messages (lines 3–4 above) are declared as **lone** (a multiplicity keyword in Alloy meaning 0 or 1), while others are **one** (exactly one). This has to do with the fact that messages within an alternative fragment are not guaranteed to occur. We will explain this in more detail later on.

```
6  lone sig e2 extends Event{}
7  lone sig e3 extends Event{}
8  lone sig e6 extends Event{}
9  lone sig e7 extends Event{}
10 lone sig e9 extends Event{}
11 lone sig g2 extends Event{}
12 lone sig g3 extends Event{}
13 lone sig g6 extends Event{}
14 lone sig g7 extends Event{}
15 lone sig g9 extends Event{}
16
17
18 //assigning events to messages
19 fact {sd1_i.send=e2 and sd1_i.receive=g2 and
20       sd1_m1.send=e3 and sd1_m1.receive=g3 and
21       sd1_j.send=e6 and sd1_j.receive=g6 and
22       sd1_m2.send=e7 and sd1_m2.receive=g7 and
23       sd1_m3.send=e9 and sd1_m3.receive=g9}
```

Lines 6–15 above declare the **sd1** events corresponding to sending/receiving a message. All events are declared as **lone** as their occurrence is dependent on whether the associated message is sent/received. For consistency, we use the same event names as used in our semantic model for the same diagram (see Fig. 3). Incidentally, we do not need to duplicate events **e9** and **g9** since Alloy will produce two solutions to represent the two possible alternative executions. In order to associate messages and events, we add a **fact** in line 19 to specify this. The following **fact EventToLifeline** connects the model events to the lifelines.

```
25 fact EventToLifeline{
26    e2.cover=L1 and g2.cover=L2 and e3.cover=L1
27    ...
28    e9.cover =L1 and g9.cover =L2  }
```

Rule 1 - Combined Fragment: A combined fragments has an interaction operator (given by `type`) and one or more interaction operands. An interaction operand covers a set of Events, CombinedFragments, or both.

```
29  abstract sig CombinedFragment{
30      operand:set InteractionOperand,type:one CF_TYPE}
31
32  abstract sig InteractionOperand
33  {cover:set Event + CombinedFragment }
34
35  fact{all e:Event| lone op:InteractionOperand |
36                    e in op.cover }
37
38  fact{all cf:CombinedFragment |
39     lone op:InteractionOperand | cf in op.cover }
40
41  fact{all op:InteractionOperand |
42     one cf:CombinedFragment | op in cf.operand }
```

Lines 29–33 define the abstract signatures for combined fragments and interaction operators with the fields mentioned. Fragment nesting is given by the fact that an `InteractionOperator` may cover a `CombinedFragment`. In addition, three facts impose further constraints on the elements of these domains. Fact on line 35 states that every event `e` belongs to at most one `InteractionOperand`, and fact on line 38 states that every combined fragment `cf` belongs to at most one interaction operand (indicating fragment nesting). Finally, fact in line 41 states that all interaction operands are operands of a combined fragment.

Rule 2 - Alternative Fragment:

```
43  // alt: exactly one operand will be executed
44  fact Alt-Execution {all cf: CombinedFragment |
45  (cf.TYPE = cf_TYPE_ALT) => # cf.operand = 1}
```

In order to preserve the semantics of alternative combined fragments, the fact above states that exactly one operand is executed. Note the `#` in line 44 corresponds to Alloy's cardinality operator. A consequence of this fact is that every time we run the code a different set of events (associated with a particular operand) may be executed, but every time we only execute one operand of an alternative fragment.

The Alloy code lines below describe an alternative fragment with two operands and no guards, as is the case of the second combined fragment from `sd1` of Fig. 1.

```
46  one sig sd1_CF2 extends CombinedFragment{}
47  lone sig sd1_CF2_Op1 extends InteractionOperand{}
48  lone sig sd1_CF2_Op2 extends InteractionOperand{}
49  fact{all cf: sd1_CF2 | cf.TYPE = CF_TYPE_ALT }
```

At the model elements level, the first step is to define the combined fragment and its operands (lines 46–49). Notice the `lone` keyword at the beginning of the operand signatures. This is necessary as only one operand will be able to execute in accordance with the fact `Alt-Execution` (line 44). Line 48 specifies the type of `sd1_CF2` (the second combined fragment of `sd1`) as an alternative fragment.

```
50 fact OperandToCF{
51 sd1_CF2_Op1 in sd1_CF2.operand
52 sd1_CF2_Op2 in sd1_CF2.operand }
53
54 fact  EventToCF{
55 e6 in sd1_CF2_Op1.cover and g6 in sd1_CF2_Op1.cover
56 and e7 in sd1_CF2_Op2.cover and
57 g7 in sd1_CF2_Op2.cover}
```

The fact `OperandToCF` connects each operand of the second combined fragment of `sd1` to its combined fragment, while the fact `EventToCF` connects the events declared earlier belonging to this combined fragment to the corresponding operands.

Rule 3 - Parallel Fragment: The representation of a parallel combined fragment is similar to that of an alternative combined fragment, but without the fact `Alt-Execution`. The Alloy model for `sd1`, which contains a parallel combined fragment, must show a parallel execution of its operands. In other words, the events covered by different operands can occur in an arbitrary order in accordance with our LES interpretation.

To capture the notion of `GeneralOrdering` from the metamodel where it captures a binary relationship between two instances of `OcurrenceSpecification`, here events, is as follows.

Rule 4 - GeneralOrder: A GeneralOrdering represents a binary relationship between two events. This is specified in Alloy by a fact specifying the order in which all messages and their underlying events occur along the lifelines of the corresponding object instances. The transitive closure of the general ordering is irreflexive.

```
58 fact GeneralOrder {
59
60 all   l: L1 + L2, ev1:sd1_cf1.operand.cover,
61         ev2:sd1_cf2.operand.cover | ev1.cover = l
62           and ev2.cover = l => ev2 in ev1.^next
63 and
64 all   l: L1,   ev1:sd1_cf2.operand.cover,
65    ev2:e9 |   ev1.cover = l =>   ev2 in  ev1.^next
66 and
67 all   l: L2,   ev1:sd1_cf2.operand.cover,
68    ev2:g9 |   ev1.cover = l => ev2 in   ev1.^next
69 }
```

In the above fact we make use of the unary operator $^\wedge$c to denote the transitive closure of c. The fact `GeneralOrder` depicts the order of the element in the `sd1` Fig. 1. Lines 60–62 state that all events `ev1` and `ev2` such that `ev1` belongs to the first combined fragment and `ev2` belongs to the second combined fragment, if they cover the same lifeline then `ev2` belongs to the transitive closure of `ev1.next`, that is, it necessarily occurs after `ev1`. Note that `ev1` $\neq$ `ev2` since they are elements from different extensions of `CombinedFragment` and necessarily disjoint in Alloy. Lines 64–68 show that the occurrence of an event `e9` or `g9` must be preceded by the occurrence of events covered by the second combined fragment. In other words, sending/receiving message `m3` can only occur if the combined fragments have executed beforehand.

5   Semantics of Composition

We define the semantics of composition for sequence diagrams in the context of labelled event structures. We restrict ourselves to the composition of two diagrams. The case for the composition of a finite number of diagrams can be generalised from here. In the sequel, let SD_1 and SD_2 be two sequence diagrams, with sets of instances and messages given by I_1, I_2, Mes_1 and Mes_2 respectively.

When composing diagrams SD_1 and SD_2 we consider *interleaving* and *shared behaviour*. In the case of interleaving, the diagrams evolve completely autonomously of one another. That is, the *interleaving* of diagrams SD_1 and SD_2 is written $SD_1 \parallel SD_2$ and equivalent to $par(SD_1, SD_2)$. In other words, the composition is behaviourally equivalent to a diagram with a par fragment and two operands where each operand contains the behaviour described in SD_1 and SD_2 respectively.

The model for $SD_1 \parallel SD_2$, $M_{SD_1 \parallel SD_2} = (E, \mu)$, is an event structure where $Ev = Ev_1 \cup Ev_2$, all relations are preserved, and $\mu(e)$ is defined for all e iff $\mu_i(e)$ is defined for some $i \in \{1, 2\}$ in which case $\mu(e) = \mu_i(e)$. For shared instances $o \in I_1 \cap I_2$ we further match the initial events for o in Ev_1 and Ev_2. Recall that an *initial event* for an object is an event for which $\downarrow e = \{e\}$ which means that the local configuration only contains itself (cf. Sect. 3). We use $\downarrow Ev_o$ to indicate the singleton containing the initial event of instance o.

The composition of diagrams with *shared behaviour* is written $SD_1 \parallel_G SD_2$ where G indicates the *composition glue*. In this paper we go beyond a syntactic matching of objects and/or messages from the different diagrams. We assume that the composition glue can in addition impose restrictions on the occurrences of messages, their ordering, and so on. The case of basic syntactic matching was treated informally in [2] and we cover *behavioural* composition glue here which subsumes syntactic matching.

We define the composition of two models formally in two stages. First we define the model obtained by syntactic matching of objects and messages of both models. We then take the glue constraints and apply a restriction on the matched composed model that satisfies the glue constraints.

Let $\Delta \subseteq L_1 \times L_2 \cup I_1 \times I_2$ be a binary relation over labels or instances satisfying if $(l, l') \in \Delta$ and $(l, l'') \in \Delta$ then $l' = l''$; and if $(l', l) \in \Delta$ and $(l'', l) \in \Delta$ then $l' = l''$. We call Δ a *matching* over labels and instances. Let $\overline{Ev_1}$ (and similarly $\overline{Ev_2}$) correspond to the set of events in Ev_1 with a label not matched in Δ.

Definition 4. *Let* $M_1 = (E_1, \mu_1)$ *and* $M_2 = (E_2, \mu_2)$ *be models for sequence diagrams* SD_1 *and* SD_2, *and* Δ *be a matching over labels and instances.* $SD_1 \parallel_\Delta SD_2$ *is a* matched composition model *for* Δ *given by* $M_\Delta = (E, \mu)$ *such that events in* M_Δ *are given by*

$$Ev = \overline{Ev_1} \cup \overline{Ev_2} \cup$$

$$\{(e_1, e_2) | (L(e_1), L(e_2)) \in \Delta\} \cup$$

$$\{(e_1, e_2) | (e_1 \in \downarrow Ev_{i_1}, e_2 \in \downarrow Ev_{i_2} \text{ and } (i_1, i_2) \in \Delta)\}$$

The labels are unchanged, that is, $\mu(e) = \mu_i(e)$ for $e \in \overline{Ev}_i$ with $i \in \{1,2\}$ and $\mu(e_1, e_2) = \mu_1(e_1) = \mu_2(e_2)$. Event relations in M_Δ are derived from the relations in M_1 and M_2 as follows $(e_1, e_2) \rightarrow^* e$ iff $(e_1 \rightarrow_1^* e$ or $e_2 \rightarrow_2^* e)$; $e_i \rightarrow e_i'$ iff $e_i \rightarrow_i^* e_i'$; and $(e_1, e_2) \rightarrow^* (e_1', e_2')$ iff $(e_1 \rightarrow_1^* e_1'$ and $e_2 \rightarrow_2^* e_2')$. Similarly for the conflict relation with additional conflict derived from propagation over causality.

According to the above definition, the event pairs (e_1, e_2) in Ev correspond to events matched by Δ or denoting initial events for shared objects. Relations and labels are preserved in the composition as expected.

If the model obtained above is a valid labelled event structure then a composition for SD_1 and SD_2 according to Δ exists. Otherwise the models are not composable.

Proposition 1. *Let $M_1 = (E_1, \mu_1)$ and $M_2 = (E_2, \mu_2)$ be models for sequence diagrams SD_1 and SD_2, and Δ be a matching over instances and labels. The diagrams are* composable *according to Δ iff the matched composition model $M_\Delta = (E, \mu)$ is a well defined labelled event structure.*

A case that illustrates a non composable model is one where the same two messages (say m_1 and m_2) are sent in the reverse order in two diagrams. The model obtained by matching the respective send/receive events in both diagrams would lead to an invalid labelled event structure as the model would contain a cycle which is not allowed. We illustrate the idea of shared behaviour further with the example from Sect. 2 to obtain the composition of **sd1** of Fig. 1. We consider the matching of messages and lifelines with the same name, i.e., messages **m1** and **m2**, and lifelines for object **a** and object **b**. There is a matched composition model M_Δ for **sd1** and **sd2** as shown in Fig. 4. It shows the matched initial events (e.g., (e_0, f_0)) and events matched by Δ (e.g., (e_3, f_1) for label (m_1, s)). Event relations are derived from the original relations and any conflict that arises from propagation over the extended causality relation. In this case, $e_6 \#(e_7, f_3)$ since $e_6 \# e_7$ and consequently also $e_6 \# f_4$, and so on.

We want to allow a designer to add further constraints on the expected composition by for example specifying behaviour that should never occur (forbidden events) or sequences of events that must occur in a given order, and so on. This can be seen as a way to give priority to certain specified interactions, and eliminates some of the possible traces in the composed model.

In the following, let $M_1 = (E_1, \mu_1)$ and $M_2 = (E_2, \mu_2)$ be composable models over Δ for sequence diagrams SD_1 and SD_2 with Δ a matching over labels and instances. Let $M_\Delta = (E, \mu)$ be the matched composed model obtained, and Γ be the set of maximal configurations (traces) in M_Δ.

Definition 5. *A behavioural glue for $M_\Delta = (E, \mu)$ is given by $G = (Ev_g, \rightarrow_g^*, \#_g, Fv_g)$ where $Ev_g, Fv_g \subseteq Ev$ are subsets of events that occur in E, and $\rightarrow_g^*, \#_g \subseteq Ev_g \times Ev_g$ are binary relations (causality and conflict) defined over the events in Ev_g. Events in Fv are forbidden events.*

A behavioural glue G as defined above may contain relations over events which disagree with the relations in M_Δ. However, we can always obtain an

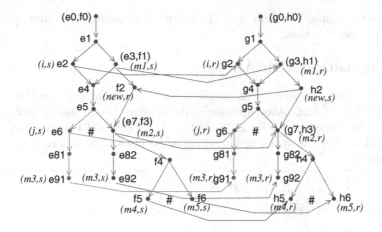

Fig. 4. Matched composition model.

equivalent glue G' that preserves the relations in $M_\Delta = (E, \mu)$ by considering all the events that violate the original relations as forbidden events. We omit a formal proof here, but illustrate the idea with an example.

Definition 6. *A composed model* $SD_1 \|_G SD_2$ *for relation preserving glue* G *is given by* $M_G = (E_G, \mu_G)$ *such that it corresponds to* M_Δ *by removing all traces* $t \in \Gamma$ *such that* $Fv \cap t \neq \emptyset$.

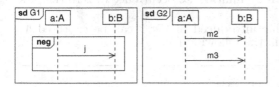

Fig. 5. Examples of behavioural glue.

Consider the two cases of behavioural glue as shown in Fig. 5. The behavioural glue G1 imposes that the occurrence of message j is forbidden in the composed model. Glue G2 imposes that for m3 to occur, m2 must have happened before.

For G1 we have $G_1 = (\emptyset, \emptyset, \emptyset, \{e_6, g_6\})$ where the events associated to message j are forbidden. This means that the composed model for sd1 and sd2 wrt G1 removes all traces which contain events e_6 and g_6 from the matched composition model shown in Fig. 4. Since the events in $\downarrow e_5$ (and similarly $\downarrow g_5$) belong to another valid trace they are not removed. We obtain a composed model which is identical to the matched composition model but where the highlighted relations and events have been removed (i.e., events $e_6, e_{81}, e_{91}, g_6, g_{81}, g_{91}$ and relations).

For G2 we consider an equivalent glue which preserves the relations, namely $G_2 = (Ev_{g2}, \to^*_{g2}, \emptyset, Fv_{g2})$ where $Ev_{g2} = \{(e_7, f_3), (g_7, h_3), e_{92}, g_{92}\}$, $Fv_{g2} = \{e_{91}, g_{91}\}$ and the causality relation is such that $\to^*_{g2} = \{((e_7, f_3), e_{92}), ((g_7, h_3), g_{92})\}$. In this case we need to remove all traces which contain e_{91} and g_{91} from the matched composition model shown in Fig. 4. The composed model for sd1 and sd2 wrt G2 coincides with the composed model wrt G1 described earlier. This follows because the traces affected by the forbidden

events are the same. We show how the model is generated automatically with
Alloy in the next section.

6 Composition with Alloy

We describe how the formal composition semantics from the previous section
is integrated in our SD2Alloy approach. We capture the syntactic matching of
labels and instances (given by Δ in Sect. 5) by additional axioms (facts). The
following describes the syntactic matching of labels and instances (lifelines) for
our example.

```
fact LifelineMatching{
//matching lifelines from sd1 and sd2
all l1:sd1_L1, l2:sd2_L2 |
(l1.name=l2.name && l1.class=l2.class) => #l2=0
}
fact  MessageMatching{
//matching message sd1_m1 and sd2_m1
all m:sd1_m1, n: sd2_m1 |
(m.name=n.name) => #n=0 and #sd2_e3=0 and #sd2_g3=0

//matching message sd1_m2 and sd2_m2
all m:sd1_m2, n:sd2_m2 |
(m.name =n.name) => #n= 0 and #sd2_e7=0 and #sd2_g7=0
}
```

The fact `LifelineMatching` matches the shared lifelines in both diagrams,
and the fact `MessageMatching` matches the messages with the same name. The
idea in Alloy is that the messages and events from one of the models are kept
(here `sd1`) and the others are hidden by limiting its occurrence to zero (i.e., its
cardinality is zero).

The examples of behavioural glue introduced in Fig. 5 can be captured as
facts in Alloy. `G1` and `G2` are given in the following facts.

```
fact Glue1{#sd1_j=0
all sd1_j_send:sd1_e6, sd1_j_receive:sd1_g6 |
 #sd1_j_send=0 and #sd1_j_receive=0}

fact Glue2{
#sd1_m3=#sd1_m2
all sd1_m2_send:sd1_e7, sd1_m3_send:sd1_e9 |
 sd1_m3_send in sd1_m2_send.^next

all sd1_m2_receive:sd1_g7, sd1_m3_receive:sd1_g9 |
 sd1_m3_receive in sd1_m2_receive.^next
}
```

`Glue1` states that j does not occur and in addition the associated events also
do not occur. `Glue2` states that every time m3 occurs it must occur with m2. In
other words, m2 must have happened before. Again, we control occurrence with
the cardinality operator #. In addition, the behavioural glue for G2 also defines
the order between m3 and m2 and underlying send and receive events.

As we have seen in the previous section, the effect of each behavioural glue in
the composed model is identical. This has been checked with Alloy, and message
j does not occur in any solution obtained. Traces obtained with our tool have a
direct correspondence with the traces of our semantic model.

7   Related Work

Zhang et al. [23] and Rubin et al. [19] use Alloy for the composition of class diagrams. They transform UML class diagrams into Alloy and compose them automatically. They focus on composing static models and the composition code is produced manually. Widl et al. [21] deal with composing concurrently evolved sequence diagrams in accordance to the overall behaviour given in state machine models. They make direct use of SAT-solvers for the composition. Liang et al. [15] present a method of integrating sequence diagrams based on the formalisation of sequence diagrams as typed graphs. Both these papers focus on less complex structures. For example, they do not deal with combined fragments which can potentially cause substantial complexity.

Composition is also important in other domains such as aspect-oriented modelling. Whittle and Jayaraman [3] introduce a tool called MATA for weaving based on sequence diagrams. They put less emphasis on the semantics of the composition. Grønmo et al. [10] propose a semantics-based technique for weaving behavioural aspects into sequence diagrams. The example we use in this paper is an adaptation of the example introduced there. However, we have a true-concurrent semantics and consider and treat parallelism in interactions. In subsequent work, Grønmo et al. [9] propose the conformance issue for aspects in ensuring that the woven always leads to the same result regardless of the order in which aspects are applied. When looking at the integration of several model views or diagrams, Bowles and Bordbar [6] present a method of mapping a design consisting of class diagrams, OCL constraints and sequence diagrams into a mathematical model for detecting and analysing inconsistencies.

Checkik et al. [7] identify model integration operators, such as merge, weave, and composition, and describe each operator along with its applicability. In addition, they provide a set of desirable criteria (completeness, non-redundancy, minimality, totality, soundness) to evaluate the merge operator. This is a direction orthogonal to our research and remains an area for future investigation.

8   Conclusion

This paper presents an automated method for sequence diagram composition. The outline of the method involves the creation of logical constraints that uniquely identify each component sequence diagram as an instance of the meta-model. To combine the models, logical constraints that synchronise the two models are produced. Some of these logical constraints declare matching elements and some are to enforce behaviour involved in the composition, such as specifying behaviour that should never occur or sequences of events that must occur in a given order. This makes it possible for a designer to give priority to certain specified interactions, which is considered in the solution by eliminating unwanted traces from an initial matched model obtained.

To ensure correctness of the composition process, we have formalised the semantics of the composition with the help of labelled event structures. The result obtained automatically with Alloy preserves our formal interpretation of parallel composition with synchronisation glue. Our Alloy-based automated method of composition has been implemented as an Eclipse plugin for the composition of sequence diagrams. Throughout the paper a small example of composing sequence diagrams inspired by an example from [10] related to weaving aspects is used.

References

1. Allen, R., Garlan, D.: Formalizing architectural connection. In: ICSE 1994, pp. 71–80. IEEE Computer Society Press (1994)
2. Alwanain, M., Bordbar, B., Bowles, J.: Automated composition of sequence diagrams via alloy. In: Pires, L., Hammoudi, S., Filipe, J., das Neves, R. (eds.) MODELSWARD 2014, pp. 384–391. SciTePress (2014)
3. Araújo, J., Whittle, J.: Aspect-oriented compositions for dynamic behavior models. In: Moreira, A., Chitchyan, R., Araújo, J., Rashid, A. (eds.) Aspect-Oriented Requirements Engineering, pp. 45–60. Springer, Heidelberg (2013)
4. Araújo, J., Whittle, J., Kim, D.: Modeling and composing scenario-based requirements with aspects. In: RE 2004, pp. 58–67. IEEE Computer Society Press (2004)
5. Berre, D.L., Parrain, A.: The SAT4j library, release 2.2 - system description. J. Satisfiability, Boolean Model. Comput. **7**, 59–64 (2010)
6. Bowles, J., Bordbar, B.: A formal model for integrating multiple views. In: ACSD 2007, pp. 71–79. IEEE Computer Society Press (2007)
7. Chechik, M., Nejati, S., Sabetzadeh, M.: A relationship-based approach to model integration. Innovations Syst. Softw. Eng. **8**(1), 3–18 (2012)
8. Fiadeiro, J.L., Lopes, A., Wermelinger, M.: Chapter 5. A mathematical semantics for architectural connectors. In: Backhouse, R., Gibbons, J. (eds.) Generic Programming. LNCS, vol. 2793, pp. 178–221. Springer, Heidelberg (2003)
9. Grønmo, R., Runde, R., Møller-Pedersen, B.: Confluence of aspects for sequence diagrams. Softw. Syst. Model. **12**(4), 789–824 (2013)
10. Grønmo, R., Sørensen, F., Møller-Pedersen, B., Krogdahl, S.: Semantics-based weaving of UML sequence diagrams. In: Vallecillo, A., Gray, J., Pierantonio, A. (eds.) ICMT 2008. LNCS, vol. 5063, pp. 122–136. Springer, Heidelberg (2008)
11. Harel, D., Marelly, R.: Come, Let's Play: Scenario-Based Programming Using LSCs and the Play-Engine. Springer, Heidelberg (2003)
12. Jackson, D.: Software Abstractions: Logic. Language and Analysis. MIT Press, Cambridge (2006)
13. Klein, J., Hélouët, L., Jézéquel, J.: Semantic-based weaving of scenarios. In: AOSD 2006, pp. 27–38. ACM (2006)
14. Küster-Filipe, J.: Modelling concurrent interactions. Theoret. Comput. Sci. **351**, 203–220 (2006)
15. Liang, H., Diskin, Z., Dingel, J., Posse, E.: A general approach for scenario integration. In: Czarnecki, K., Ober, I., Bruel, J.-M., Uhl, A., Völter, M. (eds.) MODELS 2008. LNCS, vol. 5301, pp. 204–218. Springer, Heidelberg (2008)
16. Micskei, Z., Waeselynck, H.: The many meanings of UML 2 sequence diagrams: a survey. Softw. Syst. Model. **10**, 489–514 (2011)
17. OMG: UML: Superstructure. Version 2.4.1. OMG, document id: formal/2011-08-06 (2011). http://www.omg.org. Accessed 6 January 2012

18. Reddy, R., Solberg, A., France, R., Ghosh, S.: Composing sequence models using tags. In: Proceedings of MoDELS Workshop on Aspect Oriented Modeling (2006)
19. Rubin, J., Chechik, M., Easterbrook, S.: Declarative approach for model composition. In: MiSE 2008, pp. 7–14. ACM (2008)
20. Whittle, J., Araújo, J., Moreira, A.: Composing aspect models with graph transformations. In: Proceedings of the 2006 International Workshop on Early Aspects at ICSE, pp. 59–65. ACM (2006)
21. Widl, M., Biere, A., Brosch, P., Egly, U., Heule, M., Kappel, G., Seidl, M., Tompits, H.: Guided merging of sequence diagrams. In: Czarnecki, K., Hedin, G. (eds.) SLE 2012. LNCS, vol. 7745, pp. 164–183. Springer, Heidelberg (2013)
22. Winskel, G., Nielsen, M.: Models for concurrency. In: Abramsky, S., Gabbay, D., Maibaum, T. (eds.) Handbook of Logic in Computer Science, Semantic Modelling, vol. 4, pp. 1–148. Oxford Science Publications, Oxford (1995)
23. Zhang, D., Li, S., Liu, X.: An approach for model composition and verification. In: NCM 2009, pp. 1102–1107. IEEE Computer Society Press (2009)

Formal Analysis of Power Electronic Systems

Sidi Mohamed Beillahi[(✉)], Umair Siddique, and Sofiène Tahar

Department of Electrical and Computer Engineering,
Concordia University, Montreal, QC, Canada
{beillahi,muh_sidd,tahar}@ece.concordia.ca

Abstract. Power electronics is an active area of research which has widespread applications in safety and cost critical domains such as power grids, biomedical devices and avionics systems. The complexity of power electronic systems is rapidly reaching a point where it will become difficult to verify the correctness and robustness of underlying designs. In this paper, we propose to use a recent formalization of signal-flow-graphs in higher-order-logic for the formal analysis of power electronic converters, which are the foremost components of modern power electronic systems. In particular, we demonstrate the necessary steps to formally reason about the critical properties (e.g., efficiency, stability and resonance) of power electronic converters by using their corresponding signal-flow-graph based high-level models. In order to demonstrate the utilization of the proposed infrastructure, we present the formal analysis of a couple of widely used power converters, namely a pulse width modulation push-pull DC-DC converter and a 1-boost cell DC-DC converter.

1 Introduction

Power electronic circuits are networks composed of electronic components and semiconductor devices which are connected together to form a functioning machine or an operational procedure. Nowadays, power electronics is a rapidly expanding field in electrical engineering, where power electronic devices are integral part of our everyday tasks at home, at work and in industrial settings [17]. For example, power electronic converters have found widespread applications in petrochemical [18], water-power stations [17], transportation [3], renewable-energy sources [4] and reactive-power compensators [17]. In the last few decades, high-power devices have been one of the most active areas in research and development of power electronics. Several industrial processes have increased their power needs which are mainly driven by the economy of scale (i.e., production levels and efficiency). In order to cope with future challenges, new paradigms have been developed such as power semiconductors, converter topologies and control methods. As a result, the verification and validation of such systems have become challenging due to the increased design complexities and shorter time-to-market.

One of the core steps in power electronic systems design process is the physical modeling of the circuit components. A significant portion of time is spent

© Springer International Publishing Switzerland 2015
M. Butler et al. (Eds.): ICFEM 2015, LNCS 9407, pp. 270–286, 2015.
DOI: 10.1007/978-3-319-25423-4_17

finding bugs through the validation of such models in order to minimize the failure risks and monetary loss. In particular, this step is more important in the applications, where failures directly lead to monetary loss and safety issues. For example, power electronic convertors are used for pipeline pumps in the petrochemical industry [18] and in grid integration of renewable-energy sources [4]. Generally, there are several kinds of power electronic systems which need to be analyzed; however, the focus of this paper is DC-DC power converts which form the core of power electronic systems. The first step to analyze the behavior of power electronic systems is to obtain the transfer function which relates the input and output signals (voltage or current). Consequently, the test for the stability (which ensures that the system output is always finite) and resonance (which ensures the oscillation of input alternating current at certain frequencies) conditions of the circuit are the foremost design criterion.

Once the stability and resonance of a circuit have been determined, the final step is to obtain the circuit efficiency which is a ratio of output and input powers. One primary analytical approach is to compute the transfer function by explicitly writing node and loop equations which can further be utilized to analyze some physical aspects of power electronic systems. Signal-flow graph (SFG) theory (originally proposed by Mason [13]) has also been used to compute the transfer function of power electronic systems. The main motivation of this choice is inspired by its successful applications to model control systems with minimum mathematical manipulations. Indeed, the problem of finding the transfer function reduces to the identification of forward paths and loops which further can be plugged into the Mason's gain formula (MSG) [14] (which provides an easy way to find the transfer function). Traditionally, the analysis of complex power electronic systems is performed using numerical simulation [24]. To measure the effect of different initial conditions or parametric variation over the circuit operation, it is necessary to perform exhaustive simulations and tests. However, even by doing this, there is no guarantee about the correctness of results, because it is impossible to simulate the system for an infinite number of operating conditions. Another issue of such analysis methods is the approximations in terms of numerical accuracy and types (e.g., real or complex) of variables used to encode the algorithms. For example, a MATLAB program [7] for computing transfer functions treats system parameters as a string of characters; which is indeed a complex-valued function. Considering the above mentioned verification and analysis constraints, we believe that there is a dire need to build a framework which can assist in designing accurate and high assurance power electronic systems.

In recent years, formal methods based techniques (in particular model checking and theorem proving) have been proven to be an effective approach to analyze physical, hybrid and digital engineering systems (e.g., [12]). Despite the fact that formal methods based techniques have the potential to analyze various aspects of physical systems, it is rare to find the usage of formal methods to analyze power electronic systems. The most relevant work for analyzing and modelling power electronic systems using model checking is reported in [15]. However, the authors do not study the stability and resonance which are critical requirements in designing power electronic systems. Therefore, the main motivation of our work is to fill this gap by proposing a generic framework to analyze power converters. In particular, we review the main functions of our higher-order logic formalization of signal-flow-graph theory along and the Mason's gain formula [2]. We also formalize the notion of stability and resonance along with the formal verification of some important properties such as the finiteness and the cardinality of the set of poles (complex-valued parameters at which the system becomes unstable) and zeros (parameters which determine the resonance condition in the system). In order to demonstrate the practical utilization of our work, we formally verify the transfer functions of 1-boost cell DC-DC converter [24] and push-pull pulse-width-modulation (PWM) DC-DC converter [9]. Consequently, we derive the general stability and resonance conditions, which greatly simplifies the verification for any given circuit configuration. Next, we verify the efficiency of 1-boost cell DC-DC converter circuit. In our work, we use the HOL Light theorem prover [8] due to its rich multivariate analysis libraries and interesting related formalizations about Laplace transform [21] and Z-transform [20]. The source code of our formalization is available for download [1] and can be utilized by other researchers and engineers for further developments and the analysis of various types of power engineering systems.

The rest of the paper is organized as follows: some fundamentals of signal-flow-graph theory and the Mason's gain formula are described in Sect. 2. In Sect. 3, we highlight some definitions of our formalization of signal-flow-graph theory and Mason's gain formula along with the system properties. We present the analysis of the 1-boost cell DC-DC and push-pull PWM DC-DC converters in Sect. 4. Finally, we conclude the paper in Sect. 5.

2   Signal-Flow-Graph Theory and Mason's Gain Formula

A signal-flow-graph (SFG) [13] is a special kind of directed graph which is widely used to model engineering systems. Mathematically, it represents a set of linear algebraic equations of the corresponding system. An SFG is a network in which nodes are connected by directed branches. Every node in the network represents a system variable and each branch represents the signal transmission from one node to the other under the assumption that signals flow only in one direction. An example of an SFG is shown in Fig. 2 consisting of five nodes. An input or *source node* and an output or *sink node* are the ones which only have outgoing branches and incoming branches, respectively (e.g., nodes 1 and 5 in Fig. 2). A branch is a directed line from node i to j and the gain of each branch is called the *transmittance*. A *path* is a traversal of connected branches from one node to the other and if no node is crossed more than once and connects the input to the output, then the path is called *forward path*, otherwise if it leads back to itself without crossing any node more than once, it is considered as a *closed path* or a *loop*. A loop containing only one node is called *self loop* and any two loops in the SFG are said to be *touching loops* if they have any common node.

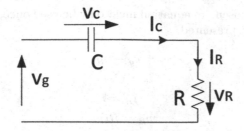

Fig. 1. RC circuit

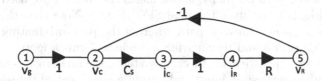

Fig. 2. Signal-flow-graph of RC circuit

The total gain of forward path and a loop can be computed by multiplying the transmittances of each traversed branch.

The procedure for transforming power electronic circuits into a signal-flow-graph is straightforward. We start by representing each variable of the circuit as a node in the graph. Next, these nodes are interconnected depending upon their physical behavior in a specific system configuration. The technique of driving-point impedance (DPI) [19] is used to derive the transmittance of the graph branches (capacitor or resistor). Indeed, the DPI analysis is based on the transformation of circuit nodes to their Norton's or Thevenin's equivalent representation along with the application of the principal of superposition [6]. Moreover, Kirchhoff's voltage and current laws are used to derive the relations between voltage and current. Kirchhoff's current law or principle of conservation of electric charge states that at any node (junction) in an electrical circuit, the sum of the currents flowing into that node is equal to the sum of currents flowing out of that node. Kirchhoff's voltage law or the principle of conservation of energy implies that the directed sum of the potential differences around any closed network is zero. For example, consider a simple RC circuit as shown in Fig. 1, where v_g is the input voltage, v_c is the voltage across the capacitor, i_c is the capacitor current, i_R is the resistor current, and v_R is the output voltage. We can transform this circuit into its equivalent signal-flow-graph by finding the set of equations from the physical network of the circuit by first using: Kirchhoff's voltage and current laws for Eqs. 1 and 3, then the branch equations for the capacitor and resistor for Eqs. 2 and 4. The next step consists in assigning to each equation a signal (voltage or current) that will be represented as a node representing each variable of the circuit as a node in the graph. Next, these nodes are interconnected depending upon their physical behavior in a specific system configuration. Note that for each signal-flow-graph a set of independent equations must be chosen, an equation must only be used once, and the variables of interest must be represented.

$$v_c = v_g - v_R \tag{1}$$
$$i_c = Csv_c \tag{2}$$
$$i_R = i_c \tag{3}$$
$$v_R = Ri_R \tag{4}$$

where C is the capacitance, R is the resistance, and s is the Laplace Transform variable (i.e., $s = \sigma + jw$). Finally, above mentioned results are used to connect the nodes in Fig. 1, to produce the final SFG (Fig. 2). Note that the path from node v_g to node v_R is a forward path whereas the path originating from node v_c, traversing i_c, i_R, v_R and terminating at node v_c forms a loop.

In the analysis of practical engineering systems, the main task is to characterize the relation among system input and output which is called transfer function. The total transmittance or gain between two given nodes (usually input and output) describes the transfer function of the corresponding system. In 1953, Mason [13] proposed a computational procedure (also called Mason's gain formula) to obtain the total gain of any arbitrary signal-flow-graph. The formula is described as follows [14]:

$$G = \sum_k \frac{G_k \Delta_k}{\Delta} \tag{5}$$

$$\Delta = 1 - \sum_m P_{m1} + \sum_m P_{m2} - \sum_m P_{m3} + \ldots + (-1)^n \sum \ldots \tag{6}$$

where Δ represents the determinant of the graph, Δ_k represents the value of Δ for the part of the graph that is not touching the kth forward path and it is called the cofactor of forward path k, P_{mr} is the gain product of mth possible combination of r non-touching loops. The gain of each forward path is represented by G_k.

For example, we can find the input to output transfer function for the SFG of Fig. 2 using the MGF as follows:

$$\frac{v_R}{v_g} = \frac{RCs}{1 + RCs} \tag{7}$$

3 Formalization of Signal-Flow-Graph and Mason's Gain

We model a single branch as a triplet (a, t_{ab}, b), where a, t_{ab} and b represent the start node, the transmittance and the end node, respectively. Consequently, a path can be modeled as a list of branches and furthermore an SFG can be defined as a composition of a path along with the information about the total number of nodes in the circuit and the source and the sink nodes at which we want to compute the transfer function. As mentioned before, nodes and transmittance represent the system variables and gain, respectively. These parameters are indeed complex valued, i.e., $a, t_{ab}, c \in \mathbb{C}$ in the context of power electronic systems. However, the information about the nodes is just used to find properties of signals (current) transmission and they do not appear in the gain and transfer function computation using Mason's gain formula. So, we adapted the same approach as proposed by Mason [13], where nodes of an SFG are represented by natural numbers ($\mathbb{N}$). In order to simplify the reasoning process, we encode the above information by defining three type abbreviations in HOL Light[1], i.e., branch, path and signal-flow-graph as follows:

Definition 1 (Branch, Path and SFG).

```
new_type_abbrev ("branch", ':N × C × N')
new_type_abbrev ("path", ':(branch)list')
new_type_abbrev ("sfg", ':path × N × N × N')
```

where the second, third, and the fourth elements of sfg represent the size, the output node and the input node of a signal-flow-graph, respectively.

Our next main task is to find all the forward paths and loops from the source node to the sink node given by the user. We implemented a search algorithm proposed in [23] which considers each path only once during the search.

In our formalization, we add a skipping function which helps to ignore the nodes which do not have any incoming branches. Indeed, we cannot find a loop which contains a node that does not have incoming branches from the definition of a feedback loop. Hence, the skipping function greatly improves the performance of the search algorithm. Briefly, in our formalization, we take an SFG and generate a matrix in which nodes are arranged in the first column and each row represents the branches of the node under consideration. For feedback loops extraction, we start the process by the first node of the SFG and we go through all possible paths which start from the node under consideration and test for each path whether it is a loop or not. In the next iteration, we go to the next node of the graph and repeat the same process. For forward paths extraction, we repeat a similar process, but we only consider the paths starting from the source node rather than exploring all the nodes.

For the sake of conciseness, we present a list of some of the main functions of our formalization of signal-flow-graph theory with a brief description in Table 1, while more details can be found in [2].

Finally, we utilize the definitions described in Table 1 to formalize the Mason's gain formula given in Eq. 5, as follows:

Definition 2 (Mason's gain formula).
⊢ ∀(system : sfg). Mason_Gain system =

$$\frac{\text{PRODUCT\_FORWARD\_DELTA (EC system) (FC system)}}{\text{DETERMINANT (EC system)}}$$

---

[1] In this paper, we use minimal HOL Light syntax in the presentation of definitions and theorems to improve the readability.

Table 1. Some important functions of SFG formalization

Definition	Description	Formalization
ECSKIP	Skip the process of finding loops of nodes that do not have incoming branches	⊢ ∀ (p:N) (G:(N list) list) (n:N) (m:N). ECSKIP p G m n = if($m = n$) then F else if(p ∈ $G[m]$) then T else (ECSKIP p G (m+1) n)
EC_POINT	Extract all the feedback loops which start from a given point of the graph	⊢ ∀ (l:KPH) (G:(N list) list) (t:N list). EC_POINT l G [ ] = [ ] ∧ EC_POINT l G (CONS e t) = if((fst_of_trpl l = 0) ∧ (¬(EC_TEST (snd_of_trpl l) (fst_of_trpl l) G))) then [ ] else (APPEND (if(EC_TEST (snd_of_trpl l)(fst_of_trpl l) G) then [(EC_add_node (snd_of_trpl l))] else [ ]) (EC_POINT (EC_POINT_AID l G) G t3))
FC	Extract all the forward paths in a given SFG	⊢ ∀ (l:path) (size:N) (stop:N) (start:N). FC l size stop start = if(l = [ ]) then [ ] else FC_REWRITING (FC_MAIN l size stop start) l
IS_TOUCHING	Check if two paths have common nodes	⊢ ∀ (t1:path) (t2:path). IS_TOUCHING [ ] [ ] = F ∧ IS_TOUCHING t2 [ ] = F ∧ IS_TOUCHING [ ] t1 = F ∧ IS_TOUCHING (CONS a t1) (CONS b t2) = if ((RIGHT (CONS a t1) b) ∨ (LEFT a (CONS b t2))) then T else IS_TOUCHING t1 t2
DETERMINANT	Compute the determinant of the given graph	⊢ ∀ (t:(path) list). DETERMINANT t = 1 + (DELTA_MINUS_ONE t (TOUCHING_LOOP_MAIN t) t (TOUCHING_LOOP_MAIN t))
PRODUCT_FORWARD_DELTA	Compute the numerator of the graph according to Mason's gain formula	⊢ ∀ (t1:(path)list) (t2:(path)list). PRODUCT_FORWARD_DELTA [ ] t2 = Cx(&0) ∧ PRODUCT_FORWARD_DELTA (CONS f t1) t2 = ((GAIN f) * (1 + FORWARD_DELTA_MINUS f t2 + PRODUCT_FORWARD_DELTA t1 t2)

where the function Mason_Gain accepts an SFG (i.e., system, which is a model of the given system in our case) and computes the Mason's gain as given in Eq. 5. Note that the function PRODUCT_FORWARD_DELTA accepts the list of loops (computed by EC) and forward paths (computed by FC) in the system and computes $\sum_{k \in system} G_k \Delta_k$, where G_k and Δ_k represent, respectively, the product of all forward path gains and the determinant of the kth forward path considering the elimination of all loops touching the kth forward path as described in Sect. 2. The function DETERMINANT takes the list of loops and gives the determinant of the system as described in Eq. (6).

In practice, the physical behavior of any power electronic system is described by the transmittance of each path (or a single branch) involved in the signal-flow-graph. We can consider each path as a system component which processes the input current signal to achieve the desired functionality. Indeed, the SFG of the given power electronic system is expressed as a function of the parameter "s" and we need to consider this physical aspect in the formalization of the transfer function which describe the overall behavior of the system. It is mentioned in Sect. 2 that the Mason's gain formula describes the total gain between the input and the output of the system and hence it can be used to describe the transfer function of the power electronic system provided the given signal-flow-graph can be described as a function of a complex parameter "s". We use the Mason's gain formalization and the above description to formalize the transfer function of a given power electronic system as follows:

Definition 3 (System Transfer Function).

⊢ ∀ system. transfer_function system = Mason_Gain (λs. system s)

where the function `transfer_function` accepts a `system` which has type
$\mathbb{C} \rightarrow$ `sfg` and returns a complex ($\mathbb{C}$) number which represents the transfer function of the power electronic system (i.e., `system`).

We have automatized the different steps for finding the transfer function of any arbitrary signal-flow-graph by developing some new simplification tactics using derived rules and tactics of HOL Light. In terms of automation, these tactics can be divided into three varieties: the first proves the extracted list of feedbacks, the second proves the extracted list of forward paths, and the third proves Mason's gain formula. In Table 2, we provide some of these tactics with corresponding descriptions. Using these tactics we prove all transfer functions given in [1]. The availability of these tactics provides the effective automation to the user, so that an application to a particular system does not involve the painful manual proofs often required with interactive theorem proving. Developing such tactics represents a first step towards building an automated tool to carry the verification of transfer functions of power electronic circuits on the basis of their signal-flow-graphs representations.

Table 2. HOL automation tactics

Tactic	Description
TAC_FC	Simplify the function which computes the entire list of forward paths.
TAC_EC	Simplify the function which computes the entire list of feedback paths.
MASON_SIMP_TAC	Simplify the function which computes the transfer function using MGF.
COMPLEX_DIV_TAC	Simplify a goal which is expressed as a fractional expression.
SFG_TAC	Main tactic for simplifying the transfer function of a given SFG.

3.1 Formalization of System Properties

In order to verify that the given model meets its specification, we need to build the foundations based on which we can formally describe the main system properties (i.e., stability, resonance) in HOL. Physically, the stability and resonance are concerned with the identification of all the values of s for which the system transfer function becomes infinite and zero, respectively. In the control theory literature, these values are called *system poles* and *system zeros* which can be computed by the denominator and numerator of the transfer function, respectively. Furthermore, all poles and zeros need to be inside the unit circle which means that their magnitude should be less or equal to 1. We formalize the above mentioned informal description of the system properties in HOL as follows:

Definition 4 (System Poles).
$\vdash \forall$ system. poles system $=$ $\{s \mid$ denominator (system s) $= 0\}$
$\vdash \forall$ system. zeros system $=$ $\{s \mid$ numerator (system s) $= 0\}$

where the functions poles and zeros take the system as a parameter and return the set of poles and zeros, respectively. Next, we formalize the notion of stability and resonance as follows:

Definition 5 (System Stability and Resonance).

$\vdash \forall$ system. is_stable system $[p_0, ..., p_n] \Leftrightarrow$

$$\forall p_i. \ p_i \in (\text{poles system}) \ \wedge \ \| \ p_i \ \| \leq 1$$

$\vdash \forall$ system. is_resonant system $[z_0, ..., z_n] \Leftrightarrow$

$$\forall z_i. \ z_i \in (\text{zeros system}) \ \wedge \ \| \ z_i \ \| \leq 1$$

where the predicate is_stable accepts the power electronic system signal-flow-graph model (i.e., system) and a list of poles $[p_0, ..., p_n]$ and verifies that each element p_i is indeed a pole of the system and its corresponding magnitude (i.e., norm of a complex number, $\| \ p_i \ \|$) is smaller or equal to 1. The predicate is_resonant is defined in a similar way by considering the list of zeros instead of the list of poles of the system.

Next, we verify an important theorem which describes that if the denominator or the numerator of the transfer function is a polynomial of order n, it will always have a finite number of poles or zeros and the cardinality of the set of poles and zeros can only be equal or less than n.

Theorem 1 (Finiteness and Cardinality of poles and zeros).

$\vdash \forall n \ c \ \text{system}. \ \neg(\forall \ i. \ i \ \in \{0, 1, ..., n\} \ \Rightarrow c \ i = 0) \wedge$
$(\forall \ z. \ \text{denominator (system z)} = \ \sum_{i \in \{0,1,...,n\}} (\lambda i. \ c \ i * z^i)) \implies$
FINITE (poles (system z)) $\wedge$ CARD (poles (system z)) $\leq n$

where n represents the order of the complex polynomial function c. The functions FINITE and CARD, represent the finiteness and cardinality of a set, respectively. We also prove the same theorem for the set of zeros of a system, where more details can be found at [1].

This concludes the signal-flow-graph formalization and system properties. In the next section, we will show how to apply our formalization in practice by presenting the formal analysis of two important topologies of power converters using the previously presented theorems and definitions.

4   Application: Power Electronics Systems

Power electronics has found an important place in modern technology being a core of power and energy control. Generally, the interaction between the utility and the load depends on the topology of the power system. Most of electronic supplies are switching semiconductor converters thanks to theirs efficiency. Power electronic converters are constructed by electronic devices, driving, protection and control circuits. In particular, DC-DC converters change the DC voltage and current levels using the switching mode of semiconductor devices. As a rule, they provide means for changing and stabilizing the output DC voltage. A DC-DC converter consists of the switching circuitry and the filter section, and power converters with feedback are known as regulators. Power electronics converters must be suitably controlled to supply the voltages, currents, or frequency ranges needed for the load and to guarantee the requested power quality. In the following subsections, we present the formal analyses of two topologies of power electronic circuits in higher-order-logic using the previous formalization.

4.1   1-Boost Cell Interleaved DC-DC Converter

Interleaved DC-DC converters are composed of N-boost cells connected in parallel which operate in an interleaved fashion. The elementary cell can be a two-level or multi-level DC-DC converter. The elementary DC-DC cells are driven with pulse width modulation in which pulses are shifted by $\frac{2\pi}{N}$ radians. Some of the advantages of interleaved parallel converters are the ripple cancellation both in the input and output waveforms and lower value of ripple amplitude. Interleaved DC-DC converter are widely used in various critical power conversion applications, such as voltage regulation modules [10], and automotive applications. Thus they have been used in aircrafts, to increase flight performance (e.g., thrust and maneuverability) and enhance onboard mission capability (e.g., sensors, weapons and communication) [11].

In [24], the authors proposed to use SFG to model N-boost cells interleaved DC-DC converters and they illustrate the analysis for the case of 1-boost cell, 2-boost cells and 3-boost cells interleaved parallel converters. We use our proposed framework to formally analyze 1-boost cell, 2-boost cells, and 3-boost cells interleaved parallel converters. For the sake of conciseness, we present the analysis of a 1-boost cell interleaved parallel converter only and more details about the 2-boost and 3-boost cells interleaved converters can be found in [1].

The circuit representation of 1-boost cell interleaved parallel DC-DC converter system is shown in Fig. 3. The circuit parameters L_1, D_1, and r_1 represent the inductance of individual boost cell, the duty ratios of the 1st state, and the inductor series resistance, respectively. The parameters R and C are the load resistance and the circuit capacitor, respectively. The parameters V_g, I_g and V_1 are the supply voltage, the source current and the voltage across inductor, respectively. Similarly, V_0 and I_0 are the output voltage and the output current, respectively. The SFG model of 1-boost cell interleaved parallel DC-DC converter is shown in Fig. 4.

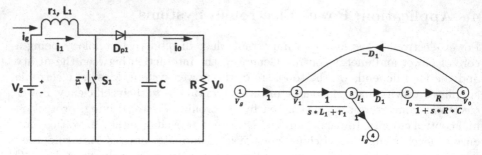

Fig. 3. 1-Boost Cell DC-DC Converter   **Fig. 4.** SFG of 1-Boost Cell DC-DC Converter

Our main interest is to evaluate the circuit behavior at the output node which is represented by node ⑥[2], when the signal is applied at the input, i.e., node ①. We keep all above mentioned parameters in the general form which further can be used to model different 1-boost cell DC-DC converter circuit configurations. We formally define 1-boost cell DC-DC converter in HOL as follows:

Definition 6 (1-Boost Cell DC_DC Converter Model).

$\vdash \forall$ C R D_1 r_1 L_1 s $\in \mathbb{C}$.
   DC_model R C D_1 r_1 L_1 s $=$
$([(1,1,2);(2, \frac{1}{s*L_1+r_1},3);(3,1,4);(3,D_1,5);(5, \frac{R}{1+s*R*C},6);(6,-D_1,2)],6,6,1)$

where DC_model accepts complex-valued circuit parameters, and returns the signal-flow-graph which has 6 nodes, where the output node is ⑥ and the input node is ① as shown in Fig. 4. Next, we verify the transfer function of the 1-boost cell DC-DC converter circuit as follows:

Theorem 2 (Transfer Function of 1-Boost Cell DC_DC Converter).

$\vdash \forall$ C R D_1 r_1 L_1 s $\in \mathbb{C}$.
   $(1 + s*R*C \neq 0) \land (s*L_1 + r_1 \neq 0) \implies$
   transfer_function (DC_model R C D_1 r_1 L_1 s) $=$
$$\frac{D_1 * R}{R*C*L_1*s^2 + (R*C*r_1 + L_1)*s + r_1 + D_1^2*R}$$

The proof of this theorem is mainly based on the extraction of forward paths and feedback loops in the circuit and then using the Mason's gain formula. We have

---

[2] Here the output node has an outgoing branch that does not follow the conventional designation of output (e.g., no outgoing branches). However, the transfer function is the same as the one obtained by adding a new output node and connecting it to the node ⑥ with transmittance equal to 1. Therefore, for the sake of simplicity, we did not add a new node that does not have physical meaning in the circuit.

made efforts to provide the effective automation using derived rules and tactics, so that the application to a particular system does not involve the painful manual proofs often required with interactive (higher-order logic) theorem proving. For example, the formal proof of Theorem 2 requires only three lines of HOL light code. A brief summary of developed tactics can be found in [2] (Appendix I).

The efficiency of any system is the useful power output divided by the total electrical power consumed. As the power in electronic circuit is the product of the voltage (V) and current (I), we can define the 1-boost cell DC-DC converter efficiency as follows:

Definition 7 (1-Boost Cell DC_DC Converter Efficiency).

$\vdash \forall$ R C D_1 r_1 L_1 s $\in \mathbb{C}$.

$\qquad$ Efficiency (DC_model R C D_1 r_1 L_1 s) $= \dfrac{I_0 * V_0}{I_g * V_g} = \dfrac{V_0}{V_g} * \dfrac{V_g}{I_g} * \dfrac{I_0}{V_g}$

Repeating the same process for calculating the transfer function in Theorem 2 we can compute the transfer functions of $\frac{I_g}{V_g}$ and $\frac{I_0}{V_g}$ by replacing the output node ⑤ by ④ and ⑥, respectively.

Based on the three transfer functions and the Definition 7 of the efficiency, we can prove the expression of the efficiency of 1-boost cell converter as follows:

Theorem 3 (1-Boost Cell DC_DC Converter Efficiency).

$\vdash \forall$ C R D_1 r_1 L_1 s $\in \mathbb{C}$.

$\qquad (1 + s * R * C \neq 0) \wedge (s * L_1 + r_1 \neq 0) \wedge$

$\qquad (R * C * L_1 * s^2 + (R * C * r_1 + L_1) * s + r_1 + D_1^2 * R \neq 0) \Longrightarrow$

$\qquad$ Efficiency (DC_model R C D_1 r_1 L_1 s) $=$

$$\frac{D_1^2 * R}{R * C * L_1 * s^2 + (R * C * r_1 + L_1) * s + r_1 + D_1^2 * R}$$

The denominator of the transfer function of 1-boost cell DC-DC converter can be represented as a second order polynomial which leads to the useful information that the 1-boost cell DC-DC circuit can only have 2 poles at maximum according to Theorem 1. Next, we present the verification of the stability conditions of the 1-boost cell DC-DC convertor circuit as follows:

Theorem 4 (Stability Conditions for 1-Boost Cell DC_DC Converter).

$\vdash \forall G_1$ G_2 G_3 k_1 k_2 $\in \mathbb{C}$.

$\left\| \dfrac{-(R*C*r_1+L_1) \pm \sqrt{(R*C*r_1+L_1)^2 - 4*R*C*L_1*(r_1+D_1^2*R)}}{2*R*C*L_1} \right\| \leq 1 \wedge$

$\dfrac{(R*C*r_1-L_1) \pm \sqrt{(R*C*r_1+L_1)^2 - 4*R*C*L_1*(r_1+D_1^2*R)}}{2*R*C*L_1} \neq 0 \wedge$

$\dfrac{(L_1-R*C*r_1) \pm \sqrt{(R*C*r_1+L_1)^2 - 4*R*C*L_1*(r_1+D_1^2*R)}}{2*R*C*L_1} \neq 0 \wedge$

$\Longrightarrow$ is_stable $(\lambda s.$ (DC_model R C D_1 r_1 L_1 s)

$$\left[\frac{-(R*C*r_1+L_1)-\sqrt{(R*C*r_1+L_1)^2-4*R*C*L_1*(r_1+D_1^2*R)}}{2*R*C*L_1};\right.$$

$$\left.\frac{-(R*C*r_1+L_1)+\sqrt{(R*C*r_1+L_1)^2-4*R*C*L_1*(r_1+D_1^2*R)}}{2*R*C*L_1}\right]$$

where $\|\,.\,\|$ and $\sqrt{\cdot}$ represent the complex norm and complex square root, respectively. The first assumption is required to prove that both poles are inside the unit circle, and the following two assumptions ensure that poles are not equal to $-\frac{r_1}{L_1}$, $-\frac{1}{R*C}$, respectively.

This concludes our HOL formal analysis of the 1-boost cell DC-DC converter circuit. The source code of the circuit formalization and the analysis of the 2-boost and 3-boost cells DC-DC converters circuits can be found in [1].

4.2   Pulse Width Modulation Push-Pull DC-DC Converter

Pulse width modulated (PWM) push-pull DC-DC converters are very popular in modern power electronic supplies. They have many applications in some sensitive and critical areas such as aerospace, transportation, and renewable energy [4]. Hence, a robust and secure stability analysis of this type of converter is extremely important. A PWM constant-frequency control technique is considered as one of the most widely used component in switched-mode DC-DC power supplies. Voltage-mode and current-mode controllers allow for achieving a satisfactory dynamic performance of DC-DC converters is considered as a DC-DC converter operating under switched-load conditions.

The circuit of linearized model of the power stage with a variable load current of PWM push-pull converter is shown in Fig. 5. In the circuit, v_c is the voltage across the capacitor C, v_T is the averaged control voltage (input voltage), i_o is the converter output current, v_o is the converter output voltage, L is the indicator, r is the equivalent averaged resistance in series with the inductor, and r_c is the equivalent series resistance of the capacitor.

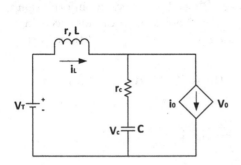

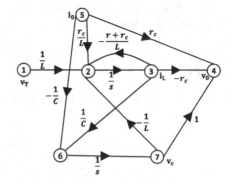

Fig. 5. Linearized model of PWM Push Pull DC-DC Converter

Fig. 6. SFG of PWM Push Pull DC-DC Converter

In [9], the authors proposed a block diagram of closed-loop of the circuit (circuit with the gains of compensation and feedback loop from the output to the input). The block diagram equivalent signal-flow-graph of PWM push-pull converter without the control part is shown in Fig. 6. The SFG is composed of 7 nodes the input node is 1 (V_T in [9]) and the output node is 4 (V_o in [9]).

Definition 8 (PWM Push Pull DC-DC Converter Model).

$\vdash \forall$ C L r k_y r_c k_i k_v s $\in \mathbb{C}$.

PWM_model C L r k_y r_c k_i k_v s $=$

$([(1, \frac{1}{L}, 2); (2, \frac{1}{s}, 3); (3, \frac{-(r+r_c)}{L}, 2); (3, -r_c, 4); (3, \frac{1}{C}, 6); (5, r_c, 4);$
$(5, -\frac{1}{C}, 6); (5, \frac{r_c}{L}, 2); (6, \frac{1}{s}, 7); (7, -\frac{1}{L}, 2); (7, 1, 4)], 7, 4, 1)$

where PWM_model accepts complex-valued circuit parameters, and returns the signal-flow-graph which has a total number of 7 nodes where the output node is ④ and the input node is ① as shown in Fig. 6.

Next, we verify the transfer function of the PWM push-pull DC-DC converter circuit as follows:

Theorem 5 (Transfer Function of PWM).

$\vdash \forall$ C L r r_c s $\in \mathbb{C}$.

$(L * C \neq 0) \implies$

transfer_function PWM_model C L r r_c s $=$

$$\frac{1 - s * C * r_c}{C * L * s^2 + (r_c + r) * C * + 1}$$

Next, we present the verification of the stability conditions of the PWM push-pull DC-DC converter circuit under the circuit global parameters as follows:

Theorem 6 (Stability Conditions for PWM).

$\vdash \forall$ C L r r_c $\in \mathbb{C}$.

$\left\| \frac{-(r+r_c)*C \mp \sqrt{((r+r_c)*C)^2 - 4*C*L}}{2*C*L} \right\| \leq 1 \wedge$

$\frac{-(r+r_c)*C \pm \sqrt{((r+r_c)*C)^2 - 4*C*L}}{2*C*L} \neq 0 \wedge L*C \neq 0 \implies$

is_stable (λs. PWM_model C L r r_c s) s

$\left[\frac{-(r+r_c)*C + \sqrt{((r+r_c)*C)^2 - 4*C*L}}{2*C*L} ; \frac{-(r+r_c)*C - \sqrt{((r+r_c)*C)^2 - 4*C*L}}{2*C*L} \right]$

The first assumption ensures that both poles are inside the unit circle, whereas the second assumption is required to prove that the poles are not equal to zero. Similarly, we verify the resonance condition for the PWM push-pull DC-DC converter circuit as follows:

Theorem 7 (Resonant Conditions for PWM).

$\vdash \forall$ C L r r_c $\in \mathbb{C}$.

$\left\| \frac{1}{C*r_c} \right\| \leq 1 \wedge r_c \neq 0 \wedge L*C \neq 0 \implies$

is_resonant (λs. PWM_model C L r r_c s) s $\left[\frac{1}{C * r_c} \right]$

The assumptions in theorem ensure that the systems zero is inside the unit circle and it is not equal to zero.

Note that the stability and resonance conditions are verified under the general parameters of the PWM circuit (e.g., r, r_c, L,...) and 1-boost cell circuit (e.g., L_1, D_1, r_1,...) which is not possible in the case of simulation. One of the main strengths of the theorem proving based approach is to unveil all the assumptions under which a theorem can be verified. For example, most of the assumptions in Theorems 4, 6, and 7 are not mentioned in the paper-and-pencil analyses reported in [9,24]. However, without these assumptions these theorems cannot be verified. Moreover, our results are verified under universal quantifiers and the problem of finding the stability and resonance conditions reduces to just ensuring that the values of the system parameters satisfy the assumptions. Remark that the signal-flow-graph models of the two applications involve, respectively, 6 and 8 nodes SFGs, however, our formalization is general and can be applied for an arbitrary number of nodes. For example, in [5] we have formally verified the transfer function of an application which consists of 20 nodes and 14 complex-valued parameters.

We believe that the formal analysis of above mentioned two real-world power electronic systems provides two main indications: theorem proving systems have reached to the maturity, where complex physical models can be expressed with less efforts than ever before; and formal methods can assist in the verification of power electronic systems which are rapidly reaching a point where it will be impossible to verify correctness of the design and its robustness. In reality, verification tools must be largely automatic to be effectively adopted which limits the usage of interactive theorem prover in industry. On the other hand, computer algebra systems (CASs), e.g., Mathematica, are more popular than theorem provers. The most important reason is that CAS tools are easier to use, and are also increasingly applied in education, which is not the case for theorem provers. Another important factor is the rapidity of CAS tools compared to theorem provers. However, higher-order-logic theorem proving systems are more precise and reliable. Our reported work can be considered as a one step towards an ultimate goal of building automatic tools which make use of HOL theorem provers as a certification tool in the design and analysis cycles of safety-critical real-world systems from different engineering and physical science disciplines (e.g., signal processing, control systems, power electronics, biology, optical and mechanical engineering).

5   Conclusion

In this paper, we reported a new application of formal methods in the domain of power electronics. We presented a formal analysis framework based on higher-order logic which provides the required expressiveness and soundness to formally model and verify physical aspects of power electronic systems. In particular, we presented an overview of our formalization of the signal-flow-graph theory along with the Mason's gain formula and transfer functions. Similarly, we presented the formalization of the properties of the power electronic systems. Consequently, we derive the transfer function of two real-world power electronic applications which are 1-boost cell DC-DC converter and PWM push pull DC-DC converter. Finally, we described the formal analysis of the stability and resonance conditions of these two applications.

Our immediate future work is to formally verify a couple of key properties about the forward and feedback paths extraction: (1) each path is extracted only once; (2) the transfer function of transposed SFG [16] is the same as the original one. This requires the formalization of undirected signal-flow-graph [22]. We also plan to verify more complex power electronic engineering systems along with the formal relation among the signal-flow-graph representation and the Z-transform [20] and the Laplace Transform [21]. A potential utilization of our formalization and developed automation tactics is to build a framework to certify the results produced by informal tools such as MATLAB based SFG analysis program (available at [7]).

References

1. Beillahi, S.M., Siddique, U.: Formal Analysis of Power Electronic Systems (2015). http://hvg.ece.concordia.ca/projects/optics/pe.html
2. Beillahi, S.M., Siddique, U., Tahar, S.: On the Formalization of Signal-Flow-Graphs in HOL. Technical report, ECE Department, Concordia University, Montreal, QC, Canada, November 2014
3. Bernet, S.: Recent developments of high power converters for industry and traction applications. IEEE Trans. Power Electron. **15**(6), 1102–1117 (2000)
4. Carrasco, J.M., Franquelo, L.G., Bialasiewicz, J.T., Galvan, E., Guisado, R.C.P., Prats, M.A.M., Leon, J.I., Moreno-Alfonso, N.: Power-electronic systems for the grid integration of renewable energy sources: a survey. IEEE Trans. Industr. Electron. **53**(4), 1002–1016 (2006)
5. Dey, S., Mandal, S.: Modeling and analysis of quadruple optical ring resonator performance as optical filter using Vernier principle. Optics Commun. **285**(4), 439–446 (2012)
6. Dorf, R.C., Svoboda, J.A.: Introduction to Electric Circuits. Wiley, New York (2009)
7. Signal Flow Graph Similification Program for MATLAB (2014). http://www.mathworks.com/matlabcentral/fileexchange/22-mason-m
8. Harrison, J.: HOL light: a tutorial introduction. In: Srivas, M., Camilleri, A. (eds.) FMCAD 1996. LNCS, vol. 1166, pp. 265–269. Springer, Heidelberg (1996)
9. Hote, Y.V., Choudhury, D.R., Gupta, J.R.P.: Robust stability analysis of the PWM push-pull DC-DC converter. IEEE Trans. Power Electron. **24**(10), 2353–2356 (2009)
10. Schultz, A., Li, J., Sullivan, C.R.: Coupled-inductor design optimization for fast-response low-voltage DC-DC converters. In: Proceeding of the IEEE Applied Power Electronics Conference and Exposition, vol. 2, pp. 817–823 (2002)
11. Scofield, J., McNeal, S., Jordan, B., Kosai, H., Ray, B.: Studies of Interleaved DC-DC Boost Converters with Coupled Inductors, April 2011. http://www.dtic.mil/dtic/tr/fulltext/u2/a542736.pdf

12. Kowalewski, S.: Introduction to the analysis and verification of hybrid systems. In: Engell, S., Frehse, G., Schnieder, E. (eds.) Modelling, Analysis and Design of Hybrid Systems. LNCIS, vol. 279, pp. 153–171. Springer, Heidelberg (2002)

13. Mason, S.J.: Feedback theory, some properties of signal flow graphs. In: Proceedings of Institute of Radio Engineers, vol. 41, pp. 1144–1156, September 1953

14. Mason, S.J.: Feedback theory, further properties of signal flow graphs. In: Proceedings of Institute of Radio Engineers, vol. 44, pp. 920–926 (1956)

15. Miranda, M.V.C., Lima, A.M.N.: Formal verification and controller redesign of power electronic converters. In: IEEE International Symposium on Industrial Electronics, vol. 2, pp. 907–912, May 2004

16. Ochoa Jr., A.: A systematic approach to the analysis of general and feedback circuits and systems using signal flow graphs and driving-point impedance. IEEE Trans. Circuits Syst. II Analog Digit. Sign. Process. 45(2), 187–195 (1998)

17. Rodriguez, J., Bernet, S., Wu, B., Pontt, J.O., Kouro, S.: Multilevel voltage-source-converter topologies for industrial medium-voltage drives. IEEE Trans. Industr. Electron. 54(6), 2930–2945 (2007)

18. Rossmann, W.C., Ellis, R.G.: Retrofit of 22 pipeline pumping stations with 3000-hp motors and variable-frequency drives. IEEE Trans. Industr. Electron. 34(1), 178–186 (1998)

19. Rowell, D.: Impedance-Based Modeling Methods, February 2003. http://web.mit.edu/2.151/www/Handouts/Impedances.pdf

20. Siddique, U., Mahmoud, M.Y., Tahar, S.: On the formalization of Z-transform in HOL. In: Klein, G., Gamboa, R. (eds.) ITP 2014. LNCS, vol. 8558, pp. 483–498. Springer, Heidelberg (2014)

21. Taqdees, S.H., Hasan, O.: Formalization of Laplace transform using the multivariable calculus theory of HOL-light. In: McMillan, K., Middeldorp, A., Voronkov, A. (eds.) LPAR-19. LNCS, vol. 8312, pp. 744–758. Springer, Heidelberg (2013)

22. Tarjan, R.: Depth first search and linear graph algorithms. SIAM J. Comput. 1(2), 146–160 (1972)

23. Tiernan, J.C.: An efficient search algorithm to find the elementary circuits of a graph. Commun. ACM 13(12), 722–726 (1970)

24. Veerachary, M., Senjyu, T., Uezato, K.: Signal flow graph nonlinear modelling of interleaved converters. IEE Proc. Electr. Power Appl. 148(5), 410–418 (2001)

Practical Analysis Framework for Component Systems with Dynamic Reconfigurations

Olga Kouchnarenko[1,2] and Jean-François Weber[1(✉)]

[1] FEMTO-ST CNRS and Bourgogne Franche-Comté University, Besançon, France
[2] Inria/Nancy-Grand Est, Villers-lès-Nancy, France
{okouchnarenko,jfweber}@femto-st.fr

Abstract. Dynamic reconfigurations that modify the architecture of component-based systems without incurring any system downtime need to preserve the architectural consistency. In this context, we propose a reconfiguration model based on Hoare logic using sequences and (unlike most of the related work on reconfigurations) the alternative and the repetitive constructs.Using primitive reconfiguration operations as building blocks, this model takes advantage of the predicate-based semantics of programming language constructs and weakest preconditions to treat dynamic reconfigurations in a manner that preserves configuration consistency. Then, after enriching the model with interpreted configurations and reconfigurations in a consistency compatible manner, a conformance relation is exploited to validate component systems' implementations within the environment supporting the Fractal and FraSCAti frameworks. A practical contribution consists of promising experimental results obtained thanks to our implementations, notably on a cloud-based multi-tier hosting environment model managed as a component system.

1 Introduction

Dynamic reconfigurations that modify the architecture of self-adaptive [1] component-based systems without incurring any system downtime must happen not only in suitable circumstances, but also need to preserve the architectural consistency. Whereas the former can be ensured by adaptation policies [1,2], the latter is directly related to the definition of reconfigurations and to the reconfiguration ordering/protocol [3,4].

In [3], it is assumed that the reconfigurations always make the component assembly evolve from one consistent architecture to another consistent architecture, only through a path of architecturally consistent architectures. However, primitive reconfigurations like *unbind, stop,* etc. may disrupt such a path. With relation to consistency constraints defined in [5] over component-based architectures, their preservation of the system under scrutiny was uneasy to prove, mostly because of the lack of precise semantics for primitive reconfiguration operations. Therefore, when considering more complicated reconfigurations composed

---

This work has been partially funded by the Labex ACTION, ANR-11-LABX-0001-01.

M. Butler et al. (Eds.): ICFEM 2015, LNCS 9407, pp. 287–303, 2015.
DOI: 10.1007/978-3-319-25423-4_18

of sequences, repetitions, or choices over primitive reconfiguration operations, to address the above-mentioned issue, we propose to express reconfigurations' preconditions and postconditions using the concept of *weakest precondition* [6]. This precise and concise formalism allows us to express primitive and non primitive *guarded reconfigurations*; this is the first contribution simplifying both reconfiguration protocols and adaptation policies.

Then, after enriching the model with interpreted configurations and reconfigurations in a consistency-compatible way, a conformance relation is exploited to validate implementations of a component architectural model developed within our architecture manager supporting the Fractal [7] and FraSCAti [8] frameworks.

This second practical contribution allows us, not only, to simulate a desired run of a system being reconfigured, but, also, to generate all (or a subset of the) possible reconfiguration combinations useful, for example, for a (bounded) reachability analysis. The paper reports on promising experimental results obtained thanks to our implementations, notably on a cloud-based multi-tier application hosting environment model managed as a component software architecture.

The paper is organised as follows: Sect. 2 presents, as a case study, a cloud-based multi-tier application hosting environment managed as a component-based system. Background information on our component-based reconfiguration model, as well as elements of operational semantics are given in Sect. 3. In Sect. 4 a richer interpreted reconfiguration model is shown to be weakly simulated by the more abstract model; nevertheless, this simulation respects non-divergency. Using several case studies, Sect. 5 describes conformant implementations of the interpreted model within different environments. Section 6 presents related work and our conclusion.

2   Case Study

Internet service providers and telecommunications operators tend more and more to define themselves as cloud providers. In this context, automation of software and (virtual) hardware installation and configuration is paramount. It is not enough for an application to be cloud-ready; it has to be scalable and scalability mechanisms need to be integrated in the core of the cloud management system.

We consider a typical three-tier web application using a front-end web server, a middle-ware application server, and a back-end data providing service such as a database or a data store. Figure 1 shows a single virtual machine (or *VM*) hosting together the three services of such an application. The VM is represented as a composite

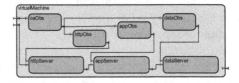

Fig. 1. Managed Virtual Machine with Three-tier Application Components

component *virtualMachine* containing sub-components representing each service (*httpServer*, *appServer*, and *dataServer*) of the application. Each of the service sub-component has two provided interfaces: one to provide its service and another one used to monitor the service.

Furthermore, the VM of Fig. 1 also contains four *observers*, that are sub-components used to monitor services. The sub-component *osObs* is used to monitor the Operating System of the VM. It is also bound to the sub-components *httpObs*, *appObs*, and *dataObs* used respectively to monitor the services of the *httpServer*, *appServer*, and *dataServer* sub-components. Finally, the VM composite component itself has two provided interfaces: one used to provide services and a second one used for monitoring.

Of course, a VM does not have to be monitored, nor have to host the three types of services. Figure 2 illustrates a *cloud environment*, *clouEnv*, containing a VM used for development purpose (*vmDev*) that contains the three tiers of the application without being monitored; such a VM is called *unmanaged*. The three other VM are all monitored, i.e., *managed*, and each contains a tier of the application. The reader can note that each of the managed VM contains only the observers responsible for monitoring the operating system and the type of service provided. The cloud environment has three provided interfaces: two to provide its service, whether it is or not in a development version, and another one, used for monitoring, connected to a sub-component *monitorObs* bound to all the monitoring interfaces of the managed VM.

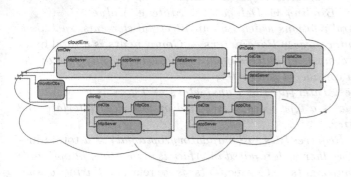

Fig. 2. Cloud Environment Example

A cloud provider must be able to provide on-demand (sets of) VMs configured with the right service components and the appropriate monitoring. In this context, we study the provisioning of a single VM as illustrated in Fig. 1. Depending on the services to provide and the monitoring state (managed vs unmanaged) the necessary components should be added. During the life cycle of the VM some configuration changes can happen; we consider them as reconfigurations of a component-based system. In this context, the challenge consists in performing adequate dynamic reconfigurations with minimum communication overhead, while avoiding reconfigurations that would lead to unwanted behaviours.

3   Component-Based Architecture

3.1   Configurations and Reconfigurations

Component models can be very heterogeneous. Most of them consider software components that can be seen as black boxes (or grey boxes if some of their inner features are visible) having fully-described interfaces. Behaviours and interactions are specified using components' definitions and their interfaces. In this section, we revisit the architectural reconfiguration model introduced in [5,9]. In general, the system configuration is the specific definition of the elements that define or prescribe what a system is composed of, while a reconfiguration can be seen as a transition from a configuration to another.

Following [9], a configuration is defined to be a set of architectural elements (components, required or provided interfaces, and parameters) together with relations to structure and to link them.

Definition 1 (Configuration). *A configuration c is a tuple $\langle Elem, Rel \rangle$ where*

- *$Elem = Components \uplus Interfaces \uplus Parameters \uplus Types$ is a set of architectural elements, such that*
    - *$Components$ is a non-empty set of the core entities, i.e. components;*
    - *$Interfaces = RequiredInts \uplus ProvidedInts$ is a finite set of the (required and provided) interfaces;*
    - *$Parameters$ is a finite set of component parameters;*
    - *$Types = ITypes \uplus PTypes$ is a finite set of the interface types and the parameter data types;*
- *$Rel = \begin{cases} Container \uplus ContainerType \uplus Contingency \\ \uplus Parent \uplus Binding \uplus Delegate \uplus State \uplus Value \end{cases}$*
  is a set of architectural relations which link architectural elements, such that
    - *$Container : Interfaces \uplus Parameters \to Components$ is a total function giving the component which supplies the considered interface or the component of a considered parameter;*
    - *$ContainerType : Interfaces \uplus Parameters \to Types$ is a total function that associates a type to each (required or provided) interface and to each parameter;*
    - *$Contingency : RequiredInts \to \{mandatory, optional\}$ is a total function indicating whether each required interface is mandatory or optional;*
    - *$Parent \subseteq Components \times Components$ is a relation linking a subcomponent to the corresponding composite component[1];*
    - *$Binding : ProvidedInts \to RequiredInts$ is a partial function which binds together a provided interface and a required one;*
    - *$Delegate : Interfaces \to Interfaces$ is a partial function to express delegation links;*
    - *$State : Components \to \{started, stopped\}$ is a total function giving the status of instantiated components;*
    - *$Value : Parameters \to \{t | t \in PType\}$ is a total function which gives the current value (of type $t \in PType$) of each parameter.*

We also introduce a set CP of configuration propositions which are constraints on the architectural elements and the relations between them. These

---

[1] For any $(p,q) \in Parent$, we say that q has a sub-component p, i.e. p is a child of q. Shared components (sub-components of multiple enclosing composite components) can have more than one parent.

propositions are specified using first-order logic formulae [10]. The interpretation of functions, relations, and predicates over $Elem$ is done according to basic definitions in [10] and Definition. 1. The interested reader is referred to [5].

Let $C = \{c, c_1, c_2, \ldots\}$ be a set of configurations. An *interpretation* function $l : C \to CP$ gives the largest conjunction of $cp \in CP$ evaluated to true on $c \in C$. We say that a configuration $c = \langle Elem, Rel \rangle$ satisfies $cp \in CP$, when $l(c) \Rightarrow cp$; in this case, cp is valid on c, otherwise, c does not satisfy cp.

Among the configuration propositions, the architectural *consistency constraints* CC in Table 1 express requirements on component assembly common to all the component architectures [5]. Intuitively,

- a component *supplies*, at least, one provided interface (**CC.1**);
- the composite components have no parameter (**CC.2**);
- a sub-component must not include its own parent component (**CC.3**);
- two bound interfaces must have the same interface type (**CC.4**) and their containers are sub-components of the same composite (**CC.5**);
- when binding two interfaces, there is a need to ensure that they have not been involved in a delegation yet (**CC.6**); similarly, when establishing a delegation link between two interfaces, the specifier must ensure that they have not yet been involved in a binding (**CC.7**);
- a provided (resp. required) interface of a sub-component is delegated to at most one provided (resp. required) interface of its parent component (**CC.8**), (**CC.9**) and (**CC.11**); the interfaces involved in the delegation must have the same interface type (**CC.10**); and
- a component is *started* only if its mandatory required interfaces are bound or delegated (**CC.12**).

Definition 2 (Consistent configuration). *Let $c = \langle Elem, Rel \rangle$ be a configuration and CC the consistency constraints. The configuration c is* consistent, *written* consistent(c), *if $l(c) \Rightarrow CC$. We write* consistent(C) *when $\forall c \in C$.* consistent(c).

Table 1. Consistency Constraints

$$\forall c.(c \in Components \Rightarrow (\exists ip.(ip \in ProvidedInts \wedge Container(ip) = c))) \ (\mathbf{CC.1})$$

$$\forall c, c' \in Components.((c, c') \in Parent \Rightarrow \forall p.(p \in Parameters \Rightarrow Container(p) \neq c')) \ (\mathbf{CC.2})$$

$$\forall c, c' \in Components.((c, c') \in Parent^+ \Rightarrow c \neq c') \ (\mathbf{CC.3})$$

$$\begin{matrix} \forall ip \in ProvidedInts, \\ \forall ir \in RequiredInts \end{matrix} \cdot \left(Binding(ip) = ir \Rightarrow \begin{matrix} ContainerType(ip) = ContainerType(ir) \\ \wedge Container(ip) \neq Container(ir) \end{matrix} \right) (\mathbf{CC.4})$$

$$\begin{matrix} \forall ip \in ProvidedInts, \\ \forall ir \in RequiredInts \end{matrix} \cdot \left(Binding(ip) = ir \Rightarrow \exists c \in Components. \left(\begin{matrix} (Container(ip), c) \in Parent \\ \wedge (Container(ir), c) \in Parent \end{matrix} \right) \right) (\mathbf{CC.5})$$

$$\forall ip \in ProvidedInts, \forall ir \in RequiredInts. \left(Binding(ip) = ir \Rightarrow \begin{matrix} ip \notin dom(Delegate) \\ \wedge ir \notin dom(Delegate) \end{matrix} \right) (\mathbf{CC.6})$$

$$\forall i, i' \in Interfaces.(Delegate(i) = i' \Rightarrow i \notin dom(Binding) \wedge i \notin codom(Binding)) \ (\mathbf{CC.7})$$

$$\forall i, i' \in Interfaces.(Delegate(i) = i' \wedge i \in ProvidedInts \Rightarrow i' \in ProvidedInts) \ (\mathbf{CC.8})$$

$$\forall i, i' \in Interfaces.(Delegate(i) = i' \wedge i \in RequiredInts \Rightarrow i' \in RequiredInts) \ (\mathbf{CC.9})$$

$$\forall i, i' \in Interfaces. \left(Delegate(i) = i' \Rightarrow \begin{matrix} ContainerType(i) = ContainerType(i') \\ \wedge (Container(i), Container(i')) \in Parent \end{matrix} \right) (\mathbf{CC.10})$$

$$\forall i, i', i'' \in Interfaces. \left(\begin{matrix} (Delegate(i) = i' \wedge Delegate(i) = i'' \Rightarrow i' = i'') \\ \wedge (Delegate(i) = i'' \wedge Delegate(i') = i'' \Rightarrow i = i') \end{matrix} \right) (\mathbf{CC.11})$$

$$\forall ir \in RequiredInts. \begin{pmatrix} State(Container(ir)) = started \\ \wedge Contingency(ir) = mandatory \end{pmatrix} \Rightarrow \exists i \in Interfaces. \begin{pmatrix} Binding(i) = ir \\ \vee Delegate(ir) = i \end{pmatrix} \end{pmatrix} (\mathbf{CC.12})$$

3.2   Reconfiguration Model and Consistency Propagation

Reconfigurations make the component-based architecture evolve dynamically. They are composed of primitive operations such as instantiation/destruction (*new/destroy*) of components; addition/removal (*add/remove*) of components; binding/unbinding (*bind/unbind*) of component interfaces; starting/stopping (*start/stop*) components; setting components' parameters values (*update*). These primitive operations obey pre/post predicates. For example, before adding a sub-component $comp_1$ to a composite $comp_2$, one must verify, as in Table 2, that (*a*) $comp_1$ and $comp_2$ exist (2) and are different (3), (*b*) $comp_2$ is not a descendant of $comp_1$ (4), and (*c*) $comp_2$ has no parameter (5). When these preconditions are met, the postcondition consists in adding $(comp_1, comp_2)$ to the *Parent* relation, as expressed by $R_{add} = Parent \cup \{(comp_1, comp_2)\}$ (1).

Table 2. Preconditions of the *add* primitive reconfiguration operation

| $comp_1, comp_2 \in Components$ (2) | $(comp_2, comp_1) \notin Parent^+$ (4) |
| $comp_1 \neq comp_2$ (3) | $\forall p \in Parameters.Container(p) \neq comp_2$ (5) |

Inspired by the predicate-based semantics of programming language constructs [11], we consider a reconfiguration operation *ope*, and two configurations c and c' such that the transition between c and c' is performed using *ope* (denoted by $c \xrightarrow{ope} c'$). Then, given R, some conditions on the configuration of the system under scrutiny, the notation $wp(ope, R)$ denotes, as in [6], the *weakest precondition* for the configuration c such that activation of *ope* can occur and, if so, is guaranteed to lead to c' satisfying the postcondition R. More formally, in our case, if $l(c) \Rightarrow wp(ope, R)$ and $c \xrightarrow{ope} c'$ then $l(c') \Rightarrow R$. Therefore, considering the *add* primitive reconfiguration operation whose preconditions are displayed in Table 2, the weakest precondition $wp(add, R_{add})$ is the conjunction of preconditions (2) to (5).

Inspired by [6] and using the same notations, we propose in Table 3 the grammar of axiom <guarded reconfiguration> for *guarded reconfigurations*. Let <*ope*> represent a primitive reconfiguration operation, also called *primitive statement*. We extend the set of primitive reconfiguration operations with the *skip* operation, which does not induce any change on a given configuration. Hence, for any postcondition R, we have $wp(skip, R) = R$. Afterwards, like in [6], the semantics of the ";" operator is given by $wp(S_1; S_2, R) = wp(S_1, wp(S_2, R))$ where S_1 and S_2 are statements.

Guarded reconfiguration sets are used to define the alternative and the repetitive constructs; these sets are not statements. In a nutshell, the alternative construct selects for execution only guarded lists with a true guard, whereas, the repetitive construct selects for execution guarded lists with a true guard and is

Table 3. Guarded reconfigurations grammar

<guarded reconfiguration>	::=	<guard> → <guarded list>
<guard>	::=	<boolean expression>
<guarded list>	::=	<statement> {; <statement>}
<guarded reconfiguration set>	::=	<guarded reconfiguration> {‖ <guarded reconfiguration>}
<alternative construct>	::=	**if** <guarded reconfiguration set> **fi**
<repetitive construct>	::=	**do** <guarded reconfiguration set> **od**
<statement>	::=	<alternative construct> | <repetitive construct> | < ope >

repeated until none of the guards is true. If a guarded reconfiguration set is made of more than one guarded reconfiguration, they are separated by the ‖ operator[2]

To present the semantics of the alternative construct, let IF denote **if** $B_1 \rightarrow S_1 \| \ldots \| B_n \rightarrow S_n$ **fi** and BB denote $(\exists i : 1 \leq i \leq n : B_i)$, then $wp(IF, R) = BB \wedge (\forall i : 1 \leq i \leq n : B_i \Rightarrow wp(S_i, R))$. For the repetitive construct, let DO denote **do** $B_1 \rightarrow S_1 \| \ldots \| B_n \rightarrow S_n$ **do**. Let $H_0(R) = R \wedge \neg BB$ and for $k > 0$, $H_k(R) = wp(IF, H_{k-1}(R)) \vee H_0(R)$, then $wp(DO, R) = \exists k : k \geq 0 : H_k(R)$. Intuitively, $H_k(R)$ is the weakest precondition guaranteeing termination after at most k selections of a guarded list, leaving the system in a configuration such that R holds. Let $\mathcal{R}_{run} = \mathcal{R} \cup \{run\}$ be a set of operations, where $\mathcal{R}$ is a finite set of guarded reconfigurations instantiated wrt. the system under consideration, and run is the name of a generic action representing all the running operations[3] of the component-based system.

Definition 3 (Reconfiguration model). *The operational semantics of a component-based system is defined by the labelled transition system $S = \langle \mathcal{C}, \mathcal{C}^0, \mathcal{R}_{run}, \rightarrow, l \rangle$ where $\mathcal{C} = \{c, c_1, c_2, \ldots\}$ is a set of configurations, $\mathcal{C}^0 \subseteq \mathcal{C}$ is a set of initial configurations, $\rightarrow \subseteq \mathcal{C} \times \mathcal{R}_{run} \times \mathcal{C}$ is the reconfiguration relation obeying $wp()$ predicates, and $l : \mathcal{C} \rightarrow CP$ is a total interpretation function.*

Let us note $c \overset{ope}{\rightarrow} c'$ for $(c, ope, c') \in \rightarrow$. Given the model $S = \langle \mathcal{C}, \mathcal{C}^0, \mathcal{R}_{run}, \rightarrow, l \rangle$, a path σ of S is a sequence of configurations $c_0, c_1, c_2, \ldots$ such that $\forall i \geq 0. \exists ope_i \in \mathcal{R}_{run}.(c_i \overset{ope_i}{\rightarrow} c_{i+1})$. An execution is a path σ in Σ s.t. $\sigma(0) \in \mathcal{C}^0$. We write $\sigma(i)$ to denote the i-th configuration of σ. The notation σ_i denotes the suffix path $\sigma(i), \sigma(i+1), \ldots$, and σ_i^j denotes the segment path $\sigma(i), \sigma(i+1), \ldots, \sigma(j-1), \sigma(j)$. Let Σ denote the set of paths, and $\Sigma^f (\subseteq \Sigma)$ the set of finite paths. A configuration c' is reachable from c when there is a path $\sigma = c_0, c_1, \ldots, c_n$ in Σ^f s.t. $c = c_0$ and $c' = c_n$ with $n \geq 0$. Let c be a configuration, the set of all configurations reachable from c is denoted $reach(c)$. This notion can be lifted from configurations to sets of configurations by $reach(\mathcal{C}) = \{reach(c) \mid c \in \mathcal{C}\}$.

Proposition 1 (Consistency propagation). *Given $\mathcal{C}^0 \subseteq \mathcal{C}$, consistent($\mathcal{C}^0$) implies consistent(reach($\mathcal{C}^0$)).*

---

[2] As in [6], the order in which guarded reconfigurations appear is semantically irrelevant.
[3] The normal running of different components also changes the architecture, e.g., by modifying parameter values or stopping components.

Proof (sketch). We start the proof (see [12] for a more complete proof) by showing that each primitive operation *ope* preserves configuration consistency. We use this result to establish (by induction) that a guarded reconfiguration having a sequence of primitive statements in its guarded list also preserves consistency.

This allows us to show that guarded reconfigurations having a statement based on a guarded reconfiguration set made only of primitive statements ($G \rightarrow$ **fi** grs **fi** or $G \rightarrow$ **do** grs **od**, where grs denotes $B_0 \rightarrow ope_0 \| B_1 \rightarrow ope_1 \| \ldots \| B_n \rightarrow ope_n$) also preserve consistency using only hypothesis on the statements' preconditions and postconditions.

Therefore, with the same reasoning, considering general (i.e., primitive or non primitive) statements instead of only primitive ones and using only hypothesis on statements' preconditions and postconditions, we can prove that consistency is preserved *a)* for guarded reconfigurations having a guarded list composed of a sequence of (non primitive) statements ($G \rightarrow S_0; S_1; \ldots; S_n$) and *b)* for guarded reconfigurations having as guarded list a statement ($G \rightarrow$ **fi** grs **fi** or $G \rightarrow$ **do** grs **od**, where grs denotes $B_0 \rightarrow S_0 \| B_1 \rightarrow S_1 \| \ldots \| B_n \rightarrow S_n$).   □

4   Interpreted Architecture Model

In the specification model, primitive operations and guarded reconfigurations were left abstract enough and *run* was uninterpreted. A formal semantics for the component-based system with interpreted operations can be obtained by enriching the configurations with more precise memory states and the effect of these actions upon memory.

4.1   Interpreted Configurations and Reconfigurations

Let us consider a set (infinite, in general) $GM = \{u, ...\}$ of shared global memory states, and a set (infinite, in general) $LM = \{v, ...\}$ of memory states local to a given component. These memory states are read and modified by the primitive and non-primitive reconfigurations, and also by actions implementing *run*.

Interpreted configurations. In addition to already interpreted parameters and interfaces (cf. [5] for more detail), the state of components can be described more precisely by using local memory states. The set of the interpreted states of components is the least set $State_{\mathcal{I}}$ s.t. if $s_1, \ldots, s_n$ are elements in $State_{\mathcal{I}}$[4], $v_1, \ldots, v_n \in LM$ are local memory states, then $((s_1, v_1), \ldots, (s_n, v_n))$ is in $State_{\mathcal{I}}$. Then, the set of the interpreted configurations $\mathcal{C}_{\mathcal{I}}$ is defined by $GM \times State_{\mathcal{I}}$.

Interpreted transitions. Our basic assumption is that all primitive actions have a deterministic effect upon the local and global memory, always terminate (either normally or exceptionally), and are effective. For each primitive reconfiguration operation *ope*, the corresponding interpreted reconfiguration, denoted by $\overline{ope}$, has equivalent or stronger preconditions, such that all constructs behave deterministically. A non-deterministic global behaviour is produced by the arbitrary interleaving of components.

---

[4] Viewed as a relation.

Formally, all the actions $ope \in \mathcal{R}_{run}$ are interpreted as mappings $\overline{ope}$ from $GM \times LM$ into itself. Additionally, there are some actions specific to the interpretation, $\mathcal{R}_{int}$, for example for testing guards. We say that $\mathcal{I} = (GM, LM, (\overline{ope})_{ope \in \mathcal{R}_{run} \cup \mathcal{R}_{int}})$ is an interpretation of the underlying $\mathcal{R}_{run}$. Let $\mathcal{I}_{\mathcal{R}_{run}}$ denote the class of all interpretations. This construction leads to

Definition 4 (Interpreted reconfiguration model). *The interpreted operational semantics of component-based system is defined by the labelled transition system $S_{\mathcal{I}} = \langle \mathcal{C}_{\mathcal{I}}, \mathcal{C}_{\mathcal{I}}^{0}, \mathcal{R}_{run_{\mathcal{I}}}, \rightarrow_{\mathcal{I}}, l_{\mathcal{I}} \rangle$ where $\mathcal{C}_{\mathcal{I}}$ is a set of configurations together with their memory states, $\mathcal{C}_{\mathcal{I}}^{0}$ is a set of initial configurations, $\mathcal{R}_{run_{\mathcal{I}}} = \{\overline{ope} \mid ope \in \mathcal{R}_{run} \cup \mathcal{R}_{int}\}$, $\rightarrow_{\mathcal{I}} \subseteq \mathcal{C}_{\mathcal{I}} \times \mathcal{R}_{run_{\mathcal{I}}} \times \mathcal{C}_{\mathcal{I}}$ is the interpreted reconfiguration relation, and $l_{\mathcal{I}} : \mathcal{C}_{\mathcal{I}} \rightarrow CP$ is a total interpretation function.*

It is easy to see that, by construction, $\mathtt{consistent}(\mathcal{C}_{\mathcal{I}}^{0})$. Moreover, if $\mathtt{consistent}(c)$ and $c \xrightarrow{\overline{ope}}_{\mathcal{I}} c'$ then $\mathtt{consistent}(c')$.

4.2   Compatible Interpretation

To establish links between the reconfiguration model and the corresponding interpreted model, we propose to use a version of the classical τ-simulation quasi-ordering [13], while relabeling the operations in $\mathcal{R}_{int}$ by τ. For all $ope \in \mathcal{R} \cup \{\epsilon\}$, where ϵ denotes the empty word, we write $c \xoverset{ope}{\Rightarrow} c'$ when there are $n, m \geq 0$ such that $c \xrightarrow{\tau^{n} ope \tau^{m}} c'$.

Definition 5 (d-simulation). *Let $S_1 = \langle \mathcal{C}_1, \mathcal{C}_1^{0}, \ldots \rangle$ and $S_2 = \langle \mathcal{C}_2, \mathcal{C}_2^{0}, \ldots \rangle$ be two models over $\mathcal{R}$. A binary relation $\sqsubseteq_d \subseteq \mathcal{C}_1 \times \mathcal{C}_2$ is a d-simulation iff, for all ope in $\mathcal{R} \cup \{\epsilon\}$, $(c_1, c_2) \in \sqsubseteq_\tau$ implies (1) whenever $c_1 \xRightarrow{ope}_1 c_1'$, then there exists $c_2' \in \mathcal{C}_2$ such that $c_2 \xRightarrow{ope}_2 c_2'$ and $(c_1', c_2') \in \sqsubseteq_d$, and (2) $c_1 \xnRightarrow{ope}$ implies $c_2 \xnRightarrow{ope}$.*

We write $S_1 \sqsubseteq_d S_2$ when $\forall c_1^{0} \in \mathcal{C}_1^{0} \exists c_2^{0} \in \mathcal{C}_2^{0}.(c_1^{0}, c_2^{0}) \in \sqsubseteq_d$.

Let us consider interpreted reconfiguration operations in $\mathcal{R}_{run_{\mathcal{I}}}$ and the corresponding non-interpreted counterpart in $\mathcal{R}_{run}$. When relabelling the operations in $\mathcal{R}_{int}$ by τ, we can state–modulo the overline notation–that the more abstract model τ-simulates the interpreted model (because of the non-determinism when testing guards in the non-interpreted model); nevertheless, this simulation respects non-divergency.

Theorem 1 (Compatibility). $S_{\mathcal{I}} \sqsubseteq_d S$.

Proof (sketch). There are two cases for $ope \in \mathcal{R}_{run} \cup \mathcal{R}_{int}$. As τ's covering operations in $\mathcal{R}_{int}$ are introduced to evaluate guards of sequences of guarded reconfigurations, they do not form infinite cycles of τ-transitions. So, there always must be a way out of these cycles, if any, by a transition of label $\overline{ope}$.

By construction any primitive reconfiguration operation of the interpreted model has preconditions equivalent to or stronger than its counterpart in the non-interpreted model. This way, by using hypothesis on weakest preconditions in [6], we can prove that guarded reconfigurations composed of primitive statements, $G \to \bar{s}$, with $\bar{s} \in \mathcal{R}_{run_\mathcal{I}} \backslash \mathcal{R}_{int}$ have preconditions equivalent to or stronger than the corresponding statement $s \in \mathcal{R}_{run}$. Consequently, starting from initial configurations, for any $c_1 \in \mathcal{C}_\mathcal{I}$, if $\mathtt{consistent}(c_1)$ there is $c_2 \in \mathcal{C}$ s.t. $\mathtt{consistent}(c_2)$, and if a guarded reconfiguration $G \to \bar{s}$ is applied to c_1 there exists a guard G', s.t. $G \Rightarrow G'$ and $G' \to s$ applies to c_2. Moreover, the consistent target configurations are in $\sqsubseteq_d$ too because of their guards.

If no ope can be performed in $c_1 \in \mathcal{C}_\mathcal{I}$ after having tested some guards covered by τ, c_1 is not consistent, and consequently neither is $c_2 \in \mathcal{C}$. At this step, only several primitive reconfigurations can be applied, as their preconditions are equivalent, no ope can be performed in c_2 either.   □

4.3   Property Preservation

Theorem 1 can be exploited for property preservation. For example, as the reachability properties are compatible with $\sqsubseteq_d$, this leads us, consequently, to:

Proposition 2. *If configuration c is not reachable in S, it is not reachable in any $S_\mathcal{I}$. Conversely, if configuration c is reachable in S, there exists an interpretation $\mathcal{I}$ such that c is reachable in $S_\mathcal{I}$.*

In addition, safety properties expressed via non-reachability properties can be ensured. Moreover, as a consequence of Theorem 1 and Propositions 1 and 2, we can state:

Proposition 3. *Let $S_\mathcal{I} = \langle \mathcal{C}_\mathcal{I}, \mathcal{C}_\mathcal{I}^0, \mathcal{R}_{run_\mathcal{I}}, \to_\mathcal{I}, l_\mathcal{I} \rangle$ be the interpreted model and $S = \langle \mathcal{C}, \mathcal{C}^0, \mathcal{R}_{run}, \to, l \rangle$ the specification model. Given $\mathcal{C}_\mathcal{I}^0 \subseteq \mathcal{C}_\mathcal{I}$, if $S_\mathcal{I} \sqsubseteq_d S$ then $\mathtt{consistent}(\mathcal{C}_\mathcal{I}^0)$ implies $\mathtt{consistent}(reach(\mathcal{C}_\mathcal{I}^0))$.*

It must be noticed that differently from [3], we do not assume that the reconfigurations always make evolve the component assembly from one consistent architecture to another consistent architecture, only through a path of consistent configurations. Indeed, this assumption seems to be too strong notably wrt. primitive reconfigurations.

5   Implementation and Architecture Conformance

5.1   Implementation Protocol

We developed a prototype tool, contained in a java package named $cbsdr$[5], supporting the interpreted reconfiguration model to design and simulate component-based systems with dynamic reconfigurations. Using generic java classes, we can use our implementation to perform reconfigurations on applications deployed using Fractal [7] or FraSCAti [8]. The Fractal framework is based on a hierarchical and reflective component model. Its goal is to reduce the development, deployment, and maintenance costs of software systems in general[6]. FraSCAti is an open-source implementation of the *Service Component Architecture*[7] (SCA).

---

[5] $cbsdr$ stands for Component-Based System Dynamic Reconfiguration.
[6] http://fractal.ow2.org/tutorial/index.html.
[7] http://www.oasis-opencsa.org/sca.

It can be seen as a framework having a Fractal base with an extra layer implementing SCA specifications. In [8], a smart home scenario illustrates the capabilities and the various reconfigurations of the FraSCAti platform.

Figure 3 shows the *cbsdr* interface displaying a given state of the VM from our running example developed using Fractal (top frame). The left frame shows the various states of the run under scrutiny, whereas the bottom frame can be used to display various information such as the evolution of parameters of the model, console output, or the outcome of reconfigurations performed.

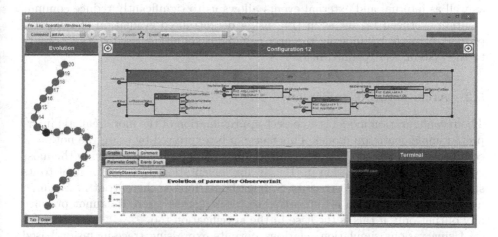

Fig. 3. Model of the VM component-based system displayed in our interface

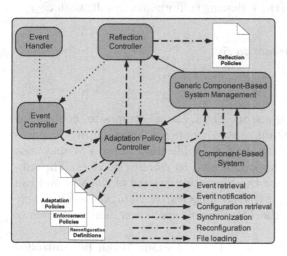

Fig. 4. *cbsdr* Implementation Architecture

This interface allows the monitoring of a component-based system and the generation of (external) events during a run of *cbsdr*, but can also be used to analyse the logs of a run already performed. It is interesting to note that primitive, as well as, non primitive reconfiguration operations can be performed and analysed.

Thanks to this application, in addition to the abovementioned functionalities, we are able to perform adaptations using dynamic reconfigurations triggered by temporal properties at runtime, as described in [2]. In this case, the implementation (see Fig. 4) works as follows: (*a*) adaptation polices are loaded and applied using a control

loop, (b) FTPL[8] expressions are evaluated and (if any) candidate reconfigurations are ordered by priority using fuzzy logic values embedded in adaptation
policies, (c) candidate reconfigurations are applied to the component-based system model using our reconfiguration semantics in order to verify that the corresponding target configuration does not violate any of the properties to enforce,
and (d) the target configuration obtained using the reconfiguration with highest
priority that does not violate any of the properties to enforce is applied to the
component based system using a protocol similar to the one described in [3].
The fact that we are using temporal properties based on architectural relations
as well as internal and external events allows us to significantly reduce communication overhead (a) by, as in [14], using decentralised evaluation of temporal
properties or (b) by allowing the user to submit simultaneous (external) events
to the system, as explained below.

5.2   Architecture Conformance

The reconfiguration model is a correct approximation of the more realistic interpreted implementation model. This fact can be expressed by using the notion of
conformance of the component architecture model. Basically, following the most
commonly used *ioco* relation in [15], an implementation $S_{\mathcal{I}}$ is conformant to its
specification S if, after a trace of S, one should foresee the output of $S_{\mathcal{I}}$ in S,
and the implementation is authorised to reach a state where it cannot produce
any output only if this is the case in the specification too.

Using various simulation relations permits expressing trace-inclusion-based
conformance and stronger conformance relations at the level of transition systems. Thus, thanks to the proof arguments of Theorem 1, and the subsequent
trace inclusion modulo τ, we have the following conformance result, with $S_{\mathcal{I}_{cbsdr}}$
being the *cbsdr* implementation.

Proposition 4. $S_{\mathcal{I}_{cbsdr}}$ *is conformant to* S.

5.3   Running Example

We consider a VM represented, as in Fig. 1, as a composite component
virtualMachine that may contain sub-components representing services
httpServer, *appServer*, or *dataServer* of an application. This VM may also
contain *observers* that are sub-components used to monitor services. The sub-
component *osObs* is used to monitor the Operating System of the VM and can
be bound to the sub-components *httpObs*, *appObs*, or *dataObs* used respectively to monitor the services of the *httpServer*, *appServer*, and *dataServer*
sub-components.

The Fractal and FraSCAti versions of the VM example can be controlled
by our implementation using external events as *init*, *manage*, *setdata*, etc., to

---

[8] FTPL stands for TPL (Temporal Pattern Language) prefixed by 'F' to denote its
relation to Fractal-like components and to first-order integrity constraints over them.

(respectively) initialise the VM, monitor the VM, or set the data server of the VM up. If the VM is monitored, it is described as *managed*, otherwise it is said to be *unmanaged*. Depending of the service to provide and the state of the VM (managed vs. unmanaged), only the necessary component should be added.

For example, let us consider a managed VM providing only the HTTP service: it contains the *httpServer* component and, since it is managed, it also contains the *osObs* and the *httpObs* components. Therefore, the generation of the *setdata* external event triggers (via adaptation policies) the addition of the *dataServer* and *dataObs* components. Of course, if the initial VM was unmanaged, the generation of the *setdata* external event would only result in the addition of the *dataServer* component. Nevertheless, in this case (unmanaged HTTP VM), the generation of the *setdata* and *manage* external events would result in a VM containing all the components pertaining to a managed VM providing the HTTP and the DATA services (i.e., *httpServer*, *dataServer*, *osObs*, *httpObs*, and *dataObs*).

This is due to the fact that we use FTPL temporal logic expressions as "**after** *unsetdata* ((**always** ⊤) **until** *setdata*)" to guarantee that, in case of opposite events like *setdata* and *unsetdata*, the corresponding expression is potentially true until the occurrence of the opposite events. This way, the ordered sequence of events *init*, *manage*, *sethttp*, *setapp*, and *setdata* is equivalent to a single communication containing all these events at once; this significantly reduces communication overhead.

5.4   Other Examples

To illustrate how the *cbsdr* tool works, we present below two examples: a small http server, and a model of the location component of the *cycab*, an autonomous vehicle. This latter example confirms that not only pertinent reconfigurations can be triggered, but also reconfigurations leading to unwanted behaviours are avoided. Finally, we conclude this section by presenting some results about the CPU consumption of the *cbsdr* tool used with both Fractal and FraSCAti frameworks.

Http Server. Figure 5 shows an experimentation with the http server composite component during which, as in [16], http requests were simulated. Depending on the *load* and *request deviation* to measure whether or not requests are similar, it may make sense to add a cache (the need can be *low*, *medium*, or *high* determining the size of the cache) or an additional file server.

Interestingly, response times measured when our http server is controlled and adapted by the *cbsdr* application match almost exactly the times measured (under similar load and request deviation patterns) for a http server having a cache (of size *high*) and two file servers. No memory nor disk overhead were noted.

Cycab. Figure 6 uses the model of the location system of an autonomous car. Thanks to adaptation using temporal properties at runtime, we can remove

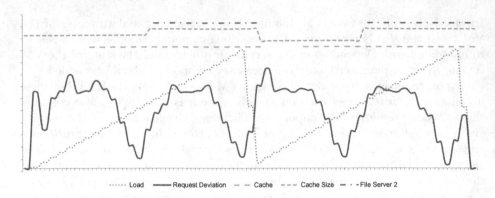

Fig. 5. Experiment with the http server composite component

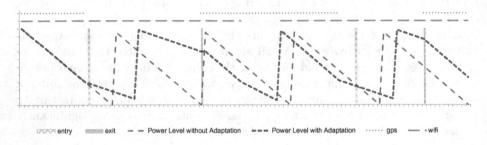

Fig. 6. Experiment with the cycab location composite component

the *gps* or *wifi* location components to save energy when needed (e.g., the *gps* component does not work in tunnels — between *entry* and *exit*).

The run represented in Fig. 6 shows a consumption of energy around 32 % lower using adaptation (empty dashed red graph) compared to a run not using it (full dashed blue graph). It is important to notice that when the vehicle is in a tunnel, the *cbsdr* tool prevents the occurrence of the reconfiguration that would normally add the *gps* component when the power level is high. The reader interested in a more detailed description is referred to [2].

CPU Overhead. We tested our implementation on the above-mentioned examples using both Fractal and FraSCAti framework. More than 300 tests were performed to assess the resources overhead caused by our implementation. Table 4 summarises the increase of CPU usage when

Table 4. Measured increase of CPU usage expressed in percent ($\bar{\mu} \pm \sigma$)

Framework	Fractal	FraSCAti
CPU User time	17 ± 3	11 ± 2
CPU System time	2 ± 2	14 ± 2
Percent of CPU	17 ± 2	15 ± 7

adaptation is used compared to similar runs not using any adaptation mechanism. CPU overhead is expressed in Table 4 in the format $\bar{\mu} \pm \sigma$ with $\bar{\mu}$ being the average and σ the standard deviation.

6   Related Work and Conclusion

6.1   Related Work

Self-adaptation is an important and active research field with applications in various domains [1]. This roadmap emphasises an important challenge consisting in bridging the gap between the design and the implementation of self-adaptive systems. In [2] component-based systems reconfiguration was performed at runtime using adaptation policies triggered by temporal patterns. The reconfigurations considered, however, were merely sequences of primitive reconfiguration operations. In the present paper, since we use the alternative and the repetitive constructs to compose reconfigurations, a given reconfiguration can have different outcomes, depending on the context, or due to non-deterministic mechanisms. It is not only a static sequence of reconfiguration instructions (as it is the case in [2,7,8,17]), but a truly *dynamic* reconfiguration. Differently from [3], we do not assume that the reconfigurations always lead the component assembly to evolve from one consistent architecture to another consistent architecture.

Version consistency was introduced in [17] to minimise the interruption of service (*disruption*) and the delay with which component-based (distributed) systems are updated (*timeliness*) by means of reconfigurations. It qualifies a state where transactions within the system are such that a given reconfiguration may not disrupt the system and occur in bounded time; version consistency was inspired by *quiescence* [18] and *tranquility* [19] with the intent to gather the best of both notions. Unlike [17–19], we only consider architectural constraints as preconditions to apply guarded reconfigurations; this way, by considering components as black boxes, the separation of concerns principle is respected. The applicative consistency (related to transactions within the system or external events) can be maintained at runtime using adaptation policies mechanisms as in [2] for centralised system and in [14] for decentralised or distributed systems.

Following [20], our notion of consistency can be viewed as a specific architecture style. Nevertheless, when using graph grammars, we represent interfaces types of the component-based systems by specific graph nodes, this way, like in [21], we can monitor (temporal) properties at the interface level.

Let us remark that the present work is motivated by other frameworks that support the development of components. For example, experimenting with our VM example within the *GROOVE* environment [22] leads us to the presentation of paths with transitions labelled by the primitive reconfiguration operations being performed. Consequently, consistency and conformity issues are pertinent to *GROOVE* too.

6.2   Conclusion

Inspired by [6], we proposed a grammar for guarded reconfigurations. This allowed us to build reconfigurations based on primitive reconfiguration operations using sequences of reconfigurations as well as the alternative and the repetitive constructs. The ability to determine weakest preconditions for the application of reconfigurations enabled us to prove that these guarded reconfigurations preserve configuration consistency.

This way, a conformance relation can be established to validate implementations of component-based systems architectural models using either our java-based *cbsdr* application or the *GROOVE* graph transformation tool. This makes these tools applicable to build some parts of state space of reachable graphs, i.e., configurations, and thereby derive information about the system. Furthermore, one of the key advantages of this work is that it is readily applicable to practical reconfiguration operations.

As a future work, we intend to exploit the results of the present paper to extend adaptation policies defined in [2] with guarded reconfigurations. Then, we could aim to perform sound and complete compositions of such adaptation policies. This would permit us to move further toward our overall goal, which is the adaptation of component-based system at runtime using adaptation policies based on temporal logic properties.

References

1. de Lemos, R., et al.: Software engineering for self-adaptive systems: a second research roadmap. In: de Lemos, R., Giese, H., Müller, H.A., Shaw, M. (eds.) Software Engineering for Self-Adaptive Systems. LNCS, vol. 7475, pp. 1–32. Springer, Heidelberg (2013)
2. Kouchnarenko, O., Weber, J.-F.: Adapting component-based systems at runtime via policies with temporal patterns. In: Fiadeiro, J.L., Liu, Z., Xue, J. (eds.) FACS 2013. LNCS, vol. 8348, pp. 234–253. Springer, Heidelberg (2014)
3. Boyer, F., Gruber, O., Pous, D.: Robust reconfigurations of component assemblies. In: International Conference on Software Engineering, ICSE 2013, pp. 13–22. IEEE Press, Piscataway (2013)
4. Myllärniemi, V., Ylikangas, M., Raatikainen, M., Pääkkö, J., Männistö, T., Aaltonen, T.: Configurator-as-a-service: tool support for deriving software architectures at runtime. In: The WICSA/ECSA 2012 Companion Volume, pp. 151–158. ACM (2012)
5. Lanoix, A., Dormoy, J., Kouchnarenko, O.: Combining proof and model-checking to validate reconfigurable architectures. ENTCS **279**, 43–57 (2011)
6. Dijkstra, E.W.: Guarded commands, nondeterminacy and formal derivation of programs. Commun. ACM **18**, 453–457 (1975)
7. Bruneton, E., Coupaye, T., Leclercq, M., Quéma, V., Stefani, J.B.: The fractal component model and its support in java. Soft. Pract. Experience **36**, 1257–1284 (2006)
8. Seinturier, L., Merle, P., Rouvoy, R., Romero, D., Schiavoni, V., Stefani, J.B.: A component-based middleware platform for reconfigurable service-oriented architectures. Softw. Pract. Experience **42**, 559–583 (2012)
9. Dormoy, J., Kouchnarenko, O., Lanoix, A.: Using temporal logic for dynamic reconfigurations of components. In: Barbosa, L.S., Lumpe, M. (eds.) FACS 2010. LNCS, vol. 6921, pp. 200–217. Springer, Heidelberg (2012)
10. Hamilton, A.G.: Logic for mathematicians. Cambridge University Press, England (1988)

11. Hoare, C.A.R.: An axiomatic basis for computer programming. Commun. ACM **12**, 576–580 (1969)
12. Kouchnarenko, O., Weber, J.F.: Practical Analysis Framework for Component Systems with Dynamic Reconfigurations (2015) Long version of the present paper – https://hal.archives-ouvertes.fr/hal-01135720
13. Milner, R.: Communication and concurrency. Prentice-Hall, Inc., Upper Saddle River (1989)
14. Kouchnarenko, O., Weber, J.-F.: Decentralised evaluation of temporal patterns over component-based systems at runtime. In: Lanese, I., Madelaine, E. (eds.) FACS 2014. LNCS, vol. 8997, pp. 108–126. Springer, Heidelberg (2015)
15. Tretmans, J.: Test generation with inputs, outputs and repetitive quiescence. Softw. Concepts Tools **17**, 103–120 (1996)
16. Chauvel, F., Barais, O., Plouzeau, N., Borne, I., Jézéquel, J.M.: Composition et expression qualitative de politiques d'adaptation pour les composants Fractal. In: Actes des Journées nationales du GDR GPL (2009)
17. Ma, X., Baresi, L., Ghezzi, C., Panzica La Manna, V., Lu, J.: Version-consistent dynamic reconfiguration of component-based distributed systems. In: The 19th ACM SIGSOFT Symposium and the 13th European Conference on Foundations of software engineering, pp. 245–255. ACM (2011)
18. Kramer, J., Magee, J.: The evolving philosophers problem: dynamic change management. IEEE Trans. Software Eng. **16**, 1293–1306 (1990)
19. Vandewoude, Y., Ebraert, P., Berbers, Y., D'Hondt, T.: Tranquility: a low disruptive alternative to quiescence for ensuring safe dynamic updates. IEEE Trans. Software Eng. **33**, 856–868 (2007)
20. Le Metayer, D.: Describing software architecture styles using graph grammars. IEEE Trans. Software Eng. **24**, 521–533 (1998)
21. Kähkönen, K., Lampinen, J., Heljanko, K., Niemelä, I.: The LIME interface specification language and runtime monitoring tool. In: Bensalem, S., Peled, D.A. (eds.) RV 2009. LNCS, vol. 5779, pp. 93–100. Springer, Heidelberg (2009)
22. Ghamarian, A.H., de Mol, M., Rensink, A., Zambon, E., Zimakova, M.: Modelling and analysis using GROOVE. Int. J. Softw. Tools Technol. Transfer **14**, 15–40 (2012)

DFTCalc: Reliability Centered Maintenance via Fault Tree Analysis (Tool Paper)

Dennis Guck[✉], Jip Spel, and Mariëlle Stoelinga

Formal Methods and Tools, University of Twente, Enschede, The Netherlands
{d.guck,m.i.a.stoelinga}@utwente.nl, j.j.spel@student.utwente.nl

Abstract. Reliability, availability, maintenance and safety (RAMS) analysis is essential in the evaluation of safety critical systems like nuclear power plants and the railway infrastructure. A widely used methodology within RAMS analysis are fault trees, representing failure propagations throughout a system. We present DFTCALC, a tool-set to conduct quantitative analysis on dynamic fault trees including the effect of a maintenance strategy on the system dependability.

Keywords: Dynamic fault trees · Maintenance · Reliability · Context-dependent reduction

1 Introduction

Maintenance is a crucial aspect in reliability engineering: good maintenance, consisting of timely inspections, spare management, renewals and repairs, reduces the number of failures and extends the system life time. The trend in maintenance is reliability-centered. To achieve higher reliability and reduce costs, it is commonly agreed that essential components should be maintained more intensively than less crucial ones, rather than the usual practice of subjecting all components the same maintenance regime. Challenge here is to identify the crucial components and determine the optimal maintenance strategy. The tool DFTCALC provides important support here: given an advanced maintenance strategy and a system model given as a fault tree, DFTCALC computes standard reliability measures like the system reliability, availability, and mean time to failures.

Technically, DFTCALC is realized via stochastic model checking of interactive Markov chains, yielding a flexible and efficient framework by exploiting state space generation via bisimulation minimisation. A first version of DFT-CALC was reported in [1] concerning fault tree analysis only. This paper reports the extensions of DFTCALC with preventive and corrective maintenance models and their analysis. To handle the additional complexity, we have implemented context-dependent model-generation, which significantly reduces the state space. We show the application of DFTCALC on standard case studies from the literature, as well as industrial cases from railway engineering.

© Springer International Publishing Switzerland 2015
M. Butler et al. (Eds.): ICFEM 2015, LNCS 9407, pp. 304–311, 2015.
DOI: 10.1007/978-3-319-25423-4_19

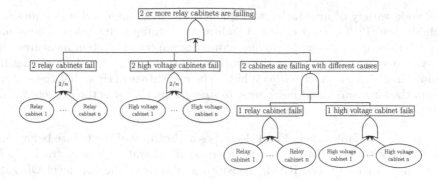

Fig. 1. Example FT of relay cabinet failures.

Paper organization. Section 2 introduces fault trees and maintenance, Sect. 3 their analysis in DFTCALC, Sect. 4 the case studies, and Sect. 5 concludes the paper.

2   Fault Trees and Maintenance

Fault trees. Fault trees are a popular graphical method for RAMS (reliability, availability, maintenance, and security) analysis [14]. A fault tree (FT) is a tree (or rather a directed acyclic graph, since sub-trees can be shared) describing how component failures propagate through a system and may lead to system failures. The FT leaves represent component failures, called *basic events* (BEs), and are equipped with probability distributions modelling the component's failure behaviour over time. Failure times are often modelled as exponential probability distributions; that is, the probability that the component fails within time t is given by $\mathbf{P}[X < t] = 1 - e^{-\lambda t}$. Here, the parameter $\lambda \in \mathbb{R}^+$ is known as the component's *failure rate*. Additionally, leaves are given a dormancy factor $\alpha \in [0, 1]$ that reduces the failure rate of a component when dormant, i.e. not in use. Thus, the probability for dormant component to fail within time t is given by $\mathbf{P}[X < t] = 1 - e^{-\alpha \lambda t}$. Apart from exponential distributions, DFTCALC supports phase-types, i.e., probability distributions given by absorption times in Markov chains, which can be used to approximate any probability distributions with arbitrary precision.

The FT *gates* model failure propagation. The static gates OR, AND, VOT(k) model respectively that a gate fails if one, all, or k of their inputs fail. The dynamic gates PAND, SPARE, FDEP provide support for common reliability patterns like sequencing, spare management and functional dependencies, and are known as dynamic fault trees (DFTs). Their behaviour is as follows: A PAND-gate fails if the inputs fail from left to right, otherwise no failure occurs. A SPARE-gate contains a primary input, and one or more spare inputs. If the primary input fails, then a spare gets activated and takes over its functionality. If all spares have failed as well, then the SPARE-gate fails. An FDEP-gate contains a trigger input, which triggers the failure of all its dependent events.

A wide variety of qualitative and quantitative DFT analysis techniques are available, see [12] for an overview. Qualitative techniques include cut sets and cut sequences; quantitative techniques compute important system measures like the system *reliability* (What is the probability that the system fails during its mission time T?); the *availability* (What is the percentage of time that the system is up in the long run?), and *mean time to first failure* (What is the expected time until the first failure occurs?).

Example 1. The fault tree in Fig. 1 describes an instance of the failure behaviour of a redundant relay cabinet system, used on an operated railway track [7]. It has been provided by the RAMS consultant Movares. The top level OR-gate describes the disruption of several relays on an operated track. The system fails, if there are at least 2 relay or high voltage cabinet failures, as modelled by the VOT(2)-gates. Besides, the system can also fail if a combination of one relay and high voltage cabinet failure occurs, as modelled by the AND-gate.

Maintenance. Maintenance comprises a combination of inspections, repairs, renewals and spare management. Two types are distinguished: *preventive maintenance* refers to actions that prevent failures. Components are inspected, and based on their condition, (partial) renewals or repairs are performed, putting the component in a better condition. Preventive maintenance can be further divided into condition-based (e.g., the replacement of car tires when their profile is too low) and usage-based maintenance (e.g. inspection every 10.000 car miles). *Corrective maintenance* is carried out after a failure has occurred, replacing or repairing the broken component. Corrective maintenance may trigger preventive maintenance. For example, when a broken train is in the garage, additional inspections commonly take place. Regular fault trees, whether static or dynamic, do not incorporate such maintenance strategies: the component failure rates assume a certain maintenance regime and once a BE fails, it remains failed.

3   DFTCalc

DFTCALC provides efficient tool support for quantitative analysis of dynamic fault trees and is available at http://fmt.ewi.utwente.nl/puptol/dftcalc via a web interface, depicted in Fig. 2. The tool takes as inputs a DFT in Galileo format [13] and a maintenance model. It computes the most common dependability metrics, being the system reliability over a time interval $[T_1, T_2]$, the system availability, and the mean time to first failure, which are outputted textually as well as graphically. Technically, DFTCALC is realized via stochastic model checking, via a compositional translation of each DFT element to an input/output interactive Markov chain where the dependability metrics are internally expressed as CSL formulas.

Maintenance in DFTCalc. We include maintenance in the FT framework by redefining the BEs behaviour. We handle condition-based maintenance, inspections, repairs, and spare management.

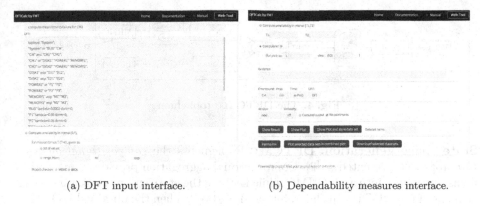

(a) DFT input interface.   (b) Dependability measures interface.

Fig. 2. DFTCALC web interface.

The *condition* of a component is modelled by different degeneration phases, similar to extended fault trees [5]. In Fig. 3(a), the first phase s_1 represents the component in perfect condition; subsequent phases represent degraded conditions, until the component is broken in s_n. A threshold is given after which an inspection will trigger a maintenance procedure. *Inspections* are modelled by an inspection module (IM), which handles several BEs, see Fig. 3(b). Thus, if the IM inspects a BE and applies a maintenance procedure, then the BE is set back to a less degraded mode — in Fig. 3(a) to its initial condition. We handle *repairs* via repair units (RUs) as presented in [7]. A RU caters for several BEs, and determines in which order the BEs are getting repaired. Further, the BE gets a repair time assigned which is described by an exponential distributed delay.

Analysis. As formal semantics of DFTs, and thus the basis for the quantitative analysis, input/output interactive Markov chains (I/O-IMCs) are used. I/O-IMCs are an extension of interactive Markov chains (IMCs) [9] by adding input and output signals to the action set. An I/O-IMC consists of a number of states which are connected via two types of transitions, interactive and Markovian. The interactive transitions are labelled with signals, which are used to communicate between components. The Markovian transitions are labelled with rates λ representing an exponential distributed delay.

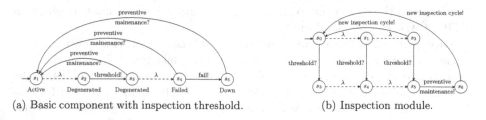

(a) Basic component with inspection threshold.   (b) Inspection module.

Fig. 3. Inspection modules as I/O-IMCs.

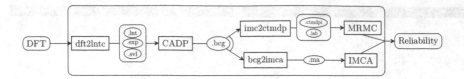

Fig. 4. The DFTCALC tool-chain.

State space generation. DFTCALC implements the *compositional aggregation* approach presented in [2]. Compositional aggregation provides a method to translate a DFT into an I/O-IMC while keeping the state space small. First, each element of the DFT is translated into an I/O-IMC. Then the obtained I/O-IMCs are iteratively composed and minimised until a single I/O-IMC remains.

This approach enables us to define I/O-IMCs for corrective and preventive maintenance. The repairable BEs as well as the RU are equivalent to the models presented in [7]. The IM as well as the new BEs for preventive maintenance are depicted in Fig. 3.

Context-dependent state space generation. The state space generation by compositional aggregation provides already a scalability of several orders of magnitude [2]. However, for large industrial case studies there is a demand for even more reduction. Therefore, we investigate context-dependencies in the component translation from DFT modules to I/O-IMCs. Instead of translating a DFT element directly into an I/O-IMC based on the semantics from [2], we differentiate between active and inactive elements and eliminate superfluous signals beforehand. Consider an AND-gate with two inputs. In the standard semantics, the full behaviour will be described, including the inactive behaviour of the components. However, if the component is active from the start, all the inactive behaviour can be discarded, which reduces the state space of the component.

Implementation. DFTCALC combines several state-of-the-art model checkers to provide a DFT analysis tool, see Fig. 4. The generation of the DFT, including the compositional aggregation, is done using the CADP tool set [6]. The generated I/O-IMC can be translated to the Markov Reward Model Checker (MRMC) [10], or to the Interactive Markov Chain Analyzer (IMCA) [8]. Finally, the requested dependability metrics, which are (a) the reliability for one or more mission times T, or (b) the probability on a system failure during an interval $[T_1, T_2]$, or (c) the mean time to failure, can be computed. A complete description of DFTCALC can be found in [1].

We exploit the modular framework of DFTCALC and provide new templates for the IM, RU, and BEs with phases, inspection signals, repair functionality and context-dependencies. Further, we adapted the generation of those FTs in the `dft2lntc` tool. The inspection and repair functionality is implemented for static FTs, with AND- OR- and VOT(k)-gates. The context-dependent behaviour detection based on the active and inactive modes works for DFTs without maintenance. The RU is defined by the new keyword `ru`, and the corresponding repair time of a BE is specified with `repair=`μ, where μ is the repair rate. The IM has the keyword `KinspN` where K is defined as the number of inspection phases and N the rate of each phase. The threshold in the BE is specified with `interval=`n, where n is the threshold. Further, each BE has a keyword `phases=`k, where k represents the number of degeneration phases.

4   Experiments

We have conducted several case studies to demonstrate the applicability of DFT-CALC; all were run on a single core of a 2 GHz Intel Xeon with 22GB RAM running on Linux.

Modelling of maintenance strategies. Figure 5 shows the effect of different maintenance strategies on a set of FTs constructed by the RAMS consultancy firm Movares, concerning a part of a major railway corridor in the Netherlands [7]. We consider two systems, the relay cabinet whose abstract version is given in Fig. 1, and a railway switch. To investigate the effect of corrective and preventive maintenance, each group of cabinets is assigned to either a RU or a IM, following the following strategies: (a) without maintenance; (b) corrective maintenance with repair times of one, two and seven days; (c) preventive maintenance with inspection frequencies of once, twice, and four times a year. We calculated the system reliability for a mission time of 10 years. The results depicted in Fig. 5 show that increasing the inspection frequency significantly improves the reliability. Lowering the repair times helps as well, but with less effect.

Analysis efficiency. Table 1 shows the impact of context-dependent state-space generation. Here, we use standard DFTs from literature: the multiprocessor computing system (MCS) [11], the cardiac assist system (CAS) [3], the fault-tolerant parallel processor (FTPP) [2], cascaded PAND system (CPS) [2] and an instance

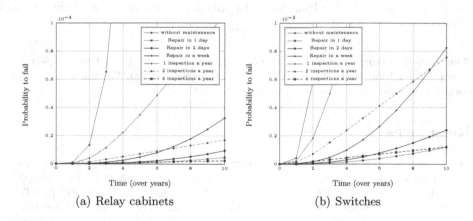

(a) Relay cabinets   (b) Switches

Fig. 5. System reliability over time for different inspection intervals.

Table 1. Context-dependent state space reductions.

Model	Gates	BEs	Smart detection	States	Transitions	Max States	Max transitions
CAS	10	10	without	16	36	84	304
			with	14	34	49	133
MCS	10	11	without	18	37	6438	32202
			with	12	31	220	803
FTPP-4	21	20	without	72	312	45823	230596
			with	66	306	7020	32200
CPS	5	12	without	39	71	918	3140
			with	38	70	134	291
SF	6	7	without	15	36	383	1500
			with	14	35	64	138

of a Sensorfilter (SF) [4] case study. The results are shown in Table 1. While the final state spaces are small, it is the size of the largest intermediate models that matter, since these determine the amount of memory required. We observe that the maximal state space reduction for the intermediate state space during generation lies between 72 % and 96 %, and the state space reduction for the final state space lies between 3 % and 33 %. This points the significance of distinguishing the active and inactive DFT part beforehand.

5   Conclusions and Future Work

This paper presented an extension of DFTCALC with preventive and corrective maintenance as well as a way to reduce the state space w.r.t. context-dependent reductions. We believe that the context-dependent generation will also have a high impact on the state space of DFTs with maintenance. Further, future work is needed to apply maintenance modules to the dynamic gates as well as to incorporate costs into the framework, to optimise maintenance strategies w.r.t. reliability as well as costs.

Acknowledgement. This work has been supported by the STW-ProRail partnership program ExploRail under the project ArRangeer (12238). We acknowledge our cooperation with Movares in the ArRangeer project.

References

1. Arnold, F., Belinfante, A., Van der Berg, F., Guck, D., Stoelinga, M.: DFTCALC: a tool for efficient fault tree analysis. In: Bitsch, F., Guiochet, J., Kaâniche, M. (eds.) SAFECOMP. LNCS, vol. 8153, pp. 293–301. Springer, Heidelberg (2013)
2. Boudali, H., Crouzen, P., Stoelinga, M.: A rigorous, compositional, and extensible framework for dynamic fault tree analysis. IEEE Trans. Dependable Secure Comput. **7**, 128–143 (2010)

3. Boudali, H., Dugan, J.B.: A Bayesian network reliability modeling and analysis framework. IEEE Trans. Reliab. **55**, 86–97 (2005)
4. Bozzano, M., Cimatti, A., Katoen, J.-P., Nguyen, V.Y., Noll, T., Roveri, M.: Safety, dependability and performance analysis of extended AADL models. Comput. J. **54**, 754–775 (2011)
5. Buchacker, K.: Modeling with extended fault trees. In: Proceeding of the 5th International Symposium on High Assurance Systems Engineering (HASE), pp. 238–246, November 2000
6. Garavel, H., Lang, F., Mateescu, R., Serwe, W.: CADP 2011: a toolbox for the construction and analysis of distributed processes. Int. J. Softw. Tools Technol. Transfer **13**, 1–19 (2012)
7. Guck, D., Katoen, J.P., Stoelinga, M.I.A., Luiten, T., Romijn, J.: Smart railroad maintenance engineering with stochastic model checking. In: Railway Technology: Research, Development and Maintenance. Civil-Comp, vol. 104, p. 299 (2014)
8. Guck, D., Timmer, M., Hatefi, H., Ruijters, E., Stoelinga, M.: Modelling and analysis of Markov reward automata. In: Cassez, F., Raskin, J.-F. (eds.) ATVA 2014. LNCS, vol. 8837, pp. 168–184. Springer, Heidelberg (2014)
9. Hermanns, H.: Interactive Markov Chains: The Quest for Quantified Quality. Springer, Heidelberg (2002)
10. Katoen, J.-P., Zapreev, I.S., Hahn, E.M., Hermanns, H., Jansen, D.N.: The ins and outs of the probabilistic model checker MRMC. Perf. Eval. **68**(2), 90–104 (2011)
11. Montani, S., Portinale, L., Bobbio, A., Varesio, M., Codetta-Raiteri, D.: A tool for automatically translating dynamic fault trees into dynamic Bayesian networks. In: RAMS, pp. 434–441 (2006)
12. Ruijters, E.J.J., Stoelinga, M.I.A.: Fault tree analysis: a survey of the state-of-the-art in modeling, analysis and tools. Elsevier Computing Surveys (2015)
13. Sullivan, K.J., Dugan, J.B., Coppit, D.: The Galileo fault tree analysis tool. In: 29th Annual International Symposium on Fault-Tolerant Computing, pp. 232–235. IEEE (1999)
14. Vesely, W.E., Goldberg, F.F., Roberts, N.H., Haasl, D.F.: Fault Tree Handbook. U.S. Nuclear Regulatory Commision, Office of Nuclear Regulatory Reasearch (1981)

B for Modeling Secure Information Systems
The B4MSecure Platform

Akram Idani[1,2]([⊠]) and Yves Ledru[1,2]

[1] University of Grenoble Alpes, LIG, 38000 Grenoble, France
[2] CNRS, LIG, 38000 Grenoble, France
{Akram.Idani,Yves.Ledru}@imag.fr

Abstract. Several approaches dedicated to model access control policies (*e.g.* MDA-Security, SecureUML, UMLSec, etc.) have used the Model Driven Engineering paradigm in order to ensure a clear separation of business rules and constraints specific to a target technology. Their supporting techniques mainly focus on modeling and verification of security rules without taking into account the functional model of the application and its interaction with the security model. In order to take into account both models, we developed the B4MSecure platform. It is a Model Driven Engineering platform that allows to graphically model and formally reason on both functional and security models. It translates a UML class diagram associated to a SecureUML model into formal B specifications. The resulting B specifications follow the separation of concerns principles in order to be able to validate both models separately and then validate their interactions. This paper gives an overview of our platform.

Keywords: Formal methods · Security · RBAC · SecureUML

1 Introduction

In software engineering, method integration has been a challenge since several years. The objective is to link formal and graphical paradigms in order to guarantee the quality of specifications. Indeed, on the one hand, graphical languages (such as UML) have been widely used for specifying, visualizing, understanding and documenting software systems, but they suffer from the lack of precise semantical basis. On the other hand, formal methods (such as B [1]) are specifically used for safety critical systems in order to rigorously check their correctness but they lead to complex models which may be difficult to read and understand. These complementarities between formal and graphical languages motivate a lot of research teams to develop tools which combine both languages.

As far as secure information systems are concerned, existing research works in this context mainly focus, on the one hand, on modeling and verification of functional models without taking into account useful non-functional rules like access control policies. On the other hand, works dedicated to model access control policies (*e.g.* MDA-Security, SecureUML, UMLSec, etc.) do not address the

© Springer International Publishing Switzerland 2015
M. Butler et al. (Eds.): ICFEM 2015, LNCS 9407, pp. 312–318, 2015.
DOI: 10.1007/978-3-319-25423-4_20

fact that the security model also refers to information of the functional model. Hence, evolutions of the functional state may influence the security behaviour and then open security flaws. Some well known insider attacks which were possible due to evolutions of the functional state can be cited:

- The account manager who creates a spurious account and adds himself to the system as a normal customer in order to transfer money into (or from) this spurious account. The access control policy should then forbid the account manager to evolve the functional entities Customer and Account whereby this malicious scenario could not take place.
- The attack of "Société Générale" in which the insider, through authorized actions, was able to conceal operations he has made on the market by introducing into the functional system fictive offsetting inverse operations.

2   B4MSecure Overview

The B4MSecure tool is intended to model the information system as a whole by covering its functional description, and its security policy. The supporting models are based on UML for the functional description and SecureUML for the access control rules. A formal B specification is generated automatically from these models (Fig. 1). The resulting formal B specification allows then to formally reason on the whole system: functional and security models can be first validated separately, and then integrated in order to verify their interactions.

B4MSecure applies the model driven engineering (MDE) approach [11] in order to ensure a clear separation of business rules and their corresponding models. Semantics of the various models are defined on basis of UML, SecureUML and B methods meta-models and the various transformation rules are encoded by a set of mappings between these meta-models. The tool has several advantages:

- *(i)* it clarifies and delineates a subset of source model structures for which the transformations are applicable;
- *(ii)* it has a catalog of transformation rules expressed in a single transformation language; and
- *(iii)* it provides a structured framework, based on meta-models, which clearly describes the semantics of the various models.

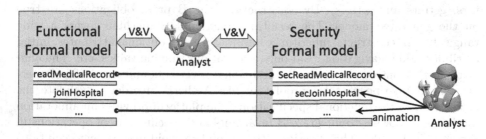

Fig. 1. Formal V&V activities of functional and security models

The tool is open source and available at http://b4msecure.forge.imag.fr. A video demo is also provided.

3   Translation of Functional Models

The translation of a UML diagram into a B specification is intended to take advantage of the B method tools in order to validate, by proofs and animations, the initial UML diagram. Several teams worked on this research problem and defined different kinds of mappings from UML into B: UML2B [3], UML2SQL [4], U2B [13] and ArgoUML+B [9]. Analysis of these various approaches show that each kind of UML-to-B mapping has its own objectives and characteristics:

- UML2SQL [4,5]: B specifications are obtained by translating a set of UML diagrams which describe a database application.
- U2B [13,14]: this work was intended to produce a B specification (so-called "natural") exempt from constructions related to the translation mechanism and which can complicate formal proofs.
- ArgoUML+B [6,9]: this work tried to take into account complex UML features. It proposed, on the one hand, solutions for the translation of the UML inheritance mechanism, and on the other hand, a new formalization of state/ transition diagrams.

Most of these tools except U2B are not publicly available despite the interest of their contributions. The B4MSecure tool encodes these mappings and then allows to reuse and combine rules issued from different UML-to-B approaches. In order to fit this need we have reimplemented existing translations using the java language. The advantage of our MDE architecture compared with existing UML-to-B tools (U2B, ArgoUML + B, UML2SQL) is its extensibility. In fact, in order to cover the transformation of UML constructs that have not been considered by the existing approaches, the rule-writer simply encodes in Java new rules and adds them to the catalog of transformations that we have implemented. Transformation from UML class diagrams into B is guided by their respective meta-models. The various java rules provided in the platform get UML concepts issued from the UML meta-model and produce instances of concepts issued from the B meta-model.

The tool produces one B model, from the functional UML class diagram, gathering its structural properties and all basic operations (constructors, destructors, getters and setters). By construction, the B proof obligations are true on the generated model. The resulting functional B machine covers a wide range of UML constructs: inheritance, mandatory and optional attributes, initial attribute value, navigation, read-only associations, unique values, etc. The analyst can then introduce, manually, additional invariants and user-defined operations and take benefit of a proof tool like AtelierB in order to validate the consistency of the functional specification. The platform provides an annotation mechanism allowing to integrate B invariants and specification of operations in the graphical model. This functionality is useful to avoid inconsistent evolutions of the graphical and formal methods.

4   Extraction of An RBAC Filter from the Security Model

4.1   A Brief Overview

In order to express a security policy, the Role-Based Access Control (RBAC) model provides a powerful mechanism for reducing the complexity, cost, and potential for error of assigning and managing users and permissions. It is supported by several software products like popular commercial database management systems (*e.g.* Oracle, Sybase, ...) or webservers (*e.g.* JBoss). The available implementations of this model act like a filter which intercepts a user request to a resource in order to permit or deny the access to associated functional actions (*e.g.* transactions on databases, file operations, ...). Our tool is based on the same principle at a modeling level. Each functional operation is encapsulated in a secure operation which checks that the current user is authorized to call it.

The tool is based on the eclipse Topcased environment. Graphical modeling of a RBAC policy in B4MSecure is done using a UML profile inspired by SecureUML [2]. Figure 2 gives a screenshot of the graphical modeler applying this security profile.

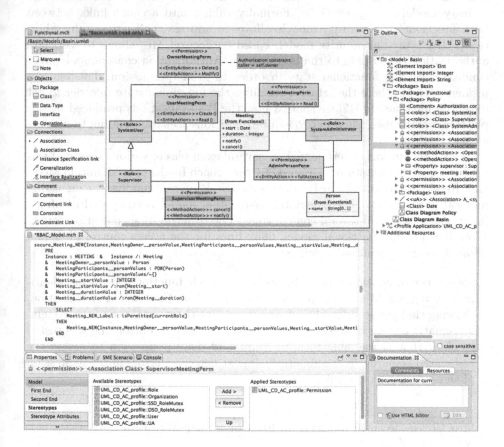

Fig. 2. B4MSecure screenshot

The tool produces a B specification gathering a set of secured operations which filter the access to the functional model. Proof-based validation of this specification should automatically succeed provided the SecureUML model is conformant to structural invariants: no cycles in role-hierarchy, no static separation of duties violation, etc. We note that the tool does not produce administrative operations allowing to modify dynamically the policy and hence validation of this model is only based on well-formedness properties.

Animation of secured operations gives access only to the authorized functional operations for the user who is trying to execute them. This approach allows to validate the functional model as well as the security policy. In fact, animation of an authorized operation changes the state of the functional model and hence allows the analyst to validate both models.

4.2   Case Studies

In [10] we discussed the benefits of the resulting B specifications and how the expected validation activities can be done. These validation activities include classical proof obligations, but also the animation and test of functional and security models, using ProB [8]. Formally taking into account links between both functional and security models allows to address challenging vulnerabilities [7]. Actually our security model, based on SecureUML, allows to associate authorisation constraints to the permissions. Authorisation constraints express conditions on the functional state in order to grant permission. This enables insiders attacks where the attacker modifies the functional state in order to get illegal permissions. In [12] we showed how the B specifications produced by our platform can be useful in order to exhibit malicious scenarios leading to insiders attacks.

The platform was experimented on several examples of various sizes and was applied on a real case study[1] proposed by the French Institute of Mountain Medicine Research (Ifremmont[2]). It is a pre-hospital information system managing medical patient data. The associated conceptual model is composed of fifteen functional classes and several control rules. The resulting B specification counts 1730 lines for the functional model, 2652 lines for the access control filter and allowed several validation activities:

- acceptance validation guided by use-cases: each functional use case identified during requirements analysis was animated on the secured specification, showing that the security filter does not prevent the normal use of the system.
- systematic testing of access control rules: each access control rule was tested to show that it was able to both grant and deny permission to access the associated resource. This animation aims at detecting errors in the expression of these access control rules.

---

[1] http://telemedecine.ifremmont.com/ifrelab/index.php?Wwwresamuorg.
[2] http://www.ifremmont.com.

– search for malicious insider scenarios: several attack scenarios were designed manually and animated on the formal model, showing its robustness against these attacks. Current work in our team tries to automatically synthesize such attacks by exploration of the specification.

This case study showed the usefulness of the tool while designing a security policy. It supports this design at a level which abstracts away implementation details such as authentification mechanisms and cryptography, and concentrates on the consistency of the set of access control rules.

5   Conclusion

In most existing Information Systems, functional and security requirements are mixed in the application code. It is, therefore, difficult to understand these systems and modify them in order to maintain, evolve and correct the security policy. In order to master complexity of systems, the MDE paradigm advocates for a separation of concerns and the use of models throughout the development process. Therefore, Information Systems security is a domain where the potential of the MDE approach is highly useful. Indeed, modeling separately functional and security models allows to better understand, validate and maintain these models.

Although it is useful to analyse and validate both models in isolation, which is addressed by several works, interactions between these models must also be taken into account. Such interactions result from the fact that constraints expressed in the security model also refer to information of the functional model. Hence, evolutions of the functional state have an impact on the security behaviour.

Conversely, security constraints often depend on the functional behaviour. The B4MSecure platform allows, on the one hand, this separation of concerns, and on the other hand, the investigation of links between both functional and security models. The platform allows: a graphical modeling of a functional UML class diagram, a graphical modeling of an access control policy using a UML profile for RBAC (Role Based Access Control) and which is inspired by SecureUML, and the translation of both models into B specifications in order to formally reason about them.

The various B specifications extracted from functional and security models allow several kinds of validation. This paper addressed mainly the principles of the tool and discussed some validation activities that we have done on several case studies. Other kinds of validation can be addressed such as the use of a constraint solver, or symbolic animation, etc.

In the future, we plan to take into account translation of other UML diagrams like state/transition and activity diagrams. Currently, the platform only deals with structural aspects of an Information System. We also plan to cover translation of other security models. Our interest is directed to attribute-based access control models.

References

1. Abrial, J.-R.: The B-book: Assigning Programs to Meanings. Cambridge University Press, New York (1996)
2. Basin, D.A., Clavel, M., Doser, J., Egea, M.: Automated analysis of security-design models. Inf. Soft. Technol. **51**(5), 815–831 (2009)
3. Hazem, L., Levy, N., Marcano-Kamenoff, R.: UML2B: un outil pour la génération de modèles formels. In: Julliand, J. (ed.) AFADL 2004 - Session Outils (2004)
4. Laleau, R., Mammar, A.: An overview of a method and its support tool for generating B specifications from UML notations. In: 15th IEEE International Conference on Automated Software Engineering, pp. 269–272. IEEE Computer Society Press (2000)
5. Laleau, R., Polack, F.A.C.: Coming and going from UML to B: a proposal to support traceability in rigorous IS development. In: Bert, D., Bowen, J.P., C. Henson, M., Robinson, K. (eds.) B 2002 and ZB 2002. LNCS, vol. 2272, pp. 517–534. Springer, Heidelberg (2002)
6. Ledang, H.: Automatic translation from UML specifications to B. In: Automated Software Engineering, p. 436. IEEE Computer Society (2001)
7. Ledru, Y., Idani, A., Milhau, J., Qamar, N., Laleau, R., Richier, J.-L., Labiadh, M.-A.: Taking into account functional models in the validation of IS security policies. In: Salinesi, C., Pastor, O. (eds.) CAiSE Workshops 2011. LNBIP, vol. 83, pp. 592–606. Springer, Heidelberg (2011)
8. Leuschel, M., Butler, M.: ProB: a model checker for B. In: Araki, K., Gnesi, S., Mandrioli, D. (eds.) FME 2003. LNCS, vol. 2805, pp. 855–874. Springer, Heidelberg (2003)
9. Meyer, E.: Développements formels par objets: utilisation conjointe de B et d'UML. Ph.D. thesis, Université de Nancy 2, Mars 2001
10. Milhau, J., Idani, A., Laleau, R., Labiadh, M.-A., Ledru, Y., Frappier, M.: Combining UML, ASTD and B for the formal specification of an access control filter. ISSE **7**(4), 303–313 (2011)
11. OMG: Mda guide version 1.0.1, June 2003. http://www.omg.org/mda/
12. Radhouani, A., Idani, A., Ledru, Y., Rajeb, N.B.: Extraction of insider attack scenarios from a formal information system modeling. In: Proceedings of the Formal Methods for Security Workshop Co-located with the PetriNets-2014 Conference. CEUR Workshop Proceedings, vol. 1158, pp. 5–19. CEUR-WS.org (2014)
13. Snook, C., Butler, M.: U2B-A tool for translating UML-B models into B. In: Mermet, J. (ed) UML-B Specification for Proven Embedded Systems Design (2004)
14. Snook, C., Butler, M.: UML-B: formal modeling and design aided by UML. ACM Trans. Soft. Eng. Methodol. (TOSEM) **15**(1), 92–122 (2006)

Enhanced Distributed Behavioral Cartography of Parametric Timed Automata

Étienne André$^{(\boxtimes)}$, Camille Coti, and Hoang Gia Nguyen

Université Paris 13, Sorbonne Paris Cité, LIPN, CNRS, UMR 7030,
93430 Villetaneuse, France

Abstract. Parametric timed automata (PTA) allow the specification and verification of timed systems incompletely specified, or subject to future changes. The behavioral cartography splits the parameter space of PTA in tiles in which the discrete behavior is uniform. Applications include the optimization of timing constants, and the measure of the system robustness w.r.t. the untimed language. Here, we present enhanced distributed algorithms to compute the cartography efficiently. Experimental results show that our new algorithms significantly outperform previous distribution techniques.

1 Introduction

Systems combining concurrent aspects with real-time constraints are notoriously difficult to exhaustively test, and their failure due to unsuspected bugs may lead to dramatic consequences. Model checking concurrent real-time systems aims at formally verifying the correctness of the system model w.r.t. a property.

The notion of timed automata (TA) is a well-known formalism for specifying and verifying concurrent real-time systems. TA extend finite-state automata with a set of clocks (real-time variables growing linearly) that can be compared with integer constants. TA are used in several powerful tools such as UPPAAL [16] or PAT [18]. However, the binary answer ("yes" or "no") output by model checking is not always satisfactory: indeed, it does not allow to change or optimize some values of the system constants, nor (in general) to evaluate the system robustness, *i.e.* the infinitesimal variation of timing constants while preserving the reachability or language. Parametric timed automata (PTA) [1] extend TA with rational-valued parameters allowed in place of constants.

In [3], the behavioral cartography (BC) of PTA was proposed: given a bounded parameter domain D, BC partitions D in *tiles*, *i.e.* in parameter subspaces where the discrete (untimed) behavior is uniform. That is, the set of satisfied linear time properties is the same for any rational-valued parameter valuation ("point") in a tile. This helps to identify robust subspaces, in which the timing constants can vary with no harm w.r.t. the system correctness expressed

---

This work was partially supported by the ANR national research program "PACS" (ANR-2014), and the INS2I PEPS JCJC 2015 "PSyCoS" project.

M. Butler et al. (Eds.): ICFEM 2015, LNCS 9407, pp. 319–335, 2015.
DOI: 10.1007/978-3-319-25423-4_21

in terms of the untimed language. In [2], we sketched two master-worker point distribution algorithms to compute BC in a distributed fashion.

Contribution. The goal of this paper is to propose efficient distributed algorithms to compute BC efficiently using parallel, distributed computing resources. We formalize the existing point-by-point distribution algorithms (Seq and Random), that were only informally sketched in [2].[1] Then, our main contribution is to propose three new distributed algorithms to speed up the cartography: the first one (Static) is a static domain decomposition scheme, where each node works independently on its own parameter subdomain; the second one (Shuffle) addresses the drawbacks of Seq and Random; finally, the third one (Subdomain) is a new master-worker, dynamic, distributed domain decomposition process. We then evaluate our algorithms on real-time case studies. In all cases, our new algorithms Shuffle and (a variant of) Subdomain outperform the algorithms of [2]. We also discuss how to choose the appropriate algorithm depending on the case study.

Related works. The design of efficient parameter synthesis techniques has been tackled in various works, *e.g.* using SMT-based model checking techniques [9], or using symbolic techniques for integer synthesis [13]. BC helps to quantify the system robustness; this has also been tackled using the "ASAP" semantics [10] (see, *e.g.* [17] for a survey), but usually in only one dimension (a single variation δ of the timing delays is considered, whereas BC allows as many dimensions as parameters). To the best of our knowledge, with the exception of [2], distributed computing techniques were not applied yet to parameter synthesis for PTA.

Formal verification can be made in parallel in two ways: modeling languages can be designed to be easy to use in a distributed fashion, or the verification algorithms themselves can be parallelized. Our approach fits in the second category. In recent years, some model checkers were extended to parallel computing, *i.e.* running on multicore computers. This is the case of PKind [14], APMC (a probabilistic model checker) [12], and FDR3 (for CSP refinement checking). More recently, two algorithms were proposed to address multi-core LTL verification [11] and emptiness checking of timed Büchi automata [15]. However, with the exception of FDR3 (that can run either on multicore or on clusters), these works run verification on multicore computers (with a shared memory) whereas our primary goal is to run verification on a cluster (where each node has its own memory). Furthermore, none of these works considered parameter synthesis.

Outline. We introduce the necessary notations in Sect. 2. We briefly define in Sect. 3 the static domain decomposition algorithm (Static). Then, we formalize in Sect. 4 the master-worker scheme and the two point distribution algorithms of [2]; we also introduce a third point distribution algorithm (Shuffle). We introduce in Sect. 5 our new dynamic domain decomposition algorithm (Subdomain). We conduct experiments in Sect. 6 and conclude in Sect. 7.

---

[1] [2] was published in a distributed computing community and focused on the parallelization technique used for this particular application, and the paper did not go into formal details. This is not an actual contribution of the current paper, but makes it standalone.

2   Preliminaries

Parameter Constraints. We assume here a set $X = \{x_1, \ldots, x_H\}$ of *clocks*, *i.e.* real-valued variables that evolve at the same rate. A clock valuation w is a function $w : X \to \mathbb{R}_+$. We denote by $X = 0$ the conjunction of equalities that assigns 0 to all clocks in X.

We assume a set $P = \{p_1, \ldots, p_M\}$ of *parameters*, *i.e.* unknown constants. A *parameter valuation* v is a function $v : P \to \mathbb{Q}_+$. We will often identify a valuation v with the *point* $(v(p_1), \ldots, v(p_M))$. An *integer* point is a valuation $v : P \to \mathbb{N}$. We denote by $\mathbf{0}$ the valuation assigning 0 to all parameters.

An *inequality* over X and P is $e \prec 0$, where $\prec \in \{<, \leq, \geq, >\}$, and e is a linear term $\sum_{1 \leq i \leq N} \alpha_i z_i + d$ for some $N \in \mathbb{N}$, where $z_i \in X \cup P$, $\alpha_i \in \mathbb{Q}$, for $1 \leq i \leq N$, and $d \in \mathbb{Q}$. A (linear) constraint over X and P is a set of inequalities over X and P. We define in a similar manner inequalities and constraints over P. A *guard* is a set of inequalities each of them referring to at most one clock.

Given a parameter valuation v, $C[v]$ denotes the constraint over X obtained by replacing each parameter p in C with $v(p)$. We say that v *satisfies* C, denoted by $v \models C$, if the set of clock valuations satisfying $C[v]$ is nonempty.

We denote by $C \!\downarrow_P$ the projection of C onto P, *i.e.* obtained by eliminating the clock variables (using existential quantification). We define the *time elapsing* of C, denoted by $C^{\nearrow}$, as the constraint over X and P obtained from C by delaying an arbitrary amount of time. Given $R \subseteq X$, we define the *reset* of C, denoted by $[C]_R$, as the constraint obtained from C by resetting the clocks in R, and keeping the other clocks unchanged.

Definition 1. *A PTA $\mathcal{A}$ is a tuple $\mathcal{A} = (\Sigma, L, l_0, X, P, I, E)$, where: (1) Σ is a finite set of actions, (2) L is a finite set of locations, (3) $l_0 \in L$ is the initial location, (4) X is a set of clocks, (5) P is a set of parameters, (6) I is the invariant, assigning to every $l \in L$ a guard $I(l)$, and (7) E is a set of edges (l, g, a, R, l') where $l, l' \in L$ are the source and destination locations, g is the transition guard, $a \in \Sigma$, and $R \subseteq X$ is a set of clocks to be reset.*

Given a PTA $\mathcal{A} = (\Sigma, L, l_0, X, P, I, E)$, and a parameter valuation v, $\mathcal{A}[v]$ denotes the TA obtained from $\mathcal{A}$ by substituting every occurrence of a parameter p_i by the constant $v(p_i)$ in the guards and invariants.

Symbolic Semantics. A symbolic state is a pair (l, C) with l a location, and C a constraint over $X \cup P$. The initial state of $\mathcal{A}$ is $s_0 = (l_0, (X = 0)^{\nearrow} \wedge I(l_0))$, *i.e.* clocks are initially set to 0, and can evolve as long as $I(l_0)$ is satisfied. The computation of the state space is as follows: Given a symbolic state $s = (l, C)$,
$$\mathsf{Succ}(s) = \{(l', C') \mid \exists (l, g, a, R, l') \in E \text{ s.t. } C' = ([(C \wedge g)]_R)^{\nearrow} \cap I(l')\}.$$
A symbolic run of a PTA is an alternating sequence of symbolic states and actions of the form $s_0 \overset{a_0}{\Rightarrow} s_1 \overset{a_1}{\Rightarrow} \cdots \overset{a_{m-1}}{\Rightarrow} s_m$, such that for all $i = 0, \ldots, m - 1$, $a_i \in \Sigma$, and $s_i \overset{a_i}{\Rightarrow} s_{i+1}$ is such that s_{i+1} belongs to $\mathsf{Succ}(s_i)$ and is obtained via action a_i. In the following, we simply refer to the symbolic states belonging to a run of $\mathcal{A}$ starting from s_0 as states of $\mathcal{A}$. Given a run $(l_0, C_0) \overset{a_0}{\Rightarrow} (l_1, C_1) \overset{a_1}{\Rightarrow}$

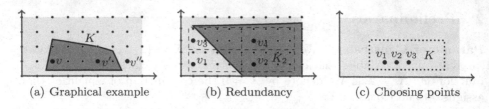

(a) Graphical example   (b) Redundancy   (c) Choosing points

Fig. 1. Graphical representations and challenges

$\cdots \overset{a_{m-1}}{\Rightarrow}{}^1 (l_m, C_m)$, its corresponding *trace* is $l_0 \overset{a_0}{\Rightarrow} l_1 \overset{a_1}{\Rightarrow} \cdots \overset{a_{m-1}}{\Rightarrow}{}^1 l_m$. The set of all traces of a TA is called its *trace set*.

The Inverse Method. The *inverse method* (IM) [7] generalizes the behavior of $\mathcal{A}[v]$ in the form of a *tile*, *i.e.* a parameter constraint K where the discrete behavior is uniform (see Fig. 1a, where $K = \mathsf{IM}(\mathcal{A}, v)$). That is, for any point v' satisfying K, the trace sets of $\mathcal{A}[v']$ and $\mathcal{A}[v]$ are equal. Hence any linear-time property (expressed in, *e.g.* LTL) valid in $\mathcal{A}[v]$ is also valid in $\mathcal{A}[v']$. Note that, in general, tiles have no predefined "shape": they are general polyhedra in $|P|$ dimensions that can have arbitrary size, number of vertices, and edge slope. The computation time of IM also greatly varies, from milliseconds to several hours, depending on the complexity of the model, and the size of the trace set.

The Behavioral Cartography. Given a PTA $\mathcal{A}$ and a bounded parameter domain D (usually a hyperrectangle in $|P|$ dimensions), the *behavioral cartography* (BC) [3] repeatedly calls IM on (some of the) integer points of D (of which there is a finite number), so as to cover D with tiles. The result gives a tiling of D such that the discrete behavior (trace set) is uniform in each tile.

In Fig. 1a, BC first considers point v, and computes $K = \mathsf{IM}(\mathcal{A}, v)$. Then, BC iterates on the subsequent points, all already covered by K, until it meets v'', that is not yet covered. Hence, BC will then compute $\mathsf{IM}(\mathcal{A}, v'')$, and so on, until all integer points in D are covered.

BC can be used for several applications: first, it identifies the system robustness in the sense that, in each tile, parameters can vary as long as they remain in the tile, without impacting the system's discrete behavior. Second, BC can be used to perform parameter optimization; the weakest conditions of the input signal of an industrial asynchronous memory circuit (SPSMALL) were derived using BC [7]. Third, given a set of linear time properties (*i.e.* that can be verified on the trace set), it suffices to compute only once BC, and then to check each property on the trace set generated for each tile in order to know a complete (or nearly complete) set of parameter valuations satisfying each property.

Remark 1. BC does not guarantee the full, dense coverage of D for two reasons. (1) IM may not terminate, as the corresponding problem is undecidable [6]. In our implementation of BC, this is addressed using a timeout: if $\mathsf{IM}(\mathcal{A}, v)$ does not terminate within some time bound, BC switches to the next integer point, and v

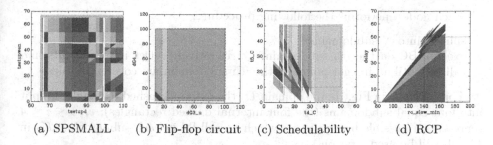

(a) SPSMALL   (b) Flip-flop circuit   (c) Schedulability   (d) RCP

Fig. 2. Examples of graphical behavioral cartographies in 2 dimensions

will (most probably) never be covered. However, although it was shown possible in theory, this never happened in any of our experiments. (2) IM generalizes integer points in the form of dense, rational-valued constraints, but it could happen in rare cases that some tiles do not contain any integer points. This sometimes happened in our experiments (*e.g.* in Fig. 2a around $x = 100$ and $y = 55$); usually, calling BC on multiples of $\frac{1}{3}$ instead of integers was empirically shown to be sufficient in most cases (although in theory there might be an infinite number of tiles in a bounded domain). Conversely, note that BC frequently covers (parts of) the parametric space beyond D; this is the case in Figs. 2b to d (in Fig. 2b, the entire parametric space is even covered).

Also note that the motivation for considering integer points is that, in most cases, considering integers is sufficient to cover entirely (or almost entirely) the domain D. However, as said above, our implementation allows any "step" instead of integers (*e.g.* multiples of $\frac{1}{3}$).

3   Static Domain Decomposition

In order to tackle larger case studies, our objective is to take advantage of the iterative nature of the cartography (in contrast to most, if not all, other known parameter synthesis algorithms), and to distribute it on N processes. There is no theoretical obstacle in doing so, since all calls to IM are independent from each other. The challenge is rather to select efficiently the points on which IM is called, so that as few redundant constraints as possible are computed.

In this section, we briefly describe a static domain decomposition ("Static"). That is, the rectangle D is split into N subdomains, and then each process is responsible for handling its own subdomain in an independent manner (with no communication). This domain decomposition method is often used for regular data distributions, where all subdomains require the same processing time, and preferably on domain shapes such as rectangles or hypercubes, that can easily be mapped on a grid of processes.

Each node i performs the following procedure:

1. split D into N subdomains;[2]
2. execute BC on the ith subdomain, *i.e.* iteratively select integer points and call IM until all integer points in the ith subdomain are covered by tiles.

For example, in Fig. 1b, the domain D (the external dashed rectangle) is split into four equal subdomains (the four internal dashed rectangles); v_i, $1 \le i \le 4$ represents a possible first point on which to call IM in each subdomain. (K_2 in Fig. 1b will be used later on.)

This static decomposition is straightforward but is not satisfactory for BC for three main reasons.

First, the general "shape" of the cartography is entirely arbitrary and unknown beforehand, since tiles can themselves have any shape. Figure 2 gives examples of cartographies in 2 parameter dimensions: although the geometrical distribution of the tiles of Fig. 2a within D is rather homogeneous, this is not true at all for the others. For example, splitting the domain of Fig. 2b (resp. Fig. 2d) into four equal parts would be very unfair for the node responsible of the lower-left (resp. upper-right) subdomain, since most tiles are concentrated there; this would also be inefficient, since the other nodes will rapidly become idle.

Second, the geometrical distribution of the tiles says nothing on the *time* necessary to compute each tile. Recall that the computation of IM can be very long (up to several hours). Even when the tiles are homogeneously located within D, some tiles may require much more time than others. For example, in Fig. 2a (where the geometrical distribution of the tiles is rather homogeneous), it could happen that the bottom-left tiles require much more time than others, resulting in this node to work much longer, while the other nodes would rapidly finish their duty. Again, this would result in a loss of efficiency due to load unbalance since not all of the nodes are working actively.

Third, the absence of communication between nodes may result in redundant computations. Let us go back to the example of cartography in Fig. 1b. Assume that node 2 finished first to compute a tile, say K_2. This tile not only covers the entire subdomain of node 2, leading to the termination of process 2, but it also covers node 4's subdomain entirely and a large part of node 2's subdomain. Without communication, these nodes will keep working without knowing that their subdomain has already been covered. In contrast, a smarter distribution scheme should be such that, in this situation, nodes 2, 3 and 4 would go to help node 1 finish its (not much covered yet) subdomain. We will address this efficiency issue in the remainder of this paper.

4   Master-Worker Point Distribution Algorithms

We first recall our master-worker scheme (Sect. 4.1); then, we formalize the abstract algorithm for the master (Sect. 4.2), the Seq (Sect. 4.3) and the Random

---

[2] Alternatively, a single node could perform the split and then send to each other node its own subdomain (at the cost of additional communications).

Table 1. Tags for master-worker communications

Master tag	Argument	Worker tag	Argument
POINT(v)	parameter valuation	COMPLETED	-
STOP	-	NOTIFYPOINT(v)	parameter valuation
SUBDOMAIN(sd)	new subdomain	REQTILES	-
TILES(T)	latest tiles	RESULT(K)	constraint computed

point distribution (Sect. 4.4) – only informally described in [2]. Additionally, we introduce a new point distribution Shuffle (Sect. 4.5).

4.1 Principle: Master-Worker

Workers ask the master for a point v, then execute $IM(\mathcal{A}, v)$, and finally send the corresponding result K to the master. The master does not call IM itself, but instead distributes points to the workers. Whereas this may be a loss of efficiency for few processes, this shall be compensated for a large number of processes. Moreover, this parallel computation scheme balances the load between workers automatically.

The master and workers communicate with each other by sending messages that are labeled using *tags*, using two asynchronous functions *send*(n, msg) and *receive*(). Function *send*(n, msg) sends a tagged message msg to node n. Function *receive*() is a blocking function that waits until a message is received, and returns a pair (n, msg), where msg is the tagged message that has been received from node n. Based on the tag of the message, receiving processes can decide what to do with the message itself. Note that workers never communicate with each other. We assume that messages are made of a tag and zero or one argument: for example, POINT(v) sends a POINT tag together with the parameter valuation v. We give the list of tags used throughout this paper in Table 1.

4.2 An Abstract Algorithm for the Master

We first formalize in Algorithm 1 the "abstract" master algorithm sketched in [2]; this algorithm contains variation points that can be instantiated to give birth to concrete master algorithms. In this section, we only use the worker tag RESULT and the master tags POINT and STOP. The workers only call the inverse method on the point they receive from the master, and send the result back, until a STOP tag is received.

Algorithm 1 takes as input a PTA $\mathcal{A}$ and a parameter domain D; it is also parameterized by a *point distribution mode* M. Each mode is responsible for instantiating the variation points to give birth to a concrete algorithm. The master starts by creating an empty set of tiles and then calls the mode initialization function M.*initialize*(), that initializes the various variables needed by the concrete algorithms (line 1). Then, the master sends a point to each node n; the way these points are chosen among D (M.*choosePoint*()) is decided by the

---

Algorithm 1. Abstract algorithm for the master

    input   : PTA $\mathcal{A}$, domain D, number of processes N, mode M
    output : Set of tiles T
    // Initialization phase
1 $T \leftarrow \emptyset$;   M.*initialize*()
2 **foreach** *process* $n \in \{1, \dots, N\}$ **do** *send*(n, POINT(M.*choosePoint*())) ;
    // Main phase
3 **while** *there are uncovered integer points in* D **do**
4 | $n, \text{RESULT}(K) \leftarrow$ *receive*(); $T \leftarrow T \cup \{K\}$
5 |___ *send*(n, POINT(M.*choosePoint*()))

    // Finalization phase
6 **foreach** *process* $n \in \{1, \dots, N\}$ **do**
7 |___ $n, \text{RESULT}(K) \leftarrow$ *receive*(); $T \leftarrow T \cup \{K\}$;   *send*($n$, STOP)

8 **return** T

---

mode (line 2). Then the master enters the main loop (line 3 to line 4): while there are uncovered points, every time a node n sends a constraint K and asks for work, the master stores the result in its list of tiles; then, it selects a point according to M and sends it to n. Finally, once all integer points are covered, the master receives results from the remaining nodes and sends STOP tags (line 6–line 7).

The way points are picked by the master to be distributed to the workers is a highly critical question. Choosing points in a wrong manner can lead to a dramatic loss of efficiency. For example, choosing points very close to each other would most probably lead to the (redundant) computation of the same tile. This situation is depicted graphically in Fig. 1c, where points v_1, v_2, v_3 may yield the same tile K. In the next three subsections, we formalize three master modes; these modes will define additional global variables and must instantiate *initialize*() and *choosePoint*().

4.3 Sequential Point Distribution

The first point distribution algorithm (Seq) is a direct extension of the monolithic (*i.e.*, non-distributed) algorithm: as in the non-distributed BC, it enumerates all the points of D in a sequential manner starting from **0**. Seq assumes a function *nextPoint* that, given a parameter valuation v and a parameter domain D, returns the next point in D for some lexicographic order on the points of D. Seq maintains a single global variable v_{prev}, storing the latest point sent to a worker. The initialization function Seq.*initialize*() sets v_{prev} to a special value $\bot$ such that *nextPoint*($\bot$) returns the smallest point in D (*e.g.* **0** if $\mathbf{0} \in D$). Seq.*choosePoint*() (given in Algorithm 2) returns the next point of D not covered yet by any tile.

The main advantage of Seq is that it is inexpensive on the master's side. Its main drawback is the risk of redundant computations by the workers, due to the

---

Algorithm 2. Seq.*choosePoint*()

---
    variables : Point v_{prev}
    output   : Point v
1   $v \leftarrow v_{prev}$
2   **repeat** $v \leftarrow nextPoint(v, D)$ **until** v *is not covered by any tile in* T;
3   $v_{prev} \leftarrow v$; **return** v

---

situation depicted graphically in Fig. 1c: for instance, at the beginning, the N processes will ask for work, and the master will give them the first sequential N points, all very close to each other, with a high risk of redundant computation.

4.4 Random + Sequential Point Distribution

The second point distribution algorithm (Random) selects points randomly, and then in a second phase performs a sequential enumeration to check the full coverage of integers in D. This second phase is necessary to guarantee that all the integer points have been covered. The second phase starts after a given number MAX of consecutive failed attempts to find an uncovered point randomly. Indeed, simply stopping BC after MAX tries could give a probabilistic coverage (*e.g.* 99 %) of integer points, but cannot guarantee the full coverage. Since finding the points not covered by a list of tiles has no efficient practical solution, this sequential check is the only concrete option we have.

    Random maintains two global variables. First, *seqPhase* acts as a flag to remember whether the algorithm is in the first or second phase. Second, v_{prev} stores the latest point sent to a worker (just as in Seq). Random.*initialize*() initially sets *seqPhase* to **false** and v_{prev} to $\perp$.

    We give Random.*choosePoint*() in Algorithm 3. In the first phase (line 1 to line 7), Random.*choosePoint*() randomly computes a point, and then checks whether it is covered by any tile; if not, it is returned. Otherwise, a second try is made, and so on, until the maximum number MAX of attempts is reached. In that latter case, it switches to the second phase (line 8 to line 11), consisting in a sequential enumeration of all the points just as in Seq.*choosePoint*().

4.5 Shuffle Point Distribution

The main problem of Random is the fact that the second phase, necessary to check the full coverage of integers, may be costly and even useless if almost all the points have already been covered. To alleviate this problem, we propose a new algorithm Shuffle that first computes statically a list of all integer points in D, then shuffles this list, and then selects the points of the shuffled list in a sequential manner. The sequential phase of Random is then dropped, at the cost of being able to compute, store statically and shuffle a large quantity of points.

    Shuffle maintains a single global variable, *i.e.* the list *allPoints* of all the points in D that has been shuffled. The Shuffle.*initialize*() function

---

Algorithm 3. Random.*choosePoint*()

---

variables : Point v_{prev}, flag *seqPhase*
output   : Point v
// First phase
1 if ¬*seqPhase* then
2 | *nbTries* ← 0
3 | **while** *nbTries* < *MAX* **do**
4 | | v ← *randomPoint*(D)
5 | | **if** v *is not covered by any tile in* T **then** **return** v;
6 | | *nbTries* ← *nbTries* + 1
7 | *seqPhase* ← **true**

// Second phase
8 if *seqPhase* then
9 | v ← v_{prev}
10 | **repeat** v ← *nextPoint*(v) **until** v *is not covered by any tile in* T;
11 | v_{prev} ← v; **return** v

---

assigns *shuffle*(*allIntegers*(D)) to *allPoints*. (We assume here that function *allIntegers*(D) returns the list of all the integer points of D, and function *shuffle*(L) shuffles the elements of a list L).

Then, the Shuffle.*choosePoint*() function simply consists in selecting the next uncovered point in *allPoints*. That is, it performs *pop*(*allPoints*), until the point output is not covered by any tile, in which case it returns it (we assume here that function *pop*(L) pops the first element of the list L and returns it).

5   Dynamic Domain Decomposition

The most intuitive solution for distributing BC is the Static distribution scheme of Sect. 3, *i.e.* to split D into N subdomains, and then ask each process to handle its own subdomain in an independent manner. As said in Sect. 3, this may lead to inefficient computations (which will be confirmed by our experiments in Sect. 6). Still, we use this idea to set up a *dynamic* domain decomposition algorithm. This algorithm is different from the previous ones, in the sense that it does not fit in the abstract master algorithm formalized in Sect. 4.2.

Initially, the master splits in D into N subdomains, and distributes the subdomains to the workers. In contrast to the algorithms of Sect. 4, the workers are now responsible for checking whether all the points in their subdomain have been covered yet or not. This mechanism reduces the load on the master without leading to redundant point coverage checks. Then, when a worker has covered all the integer points in its subdomain (because the points are covered by tiles computed either by this worker, or by other workers), it informs the master; the master dynamically splits a subdomain (typically, one that has only been covered a little) and sends it back to the idle worker.

Algorithm 4. Subdomain: Master

input   : PTA $\mathcal{A}$, domain D, number of processes N
output   : Set of tiles T
// Initialization phase

1 $T \leftarrow \emptyset$; $SD, currentPoints \leftarrow initialSplit(D, N)$
2 **foreach** *process* $n \in \{1, \ldots, N\}$ **do** $send(n, \text{SUBDOMAIN}(SD[n]))$;
   // Main phase
3 **while** *a subdomain in SD can be split* **do**
4 | **switch** *receive()* **do**
5 | | **case** $n, \text{NOTIFYPOINT}(v)$: $currentPoints[n] \leftarrow v$;
6 | | **case** $n, \text{RESULT}(K)$: $T \leftarrow T \cup \{K\}$;
7 | | **case** $n, \text{REQTILES}$: $send(n, \text{TILES}(T))$;
8 | | **case** $n, \text{COMPLETED}$:
9 | | | $n', sd_1, sd_2 \leftarrow split(SD, currentPoints, n)$
10 | | | $send(n, \text{SUBDOMAIN}(sd_1))$; $send(n', \text{SUBDOMAIN}(sd_2))$

   // Finalization phase
11 **switch** *receive()* **do**
12 | **case** $n, \text{RESULT}(K)$: $T \leftarrow T \cup \{K\}$;
13 | **case** $n, \text{COMPLETED}$: $send(n, \text{STOP})$;
14 **return** T

The main idea is that the master is responsible for handling the dynamic distribution of the subdomains (including detecting the slowest workers to split their subdomain), whereas the workers are responsible for covering all the points in their subdomain in a sequential manner. There is no need for more complex algorithms, since each worker is working on its own in its own subdomain.

5.1   Master Algorithm

In the following, we assume several functions. We believe that understanding the role of these functions is straightforward; in practice, they lead to very tricky implementation issues (especially for the *split* function with arbitrary numbers of processes and parameter dimensions).

We give the master algorithm in Algorithm 4. Besides the list of tiles T, the master maintains two arrays of size N: the array SD associating with each node its current subdomain, and the array $currentPoints$ associating with each node its latest known point (used to understand how advanced a worker is in its subdomain). These two arrays are initialized using the function *initialSplit* that splits D into N subdomains (line 1). Then the master sends its subdomain (line 2) to each node.

The algorithm then enters its main phase (line 3 to line 10). The master waits for incoming messages received via the asynchronous, blocking function *receive()*. If a new point is received (line 5), the master updates the *currentPoints* array (this is needed to perform splits using the most up-to-date data). If a result is received (line 6), the master stores it. If a request for tiles is received (line 7), the master sends all the tiles back so that n can update its local list.[3,4] If the master is notified that a worker n has completed its subdomain, $i.e.$ all of its points have been covered (line 8), the master finds out which subdomain is the least covered, $i.e.$ which workers are the most in need for assistance; this is performed by $split(SD, currentPoints, n)$, that returns the node n' needing help, and two new subdomains sd_1 and sd_2 split from n''s former subdomain, while updating SD (line 9). The master then informs both nodes of the split (line 10).

Finally, when no subdomain can be split ($i.e.$ all non-completed subdomains contain only one point), the master stores the last tiles it receives (line 12) and sends a STOP signal to the workers (line 13).

5.2   Worker Algorithm

We give the Subdomain worker algorithm in Algorithm 5. Each worker waits for messages from the master: whenever a STOP signal is received from m (m stands for the master node id), the worker terminates (line 3). Otherwise, a subdomain sd is received (line 5):the worker then covers sd with tiles (line 5 to line 11) by calling IM sequentially on consecutive integers as in the Seq (master) algorithm. The worker selects a point, sends it to the master for update purpose, calls IM on that point, sends the result to the master, asks for an update of the list of tiles, and so on. When sd is covered, the worker notifies the master (line 12), and then waits again for a new message from the master until termination.[5]

5.3   An Additional Heuristic

It may happen that, while a node is calling IM on a point v, another node has covered v with its own tile. For example, in Fig. 1b, node 2 calls IM on point v_2, while node 4 calls IM on point v_4. Assume calling IM on point v_2 yields K_2, that incidentally covers v_4. It is more efficient to stop the computation of IM on v_4, so that node 4 moves to another point instead of computing a redundant tile. We hence improve Subdomain by adding a heuristic that prevents this situation as follows: the master keeps track of all the points currently processed by each node; whenever a constraint computed by a node i covers the current node processed by another node j, the master informs immediately node j, and this node stops its computation to move to the next point. We refer to Subdomain augmented with this heuristics as Subdomain + H. This heuristic might be expensive, both

---

[3] For efficiency purpose, in our implementation, the master only sends the new tiles since n's latest request (which is ensured using additional queue data structures).

[4] The local list is necessary to detect whether a point in the worker's subdomain is covered by a tile computed by another worker.

[5] Additionally, the worker checks whether the master has split its subdomain, because some other worker completed its own subdomain. In our implementation, this requires on the worker's side frequent (but inexpensive) checks whether the master has split the worker's current subdomain and, if so, a simple update of the subdomain.

Algorithm 5. Subdomain: Worker n

---

    input   : PTA $\mathcal{A}$
    variables : Set of tiles T, point v_{prev}
1 **while true do**
2   **switch** *receive()* **do**
3   **case** $m,$ STOP*:* **return** ;
4   **case** $m,$ SUBDOMAIN(sd)*:*
5   **while** *there are uncovered points in sd* **do**
6                 $v \leftarrow$ Seq.*choosePoint*()
7   *send*($m,$ NOTIFYPOINT(v))
8                 $K \leftarrow$ IM($\mathcal{A}, v$)
9   *send*($m,$ RESULT(K))
10              $m,$ TILES(*receivedTiles*) $\leftarrow$ *receive*()
11              $T \leftarrow T \cup$ *receivedTiles*
12   *send*($m,$ COMPLETED)

---

on the master side and on the worker side (frequent checks to perform, and more communication), hence we will study both Subdomain and Subdomain + H.

6 Experiments

We implemented our algorithms in the working version (2.7) of IMITATOR [4].[6]

We are presenting here results using seven case studies: Flip-flop4 is a 4-parameter dimension asynchronous flip-flop circuit. RCP is a parametric model of the root contention protocol (inspired by the TREX [8] model). Sched3-2, Sched3B-2, Sched3B-3 and Sched5 are parametric schedulability problems, where the goal is to find tiles where the system is robustly schedulable. SiMoP is a parametric networked automation system [7]. We give in the "model" part of Table 2 the number of clocks, of parameters, and of integer points in D for each case study. In the "cartography" part, we give the number of tiles and the time (in seconds) to compute the non-distributed cartography ("monolithic"). Note that the number of tiles gives an upper bound on the number of nodes above which a perfect distribution algorithm cannot become more efficient: if each node computes a different tile, then using more than n nodes cannot be faster than n nodes. Hence, we bound the analysis to the smallest power of 2 greater or equal to # Tiles ("N_{max}").

Methodology. We compute BC for each algorithm, for a number of nodes from 4 to 128 . For sake of brevity, we study here the performances at $n = N_{max}$. The execution time (in seconds) is given in the third part ("Execution time") of Table 2. (The algorithm Hybrid will be explained later on.)

---

[6] Source models and results are available at www.imitator.fr/static/ICFEM15/.

We use two metrics to evaluate our algorithms. The first metric is the following ratio, that compares algorithms with each other, independently of their absolute performances: for each algorithm and each case study, we compute the time for this case study and this algorithm for N_{max} nodes divided by the maximum over all algorithms for this case study for N_{max} nodes, and multiplied by 100. A ratio equal to 100 means that this algorithm is the slowest for this case study, and a small ratio indicates a more efficient algorithm.

The second metrics is the speedup, that evaluates the scalability of each algorithm: for each algorithm and each case study, we compute the time for this case study and this algorithm for N_{max} nodes divided by the time needed for a perfect algorithm (*i.e.* the monolithic time divided by N_{max}), and multiplied by 100. Here, a number close to 100 means a very scalable algorithm, whereas a number close to 0 indicates an algorithm that does not scale well.

In the following, we describe the performance of each algorithm according to Table 2, before concluding which is the most efficient strategy.

Static. This static domain decomposition algorithm is clearly not efficient, which shows that BC cannot be efficiently distributed using classical techniques for regular data distribution. Static is the worst algorithm twice (for RCP and Sched3B-2), and never the most efficient; a surprise is the very good performance for Flip-flop4, which probably comes from the fact that the tiles are very homogeneous geometrically for this case study, making a static distribution efficient.

Seq. Although it is easy to implement, this algorithm is terribly inefficient: with 3 case studies for which it is the worst algorithm, it is also the worst in average. This comes from the fact that Seq is very likely to distribute to different nodes points that are close to each other, leading to redundant computations.

Random. This algorithm behaves well for case studies with relatively few points in D, but it is always behind Shuffle in that case. It does not perform as well on case studies with large D, most likely because of the sequential enumeration of all points in the second phase of Random.

Shuffle. With four case studies for which it is the best one, Shuffle is very efficient when D does not contain too many points; shuffling the points guarantees a good random repartition of the points, without entailing complex operations at the master side... at the cost of being able to shuffle a large quantities of points. This latter aspect certainly explains the low performances for Flip-flop4 and Sched3B-3.

Subdomain. This algorithm is always outperformed by its variant Subdomain + H; it seems that the cost of checking which node is computing which point and the additional necessary communications are largely compensated by the benefit of preventing redundant computations brought by stopping ongoing executions.

Subdomain + H. This algorithm has the best average speedup (17 %). Although it clearly outperforms Shuffle for only two experiments (Flip-flop4 and Sched3B-3), Subdomain + H is for no case study very far from the best algorithm. This could

Table 2. Summary of experiments

Case study	Flip-flop4	RCP	Sched3-2	Sched3B-2	Sched3B-3	Sched5	SiMoP	Average
Model								
Clocks	5	6	13	13	13	21	8	
Parameters	4	2	2	2	3	2	2	
$|D|$	386400	3050	286	14746	530856	1681	10201	
Cartography								
# Tiles	190	19	59	71	378	177	48	
N_{max}	128	32	64	128	128	128	64	
Monolithic	1341.0	1992.0	46.0	61.2	865.0	3593.0	111.6	
Execution time at N_{max} (s)								
Static	33.0	2108.0	4.0	26.6	181.0	213.0	21.4	
Seq	2059.0	653.0	4.6	11.0	810.0	219.0	36.1	
Random	652.0	635.0	3.6	8.4	524.0	148.0	23.6	
Shuffle	670.0	624.0	3.1	7.6	243.0	140.0	18.7	
Subdomain	48.0	1286.0	7.2	15.8	217.0	273.0	32.4	
Subdomain + H	24.0	622.0	4.0	11.0	81.0	199.0	23.2	
Hybrid	24.0	624.0	3.1	7.6	81.0	140.0	18.7	
Ratio at N_{max} w.r.t. slowest at N_{max} (%)								
Static	2	100	56	100	22	78	59	60
Seq	100	31	64	41	100	80	100	74
Random	32	30	50	32	65	54	65	47
Shuffle	33	30	43	29	30	51	52	38
Subdomain	2	61	100	59	27	100	90	63
Subdomain + H	1	30	56	41	10	73	64	39
Hybrid	1	30	43	29	10	51	52	31
Speedup at N_{max} (%)								
Static	32	5	19	3	4	13	11	12
Seq	1	16	17	8	1	13	6	9
Random	2	17	22	10	1	19	10	11
Shuffle	2	17	25	11	3	20	12	13
Subdomain	22	8	11	5	3	10	7	10
Subdomain + H	44	17	19	8	8	14	10	17
Hybrid	44	17	25	11	8	20	12	20

make a good candidate for the best distribution algorithm – but we advocate in the following for a better proposition.

Conclusion: Hybrid. From the experiments, we notice that Subdomain + H is always among the most efficient, but is outperformed by Shuffle for case studies with relatively few points in D. Hence, we propose the following "algorithm": if D contains relatively few points (say, less than 100,000), use Shuffle, otherwise use Subdomain + H. Note that the condition (number of points in D) only depends on the input of the analysis, and can be checked very easily. This new algorithm "Hybrid" is always the best one – except for RCP, for which it is very slightly slower than Subdomain + H despite a small number of points (3,050). In addition, Hybrid gets the smallest average ratio (31 %) and the highest speedup (20 %).

Discussion. An average speedup of 20 % at N_{max} for Hybrid can seem relatively low; this means that a perfect distribution algorithm (that would always divide the monolithic computation time by N) would be 5 times faster. Still, we find it promising. First, all distributed algorithms suffer from the time spent in communication, which always lowers the speedup. Second, this confirms that distributing BC is far from trivial, due to the unknown shape of the cartography, the unknown computation time for each tile, and the risk for redundant computations.

Third, and most importantly, a speedup of 20 % means that, when using 128 nodes, the computation time is still divided by more than 25 – which leads to an impressive decrease of the verification time.

7   Final Remarks

We proposed here distribution algorithms to compute the cartography relying on the inverse method. In fact, one can use other algorithms than IM to obtain different "cartographies"; this is the case of [5] where we use a reachability preservation algorithm ("PRP") instead of IM so as to obtain, not a behavioral cartography, but a simple "good/bad" partition with respect to a reachability property. Distributing PRP using Subdomain often outperforms the monolithic bad-state reachability synthesis (e.g. [1,13]). Hence, we believe that our point distribution algorithms can be reused for different purposes than just BC.

In addition to using distributed computing resources, our aim is to design multicore algorithms for parameter synthesis, in the line of [11,15] – and then combine both approaches.

Finally, we would like to formally verify the master-worker communication scheme of Sects. 4 and 5, so as to avoid potential deadlocks caused by a node waiting for a message that cannot arrive at that point.

References

1. Alur, R., Henzinger, T. A., Vardi, M.Y.: Parametric real-time reasoning. In: STOC, pp. 592–601. ACM (1993)
2. André, É., Coti, C., Evangelista, S.: Distributed behavioral cartography of timed automata. In: EuroMPI/ASIA, pp. 109–114. ACM (2014)
3. André, É., Fribourg, L.: Behavioral cartography of timed automata. In: Kučera, A., Potapov, I. (eds.) RP 2010. LNCS, vol. 6227, pp. 76–90. Springer, Heidelberg (2010)
4. André, É., Fribourg, L., Kühne, U., Soulat, R.: IMITATOR 2.5: a tool for analyzing robustness in scheduling problems. In: Giannakopoulou, D., Méry, D. (eds.) FM 2012. LNCS, vol. 7436, pp. 33–36. Springer, Heidelberg (2012)
5. André, É., Lipari, G., Nguyen, H.G., Sun, Y.: Reachability preservation based parameter synthesis for timed automata. In: Havelund, K., Holzmann, G., Joshi, R. (eds.) NFM 2015. LNCS, vol. 9058, pp. 50–65. Springer, Heidelberg (2015)
6. André, É., Markey, N.: Language preservation problems in parametric timed automata. In: Sankaranarayanan, S., Vicario, E. (eds.) FORMATS 2015. LNCS, vol. 9268, pp. 27–43. Springer, Heidelberg (2015)
7. André, É., Soulat, R.: The Inverse Method. ISTE Ltd and Wiley & Sons, London, UK (2013)
8. Annichini, A., Bouajjani, A., Sighireanu, M.: TREX: a tool for reachability analysis of complex systems. In: Berry, G., Comon, H., Finkel, A. (eds.) CAV 2001. LNCS, vol. 2102, pp. 368–372. Springer, Heidelberg (2001)
9. Cimatti, A., Griggio, A., Mover, S., Tonetta, S.: Parameter synthesis with IC3. In: FMCAD, pp. 165–168. IEEE (2013)

10. De Wulf, M., Doyen, L., Raskin, J.: Almost ASAP semantics: from timed models to timed implementations. Formal Aspects Comput. **17**(3), 319–341 (2005)
11. Evangelista, S., Laarman, A., Petrucci, L., van de Pol, J.: Improved multi-core nested depth-first search. In: Chakraborty, S., Mukund, M. (eds.) ATVA 2012. LNCS, vol. 7561, pp. 269–283. Springer, Heidelberg (2012)
12. Hamidouche, K., Borghi, A., Esterie, P., Falcou, J., Peyronnet, S.: Three high performance architectures in the parallel APMC boat. In: PMDC. IEEE (2010)
13. Jovanović, A., Lime, D., Roux, O.H.: Integer parameter synthesis for timed automata. IEEE Trans. Softw.Eng. **41**(5), 445–461 (2015)
14. Kahsai, T., Tinelli, C.: PKind: a parallel k-induction based model checker. In: PDMC, vol. 72, pp. 55–62 (2011)
15. Laarman, A., Olesen, M.C., Dalsgaard, A.E., Larsen, K.G., van de Pol, J.: Multi-core emptiness checking of timed Büchi automata using inclusion abstraction. In: Sharygina, N., Veith, H. (eds.) CAV 2013. LNCS, vol. 8044, pp. 968–983. Springer, Heidelberg (2013)
16. Larsen, K.G., Pettersson, P., Yi, W.: UPPAAL in a nutshell. Int. J. Softw. Tools Technol. Transf. **1**(1–2), 134–152 (1997)
17. Markey, N.: Robustness in real-time systems. In: SIES, pp. 28–34. IEEE Computer Society Press (2011)
18. Sun, J., Liu, Y., Dong, J.S., Pang, J.: PAT: towards flexible verification under fairness. In: Bouajjani, A., Maler, O. (eds.) CAV 2009. LNCS, vol. 5643, pp. 709–714. Springer, Heidelberg (2009)

A Recursive Probabilistic Temporal Logic

Pablo F. Castro[1,2(✉)], Cecilia Kilmurray[1,2], and Nir Piterman[3]

[1] Departamento de Computación,
FCEFQyN, Universidad Nacional de Río Cuarto, Río Cuarto, Argentina
{pcastro,ckilmurray}@dc.exa.unrc.edu.ar
[2] Consejo Nacional de Investigaciones Científicas y Técnicas (CONICET),
Río Cuarto, Argentina
[3] Department of Computer Science, University of Leicester, Leicester, UK
nir.piterman@leicester.ac.uk

Abstract. In this paper we introduce recursive probabilistic computa-tion-tree logic as a restriction of μPCTL. We introduce the logic in detail and show its usefulness for verifying systems. We illustrate this by means of some examples. Roughly speaking, we include recursive operators within PCTL, which enable one to identify repeating patterns of prob-ability. This new feature seems in particular useful for expressing prop-erties regarding stability of system executions; such properties are usual, for instance, in those scenarios where one is interested to verify whether the system under verification stays in, or revisits, a subset of safe states. Also, the logic makes it possible to reason about set of executions with zero measure; something no possible in related logics.

1 Introduction

The increasing role of computing systems in critical activities has led to the use of mathematical formalisms for producing error-free software as well as reducing the occurrence of faults during the execution of systems. In the case of verifica-tion of complex and large systems, automated techniques based on mathematical formalisms have been proved to be essential. One of these techniques that has received an increasing amount of attention in the last decades is *model checking*. Model checking establishes whether a system satisfies a certain property in an automated way. For that, a representation of a system M called *model* is con-structed and contrasted with a property φ in temporal logic. Temporal logic can be used to express properties about concurrent and reactive systems [1].

Tools that implement model checking algorithms for various temporal logics have been applied to verify *hardware components*, *software programs*, and *net-work protocols* among others. Many examples of applications are reported in the literature, and we refer to [1,2] for in depth introduction to model checking.

This work was partially supported by FP7-PEOPLE-IRESES-2011 MEALS project, EPSRC EP/L007177/1 project, PICT 2013-0080 project and PICT 2012-1298 project.

© Springer International Publishing Switzerland 2015
M. Butler et al. (Eds.): ICFEM 2015, LNCS 9407, pp. 336–348, 2015.
DOI: 10.1007/978-3-319-25423-4_22

In the last years, several types of temporal logics incorporating probabilities into the picture have been proposed. These formalisms provide the basis to perform model checking in scenarios where probabilities are needed. This is the case, for instance, of randomized algorithms and distributed protocols. Such logics include, for example, PCTL, the probabilistic counterpart of CTL, and PCTL*, the probabilistic counterpart of CTL*, to name a few. Tools such as PRISM [3] and LiQuor [4] support probabilistic model checking. In particular, they allow to check the validity of PCTL and PCTL* formulas over Markov chain models.

A few years ago, there was a major effort that led to standardization of temporal hardware specification languages (cf. [5,6]). This effort was preceded by much research about the constructs that should (and should not) be included in such languages (e.g., [7,8]). Much care has been given to find the right balance between ease of specification, expressive power, and complexity of model checking. In this paper we would like to start a similar process for temporal logics intended for reasoning about probabilistic systems. The standard language for reasoning about such systems is PCTL, whose expressive power is very limited. Much effort has been recently dedicated to considering probabilistic μ-calculi [9,10] and automata [11]. These are very expressive, however, neglect the issues of usability and tractability.

We present a logic called RPCTL, which, as mentioned, extends PCTL with recursive calls. This logic is a fragment of μPCTL presented in [10]. The recursive operator is, in fact, a greatest fixpoint. However, introducing it through recursion takes advantage of the familiarity of the recursion concept to computer scientists. By not allowing nesting of different recursion schemes (least and greatest fixpoints) we bound the complexity of the logic. At the same time, our logic extends PCTL in expressive power and allows it to characterize repetition in the probabilistic system.[1]

We cast expressiveness results from [10] in the context of RPCTL and show that RPCTL is more expressive than PCTL. We show that the complexity of model checking matches that of PCTL and is polynomial in the underlying Markov chain. In fact, the algorithm repeatedly calls PCTL model checking.

We believe that a main application of RPCTL is the verification of properties related to *fault-tolerance*. A system is said *fault-tolerant* when it is able to continue working in an acceptable way even under the occurrence of faults. The grade of tolerance exhibited by a given system can be characterized by using collections of safe states. For instance, a system is said *fail-safe* if it stays in a set of safe states under the occurrence of faults [12], and it is classified as *non-masking* tolerant when it revisits infinitely often a set of safe or desirable states [12]. In the case of probabilistic systems (and probabilistic temporal logics), the characterization of such properties cannot be achieved in a direct way. This is mainly because the probability of a system to stay in a set of safe states is 0 when the occurrence of faults has a positive probability (i.e., the system will eventually escape from this set of "good" states with probability 1). We illustrate this

---

[1] We note that this extension is orthogonal to the power added by PCTL*, or other mechanisms for describing regular path properties.

point with some examples in Sect. 4. Instead of using the standard quantifier for greatest fixed point we use a syntactic sugar pointing out its recursive character, we believe this improves its usability when specifying and verifying systems, we illustrate this with two examples.

The paper is structured as follows. In Sect. 2 we introduce the basic concepts needed to tackle the ideas described in this paper. In Sect. 3 we describe the logic in detail and show how it compares to CTL and PCTL. We include two examples and show the motivation for using this logic in Sect. 4. Then, we describe the model checking algorithm in Sect. 5. Finally, we discuss some conclusions and future work.

2   Preliminaries

In this section we briefly introduce some basic concepts. A *Kripke structure* over a set AP of atomic propositions is a tuple $\langle S, \rightarrow, L, s_0 \rangle$, where S is a (finite) set of locations, $\rightarrow \subseteq S \times S$ is a relation, $L : S \rightarrow 2^{AP}$ is a labeling function and $s_0 \in S$ is an initial location. A *Markov chain* over a set AP of atomic letters is a tuple $\langle S, P, L, s_0 \rangle$, where S is a (finite) set of locations, $P : S \times S \rightarrow [0, 1]$ is a stochastic matrix, $L : S \rightarrow 2^{AP}$ is a labeling function and $s_0 \in S$ is an initial location. For a location $s \in S$ we denote by M_s the Markov chain obtained from M by setting s to the initial location.

PCTL formulas over a set AP are defined as follows:

$$J ::= \{>, \geq\} \times [0, 1]$$
$$\Phi ::= \top \mid \bot \mid p_i \mid \neg p_i \mid \Phi_1 \vee \Phi_2 \mid \Phi_1 \wedge \Phi_2 \mid \mathcal{P}_J(\Psi)$$
$$\Psi ::= \mathsf{X}\Phi \mid \Phi \, \mathcal{U} \, \Phi \mid \Phi \, \mathcal{W} \, \Phi$$

As usual we introduce the abbreviations F and G. The semantics and intuitions of PCTL formulas are as usual, see [2].

The logic μPCTL extends PCTL with the inclusion of fixpoint variables and least and greatest fixpoint operators [10]. We now describe the syntax and semantics of μPCTL. Let AP be a set $\{p_0, p_1, \dots\}$ of atomic propositions and let $\mathcal{V} = \{V_0, V_1, V_2, \dots\}$ be an enumerable set of variables; the sets Φ and Ψ of location and path formulas, respectively, are mutually recursively defined as follows:

$$J ::= \{>, \geq\} \times [0, 1]$$
$$\Phi ::= \top \mid \bot \mid p_i \mid \neg p_i \mid V_i \mid \Phi_1 \vee \Phi_2 \mid \Phi_1 \wedge \Phi_2 \mid \mathcal{P}_J(\Psi) \mid \nu V_i.\Phi \mid \mu V_i.\Phi \quad (1)$$
$$\Psi ::= \mathsf{X}\Phi \mid \Phi \, \mathcal{U} \, \Phi \mid \Phi \, \mathcal{W} \, \Phi$$

We assume that in every formula there is no repetition of bound variables; it is straightforward to see that every formula can be rewritten to satisfy this requirement. In general, we are interested in formulas in which all variables are bound.

A μPCTL formula characterizes the set of states of a Markov chain in which it holds. Consider a Markov chain $M = \langle S, P, L, s_0 \rangle$. The semantics of subformulas may depend on a valuation associating a set of states with every variable appearing in it. Formally, a valuation is a function $\tau : \mathcal{V} \to 2^S$. We denote by $\tau[S'/V]$ the valuation such that $\tau(V) = S'$ and for every $V' \neq V$ we have $\tau[S'/V](V') = \tau(V)$.

The semantics of a formula φ, denoted $[\varphi]_\tau^M$ is defined as follows:

$$[p_i]_\tau^M = L(p_i)$$
$$[\neg p_i]_\tau^M = S \setminus L(p_i)$$
$$[V_i]_\tau^M = \tau(V_i)$$
$$[\varphi_1 \wedge \varphi_2]_\tau^M = [\varphi_1]_\tau^M \cap [\varphi_2]_\tau^M$$
$$[\varphi_1 \vee \varphi_2]_\tau^M = [\varphi_1]_\tau^M \cup [\varphi_2]_\tau^M$$
$$[\mathcal{P}_J(\Psi)]_\tau^M = \{s \in S \mid measure_M(s, \Psi)J\}$$
$$[\nu V_i.\Phi]_\tau^M = \mathsf{gfp}\{S' \subseteq S \mid S' = [\Phi]_{\tau[S'/V_i]}^M\}$$
$$[\mu V_i.\Phi]_\tau^M = \mathsf{lfp}\{S' \subseteq S \mid S' = [\Phi]_{\tau[S'/V_i]}^M\}$$

We notice that 2^S is a lattice and that all operators are monotonic. It follows from the Knaster-Tarski Theorem that the greatest and least fixpoint indeed exist.

3   RPCTL

In this section we present an extension of probabilistic computation tree logic with recursive statements. We provide the fixed point operators that allow writing recursive formulas. We allow a formula to contain a recursive call by using two novel operators rec and call which are syntactic sugar for the greatest fixed point. Technically speaking, this introduces greatest fixed points in the logic, effectively making it a subset of μPCTL.

Let us start presenting the syntax of RPCTL. Let AP be a set $\{p_0, p_1, \dots\}$ of atomic propositions; the sets Φ and Ψ of location and path formulas, respectively, are mutually recursively defined as follows:

$$J ::= \{>, \geq\} \times [0, 1]$$
$$\Phi ::= \top \mid \bot \mid p_i \mid \neg p_i \mid \mathsf{call}_i \mid \Phi_1 \vee \Phi_2 \mid \Phi_1 \wedge \Phi_2 \mid \mathcal{P}_J(\Psi) \mid \mathsf{rec}_i.\Phi$$
$$\Psi ::= \mathsf{X}\Phi \mid \Phi \,\mathcal{U}\, \Phi \mid \Phi \,\mathcal{W}\, \Phi$$

In general, we are interested in formulas in which all variables are bound. Note the indexes appearing in rec and call statements, they serve mainly two purposes; firstly, they provide an enumerable collection of variables for recursion ($\mathsf{call}_0, \mathsf{call}_1, \mathsf{call}_2, \dots$); and secondly, they indicate which quantifiers bind which variables, that is, call_i is bound by rec_i, for every i.

We now describe the semantics of RPCTL. An RPCTL formula characterizes the set of states of a Markov chain in which it holds. Consider a Markov chain $M = \langle S, P, L, s_0 \rangle$. The semantics of subformulas may depend on a valuation associating a set of states with every call statement appearing in it. Formally, a valuation is $\tau : \{\mathsf{call}_0, \mathsf{call}_1, \dots\} \to 2^S$. We denote by $\tau[S'/\mathsf{call}_i]$ the valuation such that $\tau(\mathsf{call}_i) = S'$ and for every $i \neq j$ we have $\tau[S'/\mathsf{call}_i](\mathsf{call}_j) = \tau(\mathsf{call}_j)$. The semantics of a formula φ, denoted $[\varphi]_\tau^M$ is defined as follows:

$$
\begin{aligned}
[p_i]_\tau^M &= L(p_i) \\
[\neg p_i]_\tau^M &= S \setminus L(p_i) \\
[\mathsf{call}_i]_\tau^M &= \tau(\mathsf{call}_i) \\
[\varphi_1 \wedge \varphi_2]_\tau^M &= [\varphi_1]_\tau^M \cap [\varphi_2]_\tau^M \\
[\varphi_1 \vee \varphi_2]_\tau^M &= [\varphi_1]_\tau^M \cup [\varphi_2]_\tau^M \\
[\mathcal{P}_J(\Psi)]_\tau^M &= \{s \in S \mid \mathsf{measure}_M(s, \Psi)J\} \\
[\mathsf{rec}_i.\Phi]_\tau^M &= \mathsf{gfp}\{S' \subseteq S \mid S' = [\Phi]_{\tau[S'/\mathsf{call}_i]}^M\}
\end{aligned}
$$

Let us illustrate the intuition behind the operators call and rec with some examples, consider the following formula:

$$\mathsf{rec}.p \wedge \mathcal{P}_{>0}(\mathsf{Xcall}), \tag{2}$$

where, for the sake of simplicity, we avoid the indexes in rec and call. This formula holds in a location s if p *holds in s, and the probability that formula 2 holds in next locations is greater than* 0. That is, p holds in s and s has a successor satisfying p, which has a successor satisfying p, and so on. This property is in fact equivalent to the CTL property $\mathsf{EG}p$. The formula:

$$\mathsf{rec}.\mathcal{P}_{>0.5}(\mathsf{call}\,\mathcal{U}\,p), \tag{3}$$

holds in a location s if *recursively, there is a probability of more than half to continue to locations that satisfy the same property until p becomes true*. That is, every location encountered on the way to the satisfaction of p has more than half of its successors satisfying the same property. As we show below this property is not expressible in either CTL or PCTL.

Intuitively, we have to treat each bound variable call_i as a new proposition. Each location labeled by one of the new propositions needs to satisfy the PCTL formula obtained from the appropriate recursive call, where calls are replaced by the corresponding formula. We provide further intuitions with some examples below.

3.1   Expressive Power

We show that RPCTL is more expressive than PCTL and incomparable with CTL.

Theorem 1. RPCTL *is more expressive than* PCTL. *There are properties expressed by* RPCTL *that are not expressible in* CTL.

Proof. We first note that PCTL is syntactically included in RPCTL. The property $\mathsf{rec}.p \wedge \mathcal{P}_{>0.5}(\mathsf{X} \wedge \mathsf{call})$ is not expressible in either PCTL or CTL [10].

We note that including existential and universal path quantification in RPCTL would not increase the complexity of model checking algorithms. This would allow us to include CTL in RPCTL, should we wish to do so.

In Sect. 4 we use properties similar to the property in the proof of Theorem 1. That is, these properties enforce a repetition of a certain pattern of probability even if that pattern occurs in a set whose measure is zero. It would be possible to show that these properties are not expressible neither in CTL nor in PCTL. It is worth noting that this "repetition" feature of RPCTL that reasons about sets of paths of measure zero is the main novelty that is afforded by RPCTL.

4 Motivating Examples

In this section we describe two examples with the aim of illustrating the use of RPCTL in practice.

4.1 A Token Ring Network

Our first example consists of a simple system composed of three connected nodes, whose activities are regulated via a token ring protocol. The three nodes are connected to each other via a network with a ring topology; in this setting, a token is passed through by the nodes in such a way of guaranteeing the access to a particular resource to the actual owner of the node, e.g., permission to send information across the network.

Let us state a few properties which might be thought of as requirements for this system. One of these properties is: *there is always exactly one node that has the token, and whenever a node hold onto a token, it eventually passes it to the next node in the ring.* A simple fault that can be conceived in this context is one in which, due to the unreliability of the medium, the token is lost while it is being sent from one node to another one, we assign some probability to the occurrence of this event. A probabilistic abstraction of this situation, including the fault detection, is depicted in Fig. 1. In this model, the proposition n_i becomes true when the token is passed to node i. While $n_i{'}$ represents the situation in which the token stays in node i, before passing to the next one. It is simple to see that the probability that a token reaches node 1 when it is sent by node 0 is $\frac{1}{2}$. Note that for the other cases similar probabilities are obtained. Simple calculations show the following: $\mathcal{P}(n_1 \ldots n_2) = \mathcal{P}(n_2 \ldots n_0) = \frac{1}{2}$.

It is interesting to investigate the properties that hold in the non-faulty part of the system, an example is the following one.

Example Property 1. *When no faults are observed, the token could stay in a given state or move to the next one, the probability of doing this is at least one half, and this pattern can be repeated an unbounded number of times.*

Note that in this property we have an implicit notion of stability, which in some sense characterizes the normative (or expected) behavior of the system. A natural candidate to express this property is the following formula:

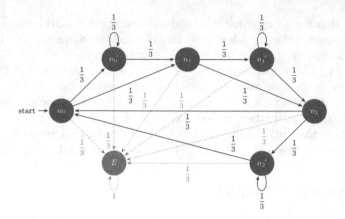

Fig. 1. A model of a token ring of nodes, where tokens can be lost.

$$\text{rec.} \begin{bmatrix} (n_0 \rightarrow \mathcal{P}_{\geq \frac{1}{2}}(\mathbf{F}(n_1 \wedge \text{call}))) \wedge \\ (n_1 \rightarrow \mathcal{P}_{\geq \frac{1}{2}}(\mathbf{F}(n_2 \wedge \text{call}))) \wedge \\ (n_2 \rightarrow \mathcal{P}_{\geq \frac{1}{2}}(\mathbf{F}(n_0 \wedge \text{call}))) \end{bmatrix} \quad (4)$$

Roughly speaking, this formula expresses that, if the token is held by node i, then the probability that the token reaches node $i+1$, and that this pattern is repeated, is one half.

If we consider the set of states that satisfy the first occurrence of call to be the state labeled by n_1, the set of states that satisfy the second appearance of call to be the state labeled by n_2, and the set of states that satisfy the last occurrence to be the state labeled by n_0, then, the PCTL property obtained by replacing bound variables by propositions denoting these sets of states, holds for states n_0, n_1, and n_2.

Let us introduce a variant of the scenario presented above. Now, when the token is held by node 2, it could stay in that state or move to node 1 or node 0, that is, now we have the possibility of returning the token to the previous node or passing it to the next one; this may be the case, for instance, in a scenario where the channel connecting node 2 with node 1 is corrupt, and the token has to be returned to the original sender. This new situation is depicted in Fig. 2. The probability of the token going from node 2 to node 0 is: $\mathcal{P}(n_2 \dots n_0) = 0.3636$.

The formula does not hold for this last model, note that state n_2 in the model does not satisfy the subformula $(n_2 \rightarrow \mathcal{P}_{\geq \frac{1}{2}}(\mathbf{F}(n_0 \wedge \text{call})))$. That is, RPCTL makes possible to distinguishing different patterns of repetition.

One may try to capture this property using the following PCTL formula:

$$\varphi = \begin{bmatrix} (n_0 \rightarrow \mathcal{P}_{\geq \frac{1}{2}}(\mathbf{F}(n_1))) \wedge \\ (n_1 \rightarrow \mathcal{P}_{\geq \frac{1}{2}}(\mathbf{F}(n_2))) \wedge \\ (n_2 \rightarrow \mathcal{P}_{\geq \frac{1}{2}}(\mathbf{F}(n_0))) \end{bmatrix} \quad (5)$$

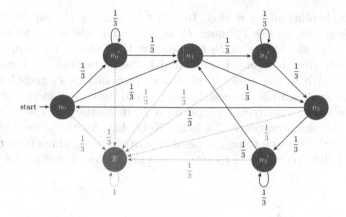

Fig. 2. Another model of a token ring of nodes, where tokens can be lost.

Fig. 3. Another model that satisfy φ.

In fact φ distinguishes the two models analyzed above, note that it is true in the model of Fig. 1, and false in the model presented in Fig. 2. However, notice that this PCTL formula does not capture the notion of repetition. Formula 5 is true in structures where the pattern of repetition is not available; an example is shown in Fig. 3, where we have $n_0 \vDash \varphi$.

Another possible way of capturing recursive properties like this one using PCTL is by using a globally operator of the kind: $\mathcal{P}_{>0}(G\varphi)$ (where φ is the property presented above). But the set of paths that satisfy these kinds of properties has measure 0; so in this model it is equivalent to $\mathcal{P}_{=0}(G\varphi)$, which prevents us from analyzing these traces.

4.2   A Mutual Exclusion Problem

Let us now consider a standard example in concurrency and fault-tolerance: the mutual exclusion problem for two processes (namely P_1 and P_2). We introduce faults in this model by allowing processes to go into an error state, in this particular case they may be down for an undetermined amount of time. The basis of this example is introduced in [13], here we add probabilities to be able to perform a quantitative analysis of this system.

In every state the probabilities of moving to its successors are distributed in a uniform way. The model that captures this scenario is shown in Fig. 4. The region M_1 (enclosed by a dashed line) contains those states that can be reached either, during the normal behavior of the system, or when P_1 is down but with a positive probability of recovering. In order to simplify the analysis, we only consider failures in process P_1, once P_1 fails, P_2 may fail too. The transitions corresponding to the failure of P_2 followed by the failure of P_1 are similar to the ones shown in that figure. In this model, the proposition N_i becomes true when process P_i is in the *non-critical* region, propositions T_i and C_i represent the situation in which the process P_i moves into its trying section, or critical region, respectively. Finally, the proposition D_i indicates that the process P_i is down, denoting the occurrence of a fault. Note that, for the sake of clarity, we have gathered the states into regions, and transitions were added from these sets of states to failure regions. Let us state some properties of this model.

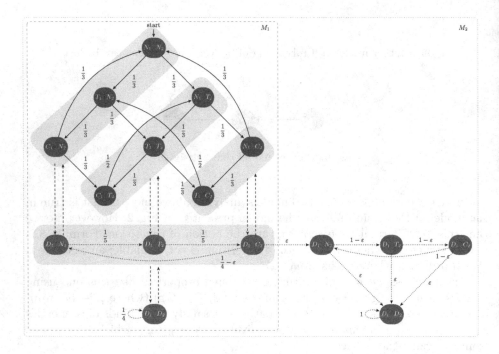

Fig. 4. Two-process mutual exclusion (Color figure online).

Example Property 2. *When there are no faults, the process P_1 stays in its safe region (N_1, T_1 or C_1) with probability greater than or equal to one half.*

This property can be expressed in RPCTL using the following formula:

$$\text{rec.}\left[\neg D_1 \; \wedge \; \mathcal{P}_{\geq \frac{1}{2}}(\mathsf{X}\ \mathsf{call})\right]$$

Observe that this formula characterizes the idea of staying in a safe set of states, we can think of this collection of states as representing the normal behavior of the system (i.e., the green states in Fig. 4), the recursive part of the formula expresses that those states will be revisited with certain probability.

As we explain in Example 1, these kinds of properties cannot be captured in PCTL. One could mix CTL and PCTL operators to express properties of traces with measure 0. Consider for instance:

$$\mathcal{P}_{\geq \frac{1}{2}}[(N_1 \vee T_1 \vee C_1)\, \mathcal{U}\, D_1] \ \wedge \ \mathsf{EG}(N_1 \vee T_1 \vee C_1) \tag{6}$$

This formula says that the probability of keeping the system in the safe zone until the process is down is at least to $\frac{1}{2}$, while the CTL subformula says that there exists an execution where the process is always up. However, note that the probability of repeating that pattern is not reflected in this formula.

Furthermore, we spice up this model with the possibility that process P_1 stays down forever, this new scenario is also depicted in Fig. 4, the region labeled M_2 represents a collection of states where process P_1 cannot recover from failures. Note that, in this modified model, we have a probability $0 < \varepsilon \leq 0.05$ representing the chance that P_i stays down forever. Another desirable property of this model is the following one.

Example Property 3. *The probability that the process P_1 is down with the possibility of getting up at some point is greater than or equal to one fifth.*

This property can be characterized with the following RPCTL formula:

$$\mathsf{rec.}\, \left[D_1 \ \wedge \ \mathcal{P}_{\geq (1-\varepsilon)}(\mathsf{F}\neg D_1) \ \wedge \ \mathcal{P}_{\geq \frac{1}{5}}(\mathsf{X\ call}) \right] \tag{7}$$

Intuitively, this formula characterizes the region of the system where the process P_1 fails, but there is a positive probability of returning to the safe zone. Graphically, it represents the notion of staying and revisiting infinitely often the set of red states in the M_1 part of the model, shown in Fig. 4.

Finally, a key feature of this model is the possibility of moving between normal regions (when no faults are present) and the idea that this behavior can be repeated an unbounded number of times with a probability greater than or equal to $\frac{1}{3}$.

Example Property 4. *When there are no faults, the probability that the process P_2 moves to the next region is greater or equal to one third.*

This property is expressed by the following RPCTL formula

$$\mathsf{rec.}\, \left[\begin{array}{l} (N_2 \rightarrow [\mathcal{P}_{\geq \frac{1}{3}}(\mathsf{X}T_2) \wedge \mathcal{P}_{\geq \frac{1}{3}}(\mathsf{X\ call})]) \ \wedge \\ (T_2 \rightarrow [\mathcal{P}_{\geq \frac{1}{3}}(\mathsf{X}C_2) \wedge \mathcal{P}_{\geq \frac{1}{3}}(\mathsf{X\ call})]) \ \wedge \\ (C_2 \rightarrow [\mathcal{P}_{\geq \frac{1}{3}}(\mathsf{X}N_2) \wedge \mathcal{P}_{\geq \frac{1}{3}}(\mathsf{X\ call})]) \end{array} \right] \tag{8}$$

Algorithm 1. Algorithm for RPCTL Model Checking.

```
let ∀ i . Wᵢ = ∅;
let ∀ i . Sᵢ = S;
do {
    let ∀ i . Wᵢ = Sᵢ;
    let ∀ i . Sᵢ =
        { s | M(S₁,...,Sₙ), s ⊨ recᵢ . φᵢ( callⱼ  ←  cⱼ | j ∈ [1..n]) };
    }
} while (∃ i . Sᵢ ≠ Wᵢ);
if (M(S₁ ,...,Sₙ), s ⊨ φ((recⱼ . φⱼ) ← cⱼ|j ∈ [1..n])) print ''Yes!'';
else print ''No!'';
```

---

5 Model Checking

In this section we consider model checking of RPCTL. We give an algorithm for model checking RPCTL on finite-state Markov chains that is polynomial in the Markov chain and the size of the formula. The algorithm is the restriction of the algorithm in [10] to the usage of just greatest fixpoints. We include it here for the sake of completeness.

Consider a Markov chain $M = \langle S, P, L, s_0 \rangle$ and an RPCTL formula φ. Suppose that the set of calls appearing in φ is $\{\mathsf{call}_1, \ldots, \mathsf{call}_n\}$, and let $\{S_1, \ldots S_n\}$ be sets of states of M. That is, for every $1 \leq i \leq n$ we have $S_i \subseteq S$. We denote by $M(S_1, \ldots, S_n)$ the structure over $AP \cup \{c_1, \ldots, c_n\}$ obtained from M by setting $L(c_i) = S_i$. For the formula $\mathsf{rec}_i.\varphi_i$, let $\mathsf{rec}_i.\varphi_i(\mathsf{call}_j \leftarrow c_j | j \in [1..n])$ be the formula obtained from φ_i, where every reference to call_j is replaced by c_j. Finally, let $\varphi(\mathsf{rec}_j.\varphi_j \leftarrow c_j | j \in [1..n])$ denote the formula obtained from φ by replacing every occurrence of $\mathsf{rec}_j.\varphi_j$ by c_j. Then, Algorithm 1 computes whether a state s of M satisfies φ. The algorithm calls PCTL model checking as a subroutine.

Theorem 2. *For a RPCTL formula ϕ, Algorithm 1 answers "yes" iff $s \in [\phi]_\tau^M$, where τ is an arbitrary valuation.*

Proof. The proof follows from the approximation of greatest fixpoints. The algorithm computes the greatest fixpoints by initializing their approximation by the set of all states and removing all states that cannot satisfy the obligation. When the fixpoint terminates the sets are the actual fixpoints.

Theorem 3. *Algorithm 1 can be computed in time polynomial in the size of M and φ.*

Proof. We rely on the fact that PCTL model checking is polynomial both in the size of the formula and in the size of the model. We note that the propositions c_j appear positively in $\varphi(\mathsf{rec}_j.\varphi_j \leftarrow c_j)$ and in $\mathsf{rec}_i.\varphi_i(\mathsf{call} \leftarrow c_j)$ Let ψ be one of these formulas. From monotonicity it follows that if $S_i \subseteq S_i'$ then $\{s \mid M(S_1, \ldots, S_i, \ldots, S_n), s \models \psi\} \subseteq \{s \mid M(S_1, \ldots, S_i', \ldots, S_n), s \models \psi\}$. Hence, the sets S_i are monotonically decreasing. If follows that after at most $n \cdot |S|$ iterations through the loop the loop exits.

We conclude that the algorithm calls a polynomial number of times the model checking procedure for PCTL and is polynomial.

6 Related Work

Over the years there have been several suggestions of probabilistic μ-calculi. Notably, the work of Huth and Kwiatkowska [14] and McIver and Morgan [15] both suggest quantitative μ-calculi that replace the Boolean interpretation of the classical μ-calculus with a quantitative interpretation. That is, the semantics of a formula instead of being a set of locations is a function associating a value with each location. These logics, however, fail to capture PCTL and do not have a means to get formulas back to the Boolean domain. Mio [9] extends these logics with different interpretations of quantitative conjunction. In order to reason about different types of conjunction he introduces parity games with independent products and tree games. Mio's quantitative μ-calculus does capture PCTL and has a fragment for which certain subformulas live in the Boolean domain and others in the quantitative domain [16]. Unfortunately, the complexity of model checking for Mio's logic is very high.

In our work [10] we introduced a well behaved subset of Mio's probabilistic μ-calculus, called μ^p-calculus. Its advantage is that its model checking procedure is in NP just like the μ-calculus. We then further suggested μPCTL, that incorporates fixpoint operators in PCTL. The disadvantage, as we have learned from the μ-calculus, is that fixpoint alternation are very hard for users to understand. A fragment of μPCTL is considered also in [17].

7 Final Remarks

In this paper we have introduced RPCTL, an extension of PCTL with recursive statements. It allows to specify properties describing possible "repetitions" in the Markov chain and the probability of events occurring within these repetitions. The extra expressive power comes at a very low price as model checking for this logic is by repeated calls to a PCTL model checker.

One of the main benefits of RPCTL is that it allows one to capture properties of internal regions of models. This is useful for instance in the case of systems where it is needed to reason about the repetition of a certain pattern with a given probability. This is the case, for example, of fault-tolerant systems where one needs to reason about the pattern of faults and the probability of avoiding them or recovering from them. We have presented some examples that show the application of this logic in practice. We leave as further work the implementation of a model checker for this logic, and the investigation of more complex case studies. We also intend to consider extensions to the types of regular properties that can be included within probability quantification.

References

1. Clarke, E., Grumberg, O., Peled, D.: Model Checking. MIT Press, Cambridge (1999)
2. Baier, C., Katoen, J.P.: Principles of Model Checking. MIT Press, Cambridge (2008)
3. Hinton, A., Kwiatkowska, M., Norman, G., Parker, D.: PRISM: a tool for automatic verification of probabilistic systems. In: Hermanns, H., Palsberg, J. (eds.) TACAS 2006. LNCS, vol. 3920, pp. 441–444. Springer, Heidelberg (2006)
4. Ciesinski, F., Baier, C.: LiQuor: a tool for qualitative and quantitative linear time analysis of reactive systems. In: QEST, pp. 131–132. IEEE Computer Society (2006)
5. Eisner, C., Fisman, D.: A Practical Introduction to PSL. Springer, New York (2006)
6. Cohen, B., Venkataramanan, S., Kumari, A., Piper, L.: System Verilog Assertions Handbook. VhdlCohen Publishing (2010)
7. Armoni, R., Fix, L., Flaisher, A., Gerth, R., Ginsburg, B., Kanza, T., Landver, A., Mador-Haim, S., et al.: The ForSpec temporal logic: a new temporal property-specification language. In: Katoen, J.-P., Stevens, P. (eds.) TACAS 2002. LNCS, vol. 2280, p. 296. Springer, Heidelberg (2002)
8. Eisner, C., Fisman, D., Havlicek, J., McIsaac, A., Campenhout, D.V.: The definition of a temporal clock operator. In: Baeten, J.C.M., Lenstra, J.K., Parrow, J., Woeginger, G.J. (eds.) ICALP 2003. LNCS, vol. 2719, pp. 857–870. Springer, Heidelberg (2003)
9. Mio, M.: Game Semantics for Probabilistic μ-Calculi. Ph.D. thesis, University of Edinburgh (2012)
10. Castro, P.F., Kilmurray, C., Piterman, N.: Tractable probabilistic μ-calculus that expresses probabilistic temporal logics. In: 32nd International Symposium on Theoretical Aspects of Computer Science. LIPIcs, Garching, Germany, pp. 211–223 (2015)
11. Huth, M., Piterman, N., Wagner, D.: p-automata: new foundations for discrete-time probabilistic verification. Perform. Eval. **69**, 356–378 (2012)
12. Arora, A., Gouda, M.: Closure and convergence: a foundation of fault-tolerant computing. TOSEM **19**, 1015–1027 (1993)
13. Attie, P., Arora, A., Emerson, A.: Synthesis of fault-tolerant concurrent programs. TOPLAS **26**, 125–185 (2004)
14. Huth, M., Kwiatkowska, M.: Quantitative analysis and model checking. In: 12th IEEE Symposium on Logic in Computer Science, pp. 111–122. IEEE Computer Society (1997)
15. McIver, A., Morgan, C.: Results on the quantitative qmμ. ACM Trans. Comput. Log. **8** (2007)
16. Mio, M., Simpson, A.: Łukasiewicz μ-calculus. In: FICS (2013)
17. Liu, W., Song, L., Wang, J., Zhang, L.: A simple probabilistic extension of model μ-calculus. In: 23rd International Joint Conference on Artificial Intelligence, Buenos Aires, Argentina. AAAI Press, pp. 882–888 (2015)

Specifying Compatible Sharing
in Data Structures

Asankhaya Sharma[1]([✉]), Aquinas Hobor[1,2], and Wei-Ngan Chin[1]

[1] School of Computing, National University of Singapore, Singapore, Singapore
[2] Yale-NUS College, National University of Singapore, Singapore, Singapore
{asankhs,hobor,chinwn}@comp.nus.edu.sg

Abstract. Automated verification of programs that utilize data structures with intrinsic sharing is a challenging problem. We develop an extension to separation logic that can reason about aliasing in heaps using a notion of *compatible sharing*. Compatible sharing can model a variety of fine grained sharing and aliasing scenarios with concise specifications. Given these specifications, our entailment procedure enables fully automated verification of a number of challenging programs manipulating data structures with non-trivial sharing. We benchmarked our prototype with examples derived from practical algorithms found in systems code, such as those using threaded trees and overlaid data structures.

1 Introduction

Systems software often uses *overlaid data structures* to utilize memory more efficiently and boost performance. Consider maintaining the set of processes in an operating system; some are running while others are sleeping. Sometimes we wish to access every process, whereas other times we only wish to access *e.g.* the running processes. To track this set efficiently we can use a "threaded list" whose nodes are defined as follows:

data node { int pid; node anext; node rnext; node snext }

Each **node** has four fields. The first two are straightforward: a process id field **pid** and a pointer to the next process (which may be running or sleeping) **anext**. The latter two are a bit trickier. When a process is running, **rnext** points to the next running process in the list, skipping over any sleeping processes in between. When a process is sleeping, **snext** points to the next sleeping process in the list. We maintain three external pointers into the structure: one for the head of the entire list **a**, the second for the head of the running sublist **r**, and the third for the head of the sleeping sublist **s**. Consider this picture:

M. Butler et al. (Eds.): ICFEM 2015, LNCS 9407, pp. 349–365, 2015.
DOI: 10.1007/978-3-319-25423-4_23

The efficiency benefits of overlaid structures can be significant: *e.g.*, we avoid representing nodes on multiple spatially-disjoint lists and can visit each running process without needing to step through the sleeping processes. The real drawback, from our perspective, is that programs utilizing overlaid structures are difficult to verify formally!

Separation logic [18] enables compositional reasoning of heap-manipulating programs and has been widely applied to automated verification [2,5,11]. Separation logic uses the separating conjunction $*$ to connect assertions valid on disjoint portions of the heap, enabling natural representations for many data structures such as lists and trees because their constituent subparts are spatially disjoint. Overlaid data structures cannot be specified so naturally because the underlying structures share nodes in memory.

We extend the notion of separation to enable local reasoning for overlaid data structures by introducing a notion of *compatibility*. Two predicates are compatible when updates to one will not affect the other despite spatial overlap. In our threaded list example above, we can imagine splitting the structure into three pseudo-disjoint/compatible lists formed by the **anext**, **rnext**, and **snext** pointer chains. A function that modifies some chains but not others can then "frame away" the part of the structure it does not use. This can happen in several steps: consider switching a process from sleeping to running. First we frame away the **anext** chain. Then we frame away the **rnext** chain, leaving only a straightforward **snext** linked list, on which we do a standard list remove. We then frame **rnext** back in and **snext** away, followed by a standard list add. Finally, we frame **snext** and **anext** back in, restoring the entire structure.

All of the above means we need field-level separation, which we get by adding annotations to fields: when a field is <u>a</u>bsent (or inaccessible) we mark it with @A; when it is present/<u>m</u>utable we mark it with @M. Here is how this looks for our threaded list:

$$\mathtt{al}\langle\mathtt{root},S\rangle \equiv (\mathtt{root} = \mathtt{null} \wedge S = \{\})$$
$$\vee\, \exists\, \mathtt{p}, \mathtt{a}, S_a \cdot (\mathtt{root}\mapsto\mathtt{node}\langle\mathtt{p@I}, \mathtt{a@M}, @\mathtt{A}, @\mathtt{A}\rangle * \mathtt{al}\langle\mathtt{a}, S_a\rangle \wedge S = S_a \cup \{\mathtt{root}\})$$
$$\mathtt{rl}\langle\mathtt{root},S\rangle \equiv (\mathtt{root} = \mathtt{null} \wedge S = \{\})$$
$$\vee\, \exists\, \mathtt{p}, \mathtt{r}, S_r \cdot (\mathtt{root}\mapsto\mathtt{node}\langle\mathtt{p@I}, @\mathtt{A}, \mathtt{r@M}, @\mathtt{A}\rangle * \mathtt{rl}\langle\mathtt{r}, S_r\rangle \wedge S = S_r \cup \{\mathtt{root}\})$$
$$\mathtt{sl}\langle\mathtt{root},S\rangle \equiv (\mathtt{root} = \mathtt{null} \wedge S = \{\})$$
$$\vee\, \exists\, \mathtt{p}, \mathtt{s}, S_s \cdot (\mathtt{root}\mapsto\mathtt{node}\langle\mathtt{p@I}, @\mathtt{A}, @\mathtt{A}, \mathtt{s@M}\rangle * \mathtt{sl}\langle\mathtt{s}, S_s\rangle \wedge S = S_s \cup \{\mathtt{root}\})$$

These predicates specify the "all list", "running list", and "sleeping list", respectively. Each list predicate is parameterized by a set of addresses S of nodes on that list. Each points-to predicate ($\mathtt{node}\langle\cdot\rangle$) annotates the ownership of its fields: *e.g.*, the points-to in **al** has full ownership @M of the first (**anext**) pointer field. This claim is compatible with the **rl** and **sl** predicates since both of them are absent in that field. An interesting case is the process id field **pid**. All three of the predicates wish to share access to this field; we still consider them to be compatible as long as the field is marked <u>i</u>mmutable @I. Our annotations are thus a kind of "poor man's fractional permissions [3]", in which @A is analogous to the empty permission, @M is analogous to the full permission, and @I is analogous to an existentialized permission. Although less precise than fractional permissions, these annotations are sufficient for some interesting examples and we avoid some of the hassles of integrating fractional permissions into a verification tool [16].

Since we have two compatible predicates we want to use $*$ to combine them:

$$\mathtt{al}\langle \mathtt{root}, S_r \cup S_1\rangle * (\mathtt{rl}\langle \mathtt{root}, S_r\rangle * \mathtt{sl}\langle \mathtt{root}, S_s\rangle)$$

Actually this is not quite right. Although adding field-level separation is not new [8], the standard way to do so introduces a subtle ambiguity. The issue is that the amount of sharing of the objects is not fully specified: in fact the two $*$ are being used quite differently. The first $*$, separating $\mathtt{al}\langle\cdot\rangle$ from the other two, is actually more like a standard classical separation logic conjunction $\wedge$. That is, every node on the left hand side is also on the right hand side, and vice versa: the fields separate, but the nodes precisely overlay one another. In contrast, the second $*$, separating $\mathtt{rl}\langle\cdot\rangle$ from $\mathtt{sl}\langle\cdot\rangle$, is much more like the standard classical field-less separating conjunction $*$. That is, the set of nodes are strictly disjoint (no running process is sleeping, and vice versa), so even if $\mathtt{rl}\langle\cdot\rangle$ and $\mathtt{sl}\langle\cdot\rangle$ had incompatible fields, they would still be separate in memory.

This ambiguity means that the traditional field-level $*$ is a bit too easy to introduce, and unnecessarily painful to eliminate. We resolve it by using two distinct operators: $\mathbb{A}$, when we mean that nodes are identical and fields must be *compatible*; and $*$, which for us means that the nodes themselves are *disjoint*. Thus, we specify our threaded list as:

$$\mathtt{al}\langle x, S_y \cup S_z\rangle \;\mathbb{A}\; (\mathtt{rl}\langle y, S_y\rangle * \mathtt{sl}\langle z, S_z\rangle)$$

We know that this predicate uses only compatible sharing because all of the fields on the lhs and rhs of the $\mathbb{A}$ are disjoint and the $*$ guarantees compatibility on the inner subformula. It may seem that $\mathbb{A}$ is very specific to this example, but that is wrong: in Sect. 6 we mention how we use it to reason about other overlaid data structures.

Contributions. We develop a specification mechanism to capture overlaid sharing, an entailment procedure to reason about such sharing, and integrate our ideas into an existing automated verification system. Our prototype, together with a web-based GUI for easy experimentation and machine checked proofs in Coq, is available at: http://loris-7.ddns.comp.nus.edu.sg/~project/HIPComp/.

2   Motivating Examples

In this section, we illustrate the difference between the various conjunction operators ($*$, $\wedge$ and $\mathbb{A}$) and give the intuition behind compatible sharing. We also show how to automatically check for compatible sharing in data structures using a notion of *memory specifications*.

2.1 From Separation to Sharing

As discussed earlier, separation logic provides a natural way to represent disjoint heaps using the separating conjunction $*$. However, if two assertions both require some shared portion of memory, then $*$ cannot easily combine them. Consider the following simple example:

$$\texttt{data pair \{ int fst; int snd \}}$$

Here **pair** is a data structure consisting of two fields, **fst** and **snd**. The following assertion[1] indicates that x points to such a structure with field values **f** and **s**:

$$\texttt{x} \mapsto \texttt{pair}\langle \texttt{f}, \texttt{s} \rangle$$

We denote two disjoint pairs x and y with the *separating* conjunction $*$, which ensures that x and y cannot be aliased:

$$\texttt{x} \mapsto \texttt{pair}\langle \texttt{f}_1, \texttt{s}_1 \rangle * \texttt{y} \mapsto \texttt{pair}\langle \texttt{f}_2, \texttt{s}_2 \rangle$$

In contrast, to capture aliased pairs we use *classical* conjunction $\wedge$ as follows:

$$\texttt{x} \mapsto \texttt{pair}\langle \texttt{f}_1, \texttt{s}_1 \rangle \wedge \texttt{y} \mapsto \texttt{pair}\langle \texttt{f}_2, \texttt{s}_2 \rangle$$

The $\wedge$ operator specifies "must aliasing", that is, $\wedge$ ensures that the pointers x and y are the equal and that the object field values are identical (*i.e.*, $\texttt{f}_1 = \texttt{f}_2$ and $\texttt{s}_1 = \texttt{s}_2$).

To support field-level framing we use the field annotations introduced in Sect. 1, to mark fields that are mutable (@M), immutable (@I) and absent (@A). Consider the following:

$$\texttt{x} \mapsto \texttt{pair}\langle \texttt{f}_1 @\texttt{M}, \texttt{s}_1 @\texttt{A} \rangle * \texttt{y} \mapsto \texttt{pair}\langle \texttt{f}_2 @\texttt{A}, \texttt{s}_2 @\texttt{M} \rangle$$

This formula asserts that the heap can be split into two disjoint parts, the first of which contains a first-half-pair pointed to by x, and the second of which contains a second-half-pair pointed to by y. Since by default fields are mutable @M, and when a field is absent @A we need not bind a variable to its value, the formula can also be written as:

$$\texttt{x} \mapsto \texttt{pair}\langle \texttt{f}_1, @\texttt{A} \rangle * \texttt{y} \mapsto \texttt{pair}\langle @\texttt{A}, \texttt{s}_2 \rangle$$

All this seems simple enough, but there is a subtle wrinkle: notice that x and y may be aliased (if the combined heap contains a single pair that has been split

---

[1] Our separation logic is both "Java-like" and "C-like". Our logic is "Java-like" in the sense that heap locations (pointers) contain (point to) indivisible objects rather than individual memory cells, avoiding the possibility of pointers pointing into the middle of a structure (*i.e.*, skewing). On the other hand, our logic is "C-like" because our formulae are given a classical rather than intuitionistic semantics, *i.e.*, $\texttt{x} \mapsto \texttt{pair}\langle \texttt{f}, \texttt{s} \rangle$ means that the heap contains **exactly** a single **pair** object at the location pointed to by x rather than **at least** a single **pair** object at x.

in half fieldwise), but need not be (if the combined heap contains two distinct half pairs). This ambiguity is inconvenient. We introduce a new operator, the *overlaid* conjunction $\mathbb{A}$ to indicate that the locations are the same although the fields are disjoint. Thus, when we write

$$x \mapsto \text{pair}\langle f_1, @A \rangle \; \mathbb{A} \; y \mapsto \text{pair}\langle @A, s_2 \rangle$$

we unambiguously mean that x and y are aliased and have been split fieldwise. On the other hand, hereafter when we use $*$, then x and y are **not** aliased, just as was the case before we added fieldwise separation. We do not use the ambiguous version of $*$.

We are now ready to give an intuition for our notion of *compatible sharing*: essentially, a conjunction ($\wedge$, $\mathbb{A}$, and $*$) expresses compatible sharing when one side can be safely framed away. Or, in other words it is possible to reason over only one side of conjunction and ignore the other since they can be combined together later without conflicts. As the simplest example, the following pairs are compatible because the separating conjunction guarantees that they exist on disjoint heaps:

$$x \mapsto \text{pair}\langle f_1, s_1 \rangle \; * \; y \mapsto \text{pair}\langle f_2, s_2 \rangle$$

Consider next the following two uses of classical conjunction $\wedge$:

$$x \mapsto \text{pair}\langle f_1, @A \rangle \wedge x \mapsto \text{pair}\langle f_2, @A \rangle$$
$$x \mapsto \text{pair}\langle f_1 @I, @A \rangle \wedge x \mapsto \text{pair}\langle f_2 @I, @A \rangle$$

The difference between the two formulae is that in the second example we have marked the field fst as immutable @I. Because fst is mutable @M in the first example, we are not able to frame away half of the conjunction, since we need to maintain the fact that $f_1 = f_2$. On the other hand, in the second example, since fst is immutable on both sides of the conjunction, we are able to frame away either side. Therefore, we deem the first example incompatible while we consider the second compatible.

Checking for compatibility is useful not only for the $\wedge$ operator but also for $\mathbb{A}$ operator in the presence of aliasing as shown in the following examples:

$$x \mapsto \text{pair}\langle f_1, @A \rangle \; \mathbb{A} \; y \mapsto \text{pair}\langle f_2, s_2 \rangle \quad (Incompatible)$$
$$x \mapsto \text{pair}\langle f_1, @A \rangle \; \mathbb{A} \; y \mapsto \text{pair}\langle @A, s_2 \rangle \quad (Compatible)$$

2.2 Shared Process Scheduler

Recall that from Sect. 1, the formula that we used to specify the threaded lists was as follows:

$$\text{al}\langle x, S_y \cup S_z \rangle \; \mathbb{A} \; (\text{rl}\langle y, S_y \rangle * \text{sl}\langle z, S_z \rangle)$$

Even though this formula uses compatible sharing of heaps, it is non-trivial to prove that automatically. Since the field annotations are hidden inside the predicate definition they cannot be exposed without doing an unfolding of the predicate. In order to expose the information about the fields inside the predicate we introduce the notion of *memory specifications*. We allow the user to specify the memory footprint of the predicate using the **mem** construct which is associated with the predicate definition. The enhanced predicate definitions for the process scheduler are shown below.

$$\mathtt{al}\langle\mathtt{root}, S\rangle \equiv (\mathtt{root}{=}\mathtt{null}{\wedge}S{=}\{\})$$
$$\vee \exists d, q, S_q \cdot (\mathtt{root}{\mapsto}\mathtt{node}\langle d@I, q, @A, @A\rangle {*} \mathtt{al}\langle q, S_q\rangle$$
$$\wedge S{=}S_q{\cup}\{\mathtt{root}\})$$
$$\mathbf{mem}\, S{\hookrightarrow}(\mathtt{node}\langle @I, @M, @A, @A\rangle)$$

$$\mathtt{rl}\langle\mathtt{root}, S\rangle \equiv (\mathtt{root}{=}\mathtt{null}{\wedge}S{=}\{\})$$
$$\vee \exists d, q, S_q \cdot (\mathtt{root}{\mapsto}\mathtt{node}\langle d@I, @A, q, @A\rangle {*} \mathtt{rl}\langle q, S_q\rangle$$
$$\wedge S{=}S_q{\cup}\{\mathtt{root}\})$$
$$\mathbf{mem}\, S{\hookrightarrow}(\mathtt{node}\langle @I, @A, @M, @A\rangle)$$

$$\mathtt{sl}\langle\mathtt{root}, S\rangle \equiv (\mathtt{root}{=}\mathtt{null}{\wedge}S{=}\{\})$$
$$\vee \exists d, q, S_q \cdot (\mathtt{root}{\mapsto}\mathtt{node}\langle d@I, @A, @A, q\rangle {*} \mathtt{sl}\langle q, S_q\rangle$$
$$\wedge S{=}S_q{\cup}\{\mathtt{root}\})$$
$$\mathbf{mem}\, S{\hookrightarrow}(\mathtt{node}\langle @I, @A, @A, @M\rangle)$$

The **mem** construct consists of a memory region along with a list of possible field annotations that the predicate unfolding would generate. It allows us to syntactically check if two predicates that share memory region have compatible field annotations. Looking at the memory specification of $\mathtt{al}$ and $\mathtt{rl}$ it is easy to see that $\mathtt{al}$ does not affect (or is compatible with) $\mathtt{rl}$. The **id** field is immutable in $\mathtt{rl}$ and the only field which is mutable in $\mathtt{al}$ is absent in $\mathtt{rl}$. Thus any updates made to the nodes in memory region S using predicate $\mathtt{al}$ will not have any effect when accessing the same memory region using predicate $\mathtt{rl}$.

To avoid writing such verbose predicates with set of addresses and to make the specifications more concise we use the overlaid conjunction operator ($\mathbb{A}$). Formulas using the $\mathbb{A}$ operator are translated automatically to those that use the $*$ operator with memory specifications. For the shared process scheduler the memory region shared by the lists $\mathtt{al}$ is same as the one shared by $\mathtt{rl}$ and $\mathtt{sl}$. The $\mathbb{A}$ operator provides the hint to the system to force the memory on both sides to be the same. Hence the key invariant of the data structure is captured more concisely as:

$$\mathtt{al}\langle x\rangle \ \mathbb{A} \ (\mathtt{rl}\langle y\rangle {*} \mathtt{sl}\langle z\rangle)$$

This formula is automatically translated by first enhancing the predicate definitions with memory specifications by using the **XMem** function from Fig. 2. (Predicate definitions also can be enchanced with other pure properties following translation technique described in Sect. 7 of [19]). And then forcing the memory region on both sides of $\mathbb{A}$ to be same. As the final translated formula is exactly the same as given before, the use of ⚖ provides a specification mechanism to precisely describe the user intention.

> //*Provided by User*
> al⟨x⟩ ⚖ (rl⟨y⟩ * sl⟨z⟩)
> //*Predicate extension with mem*
> al⟨x, S$_x$⟩ ⚖ (rl⟨y, S$_y$⟩ * sl⟨z, S$_z$⟩)
> //*Translated form*
> al⟨x, S$_x$⟩ ∧ (rl⟨y, S$_y$⟩ * sl⟨z, S$_z$⟩)∧S$_x$=S$_y$∪S$_z$

Using the ⚖ operator makes the specification of methods utilizing overlaid structures less verbose. Consider the following `insert` method which is called while scheduling a new process in the system. The new process has to be inserted into `al`, and depending on the status flag, also in `rl` or `sl`. The precondition of the method uses the ⚖ operator to specify the key safety property. The use of overlaid sharing operator allows the user to express the precondition in a concise form. Compatible sharing is used to verify this method as the inserts made to different lists can be shown to not interfere with each other.

```
void insert(int id, int status, node x, node y, node z)
requires   al⟨x⟩ ⚖ (rl⟨y⟩ * sl⟨z⟩)∧ status=1
ensures    al⟨x⟩ ⚖ (rl⟨y⟩ * sl⟨z⟩)
requires   al⟨x⟩ ⚖ (rl⟨y⟩ * sl⟨z⟩)∧ status=0
ensures    al⟨x⟩ ⚖ (rl⟨y⟩ * sl⟨z⟩)
{
    node tmp = new node(id, null, null, null);
    tmp.next = x;
    x = tmp;
    if(status == 1)
        y = rlinsert(y, tmp);
    else  z = slinsert(z, tmp);
}
```

2.3   Comparison with Fractional Permissions

In this section, we show the difficulties that arise when using separation logic with fractional permissions (SLfp) to represent overlaid data structures. We avoid these issues by using field annotations and overlaid conjunction operator while specifying compatible sharing in data structures.

Applying fractional permissions (as in SLfp) to fields inside inductive predicates can unintentionally change the meaning of the predicate. E.g consider the following predicate definition of an immutable binary tree in SLfp:

> tree⟨root⟩≡root=null
> ∨∃d, l, r · (root↦node⟨d@1/2, l@1/2, r@1/2⟩*tree⟨l⟩*tree⟨r⟩)

We restrict the use of fields in the predicate using the fraction $1/2$ to give a read-only permission. However, this predicate does not enforce a tree and is in fact a DAG. In standard SLfp the $*$ operator does not enforce strict separation, thus the left and right children can point to the same node and combine using the 1/2 permissions given to each node. A more sophisticated permission system like tree-shares [16] can avoid this problem, but it is not known how to extend a tree-shares like model to fields.

We avoid this problem by using a definition of the $*$ operator that enforces strict object level separation. Also, we use field annotations that provide a simpler way to specify mutable, immutable and absent fields. If we use $*$ for object level separation and $\wedge$ for object level sharing then it is natural to introduce another operator $\mathbb{A}$ for object level sharing and field level separation. The overlaid conjunction ($\mathbb{A}$) is also practically useful to represent several data structures as shown in Sect. 6.

3   Specification with Compatible Sharing

We extend the specification language of separation logic with *memory enhanced* predicate definitions. The specification language is as described in Fig. 1 (we use the superscript $*$ to denote a list of elements). $\Phi_{pr} * \mapsto \Phi_{po}$ captures a precondition Φ_{pr} and a postcondition Φ_{po} of a method or a loop. They are abbreviated from the standard representation **requires** Φ_{pr} and **ensures** Φ_{po}, and formalized by separation logic formula Φ. In turn, the separation logic formula is a disjunction of a heap formula and a pure formula ($\kappa \wedge \pi$). We use the set constraints for representing memory regions as shown in Fig. 1. The predicate definition allows optional **mem** construct to be specified. **mem** is useful in cases like the overlaid data structures where it is important to be able to specify that the memory regions of both overlaying structures are exactly the same.

In order to check compatible sharing between two predicates we take help of the $XMem(\kappa)$ function. The $XMem(\kappa)$ function, whose definition is given in

$$
\begin{array}{ll}
\textit{pred} & ::= p(v^*) \equiv \Phi \ [\textit{inv} \ \pi][\textit{mem} \ S \hookrightarrow ([c(@u^*)]^*)] \\
\textit{mspec} & ::= \Phi_{pr} * \mapsto \Phi_{po} \quad \Phi ::= \bigvee \ (\exists w^* \cdot \kappa \wedge \pi)^* \\
\kappa & ::= \textbf{emp} \mid v \mapsto c(v[@u]^*) \mid p(v^*) \mid \kappa_1 \natural \kappa_2 \ (\natural \in \{*, \wedge, \mathbb{A}\}) \\
\pi & ::= \alpha \mid \pi \wedge \varphi \quad \alpha ::= \beta \mid \neg \beta \\
\beta & ::= v_1 = v_2 \mid v = \textbf{null} \mid a \leq 0 \mid a = 0 \\
a & ::= k \mid k \times v \mid a_1 + a_2 \mid max(a_1, a_2) \mid min(a_1, a_2) \\
\varphi & ::= v \in S \mid S_1 = S_2 \mid S_1 \subset S_2 \mid \forall v \in S \cdot \pi \mid \exists v \in S \cdot \pi \\
S & ::= S_1 \cup S_2 \mid S_1 \cap S_2 \mid S_1 - S_2 \mid \{\} \mid \{v\} \\
u & ::= M \mid I \mid A \quad (M <: I <: A) \\
\end{array}
$$

where p is a predicate; v, w are variables; c is a data type; u is a field annotation;

Fig. 1. Specification language

$$\frac{isData(c)}{XMem(c\langle p, v@u^*\rangle) =_{df} (\{p\}, [c\langle @u^*\rangle])} \qquad \frac{isPred(c) \quad c\langle p, S, v^*\rangle \equiv \Phi[inv \; \pi][mem \; S \hookrightarrow L]}{XMem(c\langle p, S, v^*\rangle) =_{df} (S, L)}$$

$$XMem(\texttt{emp}) =_{df} (\{\}, []) \qquad \frac{XMem(\kappa_1) = (S_1, L_1) \quad XMem(\kappa_2) = (S_2, L_2)}{XMem(\kappa_1 \sharp \kappa_2) =_{df} (S_1 \cup S_2, union(L_1, L_2))}$$

Fig. 2. XMem: translating to memory form

Fig. 2, returns a sound approximation of the memory footprint of heap κ as a tuple of the form $(S, [c\langle @u^*\rangle]^*)$, which corresponds to the set of addresses and the list of field annotations used in memory specifications. The function $isData(c)$ returns **true** if c is a data node, while $isPred(c)$ returns true if c is a heap predicate. We use lists L_1 and L_2 to represent the field annotations. The function $union(L_1, L_2)$ returns the union of lists L_1 and L_2. We do not need to consider the pure formula π in $XMem$ as it doesn't correspond to any heap. In general, Φ can be disjunctive, so we can have a number of possible approximations of memory for a predicate, each corresponding to a particular disjunct. Since memory specifications are essential to check compatibility in data structures, we have machine checked the soundness proof of the $XMem$ function in Coq. We illustrate how the approximation function works on a linked list.

```
data node { int val; node next }
ll⟨root, S⟩≡(root=null∧S={})
   ∨ ∃d, q, Sq · (root↦node⟨d, q⟩*ll⟨q, Sq⟩∧S=Sq∪{root})
mem S↪(node⟨@M, @M⟩)
```

As an example consider the memory approximation of the following predicate.

$$XMem(\texttt{x} \mapsto \texttt{node}\langle \texttt{d}, \texttt{p}\rangle * \texttt{ll}\langle \texttt{y}, \texttt{S}_\texttt{y}\rangle)$$

We proceed by using the rules from Fig. 2 for the data node x and predicate ll.

$$XMem(\texttt{x} \mapsto \texttt{node}\langle \texttt{d}, \texttt{p}\rangle) = (\{\texttt{x}\}, [\texttt{node}\langle @\texttt{M}, @\texttt{M}\rangle])$$
$$XMem(\texttt{ll}\langle \texttt{y}, \texttt{S}_\texttt{y}\rangle) = (\texttt{S}_\texttt{y}, [\texttt{node}\langle @\texttt{M}, @\texttt{M}\rangle])$$
$$XMem(\texttt{x} \mapsto \texttt{node}\langle \texttt{d}, \texttt{p}\rangle * \texttt{ll}\langle \texttt{y}, \texttt{S}_\texttt{y}\rangle) = (\{\texttt{x}\} \cup \texttt{S}_\texttt{y}, [\texttt{node}\langle @\texttt{M}, @\texttt{M}\rangle])$$

As a consistency check on the memory specification we use the predicate definition to validate the user supplied memory specification. In case the user doesn't provide a memory specification (e.g. when using the $\mathbb{A}$ operator) we automatically extend the predicate definition with set of addresses returned by the $XMem$ function. We use an existing underlying [6] entailment procedure (denoted by $\vdash$) to discharge the entailment during validation of memory specifications. The rules for checking the memory specification are given in Fig. 3. In the following discussion for brevity we represent a list of field annotations used in memory specification $(c\langle @u^*\rangle^*)$ with L. We define a $subtype(L_1, L_2)$ function

$$
\begin{array}{|c|}
\hline
\text{[CHECK-MEM]}\\
\varPhi = \exists w^*\cdot\kappa\wedge\pi\\
XMem(\kappa) = (S_x, L_x)\\
\varPhi\vdash(S=S_x)*\Delta\\
subtype(L, L_x)\\
subtype(L_x, L)\\
\hline
\varPhi\vdash_{mem} S\hookrightarrow L\\
\end{array}
\qquad
\begin{array}{c}
\text{[CHECK-OR-MEM]}\\
\varPhi_1 = \exists w_1^*\cdot\kappa_1\wedge\pi_1 \quad \varPhi_2 = \exists w_2^*\cdot\kappa_2\wedge\pi_2\\
XMem(\kappa_1) = (S_1, L_1) \quad XMem(\kappa_2) = (S_2, L_2)\\
\varPhi_1\vdash(S=S_1)*\Delta \quad \varPhi_2\vdash(S=S_2)*\Delta\\
subtype(L, union(L_1, L_2)) \quad subtype(union(L_1, L_2), L)\\
\hline
\varPhi_1\vee\varPhi_2\vdash_{mem} S\hookrightarrow L\\
\end{array}
$$

Fig. 3. Validating the memory specification

on lists of field annotations. The function returns true if all the field annotations of data nodes in L_1 have a corresponding node in L_2 and their field annotations are in the subtyping relation (as defined in Fig. 1).

$$
subtype(L_1, L_2) \quad =_{df} \quad \forall\, c(@u_1^*)\ in\ L_1, \exists\, c(@u_2^*)\ in\ L_2 \quad s.t.\ u_1 <: u_2
$$

The *subtype* function is used to check the validity of the memory specification by ensuring that the field annotations defined inside the predicate are really subtype of those given by the memory specification. For a predicate $p(v^*) \equiv \varPhi$ h $S\hookrightarrow L$, the judgment $\varPhi\vdash_{mem} S\hookrightarrow L$ in Fig. 3 checks the validity of the memory specification.

Rule [CHECK-MEM] is used when the $\varPhi$ formula does not contain a disjunction, while [CHECK-OR-MEM] is used when it does. The main difference in the disjunctive case is how we handle of list of field annotations. For the set of addresses (S) we approximate the heap in each disjunctive formula. However, the field annotations have to be computed for the entire predicate as the annotations may differ in different disjuncts.

4   Verification with Compatible Sharing

To verify programs with compatible sharing we make use of an existing entailment procedure for separation logic (denoted by $\vdash$ [5]). The only additional operator we have is the *overlaid* conjunction. We first describe the automatic translation used to eliminate ⩓ operator. For *overlaid* conjunction operator (⩓), we must first identify the pairs of field annotations that are compatible. The following table can be used to look up compatible field annotations. The ⩓ operator is similar to $\wedge$, except that the shared heaps must be compatible, which can be checked using the *Compatible* function.

u_1	u_2	$Compatible_{FA}$
@M	@M	false
@M	@I	false
@M	@A	true
@I	@I	true
@I	@A	true
@A	@A	true

$$
Compatible(\kappa_1 ⩓ \kappa_2) \quad =_{df}
$$
$$
(S_1, L_1)=XMem(\kappa_1) \quad (S_2, L_2)=XMem(\kappa_2)
$$
$$
\forall\, c(@u_1^*)\ in\ L_1, \exists\, c(@u_2^*)\ in\ L_2\ s.t.\ Compatible_{FA}(u_1, u_2)
$$
$$
\forall\, c(@u_2^*)\ in\ L_2, \exists\, c(@u_1^*)\ in\ L_1\ s.t.\ Compatible_{FA}(u_2, u_1)
$$

$$[\textbf{ELIM}-\textbf{OVER}-\textbf{CONJ}]$$
$$Compatible(\kappa_1 \mathbb{A} \kappa_2)$$
$$\frac{(S_1, L_1) = XMem(\kappa_1) \quad (S_2, L_2) = XMem(\kappa_2)}{\kappa_1 \mathbb{A} \kappa_2 \rightsquigarrow \kappa_1 \wedge \kappa_2 \wedge S_1 = S_2}$$

$$[\textbf{DOWNCAST}-\textbf{FA}]$$
$$x \mapsto c(v[@u]^*) \Longrightarrow_{u <: w} x \mapsto c(v[@w]^*)$$

$$[\textbf{SPLIT}-\textbf{COMBINE}-\textbf{FA}]$$
$$x \mapsto c(v[@u]^*) \Longleftrightarrow$$
$$x \mapsto c(v[@u]^*) \wedge x \mapsto c(v[@A]^*)$$

$$[\textbf{SPLIT}-\textbf{READ}-\textbf{FA}]$$
$$x \mapsto c(v[@I]^*) \Longleftrightarrow$$
$$x \mapsto c(v[@I]^*) \wedge x \mapsto c(v[@I]^*)$$

Fig. 4. Rules with field annotations

As shown in Fig. 4, the [ELIM−OVER−CONJ] rule first checks for compatible sharing of heaps and then uses the *XMem* function to get the set of addresses S_1 and S_2 which are added to the formula when $\mathbb{A}$ operator is replaced with $\wedge$. Thus for the process scheduler example from Sect. 2 we get the following.

$$al\langle x, S_x \rangle \mathbb{A} (rl\langle y, S_y \rangle * sl\langle z, S_z \rangle) \rightsquigarrow$$
$$al\langle x, S_x \rangle \wedge (rl\langle y, S_y \rangle * sl\langle z, S_z \rangle) \wedge S_x = S_y \cup S_z$$

Figure 4 also lists the rules required during entailment with field annotations. These rules are based on the definition of field annotations and the semantic model of the specification formula (details are in Appendix 5.2). Rule [DOWNCAST−FA] says that we can always downcast a field annotation. This means that a *write* (@M) annotation can be downcast to *read* (@I) and a *read* annotation to *absent* (@A). The following examples use the [DOWNCAST−FA] rule to check validity of entailments with field annotations.

$$x \mapsto node(v@M, p@I) \vdash x \mapsto node(v@I, p@A) \quad (\textit{Valid})$$
$$x \mapsto node(v@I, p@I) \vdash x \mapsto node(v@I, p@A) \quad (\textit{Valid})$$
$$x \mapsto node(v@I, p@I) \vdash x \mapsto node(v@M, p@A) \quad (\textit{Invalid})$$

The *absent* annotation can always be split off (or combined with) any other annotation as shown in rule [SPLIT−COMBINE−FA]. Finally, as given in rule [SPLIT−READ−FA] the *read* annotation can be split into two *read* annotations. Together, these three set of rules allow exclusive write access and shared read access to fields. Entailments showing the use of [SPLIT−COMBINE−FA] rule are given below.

$$x \mapsto node(v@M, p@I) \vdash x \mapsto node(v@I, p@I) \wedge x \mapsto node(v@I, p@A)$$
$$x \mapsto node(v@M, p@M) \vdash x \mapsto node(v@M, p@A) \wedge x \mapsto node(v@A, p@M)$$
$$x \mapsto node(v@I, p@I) \vdash x \mapsto node(v@I, p@I) \wedge x \mapsto node(v@I, p@A)$$

5   Semantics and Soundness

5.1   Storage Model

The storage model is similar to classical separation logic [18], with the difference that we support field annotations, memory specifications and sharing operators.

Accordingly, we define our storage model by making use of a domain of heaps, which is equipped with a partial operator for gluing together disjoint heaps. $h_0 \cdot h_1$ takes the union of partial functions when h_0 and h_1 have disjoint domains of definition, and is undefined when $h_0(1)$ and $h_1(1)$ are both defined for at least one location $1 \in Loc$.

To define the model we assume sets Loc of locations (positive integer values), Val of primitive values, with $0 \in Val$ denoting null, Var of variables (program and logical variables), and $ObjVal$ of object values stored in the heap, with $c[f_1 \mapsto \nu_1, .., f_n \mapsto \nu_n]$ denoting an object value of data type c where $\nu_1, .., \nu_n$ are current values of the corresponding fields $f_1, .., f_n$. Each field has an attached annotation from $\{M, I, A\}$. I means that the corresponding field value cannot be modified, while M allows its mutation, and A denotes no access.

$$h \in \ Heaps \ =_{df} Loc \rightharpoonup_{fin} ObjVal \times \{M, I, A\}$$
$$s \in \ Stacks \ =_{df} Var \rightarrow Val \cup Loc$$

Note that each heap h is a finite partial mapping while each stack s is a total mapping, as in the classical separation logic [13,18].

5.2 Semantic Model of the Specification Formula

The semantics of our separation heap formula is similar to the model given for separation logic [18], except that we have extensions to handle our user-defined heap predicates together with the field annotations and new sharing operators. Let $s, h \models \Phi$ denote the model relation, i.e. the stack s and heap h satisfy the constraint Φ. Function $dom(f)$ returns the domain of function f. Now we use $\mapsto$ to denote mappings, not the points-to assertion in separation logic. The model relation for separation heap formulae is given in Definition 1. The model relation for pure formula $s \models \pi$ denotes that the formula π evaluates to true in s.

Definition 1 (Model for Specification Formula)

$s, h \models \Phi_1 \vee \Phi_2$ **iff** $s, h \models \Phi_1$ or $s, h \models \Phi_2$

$s, h \models \exists v_{1..n} \cdot \kappa \wedge \pi$ **iff** $\exists v_{1..n} \cdot s[v_1 \mapsto \nu_1, .., v_n \mapsto \nu_n], h \models \kappa$ and
                             $s[v_1 \mapsto \nu_1, .., v_n \mapsto \nu_n] \models \pi$

$s, h \models \kappa_1 * \kappa_2$ **iff** $\exists h_1, h_2 \cdot h_1 \bot h_2$ and $h = h_1 \cdot h_2$ and
                             $s, h_1 \models \kappa_1$ and $s, h_2 \models \kappa_2$

$s, h \models \kappa_1 \wedge \kappa_2$ **iff** $s, h \models \kappa_1$ and $s, h \models \kappa_2$

$s, h \models \kappa_1 \barwedge \kappa_2$ **iff** $s, h \models \kappa_1$ and $s, h \models \kappa_2$ and $Compatible(\kappa_1 \barwedge \kappa_2)$

$s, h \models$ emp   **iff** $dom(h) = \emptyset$

$s, h \models c(x, v_{1..n}@u_{1..n})$ **iff** **data** $c \ \{t_1 \ f_1, .., t_n \ f_n\} \in P$, $h = [s(x) \mapsto r]$, $dom(h) = \{x\}$
                             and $r = c[f_1 \mapsto_{w_1} s(v_1), .., f_n \mapsto_{w_n} s(v_n)]$ and $u_i <: w_i$
                             or $(c\langle x, v_{1..n}\rangle \equiv \Phi$ **inv** $\pi) \in P$ and $s, h \models [x/\text{root}]\Phi$

The last case in Definition 1 is split into two cases: (1) c is a data node defined in the program P; (2) c is a heap predicate defined in the program P. In the first case, h has to be a singleton heap. In the second case, the heap predicate c may be inductively defined. Note that the semantics for an inductively defined heap predicate denotes the least fixpoint, i.e., for the set of states (s,h) satisfying the predicate. The monotonic nature of our heap predicate definition guarantees the existence of the descending chain of unfoldings, thus the existence of the least solution.

5.3 Soundness

The soundness of rules given in Fig. 4 can be established using the semantic model and the definition of field annotations. We now present the proof of soundness of these rules, we start first with the rules for field annotations.

Rule [DOWNCAST–FA]:

$$s, h \models x \mapsto c(v[@u]^*)$$
$$\iff h=[s(x)\mapsto r]\wedge r=c[f\mapsto_w s(v)]^* \wedge u<:w \quad (\textit{Definition 1})$$
$$\implies h'=[s(x)\mapsto r]\wedge r=c[f\mapsto_w s(v)]^* \wedge h' \subset h \quad (\textit{weakening})$$
$$\iff s, h' \models x \mapsto c(v[@w]^*) \wedge h' \subset h \quad (\textit{Definition 1})$$
$$\iff s, h \models x \mapsto c(v[@w]^*)$$

$$\textit{Thus}, x \mapsto c(v[@u]^*) \implies_{u<:w} x \mapsto c(v[@w]^*) \qquad \square$$

Rule [SPLIT–COMBINE–FA]:

$$s, h \models x \mapsto c(v[@u]^*)$$
$$\iff h=[s(x)\mapsto r]\wedge r=c[f\mapsto_w s(v)]^* \wedge u<:w \quad (\textit{Definition 1})$$
$$\iff h'=[s(x)\mapsto r]\wedge r=c[f\mapsto_{@A} s(v)]^* \wedge h' \subset h \quad (\forall u \cdot u<:@A)$$
$$\iff s, h' \models x \mapsto c(v[@A]^*) \wedge h' \subset h \quad (\textit{Definition 1})$$
$$\iff s, h' \models x \mapsto c(v[@A]^*) \wedge h' \subset h$$
$$\wedge s, h \models x \mapsto c(v[@u]^*)$$
$$\iff s, h \models x \mapsto c(v[@A]^*) \wedge x \mapsto c(v[@u]^*) \quad (\textit{Definition 1})$$

$$\textit{Thus}, x \mapsto c(v[@u]^*) \iff$$
$$x \mapsto c(v[@u]^*) \wedge x \mapsto c(v[@A]^*) \qquad \square$$

Rule [SPLIT–READ–FA]:

$$s, h \models x \mapsto c(v[@I]^*)$$
$$\iff h=[s(x)\mapsto r]\wedge r=c[f\mapsto_w s(v)]^* \wedge I<:w \quad (\textit{Definition 1})$$
$$\iff h'=[s(x)\mapsto r]\wedge r=c[f\mapsto_{@I} s(v)]^* \wedge h' \subset h \quad (@I<:@I)$$
$$\iff s, h' \models x \mapsto c(v[@I]^*) \wedge h' \subset h \quad (\textit{Definition 1})$$
$$\iff s, h' \models x \mapsto c(v[@I]^*) \wedge h' \subset h$$
$$\wedge s, h \models x \mapsto c(v[@I]^*)$$
$$\iff s, h \models x \mapsto c(v[@I]^*) \wedge x \mapsto c(v[@I]^*) \quad (\textit{Definition 1})$$

$$\textit{Thus}, x \mapsto c(v[@I]^*) \iff$$
$$x \mapsto c(v[@I]^*) \wedge x \mapsto c(v[@I]^*) \qquad \square$$

Using the rules for field annotations we prove the soundness of the elimination rule as follows.

Rule [**ELIM–OVER–CONJ**]:

$$s, h \models \kappa_1 ⅋ \kappa_2 \wedge (S_1, L_1) = XMem(\kappa_1)$$
$$\wedge (S_2, L_2) = XMem(\kappa_2)$$
$$\Longleftrightarrow s, h \models \kappa_1 \wedge s, h \models \kappa_2 \wedge$$
$$Compatible(\kappa_1 ⅋ \kappa_2) \wedge s \models S_1 = S_2 (=h) \qquad (\textit{Definition } 1)$$

$case$ [**SPLIT–COMBINE–FA**]:
$$\Longleftrightarrow h = [s(\_) \mapsto r] \wedge r = c[f \mapsto_u s(\_)]^* \wedge$$
$$h' = [s(\_) \mapsto r] \wedge r = c[f \mapsto_{@A} s(\_)]^* \wedge h' \subset h \wedge$$
$$Compatible(\kappa_1 ⅋ \kappa_2) \wedge s \models S_1 = S_2$$
$$\Longleftrightarrow s, h \models \kappa_1 \wedge s, h' \models \kappa_2 \wedge h' \subset h$$
$$\wedge s \models S_1 = S_2 \qquad\qquad (\textit{Compatible}_{FA})$$
$$\Longrightarrow s, h \models \kappa_1 \wedge \kappa_2 \wedge S_1 = S_2 \qquad (\textit{Definition } 1)$$

$case$ [**SPLIT–READ–FA**]:
$$\Longleftrightarrow h = [s(\_) \mapsto r] \wedge r = c[f \mapsto_{@I} s(\_)]^* \wedge$$
$$h' = [s(\_) \mapsto r] \wedge r = c[f \mapsto_{@I} s(\_)]^* \wedge h' \subset h \wedge$$
$$Compatible(\kappa_1 ⅋ \kappa_2) \wedge s \models S_1 = S_2$$
$$\Longleftrightarrow s, h \models \kappa_1 \wedge s, h' \models \kappa_2 \wedge h' \subset h$$
$$\wedge s \models S_1 = S_2 \qquad\qquad (\textit{Compatible}_{FA})$$
$$\Longrightarrow s, h \models \kappa_1 \wedge \kappa_2 \wedge S_1 = S_2 \qquad (\textit{Definition } 1)$$

$$\textit{Thus,}\ \kappa_1 ⅋ \kappa_2 \rightsquigarrow \kappa_1 \wedge \kappa_2 \wedge S_1 = S_2 \qquad\qquad \square$$

There are two ways of splitting the *overlaid* heaps - in the first case we use the [**SPLIT–COMBINE–FA**] to combine them back as the fact that they are in compatible sharing means that the field annotations can only be from the pairs given in table for *Compatible*$_{FA}$ in Sect. 5.2 and we prove the second case similarly using the [**SPLIT–READ–FA**] rule. Soundness of the underlying entailment procedure (as shown in [5]) and the soundness of the rules given in Fig. 4 together establish the soundness of verification with compatible sharing.

6   Experiments

We have built a prototype system using Objective Caml called `HIPComp`.[2] The web interface of `HIPComp` allows testing the examples without downloading or installing the system. The proof obligations generated by `HIPComp` are discharged using off-the-shelf constraint solvers (Omega Calculator [14] and Mona [15]). In addition to the examples presented in this paper we can do automated verification of a number of challenging data structures with complex sharing. The

---

[2] http://loris-7.ddns.comp.nus.edu.sg/~project/HIPComp/.

examples are hard to reason with separation logic due to inherent sharing and aliasing in heap. For each of these examples, we verify methods that insert, find and remove nodes from the overlaid data structure.

Program	Invariant	LOC	Time [secs]	Sharing	Comp
Parameterized List	$\text{al}\langle x \rangle \; \text{Ａ} \; (\text{rl}\langle y \rangle * \text{sl}\langle z \rangle)$	30	0.28	100	40
Compatible Pairs	$x \mapsto \text{pair}\langle f_1, @A \rangle \; \text{Ａ} \; y \mapsto \text{pair}\langle @A, s_2 \rangle$	12	0.09	100	25
LL and SortedLL	$\text{ll}\langle x \rangle \; \text{Ａ} \; \text{sll}\langle y \rangle$	175	0.61	22	22
LL and Tree	$\text{ll}\langle x \rangle \; \text{Ａ} \; \text{tree}\langle t \rangle$	70	0.24	16	7
Doubly Circular List	$\text{llnext}\langle x \rangle \; \text{Ａ} \; \text{lldown}\langle y \rangle$	50	0.41	50	32
Process Scheduler	$\text{al}\langle x \rangle \; \text{Ａ} \; (\text{rl}\langle y \rangle * \text{sl}\langle z \rangle)$	70	0.47	33	23
Disk IO Scheduler	$(\text{ll}\langle x \rangle \; \text{Ａ} \; \text{tree}\langle t \rangle) * \text{ll}\langle y \rangle$	88	1.3	16	27

The above table summarises a suite of small examples verified by HIPComp. All experiments were done on a 3.20 GHz Intel Core i7-960 processor with 16 GB memory running Ubuntu Linux 10.04. The first column gives the name of the program. The second column shows how we use the overlaid conjunction Ａ to concisely specify the overlaid data structures in our experiments. As shown in the table, for the last two programs, the key invariant of the overlaid data structure can also be a composite structure which intermixes * and Ａ operators. It is essential to reason about compatible sharing when specifying and verifying such programs. The third column lists the lines of code (including specifications) in the program. The annotation burden due to specifications is about 30 % of the total number of lines of code. In the fifth column, we show the sharing degree, it is defined as the percentage of specifications that use compatible sharing using field annotations. The sharing degree varies across examples depending on the percentage of methods that use overlaid conjunction in their specifications.

As is clear from our benchmark programs, the ability to specify sharing is important to verify these data structures. The last column (Comp) is the percentage of total entailments generated that make use of compatible sharing. The compatibility percentage depends on the number of entailments that make use of the [ELIM−OVER−CONJ] rule to eliminate the overlaid conjunction. The compatibility check is essential to verify sharing in these programs.

7   Related Work and Conclusions

Our sharing and aliasing logic is most closely related to Hobor and Villard [12]; our work verifies only a subset of what they can do but we do so mechanically/automatically. The problem of sharing has also been explored in the context of concurrent data structures [7,20]. Our work is influenced by them but for a sequential setting, indeed the notion of self-stable concurrent abstract predicates is analogous to our condition for compatibility. However since we are focused on sequential programs, we avoid the use of environment actions and instead focus on checking compatibility between shared predicates. Regional logic [1] also uses set of addresses as footprint of formulas. These regions are used with dynamic frames to enable local reasoning of programs. Memory layouts [10] were used by Gast, as a way to formally specify the structure of individual memory blocks. A grammar of memory layouts enable distinguishing between variable, array, or other data structures. This shows that when dealing with shared regions of memory knowing the layout of memory can be quite helpful for reasoning. We use field annotations to specify access to memory in shared and overlaid data structures.

In the area of program analysis [4,8] the work most closely related to ours is by Lee et al. [17] on overlaid data structures. They show how to use two complementary static analysis over different shapes and combine them to reason about overlaid structures. Their shape analysis uses the $\land$ operator in the abstract state to capture the sharing of heaps in overlaid structures, but they do not provide a general way to reason with shared heaps. In contrast, we verify that the shared heaps used by the predicates are compatible with each other. Thus, we present an automated framework which can be used to reason about compatible sharing in data structures. An initial set of experiments with small but challenging programs confirms the usefulness of our method. Similarly, the recent work of Dragoi et al. [8] considers only the shape analysis of overlaid lists. In addition, Enea et al. [9] consider the compositional invariant checking of overlaid and nested lists. We extend these separation logic based techniques by going beyond shape properties and handling arbitrary data structures. Our proposal is built on top of user defined predicates with shape, size and bag properties that can express functional properties (order, sorting, height balance etc.) of overlaid data structures. A separation logic based program analysis has been used to handle non-linear data structures like trees and graphs [4]. In order to handle cycles they keep track of the nodes which are already visited using multi-sets.

We have proposed a specification mechanism to express different kinds of sharing and aliasing in data structures. The specifications can capture correctness properties of various kinds of programs using compatible sharing. We present an automated framework which can be used to reason about sharing in data structures. We have implemented a prototype based on our approach. An initial set of experiments with small but challenging programs have confirmed the usefulness of our method. For future work, we want to explore the use of memory regions and field annotations to enable automated verification of other intrinsic shared data structures that do not satisfy compatible sharing (like dags and graphs).

Acknowlegement. This work is supported by MoE 2013-T2-2-146 and Yale-NUS College R-607-265-045-121.

References

1. Banerjee, A., Naumann, D.A., Rosenberg, S.: Regional logic for local reasoning about global invariants. In: Vitek, J. (ed.) ECOOP 2008. LNCS, vol. 5142, pp. 387–411. Springer, Heidelberg (2008)

2. Berdine, J., Calcagno, C., O'Hearn, P.W.: Smallfoot: modular automatic assertion checking with separation logic. In: de Boer, F.S., Bonsangue, M.M., Graf, S., de Roever, W.-P. (eds.) FMCO 2005. LNCS, vol. 4111, pp. 115–137. Springer, Heidelberg (2006)

3. Boyland, J.T.: Semantics of fractional permissions with nesting. ACM Trans. Program. Lang. Syst. **32**(6), 22:1–22:33 (2010)

4. Cherini, R., Rearte, L., Blanco, J.: A shape analysis for non-linear data structures. In: Cousot, R., Martel, M. (eds.) SAS 2010. LNCS, vol. 6337, pp. 201–217. Springer, Heidelberg (2010)

5. Chin, W.-N., David, C., Nguyen, H.H., Qin, S.: Automated verification of shape, size and bag properties via user-defined predicates in separation logic. Sci. Comput. Program. **77**(9), 1006–1036 (2012)

6. David, C., Chin, W.-N.: Immutable specifications for more concise and precise verification. In: OOPSLA, pp. 359–374 (2011)

7. Dinsdale-Young, T., Dodds, M., Gardner, P., Parkinson, M.J., Vafeiadis, V.: Concurrent abstract predicates. In: D'Hondt, T. (ed.) ECOOP 2010. LNCS, vol. 6183, pp. 504–528. Springer, Heidelberg (2010)

8. Drăgoi, C., Enea, C., Sighireanu, M.: Local shape analysis for overlaid data structures. In: Logozzo, F., Fähndrich, M. (eds.) Static Analysis. LNCS, vol. 7935, pp. 150–171. Springer, Heidelberg (2013)

9. Enea, C., Saveluc, V., Sighireanu, M.: Compositional invariant checking for overlaid and nested linked lists. In: Felleisen, M., Gardner, P. (eds.) ESOP 2013. LNCS, vol. 7792, pp. 129–148. Springer, Heidelberg (2013)

10. Gast, H.: Reasoning about memory layouts. In: FM, pp. 628–643 (2009)

11. Gotsman, A., Berdine, J., Cook, B.: Interprocedural shape analysis with separated heap abstractions. In: Yi, K. (ed.) SAS 2006. LNCS, vol. 4134, pp. 240–260. Springer, Heidelberg (2006)

12. Hobor, A., Villard, J.: The Ramifications of sharing in data structures. In: POPL (2013)

13. Ishtiaq, S., O'Hearn, P.W.: BI as an assertion language for mutable data structures. In: ACM POPL, pp. 14–26. London, January 2001

14. Kelly, P., Maslov, V., Pugh, W., et al.: The Omega Library Version 1.1.0 Interface Guide, November 1996

15. Klarlund, N., Moller, A.: MONA Version 1.4 - User Manual. BRICS Notes Series, January 2001

16. Le, X.B., Gherghina, C., Hobor, A.: Decision procedures over sophisticated fractional permissions. In: Jhala, R., Igarashi, A. (eds.) APLAS 2012. LNCS, vol. 7705, pp. 368–385. Springer, Heidelberg (2012)

17. Lee, O., Yang, H., Petersen, R.: Program analysis for overlaid data structures. In: Gopalakrishnan, G., Qadeer, S. (eds.) CAV 2011. LNCS, vol. 6806, pp. 592–608. Springer, Heidelberg (2011)

18. Reynolds, J.: Separation aogic: a logic for shared mutable data structures. In: IEEE LICS, pp. 55–74 (2002)

19. Trinh, M.-T., Le, Q.L., David, C., Chin, W.-N.: Bi-abduction with pure properties for specification inference. In: Shan, C. (ed.) APLAS 2013. LNCS, vol. 8301, pp. 107–123. Springer, Heidelberg (2013)

20. Turon, A.J., Wand, M.: A separation logic for refining concurrent objects. In: POPL, pp. 247–258 (2011)

Delta-Oriented FSM-Based Testing

Mahsa Varshosaz$^{(\boxtimes)}$, Harsh Beohar, and Mohammad Reza Mousavi

Center for Research on Embedded Systems, Halmstad University, Halmstad, Sweden
{mahsa.varshosaz,harsh.beohar,m.r.mousavi}@hh.se

Abstract. We use the concept of delta-oriented programming to organize FSM-based test models in an incremental structure. We then exploit
incremental FSM-based testing to make efficient use of this high-level
structure in generating test cases. We show how our approach can lead
to more efficient test-case generation, both by analyzing the complexity
of the test-case generation algorithm and by applying the technique to
a case study.

Keywords: Model-based testing · FSM-based testing · HSI method ·
Software product lines · Delta-oriented programming · DeltaJava

1 Introduction

Software product lines (SPLs) have become common practice thanks to their
potential for mass production and customization of software. Testing software
product lines, and in particular, their model-based testing are topics of increasing
relevance in the research literature and also industrial practice [4,10,17]. In
this paper, we propose the formal foundations of a delta-oriented framework
for model-based testing. Delta-oriented programming (DOP) and in particular,
DeltaJava [14], is a framework for SPLs, in which a product line is specified in
terms of applications of a number of deltas (changes: additions, removals and
modifications of member objects, methods, and classes) from a core product.
The overall goal of the research commenced by this paper is to allow for efficient
test-case generation and test-case execution for delta-oriented models and their
corresponding programs. In this paper, we focus on test-case generation and
show whether and how test-case generation for delta-oriented models can be
made more efficient by benefiting from their incremental structure.

To this end, we use finite state machines (FSMs) as test models whose structure is based on DeltaJava: there is a test-model for the core product, which
includes abstraction of state valuations as its states and the method calls, their
return values and their effect on the abstract state as its transitions. Then,
test models for different products are obtained by incrementally modifying the
details of the core model (e.g., adding models for classes, member objects and

M.R. Mousavi—The work has been partially supported by the Swedish Research
Council award number: 621-2014-5057 and the Swedish Knowledge Foundation in
the context of the AUTO-CAAS HöG project.

M. Butler et al. (Eds.): ICFEM 2015, LNCS 9407, pp. 366–381, 2015.
DOI: 10.1007/978-3-319-25423-4_24

methods). In this paper, we focus on the incremental subset of DeltaJava, in which the core represents a minimal set of features and the deltas incrementally add to the core or the composition of core with other deltas (but do not remove anything from them). We also adopt the well-known Harmonized State Identification (HSI) method [13] and adapt it to the delta-oriented structure of our test models.

The remainder of this paper is organized as follows. In Sect. 2, we review several pieces of related work and identify their similarities and differences with the present paper. In Sect. 3, we recall some preliminary notions regarding FSM-based testing and the syntax of delta-oriented models. We specify the syntactic structure of our running example in Sect. 4, which we use throughout the rest of the paper to illustrate various formal definitions. Subsequently, we define the semantic domain of our test models in Sect. 5 and show how the test models of various products can be obtained from the semantics of the core model by applying a delta composition operator. In Sect. 6, we show how test cases can be generated from the test models of various products and analyze the complexity of test-case generation. In Sect. 7, we provide some empirical results obtained from comparing the effectiveness of the application of the delta-oriented testing method with the HSI-method for a case study. We conclude the paper and present the directions of our ongoing research in Sect. 8.

2   Related Work

Incremental FSM-Based Testing. The closest line of research to that of the present paper is incremental FSM-based testing, which is extensively researched in the past few years [3,6,9,11,15]. This line of research aims at modularizing the test-case generation and/or test-case execution process with respect to changes such as adding, removing, or modifying transitions or states in test models. Such a modularization should eventually lead to saving time and effort in re-generating or re-executing tests by focusing on those parts that are influenced by the change. The approaches of [3,6] differ from our approach in that they assume that the behavior of the core implementation is unchanged after each and every delta and focus on the effect of changes on the extended part of the implementation; we have no assumption about the behavior of the implementation due to the application of a delta. Our focus in this paper is on test-model semantics and test-case generation rather than test-case selection and execution. The approach of [15] is different from ours in that it aims at completing a given set of test cases, but does not per se address the changes in the test model. Our approach is mostly based on [9,11] and applies it at a higher level of abstraction to delta-oriented models inspired by the DeltaJava framework of [14].

Model-Based Testing of SPLs. In a recent survey, Oster et al. [10] observe that there is a considerable gap regarding testing in the current software engineering approaches to SPLs. Despite this gap, there is already some body of research on the theory and application of model-based testing for SPLs (see, e.g., [4,10,17] for recent surveys). Among these approaches, the closest to our approach are those developed by Malte Lochau, Ina Schaefer, et al. [8]. They propose a delta-oriented and state-machine-based testing methodology for SPLs and instantiate this methodology in a case study using IBM Rational Rhapsody and Automated Test-case Generator (ATG). Our approach follows the same structure and formalizes the part that has been implemented in IBM Rhapsody, by means of ideas from incremental FSM-based testing. This paves the way for further formal analyses of the technique proposed in [8], as well as further improvements by considering more relaxed fault models.

Object-Oriented Model-Based Testing. There is a large body of literature regarding model-based testing of object-oriented programs by using sequence- or state-diagrams as test models (see, e.g., [1,12,18]). We follow object-oriented principles such as encapsulation and data-hiding in our modeling framework and organize our test models based on specification of class instantiations and dependencies. In this sense, our work builds upon earlier work in this direction such as [5,18]; in particular, our test models are reminiscent of class state machines (CSMs) introduced in [5]. Our work differs from this line of work in two ways: firstly, our focus is on incremental changes in test models and not so much on testing object oriented programs. Secondly, in our approach the system under test need not be implemented as an object-oriented program; the abstract test-cases from our test-models can be used to test different types of implementation. This is achieved by means of adapters that turn the abstract test-cases into concrete test-cases for different programming languages and implementation platforms.

3   Preliminaries

3.1   FSM-Based Testing

In this section, we explain the basic concepts of FSM-based testing and delta-oriented modeling techniques used throughout the rest of the paper. We use the Harmonized State Identification (HSI) method [13] as the basis of our model-based testing technique. In the HSI method, test models are Finite State Machines (FSMs), specifying the desired behavior of systems. The formal definition of an FSM, borrowed from [2], is as follows.

Definition 1 (*Finite State Machine*). *A Finite State Machine (FSM) M is a 6-tuple* $(S, s_0, I, O, \mu, \lambda)$, *where S is a finite set of states,* $s_0 \in S$ *is the initial state, I and O are, respectively, finite nonempty sets of input and output symbols,* $\mu : S \times I \to S$ *is the transition function and* $\lambda : S \times I \to O$ *is the output function.*

Intuitively, whenever a machine receives input a at state s, it deterministically traverses to state $\mu(s, a)$ and generates output $\lambda(s, a)$. A transition from state s to state s' with input i and generated output o is represented by quadruple (s, i, o, s'), or alternatively by $s \xrightarrow{i/o} s'$. For a sequence $x \in I^*$, we define $\mu(s, x)$ and $\lambda(s, x)$ in the standard manner to denote, respectively, the final state that the machine ends in and the sequence of generated outputs, after receiving the input symbols in x one by one. Furthermore, we also informally recall that two states are X-equivalent ($X \subseteq I^*$) if and only if the two states produce the same output for every input sequence $\sigma \in X$ (see [2] for a formal definition). Lastly, two machines M, M' are X-equivalent, denoted by $M \equiv_X M'$, if and only if for every state of M there is an X-equivalent state of M' and vice versa. Machine M is said to conform to machine M' if and only if they are I^*-equivalent.

The main idea of the HSI method is to establish conformance between an FSM test model M and an unknown machine M', modeling the implementation, by generating a finite test case from M and applying it to M'. There are a set of assumptions that should hold for these machines, which are specified next.

Definition 2 *(HSI method assumptions). The HSI method can be applied on machines M and M', which satisfy the following assumptions:*

1. *Both M and M' are deterministic, i.e., for each state and each input i, there is at most one outgoing transition labeled with i.*
2. *Both M and M' are minimal, i.e., there are no distinct I^*-equivalent states in either of them. Note that if M is not minimal, an equivalent minimal machine can be generated using a minimization algorithm such as [7].*
3. *All states in M are reachable from its initial state s_0.*
4. *Both machines M and M' have reliable reset sequences, which take the respective machine from the current state to the initial state.*
5. *M' has at most as many states as M.*

The HSI method consists of two phases. The first phase comprises checking the existence of states in the implementation that are I^*-equivalent to the ones in the test model. In the second phase, the output and the target of the transitions for the corresponding states are tested for conformance. In order to reach all the states in the machine, the HSI method uses a set of input sequences, *state cover set*, denoted by Q, which is defined below.

Definition 3 *(State Cover Set). Consider an FSM $M = (S, s_0, I, O, \mu, \lambda)$; a state cover set of M, denoted by Q, is a set of sequences such that:*

$$\forall_{s \in S} \cdot \exists_{x \in Q} \cdot \mu(s_0, x) = s$$

A state cover set of an FSM can be obtained by building a spanning tree such that, the nodes are states of the FSM and the edges are chosen from the set of transitions in the FSM. The set of sequences obtained as the state cover set are then the paths from the initial state to the nodes in the spanning tree.

As another ingredient of the first phase, i.e., checking the existence of test-model states in the implementation, the HSI method uses a *separating family of sequences*, which is denoted by Z and comprises sets of separating sequences for all states. A set of separating sequences identifies and tests the target states after running each element of the state cover set. The separating set for a state is defined as follows.

Definition 4 *(Separating Sequences). Consider an FSM $M = (S, s_0, I, O, \mu, \lambda)$; the set of separating sequences for a state $s \in S$, is denoted by z_s and includes sequences that can distinguish s from all other states in S, that is:*

$$\forall_{s,s' \in S} \cdot s \neq s' \Rightarrow \exists_{x \in Pref(z_s) \cap Pref(z_{s'})} \cdot \lambda(s, x) \neq \lambda(s', x),$$

where $Pref(.)$ denotes the set of prefixes of a set of sequences.

A separating family of sequences for an FSM, is a set comprising the separating sequences of all states, that is $Z = \bigcup_{s \in S} \{z_s\}$.

Hence, the set of test cases executed in the first phase are generated as follows. For each state $s \in S$, let q_s and z_s denote, respectively, the sequence in the state cover set which leads to s and the set of separating sequences generated for s. Then, the test cases generated in the first phase is given by $\bigcup_{s \in S} r.q_s.z_s$, where r is the reset sequence of the FSM and for two sets A and B of sequences, $A.B$ denotes the concatenation of two sets and is defined as $\{\alpha\beta | \alpha \in A \land \beta \in B\}$. This way, in addition to checking the existence of the states, the output and target state of the transitions which are included in the spanning tree are checked for conformance to the specification.

In the second phase of the HSI method, the output and the target state of the remaining transitions, not visited while traversing the state cover set, are checked using the following set of test cases. For each of the remaining transitions such as $s \xrightarrow{i/o} s'$, the set of all $r.q_s.i.z_{s'}$ sequences is added to the set of test cases.

3.2   Delta-Oriented Syntactic Structure

Inspired by DeltaJava [14], our test-models for an SPL are structured into a *core model* and a set of *delta models*. The core model describes the correct behavior of a valid configuration in the SPL. The implementation of other products is obtained by applying delta models to the core model. The structure of our models is defined by the syntax of DeltaJava, which is described below.

A core model comprises a set of Java classes and a set of interfaces, that is:

core *⟨Feature names⟩{⟨Java classes and interfaces⟩},*

where feature names specify the set of features which are included in the configuration corresponding to the core model.

Delta models describe sets of changes to the core model. The structure of a delta in the DeltaJava language is given in Fig. 1. In this syntax, a delta model may add/remove fields, methods, or interfaces from classes in the core model. Also, it can modify the existing ones. A class can also be added or removed from a core model by applying a delta model. The keyword *after* can be used in order to specify the order of the application of a set of delta model to the core model. The *when* keyword is used to specify that this delta can be applied when a set of features are being included in the configuration. In the remainder of this paper, we only consider incremental delta-oriented models, i.e., those models that only

```
delta ⟨ name ⟩ [after ⟨ delta names ⟩]
    when ⟨application condition⟩ {
removes ⟨class  or interface name⟩
adds class ⟨ name ⟩ ⟨ standard Java class⟩
adds interface ⟨ name⟩ ⟨standard Java interface⟩
modifies interface ⟨ name ⟩
    { ⟨ (remove |  add|  rename) method header clauses⟩ }
modifies class ⟨name⟩
    { ⟨ (remove | add |  rename) field  clauses⟩ |
      ⟨ (remove | add |  rename) method  clauses ⟩} }
```

Fig. 1. DeltaJava syntax (Color figure online).

add model classes, methods or fields. In this paper, we focus on an incremental subset of the syntax, designated in blue, which assumes a minimal core and incremental additions by various deltas. Particularly, in Sect. 5, we provide a semantic domain in terms of FSMs for a subset of these syntactic structures, which covers adding classes, methods and fields to a core FSM model.

4   Running Example

In this section, we present the syntax of a DeltaJava example, which is used throughout the rest of this paper. The core model of this example consists of one class, named *Bridge*. This class has a field that represents the availability of the bridge and also a set of functions, which manipulate and report the value of this field. The syntax of the core model is given in Fig. 2.

```
Core Bridge{
    Class Bridge{
        private boolean Avl;
        public Bridge() {Avl=true;}
        public void SetAvl(){Avl=true;}
        public void ResetAvl(){Avl=false;}
        public boolean CheckAvl(){return(Avl);}
    }
}
delta DPedLight when pedestrian Light {
    modifies Class Bridge{
        adds boolean Psig
        adds boolean CheckPsig(){return(Psig);}
        adds void SetPsig(){Psig=true;}
        adds void ResetPsig(){Psig=false;}
    }
}
```

```
delta DController when controller {
    adds Class Controller{
        private boolean Lsig,Rsig;
        public bridge b;
        public controller(){
        Lsig=false; Rsig=false;}
        public int CheckLsig(){return(Lsig);}
        public int CheckRsig(){return(Rsig);}
        public void GetReq(int id){
        if(b.CheckAvl()==true){
          if(id==0){
          Lsig=true;Rsig=false;}
        else{
          Rsig=true;Lsig=false;
        }
        b. ResetAvl();}
        }
        public void SetPassed(){
        Lsig=false;Rsig=false;
        b.SetAvl();}
    }
}
```

Fig. 2. Core- and delta models of the running example.

We consider two different delta models to be added to the core model given in Fig. 2. The first delta model consists of the addition of a class. The class *controller* controls the status of the lights in both side of the bridge in order to guarantee a mutually exclusive access to the bridge. This delta is added when the feature controller is included in a product. The second delta model is added to the core model when the pedestrian light feature is included in the product. This delta model consists of adding a field to the bridge class, which represents the status of the pedestrian light, as well as two methods, which can set and reset the value of the pedestrian light.

5   Delta-Oriented FSM Modeling

In this section, we define a semantic domain based on FSMs for the syntactic structure of DeltaJava models. We assume that the transitions in our test models concern the call / return behavior of a set of modules. The states in a test model concern a symbolic aggregation of concrete states, where each concrete state corresponds to a valuation of variables. The granularity of this abstraction is modeler's choice, as long as it respects the HSI assumptions. Moreover, it is assumed that the set of fields used and manipulated by a method call, its possible return values and its effect on the value of these fields are known.

To start with, we define the following basic concepts for our semantic domain.

Definition 5 *(Abstract Valuations). Assume a set V of variables and a set D of their possible values; for simplicity, we have left out typing information here and throughout the paper. Then $Val^V \subseteq 2^{V \to D}$, is an abstract valuation (i.e., a set of valuations) of V. The set of all such abstract valuations of V is denoted by VAL^V. We remove the superscript of an abstract valuation, if the set of variables is clear. For an abstract valuation $Val^V \subseteq 2^{V \to D}$ and for $V' \subseteq V$, we write $Val \downarrow V'$ to denote element-wise domain restriction of Val to V', that is leaving out the valuation of those variables not mentioned in V'.*

Definition 6 *(Object Structure). We formalize the structure of an object obj of class c, as a 3-tuple $(Id, Flds, Mtds)$, where Id is the object's unique identifier and $Flds$ and $Mtds$, respectively, denote the set of fields and methods in the class c. (To avoid name clashes, we assume that all members of $Flds$ and $Mtds$ are prefixed with Id.) A method is represented by a 5-tuple $(Id, Inprms, Outprm, Clds, UsedVars)$, where Id, $Inprms$ and $Outprm$, respectively, denote the name of the method and the list of the input parameters and the output returned by the method; $Clds$ denotes the set of methods that are called in the body of this method and $UsedVars$ is the set of variables read from or written to in the method. Note that $UsedVars$ may comprise both members of $Flds$ and model variables. The latter are variables that the test modeler has added to the model to capture unspecified details, e.g., associations and dependencies, without cluttering the model.*

In the rest of the paper, we recognize the components of the above-given tuples, by indexing the name of the intended component with the name of the object or the method. For example, $Inprms_m$ denotes the input parameters of the method m. Next, we define the concept of post-condition for methods.

Definition 7 *(Effect and Return Value Functions). The effect of calling a method m is defined by a function $Effect_m$: $VAL^{Inprms_m \cup UsedVars_m} \rightarrow VAL^{UsedVars_m}$. Similarly, its set of admitted return values is defined by: $RetVal_m : VAL^{Inprms_m \cup UsedVars_m} \rightarrow 2^D$.*

5.1 Core Model Semantics

In this section, we define the semantic domain for core models. The behavior of a core model results from execution of the methods called in the objects instantiated from the core model classes (A conscious choice is to be made by the modeler as to which methods from which abstract states are included in the model.). Hence, the finite state machine describing the behavior of a set of objects is defined as follows.

Definition 8 *(Object FSM). An FSM $M(\mathcal{O}) = (S, s_0, I, O, \mu, \lambda)$ is a semantic model for a set $\mathcal{O}$ of objects from the set C of classes, if it satisfies the following conditions:*

- *$S \subseteq VAL^V$ where $V \subseteq \bigcup_{o \in \mathcal{O}, m \in Mtds_o} UsedVars_m$ is a subset of model variables and fields in $\mathcal{O}$; this means that each state in S is an abstract valuation of a subset of model variables and fields.*
- *$I \subseteq \bigcup_{o \in \mathcal{O}, m \in Mtds_o} \{Id_m\} \times VAL^{Inprms_m}$; this means that each input in the input symbols set comprises a method name and a set of passed arguments.*
- *$O \subseteq D$ is the set of possible return values of the method calls in I.*
- *$\mu : S \times I \rightarrow S$, is a transition function satisfying the following conditions:*

    (1) $\forall_{o \in \mathcal{O}, \ m \in Mtds_o, \ val \in VAL^{Inprms_m}, \ i \in I, \ s,s' \in S} \cdot \mu(s, i) = s' \wedge i = (Id_m, val)$
    $\Rightarrow Effect_m(s \downarrow UsedVars_m \times val) \subseteq s' \downarrow UsedVars_m,$
    (2) $\forall_{s \in S} \cdot \exists_{x \in I^*} \cdot \ (s_0, x) = s$
    (3) $\exists_{r \in I^*} \cdot \forall_{s \in S} \cdot \ \mu(s, r) = s_0$

- *$\lambda : S \times I \rightarrow O$ is an output function satisfying the following condition:*

    $\forall_{o \in \mathcal{O}, \ m \in Mtds_o, \ val \in VAL^{Inprms_m}, \ i \in I, \ o \in O, \ s \in S} \cdot \lambda(s, i) = o \wedge$
    $i = (Id_m, val) \Rightarrow RetVal_m(s \downarrow UsedVars_m \times val) = o.$

Our notion of abstract states are reminiscent of similar notions (based on the category-partition method) in the literature [19]. Regarding the transition function, condition (1) specifies that there can be a transition from one state to another, labeled with a method call as input, only if this method call maps one of the concrete evaluations of the used variables in the source to another concrete valuation in the target state. Condition (2) requires that all states included in the set of states are reachable from the initial state. Condition (3) postulates that the given FSM has a reset sequence r. Regarding the output function, the

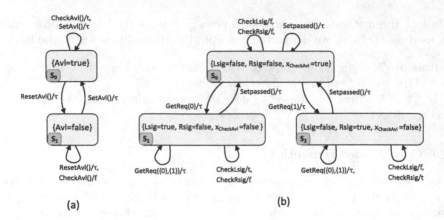

Fig. 3. (a) FSM modeling the bridge class, (b) FSM modeling the controller class

condition specifies that the output of the FSM for each given input is exactly the set of admitted outputs for the corresponding method.

A test model for core, defined below, is then an object FSM comprising a set of objects from the core model classes.

Definition 9 *(Test Model for Core). A test model for core is a minimal object FSM $M(\mathcal{O})$ such that each object in $\mathcal{O}$ is instantiated from a class in the core model.*

For example the FSM corresponding to the core model in the running example is demonstrated in Fig. 3(a). This FSM is minimal and it satisfies the reachability condition. The reset sequence of this FSM is *SetAvl()*.

5.2   Delta Application

In this section, we define the semantic domain for delta models and the application of a delta to a core model. As mentioned in Sect. 3.2, a delta comprises a set of operations applying changes to the core model. In order to give a practical definition to a delta model and the type of changes that it can make to the core model, we focus on adding a class, on one hand and adding a set of fields and methods, on the other hand. The reason we combine adding fields and methods in one step is that often adding new methods requires some additional fields. Moreover, in several cases the new abstract valuations (additional state-partitions) due to the additional fields can only preserve minimality, if new methods are also added to tell them apart. We leave the deltas concerning removals and modifications of methods and removal of fields for future work. Hence, for now we are assuming that the core model comprises the least mandatory set of features and the model regarding each product is generated incrementally from the core model.

We proceed by defining the effect of applying a delta containing each of the above-mentioned changes on the core model's FSM.

Adding a Class. The test model for the added class has the structure and abides by the constraints of object FSMs given in Definition 8. Hence, we assume that the test model for the added class c is given as a minimal object FSM $M_d(\mathcal{O}_d)$ where $\mathcal{O}_d$ only contains objects of class c with a fresh identifier (not mentioned among the identifier of core objects and other deltas).

For example, the FSM describing the behavior of an object of the controller class is depicted in Fig. 3(b). In this figure, $x_{CheckAvl}$ is an extra model variable included in the state, representing the returned value of $CheckAvl()$ and cutting the dependency with the core model. The result of adding a class to the core model is defined as follows.

Assume that the test models for the core and the delta models are object FSMs $M(\mathcal{O}) = (S, s_0, I, O, \mu, \lambda)$ and $M_d(\mathcal{O}_d) = (S_d, s_0^d, I_d, O_d, \mu_d, \lambda_d)$, respectively. In order to define the composition of the core and the delta, we first specify the possible connections between the model variables of delta and core. Assuming that V and V_d, respectively, denote the variables in the domain of the states in S and S_d, then, the (partial) composition function $\gamma : V_d \to V$ specifies which (model) variables in V_d should match which variables in V. Moreover, the methods of the delta class can initiate method calls to instances of the core class included in the delta class (if any). Here, for the sake of simplicity, we consider that each delta method can contain at most one method call to the core, but the generalization to a sequence of core method calls is straightforward. We assume that the set of methods in the core model and the set of methods in the delta model are denoted, respectively, by MTD and $Mtds$.

Definition 10. *The result of composing the above-given models M and M_d with regards to γ is an FSM $M'(\mathcal{O}') = (S', s_0', I', O', \mu', \lambda')$, where:*

- *$S' = \{val \in VAL^{V \cup V_d} \mid val \downarrow V \in S \land val \downarrow V_d \in S' \land \forall_{v_d \in V_d, v \in V} \cdot \gamma(v_d) = v \Rightarrow val \downarrow \{v_d\} = val \downarrow \{v\}\}$; for the composition to be well-defined, we assume V and V_d to be disjoint,*
- *s_0' is the initial state such that $s_0' \downarrow V = s_0$ and $s_0' \downarrow V_d = s_0^d$,*
- *$I' = I \cup I_d$*
- *$O' = O \cup O_d$*
- *$\mu' : S' \times I' \to S'$, is the transition function. For each $i \in I'$, we distinguish the following three cases:*
  - *$i \in I$ concerns a method call from the core; then, the following condition should be satisfied*

$$\forall_{m \in MTD, \ s_1', s_2' \in S'} \cdot i = (Id_m, val) \Rightarrow \big(\ \mu'(s_1', i) = s_2' \Leftrightarrow$$
$$\exists_{s_1, s_2 \in S} \cdot s_1 \downarrow UsedVars_m = s_1' \downarrow UsedVars_m \land$$
$$s_2 \downarrow UsedVars_m = s_2' \downarrow UsedVars_m \ \land \ \mu(s_1, i) = s_2 \ \big)$$

  - *$i \in I_d$ concerns a method call from delta that does not have any nested call to the core; then, the following condition should be satisfied*

$$\forall_{m \in Mtds, \ s_1', s_2' \in S'} \cdot i = (Id_m, val) \Rightarrow \big(\mu'(s_1', i) = s_2' \Leftrightarrow$$
$$\exists_{s_1^d, s_2^d \in S_d} \cdot s_1^d \downarrow UsedVars_m = s_1' \downarrow UsedVars_m \land$$
$$s_2^d \downarrow UsedVars_m = s_2' \downarrow UsedVars_m \ \land \ \mu_d(s_1^d, i) = s_2^d \big)$$

- $i \in I_d$ concerns a method call from delta that has a nested method call n_i to the core; then the following condition should hold:

$$\forall_{m \in Mtds, n \in MTD, s_1', s_2' \in S'} \cdot i = (Id_m, val) \wedge n_i = (Id_n, val_n) \Rightarrow$$
$$\mu'(s_1', i) = s_2' \Leftrightarrow \exists_{s_1^d, s_2^d \in S^d} \cdot s_1^d \downarrow UsedVars_m = s_1' \downarrow UsedVars_m \wedge$$
$$s_2^d \downarrow UsedVars_m = s_2' \downarrow UsedVars_m \wedge \mu_d(s_1^d, i) = s_d^2 \wedge$$
$$\exists_{s_1, s_2 \in S} \cdot s_1 \downarrow UsedVars_n = s_1' \downarrow UsedVars_n \wedge$$
$$s_2 \downarrow UsedVars_n = s_2' \downarrow UsedVars_n \wedge \mu(s_1, n_i) = s_2'$$

- $\lambda' : S' \times I' \to O'$ is the output function; for each $i \in I'$, we distinguish the following two cases:
  - either $i \in I$, then the following condition should hold:

$$\forall_{m \in MTD, o \in O', s' \in S'} \cdot i = (Id_m, val) \Rightarrow \lambda'(s', i) = o \Leftrightarrow$$
$$\exists_{s \in S} \cdot s \downarrow UsedVars_m = s' \downarrow UsedVars_m \wedge \lambda(s, i) = o$$

  - or $i \in I_d$, then the following condition should hold:

$$\forall_{m \in Mtds, o \in O', s' \in S'} \cdot i = (Id_m, val) \Rightarrow \lambda'(s', i) = o \Leftrightarrow$$
$$\exists_{s_d \in S_d} \cdot s_d \downarrow UsedVars_m = s' \downarrow UsedVars_m \wedge \lambda_d(s_d, i) = o$$

In the definition of transition function, a case distinction is made based on whether the method calls (in the delta model) have a nested method call or not. In the former case the valuations of the variables belonging to both core and delta models can change in the target state while in the latter case only the valuation of the variables belonging to the delta model can change. In the definition of output function these two cases are defined as one since the effect of the output of the inner method calls, if any, of a method call in the delta model is captured by the corresponding model variables which are included in the states of the delta model.

Figure 4(a) demonstrates the FSM resulting from the addition of the controller class to the bridge class. Note that the γ function is defined to match the valuation of the model variable $x_{CheckAvl}$ in the delta with the variable Avl in the core.

Theorem 1. *Based on the assumptions made about the core model and the delta model, the resulting FSM of Definition 10 satisfies the assumptions (1)–(4) of Definition 2.*

Note that the last constraint of Definition 10 is implementation-dependent and hence, it can only proven without sufficient assumptions on the implementation. This is out of the scope of the present paper.

Adding Fields and Methods. In this section, we discuss the effect of adding a set of fields and methods to the core module.

Let X and E, respectively, denote the set of fields and methods added by a delta. Also, assume that V denotes the variables in the domain of the states in

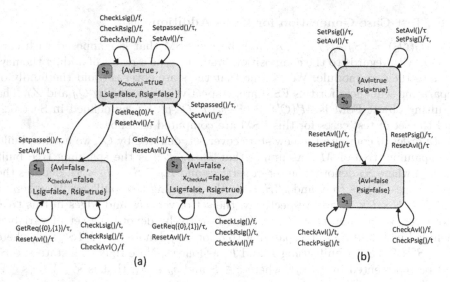

Fig. 4. (a) FSM resulted from adding the delta model *DController*, to the core model, (b) FSM resulting from adding delta *DPedLight* to the core model

the core model, and that a method can comprise method calls. The addition of X and E to the core FSM results in another FSM in which the abstract states and transitions accommodate X and E. The formal definition of the application function has a similar structure to the case of adding a class.

Theorem 2. *Assumptions (1)–(4) of Definition 2 are preserved under the addition a set of fields and methods to a core FSM model.*

As an example, Fig. 4(b) demonstrates the FSM resulting from the addition of the delta *DPedLight*, to the core model. This delta adds a new field, namely, *Psig*, and two methods, namely, *SetPsig* and *ResetPsig*, to the class *Bridge*.

6   Delta-Oriented Testing

In this section, we explain the incremental test-case generation method. In the remainder of this section, we assume that the core model is an object FSM such as $M(\mathcal{O}) = (S, s_0, I, O, \mu, \lambda)$ and the set of all methods of the classes in this core model are denoted by MTD. The state cover set and the separating family of sequences computed for M are, respectively, denoted by Q and Z. We assume that $q_s \in Q$ denotes a sequence in the state cover set that ends in state s and z_s denotes the set of sequences which separate s from other states. For example, the state cover set and the separating family of sequences for the core model represented in Fig. 3 are, respectively, $Q = \{\varepsilon, ResetAvl()\}$ and $Z = \{z_{s_0}, z_{s_1}\}$ $= \{\{CheckAvl()\}, \{CheckAvl()\}\}$.

6.1 Test-Case Generation for Class Addition

Let $M_d(\mathcal{O}_d) = (S_d, s_0^d, I_d, O_d, \mu_d, \lambda_d)$, be the FSM that is composed with core model, with regards to the composition function γ, as a result of adding the new class to the core module. We assume that the state cover set and the family of separating sequences for this FSM are, respectively, denoted by Q_d and Z_d. The resulting object FSM is $M'(\mathcal{O}') = (S', s_0', I', O', \mu', \lambda')$, as defined in Sect. 5.2, and the set of test cases for this FSM are computed as follows.

In order to compute the new state cover set, denoted by Q', we need to build the spanning tree of M'. Assuming that $P_d(S_d, E_d)$ is the spanning tree built for M_d, where S_d denotes the set of vertices and $E_d \subseteq S_d \times I_d \times S_d$, denotes the set of edges in this tree, and $P(S, E)$ is the spanning tree built for M, where S and $E \subseteq S \times I \times S$, are, respectively, the set of vertices and edges in this tree. Moreover, we assume that V and V_d, respectively, denote the set of variables included in S and S_d. The spanning tree for M', denoted by $P'(S', E')$, where $E' \subseteq S' \times I' \times S'$, is built using P and P_d as follows. Note that each state $s' \in S'$ can be represented by (s, s_d), where $s \in S$ and $s_d \in S_d$, that is $s' \downarrow V = s \downarrow V$ and $s' \downarrow V_d = s_d \downarrow V_d$.

Starting from the root of the tree, that is (s_0, s_0^d), for each state such as (s, s_d), we add the following child nodes:

1. (s', s_d), where for some $i \in I$, we have $(s, i, s') \in E$
2. (s, s_d'), where for some $i \in I'$ which is corresponding to a method call that does not contain any nested method calls, we have $(s_d, i, s_d') \in E_d$
3. (s', s_d'), where for some $i \in I'$ that contains a method call denoted by $j \in I$, we have $(s_d, i, s_d') \in E$ and $\mu(s, j) = s'$.

Assuming that $|S| = n$, $|S_d| = m$ and $|S'| = n'$, then the worst-case complexity of computing the spanning tree is $O(n'(m + n))$. The state cover set is computed by traversing the resulting spanning tree.

The family of separating sequences Z' is defined as $\bigcup_{s' \in S}\{z_{s'}'\}$, where for each state $s' = (s, s_d) \in S'$, we have that $z_{s'}' = z_s \cup z_{s_d}$.

For example, the state cover set and the family of separating sequences for the FSM corresponding to the *controller* class in Fig. 4(b) are as follows: $Q_d = \{\varepsilon, GetReq(0), GetReq(1)\}$, $Z_d = \bigcup_{i=0}^{2} (z_{s_i} = \{CheckLsig(), CheckRsig()\})$.

Hence, the state cover set and the family of separating sequences for the FSM resulted adding the class are: $Q' = Q = \{\varepsilon, ResetAvl()\}$, $Z' = \bigcup_{i=0}^{2} (z_{s_i} = \{CheckAvl(), CheckLsig(), CheckRsig()\})$, respectively.

A special case of adding a class is when there are no nested method calls. In such a case the state cover set is equal to the state cover set of the core model that is $Q = Q'$. The computation of separating sequences remains intact with respect to the general case.

Complexity Analysis. The difference of complexity of the delta-oriented testing approach compared to the HSI method, in this case, is in the computation of the family of separating sequences. As explained above, in this case the delta-oriented approach obtains the family of the separating sequences for the new

FSM, just using Z_d and Z. Hence, defining $m = |S_d|$, and $q = |I_d|$, the complexity of computing Z', using the delta-oriented approach, is $O(qm^2) + f_u$, where f_u is the complexity of computing the union of two sets. Assuming that the delta has n' states where $n' \leq m \cdot n$, and $p = |I'|$, the complexity of computing the family of separating sequences, using the HSI method, for this FSM is $O(pn'^2)$. It should be noticed that this computation is done for each product in a product line separately, where the number of the products can increase exponentially in terms of the features. Practically, in a product line we have $m \ll n$, hence $O(qm^2) + f_u \ll O(pn'^2)$. In other word, there can be a substantial gain in calculating the separating sequences using the delta-oriented approach.

7 Empirical Results

In order to check the efficiency of the proposed algorithm, we applied our method to a software system from the health-care domain. In order not to reveal the structure of the commercial system, we dispense with the details that are not necessary for understanding the experimental results. The core logic of this system includes six classes and its main functionality is to detect devices in the surroundings and control users' access to them. Each user can create and complete a set of tasks after accessing a device. We considered the proportion of time required to generate test cases for 4 different models in two cases: using the delta-oriented approach, and using the plain monolithic HSI method (In this work, we only consider the reduction in the test-case-generation time; we leave the study of the test-case-execution time as future work).

In order to compute the test-case generation time, we performed the algorithms in both methods in a step-by-step manner and manually, while counting the basic computation steps in these algorithms. Because these basic steps are common to both methods and consume a constant amount of time, we could hence come up with a precise comparison of the time required for test-case generation.

First, we considered a core FSM with 11 abstract states and 74 transitions. This core model included a set of objects, which model a group of users, devices and tasks created by users. Then, we applied a delta which comprised the addition of a method to a class in order to enable modification of a field in the core model. The result of applying this delta is another FSM with the same number of states and 85 transitions. Using the delta-oriented approach for generating test cases resulted in a 50 % reduction in test-case generation time. This difference is due to that the spanning tree and the family of separating sequences are computed anew in the HSI method, while the delta oriented approach reuses the sequences computed for the core model.

We also applied a delta concerning the addition of an object of a task to the core model which resulted in another FSM with 16 states and 89 transitions. In this case, applying the delta-oriented approach resulted in a 40 % reduction in test-case generation time (For more detailed data, we refer to Fig. 5.).

Subsequently, we considered another core model including 21 abstract states and 167 transitions. We applied a delta comprising the addition of the same

Core Model		After Applying Delta		HSI Test Case	Delta-Oriented Test	Reduction
Num. States	Num. Trans.	Num. States	Num. Trans	Generation Steps	Case Generation Steps	
11	74	11	85	194	388	50
11	74	16	89	253	421	40
21	167	21	188	419	824	50
21	167	37	215	731	1043	30

Fig. 5. Results obtained from test-case generation for the case study

method as above to the core model, which resulted in the same number of states and 188 transitions. Applying the delta-oriented approach results in a 50 % reduction in the test-case generation time.

The last delta in this software product line comprised the addition of an object of a device to the last core model, with 37 states and 215 transitions. The reduction in the test-case generation time in this latter case is 30 %.

The results show that in cases that we can reuse the separating sequences and the state cover set of the core model, such as the addition of a set of methods that do not change the number of states, the delta-oriented approach can be very efficient. The above-mentioned results are summarized in Fig. 5.

8   Conclusions and Future Work

In this paper, we introduced test models and test-case generation methods for delta-oriented FSM-based testing, based on the DeltaJava syntax. Our test-case generation method is a lifting of the incremental test-case generation for the HSI method, using a higher level of abstraction suitable for our DeltaJava-based models. We showed, both using complexity analysis and by application to a case study, that the delta-oriented approach can increase the efficiency of test-case generation.

We are studying realistic, yet more relaxed fault models (than those underlying the HSI method). Such a fault model can capture the possible mutual effects of different behavior in deltas and core. Then, we will identify parts of test cases that need not be re-executed and also independent pieces of behavior that can be reduced, e.g., using partial-order reduction [16]. Moreover, we intend to extend our approach to the full syntax of DeltaJava and in particular, consider modifying and removing methods, building upon the results of [9,11]. Finally, we plan to implement our approach in a programming environment and organize more extensive experiments with our industrial partner.

References

1. Binder, R.: Testing object-oriented systems: models, patterns, and tools. Addison-Wesley, Reading (2000)
2. Broy, M., Jonsson, B., Katoen, J.-P., Leucker, M., Pretschner, A. (eds.): Model-Based Testing of Reactive Systems. LNCS, vol. 3472. Springer, Heidelberg (2005)

3. El-Fakih, K., Yevtushenko, N., von Bochmann, G.: FSM-based incremental conformance testing methods. IEEE TSE **30**(7), 425–436 (2004)
4. Engström, E., Runeson, P.: Software product line testing - a systematic mapping study. Inf. Softw. Technol. **53**(1), 2–13 (2011)
5. Hong, H.S., Kwon, Y.R., Cha, S.D.: Testing of object-oriented programs based on finite state machines. In: Proceedings of APSEC 1995, pp. 234–241. IEEE CS (1995)
6. Jääskeläinen, A.: Filtering test models to support incremental testing. In: Bottaci, L., Fraser, G. (eds.) TAIC PART 2010. LNCS, vol. 6303, pp. 72–87. Springer, Heidelberg (2010)
7. Lee, D., Yannakakis, M.: Principles and methods of testing finite state machines-a survey. Proc. IEEE **84**(8), 1090–1123 (1996)
8. Lochau, M., Schaefer, I., Kamischke, J., Lity, S.: Incremental model-based testing of delta-oriented software product lines. In: Brucker, A.D., Julliand, J. (eds.) TAP 2012. LNCS, vol. 7305, pp. 67–82. Springer, Heidelberg (2012)
9. Németh, G.A., Pap, Z.: The incremental maintenance of transition tour. Fund. Inf. **129**, 279–300 (2014)
10. Oster, S., Wübbeke, A., Engels, G., Schürr, A.: Model-based software product lines testing survey. In: Model-based Testing for Embedded Systems, pp. 339–381. CRC Press (2011)
11. Pap, Z., Subramaniam, M., Kovács, G., Németh, G.A.: A bounded incremental test generation algorithm for finite state machines. In: Petrenko, A., Veanes, M., Tretmans, J., Grieskamp, W. (eds.) TestCom/FATES 2007. LNCS, vol. 4581, pp. 244–259. Springer, Heidelberg (2007)
12. Rumpe, B.: Model-based testing of object-oriented systems. In: de Boer, F.S., Bonsangue, M.M., Graf, S., de Roever, W.-P. (eds.) FMCO 2002. LNCS, vol. 2852, pp. 380–402. Springer, Heidelberg (2003)
13. Sabnani, K., Dahbura, A.: A protocol test generation procedure. Comput. Netw. ISDN Syst. **15**(4), 285–297 (1988)
14. Schaefer, I., Bettini, L., Bono, V., Damiani, F., Tanzarella, N.: Delta-oriented programming of software product lines. In: Bosch, J., Lee, J. (eds.) SPLC 2010. LNCS, vol. 6287, pp. 77–91. Springer, Heidelberg (2010)
15. Simão, A., Petrenko, A.: Fault coverage-driven incremental test generation. Comput. J. **53**, 1508–1522 (2010)
16. Tasharofi, S., Karmani, R.K., Lauterburg, S., Legay, A., Marinov, D., Agha, G.: TransDPOR: a novel dynamic partial-order reduction technique for testing actor programs. In: Giese, H., Rosu, G. (eds.) FORTE 2012 and FMOODS 2012. LNCS, vol. 7273, pp. 219–234. Springer, Heidelberg (2012)
17. Thüm, T., Apel, S., Kästner, C., Kuhlemann, M., Schaefer, I., Saake, G.: Analysis strategies for software product lines. Technical report FIN-004-2012, School of Computer Science, University of Magdeburg (2012)
18. Utting, M., Legeard, B.: Practical Model-Based Testing: A Tools Approach. Morgan Kaufmann, San Francisco (2010)
19. Grieskamp, W., Gurevich, Y., Schulte, W., Veanes, M.: Generating finite state machines from abstract state machines. In: Proceedings of the 2002 ACM SIGSOFT International Symposium on Software Testing and Analysis (ISSTA 2002), pp. 112–122. ACM (2002)

An Improved HHL Prover: An Interactive Theorem Prover for Hybrid Systems

Shuling Wang(✉), Naijun Zhan, and Liang Zou

State Key Laboratory of Computer Science,
Institute of Software, Chinese Academy of Sciences, Beijing, China
wangsl@ios.ac.cn

Abstract. Hybrid systems are integrations of discrete computation and continuous physical evolution. To guarantee the correctness of hybrid systems, formal techniques on modelling and verification of hybrid systems have been proposed. Hybrid CSP (HCSP) is an extension of CSP with differential equations and some forms of interruptions for modelling hybrid systems, and Hybrid Hoare logic (HHL) is an extension of Hoare logic for specifying and verifying hybrid systems that are modelled using HCSP. In this paper, we report an improved *HHL prover*, which is an interactive theorem prover based on Isabelle/HOL for verifying HCSP models. Compared with the prototypical release in [22], the new HHL prover realises the proof system of HHL as a shallow embedding in Isabelle/HOL, rather than deep embedding in [22]. In order to contrast the new HHL prover in shallow embedding and the old one in deep embedding, we demonstrate the use of both variants on the safety verification of a lunar lander case study.

1 Introduction

Hybrid systems are fusions of discrete dynamic systems and continuous dynamic systems, many of which are safety-critical, e.g., transportation, healthcare, spacecrafts, *etc.* In order to ensure the correct functioning of hybrid systems, formal techniques on modelling and verification have been proposed. Among them, the most popular model is hybrid automata [2,10], with the subsequent temporal logic based specification languages and model checkers [1,8,13]. However, due to the undecidable reachability problem of hybrid systems, various abstractions or (numeric) approximations for hybrid automata are required [3,4]. This leads to incomplete coverage of the system dynamics or loss of precision of proof results.

Alternatively, the deductive approach has been proposed, which verifies systems by proofs rather than state space exploration in model checking. This approach asks for a formal modelling language with (de-)compositionality and meanwhile a specification logic for verifying the corresponding models. Following this research line, we extended Hoare Logic to hybrid systems and established Hybrid Hoare Logic (HHL) [11]. In HHL, a hybrid system is modeled by Hybrid CSP (HCSP) process. HCSP is a formal modeling language for hybrid systems,

© Springer International Publishing Switzerland 2015
M. Butler et al. (Eds.): ICFEM 2015, LNCS 9407, pp. 382–399, 2015.
DOI: 10.1007/978-3-319-25423-4_25

due to He, Zhou *et al.* [9,21], which is an extension of CSP by introducing differential equations for representing continuous evolution. HCSP inherits from CSP the compositional process algebra constructs including communication-based synchronization and concurrency, thus it is expressive enough for describing distributed components and the interactions between them. Moreover, it extends CSP with several forms of interrupts to continuous evolution for realizing communication-based discrete control. To capture both discrete and continuous behavior of HCSP, the assertion languages of HHL include two parts: one is first-order logic (FOL), used for specifying properties of discrete processes, and the other is a subset of Duration Calculus (DC) [19,20], called history formulas, for specifying the execution history for continuous processes. A proof system for HHL was provided in [11]. In particular, the notion of differential invariant [12,14] is used to characterize the behavior of differential equations.

In [22], a prototypical implementation for HHL verification framework in proof assistant Isabelle/HOL, called *HHL prover*, was reported. In the HHL prover of [22], HHL was realised in a deep embedding style, i.e., the assertion languages of HHL including FOL and DC are defined as new datatypes of Isabelle/HOL. Since then, the HHL prover has been successfully applied to the verification of some real-world hybrid systems, e.g., Chinese train control systems [23,24] and the GNC control program of a lunar lander [18].

The disadvantage of the prototypical HHL prover is very obvious: due to the deep embedding of the HHL assertions, the proof of FOL and DC formulas needs to be conducted by the user completely, to apply the deductive rules for FOL and DC manually, thus the proof effort is very high. The main contribution of this paper is to implement the proof system for HHL in shadow embedding [1]. In addition, to demonstrate the efficiency of the improved HHL prover, we apply the prover in both embeddings to the safety verification of the slow descent guidance control program of a lunar lander, which is a closed-loop dynamic system composed of a physical plant and an embedded control program. We make a comparison between the proof results obtained from both embeddings, which indicates that the shallow embedding has better performance than the deep embedding.

Related Work. There are some tools on formal modelling and verification of hybrid systems. The tool d/dt [5] provides reachability analysis and safety verification of hybrid systems with linear continuous dynamics and uncertain bounded input. iSAT-ODE [7] is a numerical SMT solver based on interval arithmetic that can conduct bounded model checking for hybrid systems. Flow* [6] computes over-approximations of the reachable sets of continuous dynamical and hybrid systems in a bounded time. However, due to the undecidable reachability problem of hybrid systems, the above tools based on model checking are incomplete. Based on the alternative deductive approach, the theorem prover KeYmaera [15] is proposed to verify hybrid systems specified using differential dynamic logic.

---

[1] The HHL prover in both embeddings, plus the corresponding models and proofs related to the case study, can be found at https://github.com/wangslyl/hhlprover.

Compared to our work, it supports a simple set of hybrid constructs that do not cover communications and parallel composition.

Organization. The rest of the paper is organized as follows: Sects. 2 and 3 introduce briefly the proof assistant Isabelle/HOL, and the modelling language HCSP and its specification logic HHL, respectively; Sects. 4 and 5 present the HHL prover in shallow and deep embeddings respectively; Sect. 6 presents the lunar lander case study; and Sect. 7 concludes the paper.

2   Isabelle/HOL

In this section, we give a brief introduction of Isabelle/HOL, based on which the modelling and verification framework of hybrid systems is mechanized. Isabelle/HOL is a proof assistant for Higher-Order Logic (HOL). It supports functional modeling of systems by providing datatypes, functions, terms and formulas; and meanwhile, it enables proof of properties by construction by providing a set of built-in inference rules and proof tactics. Except for basic types such as *bool*, nat, etc., Isabelle/HOL provides the way to define a recursive datatype, for instance, a list of elements of type 'a can be defined by 'a list:

datatype 'a list = Nil | Cons 'a 'a list

where Nil, referring to the empty list, and Cons, adding an element to the front of a list, are the two constructors respectively. A type can also be constructed from existing ones by using types, e.g. types nlist = nat list. With the existence of types, functions are used to describe the relations between values of different types. A recursive function can be defined with respect to the constructors for the involved datatypes, e.g., the function len returns the length of a list:

primrec len :: 'a list $\Rightarrow$ nat **where**
len Nil = 0 |
len Cons x xs = 1 + len xs

Non-recursive functions can be defined with the **definition** command, and more general cases for both recursive and non-recursive functions can be defined by means of **fun**. By applying functions to arguments, terms are formed, and in particular, a special class of terms with type *bool* are formulas. The compound formulas can be formed by applying logical connectives, such as $\land$, $\neg$, $\forall$, *etc.*

Isabelle can prove facts directly based on induction and simplications. Besides, it supports more complicated verification by applying HOL inference rules for classical reasoning, e.g. the introduction or elimination rules for conjunction $\land$ or disjunction $\lor$, *etc.* It provides a set of methods to automate classical reasoning, such as blast, auto, arith and so on. Isabelle also includes some high-level proof tactics. In particular, the tool sledgehammer is a certified integration of third-party automated theorem provers and SMT solvers including Alt-Ergo, Z3, CVC3, and so on, and nitpick is a counterexample generator. For HHL prover in shallow embedding, all the proof obligations are reduced to HOL formulas at the end, for which sledgehammer can be used to search the proofs automatically.

3   Hybrid CSP

This section will give a brief introduction of Hybrid CSP (HCSP) and the specification logic Hybrid Hoare Logic for reasoning about HCSP processes. They constitute the theoretical basis on the modelling language and the safety logic of HHL prover.

3.1   Syntax

Hybrid CSP [9,21] is an extension of CSP by introducing differential equations for representing continuous evolution and several forms of interruptions to continuous evolution. The syntax of a subset of HCSP is given as follows:

$$P ::= \text{skip} \mid x := e \mid ch?x \mid ch!e \mid P; Q \mid B \to P \mid P \sqcup Q \mid P^*$$
$$\mid \langle \dot{s} = e\&B \rangle \mid \langle \dot{s} = e\&B \rangle \trianglerighteq []_{i \in I}(io_i \to Q_i)$$
$$S ::= P \mid S\|S$$

where P, Q, Q_i, S are HCSP processes, x and s stand for process variables, ch for channel name, io_i for a communication event (either input $ch?x$ or output $ch!e$), B and e for Boolean and arithmetic expressions, and I for a non-empty set of indices of communications, respectively. A whole HCSP model S is defined as a sequential process or a parallel composition of several sequential processes at the top level.

The intuitive meaning of the individual constructs is explained as follows:

- skip, $x := e$ are defined as usual.
- The input $ch?x$ receives a value along channel ch and assigns it to x, and output $ch!e$ sends the value of e along ch. A communication takes place as soon as both the sending party (i.e. $ch!$) and the receiving party (i.e. $ch?$) are ready, and may cause one side to wait.
- The sequential composition $P; Q$ behaves as P first, and if it terminates, as Q afterwards.
- The conditional $B \to P$ behaves as P if B is true, otherwise it terminates immediately.
- The internal choice $P \sqcup Q$ behaves as either P or Q, and the non-deterministic choice is made by the system itself.
- The repetition P^* executes P for some finite number of times.
- $\langle \dot{s} = e\&B \rangle$ is the continuous evolution statement, where s represents a vector of real variables and $\dot{s}$ the first-order derivative of s. It forces s to evolve continuously according to the differential equation $\dot{s} = e$ as long as B, which defines the *domain of* s, holds, and terminates when B turns false. $\langle \dot{s} = e\&B \rangle$ is a boundary interruption.
- The communication interruption $\langle \dot{s} = e\&B \rangle \trianglerighteq []_{i \in I}(io_i \to Q_i)$ behaves like the continuous $\langle \dot{s} = e\&B \rangle$, except that it is preempted as soon as one of the communications io_i takes place, and then is followed by the respective Q_i.
- $S_1\|S_2$ behaves as if S_1 and S_2 run independently except that all communications along the common channels connecting S_1 and S_2 are to be synchronized. S_1 and S_2 in parallel can neither share variables, nor input or output channels.

Some commonly used constructs of HCSP in [9, 21] are derivable from the above syntax, e.g.,

$$\mathbf{wait}\ d \qquad \hat{=}\ t := 0; \langle \dot{t} = 1 \& t < d \rangle$$
$$\langle \dot{s} = e \& B \rangle \trianglerighteq_d Q \ \hat{=}\ t := 0; \langle \dot{s} = e \wedge \dot{t} = 1 \& t < d \wedge B \rangle; t \geq d \rightarrow Q$$

Especially the timeout $\langle \dot{s} = e \& B \rangle \trianglerighteq_d Q$ executes according to the continuous evolution $\langle \dot{s} = e \& B \rangle$ for the first d time units, and Q afterwards.

Example 1. The following presents a simple HCSP description of a continuously evolving plant with discrete control:

$$\langle \dot{x} = f(x, u) \rangle \trianglerighteq sensor!x \rightarrow actuator?u)^* \| (\mathbf{wait}\ d; sensor?s; actuator!\ Comp(s))^*$$

The plant evolves according to the dynamics $\dot{x} = f(x, u)$ that depends on a control parameter u. Every d time units, the controller samples the state of the plant x via channel *sensor*, and computes the new control parameter by *Comp*, and sends it back to the plant for the next cycle via channel *actuator*.

3.2   Operational Semantics

Let *Real* be the set of reals. A state, ranging over σ, σ', is a function that assigns a value to each variable. For simplicity, given a state σ and an expression e, we also use $\sigma(e)$ to return the value of e under σ. A flow, ranging over h, h', is a function that assigns a state to each real time point in *Real*. Each transition relation has the form $(P, now, h) \xrightarrow{a} (P', now', h')$, where P, P' are processes, a is an event, now, now' are real time, and h, h' are flows, respectively. It represents that, starting from the initial time now with the initial flow h (notice that the initial state is exactly $h(now)$), P performs event a and evolves to P' at time now' with the flow h'. The events a here can be a discrete internal event, like skip, assignment, evaluation of Boolean conditions, *etc.*, or a communication event, or a time delay. For the sake of embedding in HHL prover, we define the flows h, h' to be total on the whole real domain. For the above transition, by confining flow h' on the interval $[now, now']$, we can obtain the execution history from P to P'.

For page limit, we only present the semantics of continuous evolution here.[2] Given an initial flow h and initial time now, assume $S(t)$ is a solution of $\dot{s} = e$ defined over $[0, d]$ for some duration $d > 0$, satisfying that $S(0) = h(now)(s)$. We define flow $h\langle now, d, S \rangle$ same to h except that for all $t \in (now, now + d]$, $h\langle now, d, S \rangle(t) = h(t)[s \rightarrow S(t - now)]$, i.e., the value of s is overriden by the solution $S(t)$ over the execution interval $(now, now + d]$. The semantics of continuous evolution is then defined by the following rules:

---

[2] The full version of both the operational semantics of HCSP and the specification logic HHL to be introduced next can be found at [17].

$$\frac{\forall t \in [0, d).h\langle now, d, S\rangle(now + t)(B) = true}{(\langle \dot{s} = e\&B\rangle, now, h) \xrightarrow{d} (\langle \dot{s} = e\&B\rangle, now + d, h\langle now, d, S\rangle)}$$

$$\frac{h(now)(B) = false \text{ or}}{(h(now)(B) = true \land \forall t \in (0, d).h\langle now, d, S\rangle(now + t)(B) = false)}{(\langle \dot{s} = e\&B\rangle, now, h) \xrightarrow{\tau} (skip, now, h)}$$

The first rule indicates that, it evolves for d time units according to $\dot{s} = e$ if B evaluates to true within period $[now, now + d)$ (the right end exclusive). Otherwise, indicated by the second rule, the continuous evolution terminates at now if B evaluates to false at now, or if B evaluates to false at a positive open interval right to now (depending on whether B is open or close).

The transition closure $(P_0, now_0, h_0) \xrightarrow{a_1 \cdots a_k} (P_k, now_k, h_k)$ for some $k > 0$ is defined, iff there exists a sequence of transitions

$$(P_0, now_0, h_0) \xrightarrow{a_1} (P_1, now_1, h_1), \cdots, (P_{k-1}, now_{k-1}, h_{k-1}) \xrightarrow{a_k} (P_k, now_k, h_k)$$

When $P_k = skip$, we call the sequence of the transitions a *complete execution* of P_0, and for simplicity write it as $(P_0, now_0, h_0) \rightsquigarrow (now_k, h_k)$ by omitting the labels and the terminating process *skip*.

3.3   Hybrid Hoare Logic

In order to verify HCSP, Hybrid Hoare Logic (HHL) [11] is defined. As an extension of Hoare logic to hybrid systems, it considers both discrete and continuous properties, that correspond to an isolated time point and a time interval resp.

History Formulas. In order to describe the interval-related properties, we introduce history formulas, that are defined by duration calculus (DC) [19,20]. DC is a first-order interval-based real-time logic with one binary modality known as chop $\frown$, but is extended with a special structure of temporal variable, i.e. state durations. We define history formulas HF by the following subset of DC:

$$HF ::= \ell \circ T \mid \lceil S \rceil \mid HF_1 \frown HF_2 \mid \neg HF \mid HF_1 \lor HF_2$$

where ℓ is a temporal variable denoting the length of the considered interval, $\circ \in \{<, =\}$ is a relation, T a non-negative real, and S a first-order state formula over process variables. HF can be interpreted over flows and intervals. Let the judgement $h, [a, b] \models HF$ represent that HF holds under h and $[a, b]$, then we have

$$h, [a, b] \models \ell \circ T \text{ iff } (b - a) \circ T \qquad h, [a, b] \models \lceil S \rceil \text{ iff } b > a \land \int_a^b h(t)(S) = b - a$$
$$h, [a, b] \models HF_1 \frown HF_2 \text{ iff } \exists c.a \leq c \leq b \land h, [a, c] \models HF_1 \land h, [c, b] \models HF_2$$

As defined above, ℓ indicates the length of the considered interval. $\lceil S \rceil$ asserts that the duration of state S on interval $[a, b]$ is $b - a$, i.e. S holds almost everywhere in the considered non-point interval. Thus, based on $\lceil S \rceil$, an invariant property related to an interval can be specified. Later, we will write $\lceil S \rceil^<$ as an abbreviation for $\lceil S \rceil \vee \ell = 0$ to include the point case. Lastly, $HF_1 \frown HF_2$ asserts that the interval can be divided into two sub-intervals such that HF_1 holds for the first and HF_2 for the second. The first-order connectives $\neg$ and $\vee$ can be explained as usual.

Specification and Inference Rules. The specification for a sequential HCSP process P takes the form $\{Pre\}P\{Post; HF\}$, where the pre-/post-condition Pre and $Post$, defined by first-order logic (FOL), specify properties of variables that hold at the beginning and termination of the execution of P respectively, and the history formula HF, specifies properties of variables that hold throughout the execution interval of P. The effect of discrete processes will be specified by the pre-/post-conditions, but not recorded in the history. The specification for a parallel process $P_1 \| P_2$ is then defined by assigning to each sequential component of it the respective pre-/post-conditions and the history formula, shown as below:

$$\{Pre_1, Pre_2\}P_1 \| P_2\{Post_1, Post_2; HF_1, HF_2\}$$

In HHL, HCSP constructs are axiomatized by a set of axioms and inference rules, which constitutes a basis for implementing the verification condition generator for verifying HCSP specifications in HHL prover. We will give a more detailed explanation of HHL in next section.

4   HHL Prover: Shallow Embedding

HHL prover aims to verify whether a HCSP process conforms to a HHL specification in a machine-checkable way. The implementation of HHL prover requires to embed the whole HHL verification framework in Isabelle/HOL. There are two different ways for the embedding: shallow or deep. The shallow embedding defines the assertions of HHL (i.e. FOL and DC formulas) by HOL predicates on process states or flows, while in deep embedding, it defines the assertions as new datatypes. In this section, we will present HHL prover in shallow embedding in detail, and in next section the prover in deep embedding.

4.1   HCSP

In both embeddings, we start from encoding the bottom construct, i.e. expressions, that are represented as a datatype $\texttt{exp}$[3]:

> **datatype** exp = Con Val | RVar *string* | SVar *string* | BVar *string*
> | exp [+] exp | exp [−] exp | exp [*] exp | exp [/] exp

An expression can be a constant `Con v`, where `v` is of type `Val` for representing constants, e.g. `Con Real n`; a variable, that can be `RVar x`, `SVar x` and `BVar x`

---

[3] To distinguish from HOL, we wrap the arithmetic operators and FOL connectives with [], and DC connectives with [[]] outside. For example, $\wedge, [\wedge], [[\wedge]]$ are HOL, FOL and DC conjunctions respectively.

for real, string, and boolean variables, respectively; an arithmetic expression constructed from arithmetic operators.

Based on exp, we represent HCSP processes by a datatype proc. Each construct of HCSP defined in Sect. 3 is encoded as a corresponding constructor in datatype proc. For examples, $B \to P$ is encoded as IF B P; the continuous evolution $\langle \dot{s} = e \& B \rangle$ is encoded as <s:e&&Inv&b>, with the addition of the differential invariant Inv of the differential equation $\dot{s} = e$ for the purpose of verification; for the same reason, the repetition P^* is encoded as P*&&Inv, where the loop invariant Inv is annotated. The invariants are unknown beforehand and will be solved in the proof process by calling an external invariant generator from HHL prover.

To encode the semantics of HCSP, we first define two types, state and flow, to model states and flows respectively. Then, given a process P of type proc, time now, now' of type *real*, and h, h' of typeflow, the inductive function semB P now h now' h' returns true iff $(P, now, h) \rightsquigarrow (now', h')$ is a complete execution of P.

4.2   Assertion Languages

Two types of assertion logics are used in defining the specifications of HHL: FOL and DC. The FOL formulas are defined as predicates on states,

type_synonym fform = state $\Rightarrow bool$

We can then write arbitrary Isabelle functions from state to *bool* to describe states. Especially, the FOL constructs can be derived as syntax flavours, like,

definition [True] :: fform **where**
[True] $\equiv \lambda$ s. True
definition fImp :: fform $\Rightarrow$ fform $\Rightarrow$ fform (**infixl** "[$\to$]" 65) **where**
p [$\to$] q $\equiv \lambda$ s. p s $\to$ q s

The DC formulas are represented as predicates on flows and intervals,

type_synonym dform = flow $\Rightarrow real \Rightarrow real \Rightarrow bool$

The history formulas presented in Sect. 3 can be defined correspondingly,

definition elE :: *real* $\Rightarrow$ dform **where**
elE T $\equiv \lambda$ h n m. (m−n) = T
definition almost :: fform $\Rightarrow$ dform **where**
almost p $\equiv \lambda$ h n m. (m>n) $\land$ ($\forall$a≥n. $\forall$ b≤m. a < b $\to$ ($\exists$t. t>a $\land$ t<b $\land$ p(h(t))))
definition chop :: dform $\Rightarrow$ dform $\Rightarrow$ dform ("_[^]_" 80) **where**
H [^] M $\equiv \lambda$ h n m. ($\exists$ nm. (nm $\geq$ n $\land$ nm $\leq$ m $\land$ H h n nm $\land$ M h nm m))
definition dAnd :: dform $\Rightarrow$ dform $\Rightarrow$ dform ("[[&]]" 79) **where**
P [[&]] Q $\equiv \lambda$ h n m. P h n m $\land$ Q h n m

elE T implements $\ell = T$; almost p implements $[p]$, i.e. the duration of p is $m - n$ under flow h and interval $[n, m]$ satisfying $m > n$, iff for any positive open interval inside $[n, m]$, there always exists a point in it such that P is held; H [^] M implements $H^\frown M$.

As a consequence, the formulas can be interpreted directly, (s |= p) ≡ p s, and (h, [n, m] |= H) ≡ H h n m. Moreover, the proof of FOL and DC formulas is reduced to the proof of HOL formulas, which is supported by the built-in proof tactics of Isabelle/HOL. We have proved some of the lemmas for DC stated in [19] in Isabelle/HOL, e.g.,

$$True \Leftrightarrow \ell \geq 0 \quad \lceil S \rceil \frown \lceil S \rceil \Leftrightarrow \lceil S \rceil \quad HF \frown \ell = 0 \Leftrightarrow HF$$
$$\lceil S_1 \rceil \Rightarrow \lceil S_2 \rceil \text{ if } S_1 \Rightarrow S_2 \text{ is valid in FOL}$$

4.3 Specification and Inference Rules

With the definitions of HCSP and the assertion languages, we implement a function ValidS to represent a valid specification,

definition ValidS :: fform ⇒ proc ⇒ fform ⇒ dform ⇒ *bool* ("{ _}-{-; _}")
where ValidS p c q H ≡ ∀ now h now' h' .semB c now h now' h'→ h(now) |= p
        → (h'(now') |= q ∧ h', [now, now'] |= H)

stating that, {p} c {q;H} is valid, iff starting from flow h and time now, if c terminates with flow h' and time now', then the precondition p holds under h and now implies the postcondition q and the history formula H hold under h' and now'. Below we list some of the lemmas that correspond to the valid inference rules of HHL.

Assignment. Lemma AssignRRule presents the rule for assignment to a real variable, which indicates that {p} (RVar x := f) {q; H} holds, if p implies the weakest precondition substF ([(RVar x, f)], q) and H is implied by the strongest history formula elE 0.

lemma AssignRRule: (∀ s. (p [→]substF ([(RVar x, f)], q)) s) ∧
    (∀ h now now'. (elE 0 [[→]] H) h now now')
        ⇒ {p} RVar x := f {q; H}

Here substF ([(RVar x, f)], q) is defined in the semantic level, i.e. after substituting f for RVar x, q holds,

    substF ([(RVar x, f)], q) ≡ λ s. q (λv. **if** v=(x, R) **then** evalE f s **else** s v))

in which evalE f s returns the value of f under state s.

Continuous Evolution. Lemma ContinuousRule states the rule for continuous evolutio. Function cl(·) extends the domain defined by the corresponding formula to include the boundary, e.g. cl $(x > 2) = x \geq 2$.

lemma ContinuousRule :∀ s.((p [→] Inv) [∧]
        (exeFlow <v:E&&Inv&b> Inv [→] Inv) [∧] (Inv [∧] cl([¬]b) [→] q)) s
    ⇒ ∀ h now now'. ((elE 0[[∨]] almost (Inv [&] b)) [[→]] H) h now now'
    ⇒ {p} <v:E&&Inv&b> {q; H}

Consider the hypothesis, the FOL formula in the first two lines indicates that Inv is indeed a sufficiently strong invariant, i.e. it is satisfied by the initial state, preserved by the execution of the continuous evolution, and strong enough to guarantee the postcondition; the DC formula in the third line indicates that the evolution terminates immediately (specified by elE 0), or otherwise, if the evolution takes more than zero time, then the invariant Inv and the domain b hold almost everywhere throughout the whole execution. The lemma is proved valid, as a consequence, the proof of the specification for the continuous evolution is reduced to an equivalent differential invariant generation problem: if the Inv exists such that it satisfies the conditions in the hypothesis, then the original specification is proved. HHL prover will call an external invariant generator to solve the invariant generation problem.

Sequential Composition. As shown by Lemma SequentialRule, the postcondition of P; Q (i.e. q) is equivalent to the one of Q, and the history formula (i.e. M) is implied by the concatenation of the ones of P and Q. By recursively applying the inference rules of HHL, the two sub-specifications corresponding to P and Q can be transformed eventually to logical formulas. Notice that the intermediate formulas consisting of the postcondition of P (i.e. w), the history formula of P (i.e. H), and the hisotry formula of Q (i.e. G), are not contained in the final specification for P; Q. As a result, we need to instantiate these formulas when applying this rule in the proof process.

lemma SequentialRule : {p} P {w; H} $\Rightarrow${w} Q {q; G} $\Rightarrow$
   $\forall$ h m n. (H [^] G [[$\rightarrow$]] M) h m n $\Rightarrow${p} P; Q {q; M}

Communication and Parallel Composition. HHL [11] is not compositional with respect to parallel composition, due to the communications between processes and the complex interactions between discrete computation and continuous evolution. The HHL classifies parallel composition into three cases, which are specified by the following three rules respectively.

lemma Parallel1Rule : chanset P = {} $\wedge$ chanset Q = {} $\Rightarrow${pp} P {qp; Hp}
   $\Rightarrow$ {pq} Q {qq; Hq} $\Rightarrow${pp, pq} P||Q {qp, qq; Ⅱp, Hq}

Lemma Parallel1Rule says that, when there is no communication event in both P and Q, the specification of P||Q can be copied from the ones of P and Q accordingly.

lemma CommunicationRule : {px, py} (P || Q) {qx, qy; Hx, Hy}
   $\Rightarrow$ $\forall$ s. ((qx [$\rightarrow$] substF ([(RVar x, e)], rx)) [$\wedge$] (qy [$\rightarrow$] ry)) s
   $\Rightarrow$ $\forall$ h n m. ((Hx[^](elE 0 [[||]] almost qx) [[$\rightarrow$]] Gx)
   [[$\wedge$]] (Hy[^](elE 0 [[||]]almost qy) [[$\rightarrow$]] Gy)) h n m
$\Rightarrow${px, py} P;Cm (ch??RVar x)||Q; Cm (ch!!e) {rx, ry; Gx, Gy}

where Cm ch??RVar x and Cm ch!!e implement $ch?x$ and $ch!e$ in HCSP respectively. Lemma CommunicationRule defines the case when a communication follows, no matter whether P or Q contains communication events or not. For such case, we need to synchronize the execution time till the occurrence of ch??RVar x and ch!!e. For example, indicated by line 3, if P terminates before Q, then the input event needs to wait till Q terminates, and during the waiting time, the postcondition of P, i.e. qˣ, always holds. Notice that elE 0 is included for the case when P and Q terminate simultaneously. As soon as both parties of the communication are ready, the communication completes like an assignment assigning e to real variable RVar x (indicated by line 2).

lemma Parallel2Rule : {pp, pq} P||Q {qp, qq; Hp, Hq} ⇒
    chanset P ≠ {} ∧ chanset Q ≠ {} ∧ chanset U = {} ∧ chanset V = {}
        ⇒ {qp} U {qu; Hu} ⇒{qq} V {qv; Hv}
        ⇒ {pp, pq} P; U||Q; V {qu, qv; Hp [ˆ] Hu, Hq [ˆ] Hv}

Lemma **Parallel2Rule** defines the remaining case when processes containing no communication event follow, provided that P and Q contain communications (the contrary case when P and Q do not contain communications can be reduced to the first rule). Indicated by this rule, the parallel composition is equal to executing U and V immediately from the terminating states of P and Q respectively.

Repetition. As shown by Lemma **RepetitionRule**, Inv is a loop invariant for P*: the precondition P implies Inv, Inv gurantees the postcondition q, and Inv is preserved by one round execution of P (line 1); and H is idempotent with respect to chop (line 2). The final specification for P* is reduced to an invariant generation problem, similar to continuous evolution.

lemma RepetitionRule: ∀ s. ((p [→] Inv) [∧] (Inv [→] q)) s ⇒{Inv} P {Inv; H}
        ⇒ ∀h n m. (H[ˆ]H [[→]] H) h n m ⇒{p} P*&&Inv {q; H}

The general rules that are applicable for all HCSP constructs, like the consequene rule, the case analysis rule, and so on, can be defined as in traditional Hoare Logic. Here we will not list them all.

At the end, all the lemmas corresponding to the inference rules of HHL together constitute a verification condition generator of HHL prover for proving HCSP specifications. The proof is performed according to the following process: first, by applying the lemmas of HHL, a HCSP specification is transformed step by step to a set of HOL formulas, i.e. *verification conditions*; and then, by applying proof tactics and rules of HOL, the validity of verification conditions, that is equivalent to the correctness of the original HCSP specification, is proved.

However, when the specification to be proved contains unknown differential invariants or loop invariants, some verification conditions related to the invariants cannot be proved using HOL rules. In order to solve invariant-related constraints, we have implemented an invariant generator based on the techniques proposed in [12]. By defining an oracle inv_oracle in Isabelle/HOL to call the external invariant generator, HHL prover is able to prove the remaining invariant-related verification conditions. By now, the modelling and verification in HHL prover is completed.

5   HHL Prover: Deep Embedding

Different from the shallow embedding, the deep embedding defines the DC and FOL formulas by new datatypes and the meanings of them by the corresponding deductive rules. We present HHL prover in the deep embedding next.

5.1   Assertion Languages

FOL. The deep embedding of FOL includes the definitions of the syntax and the deductive system. FOL formulas are constructed from expressions by using relational operators for atomic cases, and inductively from sub-formulas by using logical connectives for the compound cases. In syntax, the formulas can be represented by the following datatype `fform`:

datatype fform = [False] | exp [=] exp | exp [<] exp
                | [¬] fform | fform [∨] fform | [∀] *string* fform

The other logical connectives including [∧], [→], and [∃] can be derived as traditional. As seen from type `exp`, a string may correspond to three different variables, depending on the actual type construct (that can be `RVar`, `SVar`, or `BVar`). For quantified formula [∀]*string* `fform`, we assume by default that the name represented by a string s corresponds to the real variable occurring in `fform`, i.e. `RVar s`. Thus, we only consider the quantification over *real* variables here, but this restriction can be loosen by considering quantified variables of the other two types (i.e. *string* and *bool*) without any essential difficulty.

The semantics of FOL formulas is defined by induction on the constructs. Given a state s and a formula P of type `fform`, function `evalF(s, p)` is defined to return the truth value of P under state s. We then have s |= p iff `evalF (s, p)`.

We define the deductive system for `fform` in sequent calculus style. The Isabelle library includes the pre-defined theory `LK0` for a sequent calculus system of classical FOL with equation. For instances, the following two axioms define the introduction/elimination rules for conjunction in sequent calculus style:

conjR: [| $H⊢ $E, P, $F; $H⊢ $E, Q, $ |] ⇒$H⊢ $E, P [&] Q, $F
conjL: $H, P, Q, $G ⊢$E ⇒$H, P [&] Q, $G ⊢$E

where we represent a sequence of FOL formulas by putting a $ symbol before a capital letter, e.g. $H. We define the sequent calculus for `fform` (denoted by `DLK0`) based on `LK0` directly, but `LK0` is not complete because it does not include the rules for the arithmetic formulas for reals in `fform`, e.g. the arithmetic laws. In order to solve this problem, we combine deep embedding of defining explicit formulas in syntax and shallow embedding of applying the arithmetic proof tactics of Isabelle. The main step is to define an equivalent conversion between the validity of formulas of `fform` and HOL formulas, `formT (f :,: fform)`⇔⊢f, where the recursive function `formT` transforms a formula of type `fform` to a corresponding HOL formula. For instance, to prove the commutative law of [*], we first apply `formT` to the corresponding formula,

formT (RVar x [*] Rvar y [=] RVar y [*] Rvar x)
= (rvar (x) * rvar (y) = rvar (y) * rvar (x))

where **rvar** is a constant function that maps a real variable expression to a real value. The HOL formula obtained after the conversion can be proved automatically by applying **auto** directly.

As shown above, when we prove a **fform** formula involving arithmetic, we will convert it equivalently to a HOL formula and then prove the HOL formula instead. However, to prove a **fform** formula without arithmetic occurring in it, two options are provided to users: applying FOL rules defined in **DLKO**, or converting the formula to HOL and applying HOL rules.

DC. To embed DC in deep style, we first define a datatype **dexp** to represent temporal expressions:

datatype dexp = ℓ | DR *real* | dexp [[+]] dexp | dexp [[−]] dexp | dexp [[*]] dexp

dexp defines expressions that are interval-dependent, including the only temporal variable ℓ for representing the length of the considered interval, real constants, and arithmetic expressions. Then the datatype **dform** encodes the history formulas *HF*:

datatype dform = [[True]] | dexp[[=]]dexp | dexp[[<]]dexp
  | almost fform | dform[^]dform [[¬]]dform | dform[[∨]]dform

The semantics of the history formulas is defined by induction on the constructs. Given a flow **f**, a timed interval **[c, d]**, and a temporal expression **te**, function **ievalE(f, te, c, d)** is defined to evaluate **te** under flow **f** and interval **[c, d]**; and based on this function, given a history formula **H**, function **ievalF(f, H, c, d)** is defined to return the truth value of **H** under flow **f** and interval **[c, d]**. Below show some examples:

ievalE(f, ℓ, c, d) = d−c
ievalF (f, almost S, c, d) = (c<d ∧ ∀ i, j. c≤ i < j ≤ d →
    ∃t. i < t < j → evalF (f(t), S))
ievalF (f, H1[^]H2, c, d) = ∃ k.c<=k ∧ k<=d ∧ ievalF (f, H1, c, k)
        ∧ ievalF (f, H2, k, d)

We then have **h, [n, m] |= H** iff **ievalF (h, H, n, m)**.

To establish the sequent calculus style deductive system for **dform**, we first define the deductive system for the first-order connectives of **dform**, that is similar to the one built for **fform** above; then for ℓ, **[^]** and **almost**, we transform the deductive system of DC from [19] to sequent calculus style. For instance, the axiom $\lceil S \rceil^\wedge \lceil S \rceil \leftrightarrow \lceil S \rceil$ is encoded by the following rules:

AlR   : $H ⊢ (almost S[^]almost S), $E ⇒ $H ⊢ almost S, $E
AlL   : $H, (almost S[^]almost S) ⊢ $E ⇒ $H, almost S ⊢ $E

where **$H, $E** represent arbitrary sequences of logical formulas of type **dform**. Other rules can be encoded similarly.

Inference Rules. We list the rule for assignment as an illustration. Because of the deep embedding of the assertions, the effect of assignment is expressed at the level of `fform` formulas by variable substitution. This is one main difference of using deep embedding from shallow embedding. For defining variable substitution, we implement a map as a list of pairs `(exp * exp) list`, and define two recursive functions: given a map `r` and an expression `e`, function `substE(r, e)` substitutes expressions occurring in `e` according to the map `r`; based on the definition of `substE`, given a formula `P` of type `fform`, function `substF(r, p)` substitutes expressions occurring in `P` according to the map `r`. Below we have the lemma for assignment `e:=f`:

lemma AssignRRule:

$\vdash$ p [→]substF ([(RVar x, f)], q); $\vdash$elE 0 [[→]] H $\Rightarrow$ {p} RVar x :=f {q; H}

Other rules can be defined similarly. As we can see in deep embedding, the HHL specification is transformed into a set of explicit FOL and DC formulas, which can be proved by applying the corresponding deductive systems we have built.

Discussion. The general strengths and weakness of both embeddings can be found at [16], and here we will not list them again. We will make more specific comparison between the two embeddings in the case study section.

In both embeddings, the proof in HHL prover cannot be automated due to the following reasons: first, the intermediate assertions occurring in SequentialRule, CommunicationRule, *etc*, need to be instantiated in the proof process by the user manually; second, the constraints related to unknown differential invariants and loop invariants need to be gathered manually so that they are solved by the external invariant generator as a whole; finally, in shallow embedding, because of the limitation of SMT solvers, the HOL verification conditions containing quantifiers usually cannot be proved automatically; while in deep embedding, the FOL and DC verification conditions are proved by applying their deductive rules manually.

But on the contrary, compared to other automated provers, HHL prover is capable of modelling and verifying more complex hybrid systems, because of the expressiveness of both HCSP and HHL.

6   A Case Study

We demonstrate the use of HHL prover on proving the safety of the slow descent guidance control program of a lunar lander, which provides a specific sampled-data control system composed of the physical plant and the control program.

6.1   Description of the Control Program

The lunar lander's dynamics is mathematically represented by

$$\begin{cases} \dot{r} = v \\ \dot{v} = \frac{F_c}{m} - gM \\ \dot{m} = -\frac{F_c}{Isp_1} \end{cases} , \text{ where} \tag{1}$$

- r, v and m denote the altitude relative to lunar surface, vertical velocity, and mass of the lunar lander, respectively;
- F_c is the thrust imposed on the lander, which is a constant in each sampling period of length 0.128 s;
- $gM = 1.622 \, \text{m/s}^2$ is the magnitude of the gravitational acceleration on the moon;
- Isp is the *specific impulse* of the lander's thrust engine. When F_c lies in $[1500, 3000]$, $Isp = 2548 \text{N·s/kg}$, and when F_c lies in $(3000, 5000]$, $Isp = 2842 \text{N·s/kg}$. Thus the lander's dynamics comprises two different forms depending on the values of Isp.

The sample time of the guidance control program is fixed as 0.128s. In every period, the guidance program gets the values of the altitude r and the velocity v via the sensor, and then updates mass m, calculates acceleration aIC, and calculates thrust F_c in sequence. Especially, F_c is calculated according to

$$F_c := -0.01 \cdot (F_c - m \cdot gM) - 0.6 \cdot (v - vslw) \cdot m + m \cdot gM \qquad (2)$$

where F_c on the right is the thrust of last period, and m is the updated mass in this period. The new thrust F_c will then be used for the next sampling cycle.

The safety property we want to prove for the guidance program is

(SP) $|v - vslw| \leq \varepsilon$, where $\varepsilon = 0.05 \, \text{m/s}$ is the tolerance of fluctuation of v around the target $vslw = -2 \, \text{m/s}$.

6.2   Verification in HHL Prover

First, we construct the HCSP model for the control program manually, denoted by LL, which is

definition P :: proc **where**
LL ≡ PC_Init; PD_Init; t:=(Con Real 0);(PC_Difff; t:=(Con Real 0); PD_Rep)∗

where PC_Init and PD_Init are initialization procedures for the continuous dynamics and the guidance program respectively; PC_Diff models the continuous dynamics given by (1) within a period of 0.128s; PD_Rep calculates thrust F_c according to (2) for the next sampling cycle; variable t denotes the elapsed time in each sampling cycle. Hence, process LL is initialized at the beginning by PC_Init and PD_Init, and behaves as a repetition of dynamics PC_Diff and computation PD_Rep afterwards.

Proof Result. By applying HHL prover (either in shallow or deep embedding), we have proved the following specification for process LL:

lemma goal: {fTrue} LL {safeProp; (elE 0 [[|]] almost safeProp)}

where safeProp of type fform encodes the safety property **(SP)**. Lemma goal indicates that, starting from any state, the control program satisfies the safety property almost everywhere during the whole execution.

Comparison in Different Approaches. In both embeddings, the proof for lemma `goal` is composed of a sequence of rule applications of Isabelle/HOL. But the length of the proof in shallow embedding is about one half of the one in deep embedding. In detail,

- For shallow embedding, the rules applied mainly comprise of two kinds: the inference rules of HHL and the rules for unfolding the HOL predicates of FOL and DC formulas. Fortunately, many of the rules applied are found by the built-in tool `sledgehammer` of Isabelle/HOL automatically. This alleviates users' proof burden to a big extent.
- For deep embedding, the rules applied also comprise of two kinds: the deductive rules of FOL and DC. The verification conditions generated (in the form of FOL and DC) have a much smaller size than the ones (in the form of HOL) in shallow embedding, because they are not unfolded. But meanwhile, they need to be conducted by the user completely, to apply the deductive rules of both logic manually.

7 Conclusion

HHL prover can be used for verifying hybrid systems, that combine discrete computation, continuous dynamics, communications, and parallel composition, *etc.* As an interactive theorem prover, it formalizes HCSP for modelling hybrid systems and realises the Hybrid Hoare Logic (HHL) for verifying safety of HCSP models in Isabelle/HOL. The old HHL prover implemented HHL in deep embedding, but with great proof burden. This paper presents an improved HHL prover that implements HHL in shallow embedding. In addition, to compare the two different embedding styles, we demonstrated the use of both variants on a real-life example, i.e. the slow descent control program of a lunar lander. It can be seen from the proof results that the shallow embedding has better performance in the proof size and automation than deep embedding.

Acknowledgements. This paper is supported partly by "973 Program" under grant No. 2014CB340701, by NSFC under grants 91118007 and 91418204, by CDZ project CAP (GZ 1023), and by the CAS/SAFEA International Partnership Program for Creative Research Teams.

References

1. Alur, R.: Formal verification of hybrid systems. In: EMSOFT 2011, pp. 273–278 (2011)
2. Alur, R., Courcoubetis, C., Henzinger, T.A., Ho, P.-H.: Hybrid automata: an algorithmic approach to the specification and verification of hybrid systems. In: Grossman, R.L., Ravn, A.P., Rischel, H., Nerode, A. (eds.) HS 1991 and HS 1992. LNCS, vol. 736, pp. 209–229. Springer, Heidelberg (1993)
3. Alur, R., Dang, T., Ivančić, F.: Predicate abstraction for reachability analysis of hybrid systems. ACM Trans. Embed. Comput. Syst. 5(1), 152–199 (2006)

4. Asarin, E., Bournez, O., Dang, T., Maler, O.: Approximate reachability analysis of piecewise-linear dynamical systems. In: Lynch, N.A., Krogh, B.H. (eds.) HSCC 2000. LNCS, vol. 1790, p. 20. Springer, Heidelberg (2000)

5. Asarin, E., Dang, T., Maler, O.: The d/dt tool for verification of hybrid systems. In: Brinksma, E., Larsen, K.G. (eds.) CAV 2002. LNCS, vol. 2404, p. 365. Springer, Heidelberg (2002)

6. Chen, X., Ábrahám, E., Sankaranarayanan, S.: Flow*: an analyzer for non-linear hybrid systems. In: Sharygina, N., Veith, H. (eds.) CAV 2013. LNCS, vol. 8044, pp. 258–263. Springer, Heidelberg (2013)

7. Eggers, A., Ramdani, N., Nedialkov, N., Fränzle, M.: Improving SAT modulo ODE for hybrid systems analysis by combining different enclosure methods. In: Barthe, G., Pardo, A., Schneider, G. (eds.) SEFM 2011. LNCS, vol. 7041, pp. 172–187. Springer, Heidelberg (2011)

8. Frehse, G.: PHAVer: algorithmic verification of hybrid systems past hytech. In: Morari, M., Thiele, L. (eds.) HSCC 2005. LNCS, vol. 3414, pp. 258–273. Springer, Heidelberg (2005)

9. He, J. : From CSP to hybrid systems. In: A Classical Mind, Essays in Honour of C.A.R. Hoare, pp. 171–189. Prentice Hall International (UK) Ltd. (1994)

10. Henzinger, T.A.: The theory of hybrid automata. In: Inan, M.K., Kurshan, R.P. (eds.) LICS'1996. NATO ASI Series, vol. 170, pp. 278–292. Springer, Heidelberg (1996)

11. Liu, J., Lv, J., Quan, Z., Zhan, N., Zhao, H., Zhou, C., Zou, L.: A calculus for hybrid CSP. In: Ueda, K. (ed.) APLAS 2010. LNCS, vol. 6461, pp. 1–15. Springer, Heidelberg (2010)

12. Liu, J., Zhan, N., Zhao, H.: Computing semi-algebraic invariants for polynomial dynamical systems. In: EMSOFT 2011, pp. 97–106 (2011)

13. Manna, Z., Pnueli, A.: Verifying hybrid systems. In: Grossman, R.L., Ravn, A.P., Rischel, H., Nerode, A. (eds.) HS 1991 and HS 1992. LNCS, vol. 736, pp. 4–35. Springer, Heidelberg (1993)

14. Platzer, A., Clarke, E.M.: Computing differential invariants of hybrid systems as fixedpoints. In: Gupta, A., Malik, S. (eds.) CAV 2008. LNCS, vol. 5123, pp. 176–189. Springer, Heidelberg (2008)

15. Platzer, A., Quesel, J.-D.: KeYmaera: a hybrid theorem prover for hybrid systems (system description). In: Armando, A., Baumgartner, P., Dowek, G. (eds.) IJCAR 2008. LNCS (LNAI), vol. 5195, pp. 171–178. Springer, Heidelberg (2008)

16. Wildmoser, M., Nipkow, T.: Certifying machine code safety: shallow versus deep embedding. In: Slind, K., Bunker, A., Gopalakrishnan, G.C. (eds.) TPHOLs 2004. LNCS, vol. 3223, pp. 305–320. Springer, Heidelberg (2004)

17. Zhan, N., Wang, S., Zhao, H.: Formal modelling, analysis and verification of hybrid systems. In: Liu, Z., Woodcock, J., Zhu, H. (eds.) Unifying Theories of Programming and Formal Engineering Methods. LNCS, vol. 8050, pp. 207–281. Springer, Heidelberg (2013)

18. Zhao, H., Yang, M., Zhan, N., Gu, B., Zou, L., Chen, Y.: Formal verification of a descent guidance control program of a lunar lander. In: Jones, C., Pihlajasaari, P., Sun, J. (eds.) FM 2014. LNCS, vol. 8442, pp. 733–748. Springer, Heidelberg (2014)

19. Zhou, C., Hansen, M.R.: Duration Calculus – A Formal Approach to Real-Time Systems. Monographs in Theoretical Computer Science. An EATCS Series. Springer, Heidelberg (2004)

20. Zhou, C., Hoare, C.A.R., Ravn, A.P.: A calculus of durations. Inf. Process. Lett. 40(5), 269–276 (1991)

21. Chaochen, Z., Ji, W., Ravn, A.P.: A formal description of hybrid systems. In: Alur, R., Sontag, E.D., Henzinger, T.A. (eds.) HS 1995. LNCS, vol. 1066, pp. 511–530. Springer, Heidelberg (1996)
22. Zou, L., Lv, J., Wang, S., Zhan, N., Tang, T., Yuan, L., Liu, Y.: Verifying Chinese train control system under a combined scenario by theorem proving. In: Cohen, E., Rybalchenko, A. (eds.) VSTTE 2013. LNCS, vol. 8164, pp. 262–280. Springer, Heidelberg (2014)
23. Zou, L., Zhan, N., Wang, S., Fränzle, M.: Formal verification of simulink/stateflow diagrams. In: ATVA 2015 (2015) (to appear)
24. Zou, L., Zhan, N., Wang, S., Fränzle, M., Qin, S.: Verifying simulink diagrams via a hybrid hoare logic prover. In: EMSOFT 2013, pp. 1–10 (2013)

Continuation Semantics for Concurrency with Multiple Channels Communication

Gabriel Ciobanu[1] and Eneia Nicolae Todoran[2]([⊠])

[1] Institute of Computer Science, Romanian Academy,
Blvd. Carol I No. 8, 700505 Iași, Romania
[2] Department of Computer Science, Technical University of Cluj-Napoca,
400027 Cluj-Napoca, Romania
eneia.todoran@cs.utcluj.ro

Abstract. In this paper we investigate the formal design of concurrent languages based on the concept of *continuation*. We present a denotational approach of concurrent programs by using *continuations for concurrency*. We illustrate the approach by designing a continuation semantics for a language with nondeterministic choice, sequential and parallel composition, and a mechanism of communication and synchronization on multiple channels. For our language, we also present an operational semantics, and establish the formal relation between the denotational and operational semantics. We accomplish the semantic investigation in the mathematical framework of complete metric spaces.

1 Introduction

The paper deals with semantic aspects of concurrent systems, namely systems consisting of several computing processes interacting each other. By "process" we understand the behaviour of a software system, the execution of a program. Since the concurrent systems are usually complex, it is useful to have the possibility of describing, analyzing and reasoning about the concurrent systems in a precise way. Generally, the interactions among processes cannot be predicted as the concurrent computation involves nondeterminism. The traditional view of a (sequential) computation as a function from input to output cannot deal properly with nondeterminism. For concurrent systems, formal models are provided by *process calculi* like CCS [11] and CSP [9]. These process calculi work with terms, and use an operational semantics to describe the computational dynamics. They are also called *process algebras* because they use algebraic operators and equations among terms to describe the system behaviour. In general, starting out from a given set of atomic or elementary actions, the basic operators are used to compose the actions into more complicated processes. The basic operators are + (denoting nondeterministic choice), ; (denoting sequential composition) and || (denoting parallel composition). These operators satisfy certain concurrency laws describing the actions execution explicitly.

The denotational semantics of concurrent systems use the observations of a process (e.g., traces, failures), and the meaning of a process is given by a

© Springer International Publishing Switzerland 2015
M. Butler et al. (Eds.): ICFEM 2015, LNCS 9407, pp. 400–416, 2015.
DOI: 10.1007/978-3-319-25423-4_26

collection of possible observations. These denotations are compositional, and can also provide an operational intuition. However the denotational semantics are more abstract than the operational semantics, and are not close to any specific implementation for a concurrent system or language. In this paper we present a *continuation semantics for concurrency* (shortly CSC) which satisfies the main static laws of concurrent systems. Direct denotational semantics cannot easily explain constructs that interrupt the flow of control; such constructs can be expressed denotationally using continuations. A continuation represents in fact the remaining part of a certain computation. Traditional continuations [14] can be used to model a variety of advanced control concepts, including non-local exits, coroutines and even multitasking. However, the traditional continuations do not work well enough in the presence of concurrency.

The CSC technique is a general tool for representing control in concurrent systems [6, 15]. It can be used to design denotational and operational semantics of concurrent systems. As a tool for denotational design, the distinctive characteristic of the CSC technique is the modelling of continuations as structures of computations (denotations of program statements) rather than the functions to some answer type that are used in the classic technique of continuations [14]. The computations contained in a continuation can be evaluated either in some particular order or in parallel. In practice, it is possible to establish a relation between the structure of continuations and the control concepts of the language under study. Communication and synchronization information can also be encoded in continuations. Unlike other branching-time or linear-time models of concurrency [2], in the CSC approach the final yield of the denotational mapping is a simple collection of observations, and all control and synchronization information is encoded in continuations. Following [2], in this paper we use the term *resumption* as an operational counterpart of the term *continuation*. In an operational semantics designed with CSC a resumption is a structure of program statements (syntactic constructs). The structure of continuations (and resumptions) is specific of the concurrent language under investigation.

We consider a simple imperative concurrent language that we name MCC, an abbreviation for *Multiple Channels Communication*. The communication on multiple channels is inspired by the join calculus [8]. MCC provides operators for nondeterministic choice, sequential and parallel composition. It also provides two primitives for concurrent interaction on multiple channels, namely a (sending) statement $c!e$ together with a *communication pattern* $c_1?v_1 \& \cdots \& c_n?v_n$. Synchronized execution of $n + 1$ actions $c_1!e_1, \ldots, c_n!e_n$ and $c_1?v_1 \& \cdots \& c_n?v_n$ occurring in parallel processes results in the transmission of the value of each expression e_i along the channel c_i from the process executing the $c_i!e_i$ statement to the process executing the $c_1?v_1 \& \cdots \& c_n?v_n$ statement. The value of each expression e_i is transmitted along the channel c_i and assigned to the corresponding variable v_i. The whole interaction behaves like a distributed multiassignment performed upon a synchronous rendezvous between $n + 1$ parallel components. All the $n + 1$ parallel components must be ready to interact for a communication between them to occur. When $n = 1$, the interaction is a point-to-point synchronous communication like in CSP [9].

In Sect. 3 we present a denotational model designed with CSC for MCC. The denotational model is built within the mathematical framework of 1-bounded complete metric spaces [2]. We use the general theory developed in [1], and the domain of denotations is defined as a solution of an equation in which the domain variable occurs in the left-hand side of a function space construction. The semantic operators designed with CSC obey the concurrency laws such as the associativity and the commutativity of parallel composition. The semantics of nondeterministic choice is defined based on the standard union operator, which is associative, commutative and idempotent. Other properties, e.g. the associativity of sequential and parallel execution, require more complex proofs based on the identification of behavioural invariants. In our denotational model the semantic operators obey the law for the left distributivity of nondeterministic choice over sequential composition, which is characteristic of models based on *trace semantics*. The basic idea of each of these proofs is to show that the property under consideration is preserved by the computation steps. In metric semantics it is usual to attach a $\frac{1}{2}$ contracting factor to each computation step. In each case we obtain a relation of the kind $\epsilon \leq \frac{1}{2} \cdot \epsilon$ where ϵ is the distance between two behaviourally equivalent continuations. It results that $\epsilon = 0$, and the desired property follows. In Sect. 4 we present an operational semantics also designed with CSC for MCC. We establish the mathematical relation between the denotational semantics and the operational semantics of MCC. In designing and relating the denotational and the operational semantics of MCC we follow the mathematical methodology of metric semantics [2].

In Sect. 4 we prove that the denotational semantics designed with CSC for MCC is *correct* with respect to the operational semantics. However, we do not know whether the domain of CSC is also *complete*, and so fully abstract [10]. This remains an open problem. We are not aware of any full abstractness result for a concurrent language designed with continuations, although various papers employ continuations in the denotational description of concurrent languages.

Contribution: We present the denotational semantics of a concurrent language MCC in a complete metric space obtained by solving a specific CSC domain equation. Following [6], we prove that the continuation semantics satisfies some basic laws of concurrency; these results are obtained for all the continuations containing denotations of the programs. This represents an invariant of the denotational semantics, and ensures its consistency just because the initial continuation is empty and the denotational semantics adds to the continuation only denotations of the language constructs. We also present an operational semantics for MCC, and relate formally the denotational and operational semantics following the mathematical methodology of metric semantics [2]. Certain proofs are included in the paper; others are available online in a technical report [4]. The proof technique is based on the identification of behavioural invariants given by the specific structure of continuations. This technique could be applied to every language designed by using CSC.

2 MCC Syntax and Continuation Structure

The notation $(x \in)X$ introduces the set X with typical element x ranging over X. Let $f \in X \rightarrow Y$ be a function; the function $[f \mid x \mapsto y] : X \rightarrow Y$ is defined (for $x, x' \in X, y \in Y$) by: $[f \mid x \mapsto y](x') =$ if $x'=x$ then y else $f(x')$. Instead of $[[f \mid x_1 \mapsto y_1] \cdots \mid x_n \mapsto y_n]$ we write $[f \mid x_1 \mapsto y_1 \mid \cdots \mid x_n \mapsto y_n]$. If $f : X \rightarrow X$ and $f(x) = x$ we call x a *fixed point* of f. When this fixed point is unique, we write $x = fix(f)$. We recall that if (X, d_X) and (Y, d_Y) are metric spaces, a function $f{:}X \rightarrow Y$ is a *contraction* if $\exists c \in \mathbb{R}, 0 \le c < 1, \forall x_1, x_2 \in X :$ $d_Y(f(x_1), f(x_2)) \le c \cdot d_X(x_1, x_2)$. In metric semantics, it is customary to attach a contracting factor $c = \frac{1}{2}$ to each computation step. When $c = 1$ the function f is called *non-expansive*. In what follows, we denote the set of all non-expansive functions from X to Y by $X \xrightarrow{1} Y$. The well-known theorem of Banach is essential in metric semantics; this result claims that each contraction $f : X \rightarrow X$ has a unique fixed point in a complete metric space.

We use the abbreviation $\mathcal{P}_{nco}(X)$ to denote the powerset of *non-empty and compact* subsets of X, and $\mathcal{P}_{fin}(X)$ to denote the powerset of *finite* subsets of X. We only use the powerset of finite subsets to create structures that we endow with the discrete metric (which are trivially complete ultrametric spaces). We often suppress the metric part in domain definitions and write, e.g., $\frac{1}{2} \cdot X$ instead of $(X, d_{\frac{1}{2} \cdot X})$, where, if (X, d) is a (complete) metric space, the metric $d_{\frac{1}{2} \cdot X}$ is defined by $d_{\frac{1}{2} \cdot X}(x_1, x_2) = \frac{1}{2} \cdot d(x_1, x_2)$. Other preliminaries are presented in [6].

We assume a given set $(v \in)Var$ of *variables*, a set $(e \in)Exp$ of numeric *expressions* (without side effects), a set $(c \in)Ch$ of *communication channels* and a set $(x \in)Pvar$ of *procedure variables*. We assume that the evaluation of an expression always terminates and yields an integer value $z \in \mathbb{Z}$. The syntax of MCC is provided by the following components:

(a) (Communication patterns) $j(\in J) ::= c?v \mid j \& j$
    To be valid, the channels $c_1, \ldots, c_n$ and the variables $v_1, \ldots, v_n$ of a communication pattern $j = (c_1?v_1 \& \cdots \& c_n?v_n)$ must be pairwise distinct.
(b) (Statements) Let $a ::= $ skip $\mid v := e \mid c!e \mid j$
      $s(\in Stat) ::= a \mid x \mid s + s \mid s; s \mid s\|s$
(c) (Guarded statements)
      $g(\in GStat) ::= a \mid g + g \mid g; s \mid g\|g$
(d) (Declarations) $(D \in)Decl = PVar \rightarrow GStat$
(e) (Programs) $(\rho \in)MCC = Decl \times Stat$

In MCC we have assignment $(v := e)$, recursion, sequential composition $(s; s)$, nondeterministic choice $(s + s)$, parallel composition $(s\|s)$ and a communication mechanism given by statements $c!e$ together with a communication pattern $c_1?v_1 \& \cdots \& c_n?v_n$. Synchronized execution of $n + 1$ actions $c_1!e_1, \ldots, c_n!e_n$ and $c_1?v_1 \& \cdots \& c_n?v_n$ occurring in parallel results in the transmission of the value of each expression e_i along the channel c_i from the process executing the $c_i!e_i$ statement to the process executing the $c_1?v_1 \& \cdots \& c_n?v_n$ statement. The latter assigns the received n values to the variables $v_1, \ldots, v_n$; the value of each expression e_i is transmitted along the channel c_i and assigned to the corresponding variable v_i. The whole interaction behaves like a distributed multi-assignment.

Following a standard approach, the meaning of expressions is given by a valuation $\mathcal{E}[\![\cdot]\!] : Exp \to \Sigma \to \mathbb{Z}$, where $(\sigma \in)\Sigma = Var \to \mathbb{Z}$ is a set of *states*. We employ recursion based on *declarations* and *guarded statements* [2]. In a guarded statement, each recursive call is preceded by at least one elementary action, and this guarantees that the semantic operators are contracting functions in the present metric setting. Without loss of generality, in what follows we assume a fixed declaration $D \in Decl$, and in any situation we refer to this fixed D. For inductive proofs we introduce a complexity measure $c_s : Stat \to \mathbb{N}$ that decreases upon recursive calls: $c_s(a) = 1; c_s(s_1; s_2) = 1 + c_s(s_1); c_s(x) = 1 + c_s(D(x)); c_s(s_1 \text{ op } s_2) = 1 + max\{c_s(s_1), c_s(s_2)\}$, op $\in \{+, \|\}$. The function c_s is well-defined due to our restriction to guarded recursion [2].

2.1   Continuation Structure for MCC

In the CSC approach, a continuation is an application-specific structure of computations. Continuation structures can be designed by using two abstract concepts: the *stack* to model sequential composition and the *multiset* to model parallel composition [5]. The language MCC provides a general combination of parallel and sequential composition. In order to model properly this combination of concepts, a CSC continuation must be a tree of computations with active computations at the leaves. This behaviour is inspired by the structure of a *cactus stack*, namely a stack with multiple tops that can be active concurrently [3]. The major issue that gives rise to a tree-like structure is the presence of statements such as $(s_1 \| s_2); s_3$. In such a statement, s_3 can only execute after the concurrent execution of both s_1 and s_2 has terminated. In order to define such domains of trees of computations we employ a set of *identifiers* $(\alpha \in)Id$. Id is the set of all finite, possibly empty, sequences over $\{1, 2\}$. We write $\alpha \leq \alpha'$ when α is a prefix of α' ($\leq$ is a partial ordering relation defined on Id).

In this paper we use the symbol '$\cdot$' as a concatenation operator over sequences, hence we can represent any nonempty identifier $\alpha \in Id$ by a finite sequence $\alpha = i_1 \cdot \ldots \cdot i_n$, where $i_1, \ldots, i_n \in \{1, 2\}$. We use the symbol λ to represent the empty sequence over $\{1, 2\}$ (i.e., $\lambda \in Id$).

(a) Let $(\alpha \in)Id = \{1, 2\}^*$ be a set of *identifiers*, equipped with the following partial ordering: $\alpha \leq \alpha'$ iff $\alpha' = \alpha \cdot i_1 \cdot \ldots \cdot i_n$ for $i_1, \ldots, i_n \in \{1, 2\}, n \geq 0$. We define $\alpha < \alpha'$ iff $\alpha \leq \alpha'$ and $\alpha \neq \alpha'$. If $A \in \mathcal{P}(Id)$, we denote by $\leq_A$ the restriction of $\leq$ to A.

(b) We define a function $max : \mathcal{P}(Id) \to \mathcal{P}(Id)$ by

$$max(A) = \{\alpha \mid \alpha \text{ is a maximal element of} (A, \leq_A)\}.$$

Let $A \in \mathcal{P}(Id)$. An element $\alpha \in A$ is a *maximal element* of $(A, \leq_A)$ if $\neg(\alpha < \alpha')$, for any $\alpha' \in A$. An element $\alpha \in A$ is the *least element* of $(A, \leq_A)$ if $\alpha \leq \alpha'$, for any $\alpha' \in A$. $(Id, \leq)$ is a partially ordered set ($\leq$ is a binary relation over Id which is reflexive, transitive and antisymmetric). λ is the least element of $(Id, \leq)$. The concept of a *tree* that we use in this paper is taken from set theory, where a tree is a partially ordered set in which the predecessors of each element are well-ordered. A set is well-ordered if it is linearly ordered and every nonempty subset has a least element. A set is linearly ordered if any two elements are comparable. There are several books on set theory that provide formal definitions of these concepts. Here we explain the concept of a tree by means of an example.

We only work with finite trees. Let $A \subseteq Id$ be a finite subset of Id. $(A, \leq_A)$ is a finite tree. Let $\alpha \in Id$, and $A = \{\alpha, \alpha \cdot 1, \alpha \cdot 2, \alpha \cdot 1 \cdot 1, \alpha \cdot 1 \cdot 2, \alpha \cdot 2 \cdot 1, \alpha \cdot 2 \cdot 2\}$. The *maximal elements* of $(A, \leq_A)$ are exactly the *leaves* of the tree: $max(A) = \{\alpha \cdot 1 \cdot 1, \alpha \cdot 1 \cdot 2, \alpha \cdot 2 \cdot 1, \alpha \cdot 2 \cdot 2\}$. The predecessors of each element in A are well-ordered. For example, $\alpha \cdot 1 \cdot 1 > \alpha \cdot 1$ and $\alpha \cdot 1 > \alpha$. The set of predecessors of $\alpha \cdot 1 \cdot 1$ is $\{\alpha \cdot 1, \alpha\}$, which is linearly ordered, because any two elements in $\{\alpha \cdot 1, \alpha\}$ are comparable. In general, α' and α'' are comparable iff $\alpha' \leq \alpha''$ or $\alpha'' \leq \alpha'$. Obviously, every nonempty subset of $\{\alpha \cdot 1, \alpha\}$ has a least element. In fact, every finite linearly ordered set is well-ordered.

Let $(x \in)\mathbf{X}$ be a complete metric space. Let $(\pi \in)\Pi = \mathcal{P}_{fin}(Id)$. We use the notation $\{|\mathbf{X}|\} \overset{not.}{=} \Pi \times (Id \to \mathbf{X})$. Let $\alpha \in Id$. Let $(\pi, \phi) \in \{|\mathbf{X}|\}$, where ϕ ranges over $Id \to \mathbf{X}$. We define $id : \{|\mathbf{X}|\} \to \Pi$, $id(\pi, \phi) = \pi$, and use the following abbreviations: $(\pi, \phi)(\alpha) \overset{not.}{=} \phi(\alpha)$, $(\pi, \phi) \setminus \pi' \overset{not.}{=} (\pi \setminus \pi', \phi)$, $[(\pi, \phi) \mid \alpha \mapsto x] \overset{not.}{=} (\pi \cup \{\alpha\}, [\phi \mid \alpha \mapsto x])$. We treat (π, ϕ) as a 'function' with finite graph $\{(\alpha, \phi(\alpha)) \mid \alpha \in \pi\}$, thus ignoring the behaviour of ϕ for any $\alpha \notin \pi$ (π is the 'domain' of the 'function'). With this mathematical structure we represent finite partially ordered *bags* (or multisets)[1] of computations. The set Id is used to distinguish between multiple occurrences of a computation in such a bag. We endow the sets Id and Π with discrete metrics, and so they are complete ultrametric spaces. The composed metric spaces are built up as explained in [2]. If $\mathbf{X}$ is a (complete) ultrametric space then $\{|\mathbf{X}|\}$ is also a (complete) ultrametric space. The operators behave as follows: $id(\pi, \phi)$ returns the collection of identifiers for the valid computations contained in the bag, $(\pi, \phi)(\alpha)$ returns the computation with identifier α, $(\pi, \phi) \setminus \pi'$ removes the computations with identifiers in π', and $[(\pi, \phi) \mid \alpha \mapsto x]$ replaces or adds a computation with identifier α.

By a slight abuse, we use the same notations when X is an ordinary set: $\{|X|\} = \Pi \times (Id \to X)$, using the operator id and the abbreviations $(\cdot)(\alpha), (\cdot) \setminus \pi$, and $[\cdot \mid \alpha \mapsto x]$; in this case we do not endow $\{|X|\}$ with a metric.

3   Denotational Semantics

A central idea in metric semantics is that the distance between two computations is 2^{-n}, whenever the first difference between their behaviours appears after n

---
[1] We avoid to use the notion of a *partially ordered multiset* which is a more refined structure (see Chapt. 16 of [2]).

computation steps. Each computation step produces an observation. The behaviour of concurrent processes can be described in a compositional manner. The approach is well-established in the context of CSP [2,13]. In the continuation-based approach that we present in this paper each computation step is followed by a scheduling step, which can either perform a synchronization or it can activate (in a non-deterministic manner) a computation contained in the continuation. In this way, execution traces of concurrent processes are generated incrementally, and control and synchronization information is encoded in continuations.

We present a continuation-based denotational semantics for MCC. The final yield of our denotational semantics is an element of a standard linear-time domain $(p \in)\mathbf{P} = \mathcal{P}_{nco}(\Sigma^* \cup \Sigma^* \cdot \{\delta\} \cup \Sigma^\omega)$. An element of $\Sigma^* \cup \Sigma^* \cdot \{\delta\} \cup \Sigma^\omega$ is either a finite sequence over Σ, possibly terminated with the symbol δ, or an infinite sequence over Σ. The symbol δ models *deadlock*. We also use the symbol λ to represent the empty sequence over Σ. This is a slight abuse since we also use the symbol λ to represent the empty sequence over $\{1,2\}$; however, it is always clear from the context which is the type of λ (either $\lambda \in Id = \{1,2\}^*$, or $\lambda \in \Sigma^*$). We endow $\Sigma^* \cup \Sigma^* \cdot \{\delta\} \cup \Sigma^\omega$ with the Baire metric, and so obtain a complete ultrametric space [2].

The space of the denotational semantics $\mathcal{D}$ for MCC is $Stat \to \mathbf{D}$, where

$$\mathbf{D} \cong \mathbf{Cont} \xrightarrow{1} \Sigma \to \mathbf{P},$$
$$(\gamma \in)\mathbf{Cont} = Id \times \mathbf{Kont},$$
$$(\kappa \in)\mathbf{Kont} = \{\!|\mathbf{Comp}|\!\},$$
$$\mathbf{Comp} = J^\Diamond + Snd + \tfrac{1}{2} \cdot \mathbf{D}.$$

Here $J^\Diamond = \{\Diamond\} \times J$ and $Snd = Ch \times (\Sigma \to \mathbb{Z})$. We use the notation $\langle j \rangle = (\Diamond, j)$. Also, for readability, we denote typical elements (c, ξ) of Snd by $c!\xi$.

In the domain equations given above the sets Id (and Π), $\Sigma, J^\Diamond$ and Snd are endowed with the discrete (ultra)metric, according to the standard constructions for the composed metric spaces. Notice that the recursive occurrence of the domain variable $\mathbf{D}$ is preceded by the $\frac{1}{2}$ factor and it is placed in the left-hand side of a (non-expansive) function space construction. The above domain equation can be solved by using the general method presented in [1]. The solution, which is unique up to isometry, is obtained as a complete ultrametric space.

Comp is the domain of *computations*. A computation is either a (partially evaluated) denotation or a component that participates in a synchronization between multiple processes. The construction $\{\!|\mathbf{Comp}|\!\} = \Pi \times (Id \to \mathbf{Comp})$ was already presented. In the sequel φ ranges over $Id \to \mathbf{Comp}$.

We call a *closed continuation* an element of **Kont**, and an *open continuation* an element of **Cont**. A closed continuation $\kappa \in \mathbf{Kont}$ is a configuration of computations. An open continuation $(\alpha, \kappa) \in \mathbf{Cont}$ is a semantic context for the evaluation of the denotational mapping [7]. In an expression $\mathcal{D}(s)(\alpha, \kappa)$, $\mathcal{D}(s)$ is the *active computation* which is evaluated in the context given by the continuation (α, κ). In this representation α is the identifier of the active computation. The denotational semantics preserves this invariant property: $\alpha \notin id(\kappa)$ and

$\alpha \in max(\{\alpha\} \cup id(\kappa))$. In this way the active computation is always a maximal element (i.e. a leaf) in the tree of computations representing the continuation.

The denotational function $\mathcal{D}$ given in Definition 1 is defined with the aid of a mapping kc, which is called a *scheduler*. The scheduler function manipulates the computations contained in a closed continuation. Computations of the type $\frac{1}{2} \cdot \mathbf{D}$ can be activated for evaluation. Computations of the type $J^{\diamond}$ and Snd can participate in multichannel synchronizations. If the continuation is empty the scheduler terminates the computation. If the continuation is not empty and it contains no computations that can be activated and no synchronization is possible then the scheduler detects a deadlock. Otherwise the scheduler can either activate a computation or it can perform a step of synchronization between multiple processes. In order to activate a computation the scheduler decomposes a closed continuation into a computation and a corresponding open continuation and then it executes the former with the latter as a continuation. The activation of a computation can follow after a finite number of synchronization steps.

We use three auxiliary mappings that yield finite sets of schedules. A *schedule* is a finite and non-empty set of identifiers. A schedule with only 1 element is an *activation schedule*; it contains exactly one identifier α, and the computation with identifier α is activated by the scheduler function kc. A schedule that contains more than 1 element is a *synchronization schedule*; it is used to define a pattern matching synchronization on multiple channels. Activation schedules are computed by the mapping Ω_A; synchronization schedules are computed by the mapping Ω_S. For all $\kappa \in \mathbf{Kont}$ we have $\Omega_A(\kappa) \cap \Omega_S(\kappa) = \emptyset$.

Let $(\varsigma \in)Sched = \mathcal{P}_{nfin}(Id)$ be the set of schedules. We use different symbols to represent the elements of the sets $(\varsigma \in)Sched$ and $(\pi \in)\Pi$, so it is always clear when a (non-empty and) finite set of identifiers is treated as a schedule[2]. Let $\hat{\cdot} : Sched \to \Pi$, $\hat{\varsigma} = \varsigma$. With the aid of an auxiliary predicate $Sync : (Sched \times \mathbf{Kont}) \to Bool$ we define $\Omega, \Omega_A, \Omega_S : \mathbf{Kont} \to \mathcal{P}_{fin}(Sched)$ as follows:

$$Sync(\{\alpha\}, \kappa) = false$$
$$Sync(\{\alpha, \alpha_1, \ldots, \alpha_n\}, \kappa) = (\kappa(\alpha) = \langle c_1?v_1 \& \cdots \& c_n?v_n \rangle \in J^{\diamond}) \wedge$$
$$(\kappa(\alpha_1) = c_1!\xi_1 \in Snd) \wedge \cdots \wedge (\kappa(\alpha_n) = c_n!\xi_n \in Snd)$$
$$\Omega(\kappa) = \Omega_A(\kappa) \cup \Omega_S(\kappa)$$
$$\Omega_A(\kappa) = \{\{\alpha\} \mid \alpha \in max(id(\kappa)), \kappa(\alpha) \in \tfrac{1}{2} \cdot \mathbf{D}\}$$
$$\Omega_S(\kappa) = \{\varsigma \mid \varsigma \subseteq max(id(\kappa)), Sync(\varsigma, \kappa)\}$$

We use the mapping $(\cdot \mid \cdot \Rightarrow \cdot) : (\Sigma \times \Pi \times \mathbf{Kont}) \to \Sigma$ to model the state update effect of a multichannel synchronous communication:

$$(\sigma \mid \varsigma \Rightarrow \kappa) = \begin{cases} [\sigma \mid v_1 \mapsto \xi_1(\sigma) \mid \cdots \mid v_n \mapsto \xi_n(\sigma)] \\ \quad \text{if } \varsigma \subseteq max(id(\kappa)), Sync(\varsigma, \kappa), \\ \quad \quad \varsigma = \{\alpha, \alpha_1, \ldots, \alpha_n\}, \\ \quad \quad \kappa(\alpha) = \langle c_1?v_1 \& \cdots \& c_n?v_n \rangle, \\ \quad \quad \kappa(\alpha_1) = c_1!\xi_1, \ldots, \kappa(\alpha_n) = c_n!\xi_n \\ \quad \quad \text{otherwise} \\ \sigma \end{cases}$$

---

[2] $\Pi = Sched \cup \{\emptyset\}$; the set $\Pi = \mathcal{P}_{fin}(Id)$ was introduced previously.

We also define the predicates $Terminates, Blocks : \mathbf{Kont} \rightarrow Bool$ by

$$Terminates(\kappa) = (id(\kappa) = \emptyset)$$
$$Blocks(\kappa) = (id(\kappa) \neq \emptyset) \wedge (\Omega(\kappa) = \emptyset)$$

Definition 1. *(Denotational Semantics $\mathcal{D}$)*

(a) *Let $kc : \mathbf{Kont} \rightarrow \Sigma \rightarrow \mathbf{P}$ be given by*
$$kc(\kappa)(\sigma) = \text{if } Terminates(\kappa) \text{ then } \{\lambda\}$$
$$\text{else if } Blocks(\kappa) \text{ then } \{\delta\}$$
$$\text{else } \bigcup\nolimits_{\{\alpha\} \in \Omega_A(\kappa)} \kappa(\alpha)(\alpha, \kappa \setminus \{\alpha\})(\sigma) \ \cup$$
$$\bigcup\nolimits_{\varsigma \in \Omega_S(\kappa)} (\sigma \mid \varsigma \Rightarrow \kappa) \cdot kc(\kappa \setminus \hat{\varsigma})(\sigma \mid \varsigma \Rightarrow \kappa)$$

(b) *Let $(S \in)Sem_D = Stat \rightarrow \mathbf{D}$. We define $\Phi : Sem_D \rightarrow Sem_D$ by:*

$$\Phi(S)(\text{ skip })(\alpha, \kappa)(\sigma) = \sigma \cdot kc(\kappa)(\sigma)$$
$$\Phi(S)(v := e)(\alpha, \kappa)(\sigma) = \sigma' \cdot kc(\kappa)(\sigma') \qquad \text{where } \sigma' = [\sigma \mid v \mapsto \mathcal{E}[\![e]\!](\sigma)]$$
$$\Phi(S)(c!e)(\alpha, \kappa)(\sigma) = \sigma \cdot kc[\kappa \mid \alpha \mapsto c!\mathcal{E}[\![e]\!]](\sigma)$$
$$\Phi(S)(j)(\alpha, \kappa)(\sigma) = \sigma \cdot kc[\kappa \mid \alpha \mapsto \langle j \rangle](\sigma)$$
$$\Phi(S)(x)(\alpha, \kappa)(\sigma) = \Phi(S)(D(x))(\alpha, \kappa)(\sigma)$$
$$\Phi(S)(s_1 + s_2)(\alpha, \kappa)(\sigma) = \Phi(S)(s_1)(\alpha, \kappa)(\sigma) \ \cup \ \Phi(S)(s_2)(\alpha, \kappa)(\sigma)$$
$$\Phi(S)(s_1; s_2)(\alpha, \kappa)(\sigma) = \Phi(S)(s_1)(\alpha \cdot 1, [\kappa \mid \alpha \mapsto S(s_2)])(\sigma)$$
$$\Phi(S)(s_1 \parallel s_2)(\alpha, \kappa)(\sigma) = \Phi(S)(s_1)(\alpha \cdot 1, [\kappa \mid \alpha \cdot 2 \mapsto S(s_2)])(\sigma) \ \cup$$
$$\Phi(S)(s_2)(\alpha \cdot 2, [\kappa \mid \alpha \cdot 1 \mapsto S(s_1)])(\sigma)$$

(c) *We put $\mathcal{D} = fix(\Phi)$. Also, let $\alpha_0 = \lambda$ and $\kappa_0 = (\emptyset, \varphi_0)$, where $\varphi_0(\alpha) = \mathcal{D}(\text{ skip }), \forall \alpha \in Id$. We define $\mathcal{D}[\![\cdot]\!] : Stat \rightarrow \Sigma \rightarrow \mathbf{P}$ by $\mathcal{D}[\![s]\!] = \mathcal{D}(s)(\alpha_0, \kappa_0)$, where (α_0, κ_0) is the empty (open) continuation.*

In each of the first four equations given in Definition 1(b) an elementary step is produced and next the control is transmitted to the scheduler. The first equation defines the semantics of the inoperative statement skip. The second equation defines the semantics of the assignment statement $v := e$, which updates the current state. The next two equations define the semantics of the send statement $c!e$ and the communication pattern j, respectively; in both cases a synchronization attempt is added to the continuation. Our denotational model makes a *silent step* (sometimes called a *hiaton*; see, e.g., Chapt. 9 of [2]), i.e. an elementary step that does not modify the state of the system upon the creation of each synchronization attempt. The elementary steps that precede the call to the scheduler function kc ensure the contractiveness of the higher-order mapping Φ.

In the case of our language MCC, a continuation is a tree of computations with active elements at the leaves (i.e., maximal elements with respect to order '$\leq$'). In the case of a sequential composition $(s_1; s_2)$, the computations $\mathcal{D}(s_1)$ and $\mathcal{D}(s_2)$ are using the identifiers $\alpha \cdot 1$ and α, respectively ($\alpha \cdot 1 > \alpha$). The scheduler function kc gives priority to the computations at the leaves of the tree that represents the continuation; therefore $\mathcal{D}(s_2)$ will be evaluated only after the completion of the evaluation of $\mathcal{D}(s_1)$. In the case of a parallel composition $(s_1 \parallel s_2)$, the computations $\mathcal{D}(s_1)$ and $\mathcal{D}(s_2)$ are using the identifiers $\alpha \cdot 1$ and

$\alpha \cdot 2$, respectively; $\alpha \cdot 1$ and $\alpha \cdot 2$ are incomparable with respect to $\leq$, and so the computations $\mathcal{D}(s_1)$ and $\mathcal{D}(s_2)$ are evaluated in an independent manner.

It may not be obvious that the scheduler function kc is well-defined, since it occurs in the right-hand side of its definition. The recursive occurrence of kc is preceded by the (contracting) synchronization step "$(\sigma \mid \varsigma \Rightarrow \kappa) \cdot \ldots$". We could define kc as fixed-point of an appropriate higher-order contraction. However, it is easier to define kc by induction on the number of communication patterns (of the type $J^\diamond$) that are contained in the continuation κ. A continuation is a *finite* structure of **Comp** computations (**Comp** $= J^\diamond + Snd + \frac{1}{2} \cdot \mathbf{D}$). After each synchronization step the number of $J^\diamond$ communication patterns that are contained in a continuation decreases by 1. When the continuation contains no communication pattern then $\Omega_S(\kappa) = \emptyset$. If $\Omega_S(\kappa) = \emptyset$ then the evaluation either terminates, or blocks, or $\Omega_A(\kappa) \neq \emptyset$. If $\Omega_A(\kappa) \neq \emptyset$ then a computation (of the type $\frac{1}{2} \cdot \mathbf{D}$) contained in κ is activated for evaluation.

The denotational semantics $\mathcal{D}$ is defined as the (unique) fixed point of the higher-order mapping Φ. The definition of $\Phi(S)(s)$ is organized by induction on complexity measure $c_s(s)$. In the CSC approach a computation is an element of the type $\mathbf{D}$. A computation takes as parameter a continuation. A continuation is a dynamic store of computations. Computations are stored in continuations as elements of the type $\frac{1}{2} \cdot \mathbf{D}$ (the distance between computations halves while they are stored into the continuation). Intuitively, when a computation contained in a continuation is activated for evaluation it moves from the space $\frac{1}{2} \cdot \mathbf{D}$ to the space $\mathbf{D}$. This phenomenon explains the occurrence of the multiplication factor 2 (rather than $\frac{1}{2}$) in Lemma 1(b). Also, a computation is a function that is (only) non-expansive (rather than contractive) in the continuation, as stated by Lemma 2(b). Still, the higher-order mapping Φ is $\frac{1}{2}$ contractive.

Lemma 1. (a) *The mapping kc (of Definition 1) is well-defined.*
(b) $\forall \kappa_1, \kappa_2 \in \mathbf{Kont} : d(kc(\kappa_1), kc(\kappa_2)) \leq 2 \cdot d(\kappa_1, \kappa_2)$.

Lemma 2. *For all $S \in (Stat \to \mathbf{D}), s \in Stat, \alpha \in Id, \kappa \in \mathbf{Kont}, \sigma \in \Sigma$, we have*

(a) $\Phi(S)(s)(\alpha, \kappa)(\sigma) \in \mathbf{P}$ *(it is well-defined)*,
(b) $\Phi(S)(s)$ *is non-expansive (in (α, κ)), and*
(c) Φ *is $\frac{1}{2}$ - contractive (in S)*.

Example 1. *Let $j \in J, s_1, s_2 \in Stat$, $j = c_1?v_1 \& c_2?v_2$, $s_1 = c_1!1 \parallel c_2!2$ and $s_2 = j; (v := v_1 + v_2 \parallel v := 10)$. Let also $\sigma_1 = [\sigma \mid v_1 \mapsto 1 \mid v_2 \mapsto 2]$, $\sigma_2 = [\sigma_1 \mid v \mapsto 3]$, $\sigma_3 = [\sigma_1 \mid v \mapsto 10]$ $(\sigma, \sigma_1, \sigma_2, \sigma_3 \in \Sigma)$. One can check that:*

$$\mathcal{D}[\![s_1 \parallel s_2]\!](\sigma) = \{\sigma\sigma\sigma\sigma_1\sigma_2\sigma_3, \sigma\sigma\sigma\sigma_1\sigma_3\sigma_2\}$$

The execution begins with three silent steps "$\sigma\sigma\sigma$" corresponding to three synchronization attempts, followed by a multichannel communication which modifies the state from σ to σ_1. Next, the statements $v := v_1 + v_2$ and $v := 10$ are executed in an interleaved manner, which gives rise to nondeterminism.

3.1   Concurrency Laws

The semantic operators designed with continuation semantics for concurrency (CSC) to express the behaviour of MCC programs satisfy the basic concurrency laws. Some properties, such as the commutativity, associativity and idempotency of nondeterministic choice can be proved for all continuations by simple manipulations of the semantic equations. The right distributivity of the nondeterministic choice over sequential composition is also easy to establish.

In order to prove other semantic properties one can employ the technique introduced in [6], which relies on the identification of computation invariants (expressed as relations between continuation structures) and the use of contraction $\epsilon \leq \frac{1}{2} \cdot \epsilon \Rightarrow \epsilon = 0$. Arguments of the kind $\epsilon \leq \frac{1}{2} \cdot \epsilon \Rightarrow \epsilon = 0$ are standard in metric semantics [2]. The identification of computing invariants as relations between continuation structures is specific of the CSC technique.

Theorem 2 states the main properties of the semantic operators designed with CSC for MCC. The complete proof of Theorem 2 is given in the attached technical report [4]. The semantic properties stated by Theorem 2 are preserved in any MCC syntactic context. The notion of a syntactic context for MCC is introduced in Definition 2. In Definitions 3(a) and 4 we also introduce the notion of a *resumption* as a structure of MCC statements, and a notion of *isomorphism* over resumptions, respectively. Function K introduced in Definition 3(b) maps a resumption to a corresponding continuation that contains only denotations of program statements. Following [2], the notion of a *resumption* is also used in Sect. 4 as an operational counterpart of the term *continuation*.

A continuation can contain arbitrary values of the type $\mathbf{D}$. The properties presented in Theorem 2 hold for all the isomorphic continuations containing only computations denotable by program statements. This represents an invariant of the denotational semantics and ensures its consistency just because the initial continuation is empty, and the denotational semantics adds to the continuation only denotations of the language constructs. Some properties, namely Theorem 2(a)–(d), hold for all continuations.

Definition 2. *(Contexts for MCC)*

$$C ::= (\cdot) \mid a \mid x \mid C; C \mid C + C \mid C \| C$$

We denote by $C(s)$ the result of substituting s for $(\cdot)$ in C. Formally, this substitution can be defined inductively: $(\cdot)(s) = s$, $a(s) = a$, $x(s) = x$, and $(C_1 \text{ op } C_2)(s) = C_1(s) \text{ op } C_2(s)$ where $\text{op} \in \{;, +, \|\}$.

Definition 3. *(a) Let $(\theta \in) Comp = J^\diamond \cup Snd \cup Stat$ (notice that $J \subseteq Stat$, but $J^\diamond \cap Stat = \emptyset$). We define $(k \in) KRes = \{\!|Comp|\!\}$ representing the set of closed resumptions.[3] The set $CRes$ of open resumptions is defined by*

$$CRes = \{(\alpha, k) \mid \alpha \in Id, k \in KRes, \nu(\alpha, id(k))\}$$

where $\nu : Id \times \Pi \to Bool$, $\nu(\alpha, \pi) = (\alpha \notin \pi) \wedge (\alpha \in max(\{\alpha\} \cup \pi))$.

---

[3] In this case the construct $\{\!| \cdot |\!\}$ is used to define an ordinary set.

(b) Let $\Theta : Comp \to \mathbf{Comp}$, $\Theta(\langle j \rangle) = \langle j \rangle$, $\Theta(c!\xi) = c!\xi$ and $\Theta(s) = \mathcal{D}(s)$. We define $K : KRes \to \mathbf{Kont}$ by $K(k) = (id(k), \varphi)$, where $\varphi(\alpha) = \Theta(k(\alpha)))$, $\forall \alpha \in Id$.

Definition 4. *We say that two open resumptions* $(\alpha_1, k_1), (\alpha_2, k_2) \in CRes$ *are isomorphic and we write* $(\alpha_1, k_1) \cong (\alpha_2, k_2)$ *iff there exists a bijection* $\mu : (\{\alpha_1\} \cup id(k_1)) \to (\{\alpha_2\} \cup id(k_2))$ *such that*

(i) $\mu(\alpha_1) = \alpha_2$
(ii) $\mu(\alpha') \leq \mu(\alpha'') \Leftrightarrow \alpha' \leq \alpha''$, $\forall \alpha', \alpha'' \in \{\alpha_1\} \cup id(k_1)$
(iii) $k_2(\mu(\alpha)) = k_1(\alpha)$, $\forall \alpha \in id(k_1)$

We write $s \simeq \overline{s}$ $(s, \overline{s} \in Stat)$ to express that $\mathcal{D}(C(s))(\alpha, K(k)) = \mathcal{D}(C(\overline{s}))(\overline{\alpha}, K(\overline{k}))$ for all MCC syntactic contexts C and all isomorphic resumptions $(\alpha, k) \cong (\overline{\alpha}, \overline{k})$.

Theorem 2. *For all* $s, s_1, s_2, s_3 \in Stat$, *we have*

$$
\begin{array}{lll}
(a) & s_1 + s_2 \simeq s_2 + s_1 & (commutativity\,of\ +) \\
(b) & (s_1 + s_2) + s_3 \simeq s_1 + (s_2 + s_3) & (associativity\,of\ +) \\
(c) & s + s \simeq s & (idempotency\,of\ +) \\
(d) & (s_1 + s_2); s_3 \simeq s_1; s_3 + s_2; s_3 & (right distributivity\,of\ ;\ over +) \\
(e) & s_1; (s_2 + s_3) \simeq s_1; s_2 + s_1; s_3 & (left distributivity\,of\ ;\ over +) \\
(f) & s_1; (s_2; s_3) \simeq (s_1; s_2); s_3 & (associativity\,of\ ;) \\
(g) & s_1 \parallel s_2 \simeq s_2 \parallel s_1 & (commutativity\,of\ \parallel) \\
(h) & s_1 \parallel (s_2 \parallel s_3) \simeq (s_1 \parallel s_2) \parallel s_3 & (associativity\,of\ \parallel)
\end{array}
$$

Let $s, \overline{s} \in MCC$. It is easy to show that $s \simeq \overline{s}$ implies $\mathcal{D}[\![C(s)]\!] = \mathcal{D}[\![C(\overline{s})]\!]$, for any MCC syntactic context C. We obtain the following Corollary which can be used to describe compositionally the behaviour of $\mathcal{D}[\![s]\!]$ which evaluates an MCC program s with respect to the empty continuation (α_0, κ_0).

Corollary 1. *For all* $s, s_1, s_2, s_3 \in Stat$, *and for all contexts* C, *we have*

(a) $\mathcal{D}[\![C(s_1 + s_2)]\!] = \mathcal{D}[\![C(s_2 + s_1)]\!]$;
(b) $\mathcal{D}[\![C((s_1 + s_2) + s_3)]\!] = \mathcal{D}[\![C(s_1 + (s_2 + s_3))]\!]$;
(c) $\mathcal{D}[\![C(s + s)]\!] = \mathcal{D}[\![C(s)]\!]$;
(d) $\mathcal{D}[\![C((s_1 + s_2); s_3)]\!] = \mathcal{D}[\![C((s_1; s_3) + (s_2; s_3))]\!]$;
(e) $\mathcal{D}[\![C(s_1; (s_2 + s_3))]\!] = \mathcal{D}[\![C((s_1; s_2) + (s_1; s_3))]\!]$;
(f) $\mathcal{D}[\![C(s_1; (s_2; s_3))]\!] = \mathcal{D}[\![C((s_1; s_2); s_3)]\!]$;
(g) $\mathcal{D}[\![C(s_1 \parallel s_2)]\!] = \mathcal{D}[\![C(s_2 \parallel s_1)]\!]$;
(h) $\mathcal{D}[\![C(s_1 \parallel (s_2 \parallel s_3))]\!] = \mathcal{D}[\![C((s_1 \parallel s_2) \parallel s_3)]\!]$.

4   Operational Semantics ($\mathcal{O}$): Relating $\mathcal{D}$ and $\mathcal{O}$

We define an operational semantics $\mathcal{O}$ for MCC by means of a transition relation embedded in a deductive system in the style of Plotkin's structured operational semantics [12]. The operational semantics $\mathcal{O}$ is also designed by using the continuation semantics for concurrency (CSC) technique. Following [2], we use the term *resumption* as an operational counterpart of the term *continuation*. Then we establish the formal relationship between the operational semantics given in this section and the denotational semantics $\mathcal{D}$ given in Sect. 3.

A configuration of the operational semantics is either a triple $(s, (\alpha, k), \sigma)$ consisting of a statement, an open resumption and a state, or a pair (k, σ) consisting of a closed resumption and a state.

Definition 5. *We define the set* $(t \in) Conf$ *of configurations for the operational semantics of MCC by* $Conf = (Stat \times CRes \times \Sigma) \cup (KRes \times \Sigma)$.

We use some auxiliary mappings $\omega, \omega_A, \omega_S : KRes \to \mathcal{P}_{fin}(Sched)$,[4] which we define with the aid of the predicate $sync : (Sched \times KRes) \to Bool$:

$$sync(\{\alpha\}, k) = false$$
$$sync(\{\alpha, \alpha_1, \ldots, \alpha_n\}, k) = (k(\alpha) = \langle c_1?v_1 \& \cdots \& c_n?v_n \rangle \in J^\diamond) \wedge$$
$$(k(\alpha_1) = c_1!\xi_1 \in Snd) \wedge \cdots \wedge (k(\alpha_n) = c_n!\xi_n \in Snd)$$
$$\omega(k) = \omega_A(k) \cup \omega_S(k)$$
$$\omega_A(k) = \{\{\alpha\} \mid \alpha \in max(id(k)), k(\alpha) \in Stat\}$$
$$\omega_S(k) = \{\varsigma \mid \varsigma \subseteq max(id(k)), sync(\varsigma, k)\}$$

We also define $(\cdot \mid \cdot \to \cdot) : (\Sigma \times Sched \times KRes) \to \Sigma$ as follows:

$$(\sigma \mid \varsigma \to k) = \begin{cases} [\sigma \mid v_1 \mapsto \xi_1(\sigma) \mid \cdots \mid v_n \mapsto \xi_n(\sigma)] \\ \quad \text{if } \varsigma \subseteq max(id(k)), sync(\varsigma, k), \\ \quad \varsigma = \{\alpha, \alpha_1, \ldots, \alpha_n\}, \\ \quad k(\alpha) = \langle c_1?v_1 \& \cdots \& c_n?v_n \rangle, \\ \quad k(\alpha_1) = c_1!\xi_1, \ldots, k(\alpha_n) = c_n!\xi_n \\ \sigma \qquad \text{otherwise} \end{cases}$$

$\omega, \omega_A, \omega_S$ and $(\cdot \mid \cdot \to \cdot)$ are the operational counterparts of the mappings $\Omega, \Omega_A, \Omega_S$ and $(\cdot \mid \cdot \Rightarrow \cdot)$, respectively, defined in Sect. 3.

The definition of the operational semantics of MCC is based on a transition relation $\to \subseteq Conf \times (KRes \times \Sigma)$. We write $t \to t'$ to express that $(t, t') \in \to$. The restriction to $KRes \times \Sigma$ (in the right-hand side of a transition) is justified in Lemma 3. In Definition 6 we use the following convention:

$$t_1 \nearrow t_2 \quad \text{is an abbreviation for} \quad \frac{t_2 \to t'}{t_1 \to t'}$$

Definition 6. *The transition relation for MCC is the smallest subset of* $Conf \times (KRes \times \Sigma)$ *satisfying the axioms and rules given below.*

(A1) $(\mathsf{skip}, (\alpha, k), \sigma) \to (k, \sigma)$
(A2) $(v := e, (\alpha, k), \sigma) \to (k, [\sigma \mid v \mapsto \mathcal{E}[\![e]\!](\sigma)])$
(A3) $(c!e, (\alpha, k), \sigma) \to ([k \mid \alpha \mapsto c!\mathcal{E}[\![e]\!]], \sigma)$

---

[4] $(\varsigma \in) Sched = \mathcal{P}_{nfin}(Id)$; see Sect. 3.

(A4) $(j, (\alpha, k), \sigma) \to ([k \mid \alpha \mapsto \langle j \rangle], \sigma)$
(R5) $(x, (\alpha, k), \sigma) \nearrow (D(x), (\alpha, k), \sigma)$
(R6) $(s_1; s_2, (\alpha, k), \sigma) \nearrow (s_1, (\alpha \cdot 1, [k \mid \alpha \mapsto s_2]), \sigma)$
(R7) $(s_1 + s_2, (\alpha, k), \sigma) \nearrow (s_1, (\alpha, k), \sigma)$
(R8) $(s_1 + s_2, (\alpha, k), \sigma) \nearrow (s_2, (\alpha, k), \sigma)$
(R9) $(s_1 \parallel s_2, (\alpha, k), \sigma) \nearrow (s_1, (\alpha \cdot 1, [k \mid \alpha \cdot 2 \mapsto s_2]), \sigma)$
(R10) $(s_1 \parallel s_2, (\alpha, k), \sigma) \nearrow (s_2, (\alpha \cdot 2, [k \mid \alpha \cdot 1 \mapsto s_1]), \sigma)$
(R11) $(k, \sigma) \nearrow (k(\alpha), (\alpha, k \setminus \{\alpha\}), \sigma)$ if $\{\alpha\} \in w_A(k)$
(A12) $(k, \sigma) \to (k \setminus \hat{\varsigma}, (\sigma \mid \varsigma \to k))$ if $\varsigma \in w_S(k)$

Some explanations are necessary.

- A configuration $(s, (\alpha, k), \sigma)$ contains an *active* statement s with identifier α; the rest of the program is encapsulated in the resumption k. According to rules (A1), (A2), (A3) and (A4), if s is an elementary statement, the program performs a transition step. A synchronization attempt is added to the resumption if s is a communication pattern j or a send statement $c!e$.
- The sequential execution of s_1 and s_2 is enforced in rule (R6) by the fact that the $\alpha < \alpha \cdot 1$. According to rules (R9), (R10) the statements s_1 and s_2 in a construct $s_1 \parallel s_2$ are executed in an interleaved manner because the identifiers $\alpha \cdot 1$ and $\alpha \cdot 2$ are incomparable (neither $\alpha \cdot 1 \leq \alpha \cdot 2$ nor $\alpha \cdot 2 \leq \alpha \cdot 1$).
- Rules (R6), (R9) and (R10) should be read in conjunction with (R11) and (A12). The left hand side in each of the rules (R11) and (A12) is a configuration of the form (k, σ); k is a resumption, i.e., a tree-like structure with active components at the leaves.
- Rule (R11) models the activation of an *MCC* statement. Rule (A12) captures the semantics a synchronization between a communication pattern $\langle c_1?v_1 \& \cdots \& c_n?v_n \rangle$ and n corresponding send attempts $c_1!\xi_1, \ldots, c_n!\xi_n$. In general, the state σ is modified upon synchronization.

Definition 7. *(Normal termination and deadlock)*

(a) We define the predicates $terminates, blocks : KRes \to Bool$ as follows:

$$terminates(k) = (id(k) = \emptyset)$$
$$blocks(k) = (id(k) \neq \emptyset) \wedge (w(k) = \emptyset)$$

(b) Let $t \in Conf$. We say that t terminates if $t = (k, \sigma) \in KRes \times \Sigma$ and $terminates(k)$. We say that t blocks if $t = (k, \sigma) \in KRes \times \Sigma$ and $blocks(k)$.

A configuration of the form $(k, \sigma)(\in KRes \times \Sigma)$ terminates if the resumption k is empty (i.e., $id(k) = \emptyset$). Also, (k, σ) blocks if $id(k) \neq \emptyset$ and rules (R11) and (A12) are not applicable. It is not difficult to prove the following Lemma.

Lemma 3. *Let $t \in Conf$. We write $t \not\to$ to express that t has no transitions, i.e., $\neg(\exists t' \in Conf : t \to t')$.*

(a) $t \not\to \Leftrightarrow t$ terminates or t blocks.
(b) If $t \to t'$ then $t' \in KRes \times \Sigma$ (i.e., $t' = (k, \sigma)$, for some $k \in KRes, \sigma \in \Sigma$).

Lemma 3(b) can be proved in two steps. First for all configurations of the form $(s, (\alpha, k), \sigma)$ by induction on $c_s(s)$. Next, for all configurations of the form (k, σ) as follows. If (k, σ) terminates or blocks then, according to Lemma 3(a) $(k, \sigma) \nrightarrow$. Otherwise, $\omega(k) \neq \emptyset$ and either $\omega_S(k) \neq \emptyset$ in which case the result is immediate according to rule (A12), or $\omega_A(k) \neq \emptyset$ in which case the desired result follows according to rule (R11) by using the first step of the proof.

Definition 8. *(Operational semantics $\mathcal{O}$)*

(a) *Let* $(S \in)Sem_O = Conf \rightarrow \mathbf{P}$ *(the domain* $\mathbf{P}$ *was introduced at the beginning of Sect. 3) and let* $\Psi : Sem_O \rightarrow Sem_O$ *be given by:*

$$\Psi(S)(t) = \begin{cases} \{\lambda\} & \text{if } t \text{ terminates} \\ \{\delta\} & \text{if } t \text{ blocks} \\ \bigcup\{\sigma \cdot S(k, \sigma) \mid t \rightarrow (k, \sigma)\} & \text{otherwise} \end{cases}$$

(b) *Let* $\alpha_0 = \lambda$. *Let* $k_0 \in KRes, k_0 = (\emptyset, f_0)$, *with* $f_0 \in (Id \rightarrow Comp), f_0(\alpha) =$ skip $, \forall \alpha \in Id$. *We put* $\mathcal{O} = fix(\Psi)$ *and define* $\mathcal{O}[\![\cdot]\!] : Stat \rightarrow \Sigma \rightarrow \mathbf{P}$ *by*

$$\mathcal{O}[\![s]\!](\sigma) = \mathcal{O}(s, (\alpha_0, k_0), \sigma)$$

One can check that the set $\{(k, \sigma) \mid t \rightarrow (k, \sigma)\}$ is *finite*, for any configuration $t \in Conf$. This fact can be proved in two steps. First, for all configurations $(s, (\alpha, k), \sigma)$ by induction on $c_s(s)$, and next, for all configurations (k, σ), by using the fact that $id(k)$ is a finite set, for any $k \in KRes$. The implication is that the transition system for MCC is *finitely branching*, and thus it induces a compact operational semantics [2]. The higher-order mapping Ψ is contracting (and thus it has a unique fixed point) due to the "$\sigma \cdot \ldots$"-step in its definition.

Now we show that $\mathcal{D}[\![s]\!] = \mathcal{O}[\![s]\!], \forall s \in Stat$. We introduce an auxiliary mapping $\mathcal{R} : Conf \rightarrow \mathbf{P}$ (which is defined based on the denotational mapping $\mathcal{D}$) and we show that $\mathcal{R} = \mathcal{O}$. The desired result is presented in Theorem 3.

Definition 9. *Considering the mapping* $K : KRes \rightarrow \mathbf{Kont}$, *we define* $\mathcal{R} :$ $Conf \rightarrow \mathbf{P}$ *by:*

$$\mathcal{R}(k, \sigma) = kc(K(k))(\sigma)$$
$$\mathcal{R}(s, (\alpha, k), \sigma) = \mathcal{D}(s)(\alpha, K(k))(\sigma).$$

Lemma 4. $\mathcal{R} = fix(\Psi)$.

By combining Definition 8, Lemma 4 and Banach's fixed point theorem, we obtain the main result of this section.

Theorem 3. $\mathcal{D}[\![s]\!] = \mathcal{O}[\![s]\!]$ *for all* $s \in Stat$.

The denotational model $\mathcal{D}(\cdot)$ $(\in Stat \rightarrow \mathbf{D})$ of MCC given in Definition 1 is *correct* with respect to the operational model $\mathcal{O}[\![\cdot]\!] : Stat \rightarrow \Sigma \rightarrow \mathbf{P}$ given in Definition 8. Indeed, assume that $\mathcal{D}(s_1) = \mathcal{D}(s_2)$. By the compositionality of the denotational semantics function $\mathcal{D}(\cdot)$ we obtain $\mathcal{D}(C(s_1)) = \mathcal{D}(C(s_2))$, for any MCC context $C(\cdot)$, and thus $\mathcal{D}[\![C(s_1)]\!] = \mathcal{D}[\![C(s_2)]\!]$. By using Theorem 3, we obtain $\mathcal{O}[\![C(s_1)]\!] = \mathcal{O}[\![C(s_2)]\!]$ for any MCC syntactic context $C(\cdot)$, which means that $\mathcal{D}(\cdot)$ is *correct* with respect to $\mathcal{O}[\![\cdot]\!]$.

5   Conclusion

In this paper we present a formal design of concurrent languages based on the concept of continuation. We define a denotational semantics designed with continuations for a CSP-like language extended with a mechanism for synchronization on multiple channels, and prove that the semantic operators designed with continuations satisfy the basic laws of concurrency. We established the semantic properties for all continuations that contain only denotations of program statements. We conclude that continuations are semantic evaluation contexts that preserve concurrency laws. The proof technique presented in this paper is based on the behavioural invariants given by the specific structure of continuations. We think this techniques could be generally applied to all the language designed by using CSC. For a given language, the invariant properties should be expressed in terms of the particular structure of CSC continuations that are used in the design of the language; this approach allows to interpret nontrivial constructs. For the language under investigation, we also developed an operational semantics, and we related formally the denotational and operational semantics.

Acknowledgements. This research was supported by the Romanian National Authority for Scientific Research, project number PN-II-ID-PCE-2011-3-0919.

References

1. America, P., Rutten, J.J.M.M.: Solving reflexive domain equations in a category of complete metric spaces. J. Comp. Syst. Sci. **39**(3), 343–375 (1989)
2. de Bakker, J.W., de Vink, E.P.: Control Flow Semantics. MIT Press, Cambridge (1996)
3. Bobrow, D.G., Wegbreit, B.: A model and stack implementation of multiple environments. Comm. ACM **16**(10), 591–603 (1973)
4. Ciobanu, G., Todoran, E.N.: Continuation semantics for concurrency. Technical report FML-09-02, Romanian Academy (2009). http://iit.iit.tuiasi.ro/TR/reports/fml0902.pdf
5. Ciobanu, G., Todoran, E.N.: Relating two metric semantics for parallel rewriting of multisets. In: Proceedings of the SYNASC 2012, pp. 273–281. IEEE Computer Press (2012)
6. Ciobanu, G., Todoran, E.N.: Continuation semantics for asynchronous concurrency. Fundamenta Informaticae **131**(3–4), 373–388 (2014)
7. Danvy, O.: On evaluation contexts, continuations and the rest of the computation. In: 4th ACM SIGPLAN Continuations Workshop, pp. 13–23 (2004)
8. Fournet, C., Gonthier, G.: The join calculus: a language for distributed mobile programming. In: Barthe, G., Dybjer, P., Pinto, L., Saraiva, J. (eds.) APPSEM 2000. LNCS, vol. 2395, pp. 268–332. Springer, Heidelberg (2002)
9. Hoare, C.A.R.: Communicating Sequential Processes. Prentice Hall, Upper Saddle River (1985)
10. Milner, R.: Fully abstract models of typed λ-calculi. TCS **4**, 1–22 (1977)
11. Milner, R.: A Calculus of Communicating Systems. LNCS, vol. 92. Springer, Heidelberg (1980)

12. Plotkin, G.: A structural approach to operational semantics. J. Log. Algebr. Program. **60–61**, 17–139 (2004)
13. Roscoe, A.W.: The Theory and Practice of Concurrency. Prentice Hall, Upper Saddle River (1997)
14. Stratchey, C., Wadsworth, C.: Continuations: a mathematical semantics for handling full jumps. Higher-Order Symbolic Comput. **13**, 135–152 (2000)
15. Todoran, E.N.: Metric semantics for synchronous and asynchronous communication: a continuation-based approach. ENTCS **28**, 119–146 (2000)

SysML Blocks Adaptation

Hamida Bouaziz[✉], Samir Chouali, Ahmed Hammad, and Hassan Mountassir

FEMTO-ST Institute, University of Franche-Comté, Besançon, France
{hamida.bouaziz,schouali,ahammad,hmountas}@femto-st.fr

Abstract. Regarding the increasing complexity of today's systems, system engineering domain knows a constant evolution in term of processes and paradigms (Object Oriented, Component Oriented). SysML constitutes a new trends of system engineering which allows to model the system as a set of blocks. In this paper, we propose a bottom-up approach to build a system, based on its partial specifications. Our goal consists on proposing a methodology which allows to a system architect, in order to build a reliable system, to start from an abstract specification of a system, that we model as a SysML composite block, and then select a set of suitable blocks to meet this specification. The approach is based on reusing and adapting formally SysML blocks using a converter-complement block, which plays the role of a mediator between the reused blocks and the rest part of the system.

Keywords: SysML · Block · Converter-complement

1 Introduction

How to assemble components designed in isolation? That is the major question on which components based software engineering domain (*CBSE*) tries to give more precise and adequate answers. CBSE is considered as a natural consequence to the object oriented paradigm and the emergence of platforms of components (i.e. CORBA, CCM). Its major goal is to build a market of software components (the so called COTS: Commercial-Off-The-Shelf), in which the developer finds the adequate components to integrate to its application.

System engineering also adopts the principle of using the component as the development unit. This appears clearly through SysML [1], a language that is used to design systems that include software and hardware. The System Modelling Language (*SysML*), through its diagrams, fosters the view point that takes the system as a set of components. In SysML, we call them blocks. The Block Definition Diagram (*BDD*) of SysML can be seen as a tree of blocks, where the leaf nodes are the concrete blocks and the rest nodes until the root are abstract blocks. The abstract ones are called composite blocks, they are composed by assembling a set of blocks located in a less level of hierarchy.

In this paper, we propose a bottom-up approach to build the system by adapting SysML blocks. Starting from a specification of a system part, which we consider as a SysML composite block '*B*' to build, the architect select some

© Springer International Publishing Switzerland 2015
M. Butler et al. (Eds.): ICFEM 2015, LNCS 9407, pp. 417–433, 2015.
DOI: 10.1007/978-3-319-25423-4_27

SysML blocks, and adapt them using our method to meet the specification of B. In the next step of the development, the composite block B and another set of blocks will be used to achieve the specification of their parent. So, in our approach, we build an adapter per a composite block, the sub-blocks use this adapter to interact with the rest of the system.

The adaptation concerns the interaction protocols of the blocks. In this paper, we use the interface automata [2] as formalism to formally specify the interaction protocol of the reused blocks (sub-blocks), the adapter block and the specification of the part to build (the parent block). Our notion of the adapter differs from the notion used in the existing works [3–7], which define the adaptor as a protocol converter. In fact, in our approach the adapter has two roles. It plays its role as a converter between the reused blocks on the one hand, and between the reused blocks and their future parent block on the other hand. It plays the second role as a complement by performing to the reused blocks what they require and it's not planned to be required by their parent, and to offer what the parent must provide and it's not provided by any part of it.

The remainder of this paper is organized as follows: In Sect. 2, we discuss related work. Sect. 3 presents the preliminaries about the SysML BDD, SysML IBD, the interface automata and the adaptation contract. Sect. 4, introduces our approach of adapting SysML blocks. In Sect. 5, we illustrate our approach by a case study. Finally, in Sect. 6, we conclude and we present perspectives of our work.

2   Related Work

In literature, many approaches [8–10] have been proposed to adapt components designed separately. These approaches differ, for example, in the formalism used to represent the interfaces of the components and to model their interaction protocols. In addition, the approaches which intend to assemble the components differs in the direction of the design: upstream vs downstream. We find in [11], Carrillo et al. adopt a top down approach, where they verify if a specification of a SysML composite block can be divided on a set of sub-blocks specifications, the authors didn't refer to the adaptation issue. In [3,4], authors construct the wanted system by assembling existing components. They start from existing components which represent the leaves of the system. They take components designed separately, so to allow the correct interaction between them, they synthesize a third entity called adapter.

Our approach, which we present in this paper, concerns SysML blocks, it is a bottom up approach like in [3,4]. In our process, we don't give only the mapping rules between actions like in [5,12], and we don't give the specification of the adapter as in the works already done in [6,7]. But, we give the interaction protocol of the composite block which will include the reused blocks. The specification of the composite block is built by the architect according to the interaction protocol of the system's part has already been designed, and in function of what the current composite block must perform to the system's part still to develop.

In our approach, we don't use the conditions of consistency used by Carrillo et al. in [11] concerning the inclusion relation between the set of services offered and required by the composite block vs the set of services provided and required by its sub-blocks, because in the present work we take into consideration the possibility of making an adapter as a complement to achieve the specification of the parent block.

Our notion of adapter differs from the notion used in the existing works. In the works have already done, the adapter is like a protocol converter. However, in our approach the adapter has two roles. It plays the first role as a converter between sub-blocks on the one hand, and between the rest of the system and the reused sub-blocks of the composite block on the other hand. The second role is to perform to the sub-blocks what they require and it is not planned to be required by their parent, and to provide what the parent must provide to the rest of system and it is not offered by the selected sub-blocks.

We can consider that our approach introduces a new branch to the taxonomy of component adaptation. In [7], the adapter is defined binary, and in [3] is defined system-wide. However, in our approach, the adapter is defined as a composite-block-wide adapter.

3   Background

3.1   Block Definition Diagram

The Block Definition Diagram (BDD) in SysML defines features of blocks and relationships between them such as associations, generalizations, and dependencies. It captures the definition of blocks in terms of properties and operations [1].

Formally, we define a block definition diagram by the tuple:

$$BDD = <B, R>$$

where: **B** is the blocks set that compose the system. **R** is the set of relations between blocks.

The blocks are modular units of the system description. A block may include both structural and behavioural features, such as properties and operations. To communicate with its environment, a block has a list of ports. Formally, we define a block as:

Block = < name, Values, Operations, Constraints, Parts, References, Ports >

Where: **Values** is the attributes set of the block. **Operations** describe the behaviour of the block. **Constraints** give some conditions about the values. **Parts** include the list of the blocks connected with the current block through a composition relation. **Reference** include a list of the blocks connected with the current block through a navigable association. **Ports** is the list of the ports positioned on the block.

In SysML 1.2, we distinguish flow ports and standard ports. The flow specification is deprecated in SysML 1.3. However, the standard ports still existed. Formally, we define a standard port by its name, its type and its direction. The type of the port is represented by a block containing a list of operations, we call it *"interface_Block"*. The direction specifies if the port is a required or a provided port.

We formalize a standard port as:

$$port = \langle \ name, \ type, \ Direction \ \rangle$$

A block which types a port contains a set of operations, we call it *Interface_Block*, it specifies one of the interfaces associated to the block. We define it as follows:

$$Interface\_Block = \langle name, \ Op \rangle$$

where: **name** is the name of the interface_block. **Op** is the set of provided operations by the block which has the provided port whose type is this interface_block. It can also be the set of required operations by the block which has the required port whose type is this interface_block.

3.2   Internal Block Diagram

The Internal Block Diagram (IBD) in SysML captures the internal structure of a composite block [1]. It allows to represent the relations between the required and the provided ports of blocks instances. These relations are represented using the connectors. Formally, we define an IBD as:

$$IBD = \langle Parts, \ Ports, \ Connectors \rangle$$

where: **Parts** is a set of blocks instances. **Ports** is a set of ports. Each port is assigned to a part. **Connectors** is a set of connectors linking provided ports with required ports of blocks instances.

3.3   Interface Automata

Interface automata [2] were introduced by Alfaro and Henzinger to specify component interfaces and also to verify component assembly based on their actions. The set of actions is decomposed into three groups: input actions '?', output actions '!' and internal actions ','.

Definition 1 (Interface Automaton): An *interface automaton A* is represented by the tuple: $\langle S_A, I_A, \Sigma_A^I, \Sigma_A^O, \Sigma_A^H, \delta_A \rangle$

Where: S_A is a finite set of states. $I_A \subseteq S_A$ is a set of initial states. Σ_A^I, Σ_A^O, and Σ_A^H, respectively denote the sets of input, output, and internal actions. The set of actions of A is denoted by Σ_A. The set $\delta_A \subseteq S_A \times \Sigma_A \times S_A$ is the set of transitions between states.

Definition 2 (Synchronous product): The *synchronous product* is used to capture the parallel execution of two components represented by their interface automata. Before computing the global behaviour of the two components, it is mandatory to verify if they can be assembled by testing their composability. Two interface automata A_1 and A_2 are composable if:
$\Sigma_{A_1}^I \cap \Sigma_{A_2}^I = \Sigma_{A_1}^O \cap \Sigma_{A_2}^O = \Sigma_{A_1}^H \cap \Sigma_{A_2} = \Sigma_{A_1} \cap \Sigma_{A_2}^H = \emptyset.$
The synchronous product between *two composable interface automata A_1* and A_2 is defined as: $A_1 \otimes A_2 = \langle \ S_{A_1 \otimes A_2}, I_{A_1 \otimes A_2}, \Sigma_{A_1 \otimes A_2}^I, \Sigma_{A_1 \otimes A_2}^O, \Sigma_{A_1 \otimes A_2}^H, \delta_{A_1 \otimes A_2} \ \rangle$

- $S_{A_1 \otimes A_2} = S_{A_1} \times S_{A_2}$ and $I_{A_1 \otimes A_2} = I_{A_1} \times I_{A_2}$.
- $\Sigma^I_{A_1 \otimes A_2} = (\Sigma^I_{A_1} \cup \Sigma^I_{A_2}) \setminus Shared(A_1, A_2)$.
- $\Sigma^O_{A_1 \otimes A_2} = (\Sigma^O_{A_1} \cup \Sigma^O_{A_2}) \setminus Shared(A_1, A_2)$.
- $\Sigma^H_{A_1 \otimes A_2} = \Sigma^H_{A_1} \cup \Sigma^H_{A_2} \cup Shared(A_1, A_2)$.
- $((s_1, s_2), a, (s'_1, s'_2)) \in \delta_{A_1 \otimes A_2}$ if
  - $a \notin Shared(A_1, A_2) \wedge (s_1, a, s'_1) \in \delta_{A_1} \wedge s_2 = s'_2$
  - $a \notin Shared(A_1, A_2) \wedge (s_2, a, s'_2) \in \delta_{A_2} \wedge s_1 = s'_1$
  - $a \in Shared(A_1, A_2) \wedge (s_1, a, s'_1) \in \delta_{A_1} \wedge (s_2, a, s'_2) \in \delta_{A_2}$.

We define by $Shared(A_1, A_2) = (\Sigma^I_{A_1} \cap \Sigma^O_{A_2}) \cup (\Sigma^O_{A_1} \cap \Sigma^I_{A_2})$ the set of shared actions between A_1 and A_2.

Definition 3 (Parallel composition): The composition of two interface automata A_1 and A_2 is denoted by $A_1 \| A_2$, it is computed by eliminating from the product $A_1 \otimes A_2$ the illegal states and all states reached from these illegal states by enabling output and internal actions. A_1 and A_2 are compatible iff $A_1 \| A_2 \neq \emptyset$ The set of *illegal states* of two interface automata A_1, A_2 is defined as:

$$Illegal(A_1, A_2) = \left\{ \begin{matrix} (s_1, s_2) \in S_{A_1} \times S_{A_2} \mid \exists a \in Shared(A_1, A_2). \\ \left(a \in \Sigma^O_{A_1}(s_1) \wedge a \notin \Sigma^I_{A_2}(s_2) \right) \\ \vee \\ \left(a \in \Sigma^O_{A_2}(s_2) \wedge a \notin \Sigma^I_{A_1}(s_1) \right) \end{matrix} \right\}$$

We define by $\Sigma^I_A(s_1)$, $\Sigma^O_A(s_1)$, respectively the set of input and output actions enabled at the state s_1.

Definition 4 (Refinement): The refinement relation can be defined as alternating simulation [2]. An interface automaton P refines an interface automaton Q, if all input steps of Q can be simulated by P and all the output steps of P can be simulated by Q. We need some preliminary notions:

Given an interface automaton P and a state $v \in S_P$, the set $\varepsilon\text{-closure}_P(v)$ is the smallest set $U \in S_P$ such that (1) $v \in U$ and (2) if $u \in U$ and $(u, a, u') \in \delta_P$ and $a \in \Sigma^H_P$ then $u' \in U$. The ε-closure of a state v consists of the set of states that can be reached from v by taking only internal steps.

Consider an interface automaton P, and a state $v \in S_P$. We let $ExtEn^O_P(v) = \{a \mid \exists u \in \varepsilon - closure_P(v).a \in \Sigma^O_P(u)\}$, and $ExtEn^I_P(v) = \{a \mid \exists u \in \varepsilon - closure_P(v).a \in \Sigma^I_P(u)\}$ be the sets of externally enabled output and input actions, respectively, at v.

Consider an interface automaton P and a state $v \in S_P$. For all externally enabled input and output actions $a \in ExtEn^I_P(v) \cup ExtEn^O_P(v)$, we let $ExtDest_P(v, a) = \{(u, a, u') \in \delta_P. u \in \varepsilon - closure_P(v)\}$. Using this notation, we define the alternating simulation on interface automata:

Definition 5 (Alternating simulation): Consider two interface automata P and Q. A binary relation $\succeq \subseteq S_P \times S_Q$ is an alternating simulation from Q to P if for all states $v \in S_P$ and $u \in S_Q$ such that $v \succeq u$, the following conditions hold: (1) $ExtEn^I_P(v) \subseteq ExtEn^I_Q(u)$ and $ExtEn^O_Q(u) \subseteq ExtEn^O_P(v)$. (2) For all actions $a \in ExtEn^I_P(v) \cup ExtEn^O_Q(u)$ and all states $u' \in ExtDest_Q(u, a)$, there is a state $v' \in ExtDest_P(v, a)$ such that $v' \succeq u'$.

So, there is a refinement relation between two interface automata P and Q, if there is an alternating simulation between their initial states.

3.4 Adaptation contract

When assembling two components developed separately, there is a high probability to confront the problem of mismatches between them. Essentially, the adaptation contract in CBSE is used to solve this problem of mismatch between components [13]. An adaptation contract is specified by a set of rules. A rule takes the form of a synchronous vector v_i [14] (see Fig. 4). The number of elements of each vector is the number of components. A synchronous vector v_i for a set of components ($\{C_i\}_{i \in \{1..n\}}$), is a tuple $\langle e_1, \ldots, e_n \rangle$ with e_i can belong to the actions set of the component C_i, or it can be equal to ε. ε means that the component C_i doesn't participate in this synchronization.

4 Proposed Approach

Our approach aims to provide a bottom up method to construct systems by assembling and adapting blocks designed in isolation. We show a general view of our approach in Fig. 1. We start from a specification of a system part. This part is considered as a SysML block (B) that we want to construct and to integrate to the system. However, the specification represents the interaction protocol of this part (the block B). To meet this specification, the designer selects some blocks and adapts them using our method. In the next step of the system development, the composite block B will be used to meet the specification of its parent block. So, the unit used to construct the system is the composite block, and we build an adapter per a composite block (Fig. 2).

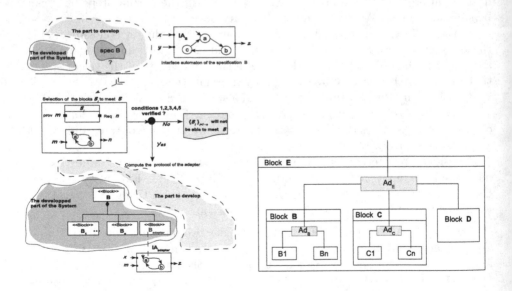

Fig. 1. The proposed approach   **Fig. 2.** Iterative process

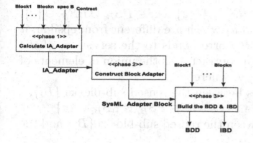

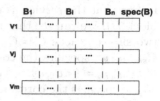

Fig. 3. Adaptation process

Fig. 4. Adaptation contract

We divide the adaptation process of a blocks set to meet the specification of their parent into three phases (see Fig. 3):

– Compute the interaction protocol of the adapter basing on the specification of the parent block and the interaction protocol of the reused blocks.
– Construct the SysML adapter block.
– Integrate the adapter block with the selected blocks to build the BDD and the IBD of the parent block.

4.1 The First Phase: Compute the Adapter Interaction Protocol

In this phase, we verify the possibility of constructing an adapter to make the set of the selected blocks able to refine the specification of the composite block B. If the case, then we compute the protocol of the adapter block.

4.1.1 The Selection of the Reused Blocks $\{B_i\}$

In this phase, the architect must select the blocks $\{B_i\}$ which will be used to meet the specification (A_{spec}) of the composite block B. The result of this phase is a set of blocks $\{B_i\}$ with their interface automata and an adaptation contract C. We need to define the sets of PS_B, RS_B and IOp_B, respectively, the set of the provided services, the set of required services and the set of internal operations of the block B.

$PS_B = \{ps \mid \exists p \in Ports(B), ps \in p.type.Op \wedge p.Direction = provided\}$

$RS_B = \{rs \mid \exists p \in Ports(B), rs \in p.type.Op \wedge p.Direction = required\}$

$IOp_B = \{o \mid o \in operations(B)\}$

The adaptation contract C is constructed incrementally. By adding a new block B_i, the architect must specify the correspondences between the services of B_i and the services of the specification on the one hand, and between the services of B_i and the services of the set of blocks already chosen ($\{B_j\}_{j<i}$) on the other hand. These correspondences represent the contract $C = \{v_i\}_{i=1..m}$. Each element v_i of the adaptation contract C takes the format of a synchronous vector:

$<a_1, a_2, \ldots, a_n, s>$, where: $s \in PS_{spec} \cup RS_{spec} \cup \{\varepsilon\} \wedge a_i \in PS_{B_i} \cup RS_{B_i} \cup \{\varepsilon\}$. Each vector contains two elements a_i and a_j which are different from epsilon, it means that the service a_i of the block B_i corresponds to the service a_j of the block B_j. We can see that the adaptation contract C is the union of elements of two sub-contracts: $C = C_{subBlocks} \cup C_{spec}$, where:

$C_{subBlocks}$: specifies the correspondences between the reused sub-blocks $\{B_i\}$,
$C_{subBlocks} = \{<a_1, a_2, \ldots, a_n, s>\}$ where $s = \varepsilon \wedge a_i \in PS_{B_i} \cup RS_{B_i} \cup \{\varepsilon\}$
C_{spec}: specifies the correspondences between the reused sub-blocks $\{B_i\}$ and the specification of the parent block,
$C_{spec} = \{<a_1, a_2, \ldots, a_n, s>\}$ where $s \neq \varepsilon \wedge a_i \in PS_{B_i} \cup RS_{B_i} \cup \{\varepsilon\}$

The sub-contract $C_{subBlocks}$ must verify the Condition 1:

Condition 1 ($C_{subBlocks}$ validity): We must verify that there is no conflict in the adaptation sub-contract $C_{subBlocks}$ which is specified by the architect.

Condition 1.1: A required service of a block corresponds at most to one provided service of another block. This means that each required service of a block appears only once in $C_{subBlocks}$.
$\forall v_i = <e_{i1}, \ldots, e_{in}, \varepsilon> \in C_{subBlocks}$, IF $e_{ik} = a, a \in RS_{B_k}$
$\Rightarrow \forall v_{j \neq i} = <e_{j1}, \ldots, e_{jn}, \varepsilon> \in C_{subBlocks}, e_{jk} \neq a$

Condition 1.2: A provided service of a block corresponds at most to one required service of another block. This means that each provided service appears only in one vector of $C_{subBlocks}$.
$\forall v_i = <e_{i1}, \ldots, e_{in}, \varepsilon> \in C_{subBlocks}$, IF $e_{ik} = a, a \in PS_{B_k}$
$\Rightarrow \forall v_{j \neq i} = <e_{j1}, \ldots, e_{jn}, \varepsilon> \in C_{subBlocks}, e_{jk} \neq a$

The sub-contract C_{spec} must verify Condition 2:

Condition 2 (C_{spec} validity): We must verify that there is no conflict in the adaptation sub-contract C_{spec}, which is made by the architect to specify the correspondences between the reused blocks and the specification of the parent block.

Condition 2.1: A provided service a of the specification can correspond at most to one provided service b of the sub-blocks. The services a and b don't correspond to any other services.
$\forall v_i = <e_{i1}, \ldots, e_{in}, a> \in C_{spec}, a \in PS_{spec} \wedge e_{ik} = b$
$\Rightarrow b \in PS_{B_k} \wedge \forall v_{j \neq i} = <e_{j1}, \ldots, e_{jn}, c> \in C, c \neq a \wedge e_{jk} \neq b$

Condition 2.2: A required service a of the specification can correspond at most to one required service b of the sub-blocks. The services a and b don't correspond to any other services.
$\forall v_i = <e_{i1}, \ldots, e_{in}, a> \in C_{spec}, a \in RS_{spec} \wedge e_{ik} = b$
$\Rightarrow b \in RS_{B_k} \wedge \forall v_{j \neq i} = <e_{j1}, \ldots, e_{jn}, c> \in C, c \neq a \wedge e_{jk} \neq b$

4.1.2   Consistency Verification
Condition 3 (Blocks interfaces Consistency):
Condition 3.1 *(Consistency verification of the selected sub-blocks):* We must verify that the blocks $\{B_i\}$ are composable:

- No shared provided services between the sub-blocks: $\forall a \in PS_{B_i}$, $a \notin \bigcup_{j \neq i} PS_{B_j}$.
- No shared required services between the sub-blocks: $\forall a \in RS_{B_i}$, $a \notin \bigcup_{j \neq i} RS_{B_j}$.
- The set of internal operations of each block is independent from the services and the internal operations of the other blocks $\{B_j\}_{j \neq i}$:
$\forall a \in IOp_{B_i}, a \notin (\bigcup_{j \neq i} PS_{B_j}) \cup (\bigcup_{j \neq i} RS_{B_j}) \cup (\bigcup_{j \neq i} IOp_{B_j})$

Condition 3.2 *(Consistency verification of the selected sub-blocks and the parent block)*: The Condition 3.2 must be verified by the interface of the parent block (B) and the interfaces of the sub-blocks ($\{B_i\}$).

- A provided service of a sub-block can not be a required service of the parent block: $\forall a \in PS_{B_i}$, $a \notin RS_{A_{spec}}$
- A required service of a sub-block can not be a provided service of the parent block: $\forall a \in RS_{B_i}$, $a \notin PS_{A_{spec}}$

4.1.3 Computing the Interaction Protocol of the Sub-blocks $\{B_i\}$

At this stage, we use only the contract $C_{subBlocks}$ to compute the global interaction protocol. For that, we need to compute the parallel composition of sub-blocks interface automata. The parallel composition is based on the shared actions between interface automata. But in our case, interface automata have corresponding actions in place of shared actions. Thus, we have adjusted the synchronous product and the parallel composition as follows:

Definition 1 *(Contract based synchronous product):* The contract based synchronous product is possible between two interface automata A_i and A_j, if they are composable ($\Sigma_{A_i}^I \cap \Sigma_{A_j}^I = \Sigma_{A_i}^O \cap \Sigma_{A_j}^O = \Sigma_{A_i}^H \cap \Sigma_{A_j} = \Sigma_{A_i} \cap \Sigma_{A_j}^H = \emptyset$), and the adaptation contract is valid (it verifies the Condition 1).

Before defining the contract based synchronous product between two interface automata A_i and A_j, we need to define $Corresponding(A_i, A_j)$, the set of corresponding actions between the interface automata A_i and A_j, and the function corresp(a) that returns the action that corresponds to the action a by referring to the adaptation contract:

$Corresponding(A_i, A_j) =$
$\{a \in \Sigma_{A_i}^I \cup \Sigma_{A_i}^O \cup \Sigma_{A_j}^I \cup \Sigma_{A_j}^O \mid \exists v = <e_1, \ldots, e_n, \varepsilon> \in C_{subBlocks}, e_k = a\}$
corresp(a) $= \{a' \mid \exists v \in C, \exists i, j \in N, v = <a_1, \ldots, a_n> \wedge a_i = a \wedge a_j = a'\}$

We define the contract based synchronous product of A_i and A_j as:
$A_i \otimes_c A_j = \langle S_{A_i \otimes_c A_j}, I_{A_i \otimes_c A_j}, \Sigma_{A_i \otimes_c A_j}^I, \Sigma_{A_i \otimes_c A_j}^O, \Sigma_{A_i \otimes_c A_j}^H, \delta_{A_i \otimes_c A_j} \rangle$

- $S_{A_i \otimes A_j} = S_{A_i} \times S_{A_j}$ and $I_{A_i \otimes_c A_j} = I_{A_i} \times I_{A_j}$;
- $\Sigma_{A_i \otimes_c A_j}^I = (\Sigma_{A_i}^I \cup \Sigma_{A_j}^I) \setminus Corresponding(A_i, A_j)$;
- $\Sigma_{A_i \otimes_c A_j}^O = (\Sigma_{A_i}^O \cup \Sigma_{A_j}^O) \setminus Corresponding(A_i, A_j)$;
- $\Sigma_{A_i \otimes_c A_j}^H = \Sigma_{A_i}^H \cup \Sigma_{A_j}^H \cup Corresponding(A_i, A_j)$;
- $((s_i, s_j), a, (s_i', s_j')) \in \delta_{A_i \otimes_c A_j}$ if:

- $a \notin Corresponding(A_i, A_j) \land (s_i, a, s_i') \in \delta_{A_i} \land s_j = s_j'$
- $a \notin Corresponding(A_i, A_j) \land (s_j, a, s_j') \in \delta_{A_j} \land s_i = s_i'$
- $a \in Corresponding(A_i, A_j) \land a \in \Sigma_{A_i}^O \land (s_i, a, s_i') \in \delta_{A_i} \land (s_j, corresp(a), s_j') \in \delta_{A_j}$.
- $a \in Corresponding(A_i, A_j) \land a \in \Sigma_{A_j}^O \land (s_j, a, s_j') \in \delta_{A_j} \land (s_i, corresp(a), s_i') \in \delta_{A_i}$.

This product absorbs the transitions $(s_i, s_j) \xrightarrow{a!} (s_i', s_j) \xrightarrow{corresp(a)} (s_i', s_j')$ and the transitions $(s_i, s_j) \xrightarrow{a!} (s_i, s_j') \xrightarrow{corresp(a)} (s_i', s_j')$ by replacing them by a single transition $(s_i, s_j) \xrightarrow{a;} (s_i', s_j')$. This absorption is helpful when we need to compute the synchronous product between multiple IAs having corresponding actions. It allows the atomic execution of the emission of an action and the reception of its corresponding action.

Definition 2 *(Contract based parallel composition):* The contract based parallel composition between two interface automata A_i and A_j is defined as: $A_i \|_c A_j = A_i \otimes_c A_j$ after removing illegal states and all states reached from these illegal states by enabling output and internal actions. The set of illegal states is defined as:

$$Illegal(A_i, A_j) = \left\{ \begin{array}{c} (s_i, s_j) \in S_{A_i} \times S_{A_j} \mid \exists a \in Corresponding(A_i, A_j). \\ \left(a \in \Sigma_{A_i}^O(s_i) \land corresp(a) \notin \Sigma_{A_j}^I(s_j) \right) \\ \lor \\ \left(a \in \Sigma_{A_j}^O(s_j) \land corresp(a) \notin \Sigma_{A_i}^I(s_i) \right) \end{array} \right\}$$

So, the global interaction protocol A_G of the sub-blocks $\{B_i\}_{i=1..n}$ is obtained by composing their interface automata $\{A_i\}_{i=1..n}$ using the contract based parallel composition:

$$A_G = A_1 \|_c A_2 \|_c \cdots \|_c A_n$$

At each given stage i of computing the composition, we must compute the composition between the interface automaton A_c (where $A_c = A_1 \|_c \cdots \|_c A_{i-1}$) and the interface automaton A_i of the block B_i. At each stage i, we must verify the Condition 4.

Condition 4: *(The blocks must be compatible)* A_c must be not empty.

4.1.4   Computing the Interaction Protocol of the Adapter

The adapter block B_{ad} having the interface automaton A_{ad} must verify this relation: $A_{spec} \succeq A_G \|_c A_{ad}$. It means that the automaton resulting from composing interface automata of the blocks $\{B_i\}$ with the adapter automaton, must refine the interface automaton of B specification. Thus, to deduce A_{ad}, we refer to the formula proposed in [15]. To compute the most general solution R where $Q \succeq P \| R$, the authors in [15] prove that $R = mirror(P \| mirror(Q))$, where P, R and Q are interface automata, and mirror(Q) is the interface automaton Q with inputs and outputs interchanged. We define formally the notion of mirror as follows:

$$mirror(Q) = \{Q' \mid \forall(s, a!, s') \in \delta_Q, \exists(s, a?, s') \in \delta_{Q'} \wedge$$
$$\forall(s, a?, s') \in \delta_Q, \exists(s, a!, s') \in \delta_{Q'} \wedge$$
$$\forall(s, a; , s') \in \delta_Q, \exists(s, a; , s') \in \delta_{Q'}\}$$

So, in our case, because we have corresponding actions between automata in place of shared actions, the A_{ad} must be computed as follows:

$$A_{ad} = mirror(A_G \|_c mirror(A_{spec})) = mirror(A_1 \|_c \cdots \|_c A_n \|_c mirror(A_{spec}))$$

Condition 5: (A_G and $mirror(A_{spec})$ must be compatible) A_{ad} is not empty

If the Condition 5 is verified, we can deduce the real interaction protocol of the adapter by applying the Algorithm 1, which allows to return transitions absorbed in the contract based synchronous product.

Algorithm 1. Deduce the interaction protocol of the adapter

INPUT: $A_{ad} = \langle\ S_{ad}, I_{ad}, \Sigma^I_{ad}, \Sigma^O_{ad}, \Sigma^H_{ad}, \delta_{ad}\ \rangle$, C
OUTPUT: $A_{adapter} = \langle S_{adapter}, I_{adapter}, \Sigma^I_{adapter}, \Sigma^O_{adapter}, \Sigma^H_{adapter}, \delta_{adapter}\rangle$

- Create a copy $A_{adapter}$ of A_{ad}.
- Construct the set T of all transitions ($s \xrightarrow{a;} s' \in \delta_{adapter}$), where a appears in the contract C.
- Replace all $s \xrightarrow{a;} s' \in \delta_{adapter}$ where $s \xrightarrow{a;} s' \in T$, by $s \xrightarrow{a?} s'' \xrightarrow{corresp(a)!} s'$.

According to the contract based synchronous product, the transitions labelled with internal actions $a;$ in A_{ad}, which appear in the contract, represent the transitions where the adapter plays the role of a converter: so each transition of this set must be replaced by two transitions. The first is labelled with the input action $a?$ and the second by the corresponding action $corresp(a)!$. This means that the adapter receives the action $a?$ from a block, after that, it converts it to the suitable input of another block and it conveys it using an output action $corresp(a)!$. The transitions which aren't selected by the Algorithm 1 are those where the adapter plays the role of a complement and not a converter.

4.2   The Second Phase: Construct the SysML Adapter Block

In this phase, we construct the SysML adapter block. We use the *Algorithm 2* to deduce the set of ports of the SysML adapter block $B_{adapter}$.

4.3   The Third Phase: Build the BDD and the IBD of the Block B

Using the *Algorithm 3*, we construct the BDD of the parent block B. The role of this algorithm is to establish the composition relations between the parent block B and its sub-blocks $\{B_i\}$, and a composition relation between the parent block B and the adapter block B_{ad}. We use the *Algorithm 4* to generate the IBD of the block B. It bases on relying the adapter block ports with the ports of the sub-blocks $\{B_i\}$ and the parent block B.

Algorithm 2. Construct the SysML adapter block

INPUT: $A_{adapter} = \langle S_{adapter}, I_{adapter}, \Sigma^I_{adapter}, \Sigma^O_{adapter}, \Sigma^H_{adapter}, \delta_{adapter} \rangle$
OUTPUT: $B_{adapter} = \langle\, 'Adapter', V, O, C, P, Ports \,\rangle$

-Create the adapter block $B_{adapter} = \langle\, 'Adapter', \emptyset, \emptyset, \emptyset, \emptyset, \emptyset \,\rangle$
// create the list of ports of the adapter that must be linked to the ports of the parent block.
if $\Sigma^I_{adapter} \cap \Sigma^I_{spec} \neq \emptyset$ **then**
    create a new provided port p which offers the services $\Sigma^I_{adapter} \cap \Sigma^I_{spec}$
    add p to the ports list of $B_{adapter}$
if $\Sigma^O_{adapter} \cap \Sigma^O_{spec} \neq \emptyset$ **then**
    create a new required port p which requires the services $\Sigma^O_{adapter} \cap \Sigma^O_{spec}$
    add p to the ports list of $B_{adapter}$
// create the list of ports of the adapter that must be linked to the ports of sub-blocks $\{B_i\}$
for all B_i in the list of sub-blocks $\{B_i\}$ **do**
    if $\Sigma^I_{adapter} \cap \Sigma^O_{B_i} \neq \emptyset$ **then**
       create a new provided port p which offers the services $\Sigma^I_{adapter} \cap \Sigma^O_{B_i}$
       add p to the ports list of $B_{adapter}$
    if $\Sigma^O_{adapter} \cap \Sigma^I_{B_i} \neq \emptyset$ **then**
       create a new required port p which requires the services $\Sigma^O_{adapter} \cap \Sigma^I_{B_i}$
       add p to the ports list of $B_{adapter}$

Algorithm 3. Construct the BDD of the parent block B

INPUT: B, $\{B_i\}$, $B_{adapter}$
OUTPUT: $BDD_B = \langle\, B, R \,\rangle$

- Set the value of the blocks set of the BDD_B to: B= $\{B_i\}_{i=1..n} \cup \{B, B_{adapter}\}$
- Create a composition relation r_i between the parent block B and each block B_i where: SourceOf(r_i) = B, TargetOf(r_i) = B_i
- Create a composition relation r_{ad} between the parent block B and the adapter block $B_{adapter}$ where: SourceOf(r_{ad}) = B, TargetOf(r_{ad}) = $B_{adapter}$
- Set the value of the relations set of BDD_B to: R= $\{r_i\}_{i=1..n} \cup \{r_{ad}\}$

---

5   Case Study

We give an example of a simple cleaning robot which moves according to a specific path, and at each given unit of time, it gives informations about its state. We consider that the robot that we want to construct and to integrate to our system (see Fig. 5), will have the interaction protocol given in Fig. 6. So, the interface automaton in Fig. 6 gives the specification of the composite block 'Robot' that we want to build.

5.1   The First Phase: Compute the IA_adapter

To build the robot, we have reused two blocks 'Controller' and 'Motor' (see Fig. 7), their interaction protocols are given in Figs. 8 and 9. To simplify we consider that the corresponding actions have the same name and we differentiate between them by adding the first letter of the block's name to each action.

Algorithm 4. Construct the IBD of the parent block B

INPUT: B, $\{B_i\}$, $B_{adapter}$

OUTPUT: $IBD_B = \langle$ Parts, Ports, Connectors $\rangle$

- Create instances $\{part_i\}_{i=1..n}$ of the blocks Set $\{B_i\}_{i=1..n}$.
- Create an instance 'ad' of the adapter block $B_{adapter}$.
- Set the set Parts of IBD_B to: $\{part_i\}_{i=1..n} \cup \{ad\}$
- Set the set Ports of IBD_B to: $\{Ports(part_i)\}_{i=1..n} \cup Ports(ad)$
//create connectors between the adapter and $\{part_i\}_{i=1..n}$.
for all $part_i \in \{part_i\}_{i=1..n}$ **do**
    for all port $p \in Ports(ad)$ **do**
        if $\exists p' \in Ports(part_i) \wedge (p.type.Op \cap p'.type.Op \neq \emptyset)$ **then**
            create a connector between p and p'
//create delegation connectors between the adapter and the parent block B.
for all port $p \in Ports(ad)$ **do**
  if $\exists p' \in Ports(B) \wedge (p.type.Op \cap p'.type.Op \neq \emptyset)$ **then**
    create a connector between p and p'

We see that the Condition 3 of consistency is verified by the interface automata of the robot, the receiver and the motor.

The contract that we use to specify the correspondences is:

$C_{subBlocks} = \{<C.on, M.on, \varepsilon>, <C.off, M.off, \varepsilon>\}$

$C_{spec} = \{<C.move, \varepsilon, R.move>, <C.stop, \varepsilon, R.stop>\}$

We see that all the conditions (Conditions 1 and 2) that the contract must respect are verified by this contract.

The global interaction protocol of the controller and the motor is given in Fig. 10, it takes the form of an interface automaton. $A_G = IA_{controler}\|_c IA_{motor}$. The Condition 4 is verified because A_G is not empty. The adapter is computed using the formula: $A_{ad} = mirror(A_G\|_c mirror(IA_{Robot}))$. The mirror of $A_G\|_c mirror(IA_{Robot})$ is presented in Fig. 11. So, the Condition 5 is verified because A_{ad} is not empty.

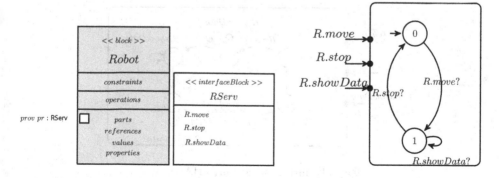

Fig. 6. The IA of the robot

Fig. 5. The robot SysML block

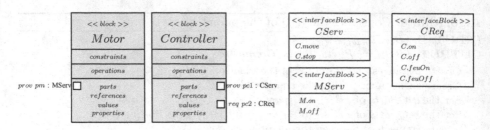

Fig. 7. SysML controller and motor blocks

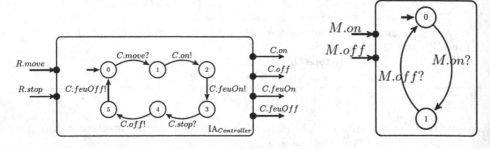

Fig. 8. IA$_{Controller}$

Fig. 9. IA$_{Motor}$

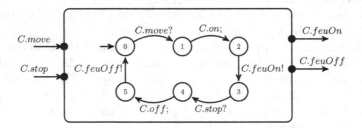

Fig. 10. A$_G$ = IA$_{controler}$ ||$_c$IA$_{motor}$

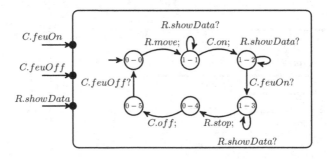

Fig. 11. mirror(A$_G$ ||$_c$ mirror(IA$_{robot}$))

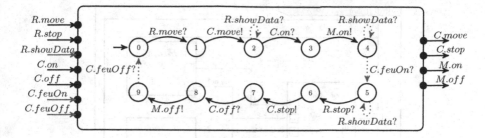

Fig. 12. The interface automaton of the adapter (Color figure online)

After applying the *Algorithm 1*, to recuperate transitions absorbed by the contract based synchronous product, we obtain the interface automaton of the adapter (Fig. 12). Dotted transitions with red colour represent where the adapter plays the role of a complement. However, transitions with black colour represent where the adapter behaves as a converter.

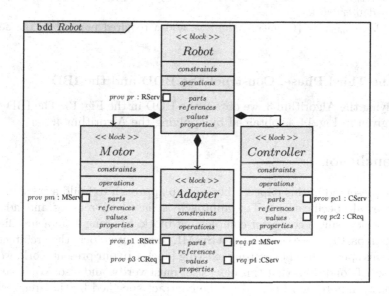

Fig. 13. BDD of the robot

5.2 The Second Phase: Construct the SysML Adapter Block

By applying the Algorithm 2, we obtain (see the adapter block in Fig. 13):

- $\Sigma_{ad}^{I} \cap \Sigma_{Robot}^{I} = \{R.move, R.stop, R.showData\} \Rightarrow$ add a provided port *p1* to the adapter

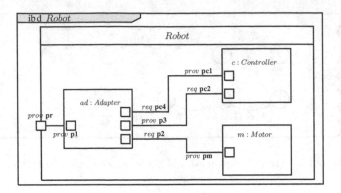

Fig. 14. IBD of the robot

- $\Sigma_{ad}^{O} \cap \Sigma_{Robot}^{O} = \emptyset, \Sigma_{ad}^{I} \cap \Sigma_{Motor}^{O} = \emptyset$
- $\Sigma_{ad}^{O} \cap \Sigma_{Motor}^{I} = \{M.on, M.off\} \Rightarrow$ add a required port $p2$ to the adapter block
- $\Sigma_{ad}^{I} \cap \Sigma_{Controller}^{O} = \{C.on, C.off, C.feuOn, C.feuOff\} \Rightarrow$ add a provided port $p3$ to the adapter block
- $\Sigma_{ad}^{O} \cap \Sigma_{Controller}^{I} = \{C.move, C.stop\} \Rightarrow$ add a required port $p4$ to the adapter block

5.3   The Third Phase: Construct the BDD and the IBD

By applying the Algorithm 3, we obtain the BDD in the Fig. 13. The IBD of the Robot, given in Fig. 14, is obtained by applying the Algorithm 4.

6   Conclusion

We have presented in this paper, a bottom-up approach to build a system, based on its partial specifications. The approach is based on reusing and adapting SysML blocks using a converter-complement block. Starting from a specification of a system part that we consider as a SysML composite block, the architect tries to meet this specification by reusing existing blocks. In our present work, we have given a set of conditions that this blocks set must verify, and also, We have given some constraints to be respected by the contract specified by the architect. We have used the interface automata as formalism to represent the blocks interaction protocols. By defining the new notion of contract based synchronous product and basing on the relation of refinement between interface automata, we deduce the interaction protocol of the converter-complement block, when the reused blocks respect the adaptation conditions. In our approach the adapter has two roles. It plays its role as a converter between the reused blocks on the one hand, and between the reused blocks and their future parent block on the other hand. It plays the second role as a complement by performing to the reused blocks what they require and it's not planed to be required by their parent, and to offer what the parent must provide and it's not provided by any part of it.

In a future work, we plan to develop a tool that support the contract-based synchronous product between interface automata, and the automatic generation of the converter-complement interaction protocol. The tool will implement all the algorithms presented in this paper.

References

1. OMG: OMG Systems Modeling Language (OMG SysML^{TM}) Version 1.3 (2012). http://www.omg.org
2. de Alfaro L., Henzinger T.A.: Interface automata. In: ESEC/SIGSOFT FSE, pp. 109–120 (2001)
3. Inverardi, P., Tivoli, M.: Software architecture for correct components assembly. In: Bernardo, M., Inverardi, P. (eds.) SFM 2003. LNCS, vol. 2804, pp. 92–121. Springer, Heidelberg (2003)
4. Poizat, P., Salaün, G., Tivoli, M.: An adaptation-based approach to incrementally build component systems. Electr. Notes Theor. Comput. Sci. **182**, 155–170 (2007)
5. Chouali, S., Hammad, A.: Formal verification of components assembly based on SysML and interface automata. ISSE **7**(4), 265–274 (2011)
6. Canal, C., Poizat, P., Salaün, G.: Adaptation de composants logiciels: une approche automatisée basée sur des expressions régulières de vecteurs de synchronisation. In: CAL, pp. 31–39. France, Nantes (2006)
7. Bracciali, A., Brogi, A., Canal, C.: A formal approach to component adaptation. J. Syst. Softw. **74**(1), 45–54 (2005)
8. Karlsson, D., Eles, P., Peng, Z.: Formal verification of component-based designs. Design Autom. Emb. Syst. **11**(1), 49–90 (2007)
9. Canal, C., Poizat, P., Salaün, G.: Synchronizing behavioural mismatch in software composition. In: Gorrieri, R., Wehrheim, H. (eds.) FMOODS 2006. LNCS, vol. 4037, pp. 63–77. Springer, Heidelberg (2006)
10. Chouali, S., Mouelhi, S., Mountassir, H.: Adaptation sémantique des protocoles des composants par les automates d'interface. TSI, Technique et Science Informatiques **31**(6), 769–796 (2012)
11. Carrillo, O., Chouali, S., Mountassir, H.: Formalizing and verifying compatibility and consistency of SysML blocks. ACM SIGSOFT Softw. Eng. Notes **37**(4), 1–8 (2012)
12. Dahmani, D., Boukala, M.C., Mountassir, H.: A petri net approach for reusing and adapting components with atomic and non-atomic synchronisation. In: Proceedings of the International Workshop on Petri Nets and Software Engineering, pp. 129–141, Tunis, Tunisia (2014)
13. Canal, C., Salaün, G.: Adaptation of asynchronously communicating software. In: Franch, X., Ghose, A.K., Lewis, G.A., Bhiri, S. (eds.) ICSOC 2014. LNCS, vol. 8831, pp. 437–444. Springer, Heidelberg (2014)
14. Canal, C., Poizat, P., Salaün, G.: Model-based adaptation of behavioral mismatching components. IEEE Trans. Software Eng. **34**(4), 546–563 (2008)
15. Bhaduri, P., Ramesh, S.: Interface synthesis and protocol conversion. Formal Asp. Comput. **20**(2), 205–224 (2008)

Author Index

Printed in the United States
By Bookmasters